F. Max (Friedrich Max)
Mu

ller

Lectures on the science of language

F. Max (Friedrich Max)
Mü
ller

Lectures on the science of language

ISBN/EAN: 9783741163463

Manufactured in Europe, USA, Canada, Australia, Japa

Cover: Foto ©Andreas Hilbeck / pixelio.de

Manufactured and distributed by brebook publishing software (www.brebook.com)

F. Max (Friedrich Max)
Mu

ller

Lectures on the science of language

LECTURES

ON

THE SCIENCE OF LANGUAGE

DELIVERED AT THE

ROYAL INSTITUTION OF GREAT BRITAIN

IN

FEBRUARY, MARCH, APRIL, AND MAY, 1863.

By MAX MÜLLER, M. A.

FELLOW OF ALL SOULS COLLEGE, OXFORD; CORRESPONDANT DE L'INSTITUT DE FRANCE.

SECOND SERIES.

WITH THIRTY-ONE ILLUSTRATIONS.

NEW YORK:
CHARLES SCRIBNER, 124 GRAND STREET.
1865.
[*Published by arrangement with the Author.*]

PREFACE.

This Second Series of Lectures on the Science of Language was delivered last year at the Royal Institution in London. Most of the topics treated in them had for many years formed the subject of my public courses at Oxford. In casting my notes into the shape of lectures to be addressed to a more advanced audience, I left out many things that were merely elementary, and I made several additions in order to show the bearing of the Science of Language on some of the more important problems of philosophy and religion.

Whilst expressing my gratitude to the readers and reviewers of the first series of my Lectures, to those who differed from me even more than to those who agreed with me, I venture to hope that this second volume may meet with as many indulgent friends and intelligent critics as the first.

MAX MÜLLER.

OXFORD; *June* 11, 1864.

CONTENTS.

LECTURE I.
INTRODUCTORY LECTURE. NEW MATERIALS FOR THE SCIENCE OF LANGUAGE, AND NEW THEORIES 9

LECTURE II.
LANGUAGE AND REASON 53

LECTURE III.
THE PHYSIOLOGICAL ALPHABET 109

LECTURE IV.
PHONETIC CHANGE 174

LECTURE V.
GRIMM'S LAW 213

LECTURE VI.
ON THE PRINCIPLES OF ETYMOLOGY 254

LECTURE VII.
ON THE POWERS OF ROOTS 313

LECTURE VIII.
METAPHOR 351

CONTENTS.

LECTURE IX.
THE MYTHOLOGY OF THE GREEKS 403

LECTURE X.
JUPITER, THE SUPREME ARYAN GOD 432

LECTURE XI.
MYTHS OF THE DAWN 481

LECTURE XII.
MODERN MYTHOLOGY 544

LECTURES.

LECTURE I.

INTRODUCTORY LECTURE.

In a course of lectures which I had the honor to deliver in this Institution two years ago, I endeavored to show that the language which we speak, and the languages that are and that have been spoken in every part of our globe since the first dawn of human life and human thought, supply materials capable of scientific treatment. We can collect them, we can classify them, we can reduce them to their constituent elements, and deduce from them some of the laws that determine their origin, govern their growth, necessitate their decay; we can treat them, in fact, in exactly the same spirit in which the geologist treats his stones and petrifactions, — nay, in some respects, in the same spirit in which the astronomer treats the stars of heaven, or the botanist the flowers of the field. There *is* a Science of Language, as there is a science of the earth, its flowers, and its stars; and though, as a young science, it is very far as yet from that perfection which — thanks to the efforts of the intellectual giants of so many ages and many countries — has been reached in Astronomy,

Botany, and even in Geology, it is, perhaps for that very reason, all the more fascinating. It is a young and a growing science that puts forth new strength with every year, that opens new prospects, new fields of enterprise on every side, and rewards its students with richer harvests than could be expected from the exhausted soil of the older sciences. The whole world is open, as it were, to the student of language. There is virgin soil close to our door, and there are whole continents still to conquer, if we step beyond the frontiers of the ancient seats of civilization. We may select a small village in our neighborhood to pick up dialectic varieties and to collect phrases, proverbs, and stories which will disclose fragments, almost ground to dust, it is true, yet undeniable fragments of the earliest formations of Saxon speech and Saxon thought.[1] Or we may proceed to our very antipodes, and study the idiom of the Hawaian islanders, and watch in the laws and edicts of Kaméhaméha the working of the same human faculty of speech which, even in its most primitive efforts, never seems to miss the high end at which it aims. The dialects of Ancient Greece, ransacked as they have been by classical scholars, such as Maittaire, Giese, and Ahrens, will amply reward a fresh *battue* of the comparative philologist. Their forms, which to the

---

[1] A valuable essay "On some leading Characteristics of the Dialects spoken in the six Northern Counties of England, or Ancient Northumbria, and on the Variations in their Grammar from that of Standard English," has lately been published by Mr. B. P. Peacock, Berlin, 1863. It is chiefly based on the versions of the Song of Solomon into many of the spoken dialects of England, which have of late years been executed and published under the auspices of H. I. H. Prince Louis-Lucien Bonaparte. It is to be hoped that the writer will continue his researches in a field of scholarship so full of promise.

classical scholar were mere anomalies and curiosities, will thus assume a different aspect. They will range themselves under more general laws, and after receiving light by a comparison with other dialects, they will, in turn, reflect that light with increased power on the phonetic peculiarities of Sanskrit and Prâkrit, Zend and Persian, Latin and French. But even were the old mines exhausted, the Science of Language would create its own materials, and as with the rod of the prophet smite the rocks of the desert to call forth from them new streams of living speech. The rock inscriptions of Persia show what can be achieved by our science. I do not wonder that the discoveries due to the genius and the persevering industry of Grotefend, Burnouf, Lassen, and last, not least, of Rawlinson, should seem incredible to those who only glance at them from a distance. Their incredulity will hereafter prove the greatest compliment that could have been paid to these eminent scholars.[1] What we at present call the Cuneiform inscriptions of Cyrus, Darius, Xerxes, Artax-

[1] A thoroughly scholar-like answer to the late Sir G. C. Lewis's attacks on Champollion and other decipherers of ancient inscriptions may be seen in an article by Professor Le Page Renouf, "Sir G. C. Lewis on the Decipherment and Interpretation of Dead Languages," in the *Atlantis*, Nos. vii. and viii. p. 23. Though it cannot be known now whether the late Sir G. C. Lewis ever modified his opinions as to the soundness of the method through which the inscriptions of Egypt, Persia, India, and ancient Italy have been deciphered, such was the uprightness of his character that he would certainly have been the first to acknowledge his mistake, had he been spared to continue his studies. Though his skepticism was occasionally uncritical and unfair, his loss is a severe loss to our studies, which, more than any others, require to be kept in order by the watchful eye and uncompromising criticism of close reasoners and sound scholars. An essay just published by Professor F. W. Newman, "On the Umbrian Language," following after a short interval on an article in *Fraser's Magazine*, Jan. 1863, does equal credit to the acumen and to the candor of its author.

erxes I., Darius II., Artaxerxes Mnemon, Artaxerxes Ochus (of which we now have several editions, translations, grammars, and dictionaries), — what were they originally? A mere conglomerate of wedges, engraved or impressed on the solitary monument of Cyrus in the Murgháb, on the ruins of Persepolis, on the rocks of Behistún near the frontiers of Media, and the precipice of Van in Armenia. When Grotefend attempted to decipher them, he had first to prove that these scrolls were really inscriptions, and not mere arabesques or fanciful ornaments.[1] He had then to find out whether these magical characters were to be read horizontally or perpendicularly, from right to left, or from left to right. Lichtenberg maintained that they must be read in the same direction as Hebrew. Grotefend, in 1802, proved that the letters followed each other, as in Greek, from left to right. Even before Grotefend, Münter and Tychsen had observed that there was a sign to separate the words. Such a sign is of course an immense help in all attempts at deciphering inscriptions, for it lays bare at once the terminations of hundreds of words, and, in an Aryan language, supplies us with the skeleton of its grammar. Yet consider the difficulties that had still to be overcome before a single line could be read. It was unknown in what language these inscriptions were composed; it might have been a Semitic, a Turanian, or an Aryan language. It was unknown to what period they belonged, and whether they commemorated the conquests of Cyrus, Darius, Alexan-

[1] *Mémoire de M. le comte de Caylus, sur les ruines de Persepolis, dans le tome XXIX des Mémoires de l'Académie des inscriptions et belles-lettres, Histoire de l'Académie*, p. 118.

der, or Sapor. It was unknown whether the alphabet used was phonetic, syllabic, or ideographic. It would detain us too long were I to relate how all these difficulties were removed one after the other; how the proper names of Darius, Xerxes, Hystaspes, and of their god Ormusd, were traced; how from them the values of certain letters were determined; how with an imperfect alphabet other words were deciphered which clearly established the fact that the language of these inscriptions was Ancient Persian; how then, with the help of the Zend, which represents the Persian language previous to Darius, and with the help of the later Persian, a most effective cross-fire was opened; how even more powerful ordnance was brought up from the arsenal of the ancient Sanskrit; how outpost after outpost was driven in, a practical breach effected, till at last the fortress had to surrender and submit to the terms dictated by the Science of Language.

I should gladly on some future occasion give you a more detailed account of this glorious siege and victory. At present I only refer to it to show how, in all quarters of the globe, and from sources where it would least be expected, new materials are forthcoming that would give employment to a much larger class of laborers than the Science of Language can as yet boast of. The inscriptions of Babylon and Nineveh, the hieroglyphics of Egypt, the records in the caves of India, on the monuments of Lycia, on the tombs of Etruria, and on the broken tablets of Umbria and Samnium, all wait to have their spell broken or their riddle more satisfactorily read by the student of language. If, then, we turn our eyes again to the yet unnumbered dialects now spoken by the nomad tribes of Asia, Africa, America, and the islands of the Pacific, no scholar need be afraid for some generations to come that there will be no language left to him to conquer.

There is another charm peculiar to the Science of Language, or one, at least, which it shares only with its younger sisters, — I mean the vigorous contest that is still carried on between great opposing principles. In Astronomy, the fundamental laws of the universe are no longer contested, and the Ptolemæan system is not likely to find new supporters. In Geology, the feuds between the Vulcanists and the Neptunists have come to an end, and no unprejudiced person doubts at the present moment whether an ammonite be a work of nature and a flint-head a work of art. It is different in the Science of Language. There, the controversies about the great problems have not yet subsided. The questions whether language is a work of nature or a work of art, whether languages had one or many beginnings, whether they can be classified in families or no, are constantly starting up, and scholars, even while engaged in the most minute inquiries, — while carrying brick and mortar to build the walls of their new science, — must have their sword girded by their side, always ready to meet the enemy. This, no doubt, may sometimes be tedious, but it has one good effect, — it leads us to examine carefully the ground on which we take our stand, and keeps us alive, even while analyzing mere prefixes and suffixes, to the grandeur and the sacredness of the issues that depend on these minutiæ. The foundations of our science do not suffer from such attacks; on the contrary, like the coral cells built up quietly and patiently from the bottom of the sea, they become more strongly cemented by these whiffs of spray that are dashed across.

Emboldened by the indulgent reception with which I met in this place, when first claiming some share of public sympathy in behalf of the Science of Language, I venture to-day to come again before you with a course of lectures on the same subject, — "on mere words, on nouns, and verbs, and particles," — and I trust you will again, as you did then, make allowance for the inevitable shortcomings of one who has to address you with a foreign accent, and on a subject foreign to the pursuits of many of the supporters of this Institution. *One* thing I feel more strongly than ever, — namely, that, without the Science of Language, the circle of the physical sciences, to which this Institution is more specially dedicated, would be incomplete. The whole natural creation tends towards man: without man, nature would be incomplete and purposeless. The Science of Man, therefore, or, as it is sometimes called, Anthropology, must form the crown of all the natural sciences. And if it is language by which man differs from all other created things, the Science of Language has a right to hold that place which I claimed for it when addressing for the first time the members and supporters of this Institution. Allow me to quote the words of one whose memory becomes more dear and sacred to me with every year, and to whose friendship I owe more than I here could say. Bunsen, when addressing, in 1847, the newly formed section of Ethnology, at the meeting of the British Association at Oxford, said: —

"If man is the apex of the creation, it seems right, on the one side, that an historical inquiry into his origin and development should never be allowed to sever itself from the general body of natural science, and in particular from physiology. But, on the other hand, if man is the apex of the creation, if he is the end to which all organic formations tend from the very beginning; if man is at once the mystery and the key of natural science; if that is the only view of natural science worthy of our age, then ethnological philology, once established on principles as clear as the physiological are, is the highest branch of that science for the advancement of which this Association is instituted. It is not an appendix to physiology or to anything else; but its object is, on the contrary, capable of becoming the end and goal of the labors and transactions of a scientific association."[1]

In my former course all that I could attempt to do was to point out the principal objects of the Science of Language, to determine its limits, and to lay before you a general map of the ground that had been explored, with more or less success, during the last fifty years. That map was necessarily incomplete. It comprehended not much more than what in an atlas of the ancient world is called "Orbis Veteribus Notus," where you distinguish names and boundaries only in those parts of Europe, Asia, and Africa which formed the primeval stage of the great

[1] *Report of the British Association for the Advancement of Science*, 1847, p. 257.

drama of history; but where beyond the Hyperboreans in the North, the Anthropophagi in the West, and the Ethiopians[1] in the South, you see but vaguely shadowed outlines, — the New World beyond the Atlantis existing as yet merely as the dream of philosophers.

It was at first my intention, in the present course of lectures, to fill in greater detail the outlines of that map. Materials for this are abundant and steadily increasing. The works of Hervas, Adelung, Klaproth, Balbi, Prichard, and Latham, will show you how much more minutely the map of languages might be colored at present than the ancient geographical maps of Strabo and Ptolemy. But I very soon perceived that this would hardly have been a fit subject for a course of lectures. I could only have given you an account of the work done by others: of explorations made by travellers or missionaries among the black races of Africa, the yellow tribes of Polynesia, and the red-skins of America. I should have had simply to copy their descriptions of the manners, customs, laws, and religions of these

[1] The Hyperboreans, known to Homer and Herodotus as a people living in the extreme north, beloved by Apollo, and distinguished for piety and happiness, were to the Greeks a mythical people, like the Uttarakurus of the Brahmans. Their name signifies "living beyond the mountains," and Boreas too, the north-wind, meant originally the wind from the mountains, and more particularly from the Rhipæan mountains. (See Preller, *Griechische Mythologie*, I. 157.) *Boras*, from which Boreas, is another form of *oros*, mountain, both derived from the same root which in Sanskrit yields *giri*, mountain, and in ancient Slavonic *gora*. (See Curtius, *Grundzüge der Griechischen Etymologie*, I. 814; ii. 67.)

The Ethiopians, equally known to Homer and Herodotus, were originally intended for dark-looking people in general. *Aithiops*, like *Aithops*, meant fiery-looking, from *aithein*, to light up, to burn, Sanskrit *idh*, to kindle. (See Curtius, l. c. I. 215.)

savage tribes, to make abstracts of their grammars
and extracts from their vocabularies. This would
necessarily have been work at second-hand, and all
I could have added of my own would have been a
criticism of their attempts at classifying some of the
clusters of languages in those distant regions, to
point out similarities which they might have over-
looked, or to protest against some of the theories
which they had propounded without sufficient evidence. All who have had to examine the accounts
of new languages, or families of languages, published
by missionaries or travellers, are aware how not
only their theories, but their facts, have to be sifted,
before they can be allowed to occupy even a temporary place in our handbooks, or before we should
feel justified in rectifying accordingly the frontiers
on the great map of the languages of mankind.
Thus I received but the other day some papers,
printed at Honolulu,[1] propounding the theory "that
all those tongues which we designate as the Indo-
European languages have their true root and origin
in the Polynesian language." "I am certain," the
author writes, "that this is the case as regards the
Greek and Sanskrit: I find reason to believe it to be
so as to the Latin and other more modern tongues,
— in short, as to all European languages, old and
young." And he proceeds: — "The second discovery which I believe I have made, and with which
the former is connected, is that the study of the Polynesian language gives us the key to the original function of language itself, and to its whole mechanism."

[1] *The Polynesian*, Honolulu, Sept. 27, Oct. 4, Oct. 11, 1862, — containing an Essay by Dr. J. Rae.

Strange as it may sound to hear the language of Homer and Ennius spoken of as an offshoot of the Sandwich Islands, mere ridicule would be a very inappropriate and very inefficient answer to such a theory. It is not very long ago that all the Greek and Latin scholars of Europe shook their heads at the idea of tracing the roots of the classical languages back to Sanskrit; and even at the present moment there are still many persons who cannot realize the fact that, at a very remote, but a very real period in the history of the world, the ancestors of the Homeric poets and of the poets of the Veda must have lived together as members of one and the same race, as speakers of one and the same idiom.

There are other theories not less startling than this, which would make the Polynesian the primitive language of mankind. I received lately a Comparative Grammar of the South-African Languages, printed at the Cape, written by a most learned and ingenious scholar, Dr. Bleek.[1] In it he proves that, with the exception of the Bushman tongue, which has not yet been sufficiently studied, the great mass of African languages may be reduced to two families. He shows that the Hottentot is a branch of the North-African class of languages,[2] and that it was sepa-

[1] *A Comparative Grammar of the South-African Languages*, by W. H. J. Bleek, Ph. D. 1862.

[2] When the Rev. R. Moffat was in England, a few years since, he met with a Syrian who had recently arrived from Egypt, and in reference to whom Mr. Moffat has the following note: — "On my giving him a specimen and a description of the Hottentot language, he remarked that he had seen slaves in the market of Cairo, brought a great distance from the interior, who spoke a similar language, and were not near so dark-colored as slaves in general. This corroborates the statement of ancient authors, whose description of a people inhabiting the interior regions of Northern

rated from its relatives by the intrusion of the second great family, the Kafir, or, as Appleyard calls them, Alliteral languages, which occupy (as far as our knowledge goes) the whole remaining portion of the South-African continent, extending on the eastern side from the Keiskamma to the equator, and on the western side from 32° southern to about 8° northern latitude. But the same author claims likewise a very prominent place for the African idioms, in the general history of human speech. "It is perhaps not too much to say," he writes (Preface, page viii), "that similar results may at present be expected from a deeper study of such primitive forms of language as the Kafir and the Hottentot exhibit, as followed, at the beginning of the century, the discovery of Sanskrit, and the comparative researches of Oriental scholars. The origin of the grammatical forms, of gender and number, the etymology of pronouns, and many other questions of the highest interest to the philologist, find their true solution in Southern Africa."

Africa answers to that of the Hottentot and Bushman." — "It may be conceived as possible, therefore, that the people here alluded to form a portion of the Hottentot race, whose progenitors remained behind in the interior country, to the south or southwest of Egypt, whilst the general emigration continued its onward course. Should this prove not incorrect, it might be reasonably conjectured that Egypt is the country from which the Hottentot tribes originally came. This supposition, indeed, is strengthened by the resemblance which appears to subsist between the Copts and Hottentots in general appearance." (Appleyard, *The Kafir Language.* 1850.) — "Since the Hottentot race is known only as a receding one, and traces of its existence extend into the interior of South Africa, it may be looked upon as a fragment of the old and properly Ethiopic population, stretched along the mountain-spine of Africa, through the regions now occupied by the Gallas; but cut through and now enveloped by tribes of a different stock." (J. C. Adamson, in *Journal of the American Oriental Society*, vol. iv. p. 449. 1854.)

But while we are thus told by some scholars that we must look to Polynesia and South Africa if we would find the clue to the mysteries of Aryan speech, we are warned by others that there is no such thing as an Aryan or Indo-European family of languages, that Sanskrit has no relationship with Greek, and that Comparative Philology, as hitherto treated by Bopp and others, is but a dream of continental professors.[1] How are theories and counter-theories of this kind to be treated? However startling and paradoxical in appearance, they must be examined before we can either accept or reject them. " Science," as Bunsen[2] said, " excludes no suppositions, however strange they may appear, which are not in themselves absurd — viz. demonstrably contradictory to its own principles." But by what tests and rules are they to be examined? They can only be examined by those tests and rules which the Science of Language has established in its more limited areas of research. " We must begin," as Leibnitz said, " with studying the modern languages which are within our reach, in order to compare them with one another, to discover their differences and affinities, and then to proceed to those which have preceded them in former ages, in order to show their filiation and their origin, and then to ascend step by step to the most ancient of tongues, the analysis of which must lead us to the only trustworthy con-

[1] See Mr. John Crawfurd's Essay *On the Aryan or Indo-Germanic Theory*, and an article by Professor T. Hewitt Key in the *Transactions of the Philological Society*, " The Sanskrit Language, as the Basis of Linguistic Science, and the Labours of the German School in that field, are they not overvalued?"

[2] *L. c.* p. 256.

clusions." The principles of Comparative Philology must rest on the evidence of the best known and the best analyzed dialects, and it is to them that we must look, if we wish for a compass to guide us through the most violent storms and hurricanes of philological speculation.[1]

I thought it best, therefore, to devote the present course of lectures to the examination of a very limited area of speech, — to English, French, German, Latin, and Greek, and, of course, to Sanskrit, — in order to discover or to establish more firmly some of the fundamental principles of the Science of Language. I believe there is no science from which we, the students of language, may learn more than from Geology. Now, in Geology, if we have once acquired a general knowledge of the successive strata that form the crust of the earth, and of the faunas and floras present or absent in each, nothing is so instructive as the minute exploration of a quarry close at hand, of a cave or a mine, in order to see things with our own eyes, to handle them, and to learn how every pebble that we pick up points a lesson of the widest range. I believe it is the same in the Science of Language. *One* word, however common, of our own dialect, if well examined and analyzed, will teach us more than the most ingenious speculations on the nature of speech and the origin of roots. We may accept it, I believe, as a general principle that what is real in modern formations is possible in more ancient formations; that what has been found to be true on a small scale

[1] *Lectures on the Science of Language*, First Series, p. 136, note (4th edition).

may be true on a larger scale. Principles like these, which underlie the study of Geology, are equally applicable to the study of Philology, though in their application they require, no doubt, the same circumspectness which is the great charm of geological reasoning.

A few instances will make my meaning clearer. They will show how the solution of some of the most difficult problems of Comparative Grammar may be found at our very door, and how theories that would seem fanciful and incredible if applied to the analysis of ancient languages, stand before us as real and undeniable facts in the very words which we use in our every-day conversation. They will at the same time serve as a warning against too rapid generalizations, both on the part of those who have no eye for distinctive features and see nothing but similarity in all the languages of the world, and on the part of those who can perceive but one kind of likeness, and who would fain confine the whole ocean of living speech within the narrow bars of Aryan or Semitic grammar.

We have not very far to go in order to hear such phrases as "he is a-going, I am a-coming," &c., instead of the more usual "he is going, I am coming." Now the fact is, that the vulgar or dialectic expression, "he is a-going," is far more correct than "he is going."[1] *Ing*, in our modern grammars, is called the termination of the participle present, but it does not exist as such in Anglo-Saxon. In Anglo-Saxon the termination of that participle is *ande* or *inde* (Gothic,

[1] Archdeacon Hare, *Words corrupted by False Analogy or False Derivation*, p. 65.

ands; Old High-German, *anter, enter;* Middle High-German, *ende;* Modern High-German, *end*). This was preserved as late as Gower's and Chaucer's time,[1] though in most cases it had then already been supplanted by the termination *ing*. Now what is that termination *ing* ?[2] It is clearly used in two different senses, even in modern English. If we say "a loving child," loving is a verbal adjective. If we say "loving our neighbor is our highest duty," loving is a verbal substantive. Again, there are many substantives in *ing*, such as *building*, *wedding*, *meeting*, where the verbal character of the substantive is almost, if not entirely, lost.

Now, if we look to Anglo-Saxon, we find the termination *ing* used —

1. To form patronymics; for instance, *Godvulfing*, the son of *Godvulf*. In the A. S. translation of the Bible, the son of *Elisha* is called *Elising*. In the plural these patronymics frequently become the names of families, clans, villages, towns, and nations, e. g. *Thyringas*, the Thuringians. Even if names in *ing* are derived from names of rivers or hills or trees, they may still be called patronymics, because in ancient times the ideas of relationship and descent were not confined to living beings.[3] People living near the Elbe might well be called the sons of the Elbe or Albings, as, for instance, the Nordalbingi in Holstein. Many of the geographical

---

[1] Pointis and sleves be wel sittánde
Full right and straight upon the hande.
Rom. of the Rose, 2264.

[2] Grimm, *Deutsche Grammatik*, II. 348-365.

[3] See Förstemann, *Die Deutschen Ortsnamen*, p. 244; and *Zeitschrift für Vergleichende Sprachforschung*, i. 109.

names in England and Germany were originally such patronymics. Thus we have the villages[1] of *Malling*, of *Billing*, &c., or in compounds, *Mallington*, *Billingborough*. In *Walsingham*, the home of the *Walsings*, the memory of the famous race of the *Wælsings* may have been preserved, to which Siegfried belonged, the hero of the Nibelunge.[2] In German names, such as *Göttingen* in Hanover, *Harlingen* in Holland, we have old genitives plural, in the sense of "the home of the Gottings, the home of the Harlings," &c.[3]

2. *Ing* is used to form more general attributive words, such as, *æpeling*, a man of rank; *lyteling*, an infant; *niðing*, a bad man. This *ing* being frequently preceded by another suffix, the *l*, we arrive at the very common derivative *ling*, in such words as *darling*, *hireling*, *yearling*, *foundling*, *nestling*, *worldling*, *changeling*. It is doubtful, in fact, whether even in such words as *æpeling*, *lyteling*, which end in *l*, the suffix is not rather *ling* than *ing*, and whether the original spelling was not *æpelling* and *lytelling*. Thus *farthing*, too, is a corruption of *feorðling*, German *vierling*.

[1] Latham, *History of the English Language*, I. p. 223; Kemble, *Saxons in England*, l. p. 59, and Appendix, p. 449.
[2] Grimm, *Deutsche Heldensage*, p. 14.
[3] Harlings, in A. S. Herelingas (*Trav. Song*, L 224); Harlonge (W. Grimm, *Deut. Heldensage*, p. 280, &c.), are found at Harling in Norfolk and Kent, and at Harlington (Herelingatûn) in Bedfordshire and Middlesex. The Wælsings, in Old Norse Völsungar, the family of Sigurdr or Siegfried, reappear at Walsingham in Norfolk, Wolsingham in Northumberland, and Woolsingham in Durham. The Billings at Billinge, Billingham, Billinghoe, Billinghurst, Billingden, Dillington, and many other places. The Þyringas, in Thoringion or Thorrington, are likely to be offshoots of the great Hermunduric race, the Thyringi or Thoringi, now Thuringians, always neighbors of the Saxons. — Kemble, *Saxons in England*, l. pp. 60, 63.

It has been supposed that the modern English participle was formed by the same derivative, but in A. S. this suffix *ing* is chiefly attached to nouns and adjectives, not to verbs. There was, however, another derivative in A. S., which was attached to verbs in order to form verbal substantives. This was *ung*, the German *ung*. For instance, *clænsung*, cleansing; *beácnung*, beaconing; &c. In early A. S. these abstract nouns in *ung* are far more numerous than those in *ing*. *Ing*, however, began soon to encroach on *ung*, and at present no trace is left in English of substantives derived from verbs by means of *ung*.

Although, as I said, it might seem more plausible to look on the modern participle in English as originally an adjective in *ing*, such popular phrases as *a-going*, *a-thinking*, point rather to the verbal substantives in *ing* as the source from which the modern English participle was derived. "I am going" is in reality a corruption of "I am a-going," i. e. "I am on going," and the participle present would thus, by a very simple process, be traced back to a locative case of a verbal noun.[1]

Let us lay it down, therefore, as a fact, that the place of the participle present may, in the progress of dialectic regeneration, be supplied by the locative or some other case of a verbal noun.

Now let us look to French. On June 3, 1679,

---

[1] Cf. Garnett's paper "On the Formation of Words from Inflected Cases," *Philological Society*, vol. III, No. 54, 1847. Garnett compares the Welsh *yn sefyll*, in standing, Ir. *ag seasamh*, on standing, the Gaelic *ag acolgadh*. The same ingenious and accurate scholar was the first to propose the theory of the participle being formed from the locative of a verbal noun.

the French Academy decreed that the participles present should no longer be declined.[1]

What was the meaning of this decree? Simply what may now be found in every French grammar, namely, that *commençant, finissant,* are indeclinable when they have the meaning of the participle present, active or neuter; but that they take the terminations of the masculine and feminine, in the singular and plural, if they are used as adjectives.[2] But what is the reason of this rule? Simply this, that *chantant,* if used as a participle, is not the Latin participle present *cantans,* but the so-called gerund, that is to say, the oblique case of a verbal noun, the Latin *cantando* corresponding to the English *a-singing,* while the real Latin participle present, *cantans,* is used in the Romance languages as an adjective, and takes the feminine termination, — for instance, "*une femme souffrante,*" &c.

Here, then, we see again that in analytical languages the idea conveyed by the participle present can be expressed by the oblique case of a verbal noun.

Let us now proceed to a more distant, yet to a cognate language, the Bengali. We there find[3] that the so-called infinitive is formed by *te,* which *te* is, at the same time, the termination of the locative singular. Hence the present, *Karitechi,* I am doing.

[1] Cf. Egger, *Notions élémentaires de Grammaire Comparée,* Paris, 1856, p. 197. — La règle est faite. On ne declinera plus les participes présents. — B. Jullien, *Cours Supérieur,* L p. 186.

[2] Diez, *Vergleichende Grammatik der Romanischen Sprachen,* ii. p. 114.

[3] M. M.'s Essay on the Relation of the Bengali to the Aryan and Aboriginal Languages of India: *Report of the British Association for the Advancement of Science,* 1847, pp. 344, 345. Cf. Garnett, L c. p. 29.

and the imperfect, *Karitechilâm*, I was doing, are mere compounds of *âchi*, I am, *âchilâm*, I was, with what may be called a participle present, but what is in reality a verbal noun in the locative. *Karitechi*, I do, means " I am on doing," or " I am a-doing."

Now the question arises, Does this perfectly intelligible method of forming the participle from the oblique case of a verbal noun, and of forming the present indicative by compounding this verbal noun with the auxiliary verb " to be," supply us with a test that may be safely applied to the analysis of languages which decidedly belong to a different family of speech? Let us take the Bask, which is certainly neither Aryan nor Semitic, and which has thrown out a greater abundance of verbal forms than almost any known language.[1] Here the present is formed by what is called a participle, followed by an auxiliary verb. This participle, however, is formed by the suffix *an*, and the same suffix is used to form the locative case of nouns. For instance, *mendia*, the mountain; *mendiaz*, from the mountain; *mendian*, in the mountain; *mendico*, for the sake of the mountain. In like manner, *etchean*, in the house; *ohean*, in the bed. If, then, we examine the verb,

    erorten niz, I fall;
    " hiz, thou fallest;
    " da, he falls;

we see again in *erorten* a locative, or, as it is called, a positive case of the verbal substantive *erorta*, the

---

[1] See Inchauspe's *Le Verbe Basque*, published by Prince Louis-Lucien Bonaparte. Bayonne, 1858.

root of which would be *eror*, falling;[1] so that the indicative present of the Bask verb does not mean

[1] Cf. *Dissertation critique et apologétique sur la Langue Basque* (par l'Abbé Darrigol), Bayonne, p. 102. "Commençons par l'expression *erortean*. Cette façon de parler signifie en tombant, mais par quel secret? La voici: le point où l'on est (abl) s'exprime par le cas positif, comme *barnean* (dans l'intérieur), *etchean* (dans la maison), *ohean* (dans le lit), &c. Or l'action que l'on fait présentement peut être envisagée comme le point où l'on est, et dès lors s'exprime aussi par le positif; de là l'expression *erortean* n'est autre chose que l'infinitif *erortea* (le tomber) mis au cas positif; elle signifie donc littéralement dans le tomber.

Cette façon de parler, qui paraît extraordinaire quand on l'entend analyser pour la première fois, n'est pas une locution propre à notre langue; on dit en hébreu *biphkad* (en visitant), et le sens littéral de ce mot est *dans visiter*: on dit en grec *en tō piptein* (en tombant, littéralement *dans le tomber*), *en tō phileis tou Theou* (mot à mot *dans l'aimer Dieu*). Quand Virgile a dit, *et centure parce, et respondere parati*, il a sous-entendu la particule *in* devant le premier infinitif, disent les commentateurs. Nous disons en français, être à manger, à boire &c., comme être à la maison, à la campagne &c.

Comme l'action sur laquelle on est présentement peut être assimilée au point de l'espace où l'on existe, où l'on agit (abl), elle peut de même représenter un point de départ (aude). C'est ainsi que nous envisageons souvent dans le français l'action exprimée par l'infinitif, puisque nous disons, *Je viens de voir la capitale*, comme *Je viens de la capitale*, *Je viens de visiter mes greniers*, comme *Je viens de mes greniers*. Les actions *voir*, *visiter* sont envisagées ici comme des points de départ, et par cette fiction elles deviennent complémens de la préposition *de*, aussi bien que les noms *capitale*, *greniers*. C'est la même fiction et la même tournure dans l'hébreu *miphphekod*, dans le latin, *à visitando*.

Ces observations faites, il est aisé de comprendre que les formes basques en *ic*, telles que *jatetic*, *edatetic*, *ikustetic*, &c. ne sont que les ablatifs des noms *jatea*, *edatea*, *ikustea*, ablatifs commandés par le point de vue sous lequel on envisage les actions qu'expriment ces mots. Ainsi cette phrase, *Çare nitarren ikustetic jiten niz* (je viens de voir votre père), signifie, mot à mot, *je viens du voir de votre père*.

Les formes *janic*, *edanic*, *ikusiric*, ont évidemment une terminaison commune avec celles dont nous venons de parler, et sont également des ablatifs qui expriment un rapport d'éloignement, ou dans l'ordre physique ou dans l'ordre moral; toute la différence des premières formes aux dernières, consiste en ce que celles-là ont un sens actif, et celles-ci un sens passif. Conséquemment cette phrase, *Çare aita ikusiric jiten niz*, signifie, comme celle de l'exemple précédent, *Je viens de voir votre père*. Mais si l'on veut rendre plus scrupuleusement la force du mot *ikusiric*, il faut dire ici, *Je viens*

either *I fall*, or *I am falling*, but was intended originally for " I (am) in the act of falling," or,

de votre père eu. Et qu'on ne dise pas que cette traduction supposerait qu'il y a *ikusitic*, et non *ikusiric* ; nous avons observé plus d'une fois que la première des deux formules est l'ablatif singulier, et l'autre l'ablatif de la section indéfinie, comme on le voit dans ces façons de parler, *Ez da eginic* (il n'y en a point de fait), *Ez da erreric* (il n'y en a point de cuit), &c.

L'action que l'on va faire peut être envisagée comme un point de l'espace où l'on se porte (*quó*); et ce rapport d'approximation, ce mouvement moral vers l'action dont il s'agit, s'exprime heureusement par le cas appelé approximatif. Conformément à cette doctrine, nous disons, *Hastera noa*, *Mintzatcera noa*, *Ikhustern noa* (*Je vais commencer, Je vais parler, Je vais voir*), ou plutôt, *Je vais au commencer, Je vais au parler* &c., comme *Je vais au jardin* &c., en hébreu *liphkod*, en latin *ad visitandum* &c.

Le lieu par où l'on passe (*quâ*), l'espace ou le *milieu* que l'on traverse (*medium*), l'instrument ou le *moyen* par lequel une chose se fait (*medium*), veulent dans le basque le cas appelé médiatif, caractérisé par la terminaison *az*, *ez*, *iz*, *oz*, *uz*. Il n'est pas difficile de reconnaître cette inflexion dans les mots *jancz*, *ikhusiz*, *baratzez*, &c. De là, quand je dis *Giçona janes bici da* (l'homme vit en mangeant), la traduction littérale est l'*homme vit par le manger*, ou plutôt l'homme vit par le mangé ; car *janes* dérive de la forme *jan*, qui est tout à la fois et le radical de cette famille, et l'inflexion passive de ce mot, comme on le voit en disant *jana* (le mangé ou la chose mangée).

Nous voici maintenant en état d'apprécier au juste une infinité de mots que l'on avait coutume d'appeler verbes. Prenons par exemple le soi-disant verbe *tomber*; il fait au présent *erorten niz* (je tombe), *erorten his* (tu tombes), *erorten da* (il tombe), *erorten girè* (nous tombons), &c. Si ce que nous avons dit de l'expression *erortean* est exact, la formule *erortean niz* doit signifier, *je suis dans le tomber*, ou *dans l'acte de tomber*. Il est vrai que nous disons, par syncope, *erorten* pour *erortean*; mais de quelle conséquence peut être la suppression de la lettre *a*, puisqu'on dit indifféremment, selon le dialecte, *etchean*, *etchen* ou *etchin* (dans la maison)? Si cependant on veut attacher quelque importance à cette voyelle, il est permis de croire que son absence dénote l'absence de l'article ; ce qui ne paraît pas invraisemblable, après ce qui a été dit à la page 46.

Il résulte de cette observation que, dans les formules du présent *erorten niz*, *erorten his*, &c., le mot *erorten*, qui exprime l'action de tomber, n'est pas un verbe, mais bien un nom au cas positif.

Le prétérit *erori niz* (je suis tombé) se compose aussi du verbe *niz* (je suis) et de la formule passive *erori*, dont le sens adjectif se manifeste encore mieux si l'on y ajoute l'article, en disant *eroria niz*, c'est à dire, mot à mot, *je suis tombé*, ou celui qui est tombé.

to return to the point from whence we started, *I am a-falling.* The *a* in *a-falling* stands for an original *on.* Thus *asleep* is *on sleep, aright* is *onrihte, away* is *onweg, aback* is *onbæc, again* is *ongén* (Ger. *entgegen*), *among* is *ongemang*, &c.

This must suffice as an illustration of the principles on which the Science of Language rests, namely, that what is real in modern formations must be admitted as possible in more ancient formations, and that what has been found to be true on a small scale may be true on a larger scale.

But the same illustration may also serve as a warning. There is much in the Science of Language to tempt us to overstep the legitimate limits of inductive reasoning. We may infer from the known to the unknown in language tentatively, but not positively. It does not follow, even within so small a sphere as the Aryan family of speech, that what is possible in French is possible in Latin, that what

---

Le futur *erorico sis* (je tomberai) offre le même verbe et la même forme passive avec la terminaison *co,* laquelle est propre à exprimer la futurition, par la vertu qu'elle a de signifier la destination *à, pour.* C'est dans ce même goût que l'on dit en espagnol, *está por llegar* (il est pour arriver).

Notre futur s'exprime encore par la désinence *en*, comme *joukeren nis* (je me lèverai), *joanen nis* (j'irai). Pour comprendre que cette formule n'exprime le futur que par une valeur empruntée de la déclinaison, il suffit d'observer que le cas destinatif *aitarentçat, aitarendaco* (pour le père), *amarentçat, amarendaco* (pour la mère), s'abrège quelquefois en cette manière, *aitaren, amaren,* &c. Cette observation faite, l'on comprend aisément que la double formule dont il s'agit n'est synonyme en cet endroit que parcequ'elle l'est aussi dans la déclinaison.

Tout ce que nous avons dit des infinitifs combinés avec le verbe *niz,* se vérifie également dans leur combinaison avec le verbe *dut*; ainsi *ikhusten dut,* pour *ikhusten dut,* répond littéralement au mauvais latin *habeo in videre; ikhusi dut* serait *habeo risum; ikhusico dut,* ou *ikhusiren dut, habeo videndum.*

explains Bengali will explain Sanskrit; nay, the similarity between some of the Aryan languages and the Bask in the formation of their participles should be considered as an entirely exceptional case. Mr. Garnett, however, after establishing the principle that the participle present may be expressed by the locative of a verbal noun, endeavors in his excellent paper to show that the original Indo-European participle, the Latin *amans*, the Greek *typtōn*, the Sanskrit *bodhat*, were formed on the same principle:— that they are all inflected cases of a verbal noun. In this, I believe, he has failed,[1] as many have failed before and after him, by imagining that what has been found to be true in one portion of the vast kingdom of speech *must* be equally true in all. This is not so, and cannot be so. Language, though its growth is governed by intelligible principles throughout, was not so uniform in its progress as to repeat exactly the same phenomena at every stage of its life. As the geologist looks for different characteristics when he has to deal with London clay, with Oxford clay, or with old red sandstone, the student of language, too, must be prepared for different formations, even though he confines himself to one stage in the history of language, the *inflectional*. And if he steps beyond this, the most modern stage, then to apply indiscriminately to the lower stages of human speech, to the *agglutinative* and *radical*, the same tests which have proved successful in the in-

[1] He takes the Sanskrit *dravat* as a possible ablative, likewise *tas-at*, and *tan-vat* (sic). It would be impossible to form ablatives in *dt* (as) from verbal bases raised by the vikaranas of the special tenses, nor would the ablative be so appropriate a case as the locative, for taking the place of a verbal adjective.

flectional, would be like ignoring the difference between aqueous, igneous, and metamorphic rocks. There are scholars who, as it would seem, are incapable of appreciating more than one kind of evidence. No doubt the evidence on which the relationship of French and Italian, of Greek and Latin, of Lithuanian and Sanskrit, of Hebrew and Arabic, has been established, is the most satisfactory; but such evidence is possible only in inflectional languages that have passed their period of growth, and have entered into the stage of phonetic decay. To call for the same evidence in support of the homogeneousness of the Turanian languages, is to call for evidence which, from the nature of the case, it is impossible to supply. As well might the geologist look for fossils in granite! The Turanian languages allow of no grammatical petrifactions like those on which the relationship of the Aryan and Semitic families is chiefly founded. If they did, they would cease to be what they are; they would be inflectional, not agglutinative.

If languages were all of one and the same texture, they might be unravelled, no doubt, with the same tools. But as they are not,—and this is admitted by all,—it is surely mere waste of valuable time to test the relationship of Tungusic, Mongolic, Turkic, Samoyedic, and Finnic dialects by the same criteria on which the common descent of Greek and Latin is established; or to try to discover Sanskrit in the Malay dialects, or Greek in the idioms of the Caucasian mountaineers. The whole crust of the earth is not made of lias, swarming with Ammonites and Plesiosauri, nor is all language made of Sanskrit, teeming with Supines and Paulo-pluperfects. Up to a certain point the method by which so great results have been achieved in classifying the Aryan languages may be applicable to other clusters of speech. Phonetic laws are always useful, but they are not the only tools which the student of language must learn to handle. If we compare the extreme members of the Polynesian dialects, we find but little agreement in what may be called their grammar, and many of their words seem totally distinct. But if we compare their numerals, we clearly see that these are common property; we perceive similarity. though at the same time great diversity: — [1]

	1	2	3	4	5
Fakaafoan	tasi	lua, ua	tolu	fa	lima
Samoan	tasi	lua	tolu	fa	lima
Tongan	taha	ua	tolu	fa	nima
New Zealand	tahi	rua	toru	wa	rima
Rarotongan	tai	rua	toru	a	rima
Mangarevan	tai	rua	toru	a	rima
Paumotuan	rari	ite	qeti	ope	qeka
Tahitian	tahi	rua, piti	toru	ha, maha	rima, pae
Hawaiian	tahi	lua	tolu	ha, tauna	lima
Nukuhivan	tahi	ua	tou	ha or fa	ima

	6	7	8	9	10
Fakaafoan	ono	fitu	valu	iva	fulu, nafulu
Samoan	ono	fitu	valu	iva	sefulu, nafulu
Tongan	ono	fitu	valu	hiva	hopofulu
New Zealand	ono	witu	waru	iwa	qaburu
Rarotongan	ono	itu	varu	iva	nauru
Mangarevan	ono	itu	varu	iva	nauru
Paumotuan	hene	hito	hawa	nipa	horihori
Tahitian	ono, fene	hitu	varu, vau	iva	ahuru
Hawaiian	ono	hitu	valu	iwa	ámi
Nukuhivan	ono	hitu, fitu	vau	iva	onohuu

[1] Hale, *United States Exploring Expedition*, vol. vii. p. 246.

PHONETIC LAWS. 35

We begin to note the phonetic changes that have taken place in one and the same numeral, as pronounced by different islanders; we thus arrive at phonetic laws, and these, in their turn, remove the apparent dissimilarity in other words which at first seemed totally irreconcilable. Let those who are inclined to speak disparagingly of the strict observance of phonetic rules in tracing the history of Aryan words, and who consider it mere pedantry to be restrained by Grimm's Law from identifying such words as Latin *cura* and *care*, Greek *kaléîn* and *to call*, Latin *peto* and *to bid*, Latin *corvus* and *crow*, look to the progress that has been made by African and Polynesian philologists in checking the wild spirit of etymology even where they have to deal with dialects never reduced as yet to a fixed standard by the influence of a national literature, never written down at all, and never analyzed before by grammatical science. The whole of the first volume of Dr. Bleek's " Comparative Grammar of the South-African Languages" treats of Phonology, of the vowels and consonants peculiar to each dialect, and of the changes to which each letter is liable in its passage from one dialect into another (see page 82, *seq.*). And Mr. Hale, in the seventh volume of the " United States Exploring Expedition " (p. 232), has not only given a table of the regular changes which words common to the numerous Polynesian languages undergo, but he has likewise noted those permutations which take place occasionally only. On the strength of these phonetic laws once established, words which have hardly one single letter in common have been traced back with perfect certainty to one and the same source.

But mere phonetic decay will not account for the differences between the Polynesian dialects, and unless we admit the process of dialectic regeneration to a much greater extent than we should be justified in doing in the Aryan and Semitic families, our task of reconciliation would become hopeless. Will it be believed that since the time of Cook five of the ten simple numerals in the language of Tahiti have been thrown off and replaced by new ones? This is, nevertheless, the fact.

> Two was *rua*; it is now *piti*.
> Four was *ha*; it is now *maha*.
> Five was *rima*; it is now *pae*.
> Six was *ono*; it is now *fene*.
> Eight was *varu*; it is now *vau*.[1]

It is clear that if a radical or monosyllabic language, like Chinese, begins to change and to break out in independent dialects, the results must be very different from those which we observe in Latin as split up into the Romance dialects. In the Romance dialects, however violent the changes which made Portuguese words to differ from French, there always remain a few fibres by which they hang together. It might be difficult to recognize the French *plier*, to fold, to turn, in the Portuguese *chegar*, to arrive, yet we trace *plier* back to *plicare*, and *chegar* to the Spanish *llegar*, the old Spanish *plegar*, the Latin *plicare*,[2] here used in the sense of

---

[1] *United States Exploring Expedition under the command of Charles Wilkes.* "Ethnography and Philology," by H. Hale. Vol. vii. p. 289.
[2] Diez, *Lexicon*, s. v. llegar; *Grammar*, i. p. 379.

plying or turning towards a place, arriving at a place. But when we have to deal with dialects of Chinese, everything that could possibly hold them together seems hopelessly gone. The language now spoken in Cochin-China is a dialect of Chinese, at least as much as Norman French was a dialect of French, though spoken by Saxons at a Norman court. There was a native language of Cochin-China, the Annamitic,[1] which forms, as it were, the Saxon of that country on which the Chinese, like the Norman, was grafted. This engrafted Chinese, then, is a dialect of the Chinese which is spoken in China, and it is most nearly related to the spoken dialect of Canton. Yet few Chinese scholars would recognize Chinese in the language of Cochin-China. It is, for instance, one of the most characteristic features of the literary Chinese, the dialect of Nankin, or the idiom of the Mandarins, that every syllable ends in a vowel, either pure or nasal.[2] In Cochin-Chinese, on the contrary, we find words ending in k, t, p. Thus, ten is *thap*, at Canton *chap*, instead of the Chinese *tchi*.[3] No wonder that the early missionaries described the Annamitic as totally distinct

---

[1] On the native residuum in Cochin-Chinese, see Léon de Rosny, *Tableau de la Cochinchine*, p. 138.

[2] Endlicher, *Chinesische Grammatik*, par. 50, 78, 96.

[3] Léon de Rosny, *Tableau de la Cochinchine*, p. 295. He gives as illustrations: —

	Annamique.	Cantonnais.
dix	thap	chap
pouvoir	dak	tak
sang	houet	hœět
forêt	lam	lam.

He likewise mentions double consonants in the Chinese as spoken in Cochin-China, namely, bl, dy, ml, ty, tv; also f, r, s. As final consonants he gives ch, k, m, n, ng, p, t. — P. 296.

from Chinese. One of them says:—" When I arrived in Cochin-China, and heard the natives speak, particularly the women, I thought I heard the twittering of birds, and I gave up all hope of ever learning it. All words are monosyllabic, and people distinguish their significations only by means of different accents in pronouncing them. The same syllable, for instance, *daï*, signifies twenty-three entirely different things, according to the difference of accent, so that people never speak without singing."[1] This description, though somewhat exaggerated, is correct in the main, there being six or eight musical accents or modulations in this as in other monosyllabic tongues, by which the different meanings of one and the same monosyllabic root are kept distinct. These accents form an element of language which we have lost, but which was most important during the primitive stages of human speech.[2] The Chinese language commands no more than about 450 distinct sounds, and with them it expresses between 40,000 and 50,000 words or meanings.[3] These meanings are now kept distinct by means of composition, as in other languages by derivation, but in the radical stage words with more than twenty significations would have bewildered the hearer entirely, without some hints to indicate their actual intention. Such hints were given by different intonations. We have something left of this faculty in the tone of our sentences. We distinguish an interrogative from a positive sentence by the raising of our voice. (Gone? Gone.) We pronounce *Yes* very differently when we

[1] Léon de Rosny, l. c. p. 301.
[2] See Beaulieu, *Mémoire sur l'origine de la Musique*, 1802. *Lectures on the Science of Language*, First Series, p. 278.

mean *perhaps* (Yes, this may be true), or *of course* (Yes, I know it), or *really* (Yes? is it true?) or *truly* (Yes, I will). But in Chinese, in Annamitic (and likewise in Siamese and Burmese), these modulations have a much wider application. Thus in Annamitic, *ba* pronounced with the grave accent means a lady, an ancestor; pronounced with the sharp accent it means the favorite of a prince; pronounced with the semi-grave accent, it means what has been thrown away; pronounced with the grave circumflex, it means what is left of a fruit after it has been squeezed out; pronounced with no accent, it means three; pronounced with the ascending or interrogative accent, it means a box on the ear. Thus —

Ba, bà, bả, bá,

is said to mean, if properly pronounced, "Three ladies gave a box on the ear to the favorite of the prince." How much these accents must be exposed to fluctuation in different dialects is easy to perceive. Though they are fixed by grammatical rules, and though their neglect causes the most absurd mistakes, they were clearly in the beginning the mere expression of individual feeling, and therefore liable to much greater dialectic variation than grammatical forms, properly so called. But let us take what we might call grammatical forms in Chinese, in order to see how differently they too fare in dialectic dispersion, as compared with the terminations of inflectional languages. Though the grammatical organization of Latin has been wellnigh used up in French, we still see in the *s* of the plural a remnant of the Latin paradigm. We can trace the one back to the other. But in Chinese, where the plural is formed by the addition of some word meaning " multitude, heap, flock, class," what trace of original relationship remains when one dialect uses one, another another word? The plural in Cochin-Chinese is formed by placing *fo* before the substantive. This *fo* means many, or a certain number. It may exist in Chinese, but it is certainly not used there to form the plural. Another word employed for forming plurals is *nung*, several, and this again is wanting in Chinese. It fortunately happens, however, that a few words expressive of plurality have been preserved both in Chinese and Cochin-Chinese; as, for instance, *choung*, clearly the Chinese *tchoung*,[1] meaning conflux, vulgus, all, and used as an exponent of the plural; and *kak*, which has been identified with the Chinese *kw*. The last identification may seem doubtful; and if we suppose that *choung*, too, had been given up in Cochin-Chinese as a term of plurality, how would the tests which we apply for discovering the original identity of the Aryan languages have helped us in determining the real and close relationship between Chinese and Cochin-Chinese?

The present indicative is formed in Cochin-Chinese by simply putting the personal pronoun before the root. Thus, —

Toy men, I love.
Mai men, thou lovest.
No men, he loves.

The past tense is formed by the addition of *da*, which means "already." Thus, —

Toy da men, I loved.
Mai da men, thou lovedst.
No da men, he loved.

[1] Endlicher, *Chinesische Grammatik*, § 182.

The future is formed by the addition of *chè*.
Thus, —

Toy chè men,	I shall love.
Mai chà men,	thou wilt love.
No chè men,	he will love.

Now, have we any right, however convinced we may be of the close relationship between Chinese and Cochin-Chinese, to expect the same forms in the language of the Mandarins? Not at all. The pronoun of the first person in Cochin-Chinese is not a pronoun, but means "servant." "I love" is expressed in that civil language by "servant loves."[1] In Chinese the same polite phraseology is constantly observed,[2] but the words used are not the same, and do not include *toy*, servant. Instead of *ngò*, I, the Chinese would use *kuà ǵin*, little man; *tcin*, subject; *tsie*, thief; *tu*, blockhead. Nothing can be more polite; but we cannot expect that different nations should hit on exactly the same polite speeches, though they may agree in the common sense of grammar. The past tense is indicated in Chinese by particles meaning "already" or "formerly," but we do not find among them the Annamitic *da*. The same applies to the future. The system is throughout the same, but the materials are different. Shall we say, therefore, that these languages cannot be proved to be related, because they do not display the same criteria of relationship as French and English, Latin and Greek, Celtic and Sanskrit?

I tried in one of my former lectures to explain some of the causes which in nomadic dialects pro-

[1] Léon de Rosny, l. c. 302.   [2] Endlicher, § 206.

duce a much more rapid shedding of words than in literary languages, and I have since received ample evidence to confirm the views which I then expressed. My excellent friend, the Bishop of Melanesia, of whom it is difficult to say whether we should admire him most as a missionary, or as a scholar, or as a bold mariner, meets in every small island with a new language, which none but a scholar could trace back to the Melanesian type. "What an indication," he writes, "of the jealousy and suspicion of their lives, the extraordinary multiplicity of these languages affords! In each generation, for aught I know, they diverge more and more; provincialisms and local words, &c. perpetually introduce new causes for perplexity."

I shall mention to-day but one new, though insignificant cause of change in the Polynesian languages, in order to show that it is difficult to overestimate the multifarious influences which are at work in nomadic dialects, constantly changing their aspect and multiplying their number; and in order to convince even the most incredulous how little we know of all the secret springs of language if we confine our researches to a comparison of the classical tongues of India, Greece, Italy, and Germany.

The Tahitians,[1] besides their mataphorical expressions, have another and a more singular mode of displaying their reverence towards their king, by a custom which they term *Te pi*. They cease to employ, in the common language, those words which form a part or the whole of the sovereign's name, or that of one of his near relatives, and invent new terms to

[1] Dale, l. c. p. 288.

supply their place. As all names in Polynesian are significant, and as a chief usually has several, it will be seen that this custom must produce a considerable change in the language. It is true that this change is only temporary, as at the death of the king or chief the new word is dropped, and the original term resumed. But it is hardly to be supposed that after one or two generations the old words should still be remembered and be reinstated. Anyhow, it is a fact that the missionaries, by employing many of the new terms, give them a permanency which will defy the ceremonial loyalty of the natives. Vancouver observes (Voyage, vol. i. p. 135) that at the accession of Otu, which took place between the visit of Cook and his own, no less than forty or fifty of the most common words, which occur in conversation, had been entirely changed. It is not necessary that all the simple words which go to make up a compound name should be changed. The alteration of one is esteemed sufficient. Thus in *Po-mare*, signifying " the night (*po*) of coughing (*mare*)," only the first word, *po*, has been dropped, *mi* being used in its place. So in *Ai-mata* (eye-eater), the name of the present queen, the *ai* (eat) has been altered to *amu*, and the *mata* (eye) retained. In *Te-arii-na-vaha-roa* (the chief with the large mouth), *roa* alone has been changed to *maoro*. It is the same as if, with the accession of Queen Victoria, either the word *victory* had been tabooed together, or only part of it, for instance *tori*, so as to make it high treason to speak during her reign of *Tories*, this word being always supplied by another; such, for instance, as Liberal-Conservative. The object was clearly to guard against the name of the sovereign being ever used, even by accident, in ordinary conversation, and this object is attained by tabooing even one portion of his name.

"But this alteration," as Mr. Hales continues, "affects not only the words themselves, but syllables of similar sound in other words. Thus the name of one of the kings being *Tu*, not only was this word, which means " to stand," changed to *tia*, but in the word *fetu*, star, the last syllable, though having no connection, except in sound, with the word *tu*, underwent the same alteration,— star being now *fetia*; *tui*, to strike, became *tiai*; and *tu pa pau*, a corpse, *tia pa pau*. So *ha*, four, having been changed to *maha*, the word *aha*, split, has been altered to *amaha*, and *murihá*, the name of a month, to *muriáha*. When the word *ai* was changed to *amu*, *maraai*, the name of a certain wind (in Rarotongan, *maranai*), became *maraamu*."

"The mode of alteration, or the manner of forming new terms, seems to be arbitrary. In many cases, the substitutes are made by changing or dropping some letter or letters of the original word, as *hopoi* for *hapai*, to carry in the arms; *ene* for *hono*, to mend; *au* for *tau*, fit; *hio* for *tio*, to look; *ea* for *ara*, path; *vau* for *varu*, eight; *vea* for *vera*, not, &c. In other cases, the word substituted is one which had before a meaning nearly related to that of the term disused,— as *tia*, straight, upright, is used instead of *tu*, to stand; *pae*, part, division, instead of *rima*, five; *piti*, together, has replaced *rua*, two, &c. In some cases, the meaning or origin of the new word is unknown, and it may be a mere invention — as *ofai* for *ohatu*, stone; *pape*, for *vai*, water; *pohe* for *mate*, dead, &c. Some have been adopted from the neighboring Paumotuan, as *rui*, night, from *ruki*, dark; *fene*, six, from *hene*; *avae*, moon, from *kawake*."

"It is evident that but for the rule by which the old terms are revived on the death of the person in whose name they entered, the language might, in a few centuries, have been completely changed, not, indeed, in its grammar, but in its vocabulary."

It might, no doubt, be said that the *Te pi* is a mere accident, a fancy peculiar to a fanciful race, but far too unimportant to claim any consideration from the philosophical student of language. I confess that at first it appeared to myself in the same light, but my attention was lately drawn to the fact that the same peculiarity, or at least something very like it, exists in the Kafir languages. "The Kafir women," as we are told by the Rev. J. W. Appleyard, in his excellent work on the Kafir language,[1] "have many words peculiar to themselves. This arises from a national custom, called *Ukuhlonipa*, which forbids their pronouncing any word which may happen to contain a sound similar to one in the names of their nearest male relations." It is perfectly true that the words substituted are at first no more than

[1] *The Kafir Language*, comprising a sketch of its history; which includes a general classification of South-African dialects, ethnographical and geographical; remarks upon its nature; and a grammar. By the Rev. J. W. Appleyard, Wesleyan missionary in British Kaffraria. King William's Town: Printed for the Wesleyan Missionary Society; sold by Godlonton and White, Graham's Town, Cape of Good Hope, and by John Mason, 66 Paternoster Row, London. 1850. Appleyard's remarks on Ukuhlonipa were pointed out to me by the Rev. F. W. Farrar, the author of an excellent work on the *Origin of Language*.

family idioms — nay, that they would be confined to the gossip of women, and not enter into the conversation of men. But the influence of women on the language of each generation is much greater than that of men. We very properly call our language in Germany our mother-tongue, *Unsere Muttersprache*, for it is from our mothers that we learn it, with all its peculiarities, faults, idioms, accents. Cicero, in his " Brutus " (c. 58), said: " It makes a great difference whom we hear at home every day, and with whom we speak as boys, and how our fathers, our tutors, and our mothers speak. We read the letters of Cornelia, the mother of the Gracchi, and it is clear from them that her sons were brought up, not in the lap, but, so to say, in the very breath and speech of their mother." And again (Rhet. iii. 12), when speaking of his mother-in-law, Crassus said, " When I hear Lælia (for women keep old fashions more readily, because, as they do not hear the conversation of many people, they will always retain what they learned at first); but when I hear her, it is as if I were listening to Plautus and Nævius."

But this is not all. Dante ascribed the first attempts at using the vulgar tongue in Italy for literary compositions to the silent influence of ladies who did not understand the Latin language. Now this vulgar Italian, before it became the literary language of Italy, held very much the same position there as the so-called Prâkrit dialects in India; and these Prâkrit dialects first assumed a literary position in the Sanskrit plays where female characters, both high and low, are introduced as speaking Prâkrit, instead of the Sanskrit employed by kings, noblemen, and priests. Here, then, we have the language of women, or, if not of women exclusively, at all events of women and domestic servants, gradually entering into the literary idiom, and in later times even supplanting it altogether; for it is from the Prâkrit, and not from the literary Sanskrit, that the modern vernaculars of India branched off in course of time. Nor is the simultaneous existence of two such representatives of one and the same language as Sanskrit and Prâkrit confined to India. On the contrary, it has been remarked that several languages divide themselves from the first into two great branches; one showing a more manly, the other a more feminine character; one richer in consonants, the other richer in vowels; one more tenacious of the original grammatical terminations, the other more inclined to slur over these terminations, and to simplify grammar by the use of circumlocutions. Thus we have Greek in its two dialects, the Æolic and the Ionic, with their subdivisions, the Doric and Attic. In German we find the High and the Low German; in Celtic, the Gadhelic and Cymric, as in India the Sanskrit and Prâkrit; and it is by no means an unlikely explanation, that, as Grimm suggested in the case of High and Low German, so likewise in the other Aryan languages, the stern and strict dialects, the Sanskrit, the Æolic, the Gadhelic, represent the idiom of the fathers and brothers, used at public assemblies; while the soft and simpler dialects, the Prâkrit, the Ionic, and the Cymric, sprang originally from the domestic idiom of mothers, sisters, and servants at home.

But whether the influence of the language of
women be admitted on this large scale or not, certain it is, that through a thousand smaller channels
their idioms everywhere find admission into the domestic conversation of the whole family, and into
the public speeches of their assemblies. The greater
the ascendency of the female element in society, the
greater the influence of their language on the language of a family or a clan, a village or a town.
The cases, however, that are mentioned of women
speaking a totally different language from the men,
cannot be used in confirmation of this view. The
Caribe women, for instance, in the Antille Islands,[1]
spoke a language different from that of their husbands, because the Caribes had killed the whole
male population of the Arawakes and married their
women; and something similar seems to have taken
place among some of the tribes of Greenland.[2] Yet
even these isolated cases show how, among savage
races, in a primitive state of society, language may
be influenced by what we should call purely accidental causes.

But to return to the Kafir language, we find in it
clear traces that what may have been originally a
mere feminine peculiarity — the result, if you like,
of the bashfulness of the Kafir ladies — extended its
influence. For, in the same way as the women
eschew words which contain a sound similar to the
names of their nearest male relatives, the men also
of certain Kafir tribes feel a prejudice against employing a word that is similar in sound to the name
of one of their former chiefs. Thus, the Amambalu

[1] Hervas, Catalogo, l. p. 212. [2] Ibid. l. p. 269.

do not use *ilanga*, the general word for *sun*, because their first chief's name was *Ulanga*, but employ *isota* instead. For a similar reason, the Amagqunukwebi substitute *immela* for *isitshetshe*, the general term for knife.[1]

Here, then, we may perceive two things: first, the influence which a mere whim, if it once becomes stereotyped, may exercise on the whole character of a language (for we must remember, that, as every woman had her own male relations, and every tribe its own ancestors, a large number of words must constantly have been *tabooed* and supplanted in these African and Polynesian dialects); secondly, the curious coincidence that two great branches of speech, the Kafir and the Polynesian, should share in common what at first sight would seem a merely accidental idiosyncrasy, a thing that might have been thought of once, but never again. It is perfectly true that such principles as the *Te pi* and the *Ukuhlonipa* could never become powerful agents in the literary languages of civilized nations, and that we must not look for traces of their influence either in Sanskrit, Greek, or Latin, as known to us. But it is for that very reason that the study of what I call *Nomad* languages, as distinguished from *State* languages, becomes so instructive. We see in them what we can no longer expect to see even in the most ancient Sanskrit or Hebrew. We watch the childhood of language with all its childish freaks, and we learn at least this one lesson, that there is more in language than is dreamt of in our philosophy.

[1] Appleyard, l. c. p. 70.

One more testimony in support of these views. Mr. H. W. Bates, in his latest work, "The Naturalist on the Amazons," writes: "But language is not a sure guide in the filiation of Brazilian tribes, seven or eight languages being sometimes spoken on the same river within a distance of 200 or 300 miles. There are certain peculiarities in Indian habits which lead to a quick corruption of language and segregation of dialects. When Indians, men or women, are conversing amongst themselves, they seem to take pleasure in inventing new modes of pronunciation, or in distorting words. It is amusing to notice how the whole party will laugh when the wit of the circle perpetrates a new slang term, and these new words are very often retained. I have noticed this during long voyages made with Indian crews. When such alterations occur amongst a family or horde, which often live many years without communication with the rest of their tribe, the local corruption of language becomes perpetuated. Single hordes belonging to the same tribe, and inhabiting the banks of the same river, thus become, in the course of many years' isolation, unintelligible to other hordes, as happens with the Collinas on the Jurúa. I think it, therefore, very probable that the disposition to invent new words and new modes of pronunciation, added to the small population and habits of isolation of hordes and tribes, are the causes of the wonderful diversity of languages in South America." — (Vol. i. pp. 329, 330.)

As I intend to limit the present course of lectures chiefly to Greek and Latin, with its Romance offshoots; English, with its Continental kith and kin;

and the much-abused, though indispensable, Sanskrit, I thought it necessary thus from the beginning to guard against the misapprehension that the study of Sanskrit and its cognate dialects could supply us with all that is necessary for the Science of Language. It can do so as little as an exploration of the tertiary epoch could tell us all about the stratification of the earth. But, nevertheless, it can tell us a great deal. By displaying to us the minute laws that regulate the changes of each consonant, each vowel, each accent, it disciplines the student, and teaches him respect for every jot and title in any, even the most barbarous, dialect he may hereafter have to analyze. By helping us to an understanding of that language in which we think, and of others most near and dear to us, it makes us perceive the great importance which the Science of Language has for the Science of the Mind. Nay, it shows that the two are inseparable, and that without a proper analysis of human language we shall never arrive at a true knowledge of the human mind. I quote from Leibniz: — " I believe truly," he says, " that languages are the best mirror of the human mind, and that an exact analysis of the signification of words would make us better acquainted than anything else with the operations of the understanding."

I propose to divide my lectures into two parts. I shall first treat of what may be called the body or the outside of language, the sounds in which language is clothed, whether we call them letters, syllables, or words; describing their origin, their formation, and the laws which determine their growth and decay. In this part we shall have to deal with some of the more important principles of Etymology.

In the second part I mean to investigate what may be called the soul or the inside of language; examining the first conceptions that claimed utterance, their combinations and ramifications, their growth, their decay, and their resuscitation. In that part we shall have to inquire into some of the fundamental principles of Mythology, both ancient and modern, and to determine the sway, if any, which language as such exercises over our thoughts.

LECTURE II.

LANGUAGE AND REASON.

THE division of my subject which I sketched out at the end of my last lecture is liable, I am aware, to some grave objections. To treat of sound as independent of meaning, of thought as independent of words, seems to defy one of the best established principles of the science of language. Where do we ever meet in reality, I mean in the world such as it is, with articulate sounds — sounds like those that form the body of language, existing by themselves, and independent of language? No human being utters articulate sounds without an object, a purpose, a meaning. The endless configurations of sound which are collected in our dictionaries would have no existence at all, they would be the mere ghost of a language, unless they stood there as the embodiment of thought, as the realization of ideas. Even the interjections which we use, the cries and screams which are the precursors, or, according to others, the elements, of articulate speech, never exist without meaning. Articulate sound is always an utterance, a bringing out of something that is within, a manifestation or revelation of something that wants to manifest and to reveal itself. It would be different if language had been invented by agreement; if certain wise kings, priests, and philosophers had put their heads together and decreed that certain conceptions should be labelled and ticketed with certain sounds. In that case we might speak of the sound as the outside, of the ideas as the inside of language; and no objection could be raised to our treating each of them separately.

Why it is impossible to conceive of living human language as having originated in a conventional agreement, I endeavored to explain in one of my former lectures. But I should by no means wish to be understood as denying the possibility of framing some language in this artificial manner, after men have once learnt to speak and to reason. It is the fashion to laugh at the idea of an artificial, still more of a universal language. But if this problem were really so absurd, a man like Leibniz would hardly have taken so deep an interest in its solution. That such a language should ever come into practical use, or that the whole earth should in that manner ever be of one language and one speech again, is hard to conceive. But that the problem itself admits of a solution, and of a very perfect solution, cannot be doubted.

As there prevails much misconception on this subject, I shall devote part of this lecture to a statement of what has been achieved in framing a philosophical and universal language.

Leibniz, in a letter to *Remond de Montmort*, written two years before his death, expressed himself with the greatest confidence on the value of what he calls his *Spécieuse Générale*, and we can hardly doubt that he had then acquired a perfectly clear in-eight into his ideal of a universal language.[1] "If he succeeded," he writes, "in stirring up distinguished men to cultivate the calculus with infinitesimals, it was because he could give palpable proofs of its use; but he had spoken to the Marquis de L'Hôpital and others, of his *Spécieuse Générale*, without gaining from them more attention than if he had been telling them of a dream. He ought to be able, he adds, to support his theory by some palpable use; but for that purpose he would have to carry out a part of his *Characteristics*, — no easy matter, particularly circumstanced as he then was, deprived of the conversation of men who would encourage and help him in this work."

A few months before this letter, Leibniz spoke with perfect assurance of his favorite theory. He admits the difficulty of inventing and arranging this philosophical language, but he maintains that, if once carried out, it could be acquired by others without a dictionary, and with comparative ease. He should be able to carry it out, he says, if he were younger and less occupied, or if young men of talent were by his side. A few eminent men might complete the work in five years, and within two years they might bring out the systems of ethics and metaphysics in the form of an incontrovertible calculus."

Leibniz died before he could lay before the world the outlines of his philosophical language, and many even among his admirers have expressed their doubts whether he ever had a clear conception of the nature of such a language. It seems hardly compatible, however, with the character of Leibniz to suppose

[1] *Guhrauer*, G. W. Freiherr von Leibnitz, 1846, vol. 1. p. 328.

that he should have spoken so confidently, that he should actually have placed this *Spécieuse Générale* on a level with his differential calculus, if it had been a mere dream. It seems more likely that Leibniz was acquainted with a work which, in the second half of the seventeenth century, attracted much attention in England, "The Essay towards a Real Character and a Philosophical Language,"[1] by Bishop Wilkins (London, 1668), and that he perceived at once that the scheme there traced out was capable of much greater perfection. This work had been published by the Royal Society, and the author's name was so well known as one of its founders, that it could hardly have escaped the notice of the Hanoverian philosopher, who was in such frequent correspondence with members of that society.

Now, though it has been the fashion to sneer at Bishop Wilkins and his Universal Language, his work seems to me, as far as I can judge, to offer the best solution that has yet been offered of a problem which, if of no practical importance, is of great interest from a merely scientific point of view; and though it is impossible to give an intelligible account of the Bishop's scheme without entering into particulars which will take up some of our time, it will help us, I believe, towards a better understanding of real language, if we can acquire a clear idea of what an artificial language would be, and how it would differ from living speech.

The primary object of the Bishop was not to in-

---

[1] The work of Bishop Wilkins is analyzed and criticised by Lord Monboddo, in the second volume of his *Origin and Progress of Language* Edinburgh, 1774.

vent a new spoken language, though he arrives at that in the end, but to contrive a system of writing or representing our thoughts that should be universally intelligible. We have, for instance, our numerical figures, which are understood by people speaking different languages, and which, though differently pronounced in different parts of the world, convey everywhere the same idea. We have besides such signs as $+$ plus, $-$ minus, $\times$ to be multiplied, $\div$ to be divided, $=$ equal, $<$ greater, $>$ smaller, ☉ sun, ☽ moon, ⊕ earth, ♃ Jupiter, ♄ Saturn, ♂ Mars, ♀ Venus, &c., which are intelligible to mathematicians and astronomers all over the world. "Now if to everything and notion," — I quote from Bishop Wilkins (p. 21), — "there were assigned a distinct mark, together with some provision to express grammatical derivations and inflections, this might suffice as to one great end of a real character, namely, the expression of our conceptions by marks, which shall signify things, and not words. And so, likewise, if several distinct words (sounds) were assigned to the names of such things, with certain invariable rules for all such grammatical derivations and inflections, and such only as are natural and necessary, this would make a much more easy and convenient language than is yet in being."

This suggestion, which, as we shall see, is not the one which *Bishop Wilkins* carried out, has lately been taken up by *Don Sinibaldo de Mas*, in his *Idéographie*.[1] He gives a list of 2600 figures, all formed

[1] *Idéographie.* Mémoire sur la possibilité et la facilité de former une écriture générale au moyen de laquelle tous les peuples puissent s'entendre mutuellement sans que les uns connaissent la langue des autres; écrit par

after the pattern of musical notes, and he assigns to each a certain meaning. According to the interval in which the head of such a note is placed, the same sign is to be taken as a noun, an adjective, a verb, or an adverb. Thus the same sign might be used to express love, to love, loving, and lovingly, by simply moving its head on the lines and spaces from f to e, d, and c. Another system of signs is then added to express gender, number, case, person, tense, mood, and other grammatical categories, and a system of hieroglyphics is thus formed, by which the author succeeds in rendering the first 150 verses of the Æneid. It is perfectly true, as the author remarks, that the difficulty of learning his 2000 signs is nothing in comparison with learning several languages; it is perfectly true, also, that nothing can exceed the simplicity of his grammatical notation, which excludes by its very nature everything that is anomalous. The whole grammatical framework consists of thirty-nine signs, whereas, as Don Sinibaldo remarks, we have in French 310 different terminations for the simple tenses of the ten regular conjugations, 1755 for the thirty-nine irregular conjugations, and 200 for the auxiliary verbs, a sum total of 2165 terminations, which must be learnt by heart.[1] It is perfectly true, again, that few persons would ever use more than 4000 words, and that by having the same sign used throughout as noun, verb, adjective, and adverb, this number might still be considerably reduced. There is, however, this fundamental difficulty, that the assignment of a certain sign to a cer-

Don Sinibaldo de Mas, Envoyé Extraordinaire et Ministre Plénipotentiaire de S. M. C. en Chine. Paris: B. Duprat, 1863.

[1] Page 99.

tain idea is purely arbitrary in this system, a difficulty which, as we shall now proceed to show, Bishop Wilkins endeavored to overcome in a very ingenious and truly philosophical way.

"If these marks or notes," he writes, " could be so contrived as to have such a dependence upon, and relation to, one another, as might be suitable to the nature of the things and notions which they represented; and so, likewise, if the names of things could be so ordered as to contain such a kind of *affinity* or *opposition* in their letters and sounds, as might be some way answerable to the nature of the things which they signified; this would yet be a farther advantage superadded, by which, besides the best way of helping the memory by natural method, the understanding likewise would be highly improved; and we should, by learning the character and the names of things, be instructed likewise in their natures, the knowledge of both of which ought to be conjoined."[1]

The Bishop, then, undertakes neither more nor less than a classification of all that is or can be known, and he makes this dictionary of notions the basis of a corresponding dictionary of signs, both written and spoken. All this is done with great circumspection, and if we consider that it was undertaken nearly two hundred years ago, and carried out by one man single-handed, we shall be inclined to judge leniently of what may now seem to us antiquated and imperfect in his *catalogue raisonné* of human knowledge. A careful consideration of his work will show us why this language, which was meant to be perma-

[1] Page 21.

nent, unchangeable, and universal, would, on the contrary, by its very nature, be constantly shifting. As our knowledge advances, the classification of our notions is constantly remodelled; nay, in a certain sense, all advancement of learning may be called a corrected classification of our notions. If a plant, classified according to the system of Linnæus, or according to that of Bishop Wilkins, has its own peculiar place in their synopsis of knowledge, and its own peculiar sign in their summary of philosophical language, every change in the classification of plants would necessitate a change in the philosophical nomenclature. The whale, for instance, is classified by Bishop Wilkins as a *fish*, falling under the division of *viviparous* and *oblong*. Fishes, in general, are classed as *substances, animate, sensitive, sanguineous*, and the sign attached to the whale, by Bishop Wilkins, expresses every one of those differences which mark its place in his system of knowledge. As soon, therefore, as we treat the whale no longer as a fish, but as a mammal, its place is completely shifted, and its sign or name, if retained, would mislead us quite as much as the names of rainbow, thunderbolt, sunset, and others, expressive of ancient ideas which we know to be erroneous. This would happen even in strictly scientific subjects.

Chemistry adopted *acid* as the technical name of a class of bodies of which those first recognized in science were distinguished by sourness of taste. But as chemical knowledge advanced, it was discovered that there were compounds precisely analogous in essential character, which were not sour, and consequently *acidity* was but an accidental quality of some of these bodies, not a necessary or universal character of all. It was thought too late to change the name, and accordingly in all European languages the term *acid*, or its etymological equivalent, is now applied to rock-crystal, quartz, and flint.

In like manner, from a similar misapplication of *salt*, in scientific use, chemists class the substance of which junk-bottles, French mirrors, windows, and opera-glasses are made, among the *salts*, while analysts have declared that the essential character, not only of other so-called salts, but of common kitchen-salt, the salt of salts, has been mistaken; that *salt is not salt*, and, accordingly, have excluded that substance from the class of bodies upon which, as their truest representative, it had bestowed its name.[1]

The Bishop begins by dividing all things which may be the subjects of language, into six classes or genera, which he again subdivides by their several differences. These six classes comprise:—

  A. Transcendental Notions.
  B. Substances.
  C. Quantities.
  D. Qualities.
  E. Actions.
  F. Relations.

In B to F we easily recognize the principal predicaments or categories of logic, the pigeon-holes in which the ancient philosophers thought they could stow away all the ideas that ever entered the human

[1] Marsh, *History of the English Language*, p. 211. Liebig, *Chemische Briefe*, 4th edit., L p. 96.

mind. Under A we meet with a number of more abstract conceptions, such as *kind, cause, condition,* &c.

By subdividing these six classes, the Bishop arrives in the end at forty classes, which, according to him, comprehend everything that can be known or imagined, and therefore everything that can possibly claim expression in a language, whether natural or artificial. To begin with the beginning, we find that his transcendental notions refer either to things or to words. Referring to things, we have:—

I. Transcendentals General, such as the notions of *kind, cause, differences, end, means, mode.* Here, under *kind,* we should find such notions as being, thing, notion, name, substance, accident, &c. Under notions of *cause,* we meet with author, tool, aim, stuff, &c.

II. Transcendentals of Mixed Relation, such as the notions of *general quantity, continued quantity, discontinued quantity, quality, whole and part.* Under *general quantity* the notions of greatness and littleness, excess and defect; under *continued quantity* those of length, breadth, depth, &c. would find their places.

III. Transcendental Relations of Actions, such as the notions of *simple action* (putting, taking), *comparate action* (joining, repeating, &c.), *business* (preparing, designing, beginning), *commerce* (delivering, paying, reckoning), *event* (gaining, keeping, refreshing), *motion* (going, leading, meeting).

IV. The Transcendental Notions of Discourse, comprehending all that is commonly comprehended under grammar and logic; ideas such as noun, verb, particle, prose, verse, letter, syllogism, question, affirmative, negative, and many more.

After these general notions, which constitute the first four classes, but before what we should call the categories, the Bishop admits two independent classes of transcendental notions, one for *God*, the other for the *World*, neither of which, as he says, can be treated as predicaments, because they are not capable of any subordinate species.

V. The fifth class, therefore, consists entirely of the idea of GOD.

VI. The sixth class comprehends the WORLD or universe, divided into *spiritual* and *corporeal*, and embracing such notions as spirit, angel, soul, heaven, planet, earth, land, &c.

After this we arrive at the five categories, subdivided into thirty-four subaltern genera, which, together with the six classes of transcendental notions, complete, in the end, his forty genera. The Bishop begins with *substance*, the first difference of which he makes to be *inanimate*, and distinguishes by the name of

VII. ELEMENT, as his seventh genus. Of this there are several differences, *fire, air, water, earth*, each comprehending a number of minor species.

Next comes SUBSTANCE INANIMATE, divided into *vegetative* and *sensitive*. The *vegetative* again he subdivides into *imperfect*, such as *minerals*, and *perfect*, such as *plants*.

The imperfect vegetative he subdivides into

VIII. STONE, and

IX. METAL.

STONE he subdivides by six differences, which, as he tells us, is the usual number of differences that he finds under every genus; and under each of these differences he enumerates several species, which seldom exceed the number of nine under any one.

Having thus gone through the *imperfect vegetative*, he comes to the *perfect*, or *plant*, which he says is a tribe so numerous and various, that he confesses he found a great deal of trouble in dividing and arranging it. It is in fact a botanical classification, not based on scientific distinctions like that adopted by Linnæus, but on the more tangible differences in the outward form of plants. It is interesting, if for nothing else, at least for the rich native nomenclature of all kinds of herbs, shrubs, and trees, which it contains.

The *herb* he defines to be a minute and tender plant, and he has arranged it according to its leaves, in which way considered, it makes his

X. Class, LEAF-HERBS.

Considered according to its flowers, it makes his

XI. Class, or FLOWER-HERBS.

Considered according to its seed-vessels, it makes his

XII. Class, or SEED-HERBS.

Each of these classes is divided by a certain number of differences, and under each difference numerous species are enumerated and arranged.

All other plants being woody, and being larger and firmer than the herb, are divided into

XIII. SHRUBS, and

XIV. TREES.

Having thus exhausted the vegetable kingdom, the Bishop proceeds to the animal or *sensitive*, as he calls it, this being the second member of his division of animate substance. This kingdom he divides into

XV. EXSANGUINEOUS.

XVI., XVII., XVIII. SANGUINEOUS, namely, FISH, BIRD, and BEAST.

Having thus considered the general nature of vegetables and animals, he proceeds to consider the parts of both, some of which are *peculiar* to particular plants and animals, and constitute his

XIX. Genus, PECULIAR PARTS;

while others are *general*, and constitute his

XX. Genus, GENERAL PARTS.

Having thus exhausted the category of *substances*, he goes through the remaining categories of *quantity*, *quality*, *action*, and *relation*, which, together with the preceding classes, are represented in the following table, the skeleton, in fact, of the whole body of human knowledge.

```
General; namely, those universal notions, whether belonging more
           properly to
                                              ( GENERAL. I.
           Things; called TRANSCENDENTAL { RELATION MIXED. II.
                                              ( RELATION OF ACTION. III.
           Words; DISCOURSE. IV.
Special; denoting either
   Creator. V.
   Creature; namely, such things as were either created or concreated by
        God, not excluding several of those notions which are framed by
        the minds of men, considered either
        Collectively; WORLD. VI.
        Distributively; according to the several kinds of beings, whether
             such as do belong to
        Substance.
             Inanimate; ELEMENT. VII.
             Animate; considered according to their several
                  Species; whether
                       Vegetative;
                            Imperfect; as Minerals { STONE. VIII.
                                                    { METAL. IX.
                                             ( HERB, considered ( LEAF. X.
                            Perfect; as Plant {     according to { FLOWER. XI.
                                             { SHRUB. XIII.      { SEED-VESSEL
                                             ( TREE. XIV.        ( XII.
                                    ( EXSANGUINEOUS. XV.
                       Sensitive {                ( FISH. XVI.
                                  { Sanguineous { BIRD. XVII.
                                                 ( BEAST. XVIII.
             Parts { PECULIAR. XIX.
                   { GENERAL. XX.
   Accident.
```

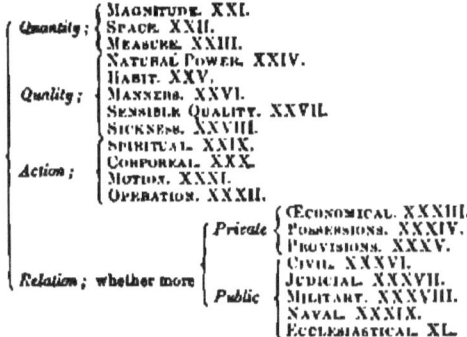

The Bishop is far from claiming any great merit for his survey of human knowledge, and he admits most fully its many defects. No single individual could have mastered such a subject, which would baffle even the united efforts of learned societies. Yet such as it is, and with all its imperfections, increased by the destruction of great part of his manuscript in the fire of London, it may give us some idea of what the genius of a Leibniz would have put in its place, if he had ever matured the idea which was from his earliest youth stirring in his brain.

Having completed, in forty chapters, his philosophical dictionary of knowledge, Bishop Wilkins proceeds to compose a philosophical grammar, according to which these ideas are to be formed into complex propositions and discourses. He then proceeds, in the fourth part of his work, to the framing of the language, which is to represent all possible notions, according as they have been previously arranged. He begins with the written language or *Real Char-*

acter, as he calls it, because it expresses things, and not sounds, as the common characters do. It is, therefore, to be intelligible to people who speak different languages, and to be read without, as yet, being pronounced at all. It were to be wished, he says, that characters could be found bearing some resemblance to the things expressed by them; also, that the sounds of a language should have some resemblance to their objects. This, however, being impossible, he begins by contriving arbitrary marks for his forty genera. The next thing to be done is to mark the differences under each genus. This is done by affixing little lines at the left end of the character, forming with the character angles of different kinds, that is, right, obtuse, or acute, above or below; each of these affixes, according to its position, denoting the first, second, third, and following difference under the genus, these differences being, as we saw, regularly numbered in his philosophical dictionary.

The third and last thing to be done is to express the species under each difference. This is done by affixing the like marks to the other end of the character, denoting the species under each difference, as they are numbered in the dictionary.

In this manner all the several notions of things which are the subject of language, can be represented by real characters. But, besides a complete dictionary, a grammatical framework, too, is wanted before the problem of an artificial language can be considered as solved. In natural languages the grammatical articulation consists either in separate particles or in modifications in the body of a word, to whatever cause such modifications may be ascribed. Bishop Wilkins supplies the former by marks denoting particles, these marks being circular figures, dots, and little crooked lines, or virgulæ, disposed in a certain manner. The latter, the grammatical terminations, are expressed by hooks or loops, affixed to either end of the character above or below, from which we learn whether the thing intended is to be considered as a noun, or an adjective, or an adverb; whether it be taken in an active or passive sense, in the plural or singular number. In this manner, everything that can be expressed in ordinary grammars, the gender, number, and cases of nouns, the tenses and moods of verbs, pronouns, articles, prepositions, conjunctions, and interjections, are all rendered with a precision unsurpassed, nay unequalled, by any living language.

Having thus shaped all his materials, the Bishop proceeds to give the Lord's Prayer and the Creed, written in what he calls his *Real Character;* and it must be confessed by every unprejudiced person that with some attention and practice these specimens are perfectly intelligible.

Hitherto, however, we have only arrived at a written language. In order to translate this written into a spoken language, the Bishop has expressed his forty genera or classes by such sounds as *ba*, *be*, *bi*, *da*, *de*, *di*, *ga*, *ge*, *gi*, all compositions of vowels, with one or other of the best-sounding consonants. The differences under each of these genera he expresses by adding to the syllable denoting the genus one of the following consonants, b, d, g, p, t, c, z, s, n, according to the order in which the differences were ranked before in the tables under each genus, *b* expressing the first difference, *d* the second, and so on.

The species is then expressed by putting after the consonant which stands for the difference one of the seven vowels, or, if more be wanted, the diphthongs.

Thus we get the following radicals corresponding to the general table of notions, as given above: —

I.	Transcen-	General	. . .	Ba
II.	dentals.	Relation Mixed	. .	Ba
III.		Relation of Action	.	Be
IV.		Discourse	. . .	Bi
V.		God	. . .	Da
VI.		World	. . .	Da
VII.		Element	. . .	De
VIII.		Stone	. . . .	Di
IX.		Metal	. . . .	Do
X.		Leaf	⎫	⎧ Ga
XI.		Flower	⎬ Herbs .	⎨ Ga
XII.		Seed-vessel	⎭	⎩ Gu
XIII.		Shrub	. . .	Gi
XIV.		Tree	. . . .	Go
XV.		Exsanguineous	.	Za
XVI.	Animals	Fish	. . .	Za
XVII.		Bird	. . .	Ze
XVIII.		Beast	. . .	Zi
XIX.	Parts	Peculiar	. . .	Pa
XX.		General	. . .	Pa
XXI.		Magnitude	.	Pe
XXII.	Quantity	Space	. . .	Pi
XXIII.		Measure	. . .	Po
XXIV.		Natural Power	.	Ta
XXV.		Habit	. . .	Ta
XXVI.	Quality	Manners	. . .	Tu
XXVII.		Quality, sensible	.	Ti
XXVIII.		Sickness	. . .	To
XXIX.		Spiritual	. . .	Ca
XXX.	Action	Corporeal	. . .	Ca
XXXI.		Motion	. . .	Ce
XXXII.		Operation	. . .	Ci

XXXIII.		Œconomical . .	Co
XXXIV.		Possessions . : .	Cy
XXXV.		Provisions . . .	Sa
XXXVI.	Relation	Civil	Se
XXXVII.		Judicial . . .	Se
XXXVIII.		Military . . .	Si
XXXIX.		Naval . . .	So
XL.		Ecclesiastical . .	Sy

The differences of the first genus would be expressed by,

B*a*b, b*a*d, b*a*g, b*a*p, b*a*t, b*a*c, b*a*z, b*a*s, b*a*n.

The species of the first difference of the first genus would be expressed by,

B*a*b*a*, b*a*b*a*, b*a*be, b*a*bi, b*a*bo, b*a*b*u*, b*a*by, b*a*byi, b*a*by*u*.

Here b*a*b*a* would mean being, b*a*b*a* thing, b*a*be notion, b*a*bi name, b*a*bo substance, b*a*b*u* quantity, b*a*by action, b*a*byi relation.

For instance, if *De* signify element, he says, then *Deb* must signify the first difference, which, according to the tables, is fire; and *Deba* will denote the first species, which is flame. *Det* will be the fifth difference under that genus, which is appearing meteor; *Deta* the first species, viz. rainbow; *Deta* the second, viz. halo.

Thus if *Ti* signify the genus of Sensible Quality, then *Tid* must denote the second difference, which comprehends colors, and *Tida* must signify the second species under that difference, viz. redness, &c.

The principal grammatical variations, laid down in the philosophical grammar, are likewise expressed by certain letters. If the word, he writes, is an adjective, which, according to his method, is always derived from a substantive, the derivation is made by the change of the radical consonant into another consonant, or by adding a vowel to it. Thus, if *Dᴀ* signifies God, *duᴀ* must signify divine; if *De* signifies element, then *due* must signify elementary; if *Do* signifies stone, then *duo* must signify stony. In like manner voices and numbers and such-like accidents of words are formed, particles receive their phonetic representatives; and again, all his materials being shaped, a complete grammatical translation of the Lord's Prayer is given by the Bishop in his own newly-invented philosophical language.

I hardly know whether the account here given of the artificial language invented by Bishop Wilkins will be intelligible, for, in spite of the length to which it has run, many points had to be omitted which would have placed the ingenious conceptions of its author in a much brighter light. My object was chiefly to show that to people acquainted with a real language, the invention of an artificial language is by no means an impossibility, nay, that such an artificial language might be much more perfect, more regular, more easy to learn, than any of the spoken tongues of man. The number of radicals in the Bishop's language amounts to not quite 3000, and these, by a judicious contrivance, are sufficient to express every possible idea. Thus the same radical, as we saw, expresses, with certain slight modifications, noun, adjective, and verb. Again, if *Dᴀ* is once known to signify God, then *idᴀ* must signify that which is opposed to God, namely, *idol.* If *dab* be spirit, *odab* will be body; if *dad* be heaven, *odad* will be hell. Again, if *saba* is king, *sava* is royalty, *salba* is reigning, *samba* to be governed, &c.

Let us now resume the thread of our argument. We saw that in an artificial language, the whole system of our notions, once established, may be matched to a system of phonetic exponents; but we maintain, until we are taught the contrary, that no real language was ever made in this manner.

There never was an independent array of determinate conceptions waiting to be matched with an independent array of articulate sounds. As a matter of fact, we never meet with articulate sounds except as wedded to determinate ideas, nor do we ever, I believe, meet with determinate ideas except as bodied forth in articulate sounds. This is a point of some importance on which there ought not to be any doubt or haze, and I therefore declare my conviction, whether right or wrong, as explicitly as possible, that thought, in one sense of the word, i. e. in the sense of reasoning, is impossible without language. After what I stated in my former lectures, I shall not be understood as here denying the reality of thought or mental activity in animals. Animals and infants that are without language, are alike without reason, the great difference between animal and infant being, that the infant possesses the healthy germs of speech and reason, only not yet developed into actual speech and actual reason, whereas the animal has no such germs or faculties, capable of development in its present state of existence. We must concede to animals " sensation, perception, memory, will, and judgment," but we cannot allow to them a trace of what the Greek called *lógos*,

i. e. reason, literally, gathering, a word which most rightly and naturally expresses in Greek both speech and reason.[1] *Lógos* is derived from *légein*, which, like Latin *legere*, means, originally, to gather. Hence *Katálogos*, a catalogue, a gathering, a list; *collectio*, a collection. In Homer,[2] *légein* is hardly ever used in the sense of saying, speaking, or meaning, but always in the sense of gathering, or, more properly, of telling, for to *tell* is the German *Zählen*, and means originally to count, to cast up. *Lógos*, used in the sense of reason, meant originally, like the English *tale*, gathering; for reason, "though it penetrates into the depths of the sea and earth, elevates our thoughts as high as the stars, and leads us through the vast spaces and large rooms of this mighty fabric,"[3] is nothing more or less than the gathering up of the single by means of the general.[4] The Latin *intelligo*, i. e. *interligo*, expresses still more graphically the interlacing of the general and the single, which is the peculiar province of the intellect. But *Lógos* used in the sense of word, means likewise a gathering, for every word, or, at least, every name is based on the same process; it represents the gathering of the single under the general.

[1] Cf. Farrar, p. 125; Heyse, p. 41.
[2] Od. xiv. 107, οὐ τι διαπρήξαιμι λέγων ἐμὰ κήδεα θυμοῦ. Ulysses says he should never finish if he were to tell the sorrows of his heart, i. e. if he were to count or record them, not simply if he were to speak of them.
[3] Locke, *On the Understanding*, iv. 17, 9.
[4] This, too, is well put by Locke (iii. 8, 20) in his terse and homely language: "I would say that all the great business of genera and species, and their essences, amounts to no more but this; that men making abstract ideas, and settling them in their minds, with names annexed to them, do thereby enable themselves to consider things, and discourse of them, as it were, *in bundles*, for the easier and readier improvement and communication of their knowledge, which would advance but slowly were their words and thoughts confined only to particulars."

As we cannot tell or count quantities without numbers, we cannot tell or recount things without words. There are tribes that have no numerals beyond four. Should we say that they do not know if they have five children instead of four? They certainly do, as much as a cat knows that she has five kittens, and will look for the fifth if it has been taken away from her. But if they have no numerals beyond four, they cannot reason beyond four. They would not know, as little as children know it, that two and three make five, but only that two and three make many. Though I dwelt on this point in the last lectures of my former course, a few illustrations may not be out of place here, to make my meaning quite clear.

Man could not name a tree, or an animal, or a river, or any object whatever in which he took an interest, without discovering first some general quality that seemed at the time the most characteristic of the object to be named. In the lowest stage of language, an imitation of the neighing of the horse would have been sufficient to name the horse. Savage tribes are great mimics, and imitate the cries of animals with wonderful success. But this is not yet language. There are cockatoos who, when they see cocks and hens, will begin to cackle as if to inform us of what they see. This is not the way in which the words of our languages were formed. There is no trace of *neighing* in the Aryan names for *horse*. In naming the *horse*, the quality that struck the mind of the Aryan man as the most prominent was its swiftness. Hence from the root *aś*,[1] to be sharp or

---

[1] Cf. Sk. âsu, quick, ὠκύς, ἀκωκή, point, and other derivatives given

swift (which we have in Latin *acus*, needle, and in the French diminutive *aiguille*, in *acuo*, I sharpen, in *acer*, quick, sharp, shrewd, in *acrimony*, and even in '*cute*), was derived *aśva*, the runner, the horse. This *aśva* appears in Lithuanian as *aszva* (mare), in Latin as *ekvus*, i. e. *equus*, in Greek as ἴκκος,[1] i. e. ἴππος, in Old Saxon as *ehu*. Many a name might have been given to the horse besides the one here mentioned, but whatever name was given it could only be formed by laying hold of the horse by means of some general quality, and by thus arranging the horse, together with other objects, under some general category. Many names might have been given to *wheat*. It might have been called eared, nutritious, graceful, waving, the incense of the earth, &c. But it was called simply the *white*, the white color of its grain seeming to distinguish it best from those plants with which otherwise it had the greatest similarity. For this is one of the secrets of *onomatopoësis*, or name-poetry, that each name should express, not the most important or specific quality, but that which strikes our fancy,[2] and seems most useful for the purpose of making other people understand what we mean. If we adopted the language of Locke, we should say that men were guided by *wit* rather than by *judgment*, in the formation of names. *Wit*, he says, lies most in the assemblage of ideas, and putting those together with quickness and variety, wherein can be found any resemblance or con-

by Curtius, *Griechische Etymologie*, I. 10). The Latin *catus*, sharp, has been derived from Sk. *ço* (*śyati*), to whet.

[1] *Etym. Magn.*, p. 474, 12., Ἴκκος σημαίνει τὸν ἵππον. Curtius, *G. E.*, ii. 48.

[2] Pott, *Etym. F.*, ii. 139.

gruity, thereby to make up pleasant pictures, and agreeable visions, in the fancy: judgment, on the contrary, lies quite on the other side, in separating carefully, one from another, ideas wherein can be found the least difference, thereby to avoid being misled by similitude, and by affinity, to take one thing for another.[1] While the names given to things according to Bishop Wilkins's philosophical method would all be founded on judgment, those given by the early framers of language repose chiefly on wit or fancy. Thus wheat was called the white plant, *hvaiteis* in Gothic, in A. S. *hvæte*, in Lithuanian *kwetys*, in English *wheat*, and all these words point to the Sanskrit *sveta*, i. e. white, the Gothic *hveits*, the A. S. *hvit*. In Sanskrit, *sveta*, white, is not applied to wheat (which is called *godhûma*, the smoke or incense of the earth), but it is applied to many other herbs and weeds, and as a compound (*svetasunga*, white-awned), it entered into the name of barley. In Sanskrit, silver is counted as white, and called *sveta*, and the feminine *sveti* was once a name of the dawn, just as the French *aube*, dawn, which was originally *alba*. We arrive at the same result whatever words we examine; they always express a general quality, supposed to be peculiar to the object to which they are attached. In some cases this is quite clear, in others it has to be brought out by minute etymological research. To those who approach these etymological researches with any preconceived opinions, it must be a frequent source of disappointment, when they have traced a word through all its stages to its first starting-point, to find in the end, or

[1] Locke, *On the Human Understanding*, II. 11, 2.

rather in the beginning, nothing but roots of the most
general powers, meaning to go, to move, to run, to
do. But on closer consideration, this, instead of being disappointing, should rather increase our admiration for the wonderful powers of language, man
being able out of these vague and pale conceptions to
produce names expressive of the minutest shades of
thought and feeling. It was by a poetical fiat that
the Greek *próbata*, which originally meant no more
than things walking forward, became in time the
name of cattle, and particularly of sheep. In Sanskrit, *sarit*, meaning *goer*, from *sar*, to go, became
the name of river; *sara*, meaning the same, what
runs or goes, was used for sap, but not for river.
Thus *dru*, in Sanskrit, means to run, *dravat*, quick;
but *drapsa* is restricted to the sense of a drop, *gutta*.
The Latin *ævum*, meaning going, from *i*, to go, became the name of time, age; and its derivative *æviternus*, or *æternus*, was made to express eternity.
Thus in French, *meubles* means literally anything
that is movable, but it became the name of chairs,
tables, and wardrobes. *Viande*, originally *vivenda*,
that on which one lives, came to mean meat. A
table, the Latin *tabula*, is originally what stands, or
that on which things can be placed (stood); it now
means what dictionaries define as "a horizontal surface raised above the ground, used for meals and
other purposes." The French *tableau*, picture, again
goes back to the Latin *tabula*, a thing stood up, exhibited, and at last to the root *stâ* of *stare*, to stand.
A *stable*, the Latin *stabulum*, comes from the same
root, but it was applied to the standing-place of animals, to stalls or sheds. That on which a thing

stands or rests is called its *base*, and *basis* in Greek meant originally no more than going, the base being conceived as ground on which it is safe to walk. What can be more general than *facies*, originally the make or shape of a thing, then the *face*? Yet the same expression is repeated in modern languages, *feature* being evidently a mere corruption of *factura*, the make. On the same principle the moon was called *luna*, i.e. *lucna* or *lucina*, the shining; the lightning, *fulmen* from *fulgere*, the bright; the stars *stellæ*, i.e. *sterulæ*, the Sanskrit *staras* from *stri*, to strew, the strewers of light. All these etymologies may seem very unsatisfactory, vague, uninteresting, yet, if we reflect for a moment, we shall see that in no other way but this could the mind, or the gathering power of man, have comprehended the endless variety of nature[1] under a limited number of categories or names. What Bunsen called "the first poesy of mankind," the creation of words, is no doubt very different from the sensation poetry of later days: yet its very poverty and simplicity render it all the more valuable in the eyes of historians and philosophers. For of this first poetry, simple as it is, or of this first philosophy in all its childishness, man only is capable. He is capable of it because he can gather the single under the general; he is capable of it because he has the faculty of speech; he is capable of it — we need not fear the tautology — because he is man.

[1] Cf. Sankara on Vedânta-Sûtra, 1, 3, 28 (Muir, *Sanskrit Texts*, iii. 67). âkritibhiś cha śabdânâm sambandho na vyaktibhih, vyaktînâm ânantyât sambandhagrahanânupapattah. "The relation of words is with the genera, not with individuals; for, as individuals are endless, it would be impossible to lay hold of relations."

NO SPEECH WITHOUT REASON.

Without speech no reason, without reason no speech. It is curious to observe the unwillingness with which many philosophers admit this, and the attempts they make to escape from this conclusion, all owing to the very influence of language which, in most modern dialects, has produced two words, one for language, the other for reason; thus leading the speaker to suppose that there is a substantial difference between the two, and not a mere formal difference. Thus Brown says: " To be without language, spoken or written, is *almost* to be without thought."[1] But he qualifies this *almost* by what follows: " That man can reason without language of any kind, and consequently without general terms, — though the opposite opinion is maintained by many very eminent philosophers, — seems to me not to admit of any reasonable doubt, or, if it required any proof, to be sufficiently shown by the very invention of language which involves these general terms, and still more sensibly by the conduct of the uninstructed deaf and dumb,[2] — to which also the evident marks of reasoning in the other animals — of reasoning which I cannot but think as unquestionable as the instincts that mingle with it — may be said to furnish a very striking additional argument from analogy."

The uninstructed deaf and dumb, I believe, have never given any signs of reason, in the true sense of the word, though to a certain extent all the deaf and dumb people that live in the society of other men catch something of the rational behavior of their neighbors. When instructed, the deaf and dumb certainly acquire general ideas without being able in

[1] Works, I. p. 475. [2] *L. c.*, ii. p. 448.

every case to utter distinctly the phonetic exponents or embodiments of these ideas which we call words. But this is no objection to our general argument. The deaf and dumb are taught by those who possess both these general ideas and their phonetic embodiments, elaborated by successive generations of rational men. They are taught to think the thoughts of others, and if they cannot pronounce their words, they lay hold of these thoughts by other signs, and particularly by signs that appeal to their sense of sight, in the same manner as words appeal to our sense of hearing. These signs, however, are not the signs of things or their conceptions, as words are: they are the signs of signs, just as written language is not an image of our thoughts, but an image of the phonetic embodiment of thought. Alphabetical writing is the image of the sound of language, hieroglyphic writing the image of language or thought.

The same supposition that it is possible to reason without signs, that we can form mental conceptions, nay, even mental propositions, without words, runs through the whole of Locke's philosophy.[1] He maintains over and over again, that words are signs *added* to our conceptions, and added arbitrarily. He imagines a state " in which man, though possessed of a great variety of thoughts, and such from which others, as well as himself, might receive profit and delight, was unable to make these thoughts appear. The comfort and advantage of society, however, not being to be had without communication of thoughts, it was necessary that man should find out some external sensible signs, whereby those in-

[1] Locke, *On the Human Understanding*, III. 2, 1.

visible ideas of which his thoughts are made up might be made known to others. For this purpose, nothing was so fit, either for plenty or quickness, as those articulate sounds, which, with so much ease and variety, he found himself able to make. Thus we may conceive how words, which were by nature so well adapted to that purpose, came to be made use of by men as the signs of their ideas; not by any natural connection there is between particular articulate sounds and certain ideas, — for then there would be but one language amongst all men, — but by a voluntary composition, whereby such a word is made arbitrarily the mark of such an idea."

Locke admits, indeed, that it is almost unavoidable, in treating of mental propositions, to make use of words. "Most men, if not all," he says, (and who are they that are here exempted?) "in their thinking and reasoning within themselves, make use of words, instead of ideas, at least when the subject of their meditation contains in it complex ideas."[1] But this is in reality an altogether different question; it is the question whether, after our notions have once been realized in words, it is possible to use words without reasoning, and not whether it is possible to reason without words. This is clear from the instances given by Locke. "Some confused or obscure notions," he says, "have served their turns; and many who talk very much of religion and conscience, of church and faith, of power and right, of obstructions and humors, melancholy and choler, would, perhaps, have little left in their thoughts and

[1] l. c., lv. 5, 4.

meditations, if one should desire them to think only of the things themselves, and lay by those words, with which they so often confound others, and not seldom themselves also."[1]

In all this there is, no doubt, great truth; yet, strictly speaking, it is as impossible to use words without thought as to think without words. Even those who talk vaguely about religion, conscience, &c., have at least a vague notion of the meaning of the words they use; and if they ceased to connect any ideas, however incomplete and false, with the words they utter, they could no longer be said to speak, but only to make noises. The same applies if we invert our proposition. It is possible, without language, to see, to perceive, to stare at, to dream about things; but, without words, not even such simple ideas as white or black can for a moment be realized.

We cannot be careful enough in the use of our words. If reasoning is used synonymously with knowing or thinking, with mental activity in general, it is clear that we cannot deny it either to the uninstructed deaf and dumb, or to infants and animals. A child *knows* as certainly before it can speak the difference between sweet and bitter (i. e. that sweet is not bitter), as it knows afterwards (when it comes to speak) that wormwood and sugar-plums are not the same thing.[2] A child receives the sensation of sweetness; it enjoys it, it recollects it, it desires it again; but it does not know what sweet is; it is absorbed in its sensations, its pleasures, its recollections; it cannot look at them from above, it can-

[1] L. c., iv. 5, 4.   [2] l. c., L 2, 15.

not reason on them, it cannot tell of them.[1] This is well expressed by Schelling. "Without language," he says, "it is impossible to conceive philosophical, nay, even any human consciousness: and hence the foundations of language could not have been laid consciously. Nevertheless, the more we analyze language, the more clearly we see that it transcends in depth the most conscious productions of the mind. It is with language as with all organic beings; we imagine they spring into being blindly, and yet we cannot deny the intentional wisdom in the formation of every one of them."[2]

Hegel speaks more simply and more boldly. "It is in names," he says, "that we think."[3]

It may be possible, however, by another kind of argument, less metaphysical, perhaps, but more convincing, to show clearly that reason cannot become real without speech. Let us take any word, for instance, *experiment*. It is derived from *experior*. *Perior*, like Greek *perân*,[4] would mean to go through. *Peritus* is a man who has gone through many things; *periculum*, something to go through, a danger. *Experior* is to go through and come out (the Sanskrit, *vyutpad*); hence *experience* and *experiment*. The Gothic *faran*, the English *to fare*, are the same words as *perân*; hence the German *Erfahrung*, experience, and *Gefahr*, periculum; *Wohlfahrt*, welfare,

[1] A child certainly knows that a stranger is not its mother; that its sucking-bottle is not the rod, long before he knows that it is impossible for the same thing to be and not to be. — Locke, *On the Human Understanding*, iv. 7, 9.
[2] *Einleitung in die Philosophie der Mythologie*, p. 52; Pott, *Etymologische Forschungen*, II. 281.
[3] Carrière, *Die Kunst im Zusammenhang der Culturentwickelung*, p. 11.
[4] Curtius, *G. E.*, i. 237.

the Greek *euporia*. As long, then, as the word experiment expresses this more or less general idea, it has a real existence. But take the mere sound, and change only the accent, and we get *experíment*, and this is nothing. Change one vowel or one consonant, *exporiment* or *esperiment*, and we have mere noises, what Heraclitus would call a mere *psóphos*, but no words. *Cháracter*, with the accent on the first syllable, has a meaning in English, but none in German or French; *charácter*, with the accent on the second syllable, has a meaning in German, but none in English or French; *charactère*, with the accent on the last, has a meaning in French, but none in English or German. It matters not whether the sound is articulate or not; articulate sound without meaning is even more unreal than inarticulate sound. If, then, these articulate sounds, or what we may call the body of language, exist nowhere, have no independent reality, what follows? I think it follows that this so-called body of language could never have been taken up anywhere by itself, and added to our conceptions from without; from which it would follow again that our conceptions, which are now always clothed in the garment of language, could never have existed in a naked state. This would be perfectly correct reasoning, if applied to anything else; nor do I see that it can be objected to as bearing on thought and language. If we never find skins except as the teguments of animals, we may safely conclude that animals cannot exist without skins. If color cannot exist by itself (ἄπαν γὰρ χρῶμα ἐν σώματι), it follows that neither can anything that is colored exist without color. A coloring substance may be added or removed; but color without some substance, however ethereal, is, *in rerum naturâ*, as impossible as substance without color, or as substance without form or weight.

Granting, however, to the fullest extent, the one and indivisible character of language and thought, agreeing even with the Polynesians, who express thinking by speaking in the stomach,[1] we may yet, I think, for scientific purposes, claim the same liberty which is claimed in so many sciences, namely, the liberty of treating separately what in the nature of things cannot be separated. Though color cannot be separated from some ethereal substance, yet the science of optics treats of light and color as if they existed by themselves. The geometrician reasons on lines without taking cognizance of their breadth, of plains without considering their depth, of bodies without thinking of their weight. It is the same in language, and though I consider the identity of language and reason as one of the fundamental principles of our science, I think it will be most useful to begin, as it were, by dissecting the dead body of language, by anatomizing its phonetic structure, without any reference to its function, and then to proceed to a consideration of language in the fulness of life, and to watch its energies, both in what we call its growth and its decay.

I tried to show in my first course of lectures, that if we analyze language, that is to say, if we trace words back to their most primitive elements, we arrive, not at letters, but at roots. This is a point which has not been sufficiently considered, and it

[1] Farrar, p. 125.

may almost be taken as the general opinion that the elements of language are vowels and consonants, but not roots. If, however, we call elements those primitive substances the combination of which is sufficient to account for things as they really are, it is clear that we cannot well call the letters the elements of language; for we might shake the letters together *ad infinitum*, without ever producing a dictionary, much less a grammar. It was a favorite idea of ancient philosophers to compare the atoms, the concurrence of which was to form all nature, with letters. Epicurus is reported to have said that — " The atoms come together in different order and position, like the letters, which, though they are few, yet, by being placed together in different ways, produce innumerable words."[1]

Aristotle, also, in his " Metaphysics," when speaking of Leucippus and Democritus, illustrates the different effects produced by the same elements by a reference to letters. "A," he says, "differs from N by its shape; AN from NA by the order of the letters; Z from N by its position."[2]

It is true, no doubt, that by putting the twenty-three or twenty-four letters together in every possible variety, we might produce every word that has ever been used in any language of the world. The number of these words, taking twenty-three letters as the basis, would be 25,852,016,738,884,976,640,000; or, if we take twenty-four letters, 620,448,401,733,-

[1] Lactantius, *Divin. Inst.*, lib. 8, c. 19. Varlo, inquit (Epicurus), ordine ac positione conveniunt atomi sicut literae, quae cum sint paucae, varie tamen collocatae innumerabilia verba conficiunt.

[2] *Metaph.*, l. 4, 11. Διαφέρει γὰρ τὸ μὲν A τοῦ N σχήματι, τὸ δὲ AN τοῦ NA τάξει, τὸ δὲ Z τοῦ N θέσει.

239,439,360,000.[1] But even then these trillions, billions, and millions of sounds, would not be words, for they would lack the most important ingredient, that which makes a word to be a word, namely, the different ideas by which they were called into life, and which are expressed differently in different languages.

"Element," Aristotle says, "we call that of which anything consists, as of its first substance, this being as to form indivisible; as, for instance, the elements of language (the letters) of which language is composed, and into which as its last component parts, it can be dissolved; while they, the letters, can no longer be dissolved into sounds different in form; but, if they are dissolved, the parts are homogeneous, as a part of water is water; but not so the parts of a syllable."

If here we take *phōnḗ* as voice, not as language, there would be nothing to object to in Aristotle's reasoning. The voice, as such, may be dissolved into vowels and consonants, as its primal elements. But not so speech. Speech is preëminently significant sound, and if we look for the elements of speech, we cannot on a sudden drop one of its two characteristic qualities, either its audibility or its significancy. Now letters as such are not significant; a, b, c, d, mean nothing, either by themselves or if put together. The only word that is formed of mere letters is "Alphabet" (ὁ ἀλφάβητος), the English ABC; but even here it is not the sounds, but the names of the letters, that form the word.

[1] Cf. Leibniz, *De Arte combinatoria, Opp.* t. II. pp. 387, 388, ed. Dutens; Pott, *Etym. Forsch.*, II. p. 9.

One other word has been supposed to have the same merely alphabetical origin, namely, the Latin *elementum*. As *elementa* is used in Latin for the ABC, it has been supposed, though I doubt whether in real earnest, that it was formed from the three letters l, m, n.

The etymological meaning of *elementa* is by no means clear, nor has the Greek *stoicheion*, which in Latin is rendered by *elementum*, as yet been satisfactorily explained. We are told that *stoicheion* is a diminutive from *stoichos*, a small upright rod or post, especially the gnomon of the sundial, or the shadow thrown by it; and under *stoichos* we find the meaning of a row, a line of poles with hunting-nets, and are informed that the word is the same as *stichos*, line, and *stóchos*, aim. How the radical vowel can change from *i* to *o* and *oi*, is not explained.

The question is, why were the elements, or the component primary parts of things, called *stoicheia* by the Greeks? It is a word which has had a long history, and has passed from Greece to almost every part of the civilised world, and deserves, therefore, some attention at the hand of the etymological genealogist. *Stoichos*, from which *stoicheion*, means a row or file, like *stix* and *stiches* in Homer. The suffix *eios* is the same as the Latin *eius*, and expresses what belongs to or has the quality of something. Therefore, as *stoichos* means a row, *stoicheion* would be what belongs to or constitutes a row. Is it possible to connect these words with *stóchos*, aim, either in form or meaning? Certainly not. Roots with i are liable to a regular change of i into *oi* or *ei*, but not into *o*. Thus the root *lip*, which appears in *élipon*, assumes the forms *leipo* and *léloipa*, and the same scale of vowel-changes may be observed in

liph, aleiphō, éloipha, and
pith, peíthō, pépoitha.

Hence *stoichos* presupposes a root *stich*, and this root would account in Greek for the following derivations : —

1, *stíx*, gen. *stichós*, a row, a line of soldiers.
2, *stíchos*, a row, a line; *distich*, a couplet.
3, *steíchō, éstichon,* to march in order, step by step; to mount.
4, *stoíchos*, a row, a file ; *stoichein*, to march in a line.

In German, the same root yields *steigen*, to step, to mount, and in Sanskrit we find *stigh*, to mount.

Quite a different root is presupposed by *stóchos*. As *tómos* points to a root *tam* (*témno, étamon*), or *bólos* to a root *bal* (*bélos, ébalon*), thus *stóchos* points to a root *stach*. This root does not exist in Greek in the form of a verb, and has left behind in the classical language this one formation only, *stóchos*, mark, point, aim, whence *stocházomai*, I point, I aim, and similar derivatives. In Gothic, a similar root exists in the verb *stiggan*, the English *to sting*.

A third root, closely allied with, yet distinct from, *stach*, has been more prolific in the classical languages, namely, *stig*, to stick.[1] From it we have *stizō, éstigmai*, I prick; in Latin, *in-stigare, stimulus*,

[1] Grimm, *Deutsche Sprache*, p. 853.

and *stilus* (for *stiglus*, like *palus* for *paglus*); Gothic *stikan*, to stick, German *stechen*.

The result at which we thus arrive is, that *stoicheion* has no connection with *stóchos*, and hence that it cannot, as the dictionaries tell us, have the primary meaning of a small upright rod or pole, or of the gnomon of the sundial. Where *stoicheion* (as in δεκάπουν στοιχείον, i. e. noon) is used with reference to the sundial, it means the lines of the shadow following each other in regular succession; the radii, in fact, which constitute the complete series of hours described by the sun's daily course. And this gives us the key to *stoicheion*, in the sense of elements. *Stoicheia* are the degrees or steps from one end to the other, the constituent parts of a whole, forming a complete series, whether as hours, or letters, or numbers, or parts of speech, or physical elements, provided always that such elements are held together by a systematic order. This is the only sense in which Aristotle and his predecessors could have used the word for ordinary and for technical purposes; and it corresponds with the explanation proposed by no less an authority than Dionysius Thrax. The first grammarian of Greece gives the following etymology of *stoicheia* in the sense of letters (§ 7):[1] — "The same are also called *stoicheia*, because they have a certain order and arrangement."[2] Why the Romans, who probably became for the first time acquainted with the idea of ele-

[1] Τὰ δὲ αὐτὰ καὶ στοιχεῖα καλεῖται διὰ τὸ ἔχειν στοιχόν τινα καὶ τάξιν.

[2] The explanation here suggested of *stoicheion* is confirmed by some remarks of Professor Pott, in the second volume of his *Etymologische Forschungen*, p. 191, 1861. The same author suggests a derivation of *elementum* from root **l**, solvere, with the preposition **è**. — *l. c.*, p. 193.

ments through their intercourse with Greek philosophers and grammarians, should have translated *stoicheia* by *elementa* is less clear. In the sense of physical elements, the early Greek philosophers used *rizómata*, roots, in preference to *stoicheia*, and if *elementa* stands for *alimenta*, in the sense of feeders, it may have been intended originally as a rendering of *rizómata*.

From an historical point of view, letters are not the *stoicheia* or *rizómata* of language. The simplest parts into which language can be resolved are the *roots*, and these themselves cannot be further reduced without destroying the nature of language, which is not mere sound, but always significant sound. There may be roots consisting of one vowel, such as *i*, to go, in Sanskrit, or 'i, one, in Chinese; but this would only show that a root may be a letter, not that a letter may be a root. If we attempted to divide roots like the Sk. *chi*, to collect, or the Chinese *tchi*, many, into *tch* and *i*, we should find that we had left the precincts of language, and entered upon the science of phonetics.

Before we do this — before we proceed to dissect the phonetic skeleton of human speech, it may be well to say a few words about *roots*. In my former Lectures I said, intentionally, very little about roots; at least very little about the nature or the origin of roots, because I believed, and still believe, that in the science of language we must accept roots simply as ultimate facts, leaving to the physiologist and the psychologist the question as to the possible sympathetic or reflective action of the five organs of sensuous perception upon the motory nerves of the organs of speech. It was for that reason that I gave a negative rather than a positive definition of roots, stating [1] that, for my own immediate purposes, I called root or radical whatever, in the words of any language or family of languages, cannot be reduced to a simpler or more original form.

It has been pointed out, however, with great logical acuteness, that, if this definition were true, roots would be mere abstractions, and as such unfit to explain the realities of language. Now, it is perfectly true, that, from one point of view, a root may be considered as a mere abstraction. A root is a cause, and every cause, in the logical acceptation of the word, is an abstraction. As a cause it can claim no reality, no vulgar reality; if we call real that only which can become the object of sensuous perception. In real language, we never hear a root; we only meet with their effects, namely, with words, whether nouns, adjectives, verbs, or particles. This is the view which the native grammarians of India have taken of Sanskrit roots; and they have taken the greatest pains to show that a root, as such, can never emerge to the surface of real speech; that there it is always a word, an effect, a substance clothed in the garment of grammatical derivatives. The Hindus call a root *dhâtu*, which is derived from the root *dhâ*,[2] to sup-

---

[1] p. 273.
[2] *Unâdi Sûtras*, l. 70, dudhâñ dhâranaposhanayoḥ. *Hetú*, the Sanskrit word for cause, cannot be referred to the same root from which *dhâtu* is derived; for though *dhâ* forms the participle *hita*, the *i* of *hi-ta* would not be liable to guṇa before *tu*. *Hetú* (*Unâdi Sûtras*, l. 73) is derived from *hi*, which Bopp identifies with *χιω* (Bopp, *Glossarium*, s. v. *hi*). This *χιω* and *χινέω* are referred by Curtius to the Latin *cio, cieo, citus, excito*, not however to the Sanskrit *hi*, but to root *śi*, to sharpen. — Cf. Curtius, *G. E.*, I. p. 118.

port or nourish. They apply the same word to their
five elements, which shows that, like the Greeks,
they looked upon these elements (earth, water, fire,
air, ether), and upon the elements of language, as the
supporters and feeders of real things and real words.
It is known that, in the fourth century B. C., the Hindus possessed complete lists, not only of their roots,
but likewise of all the formative elements, which, by
being attached to them, raise the roots into real
words.

Thus from a root *vid*, to know, they would form
by means of the suffix *ghañ*, *Veda*, i. e. knowledge;
by means of the suffix *tṛich*, *vettar*, a knower, Greek
hístōr and *ístōr*. Again, by affixing to the root certain verbal derivatives, they would arrive at *vedmi*, I
know, *viveda*, I have known, or *veda*, I know. Besides these derivatives, however, we likewise find in
Sanskrit the mere *vid*, used, particularly in compounds, in the sense of knowing; for instance, *dharmavid*, a knower of the law. Here, then, the root
itself might seem to appear as a word. But such is
the logical consistency of Sanskrit grammarians,
that they have actually imagined a class of derivative suffixes, the object of which is to be added to a
root for the sole purpose of being rejected again.
Thus only could the logical conscience of Pâṇini be
satisfied.[1] When we should say that a root is used
as a noun without any change except those that are

[1] In earlier works the meaning of *dhâtu* is not yet so strictly defined. In the *Prâtiśâkhya of the Rigveda*, xll. 5, a noun is defined as that which signifies a being, a verb as that which signifies being, and as such the verb is
identified with the root (Tan nâma yenâbhidadhâti sattvam, tad âkhyâ-
tam yena bhâvam, sa dhâtuḥ). In the *Nirukta*, too, verbs with different
verbal terminations are spoken of as dhâtus. — *Nighaṇṭu*, l. 20.

necessitated by phonetic laws (as, for instance, *dharmavit*, instead of *dharmavid*), Pâṇini says (iii. 3, 68), that a suffix (namely, *viṭ*) is added to the root *vid*. But if we come to inquire what this suffix means and why it is called *viṭ*, we find (vi. 1, 67) that a *lopa*, i. e. a lopping off, is to carry away the *v* of *viṭ*; that the final *ṭ* is only meant to indicate certain phonetic changes that take place if a root ends in a nasal (vi. 4, 41); and that the vowel *i* serves merely to connect these two algebraic symbols. So that the suffix *viṭ* is in reality nought. This is certainly strict logic, but it is rather cumbersome grammar, and from an historical point of view, we are justified in dropping these circumlocutions, and looking upon roots as real words.

With us, speaking inflectional and highly refined languages, roots are primarily what remains as the last residuum after a complete analysis of our own dialects, or of all the dialects that form together the great Aryan mass of speech. But if our analysis is properly made, what is to us a mere residuum must originally, in the natural course of events, have been a real germ; and these germinal forms would have answered every purpose in an early stage of language. We must not forget that there are languages which have remained in that germinal state, and in which there is to the present day no *outward* distinction between a root and a word. In Chinese,[1] for instance, *ly* means to plough, a plough, and an ox, i. e. a plougher; *ta* means to be great, greatness, greatly. Whether a word is intended as a noun, or a verb, or a particle, depends chiefly on the position

[1] Endlicher, *Chinesische Grammatik*, § 123.

which it occupies as a sentence. In the Polynesian[1] dialects, almost every verb may, without any change of form, be used as a noun or an adjective; whether it is meant for the one or the other must be learnt from certain particles, which are called particles of affirmation (kua), and the particles of the agent (ko). In Egyptian, as Bunsen states, there is no formal distinction between noun, verb, adjective, and particle, and a word like *an'h* might mean life, to live, living, lively.[2] What does this show? I think it shows that there was a stage in the growth of language, in which that sharp distinction which we make between the different parts of speech had not yet been fixed, and when even that fundamental distinction between subject and predicate, on which all the parts of speech are based, had not yet been realized in its fulness, and had not yet received a corresponding outward expression.

A slightly different view is propounded by Professor Pott, when he says: "Roots, it should be observed, as such, lack the stamp of words, and therefore their real value in the currency of speech. There is no inward necessity why they should first have entered into the reality of language, naked and formless; it suffices that, unpronounced, they fluttered before the soul like small images, continually clothed in the mouth, now with this, now with that form, and surrendered to the air to be drafted off in hundredfold cases and combinations."[3]

It might be said, that, as soon as a root is pronounced — as soon as it forms part of a sentence —

---

[1] Cf. Hale, p. 263.   [2] Bunsen's *Aegypten*, I. 331.
[3] *Etymologische Forschungen*, II. 95.

it ceases to be a root, and is either a subject or a predicate, or, to use grammatical language, a noun or a verb. Yet even this seems an artificial distinction. To a Chinese, the sound *ta*, even when pronounced, is a mere root; it is neither noun nor verb, distinctions which, in the form in which we conceive them, have no existence at all to a Chinese. If to *ta* we add *fu*, man, and when we put *fu* first and *ta* last, then, no doubt, *fu* is the subject, and *ta* the predicate, or, as our grammarians would say, *fu* is a noun, and *ta* a verb; *fu ta* would mean, "the man is great." But if we said *ta fu*, *ta* would be an adjective, and the phrase would mean "a great man." I can here see no real distinction between *ta*, potentially a noun, an adjective, a verb, an adverb, and *ta* in *fu ta*, used actually as an adjective or verb.

As the growth of language and the growth of the mind are only two aspects of the same process, it is difficult for us to think in Chinese, or in any radical language, without transferring to it our categories of thought. But if we watch the language of a child, which is in reality Chinese spoken in English, we see that there is a form of thought, and of language, perfectly rational and intelligible to those who have studied it, in which, nevertheless, the distinction between noun and verb, nay, between subject and predicate, is not yet realized. If a child says *Up*, that *up* is, to his mind, noun, verb, adjective, all in one. It means, "I want to get up on my mother's lap." If an English child says *ta*, that *ta* is both a noun, thanks, and a verb, I thank you. Nay, even if a child learns to speak grammatically, it does not yet think grammatically; it seems, in speaking, to wear the garments of its parents, though it has not yet grown into them. A child says, "I am hungry," without an idea that *I* is different from *hungry*, and that both are united by an auxiliary verb, which auxiliary verb again was a compound of a root *as*, and a personal termination *mi*, giving us the Sanskrit *asmi*, I am. A Chinese child would express exactly the same idea by one word, *shi*, to eat, or food, &c. The only difference would be that a Chinese child speaks the language of a child, an English child the language of a man. If, then, it is admitted that every inflectional language passed through a radical and an agglutinate stage, it seems to follow that at one time or other, the constituent elements of inflectional languages, namely, the roots, were, to all intents and purposes, real words, and used as such both in thought and speech.

Roots, therefore, are not such mere abstractions as they are sometimes supposed to be, and unless we succeed in tracing each word in English or in any inflectional language back to its root, we have not traced it back to its real origin. It is in this analysis of language that comparative philology has achieved its greatest triumphs, and has curbed that wild spirit of etymology which would handle words as if they had no past, no history, no origin. In tracing words back to their roots we must obey certain phonetic laws. If the vowel of a root is *i* or *u*, its derivatives will be different, from Sanskrit down to English, from what they would have been if that radical vowel had been *a*. If a root begins with a tenuis in Sanskrit, that tenuis will never be a tenuis in Gothic, but an aspirate; if a root begins with an aspirate in

Sanskrit, that aspirate will never be an aspirate in Gothic, but a media; if a root begins with a media in Sanskrit, that media will not be a media in Gothic, but a tenuis.

And this, better than anything else, will, I think, explain the strong objection which comparative philologists feel to what I called the Bow-wow and the Pooh-pooh theories, names which I am sorry to see have given great offence, but in framing which, I can honestly say, I thought of Epicurus [1] rather than of living writers, and meant no offence to either. "Onomatopœic" is neither an appropriate nor a pleasant word, and it was absolutely necessary to distinguish between two theories, the *onomatopœic*, which derives words from the sounds of animals and nature in general, as imitated by the framers of language, and the *interjectional*, which derives words, not from the imitation of the interjections of others, but from the interjections themselves, as wrung forth, almost against their will, from the framers of language. I did not think that the weapons of ridicule were necessary to combat theories which, since the days of Epicurus, had so often been combated, and so often been defended. I may have erred in choosing terms which, while they expressed exactly what I wished to express, sounded rather homely and undignified; but I could not plead for the terms I had chosen a better excuse than the name now suggested by the supporters of the onomatopœic theory, which, I am told, is *Insonic*, from *im* instead of *imitation*, and *son* instead of *sonus*, sound.

[1] Ὁ γὰρ Ἐπίκουρος ἔλεγεν ὅτι οὐχὶ ἐπιστημόνως οὗτοι ἔθεντο τὰ ὀνόματα, ἀλλὰ φυσικῶς κινούμενοι, ὡς οἱ βήσσοντες καὶ πταίροντες καὶ μυκώμενοι καὶ ὑλακτοῦντες καὶ στενάζοντες. — *Proclus, ad Plat. Crat.* p. 9.

That there is some analogy between the faculty of speech and the sounds which we utter in singing, laughing, crying, sobbing, sighing, moaning, screaming, whistling, and clicking, was known to Epicurus of old, and requires no proof. But does it require to be pointed out that even if the scream of a man who has his finger pinched should happen to be identically the same as the French *hélas*, that scream would be an effect, an involuntary effect of outward pressure, whereas an interjection like *alas*, *hélas*, Italian *lasso*, to say nothing of such words as *pain*, *suffering*, *agony*, &c., is there by the free will of the speaker, meant for something, used with a purpose, chosen as a sign?

Again, that sounds can be rendered in language by sounds, and that each language possesses a large stock of words imitating the sounds given out by certain things, who would deny? And who would deny that some words, originally expressive of sound only, might be transferred to other things which have some analogy with sound?

But how are all things that do not appeal to the sense of hearing — how are the ideas of going, moving, standing, sinking, tasting, thinking, to be expressed?

I give the following as a specimen of what may be achieved by the advocates of "painting in sound." *Hooiaioai* is said in Hawaian to mean to testify; and this, we are told, was the origin of the word: — [1]

"In uttering the *i* the breath is compressed into the smallest and seemingly swiftest current possible. It represents, therefore, a swift, and what we may call a sharp, movement.

[1] *The Polynesian*, Honolulu, 1862.

"Of all the vowels *o* is that of which the sound goes farthest. We have it, therefore, in most words relating to distance, as in *holo*, *lo*, long, &c.

"In joining the two, the sense is modified by their position. If we write *oi*, it is an *o* going on with an *i*. This is exemplified in *oi*, lame. Observe how a lame man advances. Standing on the sound limb, he puts the lame one leisurely out and sets it to the ground: this is the *o*. But no sooner does it get there, and the weight of the body begin to rest on it, than, hastening to relieve it of the burden, he moves the other leg rapidly forward, lessening the pressure at the same time by relaxing every joint he can bend, and thus letting his body sink as far as possible; this rapid sinking movement is the *i*.

"Again, *oi*, a passing in advance, excellency. Here *o* is the general advance, *i* is the going ahead of some particular one.

"If, again, we write *io*, it is an *i* going on with an *o*. That is to say, it is a rapid and penetrating movement — *i*, and that movement long continued. Thus we have in Hawaiian *io*, a chief's forerunner. He would be a man rapid in his course — *i*; of good bottom — *o*. In Greek, *ios*, an arrow, and *Io*, the goddess who went so fast and far. Hence *io* is anything that goes quite through, that is *thorough*, complete, real, true. Like Burns, 'facts are chiels that winna ding,' that is, cannot be forced out of their course. Hence *io*, flesh, real food, in distinction to bone, &c., and reality or fact, or truth generally.

"*Ia* is the pronoun that, analogous to Latin *is*, *ea*, *id*. Putting together these we have *o*, *ia*, *io* — Oh that is fact. Prefixing the causative *hoo*, we have 'make that to be fact;' affix *ai*, completive of the action, and we have, 'make that completely out to be a fact,' that is ' testify to its truth.'

" It is to be remarked that the stress of the voice is laid on the second *i*, the *oia* being pronounced very lightly, and that in Greek the *i* in *oíomai*, I believe, is always strongly accented, a mark of the contraction the word has suffered."

Although the languages of Europe, with their well-established history, lend themselves less easily to such speculations, yet I could quote similar passages from French, German, and English etymologists. Dr. Bolza, in his " Vocabolario Genetico-Etimologico" (Vienna, 1852), tells us, among other things, that in Italian *a* expresses light, *o* redness, *u* darkness; and he continues, " *Ecco probabilmente le tre note, che in fiamma, fuoco, e fumo, sono espresse dal mutamento della vocale, mentre la f esprime in tutti i tre il movimento dell' aria*" (p. 61, note). And again we are told by him that one of the first sounds pronounced by children is *m*: hence *mamma*. The root of this is *ma* or *am*, which gives us *amare*, to love. On account of the movement of the lips, it likewise supplies the root of *mangiare* and *masticare*; and explains besides *muto*, dumb, *muggire*, to low, *miagolare*, to mew, and *mormorio*, murmur. Now, even if *amare* could not be protected by the Sanskrit root *am*, to rush forward impetuously (according to others, *kâm*, to love), we should have thought that *mangiare* and *masticare* would have been safe against onomatopœic interference, the former being the Latin *manducare*, to chew, the latter the post-classical *masticare*, to chew. *Manducare* has a long history of its own. It descends from *mandere*, to chew, and *mandere* leads us back to the Sanskrit root *mard*, to grind, one of the numerous offshoots of the root *mar*, the history of which will form the subject of one of our later lectures. *Mûtus* has been well derived by Professor A. Weber (Kuhn's Zeitschrift, vi. p. 318) from the Sanskrit *mû*, to bind (Pâṇ. vi. 4, 20), so that its original meaning would have been "tongue-bound." As to *miagolare*, to mew, we willingly hand it over to the onomatopœic school.

The onomatopœic theory goes very smoothly as long as it deals with cackling hens and quacking ducks; but round that poultry-yard there is a dead wall, and we soon find that it is behind that wall that language really begins.

But whatever we may think of these onomatopœic and interjectional theories, we must carefully distinguish between two things. There is one class of scholars who derive all words from roots according to the strictest rules of comparative grammar, but who look upon the roots, in their original character, as either interjectional or onomatopœic. There are others who derive words straight from interjections and the cries of animals, and who claim in their etymologies all the liberty the cow claims in saying *booh, mooh*, or *ooh*, or that man claims in saying *pooh, fi, pfui*.[1] With regard to the former theory, I should wish to remain entirely neutral, satisfied with considering roots as phonetic types till some progress has been made in tracing the principal roots, not of Sanskrit only, but of Chinese, Bask, the Turanian,

[1] On the uncertainty of rendering inarticulate by articulate sounds, see Merab (4th ed.), p. 36; Sir John Stoddart's *Glossology*, p. 231; *Mélanges Asiatiques* (St. Petersbourg) iv. 1.

and Semitic languages, back to the cries of man or the imitated sounds of nature.

Quite distinct from this is that other theory which, without the intervention of determinate roots, derives our words directly from cries and interjections. This theory would undo all the work that has been done by Bopp, Humboldt, Grimm, and others, during the last fifty years; it would with one stroke abolish all the phonetic laws that have been established with so much care and industry, and throw etymology back into a state of chaotic anarchy. According to Grimm's law, we derive the English *fiend*, the German *feind*, the Gothic *fijand*, from a root which, if it exists at all in Sanskrit, Latin, Lithuanian, or Celtic, must there begin with the tenuis *p*. Such is the phonetic law that holds these languages together, and that cannot be violated with·impunity. If we found in Sanskrit a word *fiend*, we should feel certain that it could not be the same as the English *fiend*. Following this rule we find in Sanskrit the root *pîy*, to hate, to destroy, the participle of which, *pîyant*, would correspond exactly with Gothic *fijand*. But suppose we derived *fiend* and other words of a similar sound, such as *foul*, *filth*, &c., from the interjections *fi*, and *pooh* (*faugh! fo! fie!* Lith. *pui*, Germ. *pfui*), all would be mere scramble and confusion; Grimm's law would be broken; and roots, kept distinct in Sanskrit, Greek, Latin, and German, would be mixed up together. For besides *pîy*, to hate, there is another root in Sanskrit, *pûy*, to decay. From it we have Latin *pus, puteo, putridus*; Greek *pýon*, and *pýthō*; Lithuanian *pulei*, matter; and, in strict accordance with Grimm's law, Gothic *fuls*,

English *foul.* If these words were derived from *fi!* then we should have to include all the descendants of the root *bhi,* to fear, such as Lithuanian *bijau,* I fear; *biaurus,* ugly.

In the same manner, if we looked upon *thunder* as a mere imitation of the inarticulate noise of thunder, we could not trace the A. S. *thunor* back to the root *tan,* which expresses that tension of the air which gives rise to sound, but we should have to class it together with other words, such as *to din, to dun,* and discover in each, as best we could, some similarity with some inarticulate noise. If, on the contrary, we bind ourselves by definite rules, we find that the same law which changes *tan* into *than,* changes another root, *dhvan,* into *din.* There may be, for all we know, some distant relationship between the two roots *tan* and *dhvan,* and that relationship may have its origin in onomatopœia; but from the earliest beginnings of the history of the Aryan language, these two roots were independent germs, each the starting-point of large classes of words, the phonetic character of which is determined throughout by the type from which they issue. To ignore the individuality of each root in Sanskrit, Greek, and Latin, would be like ignoring the individuality of the types of the animal creation. There may be higher, more general, more abstract types, but if we want to reach them, we must first toil through the lower and more special types; we must retrace, in the descending scale of scientific analysis, every step by which, in an ascending scale, language has arrived at its present state.

The onomatopœic system would be most detrimental to all scientific etymology, and no amount of learning and ingenuity displayed in its application could atone for the lawlessness which is sanctioned by it. If it is once admitted that all words must be traced back to definite roots, according to the strictest phonetic rules, it matters little whether these roots are called phonetic types, more or less preserved in all the innumerable impressions that are taken from them, or whether we call them onomatopœic and interjectional. As long as we have definite forms between ourselves and chaos, we may build our science like an arch of a bridge, that rests on the firm piles fixed in the rushing waters. If, on the contrary, the roots of language are mere abstractions, and there is nothing to separate language from cries and interjections, then we may play with language as children play with the sands of the sea, but we must not complain if every fresh tide wipes out the little castles we had built on the beach.

LECTURE III.

THE PHYSIOLOGICAL ALPHABET.

WE proceed to-day to dissect the body of language. In doing this we treat language as a mere corpse, not caring whether it ever had any life or meaning, but simply trying to find out what it is made of, what are the impressions made upon our ear, and how they can be classified. In order to do this it is not sufficient to examine our alphabet, such as it is, though no doubt the alphabet may very properly be called the table of the elements of language. But what do we learn from our A B C? what even, if we are told that *k* is a guttural tenuis, *s* a dental sibilant, *m* a labial nasal, *y* a palatal liquid? These are names which are borrowed from Greek and Latin grammars. They expressed more or less happily the ideas which the scholars of Athens and Alexandria had formed of the nature of certain letters. But as translated into our grammatical phraseology they have lost almost entirely their original meaning. Our modern grammarians speak of *tenuis* and *media*, but they define *tenuis* not as a bare or thin letter, but on the contrary as the hardest and strongest articulation; nor are they always aware that the *mediæ* or middle letters were originally so called because, as pronounced at Alexandria, they stood half-

CLASSIFICATION OF LETTERS. 107

way between the bare and the rough letters, i. e. the aspirates, — being pronounced with less aspiration than the aspirates, with more than the tenues.[1] Plato's division of letters, as given in his *Cratylus*, is very much that which we still profess to follow. He speaks of voiced letters (φωνήεντα, vocales), our vowels; and of voiceless letters (ἄφωνα), our consonants, or mutes. But he seems to divide the latter into two classes: first, those which are voiceless, but produce a sound (φωνήεντα μὲν οὔ, οὐ μέντοι γε ἄφθογγα), afterwards called semi-vowels (ἡμίφωνα); and, secondly, the real mutes, both voiceless and soundless, i. e. all consonants, except the semi-vowels (ἄφθογγα).[2] In later times, the scheme adopted by Greek grammarians is as follows: —

I. *Phōnḗenta*, vocales, voiced vowels.
II. *Sýmphōna*, consonantes.
  II. 1. *Hēmíphōna*, semi-vocales, half-voiced,
    l, m, n, r, s: or, Hygrá, liquidæ, fluid,
    l, m, n, r.
  II. 2. *A'phōna*, mutæ, voiceless.
  a. *Psilá*, tenues b. *Mésa*, mediæ c. *Daséa*, aspiratæ.
  k, t, p.   g, d, b.   ch, th, ph.

Another classification of letters, more perfect, be-

---

[1] Schollon to Dionysius Thrax, in *Anecdota Bekk.* p. 810. Φωνητικὰ ὄργανα τρία εἰσίν, ἡ γλῶσσα, οἱ ὀδόντες, τὰ χείλη. Τοῖς μὲν οὖν ἄκροις χείλεσι πιλουμένοις ἐκφωνεῖται [τὸ π], ὥστε σχεδὸν μηδὲ ὀλίγον τι πνεῦμα παρεκβαίνειν· ὀνογομένων δὲ τῶν χειλέων πάνο καὶ πνεύματος πολλοῦ ἐξιόντος, ἐκφωνεῖται τὸ φ· τὸ δὲ β, ἐκφωνούμενον ὁμοίως ταῖς ἄκραις τῶν χειλέων, τουτέστι περὶ τὸν αὐτὸν τόπον ταῖς προλεχθεῖσι τῶν φωνητικῶν ὀργάνων, οὔτε πάνυ ἀνάγει τὰ χείλη ὡς τὸ φ, οὔτε πάνυ πιλεῖ ὡς τὸ π, ἀλλὰ μέσην τινὰ διέξοδον τῷ πνεύματι πτεισμένως δίδωσιν, κ.τ.λ. See Rudolph von Raumer, *Sprachwissenschaftliche Schriften*, p. 102; Curtius, *Griechische Etymologie*, ii. p. 80.

[2] Raumer, *l. c.*, p. 100.

cause deduced from a language (the Sanskrit) not yet reduced to writing, but carefully watched and preserved by oral tradition, is to be found in the so-called *Prâtisâkhyas*, works on phonetics, belonging to different schools in which the ancient texts of the Veda were handed down from generation to generation with an accuracy far exceeding that of the most painstaking copyists of MSS. Some of these works have lately been published and translated, and may be consulted by those who take an interest in these matters.[1]

Of late years the whole subject of phonetics has been taken up with increased ardor by scientific men, and assaults have been made from three different points by different armies, philologists, physiologists, and mathematicians. The best philological treatises I can recommend (without mentioning earlier works, such as the most excellent treatise of Bishop Wilkins, 1688), are the essays published from time to time by Mr. Alexander John Ellis,[2] by

---

[1] *Prâtisâkhya du Rig-Veda*, par M. Ad. Regnier, in the *Journal Asiatique*, Paris, 1856-'58.
Text und Uebersetzung des Prâtisâkhya, oder der ältesten Phonetik und Grammatik, in M. M.'s edition of the *Rig-Veda*, Leipzig, 1856.
Das Vâjasaneyi-Prâtisâkhyam, published by Prof. A. Weber, in *Indische Studien*, vol. iv. Berlin, 1858.
The Atharva-Veda Prâtisâkhya, by W. D. Whitney, Newhaven, 1862. The same distinguished scholar is preparing an edition of the Prâtisâkhya of the Taittirîya-Veda. As the hymns of the Sâmaveda were chanted, and not recited, no Prâtisâkhya or work on phonetics exists for this Veda.

[2] Works on Phonetics by Alexander J. Ellis.— *The Alphabet of Nature; or, contributions towards a more accurate analysis and symbolization of spoken sounds, with some account of the principal Phonetical alphabets hitherto proposed.* Originally published in the *Phonotypic Journal*, June, 1844, to June, 1845. London and Bath, 1845. 8vo, pp. viii. 104. *The Essentials of Phonetics; containing the theory of a universal alphabet, together with its practical application as an ethnical alphabet to the reduc-

far the most accurate observer and analyzer in the field of phonetics. Other works by R. von Raumer,[1] F. H. du Bois-Reymond,[2] Lepsius,[3] Thausing,[4] may be consulted with advantage in their respective spheres. The physiological works which I found most useful and intelligible to a reader not specially engaged in these studies were, Müller's "Handbook

tion of all languages, written or unwritten, to one uniform system of writing, with numerous examples, adapted to the use of Phoneticians, Philologists, Etymologists, Ethnographists, Travellers, and Missionaries. In lieu of a second edition of the *Alphabet of Nature*. London, 1846. 8vo. pp. xvi. 276. Printed entirely in a Phonetic character, with illustrations in twenty-seven languages, and specimens of various founts of Phonetic type. The *Ethnical Alphabet* was also published as a separate tract. *English Phonetics*; containing an original systematization of broken sounds, a complete explanation of the Reading Reform Alphabet, and a new universal Latinic Alphabet for Philologists and Travellers. London, 1854. 8vo. pp. 16. *Universal Writing and Printing with Ordinary Letters*, for the use of Missionaries, Comparative Philologists, Linguists, and Phonologists (Edinburgh and London, 1856, 4to. pp. 22), containing a complete Digraphic, Travellers' Digraphic, and Latinic Alphabets (of which the two first were published separately), with examples in nine languages, and a comparative table of the Digraphic, Latinic, suggested Panethnic, Prof. Max Müller's Missionary, and Dr. Lepsius's Linguistic Alphabets. *A Plea for Phonetic Spelling; or, the Necessity of Orthographic Reform*. London, 8vo. First edition, 1844. pp. 40. Second edition, 1848, pp. 180, with an Appendix, showing the inconsistencies of hetéric orthography, and the present geographical extent of the writing and printing reform. Third edition, with an Appendix, containing the above tables remodelled, an account of existing Phonetic alphabets, and an elaborate *Inquiry into the Variations in English Pronunciation during the last Three Centuries*, has been in the press in America since 1860, but has been stopped by the civil war. The whole text, pp. 151, has been printed.

[1] *Gesammelte Sprachwissenschaftliche Schriften*, von Rudolph von Raumer. Frankfort, 1863. (Chiefly on classical and Teutonic languages.)

[2] *Kadmus, oder Allgemeine Alphabetik*, von F. H. du Bois-Reymond. Berlin, 1862. (Containing papers published as early as 1811, and full of ingenious and original observations.)

[3] *Lepsius, Standard Alphabet*, second edition, 1863. (On the subject in general, but particularly useful for African languages.)

[4] *Das Natürliche Lautsystem der Menschlichen Sprache*, von Dr. M. Thausing. Leipzig, 1863. (With special reference to the teaching of deaf and dumb persons.)

of Physiology," Brücke's "Grundzüge der Physiologie und Systematik der Sprachlaute" (Wien, 1856), Funke's "Lehrbuch der Physiologie," and Czermak's articles in the "Sitzungsberichte der K. K. Akademie der Wissenschaften zu Wien."

Among works on mathematics and acoustics, I have consulted Sir John Herschel's "Treatise on Sound," in the " Encyclopædia Metropolitana"; Professor Willis's paper "On the Vowel Sound and on Reed Organ-Pipes," read before the Cambridge Physiological Society in 1828 and 1829; but chiefly Professor Helmholtz's classical work, "Die Lehre von den Tonempfindungen" (Braunschweig, 1863), a work giving the results of the most minute scientific researches in a clear, classical, and truly popular form, so seldom to be found in German books.

I ought not to omit to mention here the valuable services rendered by those who, for nearly twenty years, have been laboring in England to turn the results of scientific research to practical use, in devising and propagating a new system of "Brief Writing and True Spelling," best known under the name of the *Phonetic Reform*. I am far from underrating the difficulties that stand in the way of such a reform, and I am not so sanguine as to indulge in any hopes of seeing it carried for the next three or four generations. But I feel convinced of the truth and reasonableness of the principles on which that reform rests, and as the innate regard for truth and reason, however dormant or timid at times, has always proved irresistible in the end, enabling men to part with all they hold most dear and sacred, whether corn-laws, or Stuart dynasties, or Papal legates, or heathen idols, I doubt not but that the effete and corrupt orthography will follow in their train. Nations have before now changed their numerical figures, their letters, their chronology, their weights and measures; and though Mr. Pitman may not live to see the results of his persevering and disinterested exertions, it requires no prophetic power to perceive that what at present is pooh-poohed by the many will make its way in the end, unless met by arguments stronger than those hitherto levelled at the " Fonetic Nuz." One argument which might be supposed to weigh with the student of language, viz., the obscuration of the etymological structure of words, I cannot consider very formidable. The pronunciation of languages changes according to fixed laws, the spelling has changed in the most arbitrary manner, so that if our spelling followed the pronunciation of words, it would in reality be of greater help to the critical student of language than the present uncertain and unscientific mode of writing.

Although considerable progress has thus been made in the analysis of the human voice, the difficulties inherent in the subject have been increased rather than diminished by the profound and laborious researches carried on independently by physiologists, students of acoustics, and philologists. The human voice opens a field of observation in which these three distinct sciences meet. The substance of speech or sound has to be analyzed by the mathematician and the experimental philosopher; the organs or instruments of speech have to be examined by the anatomist; and the history of speech, the actual varieties of sound which have become typified in language, fall to the province of the student of language. Under these circumstances it is absolutely necessary that students should coöperate in order to bring these scattered researches to a successful termination, and I take this opportunity of expressing my obligation to Dr. Rolleston, our indefatigable Professor of Physiology, Mr. G. Griffith, Deputy-Professor of Experimental Philosophy, Mr. A. J. Ellis, and others, for their kindness in helping me through difficulties which, but for their assistance, I should not have been able to overcome without much loss of time.

What can seem simpler than the A B C, and yet what is more difficult when we come to examine it? Where do we find an exact definition of vowel and consonant, and how they differ from each other? The vowels, we are told, are simple emissions of the voice, the consonants cannot be articulated except with the assistance of vowels. If this were so, letters such as *s*, *f*, *r*, could not be classed as consonants, for there is no difficulty in pronouncing these without the assistance of a vowel. Again, what is the difference between *a*, *i*, *u*? What is the difference between a tenuis and media, a difference almost incomprehensible to certain races; for instance, the Mohawks and the inhabitants of Saxony? Has any philosopher given as yet an intelligible definition of the difference between whispering, speaking, singing? Let us begin, then, with the beginning, and give some definitions of the words we shall have to use hereafter.

What we hear may be divided, first of all, into *Noises* and *Sounds*. Noises, such as the rustling of leaves, the jarring of doors, or the clap of thunder, are produced by irregular impulses imparted to the air. Sounds, such as we hear from tuning-forks, strings, flutes, organ-pipes, are produced by regular periodical (isochronous) vibrations of elastic air. That sound, musical sound, or tone in its simplest form, is produced by tension, and ceases after the sounding body has recovered from that tension, seems to have been vaguely known to the early framers of language, for the Greek *tonos*, tone, is derived from a root *tan*, meaning to extend. Pythagoras[1] knew more than this. He knew that when chords of the same quality and the same tension are to sound a fundamental note, its octave, its fifth, and its fourth, their respective lengths must be like 1 to 2, 2 to 3, and 3 to 4.

When we hear a single note, the impression we receive seems very simple, yet it is in reality very complicated. We can distinguish in each note —

1. Its strength or loudness.
2. Its height or pitch.
3. Its quality, or, as it is sometimes called, *timbre*; in German *Tonfarbe*, i. e. color of tone.

Strength or loudness depends upon the *amplitude* of the excursions of the vibrating particles of air which produce the wave.

Height or pitch depends on the length of time that each particle requires to perform an excursion, i. e. on the number of vibrations executed in a given time. If, for instance, the pendulum of a clock, which oscillates once in each second, were to mark smaller portions of time, it would cause musical sounds to be heard. Sixteen double oscillations in

---

[1] Helmholtz, *Einleitung*, p. 2.

one second would be sufficient to bring out sound, though its pitch would be so low as to be hardly perceptible. For practical purposes, the lowest tone we hear is produced by 30 double vibrations in one second, the highest by 4000. Between these two lie the usual seven octaves of our musical instruments. It is said to be possible, however, to produce perceptible musical sounds through 11 octaves, beginning with 16 and ending with 38,000 double vibrations in one second, though here the lower notes are mere hums, the upper notes mere clinks. The $\scriptstyle\Lambda'$ of our tuning-forks, as fixed by the Paris Academy, requires 437·5 double, or 875 single[1] vibrations in one second. In Germany the $\scriptstyle\Lambda'$ tuning-fork makes 440 double vibrations in one second. It is clear that beyond the lowest and the highest tones perceptible to our ears, there is a progress *ad infinitum*, musical notes as real as those which we hear, yet beyond the reach of sensuous perception. It is the same with the other senses. We can perceive the movement of the pendulum, but we cannot perceive the slower movement of the hand on the watch. We can perceive the flight of a bird, but we cannot perceive the quicker movement of a cannon-ball. This, better than anything else, shows how dependent we are on our senses; and how, if our senses are our weapons for the discovery of truth, they are likewise our chains that keep us from soaring too high. Up to this point everything, though wonderful enough, is clear and intelligible.

[1] It is customary to reckon by single vibrations in France and Germany, although some German writers adopt the English fashion of reckoning by double vibrations or complete excursions backwards and forwards. Helmholtz uses double vibrations, but Scheibler uses single vibrations. De Morgan calls a double oscillation a "swing-swang."

PHONETICS. 115

As we hear a note, we know, with mathematical accuracy, to how many vibrations in one second it is due; and if we want to produce the same note, an instrument, such as the siren, which gives a definite number of impulses to the air within a given time, will enable us to do it in the most mechanical manner.

When *two* waves of one note enter the ear in the same time as *one* wave of another, the interval between the two is *an octave*.

When *three* waves of one note enter the ear in the same time as *two* waves of another, the interval between the two notes is a *fifth*.

When *four* waves of one note enter the ear in the same time as *three* waves of another, the interval between the two notes is a *fourth*.

When *five* waves of one note enter the ear in the same time as *four* waves of another, the interval between the two notes is a *major third*.

When *six* waves of one note enter the ear in the same time as *five* waves of another, the interval between the two notes is a *minor third*.

When *five* waves of one note enter the ear in the same time as *three* waves of another, the interval between the two notes is a *major sixth*.

All this is but the confirmation of what was known to Pythagoras. He took a vibrating cord, and, by placing a bridge so as to leave ⅓ of the cord on the right, ⅔ on the left side, the left portion vibrating by itself, gave him the octave of the lower note of the right portion. So, again, by leaving ⅖ on the right, ⅗ on the left side, the left portion vibrating gave him the fifth of the right.

But it is clear that we may hear the same tone, i. e. the result of exactly the same number of vibrations in one second, produced by the human voice, by a flute, a violoncello, a fife, or a double bass. They are tones of the same pitch, and yet they differ in character, and their difference is called their *quality*. But what is the cause of these various qualities? By a kind of negative reasoning, it had long been supposed that, as quality could neither arise from the amplitude nor from the duration, it must be due to the form of the vibrations. Professor Helmholtz, however, was the first to prove positively that this is the case, by applying the microscope to the vibrations of different musical instruments, and thus catching the exact outline of their respective vibrations, — a result which before had been but imperfectly attained by an instrument called the *Phonautograph*. What is meant by the form of waves may be seen from the following outlines: —

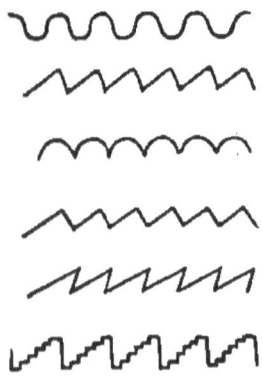

PHONETICS. 117

In pursuing these inquiries, Professor Helmholtz made another most important discovery, viz., that the different forms of the vibrations which are the cause of what he calls quality or color are likewise the cause of the presence or absence of certain harmonics, or by-notes; in fact, that varying quality and varying harmonics are but two expressions for the same thing.

Harmonics are the secondary tones which can be perceived even by the unassisted ear, if, after lifting the pedal, we strike a key on a pianoforte. These harmonics arise from a string vibrating as if its motion were compounded of several distinct vibrations of strings of its full length, and one half, one third, one fourth, &c., part of its length. Each of these shorter lengths would vibrate twice, three times, four times as fast as the original length, producing corresponding tones. Thus, if we strike c, we hear, if listening attentively, c′, g′, c″, e″, g″, b″ flat, c‴, &c.

```
 1    2    3    4    5    6    7      8
 c    c′   g′   c″   e″   g″   b″flat c‴
```

That the secondary notes are not merely imaginative or subjective can be proved by a very simple and amusing experiment. If we place little soldiers — very light cavalry — on the strings of a pianoforte, and then strike a note, all the riders that sit on strings representing the secondary tones will shake, and possibly be thrown off, while the others remain firm in their saddles, because these strings vibrate in

sympathy with the secondary tones of the string
struck. Another test can be applied by means of
resounding tubes, tuned to different notes. If we
apply these to our ear, and then strike a note the
secondary tones of which are the same as the notes
to which the resounding tubes are tuned, those notes
will sound loudly and almost yell in our ears; while
if the tubes do not correspond to the harmonics of
the note played, the resounding tubes will not answer in the same manner.

We thus see, again, that what seems to us a
simple impression, the one note struck on the pianoforte, consists of many impressions which together
make up what we hear and perceive. We are not
conscious of the harmonics which follow each note
and determine its quality, but we know, nevertheless,
that these by-notes strike our ear, and that our senses
receive them and suffer from them. The same remark applies to the whole realm of our sensuous
knowledge. There is a broad distinction between
sensation and *perception*. There are many things
which we perceive at first and which we perceive
again as soon as our attention is called to them, but
which, in the ordinary run of life, are to us as if they
did not exist at all. When I first came to Oxford, I
was constantly distracted by the ringing of bells;
after a time I ceased even to notice the dinner-bell.
There are ear-rings much in fashion just now — little
gold bells with coral clappers. Of course they produce a constant jingling which everybody hears except the lady who wears them. In these cases, however, the difference between sensation and perception
is simply due to want of attention. In other cases

our senses are really incapable, without assistance, of distinguishing the various constituents of the objective impressions produced from without. We know, for instance, that white light is a vibration of ether, and that it is a compound of the single colors of the solar spectrum. A prism will at once analyze that compound, and divide it into its component parts. To our apprehension, however, white light is something simple, and our senses are too coarse to distinguish its component elements by any effort whatsoever.

We now shall be better able to understand what I consider a most important discovery of Professor Helmholtz.[1] It had been proved by Professor G. S. Ohm[2] that there is only one vibration without harmonics, viz., the simple pendulous vibration. It had likewise been proved by Fourier, Ohm, and other mathematicians,[3] that all compound vibrations or sounds can be divided into so many simple or pendulous vibrations. But it is due to Professor Helmholtz that we can now determine the exact configuration of many compound vibrations, and determine the presence and absence of the harmonics which, as we saw, caused the difference in the quality, or color, or *timbre* of sound. Thus he found that in the violin, as compared with the guitar or pianoforte, the primary note is strong, the secondary tones from two to six are weak, while those from seven to ten are much more distinct.[4] In the clarinet[5] the odd harmonics only are perceptible, in the hautboy the even harmonics are of equal strength.

[1] Helmholtz, l. c. p. 62.   [2] l. c. p. 38.
[3] l. c. p. 54.   [4] l. c. p. 143.
[5] l. c. p. 162.

Let us now see how all this tells on language. When we are speaking we are in reality playing on a musical instrument, and a more perfect instrument than was ever invented by man. It is a wind-instrument, in which the vibrating apparatus is supplied by the *chordæ vocales*, while the outer tube, or bells, through which the waves of sound pass, are furnished by the different configurations of the mouth. I shall try, as well as I can, to describe to you, with the help of some diagrams, the general structure of this instrument, though in doing so I can only retail the scant information which I gathered myself from our excellent Professor of Physiology at Oxford, Dr. Rolleston. He kindly showed and explained to me by actual dissection, and with the aid of the newly-invented laryngoscope (a small looking-glass, which enables the observer to see as far as the bifurcation of the windpipe and the bronchial tubes), the bones, the cartilages, the ligaments and muscles, which together form that extraordinary instrument on which we play our words and thoughts. Some parts of it are extremely complicated, and I should not venture to act even as interpreter of the different and sometimes contradictory views held by Müller, Brücke, Czermak, Funke, and other distinguished physiologists, on the mechanism of the various cartilages, the *thyroid*, *cricoid*, and *arytenoid*, which together constitute the levers of the larynx. It fortunately happens that the most important organs which are engaged in the formation of letters lie above the larynx, and are so simple in their structure, and so open to constant inspection and examination, that, with the diagrams placed before you, there will be little difficulty, I hope, in explaining their respective functions.

There is, first of all, the *thorax* (1), which, by alternately compressing and dilating the lungs, performs the office of bellows.

Fig. 1.

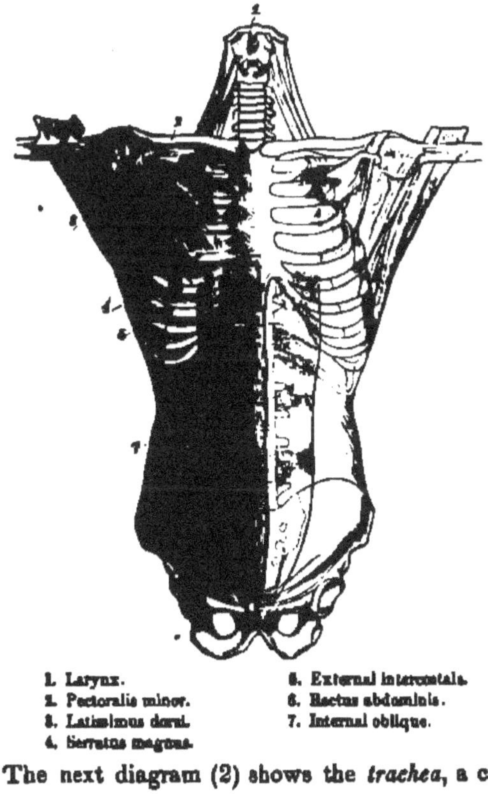

1. Larynx.
2. Pectoralis minor.
3. Latissimus dorsi.
4. Serratus magnus.
5. External intercostals.
6. Rectus abdominis.
7. Internal oblique.

The next diagram (2) shows the *trachea*, a cartilaginous and elastic pipe, which terminates in the lungs by an infinity of roots or *bronchial tubes*, its upper extremity being formed into a species of head called the *larynx*, situated in the throat, and composed of five cartilages.

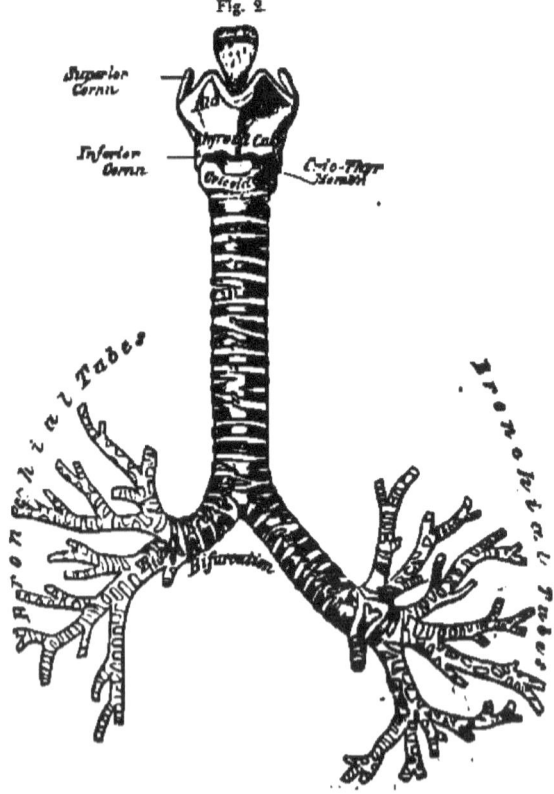

Fig. 2.

The uppermost of these cartilages, the *epiglottis* (3), is intended to open and shut, like a valve, the aperture of the *glottis*, i. e. the superior orifice of the

Fig. 3.

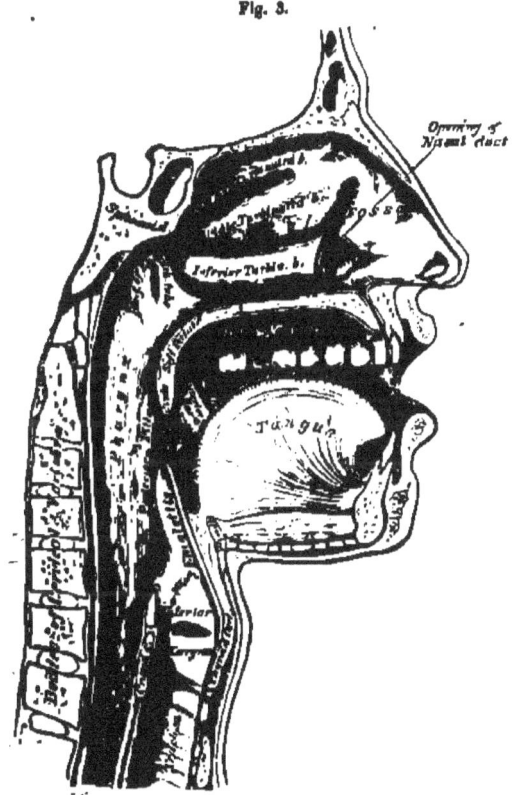

larynx (*fissura laryngea pharyngis*). The *epiglottis* is a leaf-shaped elastic cartilage, attached by its narrower end to the thyroid cartilage, and possessing a midrib overhanging and corresponding to the fissure of the glottis. The broader end of the leaf points freely upwards toward the tongue, in which direction the entire cartilage presents a concave, as towards the larynx a convex, outline. In swallowing, the epiglottis falls over the larynx, like a saddle on the back of a horse. In the formation of certain letters a horizontal narrow fissure may be produced by depressing the epiglottis over the vertical false and true vocal chords.

Within the larynx (4, 5), rather above its middle,

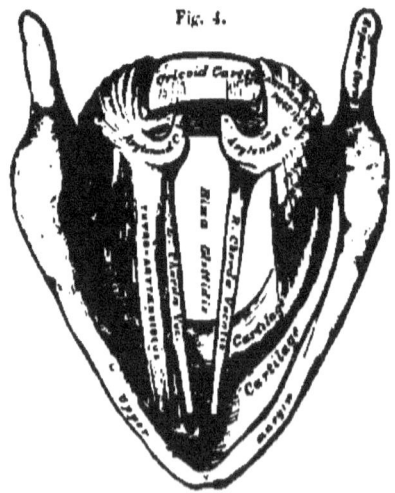

Fig. 4.

between the thyroid and arytenoid cartilages, are two elastic ligaments, like the parchment of a drum split in the middle, and forming an aperture which is called the interior or true *glottis*, and corresponds in direction with the exterior *glottis*. This aperture is provided with muscles, which enlarge and contract

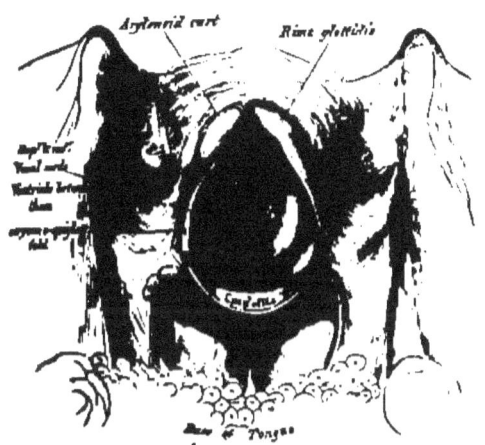

Fig. 5.

it at pleasure, and otherwise modify the form of the larynx. The three cartilages of the larynx supply the most perfect mechanism for stretching or relaxing the chords, and likewise, as it would seem, for deadening some portion of them by pressure of a protuberance on the under side of the *epiglottis* (in German, Epiglottiswulst). These chords are of different length in children and grown-up people, in man and in woman. Their average length in man is 18¾ mm. when relaxed, 23¾ mm. when stretched; in woman, 12¾ mm. when relaxed, 15¾ mm. when stretched: thus giving a difference of about one third between the two sexes, which accounts for the different pitch of male and female voices.[1]

The tongue, the cavity of the fauces, the lips, teeth, and palate, with its velum pendulum and uvula performing the office of a valve between the throat and nostrils, as well as the cavity of the nostrils themselves, are all concerned in modifying the impulse given to the breath as it issues from the larynx, and in producing the various vowels and consonants.

After thus taking to pieces the instrument, the tubes and reeds as it were of the human voice, let us now see how that instrument is played by us in speaking or in singing. Familiar and simple as singing or music in general seems to be, it is, if we analyze it, one of the most wonderful phenomena. What we hear when listening to a chorus or a symphony is a commotion of elastic air, of which the wildest sea would give a very inadequate image. The lowest tone which the ear perceives is due to about 30 vibrations in one second, the highest to about 4000. Consider, then, what happens in a *Presto* when thousands of voices and instruments are simultaneously producing waves of air, each wave crossing the other, not only like the surface waves of the water, but like spherical bodies, and, as it would seem, without any perceptible disturbance;[2] consider that each tone is accompanied by secondary tones, that each instrument has its peculiar *timbre*, due to secondary vibrations; and, lastly, let us remember that all this cross-fire of waves, all this

[1] Funke, *Lehrbuch der Physiologie*, p. 664, from observations made by J. Müller.
[2] Weber, *Wellenlehre*, p. 495.

whirlpool of sound, is moderated by laws which determine what we call harmony, and by certain traditions or habits which determine what we call melody, — both these elements being absent in the songs of birds, — that all this must be reflected like a microscopic photograph on the two small organs of hearing, and there excite not only perception, but perception followed by a new feeling even more mysterious, which we call either pleasure or pain; and it will be clear that we are surrounded on all sides by miracles transcending all we are accustomed to call miraculous, and yet disclosing to the genius of an Euler or a Newton laws which admit of the most minute mathematical determination.

For our own immediate purposes it is important to remark that, while it is impossible to sing without at the same time pronouncing a vowel, it is perfectly possible to pronounce a vowel without singing it. Why this is so we shall see at once. If we pronounce a vowel, what happens? Breath is emitted from the lungs, and some kind of tube is formed by the mouth through which, as through a clarinet, the breath has to pass before it reaches the outer air. If, while the breath passes the *chordæ vocales*, these elastic *laminæ* are made to vibrate periodically, the number of their vibrations determines the pitch of our voice, but it has nothing to do with its *timbre* or vowel. What we call vowels are neither more nor less than the qualities, or colors, or *timbres* of our voice, and these are determined by the form of the vibrations, which form again is determined by the form of the buccal tubes. This had, to a certain extent, been anticipated by Professor Wheatstone in his critique[1] on Professor Willis's ingenious experiments, but it has now been rendered quite evident by the researches of Professor Helmholtz. It is, of course, impossible to watch the form of these vibrations by means of a vibration microscope, but it is possible to analyze them by means of resounding tubes, like those before described, and thus to discover in them what, as we saw, is homologous with the form of vibration, viz. the presence and absence of certain harmonics. If a man sings the same note on different vowels, the harmonics which answer to our resounding tubes vary as they would vary if the same note was played on the violin, or flute, or some other musical instruments. In order to remove all uncertainty, Professor Helmholtz simply inverted the experiment. He took a number of tuning-forks, each furnished with a resonance box, by advancing or withdrawing which he could give their primary tones alone various degrees of strength, and extinguish their secondary tones altogether. He tuned them so as to produce a series of tones answering to the harmonics of the deepest tuning-fork. He then made these tuning-forks vibrate simultaneously by means of a galvanic battery; and by combining the harmonics, which he had first discovered in each vowel by means of the sounding tubes, he succeeded in reproducing artificially exactly the same vowels.[2]

We know now what vowels are made of. They are produced by the form of the vibrations. They vary like the *timbre* of different instruments, and we in reality change the instruments on which we speak when we change the buccal tubes in order to pro-

---
[1] *London and Westminster Review*, Oct. 1837, pp. 34, 37.
[2] L. c. p. 188.

nounce *a, e, i, o, u* (the vowels to be pronounced as in Italian).

Is it possible, then, to produce a vowel, to evoke a certain timbre of our mouth, without giving at the same time to each vowel a certain musical pitch? This question has been frequently discussed. At first it was taken for granted that vowels could not be uttered without pitch; that there could be mute consonants, but no mute vowels. Yet, if a vowel was whispered, it was easy to see that the *chordæ vocales* were not vibrating, at least not periodically; that they began to vibrate only when the whispered vowel was changed into a voiced vowel. J. Müller proposed a compromise. He admitted that the vowels might be uttered as mutes without any tone from the *chordæ vocales*, but he thought that these mute vowels were formed in the glottis by the air passing the non-sonant chords, while all consonantal noises are formed in the mouth.[1] Even this distinction, however, between mute vowels and mute consonants is not confirmed by later observations, which have shown that in whispering the vocal chords are placed together so that only the back part of the glottis between the arytenoid cartilages remains open, assuming the form of a triangle.[2] Through this aperture the air passes, and if, as happens not unfrequently in whispering, a word breaks forth quite loud, betraying our secrets, this is because the *chordæ vocales* have resumed their ordinary position and been set vibrating by the pass-

[1] Funke, *Handbuch der Physiologie*, p. 673. Different views of Willis and Brücke, p. 678.
[2] *Helmholtz*, p. 171.

ing air. Cases of aphonia, where people are unable to intone at all, invariably arise from disease of the vocal chords; yet, though unable to intone, these persons can pronounce the different vowels. It can hardly be denied, therefore, that the vowels pronounced with *vox clandestina* are mere noises, colored by the configuration of the mouth, but without any definite musical pitch; though it is equally true that, in whispering vowels, certain vague tones inherent in each vowel can be discovered, nay, that these inherent tones are invariable. This was first pointed out by Professor Donders, and afterwards corrected and confirmed by Professor Helmholtz.[1] It will be necessary, I think, to treat these tones as imperfect tones, that is to say, as noises approaching to tones, or as irregular vibrations, nearly, yet not quite, changed into regular or isochronous vibrations; though the exact limit where a noise ends and tone begins has, as far as I can see, not yet been determined by any philosopher.

Vowels in all their varieties are really infinite in number. Yet, for practical purposes, certain typical vowels have been fixed upon in all languages, and these we shall now proceed to examine.

From the diagrams which are meant to represent the configuration of the mouth requisite for the formation of the three principal vowels, you will see that there are two extremes, the *u* and the *i*, the *a* occupying an intermediate position. All vowels are to be pronounced as in Italian.

1. In pronouncing *u* we round the lips and draw down the tongue so that the cavity of the mouth as-

[1] l. c. p. 172.

VOWELS.   131

sumes the shape of a bottle without a neck. Such bottles give the deepest notes, and so does the vowel *u*. According to Helmholtz its inherent tone is F.[1]

Fig. 6.

EXAMPLES:

Open syllable, long, *who*

short, *fruition*

Closed syllable, long, *fool*

short, *full*

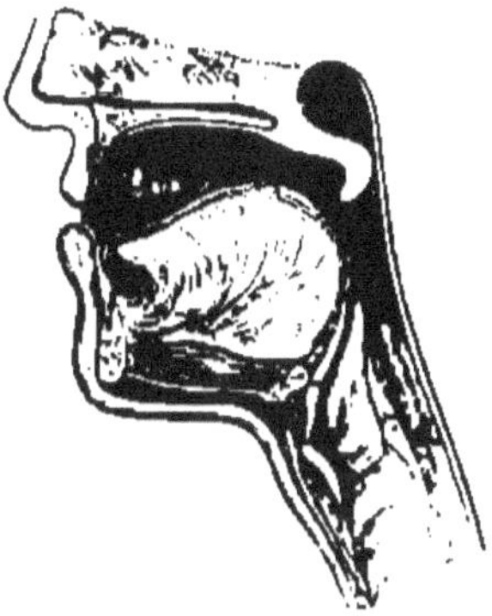

2. If the lips are opened somewhat wider, and the tongue somewhat raised, we hear the *o*. Its pitch, according to Helmholtz, B′ flat.

3. If the lips are less rounded, and the tongue somewhat depressed, we hear the *â*.

4. If the lips are wide open, and the tongue in its natural flat position, we hear *a*. Inherent pitch, according to Helmholtz, B″ flat. This seems the most natural position of the mouth in singing; yet for the higher notes singers prefer the vowels *e* and *i*, and

[1] I give instances of short and long vowels, both in open and closed syllables (i. e. not followed or followed by consonants), because in English particularly, hardly any vowels pair when free and stopped. On the qualitative, and not only quantitative, differences between long and short vowels, see Brücke, *l. c.* p. 24, *seq.*; and R. von Raumer.

132   VOWELS.

find it impossible to pronounce *a* and *u* on the highest.[1]

Fig. 7.

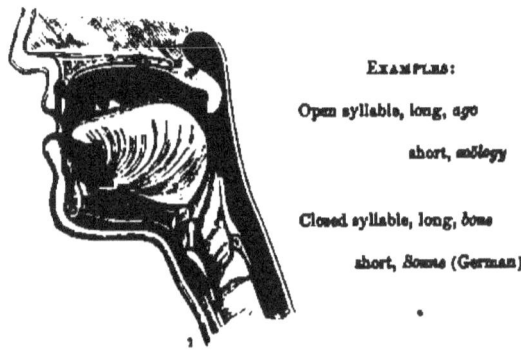

EXAMPLES:

Open syllable, long, *ago*

short, *ænlogy*

Closed syllable, long, *bone*

short, *Sonne* (German)

Fig. 8.

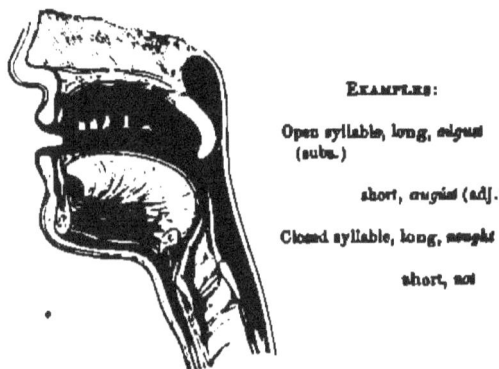

EXAMPLES:

Open syllable, long, *aught* (subs.)

short, *aught* (adj.)

Closed syllable, long, *nought*

short, *not*

5. If the lips are fairly open, and the back of the

[1] Brücke, p. 13.

VOWELS.   133

tongue raised towards the palate, the larynx being raised at the same time, we hear the sound *e*. The buccal tube resembles a bottle with a narrow neck. The natural pitch of *e* is B''' flat.

Fig. 9.

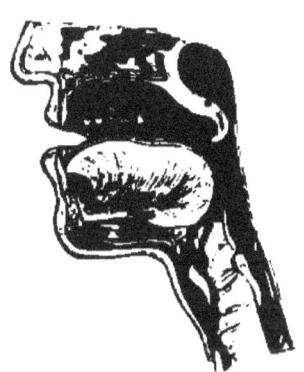

EXAMPLES:

Open syllable, long, *mowd*
  short, *pipe* [1]

Closed syllable, long, *form*
  short, It. *ballere*

Fig. 10.

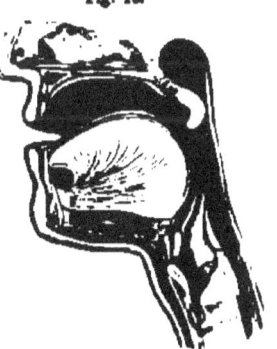

EXAMPLES:

Open syllable, long, *hey*
  short, *afraid*

Closed syllable, long, *lake*
  short, Germ. *Leck*

6. If we raise the tongue higher still, and narrow
  [1] As pronounced by children.

the lips, we hear *i*. The buccal tube represents a bottle with a very narrow neck of no more than six centimètres from palate to lips. Such a bottle would answer to c''''. The natural pitch of *i* seems to be D''''.

Fig. 11.

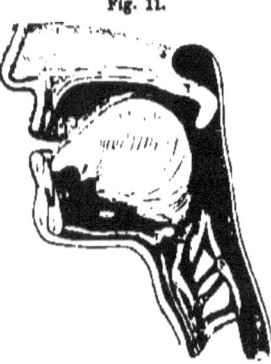

EXAMPLES:

Open syllable, long, *he*

short, *behalf*

Closed syllable, long, *been*

short, *been*

pronounced *bin*

7. There is, besides, the most troublesome of all vowels, the neutral vowel, sometimes called *Urvocal*. Professor Willis defines it as the natural vowel of the reed, Mr. Ellis as the voice in its least modified form. Some people hear it everywhere, others imagine they can distinguish various shades of it. We know it best in short closed syllables, such as *but*, *dust*, &c. It is supposed to be long in *absurd*. Sir John Herschel hears but one and the same vowel in *spurt, assert, bird, virtue, dove, oven, double, blood*. Sheridan and Smart distinguish between the vowels heard in *bird* and *work*, in *whirl'd* and *world*. There is no doubt that in English all unaccented syllables have a tendency towards it,[1] e. g. *āgainst, fīnăl, prin-*

[1] Ellis, § 29.

cipāl, ideă, captain, villăge. Town sinks to *Padding-tŏn, ford* to *Oxförd*; and though some of these pronunciations may still be considered as vulgar, they are nevertheless real.

These are the principal vowels, and there are few languages in which they do not occur. But we have only to look to English, French, and German in order to perceive that there are many varieties of vocal sound besides these. There is the French *u*, the German *ü*, which lies between *i* and *u*;[1] as in French, *du*, German, *über, Sünde*. Professor Helmholtz has fixed the natural pitch of *ü* as *o'''*.

There is the French *eu*, the German *ö*, which lies between *e* and *o*, as in French *peu*, German *König*, or short in *Böcke*.[2] Professor Helmholtz has fixed the natural pitch of *ö* as *c'''* sharp.

There is the peculiar short *a* in closed syllables in English, such as *hat, happy, man*. It may be heard lengthened in the affected pronunciation of *half*.

There is the peculiar short *i*, as heard in the English *happy, reality, hit, knit*.[3]

There is the short *e* in closed syllables, such as heard in English *debt, bed, men*, which, if lengthened, comes very near to the German *ä* in *Väter*, and the French *é* in *père*, not quite the English *there*.

Lastly, there are the diphthongs, which arise when, instead of pronouncing one vowel immediately after

---

[1] "While the tongue gets ready to pronounce *i*, the lips assume the position requisite for *u*." — Du Bois-Reymond, *Kadmus*, p. 160.

[2] The German *ö*, if shortened, seems to dwindle down to the neutral vowel, e. g. *öfen*, ovens, but *öffnen*, to open. See Du Bois-Reymond, *Kadmus*, p. 173. Nevertheless, it is necessary to distinguish between the German *Götter* and the English *gutter*.

[3] Brücke speaks of this and some other vowels which occur in English in closed syllables as imperfect vowels. — p. 23.

another with two efforts of the voice, we produce a sound *during* the change from one position to the other that would be required for each vowel. If we change the *a* into the *i* position and pronounce a vowel, we hear *ai*, as in *aisle*. A singer who has to sing *I* on a long note will end by singing the Italian *i*. If we change the *a* into the *u* position and pronounce a vowel, we hear *au*, as in *how*. Here, too, we find many varieties, such as äi, ăi, ei, and the several less perfect diphthongs, such as *oi*, *ui*, &c.

Though this may seem a long and tedious list, it is, in fact, but a very rough sketch, and I must refer to the works of Mr. Ellis and others for many minute details in the chromatic scale of the vowels. Though the tube of the mouth, as modified by the tongue and the lips, is the principal determinant in the production of vowels, yet there are other agencies at work, the *velum pendulum*, the posterior wall of the *pharynx*, the greater or less elevation of the *larynx*, all coming in at times to modify the cavity of the throat. It is said that in pronouncing the high vowels the bones of the skull participate in the vibration,[1] and it has been proved by irrefragable evidence that the *velum pendulum* is of very essential importance in the pronunciation of all vowels. Professor Czermak,[2] by introducing a probe through the nose into the cavity of the pharynx, felt distinctly that the position of the *velum* was changed with each vowel; that it was lowest for *a*, and rose successively with *e*, *o*, *u*, *i*, reaching its highest point with *i*.

[1] Brücke, p. 16.
[2] *Sitzungsberichte der K. K. Akademie zu Wien* (Mathemat.-Naturwissenschaftliche Classe), xxiv. p. 5.

He likewise proved that the cavity of the nose was more or less opened during the pronunciation of certain vowels. By introducing water into the nose he found that while he pronounced *i*, *u*, *o*, the water would remain in the nose, but that it would pass into the fauces when he came to *e*, and still more when he uttered *a*.[1] These two vowels, *a* and *e*, were the only vowels which Leblanc,[2] a young man whose larynx was completely closed, failed to pronounce.

Nasal Vowels.

If, instead of emitting the vowel sound freely through the mouth, we allow the velum pendulum to drop and the air to vibrate through the cavities which connect the nose with the pharynx, we hear the nasal vowels[3] so common in French, as *un*, *on*, *in*, *an*. It is not necessary that the air should actually pass through the nose; on the contrary, we may shut the nose, and thus increase the nasal twang. The only requisite is the removal of the velum, which, in ordinary vowels, covers the *choanæ* more or less completely.[4]

Consonants.

There is no reason why languages should not have been entirely formed of vowels. There are

---

[1] Funke, *l. c.* p. 676.
[2] Bindseil, *Abhandlungen zur Allgemeinen Vergleichenden Sprachlehre*, 1838, p. 212.
[3] Brücke, p. 27.
[4] The different degrees of this closure were tested by the experiment of Prof. Czermak with a metal looking-glass applied to the nostrils during the pronunciation of pure and nasal vowels. *Sitzungsberichte der Wiener Akademie*, xxviii. p. 575, xxix. p. 174.

words consisting of vowels only, such as Latin *eo*, I go; *ea*, she; *eoa*, eastern; the Greek ēioeis (ἠιόεις, with high banks), but for its final *s*; the Hawaiian *hooiaioai*, to testify, but for its initial breathing. Yet these very words show how unpleasant the effect of such a language would have been. Something else was wanted to supply the bones of language, namely, the consonants. Consonants are called in Sanskrit *vyanjana*, which means "rendering distinct or manifest," while the vowels are called *svara*, sounds, from the same root which yielded *susurrus* in Latin.

As scholars are always fond of establishing general theories, however scanty the evidence at their disposal, we need not wonder that languages like the Hawaiian, in which the vowels predominate to a very considerable extent, should on that very ground have been represented as primitive languages. It was readily supposed that the general progress of language was from the slightly articulated to the strongly articulated; and that the fewer the consonants, the older the language. Yet we have only to compare the Hawaiian with the Polynesian languages in order to see that there too the consonantal articulation existed and was lost; that consonants, in fact, are much more apt to be dropped than to sprout up between two vowels. Prof. Buschmann expresses the same opinion: " Mes recherches m'ont conduit à la conviction, que cet état de pauvreté phonique polynésienne n'est pas tant l'état naturel d'une langue prise à sa naissance, qu'une détérioration du type vigoureux des langues malaies occidentales, amenée par un peuple qui a peu de disposition pour varier les sons."[1] The very name of *Havai*, or more correctly *Hawai'i*, confirms this view. It is pronounced

in the Samoan dialect,	Savai'i
Tahitian,	Havai'i
Rarotongan,	Avaiki
Nukuhivan,	Havaiki
New Zealand,	Hawaiki

from which the original form may be inferred to have been *Savaiki*.[2]

All consonants fall under the category of noises. If we watch any musical instruments, we can easily perceive that their sounds are always preceded by certain noises, arising from the first impulses imparted to the air before it can produce really musical sensations. We hear the puffing and panting of the siren, the scratching of the violin, the hammering of the pianoforte, the spitting of the flute. The same in speaking. If we send out our breath, whether vocalized or not, we hear the rushing out, the momentary breathing, the impulse produced by the inner air as it reaches the outer.

If we breathe freely, the glottis is wide open,[3] and the breath emitted can be distinctly heard. Yet this is not yet our *h*, or the *spiritus asper*. An intention is required to change mere breathing into *h*; the *velum pendulum* has to assume its proper position, and the breath thus jerked out is then properly called *asper*, because the action of the abdominal muscles gives to it a certain asperity. If, on the contrary, the

[1] Buschmann, *Iles Marq.* pp. 86, 59. Pott, *Etymologische Forschungen*, ii. 46.
[2] Hale, *l. c.* p. 120.
[3] Czermak, *Physiologische Untersuchungen mit Garcia's Kehlkopfspiegel, Sitzungsberichte der K. K. Akademie der Wissenschaften*, vol. xxix. 1858, p. 563.

breath is slightly curbed or tempered by the pressure *of the glottis*, and if thus held in, it is emitted gently, it is properly called *spiritus lenis*, soft breath. We distinctly hear it, like a slight bubble, if we listen to the pronunciation of any initial vowel, as in *old, art, ache, ear*, or if we pronounce "my hand," as it is pronounced by vulgar people, "my 'and." According to some physiologists,[1] and according to nearly all grammarians, this initial noise can be so far subdued as to become evanescent, and we all imagine that we can pronounce an initial vowel quite pure.[2] Yet I believe the Greeks were right in admitting the *spiritus lenis* as inherent in all initial vowels that have not the *spiritus asper*, and the laryngoscope clearly shows in all initial vowels a narrowing of the vocal chords, quite distinct from the opening that takes place in the pronunciation of the *h*.

It has been customary to call the *h* or spiritus asper a surd, the spiritus lenis a sonant letter; and there is some truth in this distinction if we clearly know what is meant by these terms. Now, as we are speaking of whispered language, it is clear that the vocal chords, in their musical quality, can have no influence on this distinction. Nevertheless, if we may trust the laryngoscope,[3] that is to say, if we may trust our eyes, the chordæ vocales or the glottis would seem to be chiefly concerned in producing the spiritus lenis, or in mollifying the spiritus asper. It is their narrowing, though not their stretching, that tempers the impetus of the spiritus asper, and pre-

---
[1] Brücke, p. 9.
[2] Brücke, p. 83. "If in pronouncing the spiritus asper the glottis is narrowed, we hear the pure tone of the voice without any additional noise." The noise, however, is quite perceptible, particularly in the *vox clandestina*.
[3] Brücke, *Grundzüge*, p. 9.

BREATHINGS. 141

vents it from rushing straight against the faucal walls, and in this sense the noise or friction which we hear while the breath slowly emerges from the larynx into the mouth may be ascribed to them. There is another very important distinction between spiritus asper and lenis. It is quite impossible to sing the spiritus asper, that is to say, to make the breath which produces it, sonant. If we try to sing *ha*, the tone does not come out till the *h* is over. We might as well try to whistle and to sing at the same time.[1]

The reason of this is clear. If the breath that is to produce *h* is to become a tone, it must be checked

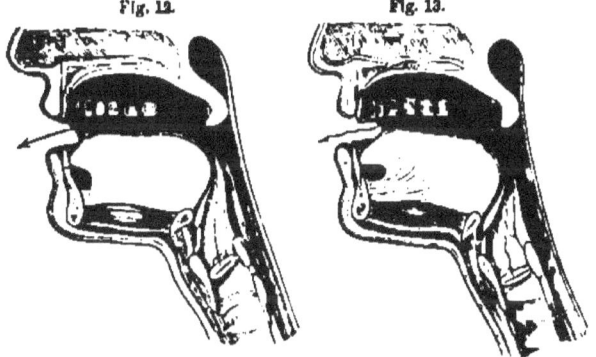

Fig. 12. Fig. 13.

[1]—(h); e. g. *hand*.   [1]—; e. g. *and*.

by the vocal chords, but the very nature of *h* consists in the noise of the breath rushing forth *unchecked*

[1] See R. von Raumer, *Gesammelte Schriften*, p. 371, note. Johannes Müller says: "The only continua which is quite mute and cannot be accompanied by the tone or the humming of the voice, is the *h*, the aspirate. If one attempts to pronounce the *h* loud, with the tone of the chordæ vocales, the humming of the voice is not synchronous with the *h*, but follows it, and the aspiration vanishes as soon as the air is changed into tones by the chordæ vocales."

from the lungs to the outer air. The spiritus lenis, on the contrary, can be sounded, because, in pronouncing it more or less distinctly, the breath is checked near the chordæ vocales, and can there be intoned.

This simplest breathing, in its double character of *asper* and *lenis*, can be modified in eight different ways by interposing certain barriers or gates formed by the tongue, the soft and hard palate, the teeth, and the lips. Before we examine these, it will be useful to say a few words on the general distinction between *asper* and *lenis*, a distinction which, as we shall see, affects every one of these breathings.

The distinction which, with regard to the first breathing or spiritus, is commonly called *asper* and *lenis*, is the same which, in other letters, is known by the names of *hard* and *soft*, *surd* and *sonant*, *tenuis* and *media*. The peculiar character meant to be described by these terms, and the manner in which it is produced, are the same throughout. The authors of the Prâtisâkhyas knew what has been confirmed by the laryngoscope, that, in pronouncing *tenues*, hard or surd letters, the glottis is open, while, in pronouncing *mediæ*, soft or sonant letters, the glottis is closed. In the first class of letters, vibration of the vocal chords is impossible; in the second, they are so close that, though not set to vibrate periodically, they begin to sound audibly, or, perhaps more correctly, they modify the sound. Anticipating the distinction between $k, t, p,$ and $g, d, b,$ I may quote here the description given by Professor Helmholtz of the general causes which produce their distinction.

"The series of the mediæ, $b, d, g,$" he says, "differs from that of the tenues, $p, t, k,$ by this, that for the former the glottis is, at the time of consonantal opening, sufficiently narrowed to enable it to sound, or at least to produce the noise of the *vox clandestina*, or whisper, while it is wide open with the tenues,[1] and therefore unable to sound.

"Mediæ are therefore accompanied by the tone of the voice, and this may even, when they begin a syllable, set in a moment before, and when they end a syllable, continue a moment after the opening of the mouth, because some air may be driven into the closed cavity of the mouth and support the sound of the vocal chords in the larynx.

"Because of the narrowed glottis, the rush of the air is more moderate, the noise of the air less sharp than with the tenues, which are pronounced with the glottis wide open, so that a great mass of air may rush forth at once from the chest."[2]

We now return to an examination of the various modifications of the breaths, in their double character of hard and soft.

If, instead of allowing the breath to escape freely from the lungs to the lips, we hem it in by a barrier formed by lifting the tongue against the uvula, we get the sound of *ch*, as heard in the German

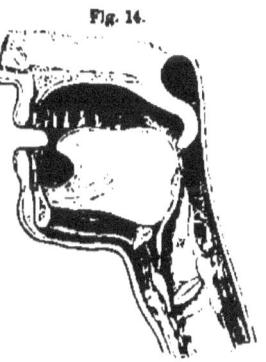
Fig. 14.

ʰ (ch); e. g. *Loch*.
ʰ (g); e. g. *Tage* (German).

[1] See Lepsius, *Die Arabischen Sprachlaute*, p. 108, line 1.
[2] This distinction is very lucidly described by R. von Raumer, *Gesammelte Schriften*, p. 144. He calls the hard letters *flatæ*, blown, the soft let-

144   BREATHINGS.

ach or the Scotch *loch*.[1] If, on the contrary, we slightly check the breath as it reaches that barrier, we get the sound which is heard when the *g* in the German word *Tage* is not pronounced as a media, but as a semi-vowel, *Tage*.

A second barrier is formed by bringing the tongue in a more contracted state towards the point where the hard palate begins, a little beyond the point where the *k* is formed. Letting the spiritus asper pass this isthmus, we produce the sound *ch* as heard in the German *China* or *ich*, a sound very difficult to an Englishman, though approaching to the initial sound of words like *hume, huge*.[2] If we soften the breath as it reaches this barrier, we arrive at the familiar sound of *y* in *year*. This sound is naturally accompanied by a slight hum arising from the check applied through the glottis, nor is there much difficulty in intoning

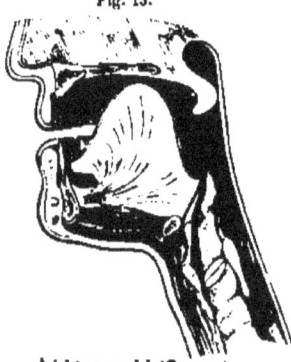

Fig. 15.

ϳ (ch); e. g. *ich* (German).
ϳ (y); e. g. *yea*.

tern *halata*, breathed. He observes that breathed letters, though always sonant in English, are not so in other languages, and therefore divides the breathed consonants, physiologically, into two classes, sonant and non-sonant. This distinction, however, is apt to mislead, and is of no importance in reducing languages to writing. See also *Investigations into the Laws of English Orthography and Pronunciation*, by Prof. R. L. Tafel. New York, 1862.

[1] The same sound occurs in some of the Dayak dialects of Borneo. See *Surat Peminyuh Daya Sarawak*, Reading-Book for Land and Hill Dayaks, in the Sentah dialect. Singapore, 1862. Printed at the Mission Press.
[2] Ellis, *English Phonetics*, § 47.

the *y*. There is no evidence whatever that the Sanskrit palatal flatus श was ever pronounced like *ch* in German *China* and *ich*. Most likely it was the assibilated sound which can be produced if, keeping the organs in the position for German *ch*, we narrow the passage and strengthen the breath. This, however, is merely an hypothesis, not a dogma.

A third barrier, produced by advancing the tongue towards the teeth, modifies the spiritus asper into *s*, the spiritus lenis into *z*, the former completely surd, the latter capable of intonation; for instance, *the rise* or *rice*; but *to rise*.

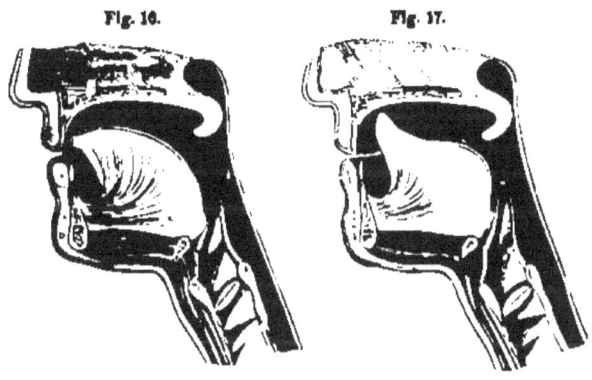

Fig. 16.   Fig. 17.

s; e. g. *the rise, rice, sin*.   s; (sh); e. g. *sharp*.
z; e. g. *to rise, zeal*.   z; e. g. *azure*.

A fourth barrier is formed by drawing the tongue back and giving it a more or less concave (retroussé) shape, so that we can distinctly see its lower surface brought in position towards the back of the upper teeth or the palate. By pressing the air through this trough, we get the letter *sh* as heard in *sharp*, and *s* as heard in *pleasure*, or *j* in the French *jamais*; the former mute, the latter intonable. The pronunciation of the Sanskrit lingual *sh* requires a very elaborate position of the tongue, so that its lower surface should really strike the roof of the palate. But a much more simple and natural position, as described above, will produce nearly the same effect.

A fifth barrier is produced by bringing the tip of the tongue almost point-blank against the back of the upper teeth, or, according to others, by placing it against the edge of the upper teeth, or even between the edges of the upper and lower teeth. If, then, we emit the spiritus asper, we form the English *th*, if we emit the spiritus lenis, the English *dh*; the former mute, as in *breath*, the latter intonable, as in *to breathe*, and both very difficult for a German to pronounce.

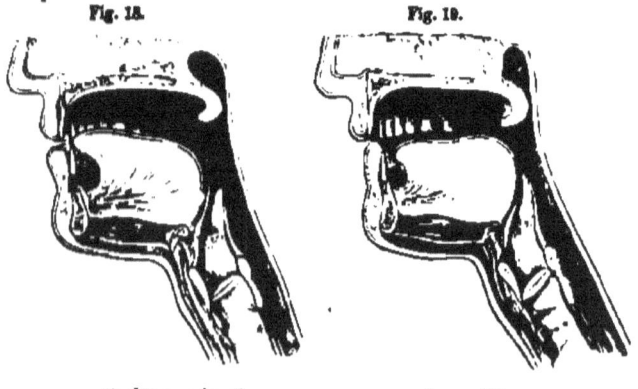

Fig. 18.   Fig. 19.

th (þ); e. g. *breath.*   f; e. g. *life.*
dh (ð); e. g. *to breathe.*   v; e. g. *to live.*

A sixth barrier is formed by bringing the lower lip against the upper teeth. This modifies the spiritus asper to *f*, the spiritus lenis to *v*, as heard in *life* and to *live*, *half* and to *halve*.

A seventh barrier is possible by bringing the two lips together. The sound there produced by the spiritus asper would be the sound which we make in blowing out a candle; it is not a favorite sound in civilized languages. The spiritus lenis, however, is very common; it is the *w* in German as heard in *Quelle*, i. e. *Kwelle*;[1] also sometimes in the German *Wind*, &c.

An eighth barrier is formed by slightly contracting and rounding the lips, instead of bringing them together flat against each other. Here the spiritus asper assumes the sound of *wh* in *wheel*, *which*; whereas the spiritus lenis is the common English double *u*, as heard in *weal*.

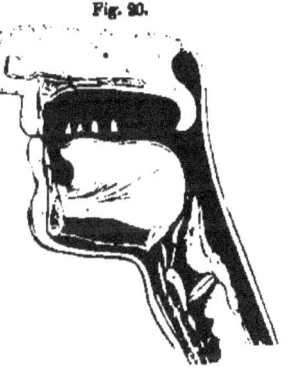

Fig. 20.

ẇ (wh); e. g. *which*.
ẇ; e. g. *we*.

We have thus examined eight modifications of spiritus asper and spiritus lenis, produced by breath emitted eruptively or prohibitively, and modified by certain narrowings of the mouth. Considering the great pliability of the muscles of the tongue and the mouth, we can easily imagine other possible narrowings; but with the exception of some peculiar letters of the Semitic and African

[1] Brücke, *l. c.* p. 34.

languages, we shall find these eight sufficient for our own immediate purposes.

The peculiar guttural sounds of the Arabs, which have given rise to so much discussion, have at last been scientifically defined by Professor Czermak. Examining an Arab by means of the laryngoscope, he was able to watch the exact formation of the Hha and Ain which constitute a separate class of guttural breathings in the Semitic languages. This is his account. If the glottis is narrowed and the vocal chords brought near together, not, however, in a straight parallel position, but distinctly notched in the middle, while, at the same time, the epiglottis is pressed down, then the stream of breath in passing assumes the character of the Arabic Hha, ح, as different from *h*, the spiritus asper, the Arabic s.

If this Hha is made sonant, it becomes Ain. Starting from the configuration as described for Hha, all that takes place in order to change it into Ain is that the rims of the apertures left open for Hha are brought close together, so that the stream of air striking against them causes a vibration in the *fissura laryngea*, and not, as for other sonant letters, in the real glottis. These ocular observations of Czermak[1] coincide with the phonetic descriptions given by Arab grammarians, and particularly with Wallin's account. If the vibration in the fissura laryngea takes place less regularly, the sound as-

[1] *Sitzungsberichte der Mathematisch - Naturwissenschaftlichen Classe der Kaiserlichen Akademie der Wissenschaften*, vol. xxix. p. 578, *seq.* Professor Lepsius, *Die Arabischen Sprachlaute*, has but partially adopted the views of Brücke and Czermak on what they call the *Gutturales Vera* in Arabic. See also the curious controversy between Professor Brücke and Professor Lepsius, in the 12th volume of the *Zeitschrift für Vergleichende Sprachforschung*.

sumes the character of a trilled r, the deep guttural r of the Low Saxons. The Arabic ح and خ I must continue to consider as near equivalents of the *ch* in *loch* and *'h* in German *tage*, though the pronunciation of the خ approaches sometimes to a trill, like the *r grasseyé*.

Trills.

We have to add to this class of letters two which are commonly called *trills*, the r and the l. They are both intonable or sonant, that is, to say, they are modifications of the spiritus lenis, but they differ from the other modifications by a vibration of certain portions of the mouth. I am unable to pronounce the different r's, and I shall therefore borrow their description from one of the highest authorities on this subject, Mr. Ellis.[1] "In the trills," he writes, "the breath is emitted with sufficient force to cause a vibration, not merely of some membrane, but of some much more extensive soft part, as the uvula, tongue, or lips. In the Arabic *grh* (grhain), which is the same as the Northumberland *burr* (burgrh, Hágrhiut for Harriot), and the French Provençal *r grasseyé* (as, Paris c'est la France, Paghri c'est la Fgrhance), the uvula lies along the back part of the tongue, pointing to the teeth, and is very distinctly vibrated. If the tongue is more raised and the vibration indistinct or very slight, the result is the English r, in *more, poor*, while a still greater elevation of the tongue produces the r as heard after palatal vowels, as *hear, mere, fire*. These trills are so vocal that they form distinct syllables, as *surf*,

[1] *Universal Writing and Printing*, by A. J. Ellis, B. A., 1856, p. 5.

serf, fur, fir, virtue, honor, and are with difficulty separable from the vowels. Hence, when a guttural vowel precedes, the effect of the *r* is scarcely audible. Thus *laud, lord, father, farther,* are scarcely distinguishable."

Professor Helmholtz describes *r* and *l* as follows: " In pronouncing *r* the stream of air is periodically entirely interrupted by the trembling of the soft palate or of the tip of the tongue, and we then get an intermittent noise, the peculiar jarring quality of which is produced by these very intermissions. In pronouncing *l*, the moving soft lateral edges of the tongue produce, not entire interruptions, but oscillations in the force of air." [1]

If the lips are trilled, the result is *brh*, a sound which children are fond of making, but which, like the corresponding spiritus asper, is of little importance in speaking. If the tongue is placed against the teeth, and its two lateral edges, or even one only, are made to vibrate, we hear the sound of *l*, which is easily intonable as well as the *r*.

We have thus exhausted one class of letters which all agree in this, that they can be pronounced by themselves, and that their pronunciation can be continued. In Greek, they are all included under the name of *Hemiphona*, or semi-vowels, while Sanskrit grammarians mention as their specific quality that, in pronouncing them, the two organs, the active and passive, which are necessary for the production of all consonantal noises, are not allowed to touch each other, but only to approach.[2]

[1] *l. c.* p. 116.
[2] In Pâṇini, l. 1, 9, y, r, l, v, are said to be pronounced with Ishatspriahtam, slight touch; i, sh, s, h, with vivṛitam, opening, or Ishadrivṛitam, slight opening, or asprishṭam, no contact.

Checks or Mutes.

We now come to the third and last class of letters, which are distinguished from all the rest by this, that for a time they stop the emission of breath altogether. They are called by the Greeks *aphōna*, mutes, because they check all voice, or, what is the same, because they cannot be intoned. They differ, however, from the hisses or hard breathings, which likewise resist all intonation; for, while the hisses are emissions of breath, they, the mutes, are prohibitions of breath. They are formed, as the Sanskrit grammarians say, by complete contact of the active and passive organs. They will require very little explanation. If we bring the root of the tongue against the soft palate, we hear the consonantal noise of *k*. If we bring the tongue against the

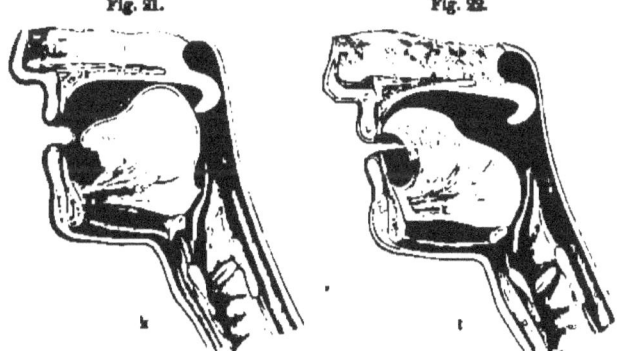

Fig. 21. Fig. 22.

teeth, we hear the consonantal noise of *t*. If we bring the lower against the upper lip, we hear the consonantal noise of *p*. The real difference between those three articulations consists in this, that in p, two flat surfaces are struck against each other; in t, a sharp against a flat surface; in k, a round against a hollow surface. These three principal contacts can be modified almost indefinitely, in some cases without perceptibly altering the articulation. If we pronounce *ku*, *ka*, *ki*, the point of contact between tongue and palate advances considerably without much influence on the character of the initial consonant. The same applies to the t contact.[1] Here the essential point is that the tongue should strike against the wall formed by the teeth. But this contact may be effected —

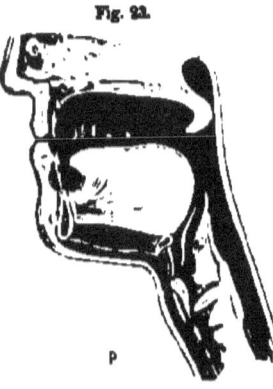

Fig. 22.

p

1. By flattening the tongue and bringing its edge against the alveolar part of the palate.

2. By making the tongue convex, and bringing the lower surface against the dome of the palate (these are the lingual or cacuminal letters in Sanskrit[2]).

3. By making the tongue convex, and bringing the upper surface against the palate, the tip against the lower teeth (dorsal *t* in Bohemian).

4. By slightly opening the teeth and stopping the aperture by the rounded tongue, or by bringing the tongue against the teeth.

[1] Brücke, p. 38.
[2] Formerly called *cerebral*, a mistranslation of *mūrddhanya*, thoughtlessly repeated by many Sanskrit scholars and retained by others, on the ground that it is too absurd to mistake. Brücke, p. 37.

Most languages have only one *t*, the first or the fourth; some have two; but we seldom find more than two sets of dentals distinguished phonetically in one and the same dialect.

If we place the tongue in a position intermediate between the guttural and dental contact, we can produce various consonantal sounds which go by the general name of *palatal*. The click that can be produced by jerking the tongue, from the position in which *ich* and *yea* are formed, against the palate, shows the possibility of a definite and simple consonantal contact analogous to the two palatal breathings. That contact, however, is liable to many modifications, and it oscillates in different dialects between *ky* and *tsh*. The sound of *ch* in *church*, or Ital. *cielo*, is formed most easily if we place the tongue and teeth in the position described above for the formation of *sh* in *sharp*, and then stop the breath by complete contact between the tongue and the back of the teeth. Some physiologists, and among them Brücke,[1] maintain that *ch* in English and Italian consists of two letters, *t* followed by *sh*, and should not be classed as a simple letter. There is some truth in this, which, however, has been greatly exaggerated from want of careful observation. *Ch* may be said to consist of half *t* and half *sh*; but half *t* and half *sh* give only one whole consonant. There is an attempt of the organs at pronouncing *t*, but that attempt is frustrated or modified before it takes effect.[2] If Sanskrit grammarians called the vowels

[1] Brücke, p. 63, *seq*. He would, however, distinguish these concrete consonants from groups of consonants, such as ξ, ψ.

[2] Du Bois-Reymond, *Kadmus*, p. 213.

é and *ó* diphthongs, because they combine the conditions of *a* and *i*, and of *a* and *u*, we might call the Sanskrit *ch* a consonantal diphthong, though even this would lead to the false supposition that it was necessarily a double letter, which it is not. That the palatal articulation may be simple is clearly seen in those languages where, as in Sanskrit, both ancient and modern, *ch* leaves a short vowel that precedes it short, whereas a double consonant would raise its quantity.

Few Sanskrit scholars acquainted with the Prâtisâkhyas, works describing the formation of letters, would venture to speak dogmatically on the exact pronunciation of the so-called palatal letters at any definite period in the history of ancient Sanskrit. They may have been pronounced as they are now pronounced, as consonantal diphthongs; they may have differed from the gutturals no more than *k* in *kaw* differs from *k* in *key*; or they may have been formed by raising the convex part of the tongue so as to flatten it against the palate, the hinder part being in the *k*, and the front part in the *y* position. The *k*, as sometimes heard in English, in *kind, card, cube, cow,* sounding almost like *kyind, cyard, cyube, cyow,* may give us an idea of the transition of *k* into *ky,* and finally into English *ch*, — a change analogous to that of *t* into *ch,* as in *natura, nature,* or of *d* into *j,* as in *soldier,* pronounced *soljer, diurnale* changed to *journal.* In the northern dialects of Jütland a distinct *j* is heard after *k* and *g* if followed by *æ, e, o, ö*; for instance, *kjæv', kjær, gjekk, kjerk, skjell,* instead of *kæv', kær,* &c.[1] However that may

[1] See Kuhn's *Zeitschrift,* xli. 147.

be, we must admit, in Sanskrit and in other languages, a class of palatals, sometimes modifications of gutturals, sometimes of dentals, varying no doubt in pronunciation, not only at different periods in the history of the same language, but also in different localities; yet sufficiently distinct to claim a place for themselves, though a secondary one, between gutturals and dentals, and embracing, as we shall see, the same number of subdivisions as gutturals, dentals, and labials.

It is not always perceived that these three consonants *k*, *t*, *p*, and their modifications, represent in reality two quite different effects. If we say *ka*, the effect produced on the ear is very different from *ak*. In the first case the consonantal noise is produced by the sudden opening of the tongue and palate; in the second, by their shutting. This is still clearer in *pa* and *ap*. In *pa* you hear the noise of two doors opening, in *ap* of two doors shutting. In *empire* you hear only half a *p*; the shutting takes place in the *m*, and the *p* is nothing but the opening of the lips. In *topmost* you hear likewise only half a *p*; you hear the shutting, but the opening belongs to the *m*. The same in *uppermost*. It is on this ground that mute letters have sometimes been called *dividuæ*, or divisible, as opposed to the first class, in which that difference does not exist; for whether I say *sa* or *as*, the sound of *s* is the same.

Soft Checks, or Mediæ.

We should now have finished our survey of the alphabet of nature, if it was not that the consonantal stops *k*, *t*, *p*, are liable to certain modifications, which, as they are of great influence in the formation of language, deserve to be carefully considered. What is it that changes *k* into *g* and *ng*, *t* into *d* and *n*, *p* into *b* and *m*? *B* is called a media, a soft letter, a sonant, in opposition to *p*, which is called a tenuis, a hard letter, or a surd. But what is meant by these terms? A tenuis, we saw, was so called by the Greeks in opposition to the aspirates, the Greek grammarians wishing to express that the aspirates had a rough or shaggy sound,[1] whereas the tenues were bald, slight, or thin. This does not help us much. "Soft" and "hard" are terms which no doubt express the outward difference of *p* and *b*, but they do not explain the cause of that difference. "Surd" and "sonant" are apt to mislead; for, as both *p* and *b* are classed as *mutes*, it is difficult to see how a mute letter could be sonant. Some persons have been so entirely deceived by the term sonant, that they imagined all the so-called sonant letters to be necessarily pronounced with *tonic* vibrations of the chordæ vocales.[2] This is physically impossible; for if we really tried to intone *p* or *b*, we should either destroy the *p* and *b*, or be suffocated in our attempt at producing voice. Both *p* and *b*, as far as tone is concerned, are aphonous or mute. But *b* differs from *p* in so far as, in order to pronounce it, the breath is for a moment checked by the glottis, just as it was in pronouncing *v* instead of *f*. What, then, is the difference between German *w* and *b*? Simply that in the former no contact takes place,

---

[1] Brücke, p. 90. τῷ πνεύματι πολλῷ, Dion Hal. R. von Raumer, *Die Aspiration*, p. 103.
[2] Funke, p. 685. Brücke, *Grundzüge*, pp. 7, 89.

and hence no cessation of breath, no silence; whereas the mute *b* requires contact, complete contact, and hence causes a pause, however short it may seem, so that we clearly hear the breath all the time it is struggling with the lips that shut in upon it. We may now understand why the terms soft and hard, as applied to *b* and *p*, are by no means so inappropriate as has sometimes been supposed. Czermak, by using his probe, as described above, found that hard consonants (mutæ tenues) drove it up much more violently than the soft consonants (mutæ mediæ).[1] The normal impetus of the breath is certainly checked, subdued, softened, when we pronounce *b*; it does not strike straight against the barrier of the lips; it hesitates, so to say, and we hear how it clings to the glottis in its slow onward passage. This slight sound, which is not caused by any rhythmic vibration, but only by a certain narrowing of the chordæ, is all that can be meant when some grammarians call these mute consonants sonant; and, physiologically, the only appreciable difference between p and b, t and d, k and g, is that in the former the glottis is wide open, in the latter narrowed, but not so far stretched as to produce musical tones.

[1] L. c. p. 9.

Nasal Checks.

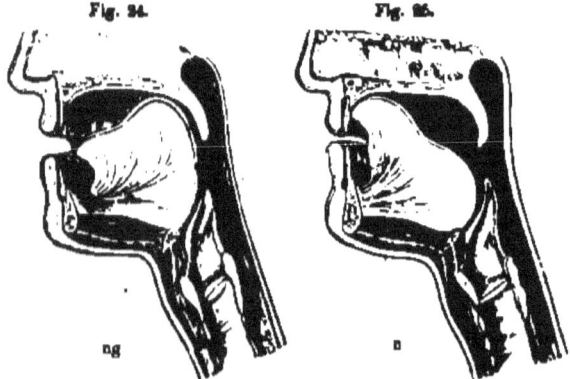

Fig. 24.   Fig. 25.

ng   n

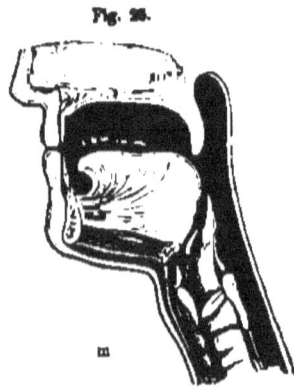

Fig. 26.

m

Lastly, g, d, b, may be modified to ng, n, m. For these three nasals a full contact takes place, but the breath is stopped, not abruptly as in the tenues, but in the same manner as with the mediæ. At the same time the breathing is emitted, not through the mouth, but through the nose. It is not necessary that breath should be propelled through the nose, as long as the veil is withdrawn that separates the nose from the pharynx. Water injected into the nose while n and m are pronounced rushes at once into the windpipe.[1] Where the withdrawal of the velum is rendered impossible by disease, — such a case came under Czermak's[2] observation, — pure nasals cannot be produced.[3]

The so-called mouillé or softened nasal, and all other mouillé consonants, are produced by the addition of a final y, and need not be classified as simple letters.

Aspirated Checks.

For most languages the letters hitherto described would be amply sufficient; but in the more highly organized forms of speech new distinctions were introduced and graphically expressed which deserve some explanation. Instead of pronouncing a tenuis as it ought to be pronounced, by cutting sharp through the stream of breath or tone which proceeds from the larynx, it is possible to gather the breath and to let it explode audibly as soon as the consonantal contact is withdrawn. In this manner we form the hard or surd aspirates which occur in Sanskrit and in Greek, kh, th, ph.

If, on the contrary, we pronounce g, d, b, and allow the soft breathing to be heard as soon as the contact is removed, we have the soft aspirates, which are of frequent occurrence in Sanskrit, gh, dh, bh.

Much discussion has been raised on these hard and soft aspirates, the question being whether their

---

[1] Czermak, *Wiener Akademie*, xxlv. p. 9.
[2] Funke, p. 68l. Czermak, *Wiener Akademie*, xxix. p. 173.
[3] Professor Helmholtz has the following remarks on M and N: "M and N resemble the vowels in their formation, because they cause no noise in the buccal tube. The buccal tube is shut, and the voice escapes through the nose. The mouth only forms a resounding cavity, modifying the sound. If we watch from below people walking up-hill and speaking together, the nasals m and n are heard longest."

first element was really a complete consonantal contact, or whether the contact was incomplete, and the letters intended were hard and soft breathings. As we have no means of hearing either the old Brahmans or the ancient Greeks pronounce their hard aspirates, and as it is certain that pronunciation is constantly changing, we cannot hope to derive much aid either from modern Pandits or from modern Greeks. The Brahmans of the present day are said to pronounce their kh, th, and ph like a complete tenuis, followed by the spiritus asper. The nearest approach to kh is said to be the English kh in *inkhorn*, though this can hardly be a good illustration, as here the tenuis ends and the aspirate begins a syllable. The Irish pronunciation of *kind, town, pig*, has likewise been quoted as in some degree similar to the Sanskrit hard aspirates. In the modern languages of India where the Sanskrit letters are transcribed by Persian letters, we actually find kh represented by two letters, k and h, joined together. The modern Greeks, on the contrary, pronounce their three aspirates as breathings, like h, th, f. It seems to me that the only two points of importance are, first, whether these aspirates in Greek or Sanskrit were formed with or without complete contact, and, secondly, whether they were classed as surd or as sonant. Sanskrit grammarians allow, as far as I can judge, of no doubt on either of these points. The hard aspirates are formed by complete contact (sprishṭa), and they belong to that class of letters for which the glottis must be completely open, i. e. to the surd or hard consonants. These two points once established put an end to all speculations on the subject. What the exact sound of these letters was is difficult to determine, because the ancient authorities vary in their descriptions, but there is no uncertainty as to their physiological character. They are said to be uttered with a strong out-breathing (mahâprâṇaḥ), but this, as it is shared by them in common with the soft aspirates and the hard breaths, cannot constitute their distinctive feature. Their technical name "soshman," i. e. "with wind," would admit of two explanations. "Wind" might be taken in the general sense of breath, or — and this is more correct — in the sense of the eight letters called "the winds" in Sanskrit, h, ś, sh, s, tongue-root breath (Jihvâmûlîya), labial breath (Upadhmânîya), neutral breath (Visarga), and neutral nasal (Anusvâra). Thus it is maintained by some ancient grammarians[1] that the hard aspirates are the hard letters k, t, p, together with the corresponding winds or homorganic winds; that is to say, kh is $= k +$ tongue-root breath, th $= t + s$, ph $= p +$ labial breath. The soft aspirates, on the contrary, of which more hereafter, are said to be produced by the union of the soft g, d, b, with the soft 'h. It is quite clear that the Sanskrit 'h, which is not the spiritus asper (though it has constantly been mistaken for that), but a sonant letter, could not possibly form the second element in the hard aspirates. They were formed, as here described, by means of complete hard contact, followed by the hard breaths of each organ. The objections which other grammarians raise against this view do not affect the facts, but only their explanation. As they look upon all letters

[1] *Survey of Languages*, p. xxxii. *Sâkala-Prâtisâkhya*, xiii. 10.

as eternal, they cannot admit their composite character, and they therefore represent the aspiration, not as an additional element, but as an external quality, and prescribe for them a quicker pronunciation in order to prevent any difference between them and other consonants. In other letters the place, the contact, and the opening or shutting of the glottis form the three constituent elements; in the aspirates a fourth, the breath, is added. The Sanskrit hard aspirates can only be considered as k, t, p, modified by the spiritus asper, which immediately follows them, and which assumes, according to some, the character of the guttural, dental, or labial breaths.

As to the Greek aspirates, we know that they belonged to the aphōna, i. e. that they were formed by complete contact. They were not originally hemiphona or breaths, though they became so afterwards. That they were hard, or pronounced with open glottis, we must gather from their original signs, such as ΠΗ, and from their reduplicated forms, *tí-thēmi*, *ké-chyka*, *pé-phyka*.[1]

It is more difficult to determine the real nature of the Sanskrit soft aspirates, gh, dh, bh. According to some grammarians they are produced by the union of g, d, b, with 'h, which in Sanskrit is a sonant letter, a spiritus lenis, but slightly modified.[2] The same grammarians, however, maintain that they are not formed entirely with the glottis closed, or as sonant letters, but that they and the h require the glottis "*both to be opened and to be closed.*" What

---

[1] Raumer, *Aspiration*, 96. Curtius, *Gr. Etymologie*, II. p. 11.
[2] If Sanskrit writing were not of so late a date, the fact that the Vedic dh or ḍh is actually represented by a combination of ḷ and h might be quoted in support of this theory (ळ् = ळ्ह).

this means is somewhat obscure. A letter may be either surd or sonant, but it can hardly be both; and the fact that not only the four soft aspirates but the simple 'h [1] also were considered as surd-sonant, would seem to show that an intermediate rather than a compound utterance is intended. One thing is certain, namely, that neither the hard nor the soft aspirates were originally mere breaths. They are both based on complete contact, and thus differ from the hard and soft breaths which sometimes take their places in cognate tongues.

We have thus finished our survey, which I have kept as general as possible, without dwelling on any of the less normal letters peculiar to every language, every dialect — nay, to the pronunciation of every individual. It is the excessive attention paid to these more or less peculiar letters that has rendered most works on Phonetics so complicated and unintelligible. If we have clearly impressed on our mind the normal conditions of the organs of speech in the production of vowels and consonants, it will be easy to arrange the sounds of every new language under the categories once established on a broad and firm basis. To do this, to arrange the alphabet of any given language according to the compartments planned by physiological research, is the office of the grammarian, not of the physiologist. But even here, too much nicety is dangerous. It is easy to perceive some little difference between k, t, p, as pronounced by an Englishman and by a German, yet each has only one set of tenues, and to class

[1] *Sâkala-Prâtisâkhya*, xlii. 1. The expression "the breath becomes both sonant and surd between the two," i. e. between the complete opening and shutting, shows that an intermediate sound is meant.

them as different and represent them by different graphic exponents would produce nothing but confusion. The Semitic nations have sounds which are absent in the Indo-European languages — the sounds which Brücke has well described as *gutturales veræ*, true gutturals; for the letters which we commonly call gutturals, k, g, have nothing to do with the guttur, but with the root of the tongue and the soft palate. But their character, if only accurately described, as it has been by Czermak, will easily become intelligible to the student of Hebrew and Arabic if he has but acquired a clear conception of what has been well called the *Alphabet of Nature*. To sum up, we must distinguish three things: —

(1) What letters are made of.
(2) How they are made.
(3) Where they are made.

(1) Letters are formed —

(a) Of vocalized breath. These I call vowels (Phōnḗenta, no contact).

(b) Of breath, not vocalized. These I call breaths or spiritus (Hēmiphōna, slight contact).

(c) Of articulate noise. These I call checks or stopping letters (Áphōna, complete contact).

(2) Letters are formed —

(a) With wide opening of the chordæ vocales. These I call *hard* letters (psila, tenues, surd, sharp; vivârasvâsâghoshâh).

(b) With a narrowing of the chordæ vocales. These I call *soft* letters (mesa, mediæ, sonant, blunt; samvâranâdaghoshâh). This distinction applies both to the breaths and to the checks, though the effect, as pointed out, is different.

(3) Letters are formed in different places by active and passive organs, the normal places being those marked by the contact between the root of the tongue and the palate, the tip of the tongue and the teeth, and the upper and lower lips, with their various modifications.

PHYSIOLOGICAL ALPHABET.

Places	Breaths			Checks		
	Hard	Soft	Trilled	Hard	Soft	Nasal
1. Glottis	˙ hand	' and				
2. Root of tongue and soft palate	h loch	h Tage, G.	r	k (kh)	g (gh)	ṅ (ng)
3. Root of tongue and hard palate	y ich, G.	y yea	.	ch (chh)	j (jh)	ñ (ny)
4. Tip of tongue and teeth	s rice	z to rise	l	t (th)	d (dh)	n
5. Tongue reversed and palate	sh sharp	s pleasure	r	ṭ (ṭh)	ḍ (ḍh)	ṇ
6. Tongue and edge of teeth	th breath	dh breathe				
7. Lower lip and upper teeth	f life	v live				
8. Upper and lower lips				p (ph)	b (bh)	m
9. Upper and lower lips rounded	wh which	w with				
	Continue.				Prohibitive sive Explosive.		

APPENDIX TO LECTURE III.

ON TRANSLITERATION.

Having on former occasions discussed the problem of transcribing languages by a common alphabet,[1] I should, for the present, have passed over that subject altogether if I had not been repeatedly urged to declare my opinion on other alphabets recommended to the public by powerful advocates. No one has worked more energetically for the propagation of a common alphabet than Professor Lepsius, of Berlin; and though, in my opinion, and in the opinion of much more competent judges, such as Brücke, the physiological basis of his alphabet is not free from error, — nay, though in the more limited field of languages on which I can form an independent opinion he has slightly misapprehended the nature of certain letters and classes of letters, — I should nevertheless rejoice in the success even of an imperfect alphabet, supposing it had any chance of general adoption. If his alphabet could become the general alphabet at least among African scholars, it would be a real benefit to that new branch of philological studies. But I regret to see that even in Africa those who, like Dr. Bleek, are most anxious to follow the propositions of Professor Lepsius, find it impossible to do so, "on account of its too great typographical difficulties."[2] If this is the case at a steam printing-

[1] Proposals for a Missionary Alphabet in M. M.'s *Survey of Languages* (2d edition), 1855.
[2] Dr. Bleek, *Comparative Grammar*, p. xlt.

office in Cape Town, what can we expect at Neu-herrnhut? Another and even more serious objection, urged likewise by a scholar most anxious to support the Church Missionary Alphabet, is that the scheme of Dr. Lepsius, as modified by the Church of England and Continental Missionary Societies, has long ceased to be a uniform system. " The Societies," says the Rev. Hugh Goldie, in his " Dictionary of the Efik Language" (Glasgow, 1862), "have not succeeded in establishing a uniform system, for which Dr. Lepsius's alphabet is taken as a base; deviations are made from it, which vary in different languages, and which destroy the claim of this system to uniformity. Marks are employed in the Church of England Society which are not employed by the continental societies, and *vice versâ*. This, I think, is fatal to the one great recommendation of the system, namely, its claim to be received as a common system. Stripped of its adventitious recommendations, and judged on its own merits, we think it deficient in simplicity."

These are serious objections; and yet I should gladly have waived them and given my support to the system of Professor Lepsius, if, during the many years that it has been before the public, I had observed any signs of its taking root, or of that slow and silent growth which alone augurs well for the future. What has been, I believe, most detrimental to its success, is the loud advocacy by which it was attempted to force that system on the acceptance of scholars and missionaries, many of them far more competent, in their own special spheres,[1] to form an

[1] Professor Lepsius has some interesting remarks on the African clicks. The Rev. J. L. Döhne, author of a *Zulu Kafir Dictionary*, expressed him-

opinion of its defects than either its author or its patrons. That my unwillingness to adopt the system of Professor Lepsius did not arise from any predilection for my own Missionary Alphabet, I have proved by adopting, when I write in English, the system of Sir William Jones. My own system was, in every sense of the word, a missionary system. My object was, if possible, to devise an alphabet capable of expressing every variety of sound that could be physiologically defined, and yet not requiring one single new or artificial type. As in most languages we find, besides the ordinary sounds that can be expressed by the ordinary types, one, or at the utmost two modifications to which certain letters or classes of letters are liable, I proposed italics as exponents of the first degree of modification, small capitals as exponents of the second degree. Thus as, besides the ordinary dentals, t, th, d, dh, we find in Sanskrit the linguals, I proposed that these should be printed as italics, *t*, *th*, *d*, *dh*, instead of the usual but more difficult types, t', th', d', dh', or T, TH, D, DH. As in Arabic we find, besides the ordinary dentals, another set of linguals, I pro-

self against Dr. Lepsius's proposal to write the clicks *before* their accompanying letters. He at the same time advanced some etymological arguments in support of his own view. How is the African missionary answered by the Berlin Professor? I quote Professor Lepsius's reply, which, if it did not convince, must have startled and stunned his humble adversary. "Equally little," he writes, "should we be justified in inferring from the fact that in the Sanskrit लेटि let'i (sic), be licks, from लिह् lih, and ति ti, t' (sic) must be pronounced not as lh (sic), but as ht (sic)." How the change of Sanskrit b and t into ḍ (ढ is ḍh, not th) has any bearing on the Rev. J. L. Döhne's argument about the clicks, I am afraid few missionaries in Africa will understand.

posed to express these too by italics. These italics were only intended to show that the dentals printed in italics were not meant for the usual dentals. This would have been sufficient for those not acquainted with Sanskrit or Arabic, while Sanskrit and Arabic scholars could have had little doubt as to what class of modified dentals was intended in Sanskrit or Arabic. If certain letters require more than one modification, — as, for instance, t, s, n, r, — then small capitals would have come in, and only in very extreme cases would an additional diacritical mark have been required for a third modification of one common type. If through the princely liberality of one opulent society, the Church Missionary Society,[1] complete founts of complicated and expensive types are to be granted to any press that will ask for them, there is no further need for italics or small capitals, — mere makeshifts that could only have recommended themselves to poor missionaries wishing to obtain the greatest results by the smallest means. It is curious, however, that, in spite of all that has been urged against a systematic use of italics, italics crop out almost everywhere both in philological works at home and in missionary publications abroad, while as yet I have very seldom met with the Church Missionary ọ for the vowel in French cœur, or with the Church Missionary ṣ for the Sanskrit sh, as written by Sir W. Jones.

Within the circle of languages in which I take a more immediate interest, the languages of India, the adoption of the alphabet advocated by the Church

[1] See Resolution 2, carried August 26, 1861, at the Church Missionary House, London.

Missionary Society seems now, after the successful exertions of Sir Charles Trevelyan, more than hopeless; nor do I think that for people situated like the modern Hindús such a *pis-aller* as italics and small capitals is likely to be popular. Living in England, and writing chiefly for England and India, I naturally decided to follow that system which was so modestly put forth by Sir William Jones in the first volume of the "Asiatic Researches," and has since, with slight modifications, not always improvements, been adopted by the greatest Oriental scholars in India, England, and the Continent. In reading that essay, written about eighty years ago, one is surprised to see how well its author was acquainted with all that is really essential either in the physiological analysis or in the philological definition of the alphabet. I do not think the criticism of Professor Lepsius quite fair when he imputes to Sir W. Jones "a defective knowledge of the general organism of sounds, and of the distinct sounds to be represented"; nor can I blame the distinguished founder of the Asiatic Society for the imperfect application of his own principles, considering how difficult it is for a scholar to sacrifice his own principles to considerations of a more practical nature.

The points on which I differ from Sir W. Jones are of very small consequence. They arise from habit rather than from principle. I should willingly give them up if by so doing I could help to bring about a more speedy agreement among Sanskrit scholars in England and India. I am glad to find that in the second edition of his "Standard Alphabet" Professor Lepsius has acknowledged the practical superiority of the system of Sir W. Jones in several important points, and I think he will find that his own system may be still further improved, or at all events have a better chance of success in Europe as well as in India, if it approaches more and more closely to that excellent standard. The subjoined table will make this clearer than any comment:—

Sanskrit Alphabet, as transcribed by Sir W. Jones, M. M., in the Missionary, and in the Church Missionary Alphabets.

Sir W. Jones. M. M.		Missionary Alphabet	Church Mis. Alphabet	Sir W. Jones. M. M.		Missionary Alphabet	Church Mis. Alphabet
अ	a	a	a	ओ	au	au	áu	áu
आ	á	á	á	क	c	k	k	k
इ	i	i	i	ख	c'h	kh	kh	k or kh
ई	í	í	í	ग	g	g	g	g
उ	u	u	u	घ	g'h	gh	gh	g or gh
ऊ	ú	ú	ú	ङ	ṅ	ṅ	n	ṅ
ऋ	ri	ṛi	ri	च	ch	ch	k	k or ŏ
ॠ	rí	ṛí	rí	छ	ch'h	chh	kh	k or ŏh
ऌ	lri	ḷi	lri	ज	j	j	g	g or j
ॡ	lrí	ḷí	lrí	झ	j'h	jh	gh	g or jh
ए	é	e	ê	ai or ē	ञ	ny	ñ	n	ń
ओ	ó	o	ô	au or ō	ट	ṭ	ṭ	t	ṭ
ऐ	ai	ai	ái	ái	ठ	t'h	ṭh	th	t' or th

TRANSLITERATION. 173

	Sir W. Jones	M. M.	Missionary Alphabet	Church Miss. Alphabet		Sir W. Jones	M. M.	Missionary Alphabet	Church Miss. Alphabet
ड	d	ḍ	d	ḍ	य	y	y	y	y
ढ	d'h	ḍh	dh	ḍ' or ḍh	र	r	r	r	r or r
ण	ń	ṇ	n	ṇ	ल	l	l	l	l
त	t	t	t	t	व	v	v	w	v
थ	t'h	t'h	th	t' or th	श	ś	ś	s	ś or ś
द	d	d	d	d	ष	sh	sh	sh	ṣ or ṣ
ध	d'h	dh	db	d' or db	स	s	s	s	s
न	n	n	n	n	ः	h (ħ)	h	h	:
प	p	p	p	p	ं	ṅ	ṁ	m	—
फ	p'h	ph	ph	p' or ph	+	—	ɤ	—	ҳ
ब	b	b	b	b	ᵡ	—	ɸ	—	ҳ
भ	b'h	bh	bh	b' or bh	ॐ	—	ḷ	ḷ	ḷ
म	m	m	m	m	ऋ	—	ḷh	—	—
ह	h	h	h	h					

LECTURE IV.

PHONETIC CHANGE.

From the investigations which I laid before you in my last Lecture, you know the materials which were at the disposal of the primitive architects of language. They may seem small compared with the countless vocables of the countless languages and dialects to which they have given rise, nor would it have been difficult to increase their number considerably, had we assigned an independent name and position to every slight variety of sound that can be uttered, or may be discovered among the various tribes of the globe. Yet small as is the number of the alphabetic elements, there are but few languages that avail themselves of all of them. Where we find very abundant alphabets, as for instance in Hindustani and English, different languages have been mixed, each retaining, for a time, its own phonetic peculiarities. It is because French is Latin as spoken not only by the Roman provincials but by the German Franks, that we find in its dictionary words beginning with *h* and with *gui.* They are due to German throats; they belong to the Teutonic, not to the Romance alphabet. Thus *hair* is to hate; *hameau*, home; *hâter*, to haste; *déguiser* points to *wise*, *guile* to *wile*, *guichet* to *wicket.* It is because

English is Saxon as spoken not only by Saxons, but likewise by Normans, that we hear in it several sounds which do not occur in any other Teutonic dialects. The sound of *u* as heard in *pure* is not a Teutonic sound. It arose from an attempt to imitate the French *u* in *pure*.[1] Most of the words in which this sound is heard are of Roman origin, e. g. d*u*ke, d*u*ring (d*u*rer), beauty (beauté, bellitas), nuisance (nocentia). This sound of *u*, however, being once naturalized, found its way into Saxon words also; that is to say, the Normans pronounced the A. S. *eów* and *eaw* like *yu*; e. g. *knew* (cneów), *few* (feawa), *dew* (deáw), *hue* (hiw).[2]

The sounds of *ch* and *j* in English are Roman or Norman rather than Teutonic sounds, though, once admitted into English, they have infected many words of Saxon descent. Thus *cheer* in *good cheer* is the ·French *chère*, the Mediæval Latin *cara*;[3] *chamber*, *chambre*, *camera*; *cherry*, A. S. *cirse*, Fr. *cerise*, Lat. *cerasus*; to *preach*, *prêcher*, *prædicare*; *forge*, *fabricare*. Or *j* in *joy*, *gaudium*, *judge*, *judex*, &c. But the same sounds found their way into Saxon words also, such as *choose* (ceósan, German *kiesen*); *chew* (ceowan, German *kauen*); particularly before *e* and *i*, but likewise before other vowels; e. g. *child*, as early as Layamon, instead of the older A. S. *cild*; *cheap*, A. S. *ceap*; *birch*, *finch*, *speech*, *much*, &c.; *thatch* (theccan), *watch* (weccan); in Scotch, *theek* and *waik*; or in *bridge* (brycg, *Brücke*), *edge* (ecg, *Ecke*), *ridge* (hrycg, *Rücken*).

[1] Fiedler, *Englische Grammatik*, I. pp. 118, 142.
[2] Cf. Marsh, *Lectures*, Second Series, p. 65.
[3] Cara in Spanish, chière in Old French, mean *face*; Nicot uses "avoir la chère baisée." It afterwards assumed the sense of welcome, and hospitable reception. Cf. Diez, *Lex. Etym.* s. v. Cara.

The soft sound of *z* in *azure* or of *s* in *vision* is likewise a Roman importation.

Words, on the contrary, in which *th* occurs are Saxon, and had to be pronounced by the Normans as well as they could. To judge from the spelling of MSS., they would seem to have pronounced *d* instead of *th*. The same applies to words containing *wh*, originally *hv*, or *ght*, originally *ht*; as in *who*, *which*, or *bought*, *light*, *right*. All these are truly Saxon, and the Scotch dialect preserves the original guttural sound of *h* before *t*.

The O Tyi-herero has neither *l* nor *f*, nor the sibilants *s r z*. The pronunciation is lisping, in consequence of the custom of the *Va-herero* of having their upper front teeth partly filed off, and four lower teeth knocked out. It is perhaps due to this that the O Tyi-herero has two sounds similar to those of the hard and soft *th* and *dh* in English (written s, z).[1]

There are languages that throw away certain letters which to us would seem almost indispensable, and there are others in which even the normal distinctions between guttural, dental, and labial contact are not yet clearly perceived. We are so accustomed to look upon *pa* and *ma* as the most natural articulations, that we can hardly imagine a language without them. We have been told over and over again that the names for *father* and *mother* in all languages are derived from the first cry of recognition which an infant can articulate, and that it could at that early age articulate none but those formed by the mere opening or closing of the lips. It is a fact, nevertheless, that the Mohawks, of whom I knew an interesting

[1] Sir G. Grey's Library, L 167.

POOR ALPHABETS. 177

specimen at Oxford, never, either as infants or as grown-up people, articulate with their lips. They have no *p, b, m, f, v, w* — no labials of any kind; and although their own name Mohawk would seem to bear witness against this, that name is not a word of their own language, but was given to them by their neighbors. Nor are they the only people who always keep their mouths open and abstain from articulating labials.[1] They share this peculiarity with five other tribes, who together form the so-called six nations, *Mohawks, Senekas, Onandagos, Oneidas, Cayugas,* and *Tuscaroras.* The Hurons likewise have no labials, and there are other languages in America with a similar deficiency.[2]

The gutturals are seldom absent altogether; in some, as in the Semitic family, they are most prominent, and represented by a numerous array of letters. Several languages do not distinguish between *k* and *g*; some have only *k*, others *g* only. The sound of *g* as in gone, of *j* as in jet, and of *z* as in zone, which are often heard in Kafir, have no place in the Sechuana alphabet.[3] There are a few dialects mentioned by Bindseil as entirely destitute of gutturals, for instance, that of the Society Islands.[4] It was unfor-

[1] Brosses, *Formation Mécanique des Langues,* I. p. 220: "La Hontan ajoute qu'aucune nation du Canada ne fait usage de la lettre *f*, que les Hurons, à qui elles manquent toutes quatre (B, P, M, F), ne ferment jamais les lèvres." *F* and *s* are wanting in Rarotongan. Hale, 232.

[2] See Bindseil, *Abhandlungen,* p. 368. The Mixteca language has no *p, b, f*; the Mexican no *b, v, f*; the Totonaca no *b, v, f*; the Kaiganí (Haidah) and Thlinkit no *b, p, f* (Pott, *E. F.* II. 63); the Hottentot no *f* or *v* (Sir G. Grey's Library, I. p. 5); the languages of Australia no *f* or *s* (*ibid.* II. 1, 2). Many of the statements of Bindseil as to the presence and absence of certain letters in certain languages, require to be reëxamined, as they chiefly rest on Adelung's Mithridates.

[3] Bindseil, l. c. 314. Mithridates, i. 632, 637.

[4] Appleyard, p. 80.

tunate that one of the first English names which the natives of these islands had to pronounce was that of Captain Cook, whom they could only call *Tute*. Besides the Tahitian, the Hawaian and Samoan[1] are likewise said to be without gutturals. In these dialects, however, the *k* is indicated by a hiatus or catching of the breath, as *ali'i* for *aliki*, *'a'no* for *kakano*.[2]

The dentals seem to exist in every language.[3] The *d*, however, is never used in Chinese, nor in Mexican, Peruvian, and several other American dialects,[4] and the *n* is absent in the language of the Hurons[5] and of some other American tribes. The *s* is absent in the Australian dialects[6] and in several of the Polynesian languages, where its place is taken by *h*.[7] Thus in Tongan we find *hahake* for *sasake*; in the New Zealand dialect *heke* for *seke*. In Rarotongan the *s* is entirely lost, as in *ae* for *sae*. When the *h* stands for an original *s*, it has a peculiar hissing sound which some have represented by *sh*, others by *zh*, others by *he* or *h'*, or simply *e*. Thus the word *hongi*, from the Samoan *songi*, meaning to salute by pressing noses, has been spelt by different writers, *shongi*, *ehongi*, *heongi*, *h'ongi*, and *zongi*.[8] But even

---

[1] Hale, p. 232.
[2] To avoid confusion, it may be stated that throughout Polynesia, with the exception of Samoa, all the principal groups of islands are known to the people of the other groups by the name of their largest island. Thus the *Sandwich Islands* are termed *Hawaii*; the *Marquesas*, *Nukuhiva*; the *Society Islands*, *Tahiti*; the *Gambier Group*, *Mangareva*; the *Friendly Islands*, *Tonga*; the *Navigator Islands*, *Samoa* (all), see Hale, pp. 4, 120; the *Hervey Islands*, *Rarotonga*; the *Low or Dangerous Archipelago*, *Paumotu*; *Bowditch Island* is *Fakaafo*.
[3] Bindseil, l. c. p. 358.
[4] Bindseil, l. c. p. 365.
[5] Bindseil, l. c. p. 334.
[6] Sir George Grey's Library, li. 1, 8.
[7] Hale, l. c. p. 232.
[8] Hale, l. c. pp. 122, 234.

POOR ALPHABETS. 179

keeping on more familiar ground, we find that so perfect a language as Sanskrit has no *f*, no soft sibilants, no short *e* and *o*; Greek has no *y*, no *w*, no *f*, no soft sibilants; Latin likewise has no soft sibilants, no θ, ϕ, χ. English is deficient in guttural breathings like the German *ach* and *ich*. High German has no *w* like the English *w* in wind, no *th, dh, ch, j*. While Sanskrit has no *f*, Arabic has no *p*. *F* is absent not only in those dialects which have no labial articulation at all, but we look for it in vain in Finnish (despite of its name, which was given it by its neighbors[1]), in Lithuanian,[2] in the Gipsy languages, in Tamil, Mongolian, some of the Tataric dialects, Burmese, &c.[3]

It is well known that *r* is felt to be a letter difficult to pronounce not only by individuals but by whole nations. No Chinese who speaks the classical language of the empire ever pronounces that letter. They say *Ki li sse tu* instead of *Christ*; *Eulopa* instead of *Europe*; *Ya me li ka* instead of *America*. Hence neither *Mandarin* nor *Sericum* can be Chinese words: the former is the Sk. *mantrin*, counsellor; the latter derived from *Seres*, a name given to the Chinese by their neighbors.[4] It is likewise absent in the language of the Hurons, the Mexicans, the Othomi, and other American dialects; in the Kafir language,[5] and

---

[1] Pott, *Etymologische Forschungen*, ii. 62.
[2] "*F* does not occur in any genuine Sclavonic word." — Brücke, *Grundzüge*, p. 34.
[3] Bindseil, p. 289.
[4] Pott, *Deutsche Morgenländische Gesellschaft*, xii. 453.
[5] Boyce's *Grammar of the Kafir Language*, ed. Davis, 1863, p. vii. The *r* exists in the Sechuana. The Kafirs pronounce *l* instead of *r* in foreign words; they have, however, the guttural trills. Cf. Appleyard, *The Kafir Language*, p. 49.

in several of the Polynesian[1] tongues. In the Polynesian tongues the name of Christ is *Kalaisi*, but also *Karaita* and *Keriso*. R frequently alternates with *l*, but *l* again is a sound unknown in Zend, and in the Cuneiform Inscriptions,[2] in Japanese (at least some of its dialects), and in several American and African tongues.[3]

It would be interesting to prepare more extensive statistics as to the presence and absence of certain letters in certain languages; nay, a mere counting of consonants and vowels in the alphabets of each nation might yield curious results. I shall only mention a few:—

Hindustani, which admits Sanskrit, Persian, Arabic, and Turkish words, has 49 consonants, of which 13 are classical Sanskrit aspirates, nasals, and sibilants, and 14 Arabic letters.

Sanskrit has 37 consonants, or, if we count the Vedic *l* and *lh*, 39.

Turkish, which admits Persian and Arabic words, has 32 consonants, of which only 25 are really Turkish.

Persian, which admits Arabic words, has 31 consonants, of which 22 are really Persian, the rest Arabic.

Arabic has 28 consonants.

The *Kafir* (Zulu) has 26 consonants, besides the clicks.

Hebrew has 23 consonants.

[1] The dialects of New Zealand, Rarotonga, Mangareva, Paumota, Tahiti, and Nukuhiva have r; those of Fakaafo, Samoa, Tonga, and Hawai, have *l*.—See Hale, *l. c.* p. 232.

[2] See Sir H. Rawlinson, *Behistun*, p. 146. Spiegel, *Parsi Grammatik*, p. 34.

[3] Bindseil, p. 318; Pott, *l. c.* xII. 453.

English has 20 consonants.
Greek has 17 consonants, of which 3 are compound.
Latin has 17 consonants, of which 1 is compound.
Mongolian has 17 or 18 consonants.
Finnish has 11.
Polynesian has 10 native consonantal sounds; no dialect has more — many have less.[1]

Some *Australian* languages have 8, with three variations.[2]

The *Melanesian* languages are richer in consonants. The poorest, the Duauru, has 12; others 13, 14, and more consonants.[3]

But what is even more curious than the absence or presence of certain letters in certain languages or families of languages, is the inability of some races to distinguish, either in hearing or speaking, between some of the most normal letters of our alphabet. No two consonants would seem to be more distinct than *k* and *t*. Nevertheless, in the language of the Sandwich Islands these two sounds run into one, and it seems impossible for a foreigner to say whether what he hears is a guttural or a dental. The same word is written by Protestant missionaries with *k*, by French missionaries with *t*. It takes months of patient labor to teach a Hawaian youth the difference between *k* and *t*, *g* and *d*, *l* and *r*. The same word varies in Hawaian dialects as much as *koki* and *hoi*, *kela* and *tea*.[4] In adopting the English word *steel*,

---

[1] Cf. Hale, p. 231; Von der Gabelentz, *Abhandlungen der Philologisch-Historischen Classe der Königlich Sächsischen Gesellschaft der Wissenschaften*, vol. iii. p. 253. Leipzig, 1861.

[2] Hale, p. 482.

[3] See Von der Gabelentz, l. c.

[4] *The Polynesian*, October, 1862.

the Hawaians have rejected the *s*, because they never pronounce two consonants together; they have added a final *a*, because they never end a syllable with a consonant, and they have changed *t* into *k*.[1] Thus steel has become *kila*. Such a confusion between two prominent consonants like *k* and *t* would destroy the very life of a language like English. The distinction between *carry* and *tarry*, *car* and *tar*, *key* and *tea*, *neck* and *net*, would be lost. Yet the Hawaian language struggles successfully against these disadvantages, and has stood the test of being used for a translation of the Bible, without being found wanting. Physiologically we can only account for this confusion by inefficient articulation, the tongue striking the palate bluntly half-way between the *k* and the *t* points, and thus producing sometimes more of a dental, sometimes more of a palatal noise. But it is curious to observe that, according to high authority, something of the same kind is supposed to take place in English and in French.[2] We are told by careful observers that the lower classes in Canada habitually confound *t* and *k*, and say *mékier*, *moikié*, for *métier* and *moitié*. Webster goes so far as to maintain, in the Introduction to his English Dictionary, that in English the letters *cl* are pronounced as if written *tl*; *clear*, *clean*, he says, are pronounced *tlear*, *tlean*; *gl* is pronounced *dl*; *glory* is pronounced *dlory*. Now Webster is a great authority on such matters, and although I doubt whether any one really

[1] Buschmann, *Iles Marq.* p. 103; Pott, *Etym. F.* II. 138. "In Hawaian the natives make no distinction between *t* and *k*, and the missionaries have adopted the latter, though improperly (as the element is really the Polynesian *t*), in the written language." — Hale, vii. p. 234.
[2] *Student's Manual of the English Language* (Marsh and Smith), p. 349.

IMPERFECT ARTICULATION. 183

says *dlory* instead of *glory*, his remark shows, at all events, that even with a well-mastered tongue and a well-disciplined ear there is some difficulty in distinguishing between guttural and dental contact.

How difficult it is to catch the exact sound of a foreign language may be seen from the following anecdote. An American gentleman, long resident in Constantinople, writes: " There is only one word in all my letters which I am certain (however they may be written) of not having spelt wrong, and that is the word *bactshtusch*, which signifies a present. I have heard it so often, and my ear is so accustomed to the sound, and my tongue to the pronunciation, that I am now certain I am not wrong the hundredth part of a whisper or a lisp. There is no other word in the Turkish so well impressed on my mind, and so well remembered. Whatever else I have written, bactshtasch! my earliest acquaintance in the Turkish language, I shall never forget you." The word intended is *Bakhshish*.[1]

The Chinese word which French scholars spell *eul*, is rendered by different writers *ôl*, *eulh*, *eull*, *r'l*, *r'll*, *urh*, *rhl*. These are all meant, I believe, to represent the same sound, the sound of a word which at Canton is pronounced *i*, in Annamitic *ñi*, in Japanese *ni*.[2]

If we consider that *r* is in many languages a guttural, and *l* a dental, we may place in the same category of wavering pronunciation as *k* and *t*, the confusion between these two letters, *r* and *l*, a confusion remarked not only in the Polynesian, but likewise in the African languages. Speaking of the

[1] *Constantinople and its Environs*, by an American long resident, New York, 1835, ii. p. 151; quoted by Marsh, *Lect.*, Second Series, p. 87.
[2] Léon de Rosny, *La Cochinchine*, p. 254.

Setshuana dialects, Dr. Bleek remarks: "One is justified to consider *r* in these dialects as a sort of floating letter, and rather intermediate between *l* and *r*, than a decided *r* sound."[1]

Some faint traces of this confusion between *r* and *l* may be discovered even in the classical languages, though here they are the exception, not the rule. There can be no doubt that the two Latin derivatives *aris* and *alis* are one and the same. If we derive *Saturnalis* from *Saturnus*, and *secularis* from *seculum*, *normalis* from *norma*, *regularis* from *regula*, *astralis* from *astrum*, *stellaris* from *stella*, it is clear that the suffix in all is the same. Yet there is some kind of rule which determines whether *alis* or *aris* is to be preferred. If the body of the words contains an *l*, the Roman preferred the termination *aris*; hence *secularis*, *regularis*, *stellaris*, the only exceptions being that *l* is preserved (1) when there is also an *r* in the body of the word, and this *r* closer to the termination than the *l*; hence *pluralis*, *lateralis*; (2) when the *l* forms part of a compound consonant, as *fluvialis*, *glacialis*.[2]

Occasional changes of *l* into *r* are to be found in almost every language, e. g. *lavender*, i. e. *lavendula*; *colonel*, pronounced *curnel* (Old French, *coronel*; Spanish, *coronel*); *rossignole* = *lusciniola*; *cæruleus* from *cælum*; *kephalargía* and *lēthargía*, but *ōtalgía*, all from *álgos*, pain. The Wallachian *dor*, desire, is supposed to be the same word as the Italian *duolo*, pain. In *apôtre*, *chapitre*, *esclandre*, the same change of *l* into *r* has taken place.[3]

[1] Sir G. Grey's Library, vol. I. p. 135.
[2] Cf. Pott, *Etymologische Forschungen*, 1st edit. II. 87 where some exceptions, such as *legalis*, *letalis*, are explained.
[3] Diez, *Vergleichende Grammatik*, I. p. 189.

On the other hand *r* appears as *l* in Italian *albero* = *arbor*; *celebro* = *cerebrum*; *mercoledi*, *Mercurii dies*; *pellegrino*, pilgrim = *peregrinus*; *autel* = *altare*.[1]

In the Dravidian family of languages the change of *l* into *r*, and more frequently of *r* into *l*, is very common.[2]

Instances of an utter inability to distinguish between two articulate sounds are, however, of rare occurrence, and they are but seldom found in languages which have received a high amount of literary cultivation. What I am speaking of here is not merely change of consonants, one consonant being preferred in one, another in another dialect, or one being fixed in one noun, another in another. This is a subject we shall have to consider presently. What I wished to point out is more than that: it is a confusion between two consonants in one and the same language, in one and the same word. I can only explain it by comparing it to that kind of color-blindness when people are unable to distinguish between blue and red, a color-blindness quite distinct from that which makes blue to seem red, or yellow green. It frequently happens that individuals are unable to pronounce certain letters. Many persons cannot pronounce the *l*, and say *r* or even *n* instead; *grass* and *crouds* instead of *glass* and *clouds*; *ritten* instead of *little*. Others change *r* to *d*, *dound* instead of *round*; others change *l* to *d*, *dong* instead of *long*. Children, too, for some time substitute dentals for gutturals, speaking of *tat* instead of *cat*, *tiss* instead of *kiss*. It is difficult to say whether their tongue is more

---
[1] Diez, *l. c.* l. p. 209.
[2] Caldwell, *Dravidian Grammar*, p. 130.

at fault or their ear. In these cases, however, a real substitution takes place; we who are listening hear one letter instead of another, but we do not hear as it were two letters at once, or something between the two. The only analogy to this remarkable imperfection peculiar to uncultivated dialects may be discovered in languages where, as in Modern German, the soft and hard consonants become almost, if not entirely, undistinguishable. But there is still a great difference between actually confounding the places of contact, as the Hawaians do in *k* and *t*, and merely confounding the different efforts with which consonants belonging to the same organic class ought to be uttered, a defect very common in some parts of Germany and elsewhere.

This confusion between two consonants in the same dialect is a characteristic, I believe, of the lower stages of human speech, and reminds us of the absence of articulation in the lower stages of the animal world. Quite distinct from this is another process which is going on in all languages, and in the more highly developed even more than in the less developed, the process of *phonetic diversification*, whether we call it growth or decay. This process will form the principal subject of our sixth Lecture, and we shall see that, if properly defined and understood, it forms the basis of all scientific etymology.

Wherever we look at language, we find that it changes. But what makes language change? We are considering at present only the outside, the phonetic body of language, and are not concerned with the changes of meaning, which, as you know, are

sometimes very violent. At present we only ask,
how is it that one and the same word assumes different forms in different dialects, and we intentionally apply the name of dialect not only to Scotch as
compared with English, but to French as compared
with Italian, to Latin as compared with Greek, to
Old Irish as compared with Sanskrit. These are all
dialects; they are all members of the same family,
varieties of the same type, and each variety may, under favoring circumstances, become a species. How
then is it, we ask, that the numeral four is *four* in
English, *quatuor* in Latin, *cethir* in Old Irish, *chatvar*
in Sanskrit, *keturi* in Lithuanian, *tettares* in Greek,
pisyres in Æolic, *fidvor* in Gothic, *fior* in Old High-
German, *quatre* in French, *patru* in Wallachian?

Are all these varieties due to accident, or are they
according to law; and, if according to law, how is
that law to be explained?

I shall waste no time, in order to show that these
changes are not the result of mere accident. This
has been proved so many times, that we may, I believe, take it now for granted.

I shall only quote one passage from the Rev. J. W.
Appleyard's excellent work, " The Kafir Language,"
in order to show that even in the changes of languages sometimes called barbarous and illiterate,
law and order prevail (p. 50) : —

" The chief difference between Kafir and Sechuana roots consists in the consonantal changes which
they have undergone, according to the habit or taste
of the respective tribes. None of these changes,
however, appear to be arbitrary, but, on the contrary,
are regulated by a uniform system of variation. The

vowels are also subject to the same kind of change; and, in some instances, roots have undergone abbreviation by the omission of a letter or syllable." Then follows a table of vowel and consonantal changes in Kafir and Sechuana, after which the author continues: "By comparing the above consonantal changes with § 42, it will be seen that many of them are between letters of the same organ, the Kafir preferring the flat sounds (*b, d, g, v, z*), and the Sechuana the sharp ones (*p, t, k, f, s*). It will be observed, also, that when the former are preceded by the nasal *m* or *n*, these are dropped before the latter. There is sometimes, again, an interchange between dentals and linguals; and there are, occasionally, other changes which cannot be so easily accounted for, unless we suppose that intermediate changes may be found in other dialects . . . . It will thus be seen that roots which appear totally different the one from the other, are in fact the very same, or rather, of the same origin. Thus no one, at first sight, would imagine that the Sechuana *reka* and the Kafir *tonga*, or the Kafir *pila* and the Sechuana *tsera*, were mere variations of the same root. Yet a knowledge of the manner in which consonants and vowels change between the two languages shows that such is the case. As corroborative of this, it may be further observed, that one of the consonants in the above and other Sechuana words sometimes returns in the process of derivation to the original one, as it is found in the Kafir root. For example, the reflective form of *reka* is *iteka*, and not *ireka*; whilst the noun, which is derived from the verb *tsera*, is *botselo*, and not *botsero*."

The change of *th* into *f*, is by many people considered a very violent change, so much so that Burnouf's ingenious identification of *Thraëtona* with *Ferīdūn*, of which more hereafter, was objected to on that ground. But we have only to look at the diagrams of *th* and *f*, to convince ourselves that the slightest movement of the lower lip towards the upper teeth would change the sound of *th* into *f*,[1] so that, in English,

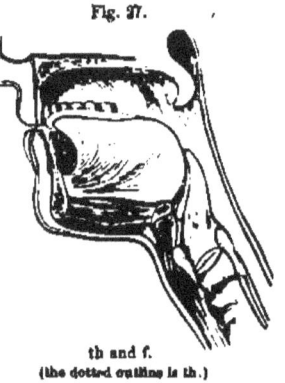

Fig. 27.

th and f.
(the dotted outline is th.)

"*nothing*," as pronounced vulgarly, sounds sometimes like "*nuffing*."

Few people, if any, would doubt any longer that the changes of letters take place according to certain phonetic laws, though scholars may differ as to the exact application of these laws. But what has not yet been fully explained is the nature of these phonetic laws which regulate the changes of words. Why should letters change? Why should we, in modern English, say *lord* instead of *hláford*, *lady* instead of *hlæfdige*? Why should the French say *père* and *mère* instead of *pater* and *mater*? I believe the laws which regulate these changes are entirely based on physiological grounds, and admit of no other explanation whatsoever. It is not sufficient to say that *l* and *r*, or *d* and *r*, or *s* and *r*, or *k* and *t*,

[1] See M. M. *On Veda and Zendavesta*, p. 32. Arendt, *Beiträge zur Vergleichenden Sprachforschung*, i. p. 425.

are interchangeable. We want to know why they are interchangeable, or rather, to use more exact language, we want to know why the same word, which a Hindu pronounces with an initial *d*, is pronounced by a Roman with an initial *l*, and so on. It must be possible to explain this physiologically, and to show, by means of diagrams, what takes place, when, instead of a *d* an *l*, instead of an *f* a *th* is heard.

And here we must, from the very beginning, distinguish between two processes, which, though they may take place at the same time, are nevertheless totally distinct. There is one class of phonetic changes which take place in one and the same language, or in dialects of one family of speech, and which are neither more nor less than the result of *laziness*. Every letter requires more or less of muscular exertion. There is a manly, sharp, and definite articulation, and there is an effeminate, vague, and indistinct utterance. The one requires a will, the other is a mere *laisser-aller*. The principal cause of phonetic degeneracy in language is when people shrink from the effort of articulating each consonant and vowel; when they attempt to economize their breath and their muscular energy. It is perfectly true that, for practical purposes, the shorter and easier a word, the better, as long as it conveys its meaning distinctly. Most Greek and Latin words are twice as long as they need be, and I do not mean to find fault with the Romance nations, for having simplified the labor of speaking. I only state the cause of what we must call *phonetic decay*, however advantageous in some respects; and I con-

sider that cause to be neither more nor less than
want of muscular energy. If the provincial of Gaul
came to say *père* instead of *pater*, it was simply
because he shrank from the trouble of lifting his
tongue, and pushing it against his teeth. *Père* required less strain on the will, and less expenditure
of breath; hence it took the place of *pater*. So in
English, *night* requires less expenditure of muscular
energy than *näght* or *Nacht*, as pronounced in Scotland and in Germany; and hence, as people always
buy in the cheapest market, *night* found more cus-
tomers than the more expensive terms. Nearly all
the changes that have taken place in the transition
from Anglo-Saxon to modern English belong to this
class. Thus:—

A. S. hafoc	became	hawk	A. S. nawiht	became	nought
" dæg	"	day	" blåford [2]	"	lord
" fæger	"	fair	" hlæfdige	"	lady
" secgan	"	say	" sælig	"	silly
" sprecan	"	speak	" bùton	"	but
" folgian	"	follow	" heáfod	"	head
" morgen	"	morrow	" nose-þyrel	"	nostril
" cyning	"	king	" wif-man	"	woman
" wöorold	"	world [1]	" Eofor-wic	"	York

The same takes place in Latin or French words
naturalized in English. Thus:—

Scutarius	escuier	= squire
Historia	histoire	= story

---

[1] Old High-German *wêr-alt* = seculum, i. e. Menschenalter. Cf. vêr-
valf, lycanthropus, werewolf, währwolf, loup-garrou(?); were-gild, mann-
geld, ransom. Cf. Grimm, *Deutsche Grammatik*, II. 480.

[2] In *hláford*, as Grimm supposes, an abbreviation of *hláf-weard*, and
hlæfdige of *hlæfweardige*, meaning loaf-ward? The compound *hláf-ord*,
source of bread, is somewhat strange, considering by whom and for whom
it was formed. But *hláf-weard* does not occur in Anglo-Saxon documents.
See *Lectures on the Science of Language*, 4th ed., vol. I. p. 216.

Egyptianus	Egyptian	= gipsy
Extraneus	estrangier	= stranger
Hydropsis	—	= dropsy
Capitulum	chapitre	= chapter
Dominicella	demoiselle	= damsel
Paralysis	paralysie	= palsy
Sacristanus	sacristain	= sexton

There are, however, some words in English which, if compared with their originals in Anglo-Saxon, seem to have added to their bulk, and thus to violate the general principle of simplification. Thus A. S. *thunor* is in English *thunder*. Yet here, too, the change is due to laziness. It requires more exertion to withdraw the tongue from the teeth without allowing the opening of the dental contact to be heard than to slur from *n* on to *d*, and then only to the following vowel. The same expedient was found out by other languages. Thus, the Greek said *ándres*, instead of *áneres*; *ambrosia*, instead of *amrosia*.[1] The French *genre* is more difficult to pronounce than *gendre*; hence the English *gender*, with its anomalous *d*. Similar instances in English are, *to slumber* = A. S. *slumerian*; *embers* = A. S. *æmyric*; *cinders* = *cineres*; *humble* = *humilis*.

It was the custom of grammarians to ascribe these and similar changes to *euphony*, or a desire to make words agreeable to the ear. Greek, for instance, it was said, abhors two aspirates at the beginning of two successive syllables, because the repeated aspiration would offend delicate ears. If a verb in Greek,

[1] In Greek, μ cannot stand before λ and ρ, nor λ before ρ, nor ν before any liquid. Hence μεσημ(ε)ρία = μεσημβρία; γαμρος = γαμβρός; ἥμαρτον = ἥμβροτον; μορτος = βροτός. See Mehlhorn, *Griechische Grammatik*, p. 54. In Tamil, *nr* is pronounced *ndr*. Caldwell, *Dravidian Grammar*, p. 138.

beginning with an aspirate, has to be reduplicated, the first syllable takes the tenuis instead of the aspirate. Thus *thē* in Greek forms *títhēmi*, as *dhá* in Sanskrit *dadhámi*. If this was done for the sake of euphony, it would be difficult to account for many words in Greek far more inharmonious than *thíthēmi*. Such words as χθών, *chthón*, earth, φθόγγος, *phthóggos*, vowel, beginning with two aspirates, were surely more objectionable than *thíthēmi* would have been. There is nothing to offend our ears in the Latin *fefelli*,[1] from *fallo*, or in the Gothic reduplicated perfect *haihald*, from *haldan*, which in English is contracted into *held*, the A. S. being *heóld*, instead of *hehold*; or even in the Gothic *faifahum*, we caught, from *fahan*, to catch.[2] There is nothing fearful in the sound of *fearful*, though both syllables begin with an *f*. But if it be objected that all these letters in Latin and Gothic are mere breaths, while the Greek χ, θ, φ are real aspirates, we have in German such words as *Pfropfenzieher*, which to German ears is anything but an unpleasant sound. I believe the secret of this so-called abhorrence in Greek is nothing but laziness. An aspirate requires

[1] It should be remarked that the Latin *f*, though not an aspirated tenuis like φ, but a labial flatus, seems to have had a very harsh sound. Quintilian, when regretting the absence in Latin of Greek φ and υ, says, "Quæ si nostris literis (*f* et *u*) scribantur, surdum quiddam et barbarum efficient, et velut in locum earum succedent tristes et horridæ quibus Græcia caret. Nam et illa quæ est sexta nostratium (*f*) pæne non humana voce, vel omnino non voce potius, inter discrimina dentium efflanda est; quæ etiam cum vocalem proxima scripsit, quassa quodammodo, utique quoties aliquam consonantem frangit, ut in hoc ipso frangit, multo fit horridior" (xii. 10). —Cf. Bindseil, p. 287.

[2]
	Pres.	Perf. Sing.	Perf. Plur.	Part. Perf. Pass.
G.	haita	haihait	haihaitum	haitan
A. S.	hâtan	hêht (hêt)	hêtcn	hâten
O. E.	hate	hight	hightan	hoten, hoot, hight

great effort, though we are hardly aware of it, beginning from the abdominal muscles and ending in the muscles that open the glottis to its widest extent. It was in order to economize this muscular energy that the tenuis was substituted for the aspirate, though, of course, in cases only where it could be done without destroying the significancy of language. Euphony is a very vague and unscientific term. Each nation considers its own language, each tribe its own dialect, euphonic; and there are but few languages which please our ear when heard for the first time. To my ear *knight* does not sound better than *Knecht*, though it may do so to an English ear, but there can be no doubt that it requires less effort to pronounce the English *knight* than the German *Knecht*.

But from this, the most important class of phonetic changes, we must distinguish others which arise from a less intelligible source. When we find that, instead of Latin *pater*, the Gothic tribes pronounced *fadar*, it would be unfair to charge the Goths with want of muscular energy. On the contrary, the aspirated *f* requires more effort than the mere tenuis; and the *d*, which between two vowels was most likely sounded like the soft *th* in English, was by no means less troublesome than the *t*. Again, if we find in Sanskrit *gharma*, heat, with the guttural aspirate, in Greek *thermós* with the dental aspirate, in Latin *formus*, adj.,[1] with the labial aspirate, we cannot charge any one of these three dialects with effeminacy, but we must look for another cause that could have produced these changes. That cause I

[1] Festus states, "forcipes dicuntur quod his *forma* id est calida capiantur."

call *Dialectic Growth*; and I feel strongly inclined
to ascribe the phonetic diversity which we observe
between Sanskrit, Greek, and Latin, to a previous
state of language, in which, as in the Polynesian
dialects, the two or three principal points of consonantal contact were not yet felt as definitely separated
from each other. There is nothing to show that in
thermós, Greek ever had a guttural initial, and to say
that Sanskrit *gh* becomes Greek *th* is in reality saying very little. No letter ever *becomes*. People pronounce letters, and they either pronounce them
properly or improperly. If the Greek pronounced
th in *thermós* properly, without any intention of pronouncing *gh*, then the *th*, instead of *gh*, requires another explanation, and I cannot find a better one than
the one just suggested. When we find three dialects,
like Sanskrit, Greek, and Latin, exhibiting the same
word with guttural, dental, and labial initials, we
gain but little if we say that Greek is a modification
of Sanskrit, or Latin of Greek. No Greek ever took
the Sanskrit word and modified it; but all three
received it from a common source, in which its articulation was as yet so vague as to lend itself to these
various interpretations. Though we do not find in
Greek the same confusion between guttural and
dental contact which exists in the Hawaian language, it is by no means uncommon to find one
Greek dialect preferring the dental[1] when another
prefers the guttural; nor do I see how this fact could
be explained unless we assume that in an earlier
state of the Greek dialects the pronunciation fluct-

[1] Doric, πόκα, ὅκα, ἄλλοκα, for πότε, ὅτε, ἄλλοτε; Doric, ὀνόφος; Æolic, γνόφος; Doric, δά for γῆ.

uated or hesitated between *k* and *t*. " No Polynesian dialect," says Mr. Hale, " makes any distinction between the sounds of *b* and *p*, *d* and *t*, *g* and *k*, *l* and *r*, or *v* and *w*. The *l*, moreover, is frequently sounded like *d*, and *t* like *k*."[1] If colonies started to-morrow from the Hawaian Islands, the same which took place thousands of years ago, when the Hindus, Greeks, and Romans left their common home, would take place again. One colony would elaborate the indistinct, half-guttural, half-dental articulation of their ancestors into a pure guttural; another into a pure dental; a third into a labial. The Romans who settled in Dacia, where their language still lives in the modern Wallachian, are said to have changed every *qu*, if followed by *a*, into *p*. They pronounce *aqua* as *apa*; *equa* as *epa*.[2] Are we to suppose that the Italian colonists of Dacia said *aqua* as long as they stayed on Italian soil, and changed *aqua* into *apa* as soon as they reached the Danube? Or may we not rather appeal to the fragments of the ancient dialects of Italy, as preserved in the Oscan and Umbrian inscriptions, which show that in different parts of Italy certain words were from the beginning fixed differently, thus justifying the assumption that the legions which settled in Dacia came from localities in which these Latin *qu*'s had always been pronounced as *p*'s?[3] It will sound to classical scholars almost like blasphemy to explain the phenomena in

---

[1] Hale, *Polynesian Grammar*, p. 233.

[2] The Macedonian (Kutzo-Wallachian) changes *pectus* into *keptu*, *pectine* into *keptina*. Cf. Pott, *Etym. F.* ii. 49. Of the Tagesa dialects, the northern entirely drops the *p*, the southern, in all grammatical terminations, either elide it or change it into *k*. Cf. Sir G. Grey's Library, i. p 130.

[3] The Oscans said *pomtis* instead of *quinque*. See Mommsen, *Unteritalische Dialekte*, p. 289.

the language of Homer and Horace, by supposing for both a background like that of the Polynesian dialects of the present day. Comparative philologists, too, will rather admit what is called a degeneracy of gutturals sinking down to dentals and labials, than look for analogies to the Sandwich Islands. Yet the most important point is, that we should have clear conceptions of the words we are using; and I confess that, without certain attenuating circumstances, I cannot conceive of a real *k* degenerating into a *t* or *p*. I can conceive different definite sounds arising out of one indefinite sound; and those who have visited the Polynesian islands describe the fact as taking place at the present day. What then takes place to-day can have taken place thousands of years ago; and if we see the same word beginning in Sanskrit, Greek, and Latin, with *k*, *t*, or *p*, it would be sheer timidity to shrink from the conclusion that there was a time in which that word was pronounced less distinctly; in short, in the same manner as the *k* and *t* in Hawaian.

There is, no doubt, this other point to be considered, that each man has his phonetic idiosyncrasies, and that what holds good of individuals, holds good of families, tribes, and nations. We saw that individuals and whole nations are destitute of certain consonants, and this defect is generally made up on the other hand by a decided predilection for some other class of consonants. The West Africans, being poor in dentals and labials, are rich in gutturals. Now if an individual, or a family, or a tribe cannot pronounce a certain letter, nothing remains but to substitute some other letter as nearly allied to it as possible. The Romans were destitute of a dental aspirate like the *th* of the Greeks, or the *dh* of the Hindus. Hence, where that letter existed in the language of their common ancestors, the Romans had either to give up the aspiration and pronounce *d*, or to take the nearest consonantal contact and pronounce *f*. Hence *fumus* instead of Sk. *dhûma*, Greek *thýmos*. It is exactly the same as what took place in English. The modern English pronunciation, owing, no doubt, to Norman influences, lost the guttural *ch*, as heard in the German *lachen*. The Saxons had it, and wrote and pronounced *hleahtor*. It is now replaced by the corresponding labial letter, namely, *f*, thus giving us *laughter* for *hleahtor*, *enough* for *genug*, &c. If we find one tribe pronounce *r*, the other *l*,[1] we can hardly accuse either of effeminacy, but must appeal to some phonetic idiosyncrasy, something in fact corresponding to what is called color-blindness in another organ of sense. These idiosyncrasies have to be carefully studied, for each language has its own, and it would by no means follow that because a Latin *f* or even *b* corresponds to a Sanskrit *dh*, therefore every *dh* in every language may lapse into *f* and *b*. Greek has a strong objection to words ending in consonants; in fact, it allows but three consonants, and all of them semivowels, to be heard as finals. We only find *n*, *r*, and *s*, seldom *k*, ending Greek words. The Roman had no such scruples. His words end with a guttural tenuis, such as *hic*, *nunc*; with a dental tenuis, such as *sunt*, *est*; and he only avoids a final labial tenuis which certainly is not melodious. We can hardly imagine Virgil, in his hexameters, uttering

[1] Pott, *Etym. Forsch.* II. 59.

PHONETIC PECULIARITIES. 199

such words as *lump, trump,* or *stump*. Such tendencies or dispositions, peculiar to each nation, must exercise considerable influence on the phonetic structure of a language, particularly if we consider that in the Aryan family the grammatical life-blood throbs chiefly in the final letters.

These idiosyncrasies, however, are quite inadequate to explain why the Latin *coquo* should, in Greek, appear as *péptō*. Latin is not deficient in labial, nor Greek in guttural sounds. Nor could we honestly say that the gutturals in Latin were gradually ground down to labials in Greek. Such forms are dialectic varieties, and it is, I believe, of the greatest importance, for the purposes of accurate reasoning, that these dialectic varieties should be kept distinct, as much as possible, from phonetic corruptions. I say, as much as possible, for in some cases I know it is difficult to draw a line between the two. Physiologically speaking, I should say that the phonetic corruptions are always the result of muscular effeminacy, though it may happen, as in the case of *thunder,* that "lazy people take the most pains." All cases of phonetic corruption can be clearly represented by anatomical diagrams. Thus the Latin *clamare* requires complete contact between root of tongue and soft palate, which contact is

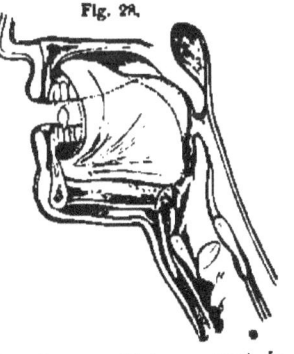

Fig. 28.

* This diagram was drawn by Professor Richard Owen.

merged by sudden transition into the dental position
of the tongue with a vibration of its lateral edges.
In Italian this lateral vibration of the tongue is
dropped, or rather is replaced by the slightest possible approach of the tongue towards the palate,
which follows almost involuntarily on the opening
of the guttural contact, producing *chiamare*, instead
of *clamare*. The Spaniard slurs over the initial
guttural contact altogether; he thinks he has pronounced it, though his tongue has never risen, and
he glides at once into the *l* vibration, the opening
of which is followed by the same sticky sound
which we observed in Italian. What applies to
the Romance applies equally to the Teutonic languages. The old Saxons said *cniht*, *cnif*, and *cneow*.
Now, the guttural contact is slurred over, and we
only hear *knight*, *knife*, *knee*. The old Saxons said
hledpan, with a distinct initial aspiration; that aspiration is given up in *to leap*. Wherever we find an
initial *wh*, as in *who*, *which*, *white*, there stood originally in A. S. *hw*, the aspirate being distinctly pronounced. That aspirate, though it is still heard in
correct pronunciation, is fast disappearing in the
language of the people except in the north, where
it is clearly sounded before, not after, the *w*. In the
interrogative pronoun *who*, however, no trace of the
w remains except in spelling, and in the interrogative adverb, *how*, it has ceased to be written (A. S.
hwû, *hu*, Goth. *hvaiva*). In *whole*, on the contrary,
the *w* is written, but simply by false analogy. The
A. S. word is *hâl*, without a *w*, and the good sense
of the people has not allowed itself to be betrayed
into a false pronunciation in spite of the false spelling enforced by its schoolmasters.

Words beginning with more than one consonant are most liable to phonetic corruption. It certainly requires an effort to pronounce distinctly two or three consonants at the beginning without intervening vowels, and we could easily understand that one of these consonants should be slurred over and be allowed to drop. But if it is the tendency of language to facilitate pronunciation, we must not shirk the question how it came to pass that such troublesome forms were ever framed and sanctioned. Strange as it may seem, I believe that these troublesome words, with their consonantal exuberances, are likewise the result of phonetic corruption, i. e. of muscular relaxation. Most of them owe their origin to contraction, that is to say, to an attempt to pronounce two syllables as one, and thus to save time and breath, though not without paying for it by an increased consonantal effort.

It has been argued, with some plausibility, that language in its original state, of which, unfortunately, we know next to nothing, eschewed the contact of two or more consonants. There are languages still in existence in which each syllable consists either of a vowel or of a vowel preceded by one consonant only, and in which no syllable ever ends in a consonant. This is the case, for instance, in the Polynesian languages. A Hawaian finds it almost impossible to pronounce two consonants together, and in learning English he has the greatest difficulty in pronouncing *cab*, or any other word ending in a consonant. *Cab*, as pronounced by a Hawaian, becomes *caba*. Mr. Hale, in his excellent " Polynesian Grammar,"[1] says: " In all the

[1] Hale, *l. c.* p. 234.

Polynesian dialects every syllable must terminate in a vowel; and two consonants are never heard without a vowel between them. This rule admits of no exception whatever, and it is chiefly to this peculiarity that the softness of these languages is to be attributed. The longest syllables have only three letters, a consonant and a diphthong, and many syllables consist of a single vowel."

There are other languages besides the Polynesian which never admit closed syllables, i. e. syllables ending in consonants. All syllables in Chinese are open or nasal,[1] yet it is by no means certain whether the final consonants which have been pointed out in the vulgar dialects of China are to be considered as later additions, or whether they do not represent a more primitive state of the Chinese language.

In South Africa all the members of the great family of speech, called by Dr. Bleek the Bâ-ntu family, agree in general with regard to the simplicity of their syllables. Their syllables can begin with only one consonant (including, however, consonantal diphthongs, nasalized consonants, and combinations of clicks with other consonants reckoned for this purpose as substantially simple). The semivowel *w*, too, may intervene between a consonant and a following vowel. No syllable, as a general rule, in these South African languages, which extend north beyond the Equator, can end in a consonant, but only in vowels, whether pure or nasal.[2] The exceptions serve but to prove the rule, for they are confined to cases where by the falling off of the

---

[1] Endlicher, *Chinesische Grammatik*, p. 112.
[2] Bleek, *Comparative Grammar*, § 259. Appleyard, *Kafir Language*, p. 89.

generally extremely short and almost indistinct terminal vowel, an approach has been made to consonantal endings.[1]

In the other family of South-African speech, the Hottentot, compound consonants are equally eschewed at the beginning of words. It is clear, too, that all radical words ended there originally in vowels, and that the final consonants are entirely due to grammatical terminations, such as *p, s, ts*, and *r*. By the frequent use of these suffixes the final vowel disappeared, but that it was there originally has been proved with sufficient evidence.[2]

The permanent and by no means accidental or individual character of these phonetic peculiarities is best seen in the treatment of foreign words. Practice will no doubt overcome the difficulty which a Hawaian feels in pronouncing two consonants together or in ending his words by consonantal checks, and I have myself heard a Mohawk articulating his labial letters with perfect accuracy. Yet if we examine the foreign words adopted by the people into their own vocabulary, we shall easily see how they have all been placed on a bed of Procrustes. In the Ewe, a West-African language, *school* is pronounced *suku*, the German *Fenster* (window) *fesre*.[3]

In the Kafir language we find	bapitizesha	—	to baptize
"	"	igolide	— gold
"	"	inkamela	— camel
"	"	ibere	— bear
"	"	umperisite	— priest
"	"	ikerike	— kirk

[1] Bleek, *Comparative Grammar*, § 257. Hahn, *Herero Grammar*, § 8.
[2] Bleek, *Comparative Grammar*, §§ 257-260.
[3] Pott, *Etymologische Forschungen*, ii. 56.

In the Kafir language we find *umposile* — *apostle*
" " *isugile* — *sugar*
" " *ama-Ngezi* — *English*[1]

If we look to the Finnish and the whole Uralic class of the Northern Turanian languages, we meet with the same disinclination to admit double consonants at the beginning, or any consonants whatever at the end of words. The German *Glas* is written *lasi* in Finnish. The Swedish *smak* is changed into *maku*, *stor* into *suuri*, *strand* into *ranta*. No genuine Finnish word begins with a double consonant, for the assibilated and softened consonants, which are spelt as double letters, were originally simple sounds. This applies equally to the languages of the Esths, Ostiaks, Hungarians, and Sirianes, though, through their intercourse with Aryan nations, these tribes, and even the Finns, succeeded in mastering such difficult groups as *pr*, *sp*, *st*, *str*, &c. The Lapp, the Mordvinian, and Tcheremissian dialects show, even in words which are of native growth, though absent in the cognate dialects, initial consonantal groups such as *kr*, *ps*, *st*, &c.; but such groups are always the result of secondary formation, as has been fully proved by Professor Boller.[2] The same careful scholar has shown that the Finnish, though preferring syllables ending in vowels, has admitted *n*, *s*, *l*, *r*, and even *t*, as final consonants. The Esthonian, Lapp, Mordvinian, Ostiakian, and Hungarian, by dropping or weakening

[1] Appleyard, *Kafir Language*, p. 69.
[2] Boller, *Die Finnischen Sprachen*, p. 19. Pott, l. c. pp. 40 and 56. See also Boehtlingk, *Ueber die Sprache der Jakuten*, § 152, " The Turko-Tataric languages, the Mongolian and Finnish show a strong aversion against double consonants at the beginning of words."

their final and unaccented vowels, have acquired a large number of words ending in simple and double consonants; but throughout the Uralic class, wherever we can trace the radical elements of language, we always find simple consonants and final vowels.

We arrive at the same result, if we examine the syllabic structure of the Dravidian class of the South Turanian languages, the Tamil, Telugu, Canarese, Malayàlam, &c. The Rev. R. Caldwell, in his excellent work, the "Dravidian Comparative Grammar," has treated this subject with the same care as Professor Boller in his Essay on the Finnish languages, and we have only to place these accounts by the side of each other, in order to perceive the extraordinary coincidences.

"The chief peculiarity of Drâvidian syllabation is its extreme simplicity and dislike of compound or concurrent consonants; and this peculiarity characterizes the Tamil, the most early cultivated member of the family, in a more marked degree than any other Drâvidian language.

"In Telugu, Canarese, and Malayâlam, the great majority of Drâvidian words, i. e. words which have not been derived from Sanskrit, or altered through Sanskrit influences, and in Tamil all words without exception, including even Sanskrit derivatives, are divided into syllables on the following plan. Double or treble consonants at the beginning of syllables, like 'str,' in 'strength,' are altogether inadmissible. At the beginning not only of the first syllable of every word, but also of every succeeding syllable, only one consonant is allowed. If, in the middle of a word of several syllables, one syllable ends with a consonant and the succeeding one commences with another consonant, the concurrent consonants must be euphonically assimilated, or else a vowel must be inserted between them. At the conclusion of a word, double and treble consonants, like 'gth,' in 'strength,' are as inadmissible as at the beginning; and every word must terminate in Telugu and Canarese in a vowel; in Tamil, either in a vowel or in a single semivowel, as 'l,' or 'r,' or in a single nasal, as 'n,' or 'm.' It is obvious that this plan of syllabation is extremely unlike that of the Sanskrit.

"Generally, 'i' is the vowel which is used for the purpose of separating inadmissible consonants, as appears from the manner in which Sanskrit derivatives are Tamilized. Sometimes 'u' is employed instead of 'i.' Thus the Sanskrit preposition 'pra' is changed into 'pira' in the compound derivatives, which have been borrowed by the Tamil; whilst 'Krishna' becomes 'Kiruttina-n' ('tt,' instead of 'sh'), or even 'Kittina-n.' Even such soft conjunctions of consonants as the Sanskrit 'dya,' 'dva,' 'gya,' &c., are separated in Tamil into 'diya,' 'diva,' and 'giya.'"[1]

It is hardly to be wondered at that evidence of this kind, which might be considerably increased, should have induced speculative scholars to look upon the original elements of language as necessarily consisting of open syllables, of one consonant followed by one vowel, or of a single vowel. The fact that languages exist, in which this simple structure has been preserved, is certainly important, nor can it be denied that out of such simple elements languages

[1] Caldwell, *Dravidian Comparative Grammar*, p. 133.

have been formed, gradually advancing, by a suppression of vowels, to a state of strong consonantal harshness. The Tcheremissian *šma*, mouth, if derived from a root *šu*, to speak, must originally have been *šuma*.

In the Aryan languages, the same process can easily be observed as producing the same effect, viz., double consonants, either at the beginning or at the end of words. It was in order to expedite the pronunciation of words that vowels were dropt, and consonants brought together: it was to facilitate the pronunciation of such words that one of the consonants was afterwards left out, and new vowels were added to render the pronunciation easier once more.

Thus, *to know* points back to Sk. *jnâ*, but this *jnâ*, the Lat. *gnô* in *gnôvi*, or *gnô* in Gr. *égnôn*, again points back to *janâ*, contracted to *jnâ*. Many roots are formed by the same process, and they generally express a derivative idea. Thus *jan*, which means to create, to produce, and which we find in Sk. *janas*, Gr. *génos*, genus, kin, is raised to *jnâ*, in order to express the idea of being able to produce. If I am able to produce music, I know music; if I am able to produce ploughing, I know how to plough, I can plough; and hence the frequent running together of the two conceptions, I can and I know, Ich kann and Ich kenne.[1] As from *jan* we have *jnâ*, so from *man*, to think (Sk. *manas*, Gr. *ménos*, mens, mind), we have *mnâ*, to learn by heart, Greek *mémnêmai*, I remember, *mimnéskô*. In modern pronunciation the *m* is

[1] Pott, E. F. II. 591, compares *quo* and *scio*, tracing them to Sanskrit *ki*. See Benfey, *Kurze Sanskrit Grammatik*, § 62, note.

dropt, and we pronounce *m-nemonics*. Again, we have in Sanskrit a root *mlai*, which means to fade; from it *mlâna*, faded, *mlâni*, fading. The Teutonic nations, avoiding the complete labial contact that is required for *m*, were satisfied with the labial approach which produces *w*, and thus pronounced *ml* like *vl*. Hence A. S. *wlæc*, tired, *wlacian*, to be tired, to flag. The Latin has *flaccus*, withered, flabby, where we should expect *blaccus*, Germ. *welk*. In German we have *flau*,[1] weak, and what seems to be merely a dialectic Low-German variety, *lau*, in the sense of luke-warm, i. e. water that is but weakly boiling. Now, whence this initial double consonant *ml*, which in German meets with the usual fate of most double initial consonants, and from *ml* sinks to *l*? The Sanskrit root *mlai* or *mlâ* is formed like *jnâ* aud *mnâ*, from a simpler root *mal* or *mar*, which means to wear out, to decay. As *jan* became *jnâ*, so *mar*, *mrâ*. This *mar* is a very prolific root, of which more hereafter, and was chiefly used in the sense of decaying or dying, *morior*, ἀμ(β)ροσια, Old Slav. *mrěti*, to die, Lith. *mirti*, to die.

These instances must suffice in order to show that in Sanskrit, too, and in the Aryan languages in general, the initial double consonants owe their existence to the same tendency which afterwards leads to their extinction. It was phonetic economy that reduced *mard* to *mrâ*; it was phonetic economy that reduced *mrâ* to *râ* and *lâ*.

The double consonants being once there, the simplest process would seem to drop one of the two.

---

[1] Cf. Leo, *Zeitschrift für Vergl. Sp.* ii. 252. Grimm (*Wörterbuch*, s. v.) traces flau to fläuen, and this to a supposed M. H. G. flou or flouwe.

This happens frequently, but by no means always. We see this process in English words like *knight*, (*h*)*ring*, &c.; we likewise observe it in Latin *natus* instead of *gnatus*, *nodus* instead of *gnodus*, English *knot*. We know that the old Latin form of *locus* was *stlocus*,[1] thus pointing to root *stâ*, whence the German *Stelle*; we know that instead of *lis*, *litis*, quarrel, litigation, the ancient Romans pronounced *stlis*, which points to German *Streit*. In all these cases the first consonant or consonants were simply dropt. But it also happens that the double consonant, which was tolerated at first, only because it was the saving of a syllable, is lengthened again into two syllables, the two syllables seeming to require less effort than the double consonant. The Semitic languages are quite free from words beginning with two consonants without an intermediate vowel or shewa. This is, in fact, considered by Ewald as one of the prominent characters of the Semitic family;[2] and if foreign words like *Plato* have to be naturalized in Arabic, the *p* has to be changed to *f*, for Arabic, as we saw, has no *p*, and an initial vowel must be added, thus changing *Plato* into *Iflatún*. We saw that the Hawaians, in adopting a word like *steel*, had to give up the initial *s* before the *t*, pronouncing *tila* or *kila*. We saw that the West-African languages met the same difficulty by making two syllables instead of one, and saying *suku* instead of *school*. The Chinese, in order to pronounce *Christ*, have to change that name into *Ki-li-sse-tu*,[3] four syllables instead of one. There are

[1] Quintil. l. 4, 16.
[2] Ewald, *Gramm. Arabica*, l. p. 23; Pott, *Etym. Forsch.* II. 66.
[3] Endlicher, *Chinesische Grammatik*, p. 22.

analogous cases nearer home. Many words in Latin begin with sc, st, sp. Some of these are found in Latin inscriptions of the fourth century after Christ spelt with an initial i : e. g. *in istatuam* (Orelli, 1120, A. D. 375) ; *Ispiritus* (Mai, Coll. Vat., t. v. p. 446, 8).[1] It seems that the Celtic nations were unable to pronounce an initial *s* before a consonant, or at least that they disliked it.[2] The Spaniards in Peru, even when reading Latin, pronounce *estudium* for *studium*, *eschola* for *schola*.[3] Hence the constant addition of the initial vowel in the Western or chiefly Celtic branch of the Romance family; French *escabeau*, instead of Latin *scabellum*; *estame* (*étaim*), Latin *stamen*; *espérer*, instead of Latin *sperare*. Then again, as it were to revenge itself for the additional trouble caused by the initial double consonant, the French language throws away the *s* which had occasioned the addition of the initial *e*, but keeps the vowel which, after the loss of the *s*, would no longer be wanted. Thus *spada* became *espée*, lastly *épée* ; *scala* became *eschelle*, lastly *échelle*. *Stabilire* became *establir*, lastly *établir*, to stablish.[4]

Now it must be clear that all these changes rest

[1] See Crecellus, in Hoefer's *Zeitschrift*, lv. 156.

[2] Richards, *Antiquæ Linguæ Britannicæ Thesaurus* (Bristol, 1753), as quoted by Pott, *E. F.* II. 67, says (after letter S): "No British word begins with s, when a consonant or w follows, without setting y before it; for we do not say Sgubor, smoden, &c., but Ysgubor, ysmoden. And when we borrow any words from another language which begin with an *s* and a consonant immediately following it, we prefix a *y* before such words, as from the Latin *schola*, ysgol; *spiritus*, yspryd; *scutum*, ysgwyd."

[3] Tschudi, *Peru*, L 176. Caldwell, *Dravidian Comparative Grammar*, p. 170: "How perfectly in accordance with Tamil this is, is known to every European resident in Southern India, who has heard the natives speak of establishing an English iskool." This *iskool* is as good as *establishing* for *stabilire*; or the Italian expressions, *con istudio, per istrada, &c.*

[4] Diez, *Grammatik*, I. p. 224.

on principles totally distinct from those which made the Romans pronounce the same word as *quatuor* which we pronounce *four*. The transition from Gothic *fidvor* to English *four* may properly be ascribed to phonetic corruption, but *quatuor* and *fidvor* together can only be explained as the result of dialectic variation. If we compare *quatuor*, *téssares*, *pisyres*, and *fidvor*, we find a change of guttural, dental, and labial contact in one and the same word. There is nothing to show that the Greek changed the guttural into the dental contact, or that the Teutonic nations considered the labial contact less difficult than the guttural and dental. We cannot show that in Greece the guttural dwindles down to a dental, or that in German the labial is later, in chronological order, than the guttural. We must look upon guttural, dental, and labial as three different phonetic expressions of the same general conception, not as corruptions of one definite original type. The guttural tenuis once fixed in any language or dialect does not in that dialect slowly dwindle down to a dental tenuis; a dental tenuis once clearly pronounced as a dental does not in the mouth of the same speaker glide into a labial tenuis. That which is not yet individualized may grow and break forth in many different forms; that which has become individual and definite loses its capability of unbounded development, and its changes assume a downward tendency and must be considered as decay. To say where growth ends and decay begins is as difficult in living languages as in living bodies; but we have in the science of language this test, that changes produced by phonetic decay must admit of a simple physiological explanation — they must be referable to a relaxation of muscular energy in the organs of speech. Not so the dialectic varieties. Their causes, if they can be traced at all, are special, not general, and in many cases they baffle all attempts at physiological elucidation.

LECTURE V.

GRIMM'S LAW.

I INTEND to devote to-day's Lecture to the consideration of one phonetic law, commonly called Grimm's Law, a law of great importance and very wide application, affecting nearly the whole consonantal structure of the Aryan languages. The law may be stated as follows:—

There are in the Aryan languages three principal points of consonantal contact, the guttural, the dental, and the labial, *k, t, p*.

At each of these three points there are two modes of utterance, the hard and the soft; each in turn is liable to aspiration, though only in certain languages.

In Sanskrit the system is complete; we have the hard checks, *k, t, p*; the soft checks, *g, d, b*; the hard aspirated checks, *kh, th, ph*; and the soft aspirated checks, *gh, dh, bh*. The soft aspirated checks are, however, in Sanskrit of far greater frequency and importance than the hard aspirates.

In Greek we find, besides the usual hard and soft checks, one set of aspirates, χ, θ, φ, which are hard, and which in later Greek dwindled away into the corresponding breathings.

In Latin there are no real aspirates; their place having been taken by the corresponding breathings. The dental breathing, however, the *s*, is never found in Latin as the representative of an original dental aspirate (*th* or *dh*).

In Gothic, too, the real aspirates are wanting, unless *th* was pronounced as such. In the guttural and labial series we have only the breathings *h* and *f*. The same seems to apply to Old High-German.

In the Slavonic languages, including Lithuanian, the aspirates were originally absent.

We see, therefore, that the aspirated letters exist only in Sanskrit and Greek, that in the former they are chiefly soft, in the latter entirely hard.

Let us now consider Grimm's Law. It is this: " If the same roots or the same words exist in Sanskrit, Greek, Latin, Celtic, Slavonic, Lithuanian, Gothic, and High-German, then wherever the Hindus and the Greeks pronounce an aspirate, the Goths and the Low-Germans generally, the Saxons, Anglo-Saxons, Frisians, &c., pronounce the corresponding soft check, the Old High-Germans the corresponding hard check. In this first change the Lithuanian, the Slavonic, and the Celtic races agree in pronunciation with the Gothic. We thus arrive at the first formula: —

		KH	TH	PH [1]
I.	Greek and Sansk.	KH	TH	PH
II.	Gothic, &c.	G	D	B
III.	Old H. G.	K	T	P

Secondly, if in Greek, Latin, Sanskrit, Lithuanian,

[1] The letters here used are to be considered merely as symbols, not as the real letters occurring in those languages. If we translate these symbols into real letters, we find, in Formula 1., instead of

	KH	TH	PH
Sanskrit	gh, h	dh, h	bh, h
Greek	χ	ϑ	φ
Latin	h, f (gv, g, v,')	f (d, b)	f (b)

Slavonic, and Celtic, we find a soft check, then we find a corresponding hard check in Gothic, a corresponding breath in Old High-German. This gives us the second formula:—

IV.	Greek, &c.	G	D	B
V.	Gothic	K	T	P
VI.	Old H. G.	Ch	Z	F (Ph)

Thirdly, when the six first-named languages show a hard consonant, then Gothic shows the corresponding breath, Old High-German the corresponding soft check. In Old High-German, however, the law holds good with regard to the dental series only, while in the guttural and labial series the Old High-German documents generally exhibit h and f, instead of the corresponding mediæ g and b. This gives us the third formula:—

VII.	Greek, &c.	K	T	P
VIII.	Gothic	H (G, F)	Th (D)	F (B)
IX.	Old H. G.	H (G, K)	D	F (B, V)

It will be seen at once that these changes cannot be considered as the result of phonetic corruption. Phonetic corruption always follows one and the same direction. It always goes downward, but it does not rise again. Now it may be true, as Grimm says, that it shows a certain pride and pluck on the part of the Teutonic nations to have raised the soft to a hard, and the hard to an aspirated letter.[1] But if this were so, would not the dwindling down of the aspirate, the boldest of the bold, into the media, the meekest of meek letters, evince the very opposite tendency? We must not forget that this phonetic law, which Grimm has well compared with a three-

[1] Cf. Curtius, *Kuhn's Zeitschrift*, II. 330.

spoked wheel, turns round completely, and that what seems a rise in one spoke is a fall in the other. Therefore we should not gain much if, instead of looking upon *Lautverschiebung* as a process of phonetic strengthening, we tried to explain it as a process of phonetic weakening.[1] For though we might consider the aspiration of the hard *t* as the beginning of a phonetic infection (*th*) which gradually led to the softening of *t* to *d*, we should have on the other side to account for the transition of the *d* into *t* by a process of phonetic reinvigoration. We are in a vicious circle out of which there is no escape unless we look at the whole process from a different point of view.

Who tells us that Greek *t* ever became Gothic *th*? What idea do we connect with the phrase, so often heard, that a Greek *t* becomes Gothic *th*? How can a Greek consonant become a Gothic consonant, or a Greek word become a Gothic word? Even an Italian word never becomes a Spanish word; an Italian *t*, as in *amato*, never becomes a Spanish *d*, as in *amado*. They both come from a common source, the Latin; and the Greek and Gothic both come from a common source, the old Aryan language. Instead of attempting to explain the differences between Greek and Gothic by referring one to the other, we ought rather to trace back both to a common source from which each may have started with its peculiar consonantal structure. Now we know from the physiological analysis of the alphabet, that three, or sometimes four, varieties exist for each of the three consonantal contacts. We may

[1] See Lottner, *Zeitschrift*, xl. p. 204; Förstemann, *ibid.* i. p. 170.

pronounce *p* as a hard letter, by cutting the breath sharply with our lips; we may pronounce it as a soft letter, by allowing the refraining pressure to be heard while we form the contact; and we may pronounce it an aspirate by letting an audible emission of breath follow immediately on the utterance of the hard or the soft letter. Thus we get for each point of consonantal contact four varieties:—

k, kh, g, gh,
t, th, d, dh,
p, ph, b, bh.

This rich variety of consonantal contact is to be found, however, in highly-developed languages only. Even among the Aryan dialects, Sanskrit alone can boast of possessing it entire. But if we look beyond the Aryan frontiers, and examine such dialects as, for instance, the Hawaian, we see, first, that even the simplest distinction, that between hard and soft contact, has not yet been achieved. A Hawaian, as we saw, not only finds it extremely difficult to distinguish between *k* and *t*; he likewise fails to perceive any difference between *k* and *g*, *t* and *d*, *p* and *b*. The same applies to other Polynesian languages. In Finnish, the distinction between *k, t, p,* and *g, d, b,* is of modern date, and owing to foreign influence. The Finnish itself recognizes no such distinction in the formation of its roots and vocables, whereas in cognate dialects, such as Hungarian, that distinction has been fully developed (Boller, *Die Finnischen Sprachen*, p. 12).

Secondly, in some of the Polynesian languages we find an uncertainty between the hard checks and their corresponding hard breaths. We find the New Zealand *poe*, ball, pronounced *foe* in Tonga,[1] just as we find the Sanskrit *pati* represented in Gothic by *fath-s*.

Now the introduction of the differences of articulation in more highly developed languages had an object. As new conceptions craved expression, the phonetic organs were driven to new devices which gradually assumed a more settled, traditional, typical form. It is possible to speak without labials, it is possible to say a great deal in a language which has but seven consonants, just as it is possible for a mollusk to eat without lips, and to enjoy life without either lungs or liver. I believe there was a far, far distant time when the Aryan nations (if we may call them so) had no aspirates at all. A very imperfect alphabet will suffice for the lower states of thought and speech; but, with the progress of the mind, a corresponding development will take place in the articulation of letters. Some dialects, as we saw, never arrived at more than one set of aspirates, others ignored them altogether, or lost them again in the course of time. But I believe it can be proved that before the Aryan nations, such as we know them, separated, some of them, at all events, had elaborated a threefold modification of the consonantal checks. The Aryans, before they separated, had, for instance, three roots, *tar*, *dar*, and *dhar*, differing chiefly by their initial consonants which represent three varieties of dental contact. *Tar* meant to cross, *dar*, to tear, *dhar*, to hold. Now although we may not know exactly how the Aryans before

[1] Hale, *Polynesian Grammar*, p. 232.

their separation pronounced these letters, the *t*, *d*, and *dh*, we may be certain that they kept them distinct. That distinction was kept up in Sanskrit by means of the hard, the soft, and the aspirated soft contact, but it might have been achieved equally well by the hard, the soft, and the aspirated hard contact, *t*, *d*, *th*, or by the hard and soft contacts together with the dental breathing. The real object was to have three distinct utterances for three distinct, though possibly cognate, expressions. Now, if the same three roots coexisted in Greek, they would there, as the soft aspirates are wanting, appear from the very beginning, as *tar* (*térma*, *terminus*), *dar* (*dérma*, skin), and *thar*.[1] But what would happen if the same three roots had to be fixed by the Romans, who had never realized the existence of aspirates at all? It is clear that in their language the distinctions so carefully elaborated at first, and so successfully kept up in Sanskrit and Greek, would be lost. *Dar* and *Tar* might be kept distinct, but the third variety, whether *dhar* or *thar*, would either be merged or assume a different form altogether.

Let us see what happened in the case of *tar*, *dar*, and *dhar*. Instead of three, as in Sanskrit, the other Aryan languages have fixed two roots only, *tar* and *dar*, replacing *dhar* by *bhar*, or some other radical. Thus *tar*, to cross, has produced in Sanskrit *tarman*,

[1] The possible corruption of *gh*, *dh*, *bh*, into *kh*, *th*, *ph*, has been explained by Curtius (*G. E.* ii. 17), under the supposition that the second element of *gh*, *dh*, *bh*, is the spiritus asper, a supposition which is untenable (Brücke, p. 84). But even if the transition of *gh* into *kh* were phonetically possible, it has never been proved that Greek ever passed through the phonetic phase of Sanskrit. See also the interesting observations of Grassmann, in Kuhn's *Zeitschrift*, xii. p. 108.

point, *tiras*, through; in Greek *tér-ma*, end; in Latin *ter-minus*, and *trans*, through; in Old Norse *thrŏ-m*, edge, *thairh*, through; in Old High-German *dru-m*, end, *durh*, through. *Dar*, to burst, to break, to tear, exists in Sanskrit *drinátti*, in Greek *deirō*, I skin; *dérma*, skin; Gothic *tairan*, to tear; Old High-German *zeran*. But though traces of the third root *dhar* may be found here and there, for instance in Persian *Dârayavus*, Darius, i. e. the holder or sustainer of the empire, in Zend *dere*, Old Persian *dar*, to hold, that root has disappeared in most of the other Aryan dialects.

The same has happened even when there were only two roots to distinguish. The two verbs, *dadámi*, I give, and *dadhámi*, I place, were kept distinct in Sanskrit by means of their initials. In Greek the same distinction was kept up between *dí-dō-mi*, I give, and *títhēmi*, I place; and a new distinction was added, namely, the *ε* and the *ō*. In Zend the two roots ran together, *dâ* meaning both *to give* and *to place*, or *to make*, besides *dâ*, to know. This is clearly a defect. In Latin it was equally impossible to distinguish between the roots *dâ* and *dhâ*, because the Romans had no aspirated dentals; but such was the good sense of the Romans that, when they felt that they could not efficiently keep the two roots apart, they kept only one, *dare*, to give, and replaced the other *dare*, to place or to make, by different verbs, such as *ponere*, *facere*. That the Romans possessed both roots originally, we can see in such words as *crédo*, *credidi*, which corresponds to Sanskrit *śrad-dadhámi*, *śrad-dadhau*,[1]

---

[1] Sanskrit *dh* appears as Latin *d* in *medius* = Sk. *madhya*, Greek μίσος or μέσος, meri-dies = μεσ·ημβρία.

but where the *dh* has of course lost its aspiration in Latin. In *condere* and *abdere* likewise the radical element is *dhâ*, to place, while in *reddo*, I give back, *do* must be traced back to the same root as the Latin *dare*, to give. In Gothic, on the contrary, the root *dâ*, to give, was surrendered, and *dhâ* only was preserved, though, of course, under the form of *dâ*.

Such losses, however, though they could be remedied and have been remedied in languages which had not developed the aspirated varieties of consonantal articulation, were not submitted to by Gothic and the other Low and High German tribes without an effort to counteract them. The Teutonic tribes were without aspirates, but when they took possession of the phonetic inheritance of their Aryan, not Indian, forefathers, they retained the consciousness of the threefold variety of their consonantal checks, and they tried to meet this threefold claim as best they could. Aspirates, whether hard or soft, they had not. Hence, where Sanskrit had fixed on soft, Greek on hard aspirates, Gothic, like the Celtic and Slavonic tongues, preferred the Latin corresponding soft checks; High-German the corresponding hard checks. High-German approached to Greek, in so far as both agreed on hard consonants; Gothic approached to Sanskrit, in so far as both agreed on some kind of aspiration. But none borrowed from the other, none was before the other. All four, according to my views of dialectic growth, must be taken as national varieties of one and the same type or idea.

So far all would be easy and simple. But now we

have to consider the common Aryan words which in Sanskrit, Greek, in fact, in all the Aryan languages, begin with soft and hard checks. What could the Goths and the High-Germans do? They had really robbed Peter to pay Paul. The High-Germans had spent their hard, the Goths their soft checks, to supply the place of the aspirates. The soft checks of the Goths, *g, d, b,* corresponding to Sanskrit *gh, dh, bh,* were never meant, and could not be allowed, to run together and be lost in the second series of soft consonants, which the Hindus, the Greeks, and the other Aryan nations kept distinct from *gh, dh, bh,* and expressed by *g, d, b.* These two series were felt to be distinct by the Goths and the High-Germans, quite as much as by the Hindus and Greeks; and while the Celtic and Slavonic nations submitted to the aspirates *gh, dh, bh,* being merged in the real mediæ *g, d, b,* remedying the mischief as best they could, the Goths, guided by a wish to keep distinct what must be kept distinct, fixed the second series, the *g, d, b'*s in their national utterance as *k, t, p.* But then the same pressure was felt once more, for there was the same necessity of maintaining an outward distinction between their *k, t, p'*s and that third series, which in Sanskrit and Greek had been fixed on *k, t, p.* Here the Gothic nations were driven to adopt the only remaining expedient; and in order to distinguish the third series both from the *g, d, b'*s and *k, t, p'*s, which they had used up, they had to employ the corresponding hard breaths, the *h, th,* and *f.*

The High-German tribes passed through nearly the same straits. What the Greeks took for hard aspirates they had taken for hard tenues. Having spent their *k, t, p's*, they were driven to adopt the breaths, the *ch, z, f*, as the second variety; while, when the third variety came to be expressed, nothing remained but the mediæ, which, however, in the literary documents accessible to us, have, in the guttural and labial scrics, been constantly replaced by the Gothic *h* and *f*, causing a partial confusion which might easily have been avoided.

This phonetic process which led the Hindus, Greeks, Goths, and Germans to a settlement of their respective consonantal systems might be represented as follows. The aspirates are indicated by I., the mediæ by II., the tenues by III., the breaths by IV.:—

$$\begin{Bmatrix} & & \text{I.} & & & \text{II.} & & & \text{III.} & \\ \text{Sanskrit} & . & gh & dh & bh & g & d & b & k & t & p \\ & & \text{II.} & & & \text{III.} & & & \text{IV.} & \\ \text{Gothic} & . & g & d & b & k & t & p & h & th & f \end{Bmatrix}$$

$$\begin{Bmatrix} & & \text{I.} & & & \text{II.} & & & \text{III.} & \\ \text{Greek} & . . & \chi & \vartheta & \varphi & g & d & b & k & t & p \\ & & \text{III.} & & & \text{IV.} & & & \text{II.} & \\ \text{High-German} & k & t & p & ch & z & f & (g)h & d & (b)f \end{Bmatrix}$$

Let us now examine one or two more of these clusters of treble roots, like *dhar, dar, tar*, and see how they burst forth under different climates from the soil of the Aryan languages.

There are three roots, all beginning with a guttural and ending with the vocalized *r*. In the abstract they may be represented as KAR, GAR, KHAR (or GHAR). In Sanskrit we meet first of all with

GHAR, which soon sinks down to HAR, a root of which we shall have to say a great deal when we come to examine the growth of mythological ideas, but which for the present we may define as meaning to glitter, to be bright, to be happy, to burn, to be eager. In Greek this root appears in *chaírein*, to rejoice, &c.

Gothic, following Sanskrit as far as it could, fixed the same root as GAR, and formed from it *geiro*, desire; *gairan* and *gairnjan*, to desire, to yearn, — derivatives which, though they seem to have taken a sense almost the contrary of that of the Greek *chaírein*, find valuable analogies in the Sanskrit *haryati*, to desire, &c.[1] The High-German, following Greek as far as possible, formed *kiri*, desire; *kerni*, desiring, &c. So much for the history of one root in the four representative languages, in Sanskrit, Gothic, Greek, and High-German.

We now come to a second root, represented in Sanskrit by GAR, to shout, to praise. There is no difficulty in Greek. Greek had not spent its mediæ, and therefore exhibits the same root with the same consonants as Sanskrit, in *gḗrys*, voice; *gērýō*, I proclaim. But what was Gothic to do, and the languages which follow Gothic, Low-German, Anglo-Saxon, Old Norse? Having spent their mediæ on *ghar*, they must fall back on their tenues, and hence the Old Norse *kalla*, to call,[2] but not the A. S. *galan*, to yell. The name for crane is derived in Greek from the same root, *géranos* meaning literally the shouter. In Anglo-Saxon *crán* we find the corresponding tenuis. Lastly, the High-German, having spent its

---

[1] See Curtius, *Griechische Etymologie*, L 168, and objections, ibid. ii. 313.
[2] Lottner, in Kuhn's *Zeitschrift*, xi. p. 165.

tenuis, has to fall back on its guttural breath; hence O. H. G. *challón*, to call, and *chránoh*, crane.

The third root, KAR, appears in Sanskrit as well as in Greek with its guttural tenuis. There is in Sanskrit *kar*, to make, to achieve; *kratu*, power, &c.; in Greek *kraínô*, I achieve; and *kratýs*, strong; *kártos*, strength. Gothic having disposed both of its media and tenuis, has to employ its guttural breath to represent the third series; hence *hardus*, hard, i.e. strong. The High-German, which naturally would have recourse to its unemployed media, prefers in the guttural series the Gothic breath, giving us *harti* instead of *garti*, and thereby causing, in a limited sphere, that very disturbance the avoidance of which seems to be the secret spring of the whole process of the so-called Dialocation of Consonants, or *Lautverschiebung*.

Again, there are in Sanskrit three roots ending in u, and differing from each other merely by the three dental initials, *dh*, *d*, and *t*. There is *dhû* (dhu), to shake; *du*, to burn; and *tu*, to grow.[1]

The first root, *dhû*, produces in Sanskrit *dhû-no-mi*, I shake; *dhû-ma*, smoke (what is shaken or whirled about); *dhû-li*, dust. In Greek the same root yields *thýô*, to rush, as applied to rivers, storms, and the passions of the mind; *thýella*, storm; *thymós*, wrath, spirit; in Latin, *fumus*, smoke.

In Gothic the Sanskrit aspirate *dh* is represented by *d*; hence *dauns*, vapor, smell. In Old High-German the Greek aspirate *th* is represented by *t*; hence *tunst*, storm.

The second root, *du*, meaning to burn, both in a

[1] See Curtius, *Griechische Etymologie*, I. 224, 196, 192.

material and moral sense, yields in Sanskrit *dava*, conflagration; *davathú*, inflammation, pain; in Greek *daíō*, *dédaumai*, to burn; and *dýē*, misery. Under its simple form it has not yet been discovered in the other Aryan dialects; but in a secondary form it may be recognized in Gothic *tundnan*, to light; Old High-German, *zünden*; English, *tinder*. Another Sanskrit root, *du*, to move about, has as yet been met with in Sanskrit grammarians only. But, besides the participle *dúna*, mentioned by them, there is the participle *dúta*, a messenger, one who is moved or sent about on business, and in this sense the root *du* may throw light on the origin of Gothic *taujan*, German *zauen*, to do quickly, to speed an act.

The third root, *tu*, appears in Sanskrit as *taviti*, he grows, he is strong; in *tavás*, strong; *tavishá*, strong; *tuvi* (in comp.), strong; in Greek, as *taýs*, great. The Latin *tótus* has been derived from the same root, though not without difficulty. The Umbrian and Oscan words for city, on the contrary, certainly come from that root, *tuta*, *tota*, from which *tuticus* in *meddix tuticus*,[1] town magistrate. In Lettish, *tauta* is people; in Old Irish, *tuath*.[2] In Gothic we have *thiuda*,[3] people; *thiudisks*, belonging to the people, *theodiscus*; *thiudiskó*, *ethnikōs*; in Anglo-Saxon, *theón*, to grow; *thedd* and *theódisc*, people; *gethedd*, language (il volgare). The High-German, which looks upon Sanskrit *t* and Gothic *th* as *d*, possesses the same word, as *diot*, people, *diutisc*, popu-

---

[1] Aufrecht und Kirchhoff, *Die Umbrischen Sprachdenkmäler*, i. p. 155.
[2] Lottner, Kuhn's *Zeitschrift*, vii. 168.
[3] Grimm, *Deutsche Grammatik*, first part, 3d edition, 1840, Einleitung, p. x. "Excurs über Germanisch und Deutsch."

laris; hence *Deutsch*, German, and *deuten*, to explain, lit. to Germanize.

Throughout the whole of this process there was no transition of one letter into another; no gradual strengthening, no gradual decay, as Grimm supposes.[1] It was simply and solely a shifting of the three cardinal points of the common phonetic horizon of the Aryan nations. While the Hindus fixed their East on the *gh, dh*, and *bh*, the Teutons fixed it on the *g, d*, and *b*. All the rest was only a question of what the French call *s'orienter*. To make my meaning more distinct, I will ask you to recall to your minds the arms of the Isle of Man, three legs on one body, one leg kneeling towards England, the other towards Scotland, the third towards Ireland. Let England, Scotland, and Ireland represent the three varieties of consonantal contact; then Sanskrit would bow its first knee to England (*dh*), its second to Ireland (*d*), its third to Scotland (*t*); Gothic would bow its first knee to Ireland (*d*), its second to Scotland (*t*), its third to England (*th*); Old High-German would bow its first knee to Scotland (*t*), its second to England (*th*), its third to Ireland (*d*). The three languages would thus exhibit three different aspects of the three points that have successively to be kept in view; but we should have no right to maintain that any one of the three lan-

[1] Grimm supposes these changes to have been very gradual. He fixes the beginning of the first change (the Gothic) about the second half of the first century after Christ, and supposes that it was carried through in the second and third centuries. "More towards the West of Europe," he says, "it may have commenced even at an earlier time, and have been succeeded by the second change (the Old High-German), the beginning of which is difficult to fix, though we see it developed in the seventh century." — *Geschichte der Deutschen Sprache*, i. 437.

guages shifted its point of view after having once assumed a settled position; we should have no right to say that *t* ever became *th*, *th d*, and *d t*.

Let us now examine a few words which form the common property of the Aryan nations, and which existed in some form or other before Sanskrit was Sanskrit, Greek Greek, and Gothic Gothic. Some of them have not only the same radical, but likewise the same formative or derivative elements in all the Aryan languages. These are, no doubt, the most interesting, because they belong to the earliest stages of Aryan speech, not only by their material, but likewise by their workmanship. Such a word as *mother*, for instance, has not only the same root in Sanskrit, Greek, Latin, German, Slavonic, and Celtic, namely, the root *mâ*, but likewise the same derivative *tar*,[1] so that there can be no doubt that in the English *mother* we are handling the same word which in ages commonly called *prehistoric*, but in reality as historical as the days of Homer, or the more distant times of the Vedic Rishis, was framed to express the original conception of *genitrix*. But there are other words which, though they differ in their derivative elements, are identical in their roots and in their meanings, so as to leave little doubt that, though they did not exist previous to the dispersion of the Aryans, in exactly that form in which they are found in Greek or Sanskrit, they are nevertheless mere dialectic varieties, or modern modifications of earlier words. Thus *star* is not exactly the same word as *stella*, nor *stella* the same as the Sk. *târâ*; yet these words show that, previous to the confusion of the Aryan tongues, the

[1] Sk. mâtâ; Greek μήτηρ; Lat. mater; O. H. G. muotar; O. Sl. mati; Lith. moti; Gaelic, mathair.

root *star*, to strew, was applied to the stars, as strewing about or sprinkling forth their sparkling light. In that sense we find the stars called *stṛi*, plural *staras*, in the Veda. The Latin *stella* stands for *sterula*, and means a little star; the Gothic *stair-no* is a new feminine derivative; and the Sanskrit *târâ* has lost its initial *s*. As to the Greek *astér*, it is supposed to be derived from a different root, *as*, to shoot, and to mean the shooters of rays, the darters of light; but it can, with greater plausibility, be claimed for the same family as the Sanskrit *star*.

It might be objected, that this very word *star* violates the law which we are going to examine, though all philologists agree that it is a law that cannot be violated with impunity. But, as in other sciences, so in the science of language, a law is not violated, on the contrary, it is confirmed, by exceptions of which a rational explanation can be given. Now the fact is, that Grimm's law is most strictly enforced on all initial consonants, much less so on medial and final consonants. But whenever the tenuis is preceded at the beginning of words by an s, h, or f, these letters protect the k, t, p, and guard it against the execution of the law. Thus the root *stâ* does not become *sthâ* in Gothic; nor does the *t* at the end of *noct-is* become *th*, night being *naht* in Gothic. On the same ground, *st* in *stâr* and *stella* could not appear in Gothic as *th*, but remain *st* as in *stairnô*.

In selecting words to illustrate each of the nine cases in which the dislocation of consonants has taken place, I shall confine myself, as much as possible, to words occurring in English; and I have to observe that, as a general rule, Anglo-Saxon stands throughout on the same step as Gothic. Consonants in the middle and at the end of words, are liable to various disturbing influences, and I shall therefore dwell chiefly on the changes of initial consonants.

Let us begin with words which in English and Anglo-Saxon begin with the soft g, d, and b. If the same words exist in Sanskrit, what should we expect instead of them? Clearly the aspirates gh, dh, bh, but never g, d, b, or k, t, p. In Greek we expect χ, θ, φ. In the other languages there can be no change, because they ignore the distinction between aspirates and soft checks, except the Latin, which fluctuates between soft checks and guttural and labial spiritus.

I. KΠ, Greek χ; Sanskrit gh, h; Latin h, f.
G, Gothic g; Latin gv, g, v; Celtic g; Slavonic g, z.
K, Old High-German k.

The English *yesterday* is the Gothic *gistra*, the Anglo-Saxon *gystran* or *gyrstandæg*, German *gestern*. The radical portion is *gis*, the derivative *tra*; just as in Latin *hes-ternus*, *hes* is the base, *ternus* the derivative. In *heri* the s is changed to r, because it stands between two vowels, like *genus, generis*. Now in Sanskrit we look for initial gh, or h, and so we find *hyas*, yesterday. In Greek we look for χ, and so we find *chthés*. Old High-German, *kestre*.

Corresponding to *gall*, bile, we find Greek *cholé*, Latin *fel* instead of *hel.*[1]

Similarly *garden*, Goth. *gards*, Greek *chórtos*, Latin *hortus*, and *cohors, cohortis*, Slavonic *gradŭ*,[2] as in *Novgorod*, Old High-German *karto*.

[1] Lottner, *Zeitschrift*, vii. 167.   [2] Grimm, *D. G.* I. 244.

The English *goose*, the A. S. *gós*, is the O. H. G. *kans*, the Modern German *Gans*.[1] (It is a general rule in A. S. that n before f, s, and ð is dropped; thus Goth. *munth* = A. S. *mudh*, mouth; Latin *dens*, A. S. *tóð*, tooth; German *ander*, Sk. *antara*, A. S. *oðer*, other.) In Greek we find *chén*, in Latin *anser*, instead of *hanser*, in Sanskrit *hansa*, in Russian *gus'*, in Bohemian *hus*, well known as the name of the great reformer and martyr.

II. TH, Greek ϑ, φ; Sanskrit dh; Latin f.
    D, Gothic d; Latin d, b; Celtic d; Slavonic d.
    T, Old High-German t.

The English *deer*, A. S. *deor*, Goth. *dius*, correspond to Greek *thér*, or *phér*; Latin, *fera*, wild beast; O. H. G., *tior*.

The English *to dare* is the Gothic *gadaursan*, the Greek *tharsein* or *tharrein*, the Sanskrit *dhṛish*, the O. Sl. *drizati*, O. H. G. *tarran*. The Homeric *Thersites*[1] may come from the same root, meaning the daring fellow. Greek, *thrasýs*, bold, is Lithuanian *drasus*.

The English *doom* means originally *judgment*; hence, "final doom," the last judgment. So in Gothic *dom-s* is judgment, sentence. If this word exists in Greek, it would be there derived from a root *dhâ* or *thê* (títhēmi), which means to place, to settle, and from which we have at least one derivative in a strictly legal sense, namely, *thémis*, law, what is settled, then the goddess of justice.

III. PH, Greek φ; Sanskrit bh; Latin f.
    B, Gothic b; Latin b; Celtic and Slavonic b.
    P, Old High-German p.

[1] Curtius, G. E. I. 229.

"I am" in Anglo-Saxon is *beom* and *eom*. *Eom* comes from the root *as*, and stands for eo(r)m, O. N. ë(r)m, Gothic i(s)m, Sanskrit *asmi*. *Beom* is the O. H. G. *pi-m*, the modern German *bin*, the Sanskrit *bhavâmi*, the Greek *phúō*, Latin *fu* in *fui*.

Beech is the Gothic *bôka*, Lat. *fagus*, O. H. G. *puocha*. The Greek *phēgós*, which is identically the same word, does not mean beech, but oak. Was this change of meaning accidental, or were there circumstances by which it can be explained? Was *phēgós* originally the name of the oak, meaning the food-tree, from *phagein*, to eat? And was the name which originally belonged to the oak (the Quercus Esculus) transferred to the beech, after the age of stone with its fir-trees, and the age of bronze with its oak-trees, had passed away,[1] and the age of iron and of beech-trees had dawned on the shores of Europe? I hardly venture to say Yes; yet we shall meet with other words and other changes of meaning suggesting similar ideas, and encouraging the student of language in looking upon these words as witnesses attesting more strikingly than flints and "tags" the presence of human life and Aryan language in Europe, previous to the beginning of history or tradition.

What is the English *brim*?[2] We say a glass is *brim full*, or we fill our glasses to the *brim*, which means simply "to the edge." We also speak of the brim of a hat, the German *Bräme*. Now originally *brim* did not mean every kind of edge or verge, but only the line which separates the land from the sea. It is derived from the root *bhram*, which, as it ought,

[1] Sir Charles Lyell, *Antiquity of Man*, p. 9.
[2] Kuhn, *Zeitschrift*, vi. 152.

exhibits *bh* in Sanskrit, and means to *whirl about*, applied to fire, such as *bhrama*, the leaping flame, or to water, such as *bhrama*, a whirlpool, or to air, such as *bhrimi*, a whirlwind. Now what was called *æstus* by the Romans, namely, the swell or surge of the sea, where the waves seemed to foam, to flame, and to smoke (hence æstuary), the same point was called by the Teutonic nations the *whirl*, or the *brim*. After meaning the border-line between land and sea, it came to mean any border, though in the expression, "fill your glasses to the brim," we still imagine to see the original conception of the sea rushing or pouring in toward the dry land. In Greek we have a derivative verb *phrimássein*,[1] to toss about; in Latin *fremo*, chiefly in the sense of raging or roaring, and perhaps *frendo*, to gnash, are akin to this root. In the Teutonic languages other words of a totally different character must be traced back to the same original conception of *bhram*, to whirl, to be confused, to be rolled up together, namely, *bramble*, *broom*, &c.[2]

We now proceed to the second class, namely, words which in Gothic and Anglo-Saxon are pronounced with k, t, p, and which, therefore, in all the other Indo-European languages, with the exception of Old High-German, ought to be pronounced with g, d, b.

IV. G, Sanskrit g; Greek, Latin, and Celtic g; Slavonic g, z.
    K, Gothic k.
    KH, Old High-German ch.

---

[1] βρίμω and βρόμος, which are compared by Kuhn, would violate the law; they express principally the sound, for instance in βροντή, ὑψιβρεμέτης, Curtius, *G. E.* II. 109. Grassmann, in Kuhn's *Zeitschrift*, xii. 93.

[2] *Broude*, sorte de broussaille dans le Berry, bruyère à balai.

(4.) The English *corn* is the Gothic *kaurn*, Slavonic *zr'no*, Lith. *žirnis*. In Latin we find *granum*, in Sanskrit we may compare *jirṇa*, ground down, though chiefly applied metaphorically to what is ground down or destroyed by old age. O. H. G. *chorn*.

The English *kin* is Gothic *kuni*, O. H. G. *chunni*. In Greek *génos*, Lat. *genus*, Sk. *janas*, we have the same word. The English *child* is in Old Saxon *kind*, the Greek *gónos*, offspring. The English *queen* is the Gothic *qinô*, or *qens*, the Old Saxon *quena*, A. S. *cven*. It meant originally, like the Greek *gyné*,[1] the Old Slavonic *žena*, the Sanskrit *janí* and *jani*, mother, just as *king*, the German *König*, the O. H. G. *chuninc*, the A. S. *cyn-ing*, meant originally, like Sk. *janaka*, father.

The English *knot* is the Old Norse *knútr*, the Latin *nodus*, which stands for *gnodus*.

V. D, Sanskrit d; Greek, Latin, Celtic, Slavonic d.
T, Gothic t.
TH, Old High-German z.

(5.) English *two* is Gothic *tvai*, O. H. G. *zuei*. In all other languages we get the initial soft d; Greek *dúo*, Latin *duo*, Lith. *du*, Slav. *dva*, Irish *do*. *Dubius*, doubtful, is derived from *duo*, two; and the same idea is expressed by the German *Zweifel*, Old High-German *zwifal*, Gothic *tveifls*.

English *tree* is Gothic *triu*; in Sanskrit *dru*, wood and tree (*dâru*, a log). In Greek *drŷs* is tree, but especially *the* tree, namely, the oak.[2] In Irish *darach* and in Welsh *derw*, the meaning of oak is said to

[1] Curtius, G. E. II. 247.
[2] Schol. ad Hom. *Il.* xi. 86. δρυτόμος, ξυλοτόμος· δρῦν γὰρ ἐκάλουν οἱ παλαιοὶ ἀπὸ τοῦ ἀρχαιοτέρου πᾶν δένδρον.

preponderate, though originally they meant tree in general. In Slavonic *drjevo* we have again the same word in the sense of tree. The Greek *dóry* meant originally a wooden shaft, then a spear.

English *timber* is Gothic *timr* or *timbr*, from which *timrjan*, to build. We must compare it, therefore, with Greek *démein*, to build, *dómos*, house, Lat. *domus*, Sanskrit, *dama*, the German *Zimmer*, room.

VI. B, Sanskrit b or v; Greek, Latin, Celtic, and Slavonic b.
P, Gothic p (scarce).
PH, Old High-German ph or f.

(6.) There are few really Saxon words beginning with p, and there are no words in Gothic beginning with that letter, except foreign words. In Sanskrit, too, the consonant that ought to correspond to Gothic p, namely b, is very seldom, if ever, an initial sound, its place being occupied by the labial spiritus v.

We now proceed to the third class, i. e. words beginning in English and Gothic with aspirates, or more properly with breathings, which necessitate in all other Aryan languages, except Old High-German, corresponding consonants such as k, t, p. In Old High-German the law breaks down. We find h and f instead of g and b, and only in the dental series the media d has been preserved, corresponding to Sanskrit t and Gothic th.

VII. K, Sanskrit k; Greek k; Latin c, qu; Old Irish c, ch; Slavonic k.
KH, Gothic h, g (f); Sanskrit h.
G, Old High-German h (g, k).

(7.) The English *heart* is the Gothic *hairtó*. Accordingly we find in Latin *cor*, *cordis*, in Greek *kardia*. In Sanskrit we should expect *kṛid*, instead of which we find the irregular form *hṛid*. O. H. G. *herza*.

The English *hart*, cervus, is the Anglo-Saxon *heorot*, the Old High-German *hiruz*. This points to Greek *keraós*, horned, from *kéras*, horn, and to *cervus* in Latin. The same root produced in Latin *cornu*, Gothic *haurn*, Old High-German *horn*. In Sk. *śiras* is head, *śṛinga*, horn.

The English *who* and *what*, though written with *wh*, are in Anglo-Saxon *hva* and *hvæt*, in Gothic *hvas*, *hvó*, *hva*. Transliterating this into Sanskrit, we get *kas*, *kâ*, *kad*; Latin *quis*, *quæ*, *quid*; Greek *kós* and *pós*.

  VIII. T, Sanskrit t; Greek, Latin, Celtic, Slavonic t.
    TH, Gothic th and d.
    D, Old High-German d.

(8.) The English *that* is the Gothic *thata*, the neuter of *sa*, *só*, *thata*; A. S. *se*, *seó*, *thæt*; German *der*, *die*, *das*. In Sanskrit *sa*, *sâ*, *tad*; in Greek *hós*, *hé*, *tó*.

In the same manner *three*, Gothic *thrais*, is Sanskrit *trayas*, High-German *drei*.

Thou, Sanskrit *tvam*, Greek *tý* and *sý*, Latin *tu*, High-German *du*.

Thin in old Norse is *thunnr*, Sanskrit *tanu-s*, Latin *tenuis*, High-German *dünn*.

  IX. P, Sanskrit p; Greek, Latin, Celtic, Slavonic p.
    PH, Gothic f and b.
    B, Old High-German f and v.

(9.) The last case is that of the labial spiritus in English or Gothic, which requires a hard labial as its substitute in Sanskrit and the other Aryan dialects, except in Old High-German, where it mostly reappears as f.

The English *to fare* in "fare thee well" corresponds to Greek *póros*, a passage. *Welfare, wohlfahrt*, would be in Greek *euporía*, opposed to *aporía*, helplessness. In Sanskrit the same word appears, though slightly altered, namely, *char*,[1] to walk.

The English *feather* would correspond to a Sanskrit *pattra*, and this means a *wing* of a bird, i. e. the instrument of flying, from *pat*, to fly, and *tra*. As to *penna*, it comes from the same root, but is formed with another suffix. It would be in Sanskrit *patana*, *pesna* and *penna* in Latin.

The English *friend* is a participle present. The verb *frijon* in Gothic means *to love*; hence, *frijond*, a lover. It is the Sanskrit *prî*, to love.

The English *few* is the same word as the French *peu*. *Few*, however, is not borrowed from Norman-French, but the two are distant cousins. *Peu* goes back to *paucus*; *few* to A. S. *feawa*, Gothic *fav-s*; and this is the true Gothic representative of the Latin *paucus*. O. H. G. *fóh*.[2]

GENERAL TABLE OF GRIMM'S LAW.

	1	2	3	4	5	6	7	8	9
Sansk.	gh (h)	dh (h)	bh (h)	g	d	b	k	t	p
Greek	χ	θ	φ	γ	δ	β	κ	τ	π
Latin	h f (g v)	f (d b)	f (b)	g	d	b	c qu	t	p
O. Irish	g	d	b	g	d	b?	c (ch)	t (th)	(p)?
O. Slav.	g z	d	b	g z	d	b	k	t	p
Lith.	g z	d	b	g z	d	b	k	t	p
Gothic	g	d	b	k	t	(p)?	h g (f)	th d	f b
O.H.G.	k	t	p	ch	z s	f ph	h g k	d	f v

[1] Cf. Grimm, s. v. fahren.
[2] Kuhn, *Zeitschrift*, l. 515. For exceptions to Grimm's law, see a learned article by Professor Lottner, in Kuhn's *Zeitschrift*, xi. 161; and Grassmann's observations in the same Journal, xii. 131.

APPENDIX.

ON WORDS FOR FIR, OAK, AND BEECH.

In the course of these illustrations of Grimm's law I was led to remark on the peculiar change of meaning in Latin *fagus*, Greek *phêgós*, and Gothic *bóka*. *Phêgós* in Greek means oak, never beech;[1] in Latin and Gothic *fagus* and *bóka* signify beech, and beech only. No real attempt, as far as I know, has ever been made to explain how the same name came to be attached to trees so different in outward appearance as oak and beech. In looking out for analogous cases, and trying to find out whether other names of trees were likewise used in different senses in Greek, Latin, and German, one other name occurred to me which in German means fir, and in Latin oak. At first sight the English word *fir* does not look very like the Latin *quercus*, yet it is the same word. If we trace *fir* back to Anglo-Saxon, we find it there under the form of *furh*. According to Grimm's law, *f* points to *p*, *h* to *k*, so that in Latin we should have to look for a word the consonantal skeleton of which might be represented as *p r c*. Guttural and labial tenues change, and as Anglo-Saxon *fif* points to *quinque*, so *furh* leads to Latin *quercus*, oak. In Old High-German, *foraha* is *Pinus silvestris*; in modern German *föhre* has the same meaning. But in a passage quoted from the Lombard laws of Rothar, *fereha*, evidently the same word, is mentioned as a name of oak (roborem aut quercum quod

[1] Theophrastus, *De Historia Plantarum*, III. 8, 2.

est *fereha*); and Grimm, in his "Dictionary of the German Language," gives *ferch*, in the sense of oak, blood, life.

It would be easy enough to account for a change of meaning from fir, or oak, or beech, to tree in general, or *vice versâ*. We find the Sanskrit *dru*, wood (cf. *druma*, tree, *dâru*, log), the Gothic *triu*, tree, used in Greek chiefly in the sense of oak, *drŷs*. The Irish *darach*, Welsh *derw*, mean oak, and oak only.[1] But what has to be explained here is the change of meaning from fir to oak, and from oak to beech — i. e. from one particular tree to another particular tree. While considering these curious changes, I happened to read Sir Charles Lyell's new work, "The Antiquity of Man," and I was much struck by the following passage (p. 8 *seq.*) : —

"The deposits of peat in Denmark, varying in depth from ten to thirty feet, have been formed in hollows or depressions in the northern drift or boulder formations hereafter to be described. The lowest stratum, two or three feet thick, consists of swamp peat, composed chiefly of moss or sphagnum, above which lies another growth of peat, not made up exclusively of aquatic or swamp plants. Around the borders of the bogs, and at various depths in them, lie trunks of trees, especially of the Scotch fir (*Pinus silvestris*), often three feet in diameter, which must have grown on the margin of the peat-mosses, and have frequently fallen into them. This tree is not now, nor has ever been in historical times, a native of the Danish Islands, and when introduced there has not thriven; yet it was evidently indigenous in

[1] Grimm, *Wörterbuch*, s. v. Elche.

the human period, for Steenstrup has taken out with his own hands a flint instrument from below a buried trunk of one of these pines. It appears clear that the same Scotch fir was afterwards supplanted by the sessile variety of the common oak, of which many prostrate trunks occur in the peat at higher levels than the pines; and still higher the pedunculated variety of the same oak (*Quercus Robur, L.*) occurs, with the alder, birch (*Betula verrucosa, Ehrh.*), and hazel. The oak has in its turn been almost superseded in Denmark by the common beech. Other trees, such as the white birch (*Betula alba*), characterize the lower part of the bogs, and disappear from the higher; while others again, like the aspen (*Populus tremula*), occur at all levels, and still flourish in Denmark. All the land and fresh-water shells, and all the mammalia as well as the plants, whose remains occur buried in the Danish peat, are of recent species.

"It has been stated that a stone implement was found under a buried Scotch fir at a great depth in the peat. By collecting and studying a vast variety of such implements, and other articles of human workmanship preserved in peat and in sand-dunes on the coast, as also in certain shell-mounds of the aborigines presently to be described, the Danish and Swedish antiquaries and naturalists, MM. Nillson, Steenstrup, Forchhammer, Thomsen, Worsäae, and others, have succeeded in establishing a chronological succession of periods, which they have called the ages of stone, of bronze, and of iron, named from the materials which have each in their turn served for the fabrication of implements.

"The age of stone in Denmark coincides with the period of the first vegetation, or that of the Scotch fir, and in part at least with the second vegetation, or that of the oak. But a considerable portion of the oak epoch coincided with 'the age of bronze,' for swords and shields of that metal, now in the Museum of Copenhagen, have been taken out of peat in which oaks abound. The age of iron corresponded more nearly with that of the beech-tree.

"M. Morlot, to whom we are indebted for a masterly sketch of the recent progress of this new line of research, followed up with so much success in Scandinavia and Switzerland, observes that the introduction of the first tools made of bronze among a people previously ignorant of the use of metals, implies a great advance in the arts, for bronze is an alloy of about nine parts of copper and one of tin; and although the former metal, copper, is by no means rare, and is occasionally found pure, or in a native state, tin is not only scarce, but never occurs native. To detect the existence of this metal in its ore, then to disengage it from the matrix, and finally, after blending it in due proportion with copper, to cast the fused mixture in a mould, allowing time for it to acquire hardness by slow cooling, all this bespeaks no small sagacity and skilful manipulation. Accordingly, the pottery found associated with weapons of bronze is of a more ornamental and tasteful style than any which belongs to the age of stone. Some of the moulds in which the bronze instruments were cast, and 'tags,' as they are called, of bronze, which are formed in the hole through which the fused metal was poured, have been found. The number and variety of objects belonging to the age of bronze indicates its long duration, as does the progress in the arts implied by the rudeness of the earlier tools, often mere repetitions of those of the stone age, as contrasted with the more skilfully worked weapons of a later stage of the same period.

"It has been suggested that an age of copper must always have intervened between that of stone and bronze; but if so, the interval seems to have been short in Europe, owing apparently to the territory occupied by the aboriginal inhabitants having been invaded and conquered by a people coming from the East, to whom the use of swords, spears, and other weapons of bronze, was familiar. Hatchets, however, of copper have been found in the Danish peat.

"The next stage of improvement, or that manifested by the substitution of iron for bronze, indicates another stride in the progress of the arts. Iron never presents itself, except in meteorites, in a native state, so that to recognize its ores, and then to separate the metal from its matrix, demands no small exercise of the powers of observation and invention. To fuse the ore requires an intense heat, not to be obtained without artificial appliances, such as pipes inflated by the human breath, or bellows, or some other suitable machinery."

After reading this extract I could hardly help asking the question, Is it possible to explain the change of meaning in one word which meant fir and came to mean oak, and in another word which meant oak and came to mean beech, by the change of vegetation which actually took place in those early ages? Can we suppose that members of the Aryan family had settled in parts of Europe, that dialects of their common language were spoken in the south and in the north of this western peninsula of the primeval Asiatic Continent, at a time which Mr. Steenstrup estimates as at least 4000 years ago? Sir Charles Lyell does not commit himself to such definite chronological calculations. "What may be the antiquity," he writes, "of the earliest human remains preserved in the Danish peat, cannot be estimated in centuries with any approach to accuracy. In the first place, in going back to the bronze age, we already find ourselves beyond the reach of history or even of tradition. In the time of the Romans, the Danish Isles were covered, as now, with magnificent beech forests. Nowhere in the world does this tree flourish more luxuriantly than in Denmark, and eighteen centuries seem to have done little or nothing towards modifying the character of the forest vegetation. Yet in the antecedent bronze period there were no beech-trees, or, at most, but a few stragglers, the country being covered with oak. In the age of stone, again, the Scotch fir prevailed, and already there were human inhabitants in these old pine forests. How many generations of each species of tree flourished in succession before the pine was supplanted by the oak, and the oak by the beech, can be but vaguely conjectured, but the minimum of time required for the formation of so much peat must, according to the estimate of Steenstrup and other good authorities, have amounted to at least 4000 years; and there is nothing in the observed rate of the growth of peat opposed to the conclusion that the number of centuries may not have been four times as great, even though the signs of man's existence have not yet been traced down to the lowest or amorphous stratum. As to the 'shell-mounds,' they correspond in date to the older portion of the peaty record, or to the earliest part of the age of stone as known in Denmark."

To suppose the presence in Europe of people speaking Aryan languages at so early a period in the history of the world, is opposed to the ordinarily received notions as to the advent of the Aryan race on the soil of Europe. Yet, if we ask ourselves, we shall have to confess that these notions themselves rest on no genuine evidence, nor is there for these early periods any available measure of time, except what may be read in the geological annals of the post-tertiary period. The presence of human life during the fir period or the stone age seems to be proved. The question whether the races then living were Aryan or Turanian can be settled by language only. Skulls may help to determine the physical character, but they can in no way clear up our doubts as to the language of the earliest inhabitants of Europe. Now, if we find in the dialects of Aryan speech spoken in Europe, if we find in Greek, Latin, and German, changes of meaning running parallel with the changes of vegetation just described, may we not admit, though as an hypothesis, and as an hypothesis only, that such changes of meaning were as the shadows cast on language by passing events?

Let us look for analogies. A word like *book*, the German *Buch*, being originally identical with *beech*, the German *Buche*, is sufficient evidence to prove that German was spoken before parchment and paper superseded wooden tablets. If we knew the time when tablets made of beech-wood ceased to be employed as the common writing-material, that date would be a *minimum* date for the existence of that language in which a book is called book, and not either *volumen*, or *liber*, or *biblos*.

Old words, we know, are constantly transferred to new things. People speak of an *engine-driver*, because they had before spoken of the driver of horses. They speak of a steel-pen and a *pen-holder*, because they had before spoken of a *pen*, *penna*. When hawks were supplanted by fire-arms, the names of the birds of prey, formerly used in hawking, were transferred to the new weapons. *Mosquet*, the name of a sparrow-hawk, so called on account of its dappled (*muscatus*) plumage, became the name of the French *mousquet*, a musket. *Faucon*, hawk, was the name given to a heavier sort of artillery. *Sacre* in French and *saker* in English, mean both hawk and gun; and the Italian *terzeruolo*, a small pistol, is closely connected with *terzuolo*, a hawk. The English expression " to let fly at a thing " suggests a similar explanation. In all these cases, if we knew the date when hawking went out and firearms came in, we should be able to measure by that date the antiquity of the language in which fire-arms were called by names originally the names of hawks.

The Mexicans called their own copper or bronze *tepuztli*, which is said to have meant originally *hatchet*. The same word is now used for iron, with which the Mexicans first became acquainted through their intercourse with the Spaniards. *Tepuztli* then became a general name for metal, and when copper had to be distinguished from iron, the former was called red, the latter black *tepuztli*.[1] The conclusion which we may draw from this, viz., that Mexican was spoken before the introduction of iron into Mexico, is one of no great value, because we know it from other sources.

But let us apply the same line of reasoning to Greek. Here, too, *chalkós*, which at first meant copper,[2] came afterwards to mean metal in general, and *chalkeús*, originally a coppersmith, occurs in the "Odyssey" (ix. 391) in the sense of blacksmith, or a worker of iron (*sidēreús*). What does this prove? It proves that Greek was spoken before the discovery of iron, and it shows that if we knew the exact date of that discovery, which certainly took place before the Homeric poems were finished, we should have in it a *minimum* date for the antiquity of the Greek language. Though the use of iron was known before the composition of the Homeric poems, it certainly was not known, as we shall see presently, previous to the breaking up of the Aryan family. Even in Greek poetry there is a distinct recollection of an age in which copper was the only metal used for weapons, armor, and tools. Hesiod[3] speaks of the third generation of men, "who had

---

[1] *Anahuac; or, Mexico and the Mexicans*, by Edward B. Tylor. 1861, p. 140.

[2] Gladstone, *Homer and the Homeric Age*, III. p. 499.

[3] Hesiod, *Op. et D.* 150 : —

Τοῖς δ' ἦν χάλκεα μὲν τεύχεα, χάλκεοι δέ τε οἶκοι,
Χαλκῷ δ' εἰργάζοντο μέλας δ' οὐκ ἔσκε σίδηρος.

Cf. Lucretius, 5, 1286.

arms of copper, houses of copper, who ploughed with copper, and the black iron did not exist." In the Homeric poems, knives, spear-points, and armor were still made of copper, and we can hardly doubt that the ancients knew a process of hardening that pliant metal, most likely by repeated smelting and immersion in water.[1] The discovery of iron marks a period in the history of the world. Iron is not, like gold, silver, and copper, found in a pure state; the iron ore has to be searched for, and the process of extracting from it the pure metal is by no means easy.[2]

What makes it likely that iron was not known previous to the separation of the Aryan nations is the fact that its names vary in every one of their languages. It is true that *chalkós*, too, in the sense of copper, occurs in Greek only, for it cannot be compared phonetically with Sanskrit *hriku*, which is said to mean tin. But there is another name for copper, which is shared in common by Latin and the Teutonic languages, *æs, æris,* Gothic *ais,* Old High-German *êr,* Modern German *Er-z,* Anglo-Saxon *âr,* English *ore.* Like *chalkós,* which originally meant copper, but came to mean metal in general, bronze or brass, the Latin *æs,* too, changed from the former to the latter meaning; and we can watch the same transition in the corresponding

---

[1] See J. P. Rossignol, Membre de l'Institut, *Les Métaux dans l'Antiquité,* Paris, 1863, pp. 215, 237. Proclus says, with regard to the passage in Hesiod, καὶ τῷ χαλκῷ πρὸς τοῦτο ἐχρῶντο, ὡς τῷ σιδήρῳ πρὸς γεωργίαν, διά τινος βαφῆς τὸν χαλκὸν στερροποιοῦντες. In Strabo, xiii. p. 610, the process of making the alloy of copper and zinc is described, and ἡ ψευδάργυρος is zinc, the result of its mixture with copper can only be brass.

[2] Rossignol, l. c. p. 216. Buffon, *Histoire Naturelle,* article du *Fer,* and article du *Cuivre.* Homer calls iron πολύκμητος σίδηρος.

words of the Teutonic languages. *Æs*, in fact, like Gothic *aiz*, meant the one metal which, with the exception of gold and silver, was largely used of old for practical purposes. It meant copper, whether in its pure state, or alloyed, as in later times, with zin (bronze) and zinc (brass). But neither *æs* in Latin nor *aiz* in Gothic ever came to mean gold, silver, or iron. It is all the more curious, therefore, that the Sanskrit *ayas*, which is the same word as *æs* and *aiz*, should in Sanskrit have assumed the almost exclusive meaning of iron. I suspect, however, that in Sanskrit, too, *ayas* meant originally the metal, i. e. copper, and that as iron took the place of copper, the meaning of *ayas* was changed and specified. In passages of the "Atharva Veda" (xi. 3, 1, 7), and the "Vâjasaneyi-sanhitâ" (xviii. 13), a distinction is made between *syâmam ayas*, dark-brown metal, and *loham* or *lohitam ayas*, bright metal, the former meaning copper, the latter iron.[1] The flesh of an animal is likened to copper, its blood to iron. This shows that the exclusive meaning of *ayas* as iron was of later growth, and renders it more than probable that the Hindus, like the Romans and Germans, attached originally to *ayas* (*æs* and *aiz*), the meaning of the metal *par excellence*, i. e. copper. In Greek, *ayas* would have dwindled to *és*, and was replaced by *chalkós*; while, to distinguish the new from the old metals, iron was called by Homer *sidéros*. In Latin, different kinds of *æs* were distinguished by adjectives, the best known being the

[1] *Lohitâyas* is given in Wilson's *Dictionary* as meaning copper. If this were right, *syâmam ayas* would be iron. The commentator to the "Vâjasaneyi-sanhitâ" is vague, but he gives copper as the first explanation of *syâmam*, iron as the first explanation of *loham*.

æs *Cyprium*, brought from *Cyprus*. Cyprus was taken possession of by the Romans in 57 B. C. *Herod* was intrusted by Augustus with the direction of the Cyprian copper-mines, and received one half of the profits. Pliny used *æs Cyprium* and *Cyprium* by itself, for copper. The popular form, *cuprum*, copper, was first used by Spartianus, in the third century, and became more frequent in the fourth.[1] Iron in Latin received the name of *ferrum*. In Gothic, *aiz* stands for Greek *chalkós*, but in Old High-German *chuphar* appears as a more special name, and *ér* assumes the meaning of bronze. This *ér* is lost in Modern German,[2] except in the adjective *ehern*, and a new word has been formed for metal in general, the Old High-German *ar-uzi*,[3] the Modern German *Erz*. As in Sanskrit *ayas* assumed the special meaning of iron, we find that in German, too, the name for iron was derived from the older name of copper. The Gothic *eisarn*, iron, is considered by Grimm as a derivative form of *aiz*, and the same scholar concludes from this that " in Germany bronze must have been in use before iron."[4] *Eisarn* is changed in Old High-German

---

[1] Rosigno1, l. c. pp. 268, 269.

[2] It occurs as late as the fifteenth century. See Grimm, *Deutsches Wörterbuch*, s. v. *erin*, and s. v. *Erz*, 4, *sub fine*.

[3] Grimm throws out a hint that *ruzi* in *aruzi* might be the Latin *radus*, or *raudus*, *rauderia*, brass, but he qualifies the idea as bold.

[4] See Grimm, *Geschichte der Deutschen Sprache*, where the first chapter is devoted to the consideration of the names of metals. The same subject has been treated by M. A. Pictet, in his *Origines Indo-Européennes*, vol. I. p. 149 *seq*. The learned author arrives at results very different from those stated above, but the evidence on which he relies, and particularly the supposed coincidences between comparatively late or purely hypothetical compounds in Sanskrit, and words in Greek and Latin, would require much fuller proofs than he has given.

to *tsarn*, later to *isan*, the Modern German *Eisen*; while the Anglo-Saxon *tsern* leads to *iren* and *iron*.

It may safely be concluded, I believe, that before the Aryan separation, gold, silver, and a third metal, i. e. copper, in a more or less pure state, were known. Sanskrit, Greek, the Teutonic and Slavonic languages, agree in their names for gold;[1] Sanskrit, Greek, and Latin in their names for silver;[2] Sanskrit, Latin, and German in their names for the third metal. The names for iron, on the contrary, are different in each of the principal branches of the Aryan family, the coincidences between the Celtic and Teutonic names being of a doubtful character. If, then, we consider that the Sanskrit *ayas*, which meant, originally, the same as Latin *æs* and Gothic *aiz*, came to mean iron, — that the German word for iron is derived from Gothic *aiz*, and that Greek *chalkós*, after meaning copper, was used as a general name for metal, and conveyed occasionally the meaning of iron, — we may conclude, I believe, that Sanskrit, Greek, Latin, and German were spoken before the discovery of iron, that each nation became acquainted with that most useful of all metals after the Aryan family was broken up, and that each of the Aryan languages coined its name for iron from its own resources, and marked it by its own national stamp, while it brought the names for gold, silver, and copper from the common treasury of their ancestral home.

Let us now apply the same line of reasoning to the names of fir, oak, and beech, and their varying signification. The Aryan tribes, all speaking dia-

---

[1] Curtius, *Griechische Etymologie*, I. 172, II. 314.
[2] Curtius, l. c. I. 141.

lects of one and the same language, who came to settle in Europe during the fir period, or the stone age, would naturally have known the fir-tree only. They called it by the same name which still exists in English as *fir*, in German as *Föhre*. How was it, then, that the same word, as used in the Lombard dialect, means oak, and that a second dialectic form exists in Modern German, meaning oak, and not fir? We can well imagine that the name of the fir-tree should, during the fir period, have become the appellative for tree in general, just as *chalkós*, copper, became the appellative for metal in general. But how could that name have been again individualized and attached to oak, unless the dialect to which it belonged had been living at a time when the fir vegetation was gradually replaced by an oak vegetation? Although there is as little evidence of the Latin *quercus* having ever meant fir, and not oak, as there is of the Gothic *aiz* having ever meant copper, and not bronze, yet, if *quercus* is the same word as *fir*, I do not hesitate to postulate for it the prehistoric meaning of fir. That in some dialects the old name of fir should have retained its meaning, while in others it assumed that of oak, is in perfect harmony with what we observed before, viz., that *æs* retained its meaning in Latin, while *ayas* in Sanskrit assumed the sense of iron.

The fact that *phēgós* in Greek means oak,[1] and oak only, while *fagus* in Latin, *boka* in Gothic, mean

[1] In Persian, too, *būk* is said to mean oak. No authority, however, has ever been given for that meaning, and it is left out in the last edition of Johnson's *Dictionary*, and in Vullers' *Lexicon Persico-Latinum*. Though the Persian *būk*, in the sense of oak, would considerably strengthen our argument, it is necessary to wait until the word has been properly authenticated.

beech, requires surely an explanation, and until a better one can be given, I venture to suggest that Teutonic and Italic Aryans witnessed the transition of the oak period into the beech period, of the bronze age into the iron age, and that while the Greeks retained *phēgós* in its original sense, the Teutonic and Italian colonists transferred the name, as an appellative, to the new forests that were springing up in their wild homes.

I am fully aware that many objections may be urged against such an hypothesis. Migration from a fir-country into an oak-country, and from an oak-country into a beech-country, might be supposed to have caused these changes of meaning in the ancient Aryan words for fir and oak. I must leave it to the geologist and botanist to determine whether this is a more plausible explanation, and whether the changes of vegetation, as described above, took place in the same rotation over the whole of Europe, or in the North only. Again, the skulls found in the peat deposits are of the lowest type, and have been confidently ascribed to races of non-Aryan descent. In answer to this, I can only repeat my old protest,[1] that the science of language has nothing to do with skulls. Lastly, the date thus assigned to the Aryan arrival in Europe will seem far too remote, particularly if it be considered that long before the first waves of the Aryan emigrants touched the shores of Europe, Turanian tribes, Finns, Lapps, and Basks, must have roved through the forests of our continent. My answer is, that I feel the same

---

[1] See M. M.'s *Lectures on the Turanian Languages*, p. 89. Ethnology *v.* Phonology.

difficulty myself, but that I have always considered a full statement of a difficulty a necessary step towards its solution. I shall be as much pleased to see my hypothesis refuted as to see it confirmed. All that I request for it is an impartial examination.

LECTURE VI.

ON THE PRINCIPLES OF ETYMOLOGY.

VOLTAIRE defined etymology as a science in which vowels signify nothing at all, and consonants very little. "*L'étymologie,*" he said, "*est une science où les voyelles ne font rien, et les consonnes fort peu de chose.*" Nor was this sarcasm quite undeserved by those who wrote on etymology in Voltaire's time, and we need not wonder that a man so reluctant to believe in any miracles should have declined to believe in the miracles of etymology. Of course, not even Voltaire was so great a sceptic as to maintain that the words of our modern languages have no etymology, i. e. no origin, at all. Words do not spring into life by an act of spontaneous generation, and the words of modern languages in particular are in many cases so much like the words of ancient languages, that no doubt is possible as to their real origin and derivation. Wherever there was a certain similarity in sound and meaning between French words and words belonging to Latin, German, Hebrew, or any other tongue, even Voltaire would have acquiesced. No one, for instance, could ever have doubted that the French word for God, *Dieu,* was the same as the Latin *Deus;* that the French *homme,* and even *on,* was the Latin *homo*; the French *femme,* the Latin *femina*. In these instances there had been no change of meaning, and the change of form, though the process by which it took place remained unexplained, was not such as to startle even the most sensitive conscience. There was indeed one department of etymology which had been cultivated with great success in Voltaire's time, and even long before him, namely, the history of the Neo-Latin or Romance dialects. We find in the dictionary of *Du Cange* a most valuable collection of extracts from mediæval Latin writers, which enables us to trace, step by step, the gradual changes of form and meaning from ancient to modern Latin; and we have in the much-ridiculed dictionary of *Menage* many an ingenious contribution towards tracing those mediæval Latin words in the earliest documents of French literature, from the times of the Crusades to the Siècle of Louis XIV. Thus a mere reference to Montaigne, who wrote in the sixteenth century, is sufficient to prove that the modern French *gêner* was originally *gehenner*. Montaigne writes: " *Je me suis contraint et gehenné*," meaning, " I have forced and tortured myself." This verb *gehenner* is easily traced back to the Latin *gehenna*,[1] used in the Greek of the New Testament and in the ecclesiastical writings of the Middle Ages not only in the sense of hell, but in the more general sense of suffering and pain. It is well known that Gehenna was originally the name of the valley of Hinnom, near Jerusalem (גֵּיהִנֹּם), the Tophet, where the Jews burnt their sons and their daughters in the fire, and of which Jeremiah prophesied that it should

[1] Molière says, " Je sens de son courroux des gênes trop cruelles."

be called the valley of slaughter: for " They shall bury in Tophet till there be no place."[1] How few persons think now of the sacrifices offered to Moloch in the valley of Hinnom when they ask their friends to make themselves comfortable, and say, " *Ne vous gênez pas.*"

It was well known, not only to Voltaire, but even to Henri Estienne,[2] who wrote in the sixteenth century, that it is in Latin we may expect to find the original form and meaning of most of the words which fill the dictionaries of the French, Italian, and Spanish languages. But these early etymologists never knew of any test by which a true derivation might be distinguished from a false one, except similarity of sound and meaning; and how

---

[1] Jeremiah vii. 31, 32.

[2] Henri Estienne, *Traicte de la Conformité du Langage Françoys avec le Grec*, 1566. What Estienne means by the *conformité* of French and Greek refers chiefly to syntactical peculiarities, common to both languages. "En une epistre Latine que je mi l'an passé auderant de quelques miens dialogues Grecs, ce propos m'eschappa, Quia multo majorem Gallica lingua cum Græcâ habet affinitatem quam Latina; et quidam tantum (absit invidia dicto) ut Gallos eo ipso quod nati sint Galli, maximum ad linguæ Græcæ cognitionem προτέρημα seu πλεονέκτημα afferre putem." Estienne's etymologies are mostly sensible and sober; those which are of a more doubtful character are marked as such by himself. It is not right to class so great a scholar as H. Estienne together with Perion, and to charge him with having ignored the Latin origin of French. (See August Fuchs, *Die Romanischen Sprachen*, 1849, p. 9.) What Estienne thought of Perion may be seen from the following extract (*Traicte de la Conformité*, p. 139): " Il trouvera assez bô nombre de telles en un livre de nostre maistre Perion: Je ne di pas seulemêt de phantastiques, mais de sottes et ineptes, et si lourdes et asnieres que n'estoyent les autres temoignages que ce povre moine nous a laissez de sa lourderie et asnerie, on pourroit penser son œuvre estre supposé." Estienne is wrongly charged with having derived admiral, French *amiral*, from ἁλμυρός. He says it is Arabic, and so it is. It is the Arab *Emir*, prince, leader, possibly with the Arabic article. French *amirail*; Span. *almirante*; It. *almiraglio*, as if from *admirabilis*. Hammer's derivation from *amir al bahr*, commander of the sea, is untenable.

far this similarity might be extended may be seen in such works as Perion's "*Dialogi de Linguæ Gallicæ Origine*" (1557), or Guichard's "*Harmonie Étymologique des Langues Hebraique, Chaldaique, Syriaque, Greque, Latine, Italienne, Espagnole, Allemande, Flamende, Angloise*" (Paris, 1606). Perion derives *brébis*, sheep (the Italian *berbice*), from *próbaton*, not from the Latin *vervex*, like *berger* from *berbicarius*. *Envoyer* he derives from the Greek *pémpein*, not from the Latin *inviare*. *Heureux* he derives from the Greek *oŭrios*.

Now, if we take the last instance, it is impossible to deny that there is a certain similarity of form and meaning between the Greek and French; and as there can be no doubt that certain French words, such as *parler, prêtre, aumône*, were derived from Greek, it would have been very difficult to convince M. Perion that his derivation of *heureux* was not quite as good as any other. There is another etymology of the same word, according to which it is derived from the Latin *hora*. *Bonheur* is supposed to be *bona hora; malheur, mala hora*; and therefore *heureux* is referred to a supposed Latin form, *horosus*, in the sense of *fortunatus*. This etymology, however, is no better than that of Perion. It is a guess, and no more, and it falls to the ground as soon as any of the more rigid tests of etymological science are applied to it. In this instance the test is very simple. There is, first of all, the gender of *malheur* and *bonheur*, masculine instead of feminine. Secondly, we find that *malheur* was spelt in Old French *mal aür*, which is *malum augurium*. (See Diez, "Etymologisches Wörterbuch der Romanischen Sprachen," 1858, s. v.) Thirdly, we find in Provençal *agur*, *augur*, and from it the Spanish *agüero*, an omen. *Augurium* itself comes from *avis*, bird, and *gur*, telling, *gur* being connected with *garrire*, *garrulus*, and the Sanskrit *gar* or *gṛi*, to shout.

We may form an idea of what etymological tests were in former times when we read in Guichard's "Harmonie Étymologique:"[1] "With regard to the derivations of words by means of the addition, subtraction, transposition, and inversion of letters, it is certain that this can and must be done, if we wish to find true etymologies. Nor is it difficult to believe this, if we consider that the Jews wrote from right to left, whereas the Greeks and the other nations, who derive their languages from Hebrew, write from left to right." Hence, he argues, there can be no harm in inverting letters or changing them to any amount. As long as etymology was carried on on such principles, it could not claim the name of a science. It was an amusement in which people might display more or less of learning or ingenuity, but it was unworthy of its noble title, "The Science of Truth."

It is only in the present century that etymology has taken its rank as a science, and it is curious to observe that what Voltaire intended as a sarcasm has now become one of its acknowledged principles. Etymology is indeed a science in which identity, or even similarity, whether of sound or meaning, is

---

[1] "Quant à la derivaison des mots par addition, substraction, transposition, et invension des lettres, il est certain que cela se peut et doit ainsi faire, si on veut trouver les étymologies. Ce qui n'est point difficile à croire, si nous considerons que les Hebreux escrivent de la droite à la senestre, et les Grecs et autres de la senestre à la droite."

of no importance whatever. Sound etymology has nothing to do with sound. We know words to be of the same origin which have not a single letter in common, and which differ in meaning as much as black and white. Mere guesses, however plausible, are completely discarded from the province of scientific etymology. What etymology professes to teach is no longer merely that one word is derived from another, but how to prove, step by step, that one word was regularly and necessarily changed into another. As in geometry it is of very little use to know that the squares of the two sides of a rectangular triangle are equal to the square of the hypotenuse, it is of little value in etymology to know, for instance, that the French *larme* is the same word as the English *tear*. Geometry professes to teach the process by which to prove that which seems at first sight so incredible; and etymology professes to do the same. A derivation, even though it be true, is of no real value if it cannot be proved, — a case which happens not unfrequently, particularly with regard to ancient languages, where we must often rest satisfied with refuting fanciful etymologies, without being able to give anything better in their place. It requires an effort before we can completely free ourselves from the idea that etymology must chiefly depend on similarity of sound and meaning; and in order to dispose of this prejudice effectually, it may be useful to examine this subject in full detail.

If we wish to establish our thesis that sound etymology has nothing to do with sound, we must prove four points: —

1. *That the same word takes different forms in different languages.*

2. *That the same word takes different forms in one and the same language.*

3. *That different words take the same form in different languages.*

4. *That different words take the same form in one and the same language.*

In order to establish these four points, we should at first confine our attention to the history of modern languages, or, as we should say more correctly, to the modern history of language. The importance of the modern languages for a true insight into the nature of language, and for a true appreciation of the principles which govern the growth of ancient languages, has never been sufficiently appreciated. Because a study of the ancient languages has always been confined to a small minority, and because it is generally supposed that it is easier to learn a modern than an ancient tongue, people have become accustomed to look upon the so-called classical languages — Sanskrit, Greek, and Latin — as vehicles of thought more pure and perfect than the spoken or so-called vulgar dialects of Europe. We are not speaking at present of the literature of Greece or Rome or ancient India, as compared with the literature of England, France, Germany, and Italy. We speak only of language, of the roots and words, the declensions, conjugations, and constructions peculiar to each dialect; and with regard to these, it must be admitted that the modern stand on a perfect equality with the ancient languages. Can it be supposed that we, who are always advancing in art, in science, in philosophy, and religion, should have allowed language, the most powerful instrument of the mind, to fall from its pristine purity, to lose its vigor and nobility, and to become a mere jargon? Language, though it changes continually, does by no means continually decay; or, at all events, what we are wont to call decay and corruption in the history of language is in truth nothing but the necessary condition of its life. Before the tribunal of the Science of Language, the difference between ancient and modern languages vanishes. As in botany aged trees are not placed in a different class from young trees, it would be against all the principles of scientific classification to distinguish between old and young languages. We must study the tree as a whole, from the time when the seed is placed in the soil to the time when it bears fruit; and we must study language in the same manner as a whole, tracing its life uninterruptedly from the simplest roots to the most complex derivatives. He who can see in modern languages nothing but corruption or anomaly, understands but little of the true nature of language. If the ancient languages throw light on the origin of the modern dialects, many secrets in the nature of the dead languages can only be explained by the evidence of the living dialects. Apart from all other considerations, modern languages help us to establish by evidence which cannot be questioned the leading principles of the science of language. They are to the student of language what the tertiary, or even more recent formations, are to the geologist. The works of Diez, his "Comparative Grammar of the Romanic

Languages" and his "Lexicon Comparativum Linguarum Romanarum," are as valuable in every respect as the labors of Bopp, Grimm, Zeuss, and Miklosich; nay, they form the best introduction to the study of the more ancient periods of Aryan speech. Many points which, with regard to Sanskrit, Greek, and Latin, can only be proved by inductive reasoning, can here be settled by historical evidence.

In the modern Romance dialects we have before our eyes a more complete and distinct picture or repetition of the origin and growth of language than anywhere else in the whole history of human speech. We can watch the Latin from the time of the first Scipionic inscription (283 B.C.) to the time when we meet with the first traces of Neo-Latin speech in Italy, Spain, and France. We can then follow for a thousand years the later history of modern Latin, in its six distinct dialects, all possessing a rich and well-authenticated literature. If certain forms of grammar are doubtful in French, they receive light from the collateral evidence which is to be found in Italian or Spanish. If the origin of a word is obscure in Italian, we have only to look to French and Spanish, and we shall generally receive some useful hints to guide us in our researches. Where, except in these modern dialects, can we expect to find a perfectly certain standard by which to measure the possible changes which words may undergo both in form and meaning without losing their identity? We can here silence all objections by facts, and we can force conviction by tracing, step by step, every change of sound and sense from Latin to French;

whereas when we have to deal with Greek and Latin and Sanskrit, we can only use the soft pressure of inductive reasoning.

If we wish to prove that the Latin *coquo* is the same word as the Greek *péptō*, I cook, we have to establish the fact that the guttural and labial tenues, k and p, are interchangeable in Greek and Latin. No doubt there is sufficient evidence in the ancient languages to prove this. Few would deny the identity of *pénte* and *quinque,* and if they did, a reference to the Oscan dialect of Italy, where *five* is not *quinque* but *pomtis*, would suffice to show that the two forms differed from each other by dialectic pronunciation only. Yet it strengthens the hands of the etymologist considerably if he can point to living languages and trace in these exactly the same phonetic influences. Thus the Gaelic dialect shows the guttural where the Welsh shows the labial tenuis. Five in Irish is *coic*, in Welsh *pimp*. Four in Irish is *cethir*, in Welsh *petwar*. Again, in Wallachian, a Latin *qu* followed by *a* is changed into *p*. Thus, *aqua* becomes in Wallachian *apă*; *equa*, *épă*; *quatuor, patru*. It is easier to prove that the French *même* is the Latin *semet ipsissimus*, than to convince the incredulous that the Latin *sed* is a reflective pronoun, and meant originally *by itself.*

Where, again, except in the modern languages, can we watch the secret growth of new forms, and so understand the resources which are given for the formation of the grammatical articulation of language? Everything that is now merely formal in the grammatical system of French can easily be proved to have been originally substantial; and after we have once become fully impressed with this fact, we shall feel less reluctance to acknowledge the same principle with regard to the grammatical system of more ancient languages. If we have learnt how the French future, *j'aimerai*, is a compound tense, consisting of the infinitive and the auxiliary verb, *avoir*, to have, we shall be more ready to admit the same explanation for the Latin future in *bo*, and the Greek future in *sō*. Modern dialects may be said to let out the secrets of language. They often surprise us by the wonderful simplicity of the means by which the whole structure of language is erected, and they frequently repeat in their new formations the exact process which had given rise to more ancient forms. There can be no doubt, for instance, about the Modern German *entzwei*. *Entzweireissen* does not mean only to tear into two parts, but it assumes the more general sense of to tear in pieces. In English, too, a servant will say that a thing came *a-two*, though he broke it into many pieces. *Entzwei*, in fact, answers exactly the same purpose as the Latin *dis* in *dissolvo, disturbo, distraho*. And what is the original meaning of this *dis*? Exactly the same as the German *entzwei*, the Low-German *twei*. In Low-German *mine Schau sint twei* means my shoes are torn. The numeral *duo*, with the adverbial termination *is*, is liable to the following changes: — *Du-is* may become *dvis*, and *dvis dbis*. In *dbis* either the d or the b must be dropped, thus leaving either *dis* or *bis*. *Bis* in Latin is used in the sense of twice, *dis* in the sense of *a-two*. The same process leads from *duellum*, Zweikampf, duel, to *dvellum, dbellum*, and *bellum*; from Greek *dyis* to *dFis* and *dis* (twice); from *duiginti* to *dvigínti* and *viginti*, twenty ; from *dyi-kosi* to *dFi-kosi*, *Fi-kosi*, and *ei-kosi*.

And what applies to the form, applies to the meaning of words. What should we say if we were told that a word which means good in Sanskrit meant bad in Greek? Yet we have only to trace the Modern German *schlecht* back through a few centuries before we find that the same word which now means *bad* was then used in the sense of *good*,[1] and we are enabled to perceive, by a reference to intermediate writers, that this transition was by no means so violent as it seems to be. *Schlecht* meant *right* and *straight*, but it also meant *simple*; *simple* came to mean *foolish* ; *foolish, useless* ; *useless, bad*. *Ekelhaft* is used by Leibnitz in the sense of fastidious, delicate;[2] it now means only what causes disgust. *Ingenium*, which meant an inborn faculty, is degraded into the Italian *ingannare*, which means to cheat. *Sælig*, which in Anglo-Saxon meant blessed, *beatus*, appears in English as *silly* ; and the same ill-natured change may be observed in the Greek *euḗthēs*, guileless, mild, silly, and in the German *albern*, stupid, the Old High-German *alawár*, verissimus, *alawári*, benignus.

Thus, a word which originally meant life or time in Sanskrit, has given rise to a number of words expressing eternity, the very opposite of life and time. *Ever* and *never* in English are derived from the same source from which we have *age*. *Age* is of course the French *âge*. This *âge* was in Old French *edage*,

---

[1] "Er (Got) enwil niht tuon wan slehtes," God will do nothing but what is good. Fridank's *Bescheidenheit*, in M. M.'s *German Classics*, p. 121.

[2] Not mentioned in Grimm's *Dictionary*.

changed into *eage* and *áge*. *Edage*, again, represents a Latin form, *ætaticum*, which was had recourse to after the original *ætas* had dwindled away into a mere vowel, the Old French *aé* (Diez, s. v.). Now the Latin *ætas* is a contraction of *ævitas*, as *æternus* is a contraction of *æviternus* (cf. sempiternus). *Ævum*, again, corresponds by its radical, though not by its derivative elements, to Greek *aiFón* and the Gothic *aiv-s*, time, and eternity. In Sanskrit, we meet with a *áyus*, a neuter, which, if literally translated into Greek, would give as a Greek form *aios*, and an adjective, *aiés*, neut. *aiés*. Now, although *aios* does not survive in the actual language of Greece, its derivatives exist, the adverbs *aiés* and *aiei*. This *aiei* is a regular dative (or rather locative) of *aiés*, which would form *aiesi*, *aiei*, like *génesi* and *ginei*. In Gothic, we have from *aivs*, time, the adverbs *aiv*, ever, the Modern German *je*; and *ni aiv*, never, the Modern German *nie*.

There is a peculiar charm in watching the various changes of form and meaning in words passing down from the Ganges or the Tiber into the great ocean of modern speech. In the eighth century B.C. the Latin dialect was confined to a small territory. It was but one dialect out of many that were spoken all over Italy. But it grew — it became the language of Rome and of the Romans, it absorbed all the other dialects of Italy, the Umbrian, the Oscan, the Etruscan, the Celtic, and became by conquest the language of Central Italy, of Southern and Northern Italy. From thence it spread to Gaul, to Spain, to Germany, to Dacia on the Danube. It became the language of law and government in the civilized portions of Northern Africa and Asia, and it was carried through the heralds of Christianity to the most distant parts of the globe. It supplanted in its victorious progress the ancient vernaculars of Gaul, Spain, and Portugal, and it struck deep roots in parts of Switzerland and Wallachia. When it came in contact with the more vigorous idioms of the Teutonic tribes, though it could not supplant or annihilate them, it left on their surface a thick layer of foreign words, and it thus supplied the greater portion in the dictionary of nearly all the civilized nations of the world. Words which were first used by Italian shepherds are now used by the statesmen of England, the poets of France, the philosophers of Germany, and the faint echo of their pastoral conversation may be heard in the Senate of Washington, in the cathedral of Calcutta, and in the settlements of New Zealand.

I shall trace the career of a few of those early Roman words, in order to show how words may change, and how they adapt themselves to the changing wants of each generation. I begin with the word *Palace*. A palace now is the abode of a royal family. But if we look at the history of the name we are soon carried back to the shepherds of the Seven Hills. There, on the Tiber, one of the seven hills was called the *Collis Palatinus*, and the hill was called Palatinus, from *Pales*, a pastoral deity, whose festival was celebrated every year on the 21st of April as the birthday of Rome. It was to commemorate the day on which Romulus, the wolf-child, was supposed to have drawn the first furrow on the foot of that hill, and thus to have laid the foundation of the most ancient part of Rome, the *Roma Quadrata*. On this hill, the Collis Palatinus, stood in later times the houses of Cicero and of his neighbor and enemy Catiline. Augustus built his mansion on the same hill, and his example was followed by Tiberius and Nero. Under Nero, all private houses had to be pulled down on the Collis Palatinus, in order to make room for the emperor's residence, the *Domus Aurea*, as it was called, the Golden House. This house of Nero's was henceforth called the *Palatium*, and it became the type of all the palaces of the kings and emperors of Europe.

The Latin *palatium* has had another very strange offspring, — the French *le palais*, in the sense of palate. Before the establishment of phonetic rules to regulate the possible changes of letters in various languages, no one could have doubted that *le palais*, the palate, was the Latin *palatum*. However, *palatum* could never have become *palais*, but only *palé*. How *palatium* was used instead is difficult to explain. It was a word of frequent use, and with it was associated the idea of vault (palais vouti). Now *vault* was a very appropriate name for the palate. In Italian the palate is called *il cielo della bocca*; in Greek, *ouranós*, *ouraniskos*. Ennius, again, speaks of the vault of heaven as *palatum cœli*. There was evidently a similarity of conception between palate and vault, and vault and palace; and hence *palatium* was most likely in vulgar Latin used by mistake for *palatus*, and thus carried on into French.[1]

Another modern word, the English *court*, the French *cour*, the Italian *corte*, carries us back to

[1] See Diez, *Lexicon Comp.* s. v.

the same locality and to the same distant past. It was on the hills of Latium that *cohors* or *cors* was first used in the sense of a *hurdle*, an *enclosure*, a *cattle-yard*. The *cohortes*, or divisions of the Roman army, were called by the same name; so many soldiers constituting a pen or a court. It is generally supposed that *cors* is restricted in Latin to the sense of cattle-yard, and that *cohors* is always used in a military sense. This is not so. Ovid (Fasti, iv. 704) used *cohors* in the sense of cattle-yard:—

"Abstulerat multas illa cohortis aves;"

and on inscriptions *cors* has been found in the sense of *cohors*. The difference between the two words was a difference of pronunciation merely. As *nihil* and *nil*, *mihi* and *mi*, *nehemo* and *nemo*, *prehendo* and *prendo*, so *cohors*, in the language of Italian peasants, glided in *cors*.

Thus *cors*, *cortis*, from meaning a pen, a cattle-yard, became in mediæval Latin *curtis*, and was used, like the German *Hof*, of the farms and castles built by Roman settlers in the provinces of the empire. These farms became the centres of villages and towns, and in the modern names of *Vraucourt*, *Graincourt*, *Liencourt*, *Magnicourt*, *Aubignicourt*, the older names of *Vari curtis*, *Grani curtis*, *Leonii curtis*, *Manii curtis*, *Albini curtis*, have been discovered.[1]

Lastly, from meaning a fortified place, *curtis* rose to the dignity of a royal residence, and became synonymous with palace. The two names having started from the same place, met again at the end of their long career.

[1] Mannier, *Études sur les Noms des Villes.* Paris, 1861, p. xxvi.

Now, if we were told that a word which in Sanskrit means *cow-pen* had assumed in Greek the meaning of *palace*, and had given rise to derivatives such as *courteous* (civil, refined), *courtesy* (a graceful inclination of the body, expressive of respect), *to court* (to pay attentions, or to propose marriage), many people would be incredulous. It is therefore of the greatest use to see with our own eyes how, in modern languages, words are polished down, in order to feel less sceptical as to a similar process of attrition, in the history of the more ancient languages of the world.

While names such as *palace* and *court*, and many others, point back to an early pastoral state of society, and could have arisen only among shepherds and husbandmen, there are other words which we still use, and which originally could have arisen only in a seafaring community. Thus *government*, or *to govern*, is derived from the Latin *gubernare*. This *gubernare* is a foreign word in Latin; that is to say, it was borrowed by the Romans from the Greeks, who at a very early time had sailed westward, discovered Italy, and founded colonies there, just as in later times the nations of Europe sailed farther west, discovered America, and planted new colonies there. The Greek word which in Italy was changed into *gubernare* was *kubernân*, and it meant originally to handle the rudder, or to steer. It was then transferred to the person or persons intrusted with the direction of public affairs, and at last came to mean to rule.

Minister meant, etymologically, a small man; and it was used in opposition to *magister*, a big man.

Minister is connected with *minus*, less; *magister* with *magis*, more. Hence *minister*, a servant, a servant of the Crown, a minister. From *minister* came the Latin *ministerium*, service; in French contracted into *métier*, a profession. A *minstrel* was originally a professional artist, and more particularly a singer or poet. Even in the *Mystery Plays*, the theatrical representations of portions of the Old or New Testament story, such as still continue to be performed at Ammergau in Bavaria, *mystery* is a corruption of *ministerium*; it meant a religious ministry or service, and had nothing to do with mystery. It ought to be spelt with an *i*, therefore, and not with a *y*.

There is a background to almost every word which we are using; only it is darkened by ages, and requires to be lighted up. Thus *lord*, which in modern English has become synonymous with *nobleman*, was in Anglo-Saxon *hláf-ord*, which is supposed by some to mean *ord*, the origin of *hláf*, loaf; while others look upon it as a corruption of *hláf-weard*, the warder of bread.[1] It corresponds to the German *Brotherr*, and meant originally employer, master, lord. *Lady* in Anglo-Saxon is *hlæfdige*, and likewise means "she who looks after the loaf," the mistress; unless it is a corruption of *hláf-weardige*, the feminine of *hláf-weard*. *Earl*, the same as the Danish *Jarl*, was, I believe, originally a contraction of *elder*; *earl*, therefore, and *alder* in *alderman* were once the same word. In Latin, *an elder* would be *senior*, and this became changed into *seigneur*, *sieur*, and at last dwindled down to *sir*. *Duke* meant originally a

[1] See Grimm, *Deutsches Wörterbuch*, s. v. Brotherr.

leader; *count*, the Latin *comes*, a companion; *baron*, the mediæval Latin *baro*, meant man; and *knight*, the German *Knecht*, was a servant. Each of these words has risen in rank, but they have kept the same distance from each other.

As families rose into clans, clans into tribes, tribes into confederacies, confederacies into nations, the elders of each family naturally formed themselves into a *senate*, *senatus* meaning a collection of elders. The elders were also called the gray-headed, or the *Greys*, and hence the German *Graf*, *gravio*, originally *der Graue*. But at the head of such senates the German nations at an early time placed a *king*. In Latin the king is called *rex*, the Sanskrit *rájan*, in *Mahárája*, and this *rex*, the French *roi*, meant originally *steersman*, from *regere*, to steer. The Teutonic nations, on the contrary, used the name *König*, or *King*, and this corresponds to the Sanskrit *janaka*. What did it mean? It simply meant father, the father of a family, "the *king* of his own *kin*," the father of a clan, the father of a people. Need I add what was the original, and what is still the true meaning of queen? In German we have simply formed a feminine of *König*, namely, *Königin*. In English, on the contrary, the old word for *mother* has been retained. In the translation of the Bible by Ulfilas, in the fourth century, we meet with *qens* and *qino*, meaning *wife* and *woman*. In the eleventh century we read in Notker, *Sol chena iro charal furhten unde minnon*, "a wife shall fear and love her husband." After the fifteenth century the word is no longer used in High-German, but in the Scandinavian languages the word still lives, *karl* and *kona* still meaning *man* and *wife*.

We thus see now languages reflect the history of nations, and how, if properly analyzed, almost every word will tell us of many vicissitudes through which it passed on its way from Central Asia to India or to Persia, to Asia Minor, Greece, and Italy, to Russia, Gaul, Germany, the British Isles, America, New Zealand; nay, back again, in its world-encompassing migrations, to India and the Himalayan regions from which it started. Many a word has thus gone the round of the world, and it may go the same round again and again. For although words change in sound and meaning to such an extent that not a single letter remains the same, and that their meaning becomes the very opposite of what it originally was, yet it is important to observe, that since the beginning of the world no new addition has ever been made to the substantial elements of speech, any more than to the substantial elements of nature. There is a constant change in language, a coming and going of words; but no man can ever invent an entirely new word. We speak to all intents and purposes substantially the same language as the earliest ancestors of our race; and, guided by the hand of scientific etymology, we may pass on from century to century through the darkest periods of the world's history, till the stream of language on which we ourselves are moving carries us back to those distant regions where we seem to feel the presence of our earliest forefathers, and to hear the voices of the earth-born sons of Manu.

Those distant regions in the history of language are, no doubt, the most attractive, and, if cautiously explored, full of instructive lessons to the historian and the philosopher. But before we ascend to those distant heights, we must learn to walk on the smoother ground of modern speech. The advice of Leibnitz that the science of language should be based on the study of modern dialects, has been but too much neglected, and the results of that neglect are visible in many works on Comparative Philology. Confining ourselves therefore for the present chiefly to the modern languages of Europe, let us see how we can establish the four fundamental points which constitute the *Magna Charta* of our science.

1. *The same Word takes different Forms in different Languages.*

This sounds almost like a truism. If the six dialects which sprang from Latin have become six independent languages, it would seem to follow that the same Latin word must have taken a different form in each of them. French became different from Italian, Italian from Spanish, Spanish from Portuguese, because the same Latin words were pronounced differently by the inhabitants of the countries conquered or colonized by Rome, so that, after a time, the language spoken by the colonists of Gaul grew to be unintelligible to the colonists of Spain. Nevertheless, if we are told that the French *même* is the same as the Italian *medesimo*, and that both are derived from the Latin *ipse*, we begin to see that even this first point requires to be carefully examined, and may help to strengthen our arguments against all etymology which trusts to vague similarity of sound or meaning.

How then can French *même* be derived from Latin

ipse? By a process which is strictly genealogical, and which furnishes us with a safer pedigree than that of the Montmorencys or any other noble family. In Old French *même* is spelt *meïsme*, which comes very near to Spanish *mismo* and Portuguese *mesmo*. The corresponding term in Provençal is *medesme*, which throws light on the Italian *medesimo*. Instead of *medesme*, Old Provençal supplies *smetessme*. In order to connect this with Latin *ipse*, we have only to consider that *ipse* passes through Old Provençal *eps* into Provençal *eis*, Italian *esso*, Spanish *ese*, and that the Old Spanish *esora* represents *ipsâ horâ*, as French *encore* represents *hanc horam*. If *es* is *ipse*, *essme* would be *ipsissimum*, Provençal *medesme*, *metipsissimum*, and Old Provençal *smetessme*, *semetipsissimum*.[1]

To a certain point it is a matter of historical rather than of philological inquiry, to find out whether the English *beam* is the German *Baum*. *Beam* in Anglo-Saxon is *beám*, Frisian *bám*, Old Saxon *bâm* and *bôm*, Middle High-German *boum*, Modern High-German *Baum*. It is only when we come to Gothic *bagms* that philological arguments come in, in order to explain the loss of *g* before *m*. This must be explained by a change of *beagm* into *beawm*, and lastly into *beam*.[2]

If we take any word common to all the Teutonic dialects, we shall find that it varies in each, and that it varies according to certain laws. Thus, *to hear* is in Gothic *hausjan*, in Old Norse *heyra*, in Old Saxon *horian*, in Anglo-Saxon *hyran*, in Old High-German *horran*, in Swedish *höra*, in Danish *hore*, in Dutch *hooren*, in Modern German *hören*.

---

[1] Diez, *Grammatik* and *Lexicon*, s. v.
[2] Grimm, *Deutsche Grammatik*, II. 66; I. 261.

We have only to remember that English ranges, as far as its consonants go, with Gothic and Low-German, while Modern German belongs to the third or High-German stage, in order to discover without difficulty the meaning of many a German word by the mere application of Grimm's Law. Thus:—

I.	II.	III.
Drei is *three*	*Zehn* is *ten*	*Tag* is *day*
Du is *thou*	*Zagel* is *tail*	*Trommel* is *drum*
Denn is *then*	*Zahn* is *tooth*	*Traum* is *dream*
Durch is *through*	*Zaun* is *town*	*T(h)euer* is *dear*
Denken is *to think*	*Zinn* is *tin*	*T(h)au* is *dew*
Drang is *throng*	*Zerren* is *to tear*	*Taube* is *dove*
Durst is *thirst*	*Zange* is *tong*	*Teich* is *dough*.

If we compare *tear* with the French *larme*, a mere consultation of historical documents would carry us from *tear* to the earlier forms, *taer*, *tehr*, *teher*, *tæher*, to Gothic *tagr*. The A. S. *tæher*, however, carries us back, even more simply than the Gothic *tagr*, to the corresponding form *dákry* in Greek, and (d)*aśru* in Sanskrit. We saw in our last Lecture how every Greek *d* is legitimately represented in Anglo-Saxon by *t*, and *k* by *h*. Hence *tæher* is *dákry*. In the same manner there is no difficulty in tracing the French *larme* back to Latin *lacruma*. The question then arises, are *dákry* and *lacruma* cognate terms? The secondary suffix *ma* in *lacruma* is easily explained, and we then have Greek *dákry* and Latin *lacru*, differing only by their initials. Here a phonetic law must remove the last difference. *D*, if pronounced without a will, is apt to lapse into *L*. *Dákry*, therefore, would become *lacru*, and both can be derived from a root *dak*, to bite.[1] Only let it

[1] See M. M. in Kuhn's *Zeitschrift*, v. 152. Pott, *Etymologische Forschungen*, II. 58–60, 442, 450.

be borne in mind, that although an original *d* may dwindle down to *t*, no *t* in the Aryan languages was ever changed into *d*, and that it would be wrong to say that *t* and *d* are interchangeable.

The following table will show at a glance a few of the descendants of the Latin preposition *ante*:—

ANTE, before.
It. *anzi*; Sp. *antes*; Old Fr. *ans, ains* (*ainsné* = *aîné*, elder).

ANTE IPSUM.
Old Fr. *ainçois*, before.
It. *anziano*; Sp. *anciano*; Fr. *ancien*, old.

ABANTE, from before.

It. *avanti*;		Fr. *avant*, before.
It. *avanzare*;	Sp. *avanzar*;	Fr. *avancer*, to bring forward.
It. *vantaggio*;	Sp. *ventaja*;	Fr. *avantage*, advantage.

DEABANTE.
It. *davanti*; Fr. *devant*, before.
Fr. *devancer*, to get before.

If instead of a Latin we take a Sanskrit word, and follow it through all its vicissitudes from the earliest to the latest times, we see no less clearly how inevitably one and the same word assumes different forms in different dialects. Tooth in Sanskrit is *dat* (nom. *dantah*, but genitive of the old base, *datah*). The same word appears in Latin as *dens, dentis,* in Gothic as *tunthus,* in English as *tooth,* in Modern German as *Zahn.* All the changes are according to law, and it is not too much to say that in the different languages the common word for tooth could hardly have appeared under any form but that in which we find it. But is the Greek *odoús, odóntos,* the same word as *dens*? And is the Greek *odóntes,* the Latin *dentes,* a mere variety of *edontes* and *eden-*

tes, the eaters? I am inclined to admit that the *o* in *odóntes* is a merely phonetic excrescence, for although I know of no other well-established case in Greek where a simple initial *d* assumes this prosthetic vowel, it would be against all rules of probability to suppose that Greek had lost the common Aryan term for teeth, *danta*, and replaced it by a new and independent word so exactly like the one which it had given up. Prosthetic vowels are very common in Greek before certain double consonants, and before *r, l, n, m*.[1] The addition of an initial *o* in *odóntes* may provisionally be admitted. But if so, it follows that *odóntes* cannot be a mere variety of *edontes*. For wherever Greek has these initial vowels, while they are wanting in Sanskrit, Latin, &c., they are, in the true sense of the word, prosthetic vowels. They are not radical, but merely adscititious in Greek, while if *odóntes* were derived from the root *ed*, we should have to admit the loss of a radical initial vowel in all the members of the Aryan family except Greek, — an admission unsupported by any analogy.[2]

In languages which possess no ancient literature the charm of tracing words back from century to century to its earliest form is of course lost. Contemporary dialects, however, with their extraordinary varieties, teach us even there the same lessons, showing that language must change and is always changing, and that similarity of sound is the same unsafe guide here as elsewhere. One instance must suffice. Man in Malay is *orang*; hence *orang utan*, the man

[1] Curtius, *Grundzüge der Griechischen Etymologie*, ii. 291. Savelsberg, in Höfer's *Zeitschrift*, iv. p. 91.
[2] See Schleicher, *Compendium*, § 43.

of the forest, the Orangutang. This *orang* is pronounced in different Polynesian dialects, *rang, oran, olan, lan, ala, la, na, da, ra.*[1]

We now proceed to a consideration of our second point.

2. *The same Word takes different Forms in the same Language.*

There are, as you know, many Teutonic words which, through two distinct channels, found their way twice into the literary language of Chaucer, Shakspeare, and Milton. They were imported into England at first by Saxon pirates, who gradually dislodged the Roman conquerors and colonists from their *castra* and *coloniæ*, and the Welsh inhabitants from their villages, and whose language formed the first permanent stratum of Teutonic speech in these islands. They introduced such words as, for instance, *weardian*, to ward, *wile*, cunning, *wise*, manner. These words were German words, peculiar to that soft dialect of German which is known by the name of Low-German, and which was spoken on those northern coasts from whence the Juts, the Angles, and Saxons embarked on their freebooting expeditions.

Another branch of the same German stem was the High-German, spoken by the Franks and other Teutonic tribes, who became the conquerors of Gaul, and who, though they adopted in time the language of their Roman subjects, preserved nevertheless in their conversational idiom a large number of their own homespun words. The French or Frankish

[1] Logan, *Journal of Indian Archipelago*, iii. p. 665.

language is now a Romanic dialect, and its grammar is but a blurred copy of the grammar of Cicero. But its dictionary is full of Teutonic words, more or less Romanized to suit the pronunciation of the Roman inhabitants of Gaul. Among warlike terms of German origin, we find in French *guerre*, the same as *war*; *massacre*, from *metzeln*, to cut down, or *metzgen*, to butcher; *maçon*, *Metze*, *Stein-metze*, i. e. stone-cutter; *auberge*, Italian *albergo*, the German *Herberge*, barracks for the army, Old High-German *heriberga*; *bivouac*, the German *Beiwacht*; *boulevard*, German *Bollwerk*; *bourg*, German *Burg*; *brèche*, a breach, from *brechen*; *havresac*, German *Hafersack*; *haveron*, Old High-German *habaro*, oats; *canapsa*, the German *Knappsack*, *Ess-sack*, from *knappen*, *knabern*, or *Schnappsack*;[1] *éperon*, Italian *sperone*, German *Sporn*; *héraut*, Italian *araldo*, German *Herold*, i. e. *Heerwalt*, or from Old High-German *harén*, French *harer*, to call; *maréchal*, Old German *mariscalco*.

Many maritime words, again, came from German, more particularly from Low-German. French *chaloupe* = Sloop, Dutch *sloep*; *cahute* = Dutch *kajuit*, German *Kaue*, or *Koje*; *stribord*, the right side of a ship, English *starboard*, Anglo-Saxon *steorbord*, *Steuerbord*; *hâvre*, *Hafen*; *Nord*, *Sud*, *Est*, *Ouest*, all come from German.

But much commoner words are discovered to be German under a French disguise. Thus, *haie*, hedge, is *Hecke*; *haïr*, to hate, Anglo-Saxon *hatian*; *hameau*, hamlet, *Heim*; *hâter*, to haste; *honnir*, to blame, Gothic *háunjan*, *höhnen*; *harangue*, (*h*)*ring*,

---

[1] Danneil, *Wörterbuch der Altmärkisch-plattdeutschen Mundart*, 1859, s. v.

as in ringleader. The initial *h* betrays the German origin of all these words. Again, *choisir*, to choose, is *kiesen*, A. S. *ceósan*, Gothic *kiusan*, or Gothic *kausjan*, to examine; *danser*, *tanzen*; *causer*, to chat, *kosen*; *dérober*, to rob, *rauben*; *épier*, to spy, *spähen*; *gratter*, *kratzen*; *grimper*, to climb, *klimmen*; *grincer*, *grinsen*, or Old High-German *grimisón*; *gripper*, *greifen*; *rôtir*, *rösten*; *tirer*, to tear; *tomber*, to tumble; *guinder*, to wind; *déguerpir*, to throw away, *werfen*.[1]

It was this language, this Germanized Latin, which was adopted by the Norman invaders of France, themselves equally Teutonic, and representing originally that third branch of the Teutonic stock of speech which is known by the name of Scandinavian. These Normans, or Northmen, speaking their newly-acquired Franco-Roman dialect, became afterwards the victors of Hastings, and their language, for a time, ruled supreme in the palaces, law-courts, churches, and colleges of England. The same thing, however, which had happened to the Frank conquerors of Gaul and the Norman conquerors of Neustria happened again to the Norman conquerors of England. They had to acquire the language of their conquered subjects; and as the Franks, though attempting to speak the language of the Roman provincials, retained large numbers of barbaric terms, the Normans, though attempting to conform to the rules of the Saxon grammar, retained many a Norman word which they had brought with them from France.

Thus the German word *wise* was common to the

[1] See Diez, *Grammatik der Romanischen Sprachen*, passim.

High and the Low branches of the German language; it was a word as familiar to the Frank invaders of Gaul as it was to the Saxon invaders of England. In the mouths of the Roman citizens of France, however, the German initial *W* had been replaced by the more guttural sound of *gu*. *Wise* had become *guise*, and in this new form it succeeded in gaining a place side by side with its ancient prototype, *wise*. By the same process *guile*, the Old French *guile*, was adopted in English, though it was the same word originally as the Anglo-Saxon *wile*, which we have in *wily*. The changes have been more violent through which the Old High-German *wetti*, a pledge (Gothic *vadi*), became changed into the mediæval Latin *wadium* or *vadium*,[1] Italian *gaggio*, and French *gage*. Nevertheless, we must recognize in the verbs *to engage* or *disengage* Norman varieties of the same word which is preserved in the pure Saxon forms *to bet* and *to wed*, literally to bind or to pledge.

There are many words of the same kind which have obtained admittance twice into the language of England, once in their pure Saxon form, and again in their Roman disguise. Words beginning in Italian with *gua*, *gue*, *gui*, are almost invariably of German origin. A few words are mentioned, indeed, in which a Latin *v* seems to have been changed into *g*. But as, according to general usage, Latin *v* remains *v* in the Romance dialects, it would be more correct to admit that in these exceptional cases Latin words had first been adopted and corrupted by the Germans, and then, as beginning with

[1] Diez, *Lexicon Comparativum*, s. v.

German *w*, and not with Latin *v*, been readopted by the Roman provincials.

These exceptional cases, however, are very few, and somewhat doubtful. It was natural, no doubt, to derive the Italian *guado*, a ford, the French *gué*, from Latin *vadum*. Yet the initial *gua* points first to German, and there we find in Old High-German *wat*, a ford, *watan*, to wade. The Spanish *vadear* may be derived from Latin, or it may owe its origin to a confusion in the minds of those who were speaking and thinking in two languages, a Teutonic and a Romanic. The Latin *vadum* and the German *wat* may claim a distant relationship.

Guère in *je ne crois guère* was for a time traced back to *purum, varium, valide, avare,* or *grandem rem*, the Provençal *granren*. But, like the Italian *guari*, it comes from *wári*, true, which gradually assumed the meaning of *very*.[1] The Latin *verus* changes to *vero* and *vrai*.

Guastare, French *gâter*, has been traced back to Latin *vastare*; but it is clearly derived from Old High-German *wastjan*, to waste, though again a confusion of the two words may be admitted in the minds of the bilingual Franks.

Guêpe, wasp, is generally derived from *vespa*; it really comes from the German *Wespe*.[2]

It has frequently been pointed out that this very fact, the double existence of the same word (*warden*

---

[1] Diez, *Lexicon Comp.*, s. v., second edition, proposes *weiger* instead of *wári*.

[2] In Ital. *golpe* and *volpe*, Span. *vulpeja*, Fr. *goupil*, Lat. *vulpecula*, and a few more words of the same kind, mentioned by Diez (p. 267), the cause of confusion is less clear; but even if admitted as real exceptions, they would in no way invalidate the very general rule.

and *guardian*, &c.), has added much to the strength and variety of English. Slight shades of meaning can thus be kept distinct, which in other languages must be allowed to run together. The English *brisk*, *frisky*, and *fresh*, all come from the same source.[1] Yet there is a great difference between a brisk horse, a frisky horse, and a fresh horse,— a difference which it would be difficult to express in any other language. It is a cause of weakness in language if many ideas have to be expressed by the same word, and *fresh* in English, though relieved by *brisk* and *frisky*, embraces still a great variety of conceptions. We hear of a fresh breeze, of fresh water (opposed to stagnant), of fresh butter, of fresh news, of a fresh hand, a freshman, of freshness of body and mind; and such a variation as a brisk fire, a brisk debate, is therefore all the more welcome. *Fresh* has passed through a Latin channel, as may be seen from the change of its vowel, and to a certain extent from its taking the suffix *ment* in *refreshment*, which is generally, though not entirely, restricted to Latin words.[2] Under a thoroughly foreign form it exists in English as *fresco*, in *fresco-paintings*, so called because the paint was applied to the walls whilst the plaster was still fresh or damp.

The same process explains the presence of double forms, such as *ship* and *skiff*, the French *esquif*; from which is derived the Old French *esquiper*, the Modern French *équiper*, the English *to equip*. Or again, *sloop* and *shallop*, the French *chaloupe*.

[1] Grimm, *Deutsche Grammatik*, ii. 63, *friskn*, *frask*, *frushn*; O. H. G. *friscing*, victima (caro recens), *frischling*, porcellus.
[2] After Saxon verbs, *ment* is found in *shipment*, *easement*, *fulfilment*, *forebodement*.

Thus *bank* and *bench* are German; *banquet* is German Romanized.

Bar is German (O. H. G. *para*); *barrier* is Romanized. Cf. Span. *barras*, a bar, French *embarras*, and English *embarrassed*.

Ball is German; *balloon* Romanized.

To pack is German; *bagage* Romanized.

Ring, a circle, is German; O. H. G. *hring*. To *harangue*, to address a ring, to act as a ringleader, is Romanized; It. *aringa*, Fr. *la harangue*.

Sometimes it happens that the popular instinct of etymology reacts on these Romanized German words, and, after tearing off their foreign mask, restores to them a more homely expression. Thus the German *Krebs*, the O. H. G. *krebiz*, is originally the same word as the English *crab*. This *krebiz* appears in French as *écrevisse*; it returned to England in this outlandish form, and was by an off-hand etymology reduced to the Modern English *crayfish*.

Thus *filibuster* seems to be derived from the Spanish *filibote* or *flibote*, but the Spanish word itself was a corruption of the English *fly-boat*.

And as the German elements entered into the English language at various times and under various forms, so did the Latin. Latin elements flowed into England at four distinct periods, and through four distinct channels.

First, through the Roman legions and Roman colonists, from the time of Cæsar's conquest, 55 B. C., to the withdrawal of the Roman legions in 412: e. g. *colonia* = *coln*; *castra* = *chester*; *stratum* = *street*.

Secondly, through the Christian missionaries and priests, from the time of St. Augustine's landing in

597 to the time of Alfred: e. g. *candela* = *candle*; *Kyriake* = *church*; *diaconus* = *dean*; *regula* = *rule*; *corona* = *crown*; *discus* = *dish*; *uncia* = *inch*.

Thirdly, through the Norman nobility and Norman ecclesiastics and lawyers, who, from the days of Edward the Confessor, brought into England a large number of Latin terms, either in their classical or in their vulgar and Romanized form.

Fourthly, through the students of the classical literature of Rome, since the revival of learning to the present day. These repeated importations of Latin words account for the coexistence in English of such terms as *minster* and *monastery*. *Minster* found its way into English through the Christian missionaries, and is found in its corrupt or Anglicized form in the earliest documents of the Anglo-Saxon language. *Monastery* was the same word, only pronounced with less corruption by later scholars, or clergymen, familiar with the Latin idiom. Thus *paragraph* is the Latin *paragraphus*, but slightly altered; *pilcrow*, *pylcrafte*, and *paraf*, are vulgar corruptions of the same word.[1] In a similar way, the verb *to blame* became naturalized in England through the Norman Conquest. The original Latin or Greek word from which the French *blâmer* was derived kept its place in the form of *to blaspheme* in the more cultivated language of the realm. *Triumph* was a Latin word, naturally used in the ecclesiastical and military language of every country. In its degraded form, *la triomphe*, it was peculiar to French, and was brought into England by the Norman nobility as *trump, trump card*.[2] We can watch the same

[1] See *Promptorium Parvulorum*, p. 398.
[2] Trench, *On Words*, p. 156.

process more fully in the history of the French language. That language teems with Latin words which, under various disguises, obtained repeated admittance into its dictionary. They came first with the legions that settled in Gaul, and whose more or less vulgar dialects supplanted the Celtic idiom of the country. They came again in the track of Christian missionaries, and not unfrequently were smuggled in for the third time by the classical scholars of a later age. The Latin *sacramentum*, in its military acceptation, became the French *serment*; in its ecclesiastical meaning it appears as *sacrement*. *Redemptio*, in its military sense, became the French *rançon*, ransom; in its religious meaning it preserved the less mutilated form of *redemption*. Other words belonging to the same class are *acheter*,[1] to buy, *accepter*, to accept, both derived from the Latin *acceptare*. *Chétif*, miserable, *captif*, both from Latin *captivus*. *Chose*, a thing, *cause*, a cause, both from Latin *causa*. *Façon* and *faction*, from Latin *factio*; meaning originally the manner of doing a thing, then peculiarity, then party. Both *fraile* and *fragile* come from *fragilis*. *On* and *l'homme*, from *homo*. *Noël*, Christmas, and *natal*, from *natalis*. *Naïf* and *natif* from *nativus*. *Parole* and *parabole* from *parabola*. *Penser*, to weigh or ponder in one's mind, and *peser*, to weigh on scales, both come from Latin *pensare*. *Pension* also is derived from *pensum*. In Latin, too, *expendo* is used in the sense of spending money, and of weighing or considering.

The Latin pronoun *ille* exists in French under two different forms. It is the *il* of the pronoun of the

[1] Fuchs, p. 125.

third person, and the *le* of the definite article. Of course it must not be supposed for a moment that by any kind of agreement *ille* was divided into two parts, *il* being put aside for the pronoun, and *le* for the article. The pronoun *il* and *elle* in French, *egli* and *ella* in Italian, *el* and *ella* in Spanish, are nothing but provincial varieties of *ille* and *illa*. The same words, *ille* and *illa*, used as articles, and therefore pronounced more rapidly and without an accent, became gradually changed from *il*, which we see in the Italian *il* to *el*, which we have in Spanish; to *lo* (illum), which exists in Provençal and in Italian (lo spirito); and to *le*, which appears in Provençal[1] dialects and in French.

As there are certain laws which govern the transition of Latin into French and Italian, it is easy to determine whether such a word as *opéra* in French is of native growth, or imported from Italian. French has invariably shortened the final *a* into *e*, and a Latin *p* in the middle of words is generally changed into French *b* or *v*. This is not the case in Italian. Thus the Latin *apis*, a bee, becomes in Italian *ape*, in French *abeille*.[2] The Latin *capillus* is the Italian *capello*, the French *cheveu*. Thus *opéra* has become *œuvre* in French, whereas in Italian it remained *opera*,[3] Spanish *obra*.

There is a small class of words in French which ought to be mentioned here, in order to show under

[1] Diez, *Romanische Grammatik*, ii. 35.
[2] Diez, *Rom. Gram.* I. 177. There are exceptions to this rule; for instance, Italian *riva*, for *ripa*; *savio*, for *sapio*; and in French, such words as *vapeur*, *stupide*, *capitaine*, Old French *chevetaine*.
[3] Diez, ii. 20. *Opera* is not the Latin *opus*, used as a feminine, but the plural of *opus*. Such neutral plurals were frequently changed into Romance feminines, and used in the singular. Thus Latin *gaudia*, plural neut.,

how many disguises words have slipped in again and again into the precincts of that language. They are words neither Teutonic nor Romance, but a cross between the two. They are Latin in appearance, but it would be impossible to trace them back to Latin unless we knew that the people who spoke this Latin were Germans who still thought in German. If a German speaks a foreign tongue, he commits certain mistakes which a Frenchman never would commit, and *vice versâ*. A German speaking English would be inclined to say *to bring a sacrifice*; a Frenchman would never make that mistake. A Frenchman, on the contrary, is apt to say that he cannot *attend* any longer, meaning that he cannot wait any longer. Englishmen, again, travelling abroad, have been heard to call for *Wächter*, meaning the waiter; they have declared, in German, *Ich habe einen grossen Geist Sie nieder zu klopfen*, meaning they had a great mind to knock a person down; and they have announced in French, *J'ai changé mon esprit autour de cette tasse de café*, meaning that they had changed their mind about a cup of coffee.

There are many more mistakes of that kind, which grammarians call Germanisms, Gallicisms, or Anglicisms, and for which pupils are constantly reproved by their masters.

Now the Germans who came to settle in Italy and Gaul, and who learnt to express themselves in Latin

is the French *joie*, fem. sing., Italian *gioja*. A diminutive of the French *joie* is the Old French *joel*, a little pleasure; the English *jewel*, the French *joyau*.

Latin *arma*, neut. plur.		Italian and Sp. *arma*	Fr. *l'arme*
" *folia*	"	It. *foglia*	Fr. *feuille*
" *vela*	"	It. and Sp. *vela*	Fr. *voile*
" *batualia*	"	It. *battaglia*	Fr. *bataille*

tant bien que mal, had no such masters to reprove them. On the contrary, their Roman subjects did the best they could to understand their Latin jargon, and, if they wished to be very polite, they would probably repeat the mistakes which their masters had committed. In this manner the most ungrammatical, the most unidiomatic phrases would, after a time, become current in the vulgar language.

No Roman would have expressed the idea of entertaining or amusing by *intertenere.* Such an expression would have conveyed no meaning at all to Cæsar or Cicero. The Germans, however, were accustomed to the idiomatic use of *unterhalten, Unterhaltung,* and when they had to make themselves understood in Latin they rendered *unter* by *inter, halten* by *tenere,* and thus formed *entretenir,* a word owned neither by Latin nor German.

It is difficult, no doubt, to determine in each case whether words like *intertenere,* in the sense of entertaining, were formed by Germans speaking in Latin but thinking in German, or whether one and the same metaphor suggested itself both to Romans and Germans. It might seem at first sight that the French *circonstance,* circumstance, was a barbarous translation of the German *Umstand,* which expresses the same idea by exactly the same metaphor. But if we consult the later Latin literature, we find there, in works which could hardly have experienced any influence of German idiom, *circumstantia,* in the sense of quality or accident, and we learn from Quintilian, v. 10, 104, that the word had been formed in Latin as an equivalent of the Greek *peristasis.*

In some cases, however, it admits of no doubt that

words now classical in the modern languages of Europe were originally the unidiomatic blunders of Germans attempting to express themselves in the Latin of their conquered provinces.

The future is called in German *Zukunft*, which means "what is to come."[1] There is no such word in ancient Latin, but the Germans again translated their conception of future time literally into Latin, and thus formed *l'avenir*, what is to come, *ce qui est à venir*.

One of the many German expressions for sick or unwell is *unpass*. It is used even now, *unpässlich*, *Unpässlichkeit*. The corresponding Latin expression would have been *æger*, but instead of this we find the Provençal *malapte*, It. *malato*, Fr. *malade*. *Malapte* is the Latin *male-aptus*, meaning *unfit*, again an unidiomatic rendering of *unpass*. What happened was this. *Male-aptus* was at first as great a mistake in Latin as if a German speaking English were to take *unpass* in the sense of *unpassend*, and were to say, "that he was unfit," meaning he was unwell. But as there was no one to correct the German lords and masters, the expression *male-aptus* was tolerated, was probably repeated by good-natured Roman physicians, and became after a time a recognized term.

One more word of the same kind, the presence of which in French, Italian, and English it would be impossible to explain except as a Germanism, as a blunder committed by people who spoke in Latin, but thought in German.

Gegend in German means region or country. It

[1] In Claus Groth's *Fir nie Leder tom Singn un Beden vær Schleswig-Holsteen*, 1864, tokum, L e. to come, is used as an adjective: "Se kamt wedder to tokam Jahr."

is a recognized term, and it signified originally that which is before or against, what forms the object of our view. Now in Latin *gegen*, or against, would be expressed by *contra*; and the Germans, not recollecting at once the Latin word *regio*, took to translating their idea of *Gegend*, that which was before them, by *contratum*, or *terra contrata*. This became the Italian *contrada*, the French *contrée*, the English *country*.[1]

And here, in discussing words which, though originally distinct in origin and meaning, have in the course of time become identical or nearly identical in sound, I ought not to pass over in silence the name of a scholar who, though best known in the

[1] Cf. M. M., *Ueber Deutsche Schattirung Romanischer Worte*, in Kuhn's *Zeitschrift*, v. 11.

I take this opportunity of stating that I never held the opinion ascribed to me by M. Littré (*Journal des Savants*, avril 1856; *Histoire de la Langue Française*, 1863, vol. I. p. 84), with regard to the origin of the Romance languages. My object was to explain certain features of these languages which, I hold, would be inexplicable if we looked upon French, Italian, and Spanish merely as secondary developments of Latin. They must be explained, as I tried to show, by the fact that the people in whose minds and mouths these modern dialects grew up, were not all Romans or Roman provincials, but tribes thinking in German and trying to express themselves in Latin. It was this additional disturbing agency to which I endeavored to call attention, without for a moment wishing to deny other more normal and generally admitted agencies which were at work in the formation of the Neo-Latin dialects, as much as in all other languages advancing from what has been called a synthetic to an analytic state of grammar. In trying to place this special agency in its proper light, I may have expressed myself somewhat incautiously; but if I had to express again my own view on the origin of the Romance languages, I could not do it more clearly and accurately than in adopting the words of my eminent critic: " A mon tour, venant, par la série de ces études, à m'occuper du débat ouvert, j'y prends une position intermédiaire, pensant que, essentiellement, c'est la tradition latine qui domine dans les langues romanes, mais que l'invasion germanique leur a porté un rude coup, et que de ce conflit où elles ont failli succomber, et avec elles la civilisation, il leur est resté des cicatrices encore apparentes et qui sont, à un certain point de vue, ces nuances germaniques signalées par Max Müller."

annals of the physical sciences, deserves an honorable place in the history of the Science of Language. Roger Bacon's views on language and etymology are strangely in advance of his age. He called etymology the tale of truth,[1] and he was probably the first who conceived the idea of a Comparative Grammar. He uses the strongest language against those who proposed derivations of words in Latin, Greek, and Hebrew without a due regard to the history of these languages. "Brito," he says, "dares to derive *Gehenna* from the Greek *ge*, earth, and *ennos*, deep, though *Gehenna* is a Hebrew word, and cannot have its origin in Greek."[2] As an instance of words becoming identical in the course of time, he quotes *kenon* as used in many mediæval compounds. In *cenotaph*, an empty tomb, *ceno* represents the Greek κενός, empty. In *cenobite*, one of a religious order living in a convent, *ceno* is the Greek κοινός, common. In *encenia*, festivals kept in commemoration of the foundation of churches, &c., *cenia* answers to the Greek καινός, new, these festivals being intended as renewals of the memory of pious founders.[3] Surely this does honor to the thirteenth century!

---

[1] Roger Bacon, *Compendium Studii*, cap. 7 (ed. Brewer, p. 449): "quoniam etymologia est sermo vel ratio veritatis."

[2] *l. c.* cap. 7, p. 450. "Brito quidem indignissimus auctoritate, pluries redit in vitium de quo reprehendit Hugutionem et Papiam. Nam cum dicit quod *Gehenna* dicitur a *ge*, quod est terra, et *ennos*, quod est profundum, Hebræum vocabulum docet oriri ex Græco; quia *ge* pro terra est Græcum, et *gehenna* est Hebræum."

[3] *l. c.* cap. 7, p. 457. "Similiter multa falsa dicuntur cum istis nominibus, *cœnobium*, *cenodoxia*, *encenia*, *cinomia*, *scenophagia*, et hujusmodi similia. Et est error in simplicibus et compositis, et ignorantia horribilis. Propter quod diligenter considerandum est quod multa istorum dicuntur a κενῷ Græco, sed non omnia. Et sciendum quod *cenon*, apud nos prolatum uno modo, scribitur apud Græcos tribus modis. Primo per e breve, sicut

Accidents like those which we have hitherto discussed are, no doubt, more frequent in the modern history of speech, because, owing to ethnic migrations and political convulsions, the dialects of neighboring or distant races have become mixed up together more and more with every century that has passed over the ethnological surface of Europe. But in ancient times also there had been migrations, and wars, and colonies causing a dislocation and intermixture of the various strata of human speech, and the literary languages of Greece and Rome, however uniform they may seem to us in their classical writings, had grown up, like French or English, by a constant process of absorption and appropriation, exercised on the various dialects of Italy and Greece. What happened in French happened in Latin. As the French are no longer aware that their *paysan*, a peasant, and *païen*, a pagan, were originally but slight dialectic varieties of the same Latin word *paganus*, a villager, the citizen of Rome used the two words *luna*, moon, and *Lucina*, the goddess, without being aware that both were derived from the same root. In *luna* the *c* belonging to the root *lucere*, to shine, is elided; not by caprice or accident, but according to general phonetic rule which requires the omission of a guttural before a liquid. Thus *lumen*, light, stands for *lucmen*; *examen* for *exagmen*; *flamma*,

kenon, et sic est inane seu vacuum, a quo *cenodoxia*, quæ est vana gloria. ... Secundo modo scribitur per diphthongum ex alpha et iota, sicut *kainon*, et tunc idem est quod novum; unde *encænia*, quod est innovatio vel dedicatio, vel nova festa et dedicationes ecclesiarum. ... Tertio modo scribitur per diphthongum ex omicron et iota, sicut *koinos*. ... Unde dicunt *cenon*, a quo *epicenum*, communis generis. ... Item a *cenon*, quod est commune, et *bios*, quod est vita, dicitur *cenobium*, et *cenobita*, quasi communiter viventes."

flame, for *flagma*, from *flagrare*, to burn; *flamen* for *flagmen*, the lighter, the priest (not *brahman*); *lanio*, a butcher, if derived from a root akin to *lacerare*, to lacerate, stands for *lacnio*. *Contaminare*, to contaminate, is certainly derived from the same verb *tango*, to touch, from which we have *contagio*, contagion, as well as *integer*, intact, entire. *Contaminare*, therefore, was originally *contagminare*. This is in fact the same phonetic rule which, if applied to the Teutonic languages, accounts for the change of German *Nagel* into *nail*, *Zagel* into *tail*, *Hagel* into *hail*, *Riegel* into *rail*, *Regen* into *rain*, *Pflegel* into *flail*, *Segel* into *sail*; and which, if applied to Greek and Latin, helps us to discover the identity of the Greek *láchnē*, wool, and Latin *lána*; of Greek *aráchnē*, a spider, and Latin *aránea*. Though a scholar like Cicero[1] might have been aware that *ala*, a wing, was but an abbreviated form of *axilla*, the arm-pit, the two words were as distinct to the common citizen of Rome as *païen* and *paysan* to the modern Frenchman. *Tela*, a web, must, on the same principle, be derived from *texela*, and this from the verb *texere*, to weave. Thus *mala*, the check, is derived from *maxilla*, the jawbone, and *velum*, a sail or veil, from *vexillum*, anything flying or moved by the wind, a streamer, a flag, or a banner. Once in possession of this rule, we are able to discover even in such modern and corrupt forms as *subtle*, the same Latin root *texere*, to weave, which appeared in *tela*. From *texere* was formed the Latin adjective *subtilis*, that which is woven under or beneath, with the same metaphor which leads us to say

[1] "Quomodo enim vester *Axilla Ala* factus est nisi fugâ literæ vastioris, quam literam etiam e *maxillis* et *taxillis* et *vexillis* et *parillo* consuetudo elegans Latini sermonis evellit." — Cicero, Orat. 45, § 153.

fose spun; and this dwindled down into the English *subtle*.

Other words in Latin, the difference of which must be ascribed to the influence of local pronunciation, are *cors* and *cohors*, *nil* and *nihil*, *mi* and *mihi*, *prendo* and *prehendo*, *prudens* and *providens*, *bruma*, the winter solstice, and *brevissima*, scil. *dies*, the shortest day.[1] Thus, again, *susum* stands for *sursum*, upward, from *sub* and *versum*. *Sub*, it is true, means generally below, under; but, like the Greek *hypó*, it is used in the sense of "from below," and thus may seem to have two meanings diametrically opposed to each other, *below* and *upward*. *Submittere* means to place below, to lay down, to submit; *sublevare*, to lift from below, to raise up. *Summus*, a superlative of *sub*, *hýpatos*, a superlative of *hypó*, do not mean the lowest but the highest.[2] As *sub-versum* glides into *sursum* and *susum*, so *retroversum* becomes *retrorsum*, *retrosum*, and *rursum*. *Proversum* becomes *prorsum*, originally *forward*, straightforward; and hence *oratio prosa*, straightforward speech or prose, opposed to *oratio vincta*, fettered or measured speech, poetry.[3]

Now as we look upon Æolic and Doric, Ionic and Attic, as dialects of one and the same language, as we discover in the Romance languages mere varieties of the Latin, and in the Scandinavian, the High-German, and Low-German, only three branches of one and the same stock, we must learn to look upon Greek and Latin, Teutonic and Celtic, Slavonic,

[1] Pott, *Etymologische Forschungen*, L p. 645.
[2] The Sanskrit *upa* and *upari* correspond to Greek *hypó* and *hypér*, Latin *sub* and *super*, Gothic *uf* and *ufar*.
[3] Quint. 9, 4, " oratio alia vincta atque contexta, alia soluta."

Sanskrit, and the ancient Persian, as so many varieties of one and the same original type of speech, which were fixed in the end as the classical organs of the literature of the world. Taking this point of view, we shall be able to understand how what happens in the modern, happened in the ancient periods of the history of language. The same word, with but slight dialectic variations, exists in Greek, Latin, Gothic, and Sanskrit, and vocables which at first sight appear totally different, are separated from each other by no greater difference than that which separates an Italian word from its cognate term in French. There is little similarity to the naked eye between *pen* and *feather*, yet if placed under the microscope of comparative grammar, both words disclose exactly the same structure. Both are derived from a root *pat*, which in Sanskrit means to fly, and which is easily recognized in the Greek *pétomai*, I fly. From this root a Sanskrit word is derived by means of the instrumental suffix *tra*, *pattra*, or *pata-tra*, meaning the instrument of flying, a wing, or a feather. From the same root another substantive was derived, which became current in the Latin dialect of the Aryan speech, *patna* or *petna*, meaning equally an instrument of flying, or a feather. This *petna* became changed into *penna* — a change which rests not merely on phonetic analogy, but is confirmed by Festus, who mentions the intermediate Italian form, *pesna*.[1] The Teutonic dialect retained the same derivative which we saw in Sanskrit, only modifying its pronunciation by

[1] Cf. Greek ἐρετμός, Latin *remus* and *remus*. *Triresmos* occurs in the inscription of the Columna Rostrata.

substituting aspirated for hard consonants, according to rule. Thus *patra* had to be changed into *phathra*, in which we easily recognize the English *feather*. Thus *pen* and *feather*, the one from a Latin, the other from a Teutonic source, are established as merely phonetic varieties of the same word, analogous in every respect to such double words as those which we pointed out in Latin, which we saw in much larger numbers in French, and which impart not only the charm of variety, but the power of minute exactness to the language of Chaucer, Shakspeare, and Milton.

3. *Different Words take the same Form in different Languages.*

We have examined in full detail two of the propositions which serve to prove that in scientific etymology identity of origin is in no way dependent on identity of sound or meaning. If words could forever retain their original sound and their original meaning, language would have no history at all; there would have been no confusion of tongues, and our language would still be the language of our first ancestors. But it is the very nature of language to grow and to change, and unless we are able to discover the rules of this change, and the laws of this growth, we shall never succeed in tracing back to their original source and primitive import the manifold formations of human speech, scattered in endless variety over all the villages, towns, countries, and continents of our globe. The radical elements of language are so extremely few, and the words which constitute the dialects of mankind so countless, that unless it had been possible to express the infinitesimal shades of human thought by the slightest differences in derivation or pronunciation, we should never understand how so colossal a fabric could have been reared from materials so scanty. Etymology is the knowledge of the changes of words, and so far from expecting identity, or even similarity of sound in the outward appearance of a word, as now used in English, and as used by the poets of the Veda, we should always be on our guard against any etymology which would fain make us believe that certain words which exist in French existed in exactly the same form in Latin, or that certain Latin words could be discovered without the change of a single letter in Greek or Sanskrit. If there is any truth in the laws which govern the growth of language, we can lay it down with perfect certainty, that words of identically the same sound in English and in Sanskrit cannot be the same words. And this leads us to our third proposition. It does happen now and then that in languages, whether related to each other or not, certain words appear of identically the same sound and with some similarity of meaning. These words, which former etymologists seized upon as most confirmatory of their views, are now looked upon with well-founded mistrust. Attempts, for instance, are frequently made at comparing Hebrew words with the words of Aryan languages. If this is done with a proper regard to the immense distance which separates the Semitic from the Aryan languages, it deserves the highest credit. But if, instead of being satisfied with pointing out the faint coincidences in the lowest and most general elements of speech, scholars imagine they can discover isolated cases of minute coincidence amidst the general disparity in the grammar and dictionary of the Aryan and Semitic families of speech, their attempts become unscientific and reprehensible.

It is surprising, considering the immense number of words that might be formed by freely mixing the twenty-five letters of our alphabet, that in languages belonging to totally different families, the same ideas should sometimes be expressed by the same or very similar words. Dr. Rae, in order to prove some kind of relationship between the Polynesian and Aryan languages, quotes the Tahitian *pura*, to blaze as a fire, the New Zealand *kapura*, fire, as similar to Greek *pyr*, fire. He compares Polynesian *ao*, sunrise, with Eos; Hawaian *mauna* with *mons*; Hawaian *ike*, he saw or knew, with Sanskrit *iksh*, to see; *manao*, I think, with Sanskrit *man*, to think; *noo*, I perceive, and *noo-noo*, wise, with Sanskrit *jnâ*, to know; *orero* or *orelo*, a continuous speech, with *oratio*; *kala*, I proclaim, with Greek *kalein*, to call; *kalanga*, continuous speech, with *harangue*; *kani* and *kakani*, to sing, with *cano*; *mele*, a chanted poem, with *mélos*.[1]

It is easy to multiply instances of the same kind. Thus in the Kafir language to beat is *beta*, to tell is *tyelo*, hollow is *uholo*.[2]

In Modern Greek, eye is *mati*, a corruption of *om-*

---

[1] See M. M., *Turanian Languages*, p. 85, *seq.* Pott, in *Deutsche Morgenländische Gesellschaft*, ix. 430, containing an elaborate criticism on M. M.'s *Turanian Languages*. The same author has collected some more accidental coincidences in his *Etymologische Forschungen*, ii. 430.

[2] Appleyard, *Kafir Language*, p. 3.

mation; in Polynesian, eye is *mata*, and in Lithuanian *matau* is to see.

And what applies to languages which, in the usual sense of the word, are not related at all, such as Hebrew and English, or Hawaian and Greek, applies with equal force to cognate languages. Here, too, a perfect identity of sound between words of various dialects is always suspicious. No scholar would nowadays venture to compare *to look* with Sanskrit *lokayati*; *to speed* with Greek *speúdō*; *to call* with Greek *kalein*; *to care* with Latin *cura*. The English sound of *i*, which in English expresses an *eye*, oculus, is used in German in the sense of *egg*, ovum; and it would not be unreasonable to take both words as expressive of roundness, applied in the one case to an *egg*, in the other to an *eye*. The English *eye*, however, must be traced back to the Anglo-Saxon *eáge*, Gothic *augô*, German *Auge*, words akin to Sanskrit *akshi*, the Latin *oculus*, the Greek *ósse*; whereas the German *Ei*, which in Old High-German forms its plural *eigir*, is identical with the English *egg*, the Latin *ovum*, the Greek *óFon*, and possibly connected with *avis*, bird. This Anglo-Saxon *eáge*, eye, dwindles down to *y* in *daisy*, and to *ow* in *window*, supposing that *window* is the Old Norse *vindauga*, the Swedish *vindöga*, the Old English *windor*.[1] In Gothic, a window is called *augadauro*, in Anglo-Saxon, *eágduru*, i. e. eye-door. In *island* (which ought to be spelt *iland*), the first portion is neither *egg* nor *eye*, but a corruption of Gothic *ahva*, i. e. *aqua*, water; hence Anglo-Saxon *eáland*, the Old Norse *aland*, waterland.

[1] Grimm, *Deutsche Grammatik*, II. pp. 192, 421.

What can be more tempting than to derive "*on the whole*" from the Greek *kath hólon*, from which *Catholic*?[1] Buttmann, in his "Lexilogus," has no misgivings whatever as to the identity of the Greek *hólos* and the English *hale* and *whole* and *wholesome*. At present, a mere reference to "Grimm's Law" enables any tyro in etymology to reject this identification as impossible. First of all, *whole*, in the sense of sound, is really the same word as *hale*. Both exist in Anglo-Saxon under the form of *hâl*, in Gothic as *hail*, German *heil*.[2] Now, an initial aspirate in Anglo-Saxon or Gothic presupposes a tenuis in Greek, and if, therefore, the same word existed in Greek, it could only have been *kólos*, not *hólos*.

In *hólos* the asper points to an original *s* in Sanskrit and Latin, and *hólos* has therefore been rightly identified with Sanskrit *sarva* and Latin *salvus* and *sollus*, in *sollers*, *sollemnis*, *solliferreus*, &c.

There is perhaps no etymology so generally acquiesced in as that which derives *God* from *good*. In Danish *good* is *god*, but the identity of sound between the English *God* and the Danish *god* is merely accidental; the two words are distinct, and are kept distinct in every dialect of the Teutonic family. As in English we have *God* and *good*, we have in Anglo-Saxon *God* and *gôd*; in Gothic, *Guth* and *god*; in Old High-German, *Cot* and *cuot*; in German, *Gott* and *gut*; in Danish, *Gud* and *god*; in Dutch, *God* and *goed*. Though it is impossible to give a satisfactory etymology of either *God* or *good*, it is clear that two words which thus run parallel in all these

[1] Pott, *Etymol. Forschungen*, i. 776, seq. "Sollum Osce totum et solidum significat."—Festus.
[2] Grimm, *Deutsche Grammatik*, i. pp. 389, 394.

dialects without ever meeting, cannot be traced back to one central point. *God* was most likely an old heathen name of the Deity, and for such a name the supposed etymological meaning of *good* would be far too modern, too abstract, too Christian.[1] In the Old Norse, *Goð* is actually found in the sense of a graven image, an idol, and is then used as a neuter, whereas, in the same language, *Guð*, as a masculine, means God. When, after their conversion to Christianity, the Teutonic races used *God* as the name of the true God, in the same manner as the Romanic nations retained their old heathen word *Deus*, we find that in Old High-German a new word was formed for false gods or idols. They were called *apcot*, as if ex-gods. The Modern German word for idol, *Götze*, is but a modified form of *God*, and the compound *Oelgötze*, which is used in the same sense, seems actually to point back to ancient stone idols, before which, in the days of old, lamps were lighted and incense burned. Luther, in translating the passage of Deuteronomy, "And ye shall hew down the graven images of their gods," uses the expression, "*die Götzen ihrer Götter*."

What thus happens in different dialects may happen also in one and the same language; and this leads us to the consideration of our fourth and last proposition.

4. *Different Words may take the same Form in one and the same Language.*

The same causes which make words which are perfectly distinct in their origin to assume the same,

---

[1] In the language of the gipsies, *devvl*, meaning God, is connected with Sanskrit *deva*. Kuhn, *Beiträge*, I. p. 147. Pott, *Die Zigeuner*, ii. p. 311.

or very nearly the same sound in English and German, may produce a similar convergence between two words in one and the same language. Nay, the chances are, if we take into account the peculiarities of pronunciation and grammar in each dialect, that perfect identity of sound between two words, differing in origin, will occur more frequently in one and the same than in different dialects. It would seem to follow, also, that these cases of verbal convergence are more frequent in modern than in ancient languages; for it is only by a constant process of phonetic corruption, by a constant wearing off of the sharp edges of words, that this verbal assimilation can be explained. Many words in Latin differ by their terminations only; these terminations were generally omitted in the modern Romance dialects, and the result is, that these words are no longer distinguishable in sound. Thus *novus* in Latin means *new*; *novem*, *nine*; the terminations being dropped, both become in French *neuf*. *Suum*, *his*, is pronounced in French *son*; *sonum*, *sound*, is reduced to the same form. In the same manner *tuum*, *thine*, and *tonus*, *tone*, become *ton*. The French *feu*, fire, is the Latin *focus*; *feu*, in the sense of late, is not exactly Latin, — at least, it is derived from Latin in the most barbarous way. In the same manner as we find in Spanish *somos*, *sois*, *son*, where *sois* stands ungrammatically for Latin *estis*; as in the same language a gerund *siendo* is formed which would seem to point to a barbarous Latin form, *essendo*, so a past participle *fuitus* may have been derived from the Latin perfect *fui*, I was; and this may have given rise to the French *feu*, late. Hence we find both *feu la reine* and *la feue reine*.

It sometimes happens that three Latin words are absorbed into one French sound. The sound of *mer* conveys in French three distinct meanings; it means sea, mother, and mayor. Suppose that French had never been written down, and had to be reduced to writing for the first time by missionaries sent to Paris from New Zealand, would not *mer*, in their dictionary of the French language, be put down with three distinct meanings, — meanings having no more in common than the explanations given in some of our old Greek and Latin dictionaries? It is no doubt one of the advantages of the historical system of spelling that the French are able to distinguish between *la mer, mare, le maire, major, la mère, mater*; yet if these words produce no confusion in the course of a rapid conversation, they would hardly be more perplexing in reading, even though written phonetically.

There are instances where four and five words, all of Latin origin, have dwindled away into one French term. *Ver*, the worm, is Latin *vermis*; *vers*, a verse, is Latin *versus*; *verre*, a glass, is Latin *vitrum*; *vert*, green, is Latin *viridis*; *vair*, fur, is Latin *varius*. Nor is there any difference in pronunciation between the French *mai*, the month of May, the Latin *majus*; *mais*, but, the Latin *magis*; *mes*, the plural of my, Latin *mei*; and *la maie*, a trough, perhaps the Latin *mactra*; or between *sang*, blood, *sanguis*; *cent*, a hundred, *centum*; *sans*, without, *sine*; *sent*, he feels, *sentit*; *s'en*, in *il s'en va*, *inde*.

Where the spelling is the same, as it is, for instance, in *louer*, to praise, and *louer*, to let, attempts have not been wanting to show that the second meaning was derived from the first; that *louer*, for instance, was used in the sense of letting, because you have to praise your lodgings before you can let them. Thus *fin*, fine, was connected with *fin*, the end, because the end occasionally expresses the smallest point of an object. Now, in the first instance, both *louer*, to let, and *louer*, to praise, are derived from Latin; the one is *laudare*, the other *locare*. In the other instance we have to mark a second cause of verbal confusion in French. Two words, the one derived from a Latin, the other from a German source, met on the neutral soil of France, and, after being divested of their national dress, ceased to be distinguishable from each other. The same applies to the French *causer*. In one sense it is the Latin *causare*, to cause; in another, the Old German *chósón*, the Modern German *kosen*. As French borrows not only from German, but also from Greek, we need not be surprised if in *le page*, page, we meet with the Greek *paídion*, a small boy, whereas *la page* is the Latin *página*, a page or leaf.

There are cases, however, where French, Italian, and Spanish words, though apparently invested with two quite heterogeneous meanings, must nevertheless be referred to one and the same original. *Voler*, to fly, is clearly the Latin *volare*; but *voler*, to steal, would seem at first sight to require a different etymology. There is, however, no simple word, whether in Latin, or Celtic, or Greek, or German, from which *voler*, to steal, could be derived. Now, as we observed that the same Latin word branched off into two distinct French words by a gradual change of pronunciation, we must here admit a similar bifurcation, brought on by a gradual change of meaning.

It would not, of course, be satisfactory to have recourse to a mere gratuitous assumption, and to say that a thief was called *volator*, a flyer, because he flew away like a bird from his pursuers. But Professor Diez has shown that in Old French, to steal is *embler*, which is the mediæval Latin *imbulare*, used, for instance, in the "Lex Salica." This *imbulare* is the genuine Latin *involare*, which is used in Latin of birds flying down,[1] of men and women flying at each other in a rage,[2] of soldiers dashing upon an enemy,[3] and of thieves pouncing upon a thing not their own.[4] The same *involare* is used in Italian in the sense of stealing, and in the Florentine dialect it is pronounced *imbolare*, like the French *embler*. It was this *involare*, with the sense of seizing, which was abbreviated to the French *voler*. *Voler*, therefore, meant originally, not to fly away, but to fly upon, just as the Latin *impetus*, assault, is derived from the root *pat*, to fly, in Sanskrit, from which we derived *penna* and *feather*. A complete dictionary of words of this kind in French has been published by M. E. Zlatagorskoi, under the title, "Essai d'un Dictionnaire des Homonymes de la Langue Française" (Leipzig, 1862), and a similar dictionary might be composed in English. For here, too, we

---

[1] "Neque enim debent (aves) ipsis nidis involare; ne, dum adsiliunt, pedibus ova confringant." — Col. 8, 3, 5.
[2] "Vix me contineo, quin involem in capillum, monstrum." — Ter. Eun. 3, 2, 20.
[3] "Adeoque improvisi castra involavere." — Tac. H. 4, 33.
[4] "Remitte pallium mihi meum quod involasti." — Cat. 25, 6. These passages are taken from White and Riddle's *Latin-English Dictionary*, a work which deserves the highest credit for the careful and thoughtful manner in which the meanings of each word are arranged and built up architecturally, story on story.

find not only Romance words differing in origin and becoming identical in form, but Saxon words likewise; nay, not unfrequently we meet with words of Saxon origin which have become outwardly identical with words of Romance origin. For instance:—

I.
- *to blow* . A. S. *bláwan*, the wind blows
- *to blow* . A. S. *blówian*, the flower blows
- *to cleave* A. S. *clífian*, to stick
- *to cleave* A. S. *clúfan*, to sunder
- *a hawk* . A. S. *hafuc*, a bird; German *Habicht*
- *to hawk* . to offer for sale, German *höken*
- *to last* . A. S. *gelæstan*, to endure
- *last* . . A. S. *latost*, latest
- *last* . . A. S. *hlæst*, burden
- *last* . . A. S. *lást*, mould for making shoes
- *to lie* . . A. S. *licgan*, to repose
- *to lie* . . A. S. *leogan*, to speak untruth
- *ear* . . A. S. *áre*, the ear; Lat. *auris*
- *ear* . . A. S. *eár*, the ear of corn; Gothic *ahs*; German *Ähre*

II.
- *count* . Latin *comes*
- *to count* . Latin *computare*
- *to repair* Latin *reparare*
- *to repair* Latin *repatriare*
- *tense* . Latin *tempus*
- *tense* . Latin *tensus*
- *vice* . . Latin *vitium*
- *vice* . . Latin *vice*

III.
- *corn* . . A. S. *corn*, in the fields
- *corn* . . Latin *cornu*, on the feet
- *sage* . . A. S. *salwige*, a plant
- *sage* . . Latin *sapius*
- *to see* . A. S. *seohan*
- *see* . . Latin *sedes*
- *scale* . A. S. *scalu*, of a balance
- *scale* . A. S. *scealu*, of a fish

scale	Latin *scala*, steps
sound	A. S. *sund*, hale
sound	A. N. *rund*, of the sea, from *swimman*
sound	Latin *sonus*, tone
sound	Latin *subundare*, to dive [1]

Although, as I said before, the number of these equivocal words will increase with the progress of phonetic corruption, yet they exist likewise in what we are accustomed to call ancient languages. There is not one of these languages so ancient as not to disclose to the eye of an accurate observer a distant past. In Latin, in Greek, and even in Sanskrit, phonetic corruption has been at work, smoothing the primitive asperity of language, and now and then producing exactly the same effects which we have just been watching in French and English. Thus, Latin *est* is not only the Sanskrit *asti*, the Greek *esti*, but it likewise stands for Latin *edit*, he eats. Now, as in German *ist* has equally these two meanings, though they are kept distinct by a difference of spelling, elaborate attempts have been made to prove that the auxiliary verb was derived from a verb which originally meant to eat, — eating being supposed to have been the most natural assertion of our existence.

The Greek *iós* means both arrow and poison; and here again attempts were made to derive either arrow from poison, or poison from arrow.[2] Though these two words occur in the most ancient Greek, they are nevertheless each of them secondary modifications

[1] Large numbers of similar words in Mätzner, *Englische Grammatik*, l. p. 187; Koch, *Historische Grammatik der Englischen Sprache*, l. p. 223.

[2] The coincidence of τόξον, a bow, and τοξικόν, poison for smearing arrows (hence *intoxication*), is curious.

of two originally distinct words. This can be seen by reference to Sanskrit, where arrow is *ishu*, whereas poison is *visha*, Latin *virus*. It is through the influence of two phonetic laws peculiar to the Greek language — the one allowing the dropping of a sibilant between two vowels, the other the elision of the initial *v*, the so-called digamma — that *ishu* and *visha* converged towards the Greek *iós*.

There are three roots in Sanskrit which in Greek assume one and the same form, and would be almost undistinguishable except for the light which is thrown upon them from cognate idioms. *Nah*, in Sanskrit, means to bind, to join together; *snu*, in Sanskrit, means to flow, or to swim; *nas*, in Sanskrit, means to come. These three roots assume in Greek the form *néō*.

Néō, fut. *nésō* (the Sanskrit NAH), means to spin, originally to join together; it is the German *nähen*, to sew, Latin *nere*. Here we have only to observe the loss of the original aspirate *h*, which reappears, however, in the Greek verb *néthō*, I spin; and the former existence of which can be discovered in Latin also, where the *c* of *necto* points to the original guttural *h*.

SNU, *snauti*, to run, appears in Greek as *néō*. This *néō* stands for *sneFō*. S is elided as in *mikrós* for *smikrós*,[1] and the digamma disappears, as usual, between two vowels. It reappears, however, as soon as it stands no longer in this position. Hence fut. *neúsomai*, aor. *éneusa*. From this root, or rather from the still simpler and more primitive root *nu*, the

---

[1] Cf. Mehlhorn, § 54. Also σφάλλω, fallo; σφόγγος, fungus. Festus mentions in Latin, smitto and mitto, stritavus and tritavus.

Aryan languages derived their word for ship, originally the *swimmer*; Sanskrit *naus, návas*; Greek *naûs, neós*; Latin *navis*; and likewise their word for snow, the Gothic *snaivs*, the Latin *nix*, but *nivis*, like *rivo, vixi*. Secondary forms of *nu* or *snu* are the Sanskrit causative *snavayati*, corresponding to the Latin *nare*, which grows again into *natare*. By the addition of a guttural, we receive the Greek *néchō*, I swim, from which *nêsos*, an island, and *Náxos*, the island. The German *Nachen*, too, shows the same tendency to replace the final *v* by a guttural.

The third root is the Sanskrit *nas*, to come, the Vedic *nasati*. Here we have only to apply the Greek euphonic law, which necessitates the elision of an *s* between two vowels; and, as our former rule with regard to the digamma reduced *ne*F*ó* to *néō*, this will reduce the original *nésō* to the same *néō*. Again, as in our former instance, the removal of the cause removed the effect, the digamma reappearing whenever it was followed by a consonant, so in this instance the *s* rises again to the surface when it is followed by a consonant, as we see in *nóstos*, the return, from *néesthai*.

If, then, we have established that sound etymology has nothing to do with sound, what other method is to be followed in order to prove the derivation of a word to be true and trustworthy? Our answer is, We must discover the laws which regulate the changes of letters. If it were by mere accident that the ancient word for *tear* took the form *asru* in Sanskrit, *dákry* in Greek, *lacruma* in Latin, *tagr* in Gothic, a scientific treatment of etymology would be an impossibility. But this is not the case. In spite of the apparent dissimilarity of the words for *tear* in English and French, there is not an inch of ground between these two extremes, *tear* and *larme*, that cannot be bridged over by Comparative Philology. We believe, therefore, until the contrary has been proved, that there is law and order in the growth of language, as in the growth of any other production of nature, and that the changes which we observe in the history of human speech are not the result of chance, but are constrained by general and ascertainable laws.

LECTURE VII.

ON THE POWERS OF ROOTS.

AFTER we have removed everything that is formal, artificial, intelligible in words, there remains always something that is not merely formal, not the result of grammatical art, not intelligible, and this we call for the present a *root* or a *radical element*. If we take such a word as *historically*, we can separate from it the termination of the adverb, *ly*, the termination of the adjective *al*. This leaves us *historic*, the Latin *historicus*. Here we can again remove the adjectival suffix *cus*, by which *historicus* is derived from *histŏr* or *historia*. Now *historia*, again, is formed by means of the feminine suffix *ia*, which produces abstract nouns, from *histŏr*. *Histŏr* is a Greek word, and it is in reality a corruption of *istŏr*. Both forms, however, occur; the spiritus asper instead of the spiritus lenis, in the beginning of the word, may be ascribed to dialectic influences. Then *istŏr*, again, has to be divided into *is* and *tŏr*, *tŏr* being the nom. sing. of the derivative suffix *tar*, which we have in Latin *dá-tor*, Sanskrit, *dâ-tar*, Greek *do-tér*, a giver, and the radical element *is*. In *is*, the *s* is a modification of *d*, for *d* in Greek, if followed immediately by a *t*, is changed to *s*. Thus we arrive at last at the root *id*, which we have in Greek *oída*, in Sanskrit *veda*, the non-reduplicated perfect of the root *vid*, the English *to wit*, to know. *Histōr*, therefore, meant originally a knower, or a finder, *historia*, knowledge. Beyond the root *vid* we cannot go, nor can we tell why *vid* means to see, or to find, or to know. Nor should we gain much if from *vid* we appealed to the preposition *vi*, which means asunder, and might be supposed to have imparted to *vid* the power of *dividing*, *singling out*, perceiving (*dis-cerno*).[1] It is true there is the same similarity of meaning in the Hebrew preposition *bin*, between, and the verb *bin*, to know, but why *bin* should mean *between* is again a question which we cannot hope to clear up by mere etymological analysis.

All that we can safely maintain with regard to the nature of the Aryan roots is this, that they have definite forms and definite meanings. However chaotic the origin of language may by some scholars be supposed to have been, certain it is that here, as in all other subjects of physical research, we must attempt to draw a line which may separate the Chaos from the Kosmos. When the Aryan languages began to assume their individuality, their roots had become typical, both in form and meaning. They were no longer mere interjections with varying and indeterminate vowels, with consonants floating about from guttural to labial contact, and uncertain between surd, sonant, or aspirated enunciation. Nor were they the expressions of mere impressions of the moment, of single, abrupt states of feeling that had no reference to other sensations of a similar or dissimilar character. Language, if it then

---

[1] On the supposed original connection between *vi* and *dvi*, see Pott, *Etym. Unters.* l. 705. *Lectures*, First Series, p. 44.

deserved that name, may at one time have been in that chaotic condition; nay, there are some small portions in almost every language which seem to date from that lowest epoch. Interjections, though they cannot be treated as parts of speech, are nevertheless ingredients of our conversation; so are the clicks of the Bushmen and Hottentots, which have been well described as remnants of animal speech. Again, there are in many languages words, if we may call them so, consisting of mere imitations of the cries of animals or the sounds of nature, and some of them have been carried along by the stream of language into the current of nouns and verbs.

It is this class of words which the Greeks meant when they spoke of *onomatopœia*. But do not let us suppose that because *onomatopœia* means making of words, the Greeks supposed all words to owe their origin to *onomatopœia*, or imitation of sound. Nothing would have been more remote from their minds. By *onomatopœia* they meant to designate not real words, but made, artificial, imitative words, — words that any one could make at a moment's notice. Even the earliest of Greek philosophers had seen enough of language to know that the key to its mysteries could not be bought so cheaply. When Aristotle[1] calls words imitations (*mimḗmata*), he does not mean those downright imitations, as when we call a cow a moo, or a dog a bow-wow. His statements and those of Plato[2] on language must be read in connection with the statements of earlier

---

[1] *Rhet.* III. 1. τὰ γὰρ ὀνόματα μιμήματά ἐστιν, ὑπῆρξε δὲ καὶ ἡ φωνὴ πάντων μιμητικώτατον τῶν μορίων ἡμῖν.

[2] Plato, *Cratylus*, 423 B. ὄνομα ἄρα ἐστίν, ὡς ἔοικε, μίμημα φωνῇ ἐκείνου ὃ μιμεῖται καὶ ὀνομάζει ὁ μιμούμενος τῇ φωνῇ, ὅταν μιμῆται.

philosophers, such as Pythagoras (540–510), Heraclitus (503), Democritus (430–410), and others, that we may see how much had been achieved before them, how many guesses on language had been made and refuted before they in turn pronounced their verdict. Although we possess but scant, abrupt, and oracular sayings which are ascribed to those early sages, yet these are sufficient to show that they had pierced through the surface of language, and that the real difficulties of the origin of speech had not escaped their notice. When we translate the enigmatic and poetical utterances of Heraclitus into our modern, dry, and definite phraseology, we can hardly do them justice. Perfect as they are when seen in their dark shrines, they crumble to dust as soon as they are touched by the bright rays of our modern philosophy. Yet if we can descend ourselves into the dark catacombs of ancient thought, we feel that we are there in the presence of men who, if they lived with us and could but speak our language, would be looked upon as giants. They certainly had this one advantage over us, that their eyes had not been dimmed by the dust raised in the wars of words that have been going on since their time for more than two thousand years. When we are told that the principal difference of opinion that separated the philosophers of old with regard to the nature and origin of language is expressed by the two words *phýsei* and *thései*, "naturally" and "artificially," we learn very little from such general terms. We must know the history of those words, which were watch-words in every school of philosophy, before they dwindled down to mere technical terms.

GREEK THEORIES ON LANGUAGE.   317

With the later sophists *thései*, "artificially," or the still earlier *nómō*, "conventionally," meant no longer what they meant with the fathers of Greek philosophy; nay, they sometimes assumed the very opposite meaning. A sophist like Hermogenes, in order to prove that language existed conventionally, maintained that an apple might have been called a plum, and a plum an apple, if people had only agreed to do so.[1] Another[2] pointed in triumph to his slave, to whom he had actually given a new name, by calling him "Yet," in order to prove that any word might be significative. Nor were the arguments in favor of the natural origin of language of a better kind, when the efficacy of curses was quoted to show that words endowed with such powers could not have a merely human or conventional origin.[3]

Such was not the reasoning of Heraclitus or Democritus. The language in which they spoke, the whole world of thought in which they lived, did not allow them to discuss the nature and origin of language after the fashion of these sophists, nor after our own fashion. They had to speak in parables, in

[1] Lersch, *Sprachphilosophie der Alten*, I. p. 28. *Ammonius Hermiae ad Aristot. de Interpr.* p. 25 A. Οἱ μὲν οὕτω τὸ θέσει λέγουσιν ὡς ἐξὸν ὁτῳοῦν τῶν ἀνθρώπων ἕκαστον τῶν πραγμάτων ὀνομάζειν ὅτῳ ἂν ἐθέλῃ ὀνόματι, καθάπερ Ἑρμογένης ἠξίου. . . . Οἱ δὲ οὐχ οὕτως, ἀλλὰ τίθεσθαι μὲν τὰ ὀνόματα ὑπὸ μόνου τοῦ ὀνομαθέτου, τοῦτον δὲ εἶναι τὸν ἐπιστήμονα τῆς φύσεως τῶν πραγμάτων, οἰκεῖον τῇ ἑκάστου τῶν ὄντων φύσει ἐπιφημίζοντα ὄνομα, ἢ τὸν ὑπηρετούμενον τῷ ἐπιστήμονι.

[2] *l. c.* l. 42. *Ammonius Hermiae ad Aristot. de Interpret.* p. 103. Εἰ δὲ ταῦτα ὀρθῶς λέγεται, δῆλον ὡς οὐκ ἀποδεξόμεθα τὸν διαλεκτικὸν Διόδωρον πάσας οἰόμενον φωνὴν σημαντικὴν εἶναι, καὶ πρὸς πίστιν τούτου καλέσαντα τῶν ἑαυτοῦ τινὰ οἰκετῶν τῷ συλλογιστικῷ συνδέσμῳ 'Ἀλλὰ μὴν' καὶ ἄλλον ἄλλῳ συνδέσμῳ· ποίαν γὰρ ἔξουσιν αἱ τοιαῦται φωναὶ σημασίαν φύσεώς τινος ἢ ἐνεργείας ἢ πάθους, καθάπερ τὰ ῥήματα χαλεπὸν καὶ πλάσαι.

[3] Lersch, p. 44.

full, weighty, suggestive poetry, poetry that cannot be translated without an anachronism. We must take their words, such as they are, with all their vagueness and all their depth, but we must not judge them by these words as if these words were spoken by ourselves. The oracle on languages which is ascribed to Heraclitus was certainly his own. Commentators may have spoiled, but they could not have invented it. Heraclitus held that words exist naturally, but he did not confine himself to that technical phraseology. Words, he said,[1] are like the shadows of things, like the pictures of trees and mountains reflected in the river, like our own images when we look into a mirror. This sounds like Heraclitus; his sentences are always like nuggets of gold, to use his own simile,[2] without any of the rubbish through which philosophers have to dig before they can bring to light solid truth. He is likewise reported to have said, that to use any words except those supplied by nature for each thing, was not to speak, but only to make a noise. What Heraclitus meant by his simile, or by the word "nature," if he used it, we cannot know definitely; but we know, at all events, what he did *not* mean, namely, that man imposed what names he pleased on the objects around him. To have perceived that at that time, to have given any thought to that problem in the days when Heraclitus lived, stamps him once for all as a philosopher, ignorant though he may have been of all the rules of our logic, and our rhetoric, and our

[1] Lersch, l. c. l. 11. *Ammonius ad Arist. de Interpret.* p. 24 B, ed. Ald.
[2] Bernays, *Neue Bruchstücke des Heraclitus von Ephesus, Rheinisches Museum für Philologie*, x. p. 242. χρυσὸν οἱ διζήμενοι γῆν πολλὴν ὀρύσσουσι καὶ εὑρίσκουσι ὀλίγον. Clemens Stromat. iv. 2, p. 565 P.

GREEK THEORIES ON LANGUAGE.   319

grammar. It is commonly supposed that, as on all other subjects, so on the subject of language, Democritus took the opposite view of the dark thinker, nor can we doubt that Democritus represented language as due to *thési*, i. e. institution, art, convention. None of these terms, however, can more than indicate the meaning of *thési*. The lengthy arguments which are ascribed to him[1] in support of his theory savor of modern thought, but the similes again, which go by his name, are certainly his own. Democritus called words *agálmata phōnéenta*, statues in sound. Here, too, we have the pithy expression of ancient philosophy. Words are not natural images, images thrown by nature on the mirror of the soul; they are statues, works of art, only not in stone or brass, but in sound. Such is the opinion of Democritus, though we must take care not to stretch his words beyond their proper intent. If we translate *thései* by artificial, we must not take artificial in the sense of arbitrary. If we translate *nómō* by conventional, we must not take it to mean accidental. The same philosopher would, for instance, have maintained that what we call sweet or sour, warm or cold, is likewise so *thései* or conventionally, but by no means arbitrarily. The war-cries of *phýsei* or *thései*, which are heard through the whole history of these distant

[1] Lersch, L p. 14. Proclus, *ad Plat. Crat.* p. 6. Ὁ δὲ Δημόκριτος θέσει λέγων τὰ ὀνόματα, διὰ τεσσάρων ἐπιχειρημάτων τοῦτο κατεσκεύαζεν· ἐκ τῆς ὁμωνυμίας· τὰ γὰρ διάφορα πράγματα τῷ αὐτῷ καλοῦνται ὀνόματι· οὐκ ἄρα φύσει τὸ ὄνομα· καὶ ἐκ τῆς πολυωνυμίας· εἰ γὰρ διάφορα ὀνόματα ἐπὶ τὸ αὐτὸ καὶ ἓν πρᾶγμα ἐφαρμόσουσιν, καὶ ἐπάλληλα, ὅπερ ἀδύνατον· τρίτον ἐκ τῆς τῶν ὀνομάτων μεταθέσεως· διὰ τί γὰρ τὸν Ἀριστοκλέα μὲν Πλάτωνα, τὸν δὲ Τύρταμον Θεόφραστον μετωνομάσαμεν, εἰ φύσει τὰ ὀνόματα; ἐκ δὲ τῆς τῶν ὁμοίων ἐλλείψεως· διὰ τί ἀπὸ μὲν τῆς φρονήσεως λέγομεν φρονεῖν, ἀπὸ δὲ τῆς δικαιοσύνης οὐκ ἔτι παρονομάζομεν; τύχῃ ἄρα καὶ οὐ φύσει τὰ ὀνόματα.

battles of thought, involved not only philosophical, but political, moral, religious interests. We shall best understand their meaning if we watch their application to moral ideas. *Philolaos*, the famous Pythagorean philosopher, held that virtue existed by nature, not by institution. What did he mean? He meant what we mean when we say that virtue was not an invention of men who agreed to call some things good and others bad, but that there is a voice of conscience within us, the utterance of a divine law, independent of human statutes and traditions, self-evident, irrefragable. Yet even those who maintained that morality was but another name for legality, and that good and bad were simply conventional terms, insisted strongly on the broad distinction between law and the caprice of individuals. The same in language. When Democritus said that words were not natural images, natural echoes, but works of art in sound, he did not mean to degrade language to a mere conglomerate of sound. On the contrary, had he, with his terminology, ascribed language to nature, nature being with him the mere concurrence of atoms, he would have shown less insight into the origin, less regard for the law and order which pervade language. Language, he said, exists by institution; but how he must have guarded his words against any possible misapprehension, how he must have protested against the confusion of the two ideas, conventional and arbitrary, we may gather from the expression ascribed to him by a later scholiast, that words were statues in sound, but statues not made by the hands of men, but by the gods themselves.[1] The boldness and pregnancy

[1] *Olympiodorus ad Plat. Philebum*, p. 242, ὅτι ἀγάλματα φωνήεντα καὶ

of such expressions are the best guaranty of their
genuineness, and to throw them aside as inventions
of later writers would betray an utter disregard of
the criteria by which we distinguish ancient and
modern thought.

Our present object, however, is not to find out what
these early philosophers thought of language, — I am
afraid we shall never be able to do that, — but only
to guard against their memory being insulted, and
their names abused for sanctioning the shallow wisdom of later ages. It is sufficient if we only see
clearly that, with the ancient Greeks, language was
not considered as mere *onomatopœia*, although that
name means, literally, making of names. I should
not venture to explain what Pythagoras meant by
saying, " the wisest of all things is Number, and
next to Number, that which gives names."[1] But
of this I feel certain, that by the Second in Wisdom
in the universe, even though he may have represented
him exoterically as a human being, as the oldest and
wisest of men,[2] Pythagoras did not mean the man
who, when he heard a cow say moo! succeeded in
repeating that sound, and fixed it as the name of the
animal. As to Plato and Aristotle, it is hardly necessary to defend them against the imputation of
tracing language back to *onomatopœia*. Even *Epicurus*, who is reported to have said that in the first
formation of language men acted unconsciously,
moved by nature, as in coughing, sneezing, lowing,

ταῦτα ἐστὶ τῶν θεῶν, ὡς Δημόκριτος. It is curious that Lersch, who quotes this passage (lit. 19), should, nevertheless, have ascribed to Democritus the opinion of the purely human origin of language (i. 13).

[1] Lersch, l. c. i. 26.
[2] Ibid. l. c. i. 27.

barking, or sighing, admitted that this would account only for one half of language, and that some agreement must have taken place before language really began, before people could know what each person meant by these uncouth utterances.[1] In this, *Epicurus* shows a more correct appreciation of the nature of language than many who profess to hold his theories at present. He met the objection that words, if suggested by nature, ought to be the same in all countries, by a remark in which he anticipated Humboldt, viz., that human nature is affected differently in different countries, that different views are formed of things, and that these different affections and views influence the formation of words peculiar to each nation. He saw that the sounds of nature would never have grown into articulate language without passing through a second stage, which he represents as an agreement or an understanding to use a certain sound for a certain conception. Let us substitute for this Epicurean idea of a conventional agreement an idea which did not exist in his time, and the full elaboration of which in our own time we owe to the genius of *Darwin*; — let us place instead of agreement, *Natural Selection*, or, as I called it in my former Lectures, *Natural Elimina-*

---

[1] Diogenes Laërtius, *Epicurus*, § 75. Ὅθεν καὶ τὰ ὀνόματα ἐξ ἀρχῆς μὴ θέσει γενέσθαι, ἀλλ' αὐτὰς τὰς φύσεις τῶν ἀνθρώπων καθ' ἕκαστα ἔθνη ἴδια πάσχουσας πάθη, καὶ ἴδια λαμβανούσας φαντάσματα, ἰδίως τὸν ἀέρα ἐκπέμπειν, στελλόμενον ὑφ' ἑκάστων τῶν παθῶν καὶ τῶν φαντασμάτων, ὡς ἄν ποτε καὶ ἡ παρὰ τοὺς τόπους τῶν ἐθνῶν διαφορὰ εἴη. Ὕστερον δὲ κοινῶς καθ' ἕκαστα ἔθνη τὰ ἴδια τεθῆναι, πρὸς τὰς δηλώσεις ἧττον ἀμφιβόλους γενέσθαι ἀλλήλοις, καὶ συντομωτέρως δηλουμένας· τινὰ δὲ καὶ οὐ συνορώμενα πράγματα εἰσφέροντας, τοὺς συνειδότας παρεγγυῆσαι τινὰς φθόγγους ὧν τοὺς μὲν ἀναγκασθέντας ἀναφωνῆσαι, τοὺς δὲ τῷ λογισμῷ ἑλομένους κατὰ τὴν πλείστην αἰτίαν οὕτως ἑρμηνεῦσαι. — Lersch, L 39.

tion, and we shall then arrive, I believe, at an understanding with *Epicurus*, and even with some of his modern followers. As a number of sensuous impressions, received by man, produce a mental image or a perception, and, secondly, as a number of such perceptions produce a general notion, we may understand that a number of sensuous impressions may cause a corresponding vocal expression, a cry, an interjection, or some imitation of the sound that happens to form part of the sensuous impressions; and, secondly, that a number of such vocal expressions may be merged into one general expression, and leave behind the root as the sign belonging to a general notion. But as there is in man a faculty of reason which guides and governs the formation of sensuous impressions into perceptions, and of perceptions into general notions, the gradual formation of roots out of mere natural cries or imitations takes place under the same rational control. General notions are not formed at random, but according to law, that law being our reason within, corresponding to the reason without — to the reason, if I may so call it, of nature. Natural selection, if we could but always see it, is invariably rational selection. It is not any accidental variety that survives and perpetuates itself; it is the individual which comes nearest to the original intention of its creator, or what is best calculated to accomplish the ends for which the type or species to which it belongs was called into being, that conquers in the great struggle for life. So it is in thought and language. Not every random perception is raised to the dignity of a general notion, but only the constantly recurring, the strong-

est, the most useful; and out of the endless number
of general notions that suggest themselves to the
observing and gathering mind, those only survive
and receive definite phonetic expression which are
absolutely requisite for carrying on the work of life.
Many perceptions which naturally present themselves to our minds have never been gathered up
into general notions, and accordingly they have not
received a name. There is no general notion to
comprehend all blue flowers or all red stones; no
name that includes horses and dogs, but excludes
oxen and sheep. The Greek language has never
produced a word to express *animal* as opposed to
man, and the word *zóon*, which, like animal, com-
prises all living creatures, is post-Homeric.[1] Locke
has called attention to the fact that in English there
is a special word for killing a man, namely, *murder*,
while there is none for killing a sheep; that there is
a special designation for the murder of a father,
namely, *parricide*, but none for the murder of a son
or a neighbor. "Thus the mind," he writes,[2] "in
mixed modes, arbitrarily unites into complex ideas
such as it finds convenient; whilst others that have
altogether as much union in nature are left loose,
and never combined into one idea because they have
no need of one name." And again, "*Colshire, drill-
ing, filtration, cohobation*, are words standing for certain complex ideas, which, being seldom in the minds
of any but the few whose particular employments do
at every turn suggest them to their thoughts, those
names of them are not generally understood but by
smiths and chemists, who having framed the com-

[1] Curtius, *Grundzüge*, L 78.
[2] Locke, *In the Understanding*, III. 6, 6.

plex ideas which these words stand for, and having
given names to them or received them from others
upon hearing of these names in communication,
readily conceive those ideas in their minds; as by
cohobation, all the simple ideas of distilling and the
pouring the liquor distilled from anything back
upon the remaining matter, and distilling it again.
Thus we see that there are great varieties of simple
ideas, as of tastes and smells, which have no names,
and of modes many more, which either not having
been generally enough observed, or else not being of
any great use to be taken notice of in the affairs and
concerns of men, they have not had names given to
them, and so pass not for species."[1]

Of course, when new combinations arise, and
again and again assert their independence, they at
last receive admittance into the commonwealth of
ideas and the republic of words. This applies to
ancient even more than to modern times — to the
early ages of language more than to its present
state. It was an event in the history of man when
the ideas of father, mother, brother, sister, husband,
wife were first conceived and first uttered. It was
a new era when the numerals from one to ten had
been framed, and when words like law, right, duty,
virtue, generosity, love, had been added to the dictionary of man. It was a revelation — the greatest
of all revelations — when the conception of a Creator, a Ruler, a Father of man, when the name of
God was for the first time uttered in this world.
Such were the general notions that were wanted and
that were coined into intellectual currency. Other

[1] Locke, l. c. ii. 18, 7.

notions started up, lived for a time, and disappeared
again when no longer required. Others will still rise
up, unless our intellectual life becomes stagnant, and
will receive the baptism of language. Who has
thought about the changes which are brought about
apparently by the exertions of individuals, but for
the accomplishment of which, nevertheless, individual exertions would seem to be totally unavailing,
without feeling the want of a word, that is to say,
in reality, of an idea, to comprehend the influence
of individuals on the world at large and of the world
at large on individuals, — an idea that should explain
the failure of a *Huss* in reforming the Church, and
the success of a *Luther*, the defeat of a *Pitt* in carrying parliamentary reform, and the success of a
Russell? How are we to express that historical
process in which the individual seems to be a free
agent and yet is the slave of the masses whom he
wants to influence, in which the masses seem irresistible, and are yet swayed by the pen of an unknown writer? Or, to descend to smaller matters,
how does a poet become popular? How does a new
style of art or architecture prevail? How, again,
does fashion change? — how does what seemed absurd last year become recognized in this, and what
is admired in this becomes ridiculous in the next
season? Or take language itself. How is it that a
new word, such as *to shunt*, or a new pronunciation,
such as *gold* instead of *goold*, is sometimes accepted,
while at other times the best words newly coined or
newly revived by our best writers are completely
ignored and fall dead? We want an idea that is
to exclude caprice as well as necessity, — that is to

include individual exertion as well as general co-operation, — an idea applicable neither to the unconscious building of bees nor to the conscious architecture of human beings, yet combining within itself both these operations, and raising them to a new and higher conception. You will guess both the idea and the word, if I add that it is likewise to explain the extinction of fossil kingdoms and the origin of new species, — it is the idea of *Natural Selection* that was wanted, and being wanted it was found, and being found it was named. It is a new category — a new engine of thought; and if naturalists are proud to affix their names to a new species which they discover, Mr. Darwin may be prouder, for his name will remain affixed to a new idea, a new genus of thought.

There are languages which do not possess numerals beyond four. All beyond four is lumped together in the general idea of *many*. There are dialects, such as the *Hawaian*, in which [1] black and blue and dark-green are not distinguished, nor bright yellow and white, nor brown and red. This arises from no obtuseness of sense, for the slightest variation of tint is immediately detected by the people, but from sluggishness of mind. In the same way the *Hawaians* are said to have but one term for love, friendship, gratitude, benevolence, esteem, &c., which they call indiscriminately *aloha*, though the same people distinguish in their dictionary between *aneane*, a gentle breeze, *matani*, wind, *puhi*, blowing or puffing with the mouth, and *hano*, blowing through the nose, asthma.[2] It is the same in the lower classes

---

[1] *The Polynesian*, September 27, 1862.
[2] Hale, *Polynesian Lexicon*, s. v.

of our own country. People who would never use
such words as quadruped, or mineral, or beverage,
have different names for the tail of a fox, the tail of
a dog, the tale of a hare.[1]

Castrèn, the highest authority on the languages,
literature, and civilization of the *Northern Turanian*
races, such as the *Finns, Lapps, Tatars*, and *Mongolians*,
speaks of tribes which have no word for *river*, though
they have names for the smallest *rivulet*; no word
for *finger*, but names for the *thumb*, the *ring-finger*,
&c.; no word for *berry*, but many names for *cranberry, strawberry, blueberry*; no word for *tree*, but
names for *birch, fir, ash*, and other trees.[2] He states
in another place (p. 18) that in Finnish the word for
thumb gradually assumed the meaning of *finger*, the
word for *waterberry* (empetrum nigrum) the meaning of *berry*.

But even these, the most special names, are really
general terms, and express originally a general quality,
nor is there any other way in which they could have
been formed. It is difficult to place ourselves in the
position of people with whom the framing of new
ideas and new words was the chief occupation of
their life.[3] But suppose we had no word for *dog*;
what could we do? If we, with a full-grown language at our command, became for the first time
acquainted with a dog, we should probably discover
some similarity between it and some other animal,
and call it accordingly. We might call it a tame
wolf, just as the inhabitants of *Mallicolo*,[4] when they

[1] Pott, *Etymologische Forschungen*, ii. 489.
[2] *Vorlesungen über Finnische Mythologie*, p. 11.
[3] Daniel Wilson, *Prehistoric Man*, Third Chapter.
[4] Pott, *Etymologische Forschungen*, ii. 138.

saw the first dogs that had been sent to them from the *Society Islands*, called them *broods*, their name for *pig*. Exactly the same happened in the island of *Tanna*. Here, too, the inhabitants called the dogs that were sent to them *pigs* (*buga*). It would, however, very soon be felt as an inconvenience not to be able to distinguish between a dog and a pig, and some distinguishing mark of the dog would have to be chosen by which to name it. How could that be effected? It might be effected by imitating the barking of the animal, and calling it *bow-wow*; yet, strange to say, we hardly ever find a civilized language in which the dog was so called. What really took place was this. The mind received numerous impressions from everything that came within its ken. A dog did not stand before it at once, properly defined and classified, but it was observed under different aspects, — now as a savage animal, now as a companion, sometimes as a watcher, sometimes as a thief, occasionally as a swift hunter, at other times as a coward or an unclean beast. From every one of these impressions a name might be framed, and after a time the process of natural elimination would reduce the number of these names, and leave only a few, or only one, which, like *canis*, would become the proper name of dog.

But in order that any such name could be given, it was requisite that general ideas, such as roving, following, watching, stealing, running, resting, should previously have been formed in the mind, and should have received expression in language. These general ideas are expressed by roots. As they are more simple and primitive, they are expressed by more

simple and primitive roots, whereas complex ideas
found expression in secondary radicals. Thus *to go*
would be expressed by *sar*, to creep by *sarp*; to shout
by *nad*, to rejoice by *nand*, to join by *yu* or *yuj*, to
glue together by *yaut*. We thus find in Sanskrit
and in all the Aryan languages *clusters of roots* expressive of one common idea, and differing from each
other merely by one or two additional letters, either
at the end or at the beginning. The most natural
supposition is that which I have just stated, namely,
that as ideas grew and multiplied, simple roots were
increased and became diversified. But the opposite
view might likewise be defended, namely, that language began with variety, that many special roots
were thrown out first, and from them the more general roots elaborated by leaving out those letters
which constituted the specific differences of each.

Much may be said in support of either of these
views, nor is it at all unlikely that both processes,
that of accretion and that of elimination, may have
been at work simultaneously. But the fact is that
we do not know even the most ancient of the Aryan
languages, the Sanskrit, till long after it had passed
through its radical and agglutinative stages, and we
shall never know for certain by what slow degrees it
advanced through both, and became settled as an
inflectional language. Chronologically speaking, the
question whether *sarp* existed before *sar*, is unanswerable; logically, no doubt, *sar* comes first, but we
have seen enough of the history of speech to know
that what ought to have been according to the strict
laws of logic is very different from what has been
according to the pleasure of language.[1]

[1] On clusters of roots, or the gradual growth of roots, see some interest-

What it is of the greatest importance to observe is this, that out of many possible general notions, and out of many possible general terms, those only become, through a process of natural selection, typical in each language which are now called the roots, the fertile germs of that language. These roots are definite in form and meaning: they are what I called *phonetic types*, firm in their outline, though still liable to important modifications. They are the "*specific centres*" of language, and without them the science of language would be impossible.

All this will become clearer by a few examples. Let us take a root and follow it through its adventures in its way through the world. There is an Aryan root *MAR*, which means to crush, to pound, to destroy by friction. I should not venture to say that those are mistaken who imagine they perceive in this root the grating noise of some solid bodies grinding against each other. Our idiosyncrasies as to the nature of certain sounds are formed, no doubt, very much through the silent influence of the languages which we speak or with which we are acquainted. It is perfectly true also that this jarring or rasping noise is rendered very differently in different languages. Nevertheless, there being such a root as *mar*, meaning to pound, it is natural to imagine that we hear in it something like the noise of two mill-stones, or of a metal-crushing engine.[1]

ing remarks by Benfey, *Kurze Sanskrit Grammatik*, § 60 seq., and Pott, *Etymologische Forschungen*, ii. p. 283. Bopp, *Vergleichende Grammatik*, § 109 a, 3, 109 b, 1.

[1] The following remarks of St. Augustine on this subject are curious: "Deinde perveniatur eo ut res cum sono verbi aliqua similitudine concinat, ut cum dicimus æris tinnitum, equorum hinnitum, ovium balatum, tubarum clangorem, stridorem catenarum (perspicis enim hæc verba ita

But let us mark at once the difference between a mere imitation of the inarticulate groaning and moaning noises produced by crushing hard substances, and the articulate sound *mar*. Every possible combination of consonants with final *r* or *l* was suggested; *kr, tr, chr, glr*, all would have answered the purpose, and may have been used, for all we know, previous to the first beginning of articulate speech. But as soon as *mr* had got the upperhand, all other combinations were discarded; *mr* had conquered, and became by that very fact the ancestor of a large family of words. If, then, we either follow the history of this root *MAR* in an ascending line and spreading direction, or if we trace its offshoots back in a descending line to that specific germ, we must be able to explain all later modifications, as necessitated by phonetic and etymological laws; in all the various settings, the jewel must be the same, and in all its various corruptions the causes must be apparent that produced the damage.

I begin, then, with the root *MAR*, and ascribe to

sonare ut ipsa res qua his verbis significantur). Sed quia sunt res quæ non sonant, in his similitudinem tactus valere, ut si leniter vel aspere sensum tangunt, lenitas vel asperitas literarum ut tangit auditum sic eis nomina peperit: ut ipsum *lene* cum dicimus leniter sonat, quis item *asperitatem* non et ipso nomine asperam judicet? Lene est auribus cum dicimus *voluptas*, asperam cum dicimus *crux*. Ita res ipsæ adficiunt, ut verba sentiuntur. *Mel*, quam suaviter gustum res ipsa, tam leniter nomine tangit auditum, *acre* in utroque asperam est. *Lana* et *vepres* ut audiuntur verba, sic illa tanguntur. Hæc quasi cunabula verborum esse crediderunt, ubi sensus rerum cum sonorum sensu concordarent. Hinc ad ipsarum inter se rerum similitudinem processisse licentiam nominandi; ut cum verbi causa *crus* propterea dicta sit, quod ipsius verbi asperitas cum doloris quem *crux* efficit asperitate concordat, *crura* tamen non propter asperitatem doloris sed, quod longitudine atque duritia inter membra cetera sint ligno similiora sic appellata sint." — Augustinus, *De dialectica*, as corrected by Crecelius in Hoefer's *Zeitschrift*, iv. 152.

it the meaning of grinding down. In all the words that are derived from *mar* there must be no phonetic change, whether by increase, decrease, or corruption, that cannot be supported by analogy; in all the ideas expressed by these words there must always be a connecting link by which the most elevated and abstract notions can be connected, directly or indirectly, with the original conception of "grinding." In the phonetic analysis, all that is fanciful and arbitrary is at once excluded; nothing is tolerated for which there is not some precedent. In the web of ideas, on the contrary, which the Aryan mind has spun out of that one homely conception, we must be prepared not only for the orderly procession of logical thought, but frequently for the poetic flights of fancy. The production of new words rests on poetry as much, if not more, than on judgment; and to exclude the poetical or fanciful element in the early periods of the history of human speech would be to deprive ourselves of the most important aid in unravelling its early beginnings.

Before we enter on our survey of this family of words, we must bear in mind (1) that *r* and *l* are cognate and interchangeable; therefore *mar* = *mal*.

2. That *ar* in Sanskrit is shortened to a simple vowel, and then pronounced *ri*; hence *mar* = *mri*.

3. That *ar* may be pronounced *ra*,[1] and *al*, *la*; hence *mar* = *mra*, *mal* = *mla*.

4. That *mra* and *mla* in Greek are changed into *mbro*, *mblo*, and, after dropping the *m*, into *bro* and *blo*.

In Sanskrit we find *malana* in the sense of rubbing

[1] In Sanskrit we have *mardita* and *mradita*, he will grind to pieces, as the future of *mard*.

or grinding, but the root does not seem in that language to have yielded any names for mill. This may be important historically, if it should indicate that real mills were unknown previous to the Aryan separation. In Latin, Greek, German, Celtic, Slavonic, the name for mill is throughout derived from the root *mar*. Thus, Latin *mola*,[1] Greek *mýlē*, Old High-German *muli*, Irish *meile*, Bohemian *mlyn*, Lithuanian *malunas*. From these close coincidences among all the members of the Northern branch of the Aryan family, it has been concluded that mills were known previous to the separation of the Northern branch, though it ought to be borne in mind that some of these nations may have borrowed the name from others who were the inventors of mills.

With the name for mill we have at the same time the names for *miller, mill-stone, milling, meal*. In Greek *mýlos*, mill-stone; *mýllō*, I mill. In Gothic *malan*, to mill; *melo*, meal; *muljan*, to rub to pieces.

What in English are called the mill-teeth are the *mylítai* in Greek; the *moláres*, or grinders, in Latin.

To any one acquainted with the living language of England, the transition from *milling* to *fighting* does not require any long explanation. Hence we trace back to *mar* without difficulty the Homeric *már-na-mai*, I fight, I pound, as applied to boxers in the "Odyssey."[2] In Sanskrit, we find *mṛi-ṇá-mi* used in the more serious sense of smashing, i. e. killing.[3] We

---

[1] See Pott, *Etym. Forsch.* (I.) L 920. Kuhn, *Indische Studien*, i. 350. Curtius, *G. E.* i. 302.

[2] *Od.* xviii. 31.

Ζώσαι νῦν, ἵνα πάντες ἐπιγνώωσι καὶ οἵδε
Μαρναμένους· πῶς δ' ἂν σὺ νεωτέρῳ ἀνδρὶ μάχοιο.

[3] *Rig-Veda*, vi. 44, 17 : "prá mṛiṇa jahí cha;" strike (them) down and kill them.

shall now understand more readily the Greek *mólos* in *mólos Áreos*, the toil and moil of war, and likewise the Greek *mólóps*, a weal, originally a blow, a contusion.

Hitherto we have treated *mar* as a transitive verb, as expressive of the action of grinding exerted on some object or other. But most verbs were used originally intransitively as well as transitively, and so was *mar*. What then would *mar* express if used as an intransitive verb, if expressive of a mere condition or status? It would mean " to be wearing away," " to be in a state of decay," " to crumble away as if ground to dust." We say in German, *sich aufreiben*, to become exhausted; and *aufgerieben* means nearly destroyed. Goethe says, " *Die Kraft der Erregbarkeit nimmt mit dem Leben ab, bis endlich den aufgeriebenen Menschen nichts mehr auf der leeren Welt erregt als die künftige;* " " Our excitability decreases with our life, till at last nothing can excite the ground-down mortal in this empty world except the world to come." What then is the meaning of the Greek *maraínó* and *marasmós*? *Maraínó*, as an intransitive verb, means to wear out; as *nósos maraínei me*, illness wears me out; but it is used also as a neuter verb in the sense of to wither away, to die away. Hence *marasmós*, decay, the French *marasme*. The adjective *mólys*, formed like *mólos*, means worn out, feeble, and a new verb, *mólýnomai*, to be worn out, to vanish.

The Sanskrit *mûrchh*, to faint, is derived from *mar* by a regular process for forming inchoative verbs; it means to begin to die.

Now let us suppose that the ancient Aryans

wanted to express for the first time what they constantly saw around them, namely, the gradual wearing away of the human frame, the slow decay which at last is followed by a complete breaking up of the body. How should they express what we call dying or death? One of the nearest ideas that would be evoked by the constant impressions of decay and death was that expressed by *mar*, the grinding of stone to dust. And thus we find in Latin *mor-i-or*, I die, *mortuus*, dead, *mors*, death. In Sanskrit, *mriye*, I die, *mritá*, dead, *mrityu*, death. One of the earliest names for *man* was *márta*, the dying, the frail creature, — a significant name for man to give to himself; in Greek *brotós*, mortal. Having chosen that name for himself, the next step was to give the opposite name to the gods, who were called *ámbrotoi*, without decay, immortal, and their food *ambrosia*, immortality. In the Teutonic languages these words are absent, but that *mar* was used in the sense, if not of dying, at least of killing, we learn from the Gothic *maurthr*, the English *murder*. In Old Slavonic we find *mréti*, to die, *morŭ*, pestilence, death; *smriti*, death; in Lithuanian, *mir-ti*, to die, *smertis*, death.

If *morior* in Latin is originally to decay, then what causes decay is *morbus*, illness.

In Sanskrit the body itself, our frame, is called *mûrti*, which originally would seem to have meant decay or decayed, a corpse, rather than a *corpus*.

The Sanskrit *marman*, a joint, a member, is likewise by Sanskrit grammarians derived from *mar*. Does it mean the decaying members? or is it derived from *mar* in its original sense of grinding, so as to express the movement of the articulated joints?

The Latin *membrum* is *memrum*, and this possibly by reduplication derived from *mar*, like *mémbletai* from *méld*, *mémblōka* from *mol* in *émolon*, the present being *bósko*.

Let us next examine the Latin *mŏra*. It means *delay*, and from it we have the French *demeurer*, to dwell. Now *mora* was originally applied to time, and in *mora temporis* we have the natural expression of the slow dying away, the gradual wasting away of time. " *Sine morâ*," without delay, originally without decay, without loss of time.

From *mar*, in the secondary but definite sense of withering, dying, we have the Sanskrit *maru*, a desert, a dead soil. There is another desert, the sea, which the Greeks called *atrýgeton*, unfruitful, barren. The Aryans had not seen that watery desert before they separated from each other on leaving their central homes. But when the Romans saw the Mediterranean, they called it *māre*, and the same word is found among the Celtic, the Slavonic, and the Teutonic nations.[1] We can hardly doubt that their idea in applying this name to the sea was the dead or stagnant water as opposed to the running streams (*l'eau vive*), or the unfruitful expanse. Of course there is always some uncertainty in these guesses at the original thoughts which guided the primitive framers of language. All we can do is to guard against mixing together words which may have had an independent origin; but if it is once established that there is no other root from which *mare* can be derived more regularly than from *mar*, to die, (Bopp's derivation from the Sk. *vári*, water, is not tenable,)

[1] Curtius, *Zeitschrift*, I. 30. Slav. *mõre*; Lith. *marios* and *mards*; Goth. *marei*; Ir. *muir*.

then we are at liberty to draw some connecting line between the root and its offshoot, and we need not suppose that in ancient days new words were framed less boldly than in our own time. Language has been called by Jean Paul "a dictionary of faded metaphors": so it is, and it is the duty of the etymologist to try to restore them to their original brightness. If, then, in English we can speak of dead water, meaning stagnant water, or if the French[1] use *eau morte* in the same sense, why should not the Northern Aryans have derived one of their names for the sea from the root *mar*, to die? Of course they would have other names besides, and the more poetical the tribe, the richer it would be in names for the ocean. The Greeks, who of all Aryan nations were most familiar with the sea, called it not the dead water, but *thálassa (tarássó)*, the commotion, *háls*, the briny, *pélagos (plázó)*, the tossing, *póntos*, the high-road.[2]

Let us now return to the original sense of *mar* and *mal*, which was, as we saw, to grind or to pound, chiefly applied to the grinding of corn and to the blows of boxers. The Greeks derived from it one of their mythological characters, namely, *Molión*, a word which, according to Hesychius, would mean a fighter in general, but which, in the fables of Greece, is chiefly known by the two *Moliónes*, the millers, who had one body, but two heads, four feet, and four hands. Even *Herakles* could not vanquish them when they fought against him in defence of their uncle *Augeias* with his herd of three thousand oxen. He killed them afterwards by surprise.

[1] Pott, Kuhn's *Zeitschrift*, ii. 107.
[2] Curtius, Kuhn's *Zeitschrift*, i. 33.

These heroes having been called originally *Moliones* or *Molionidae*, i. e. pounders, were afterwards fabled to have been the sons of *Molione*, the mill, and *Aktōr*, the corn-man. Some mythologists[1] have identified these twins with thunder and lightning, and it is curious that the name of *Thor's* thunderbolt should be derived from the same root; for the hammer of *Thor Miölnir*[2] means simply the smasher. Again, among the Slavonic tribes, *molnija* is a name for lightning; and in the Serbian songs *Munja* is spoken of as the sister of *Grom*, the thunder, and has become a mythological personage.

Besides these heroic millers, there is another pair of Greek giants, known by the name of *Aloadae*, *Otos* and *Ephialtes*. In their pride they piled Ossa on *Olympus*, and *Pelion* on *Ossa*, like another Tower of Babel, in order to scale the abode of the gods. They were defeated by *Apollo*. The name of these giants has much the same meaning as that of the *Moliones*. It is derived from *alōē'*, a threshing-floor, and means threshers. The question, then, is whether *alōē'*, threshing-floor, and *áleuron* and *tá áleura*, wheat-flour, can be traced back to the root *mal*. It is sometimes said that Greek words may assume an initial *m* for euphony's sake. That has never been proved. But it can be proved by several analogous cases that Greek words, originally beginning with *m*, occasionally drop that *m*. This, no doubt, is a violent change,

[1] Friedreich, *Realien in der Iliade und Odyssee*, p. 662. Preller, *Griechische Mythologie*, ii. 185.

[2] Grimm, *Deutsche Mythologie*, 164, 1171. "The holy mawle" (maul, maillet, malleus) is referred by Grimm to the hammer of Thor. "The holy mawle, which they fancy hung behind the church-door, which, when the father was seaventie, the sonne might fetch to knock his father on the head, as effete and of no more use." — Haupt's *Zeitschrift*, v. 72.

and a change apparently without any physiological necessity, as there is no more difficulty in pronouncing an initial *m* than in pronouncing an initial vowel. However, there is no lack of analogies; and by analogies we must be guided. Thus *móschos*, a tender shoot, exists also as *óschos* or *ósché*, a young branch. Instead of *mía*, one, in the feminine, we find *ía* in Homer. Nay, instead of our very word *áleuron*, wheaten flour, another form, *máleuron*, is mentioned by *Helladius*.[1] Again, if we compare Greek and Latin, we find that what the Romans called *mola* — namely, meal, or rather the grits of spelt, coarsely ground, which were mixed with salt, and thus strewed on the victims at sacrifices — were called in Greek *oulaí* or *olaí*, though supposed to be barley instead of spelt.[2] On the strength of these analogies we may, I believe, admit the possibility of an initial *m* being dropped in Greek, which would enable us to trace the names both of the *Moliones* and *Aloadae* back to the root *mar*. And if the *Moliones* and *Aloadae*[3] derive their names from the root *mar*, we can hardly doubt that *Mars* and *Ares*, the prisoner of the *Aloadae*, came both from the same source. In Sanskrit the root *mar* yields *Marut*, the storm, literally the pounder or smasher;[4] and in the

---

[1] μώλωψ, a weal, seems connected with οὐλαί, scars.

[2] Cf. Buttmann, *Lexilogus*, p. 460.

[3] Otos and Ephialtes, the wind (vâta) and the hurricane.

[4] Professor Kuhn takes *Marut* as a participle in *at*, and explains it as dying or dead. He considers the *Maruts* were originally conceived as the souls of the departed, and that because the souls were conceived as ghosts, or spirits, or winds, the Maruts assumed afterwards the character of storm-deities. Such a view, however, finds no support in the hymns of the Veda. In *Pitarmas*, the brother of *Picumnus*, both companions of Mars, we have a name of similar import, viz. a pounder. *Jupiter Pistor*, too, was originally the god who crushes with the thunderbolt (Preller, *Rö-*

character of the *Maruts*, the companions of *Indra* in his daily battle with *Vṛitra*, it is easy to discover the germs of martial deities. The same root would fully explain the Latin *Mars*,[1] *Martis*, and, considering the uncertain character of the initial *m*, the Greek *Árēs*, *Áreōs*. *Marmar* and *Marmor*, old Latin names for *Mars*, are reduplicated forms; and in the Oscan *Mámers* the *r* of the reduplicated syllable is lost. *Mávors* is more difficult to explain,[2] for there is no instance in Latin of *m* in the middle of a word being changed into *v*. But although, etymologically, there is no difficulty in deriving the Indian name *Marut*, the Latin name *Mars*, and the Greek name *Ares*, from one and the same root,[3] there is certainly neither in the legends of *Mars* nor in those of *Ares* any very distinct trace of their having been representatives of the storm. *Mars* at Rome and *Ares* in Thracia, though their worship was restricted to small territories, both assumed there the character of supreme tutelary deities. The only connecting

mische *Mythologie*, p. 173), and the *Mola Martis* seem to rest on an analogous conception of the nature of *Mars*.

[1] The suffix in *Mars*, *Martis*, is different from that in *Marut*. The Sanskrit *Marut* is *Mar-vat*; *Mars*, *Martis*, is formed like *pars*, *partis*, which happens to correspond with Sanskrit *par-as* or *par-van*. The Greek *Árēs* is again formed differently, but the Æolic form, *Áreus*, would come nearer to *Marut*. — Kuhn, *Zeitschrift*, i. 378.

[2] See Corssen, in Kuhn's *Zeitschrift*, ii. 1–35.

[3] That *Marut* and *Mars* were radically connected, was first pointed out by Professor Kuhn, in Haupt's *Zeitschrift*, v. 491; but he derived both words from *mar* in the sense of dying. Other derivations are discussed by Corssen, in Kuhn's *Zeitschrift*, ii. 1. He quotes Cicero (*Nat. Deor.* ii. 28): "Jam qui magna verteret Mavors;" Cedrenus (*Corp. Byz. Niebuhr*, t. l. p. 295, 31 ff.): ὅτι τὸν Μάρτεμ οἱ Ῥωμαῖοι μόρτεμ ἐκάλουν οἱανεὶ θάνατον, ἢ κινητὴν τῶν τεχνῶν, ἢ τὸν παρ' ἀρρένων καὶ μόνων τιμώμενον; Varro (L. L. v. § 73, ed. O. Müller). "Mars ab eo quod maribus in bello praeest, aut quod ab Sabinis acceptus, ibi est Mamers." See also Leo Meyer, in Kuhn's *Zeitschrift*, v. 387.

link between the classical deities *Mars* and *Ares* and the Indian *Maruts* is their warlike character; and if we take *Indra* as the conqueror of winter, as the destroyer of darkness, as the constant victor in the battle against the hostile powers of nature, then he, as the leader of the *Maruts*, who act as his army, assumes a more marked similarity with *Mars*, the god of spring, the giver of fertility, the destroyer of evil.[1] In *Ares*, Preller, without any thought of the relationship between *Ares* and the *Maruts*, discovered the personification of the sky as excited by storm.[2]

We have hitherto examined the direct offshoots only of the root *mar*, but we have not yet taken into account the different modifications to which that root itself is liable. This is a subject of considerable importance, though at the same time beset with

---

[1] See Preller, *Römische Mythologie*, pp. 300, seq.

[2] Preller, *Griechische Mythologie*, pp. 202, 203. "Endlich deuten aber auch verschiedene bildliche Erzählungen in der Ilias eine solche Naturbeziehung an, besonders die Beschreibung der Kämpfe zwischen Ares und Athena, welche als Göttin der reinen Luft und des Aethers die natürliche Feindin des Ares ist, und gewöhnlich sehr unbarmherzig mit ihm umgeht. So Il. v. 883 ff., wo sie ihn durch Diomedes verwundet, Ares aber mit solchem Getöse niederrasselt (ἰβραχε), wie neuntausend oder zehntausend Männer in der Schlacht zu lärmen pflegen, worauf er als dunkles Gewölk zum Himmel emporfährt. Ebenso Il. xxi. 400 ff., wo Athena den Ares durch einen Steinwurf verwundet, er aber fällt und bedeckt sieben Morgen Landes im Fall, und seine Haare vermischen sich mit dem Staube, seine Waffen rasseln: was wieder ganz den Eindruck eines solchen alten Naturgemäldes macht, wo die Ereignisse der Natur, Donnerwetter, Wolkenbruch, gewaltiges Stürmen und Brausen in der Luft als Acte einer himmlischen Göttergeschichte erscheinen, in denen gewöhnlich Zeus, Hera, Athena, Hephästos, Ares und Hermes als die handelnden Personen auftreten. Indessen ist diese allgemeine Bedeutung des Ares bald vor der speciellen des blutigen Kriegsgottes zurückgetreten." See also *Il.* xx. 51.

Αὖε δ' Ἄρης ἑτέρωθεν, ἐρεμνῇ λαίλαπι ἶσος. — Il. ix. 4.
Ὅς δ' ἄνεμοι δύο πόντον ὀρίνετον ἰχθυόεντα,
Βορέης καὶ Ζέφυρος, τώ τε Θρῄκηθεν ἄητον.

greater difficulties and uncertainties. I stated in a former Lecture that Hindu grammarians have reduced the whole wealth of their language to about 1700 roots. These roots once granted, there remained not a single word unexplained in Sanskrit. But the fact is that many of these roots are clearly themselves derivatives. Thus, besides *yu*, to join, we found *yuj*, to join, and *yudh*, to join in battle. Here *j* and *dh* are clearly modificatory letters, which must originally have had some meaning. Another root, *yaut*, in the sense of joining or gluing together, must likewise be considered as a dialectic variety of *yuj*.

Let us apply this to our root *MAR*. As *yu* forms *yudh*, so *mar* forms *mardh* or *mṛidh*, and this root exists in Sanskrit in the sense of destroying, killing; hence *mṛidh*, enemy.[1]

Again, as *yu* produces *yuj*, so *mar* produces *marj* or *mṛij*. This is a root of very common occurrence. It means to rub, but not in the sense of destroying, like *mṛidh*, but in the sense of cleaning or purifying. This is its usual meaning in Sanskrit, and it explains the Sanskrit name for cat, namely, *mârjâra*, literally the animal that always rubs or cleans itself. In Greek we find *omórg-ny-mi* in the same sense. But this general meaning became still more defined in Greek, Latin, German, and Slavonic, and by changing *r* into *l* the root *malg* was formed, meaning to rub or stroke the udder of the cow, i. e. to milk. Thus *mélgō*, and *amélgō*, in Greek, mean to milk; in Latin, *mulgére* has the same meaning. In Old High-German we find the substantive *milchu*,

[1] Rv. vi. 53. 4. " vi mṛidhaḥ jahi," kill the enemies.

and from it new verbal derivatives in the sense of milking. In Lithuanian, *milzti* means both to milk and to stroke. These two cognate meanings are kept asunder in Latin by *mulgēre*, as distinct from *mulcēre*, to stroke, and we thus discover a third modification of *mar* with final guttural or palatal tenuis, namely, *march*, like Sanskrit *yách*, to ask, from *yâ*, to go (ambire or adire). Formed by a similar process, though for a different purpose, is the Latin *marcus*, a large hammer or pestle, which was used at Rome as a personal name, *Marcus*, *Marcius*, *Marcianus*, *Marcellus*, and occurs again in later times in the historical name of *Charles Martel*. In Sanskrit, on the contrary, the verb *mṛiś*, with final palatal *ś*, expresses the idea of gentle stroking, and with certain prepositions comes to mean to revolve, to meditate, to think. As *mori*, to die, meant originally to wither, so *marcere* exhibits the same idea in a secondary form. It means to droop, to faint, to fade, and is supported by the adjective *marcidus*. In Greek we have to mention the adjective *malakós*. It means soft and smooth, originally rubbed down or polished; and it comes to mean at last weak, or sick, or effeminate.[1]

One of the most regular modifications of *mar* would be *mrâ*, and this, under the form of *mlâ*, means in Sanskrit to wither, to fade away. In Greek, *ml* being frequently rendered by *bl*, we can hardly be wrong in referring to this base *blâx*, meaning slack in body and in mind, and the Gothic *malsk-s*, foolish.[2] Soft and foolish are used synonymously

[1] Cf. Latin *hvis*; ἀμαλός, if for μαμαλος, soft, may belong to the same root. We have to consider, however, the Attic ἀμαλός.

[2] Curtius, G. E. I. 303.

in many languages, nor is it at all unlikely that the Greek *móros*, foolish, may come from our root *mar*, and have meant at first soft.

Here we see how different meanings play into each other; how what from one point of view is looked upon as worn down and destroyed, is from another point of view considered as smooth and brilliant, and how the creative genius of man succeeded in expressing both ideas by means of the same radical element. We saw that in *omórgnymi* the meaning fixed upon was that of rubbing or wiping clean, in *amélgō* that of rubbing or milking; and we can see how a third sense, that of rubbing in the sense of tearing off or plucking off, is expressed in Greek by *mérgō* or *amérgō*.

If we suppose our root *mar* strengthened by means of a final labial, instead of the final guttural which we have just been considering, we have *marp*, a base frequently used by Greek poets. It is generally translated by catching (and identified with *harpázō*), but we perceive traces of its original meaning in such expressions as *gêras émarpse*,[1] old age ground him down; *chthóna márpte podoïin* (Il. xiv. 228), he struck or pounded the soil with his feet.

Let us keep to this new base, *marp*, and consider that it may assume the forms of *malp* and *mlap*; let us then remember that *ml*, in Greek, is interchangeable with *bl*, and we arrive at the new base, *blap*, well known in the Greek *bláptō*, I damage, I hinder, I mar. This *bláptō* still lives in the English *to blame*, the French *blâmer*, for *blasmer*, which is a corruption of *blasphémer*. The Greek *blasphēmein*, again, stands

[1] Od. xxiv. 390.

for *blapsiphēmein*, i. e. to use damaging words; and in *blapsi* we see the verb *bláptō*, the legitimate offspring of our root *mar*.

One of the most prolific descendants of *mar* is the root *mard*. It occurs in Sanskrit as *mṛidnâti* (9th conj.), and as *mṛadati* (1st conj.), in the sense of rubbing down; but it is likewise used, particularly if joined with prepositions, in the sense of to squash, to overcome, to conquer. From this root we have the Sanskrit *mṛidu*, soft,[1] the Latin *mollis* (mard, mald, mall), the Old Slavonic *mladu* (maldu), and, though formed by a different suffix, the English *mellow*. In all these words what is ground down to powder was used as the representative of smoothness, and was readily transferred to moral gentleness and kindness. Dust itself was called by the same root in its simplest form, namely, *mṛid*, which, after meaning dust, came to mean soil in general, or earth.

The Gothic *malma*, sand, belongs to the same class of words; so does the Modern German *zermalmen*, to grind to pieces, and the Gothic *malvjan*, used by Ulfilas in the same sense.

In Latin this root has thrown out several offshoots. *Malleus*, a hammer, stands probably for *mardeus*; and even *martellus*, unless it stands for *marcellus*, claims the same kin. In a secondary form we find our root in Latin as *mordēre*, to bite, originally to grind or worry.

In English, *to smart* has been well compared with

---

[1] Curtius (*G. E.* I. 92) points out the analogous case of Greek τέρην, tender, if derived from τερ, as in τείρω. If so, *terra* also, dust, might be explained like Sanskrit *mṛid*, dust, earth.

mordére, the *s* being a formative letter with which we shall meet again. " A wound smarts," means a wound bites or hurts. It is thus applied to every sharp pain, and in German *Schmerz* means pain in general.[1]

This root *mard*, the Greek *méldô*, to make liquid, assumes in English regularly the form *malt*, or *melt*; nor is there any doubt that the English *to melt* meant originally to make soft, if not by the blows of the hammer, at least by the licking of the fire and the absorbing action of the heat. The German *schmelzen* has the same power, and is used both as a transitive and an intransitive verb. Now let us watch the clever ways of language. An expression was wanted for the softening influence which man exercises on man by looks, gestures, words, or prayers. What could be done? The same root was taken which had conveyed before the idea of smoothing a rough surface, of softening a hard substance; and, with a slight modification, the root *mard* became fixed as the Sanskrit *mrid*, or *mril*, to soften, to propitiate.[2] It was used in that sense chiefly with regard to the gods, who were to be propitiated by prayers and sacrifices. It was likewise used in an intransitive sense of the gods themselves, who were implored to melt, to become softened and gracious; and prayers which we now translate by " Be gracious to us," meant originally " Melt to us, O gods."

From this source springs the Gothic *mild*, the Eng-

[1] Cf. Ebel, in Kuhn's *Zeitschrift*, vii. 226, where σμερδαλέος is likewise traced to this root, and the Gothic *marzjan*, to mar. See also Benary, Kuhn's *Zeitschrift*, iv. 48.
[2] The lingual *d̥* appears regularly in Sanskrit *mrinmaya*, made of earth.

lish *mild*, originally soft or gentle. The Lithuanian takes from it its name for love, *meile*; and in Greek we find *meilia*, gladdening gifts or appeasements, and such derivatives as *meilissō*, to soothe, and *meilichos*, gentle.

This was one aspect of the process of melting; but there was a second, equally natural, namely, that of melting or dying away in the sense of desiring, yearning, grieving after a thing. We might say a man melts in love, in grief (in German *er zerschmilzt, er vergeht vor Liebe*), and the Greeks said in the same sense *meledainō*, I melt, i. e. I care for, *meledōnē*, anxiety, grief. *Meldómenos*, too, is explained by Hesychius in the sense of desiring.[1] But more than this. We saw before that there is sufficient evidence for the occasional disappearance of the initial *m* in the root *mar*. We therefore are justified in identifying the Greek *éldomai* with an original *méldomai*. And what does *éldomai* mean in Greek? It means to die for a thing, to desire a thing;[2] that is to say, it means exactly what it ought to mean if it is derived from the root which we have in *méldō*, I melt.

Nay, we may go still another step farther. That *mar* was raised to *marp*, we saw in Greek *márptō*, I grasp. *Mélpein*, too, is used in Greek in the sense of propitiating,[3] originally of softening or melting. If, then, we look again for corresponding forms without *m*, we should find *élpomai*, which now means I hope,

[1] Cf. Curtius, G. E. ii. 167.
[2] In Wallachian, *dor* means desire, but it is in reality the same as Italian *duolo*, pain. Cf. Diez, s. v. Analogous constructions in Latin, *Oryden ardebat Alexin.*
[3] Curtius, G. E. I. 293, μέλπειν τὸν θεόν?

but which originally would have meant I desire. It is not without importance that Hesychius mentions the very form which we should have expected, namely, *mólpis,* instead of the more usual *élpis,* hope.[1]

We have throughout these investigations met on several occasions with an *s* prefixed to *mar,* and we have treated it simply as a modificatory element added for the purpose of distinguishing words which it was felt desirable to keep distinct. Without inquiring into the real origin of this *s,* which has lately been the subject of violent disputes between Professors Pott and Curtius, we may take it for granted that the Sanskrit root *smar* is closely related to the root *mar*; nor is it difficult[2] to discover how the meaning of *smar,* namely, to remember, could have been elaborated out of *mar,* to grind. We saw over and over again that the idea of melting glided into that of loving, hoping, and desiring, and we shall find that the original meaning of *smar* in Sanskrit is to desire, not to remember. Thus Sk. *smara* is love, very much like the Lithuanian *meilė,* love, i. e. melting. From this meaning of desiring, new meanings branched off, such as dwelling on, brooding over, musing over, and then recollecting. In the other Aryan languages the initial specific *s* does not appear. We have *memor* in Latin, *memoria, memorare,* all in the special sense of remembering; but in Greek *mermairō* means simply I brood, I care, I mourn; *mérimna* is anxiety, and even *mártyr* need not necessarily mean a man who remembers, but

[1] Curtius, *G. E.* ii. 167.
[2] Curtius mentions *smar* as one of the roots which, if not from the beginning, " had, at all events before the Aryan separation, assumed an entirely intellectual meaning." — *G. E.* i. 84.

a man who cares for, who cherishes, who holds a thing.[1]

In unravelling this cluster of words, it has been my chief object to trace the gradual growth of ideas, the slow progress of the mind from the single to the general, from the material to the spiritual, from the concrete to the abstract. To rub down or to polish leads to the idea of propitiation; to wear off or to wither are expressions applied to the consuming feeling of hopes deferred and hearts sickening, and ideas like memory and martyrdom are clothed in words taken from the same source.

The fates and fortunes of this one root *mar* form but a small chapter in the history and growth of the Aryan languages; but we may derive from this small chapter some idea as to the power and elasticity of roots, and the unlimited sway of metaphor in the formation of new ideas.

[1] Cf. ἰόμωρος, ἐγχεσίμωρος, in the sense of caring for arrows, spears, &c., Benary, Kuhn's *Zeitschrift*, iv. 53; and ἴστορες θεοί, Ἀγραυλος, Ἐνυάλως, Ἄρης, Ζεύς, Preller, *Griechische Mythologie*, p. 205.

LECTURE VIII.

METAPHOR.

Few philosophers have so clearly perceived the importance of language in all the operations of the human mind, few have so constantly insisted on the necessity of watching the influence of words on thought, as *Locke* in his " Essay concerning Human Understanding." Of the four books into which this great work is divided, one, the third, is entirely devoted to Words or Language in general. At the time when Locke wrote, but little attention had been paid to the philosophy of language, and the author, afraid that he might seem to have given more prominence to this subject than it deserved, thought it necessary to defend himself against such a charge in the following words: " What I have here said concerning words in this third book will possibly be thought by some to be much more than what so slight a subject required. I allow, it might be brought into a narrower compass; but I was willing to stay my reader on an argument that appears to me new, and a little out of the way (I am sure it is one I thought not of when I began to write); that by searching it to the bottom, and turning it on every side, some part or other might meet with every one's thoughts, and give occasion to the most averse or negligent to reflect on a general miscarriage, which, though of great consequence, is little taken notice of. When it is considered what a pudder is made about essences, and how much all sorts of knowledge, discourse, and conversation are pestered and disordered by the careless and confused use and application of words, it will, perhaps, be thought worth while thoroughly to lay it open. And I shall be pardoned if I have dwelt long on an argument which I think, therefore, needs to be inculcated; because the faults men are usually guilty of in this kind are not only the greatest hindrances of true knowledge, but are so well thought of as to pass for it. Men would often see what a small pittance of reason and truth, or possibly none at all, is mixed with those huffing opinions they are swelled with, if they would but look beyond fashionable sounds, and observe what ideas are, or are not, comprehended under those words with which they are so armed at all points, and with which they so confidently lay about them. I shall imagine I have done some service to truth, peace, and learning, if, by an enlargement on this subject, I can make men reflect on their own use of language, and give them reason to suspect, that, since it is frequent for others, it may also be possible for them, to have sometimes very good and approved words in their mouths and writings, with very uncertain, little, or no signification. And, therefore, it is not unreasonable for them to be wary herein themselves, and not to be unwilling to have these examined by others."[1]

[1] Locke, *On the Understanding*, III. 6, 16.

And again, when summing up the results of his inquiries, Locke says: "For since the things the mind contemplates are none of them, besides itself, present to the understanding, it is necessary that something else, as a sign or representation of the thing it considers, should be present to it; and these are ideas. And because the scene of ideas that make one man's thoughts cannot be laid open to the immediate view of another, nor laid up anywhere but in the memory,— a no very sure repository,— therefore, to communicate our thoughts to one another, as well as record them for our own use, signs of our ideas are also necessary. Those which men have found most convenient, and therefore generally make use of, are articulate sounds. *The consideration, then, of ideas and words as the great instruments of knowledge, makes no despicable part of their consideration, who would take a view of human knowledge in the whole extent of it. And, perhaps, if they were distinctly weighed and duly considered, they would afford us another sort of logic and critic than what we have been hitherto acquainted with.*"

But, although so strongly impressed with the importance which language, as such, claims in the operations of the understanding, Locke never perceived that general ideas and words are inseparable, that the one cannot exist without the other, and that an arbitrary imposition of articulate sounds to signify definite ideas is an assumption unsupported by any evidence. Locke never seems to have realized the intricacies of the names-giving process; and though he admits frequently the difficulty, nay, sometimes the impossibility, of our handling any general ideas without the outward signs of language, he never questions for a moment the received theory that at some time or other in the history of the world men had accumulated a treasure of anonymous general conceptions, to which, when the time of intellectual and social intercourse had arrived, they prudently attached those phonetic labels which we call words.

The age in which Locke lived and wrote was not partial to those inquiries into the early history of mankind which have, during the last two generations, engaged the attention of the most eminent philosophers. Instead of gathering the fragments of the primitive language, poetry, and religion, not only of the Greeks and Romans, but of all the nations of the world, and instead of trying to penetrate, as far as possible, into the real and actual life of the fathers of the human race, and thus to learn how both in our thoughts and words we came to be what we are, the great schools of philosophy in the 18th century were satisfied with building up theories how language might have sprung into life, how religion might have been revealed or invented, how mythology might have been put together by priests, or poets, or statesmen, for the purposes of instruction, of amusement, or of fraud. Such systems, though ingenious and plausible, and still in full possession of many of our handbooks of history and philosophy, will have to give way to the spirit of what may be called the *Historical School* of the 19th century. The principles of these two schools are diametrically opposed; the one begins with theories without facts, the other with facts without theories. The systems of *Locke*, *Voltaire*, and *Rousseau*, and in later times of *Comte*, are plain, intelligible, and perfectly rational; the facts collected by men like *Wolf*, *Niebuhr*, *F. Schlegel*, *W. von Humboldt*, *Bopp*, *Burnouf*, *Grimm*, *Bunsen*, and others, are fragmentary, the inductions to which they point incomplete and obscure, and opposed to many of our received ideas. Nevertheless, the study of the antiquity of man, the Palæontology of the human mind, can never again be allowed to become the playground of mere theorizers, however bold and brilliant, but must henceforth be cultivated in accordance with those principles that have produced rich harvests in other fields of inductive research. It is no want of respect for the great men of former ages to say that they would have written differently if they had lived in our days. *Locke*, with the results of Comparative Philology before him, would have cancelled, I believe, the whole of his third book " On the Human Understanding "; and even his zealous and ingenious pupil, *Horne Tooke*, would have given us a very different volume of " Diversions of Purley." But in spite of this, there are no books which, with all their faults — nay, on account of these very faults — are so instructive to the student of language as *Locke's* "Essay," and *Horne Tooke's* " Diversions "; nay, there are many points bearing on the later growth of language which they have handled and cleared up with greater mastery than even those who came after them.

Thus the fact that all words expressive of immaterial conceptions are derived by metaphor from words expressive of sensible ideas was for the first time clearly and definitely put forward by Locke, and is now fully confirmed by the researches of comparative philologists. All roots, i. e. all the material elements of language, are expressive of sensuous impressions, and of sensuous impressions only; and as all words, even the most abstract and sublime, are derived from roots, comparative philology fully indorses the conclusions arrived at by Locke. This is what Locke says (iii. 4, 3) : —

"It may also lead us a little toward the original of all our notions and knowledge, if we remark, how great a dependence our words have on common sensible ideas; and how those, which are made use of to stand for actions and notions quite removed from sense, have their rise from thence, and from obvious sensible ideas are transferred to more abstruse significations, and made to stand for ideas that come not under the cognizance of our senses: e. g. *to imagine, apprehend, comprehend, adhere, conceive, instil, disgust, disturbance, tranquillity,* &c., are all words taken from the operations of sensible things, and applied to certain modes of thinking. *Spirit,* in its primary signification is breath; *angel,* a messenger; and I doubt not, but *if we could trace them to their sources, we should find, in all languages, the names which stand for things that fall not under our senses to have had their first rise from sensible ideas.* By which we may give some kind of guess, what kind of notions they were and whence derived, which filled their minds, who were the first beginners of languages; and how nature, even in the naming of things, unawares suggested to men the originals and principles of all their knowledge; whilst, to give names, that might make known to others any operations they felt in themselves, or any other ideas that come not under their senses, they were fain to borrow words from ordinary known ideas of sensation, by that means to make others the more easily to conceive those operations they experimented in themselves, which made no outward sensible appearances; and then, when they had got known and agreed names, to signify these internal operations of their own minds, they were sufficiently furnished to make known by words all their other ideas, since they could consist of nothing but either of outward sensible perceptions, or of the inward operations of their minds about them; we having, as has been proved, no ideas at all, but what originally came either from sensible objects without, or what we feel within ourselves from the inward workings of our own spirits, of which we are conscious to ourselves within."

This passage, though somewhat involved and obscure, is a classical passage, and has formed the subject of many commentaries, both favorable and unfavorable. Some of Locke's followers, particularly Horne Tooke, used the statement that all abstract words had originally a material meaning, in order to prove that all our knowledge was restricted to sensuous knowledge; and such was the apparent cogency of their arguments, that, to the present day, those who are opposed to materialistic theories consider it necessary to controvert the facts alleged by Locke and Horne Tooke, instead of examining the cogency of the consequences that are supposed to flow from them. Now the facts stated by Locke seem to be above all doubt. *Spiritus* is certainly derived from a verb *spirare*, which means to draw breath. The same applies to *animus*. *Animus*, the mind, as Cicero says,[1] is so called from *anima*, air. The root is *an*, which in Sanskrit means to blow, and which has given rise to the Sanskrit and Greek words for wind, *an-ila*, and *án-emos*. Thus the Greek *thymós*, the soul, comes from *thýein*, to rush, to move violently, the Sanskrit *dhu*, to shake. From *dhu* we have in Sanskrit *dhûli*, *dust*, which comes from the same root, and *dhûma*, smoke, the Latin *fumus*. In Greek, the same root supplied *thýella*, storm-wind, and *thymós*, the soul, as the seat of the passions. Plato guesses correctly when he says (Crat. p. 419) that *thymos*, soul, is so called ἀπὸ τῆς θύσεως καὶ ζέσεως τῆς ψυχῆς. *To imagine* certainly meant in its original conception to make pictures, to picture to ourselves; but even to picture is far too mixed an idea to have been expressed by a simple root. *Imago*, picture, stands for *mimago*, as *imitor* for *mimitor*, the Greek *miméomai*, all from a root *má*, to measure, and therefore meaning originally to measure again and again, to copy, to imitate. *To apprehend* and *to comprehend* meant to grasp at a thing and to grasp a thing together; *to adhere* to one's opinions was literally to stick to one's opinions; *to conceive* was to take and hold together; *to instil* was to drop or pour in; *to disgust* was to create a bad taste; *to disturb* was to throw into disorder; and *tranquillity* was calmness and particularly the smoothness of the sea.

Look at any words expressive of objects which cannot fall under the immediate cognizance of the

[1] Cicero, *Tuscul.* l. 9, sub fin. Locke, *Human Understanding*, iv. 3, 6, note (ed. London, 1836, p. 412). "Anima sit animus ignisve nescio," &c.

senses, and you will not have much difficulty in testing the truth of Locke's assertion that such words are invariably derived from others which originally were meant to express the objects of the senses.

I begin with a list of Kafir metaphors:—

Words	Literal meaning	Figurative meaning
beta	beat	punish
dhlelana	to eat together	to be on terms of intercourse
fa	to be dying	to be sick
hlala	to sit	to dwell, live, continue
ihlati	bush	refuge
ingcala	flying-ant	uncommon dexterity
incwadi	kind of bulbous plant	book, glass
inja	dog	a dependant
kolwa	to be satisfied	to believe
lila	to cry	to mourn
mnandi	sweet	pleased, agreeable
gauka	to be snapped asunder	to be quite dead
umsila	tail	court-messenger
zidhla	to eat one's self	to be proud
akasiboni	he does not see us	he is above noticing us
nikela indhlebe	give the ears	listen attentively
ukudhla ubomi	to eat life	to live
ukudhla umntu	to eat a person	to confiscate his property
ukumgekeza inkloko	to break his head	to weary one
ukunuka umntu	to smell a person	to accuse one of witchcraft [1]

Tribulation, anxiety, is derived from *tribulum*, a sledge used by the ancient Romans for rubbing out the corn, consisting of a wooden platform, studded underneath with sharp pieces of flint or with iron teeth.[2]

[1] Appleyard, *l. c.* p. 70.
[2] See White, *Latin-English Dictionary*, s. v.

The similarity between the state of mind that had to be expressed and the state of the grains of corn shaken in a *tribulum* is evident, and so striking that, if once used, it was not likely to be forgotten again. This *tribulum*, again, is derived from the verb *terere*, to rub or grind. Now suppose a man's mind so oppressed with the weight of his former misdeeds that he can hardly breathe, or look up, or resist the pressure, but feels crushed and ground to dust within himself, that man would describe his state of mind as a state of *contrition*, which means "being ground to pieces," from the same verb *terere*, to grind.

The French *penser*, to think, is the Latin *pensare*, which would mean to weigh, and lead us back to *pendere*, to hang. . "To be in suspense" literally means to be hung up, and swaying to and fro. "To suspend judgment" means to hang it up, to keep it from taking effect.

Doubt, again, the Latin *dubium*, expresses literally the position between two points, from *duo*, just as the German *Zweifel* points back to *zwei*, two.

To believe is generally identified with the German *belieben*, to be pleased with a thing, to approve of it; the Latin *libet*, it pleases. But *to believe*, as well as the German *glauben*, meant originally more than simply to approve of a thing. Both words must be traced back to the root *lubh*, which has retained its original meaning in the Sanskrit *lobha*, desire, and the Latin *libido*, violent, irresistible desire. The same root was taken to express that irresistible passion of the soul, which makes man break apparently through the evidence of the senses and the laws of reason (*credo quia absurdum*), and drives him, by a power which nothing can control, to embrace some truth which alone can satisfy the natural cravings of his being. This is belief in its truest sense, though it dwindles down in the course of time to mean no more than to suppose, or to be pleased, just as *I love*, which is derived from the same root as *to believe*, comes to mean, I like.

Truth has been explained by Horne Tooke as that which a man *troweth*. This, however, would explain very little. *To trow* is but a derivative verb, meaning to make or hold a thing true. But what is *true*? *True* is the Sanskrit *dhruva*,[1] and means firm, solid, anything that will hold; from *dhar*, to hold.

Another word for *true* in Sanskrit is *satya*, an adjective formed from the participle present of the auxiliary verb *as*, to be. *Sat* is the Latin *ens*, being; from it *satya*, true, the Greek *eteós*,[2] the English *sooth*. If I say that *sat* is the Latin *ens*, the similarity may not seem very striking. Yet Latin *ens* clearly stands for *sens*, which appears in *præ-sens*. The nominative singular of *sat* is *san*, because in Sanskrit you cannot have a word ending in *ns*. But the accusative sing. is *santam = sentem*, the nom. plur. *santas = sentes*; so that there can be no doubt as to the identity of the two words in Sanskrit and Latin.

And how did language express what, if it were a

---

[1] Kuhn's *Zeitschrift*, vii. 82.

[2] See Pott, *Etymologische Forschungen*, ii. p. 864; Kern, in Kuhn's *Zeitschrift*, viii. 400. It should be remembered that in *satya*, the *t* belongs to the base, and that the derivative element is not *tya*, Greek ουδς, but *ya*. Whether εὀς represents the same suffix as *ya* in Sanskrit may be doubtful. See, however, Bopp, *Vergleich. Gr.* (2), § 109 a, 2 (p. 212); and § 956. *Sattva* in Sanskrit means being and a being.

rational conception at all, would seem to be the most immaterial of all conceptions — namely, *nothing*? It was expressed in the only way in which it could be expressed — namely, by the negation of, or the comparison with, something real and tangible. It was called in Sanskrit *asat*, that which is not being; in Latin *nihil*, i. e. *nihilum*,[1] which stands for *nifilum*, i. e. *ne-filum*, and means "not a thread or shred." In French, *rien* is actually a mere corruption of *rem*, the accusative of *res*, and retains its negative sense even without the negative particle by which it was originally preceded. Thus *ne-pas* is *non-passum*, not a step; *ne-point* is *non-punctum*, not a point. The French *néant*, Italian *niente*, are the Latin *non ens*. And now observe for a moment how fables will grow up under the charm of language. It was perfectly correct to say, "I give you nothing," i. e. "I give you not even a shred." Here we are speaking of a relative nothing; in fact, we only deny something, or decline to give something. It is likewise perfectly correct to say, on stepping into an empty room, "There is nothing here," meaning not that there is absolutely nothing, but only that things

---

[1] Cf. Kuhn, *Zeitschrift*, I. 544. Dietrich mentions similar cases of shortening, such as *cognitus* and *nôtus*, *pejêro* and *jûro*. Bopp has clearly given up the etymology of *nihil*, which he proposed in the first edition of his *Comparative Grammar*, as it is suppressed in the second. It is to be regretted that even so careful a scholar as Mr. White, in his excellent *Latin-English Dictionary*, should still quote from the first edition only of Bopp's work. As to *h* taking the place of *f*, we know that in Spanish every Latin *f* is represented by *h*, e. g. *hablar* = *fabulari*, *hijo* = *filius*, *hierro* = *ferrum*, *hilo* = *filum*. But in Latin itself these two letters are frequently interchangeable. Instead of *hircus*, the Sabines said *fircus*; instead of *hædus*, *fædus*; instead of *harena*, *farena*. Nay, double forms are mentioned in Latin, such as *hordeum* and *fordeum*; *hostis* and *fostis*; *hariolus* and *fariolus*. See Corssen, *Aussprache der Lateinischen Sprache*, p. 48.

which we expect to find in a room are not there.
But by dint of using such phrases over and over
again, a vague idea is gradually formed in the mind
of a Nothing, and *Nihil* becomes the name of something positive and real. People at a very early time
began to talk of the Nothing as if it were something; they talked and trembled at the idea of *annihilation*, — an idea utterly inconceivable, except in
the brain of a madman. *Annihilation*, if it meant
anything, could etymologically — and in this case,
we may add, logically too — mean nothing but to
be reduced to a something which is not a shred, —
surely no very fearful state, considering that in strict
logic it would comprehend the whole realm of existence, exclusive only of what is meant by *shred*. Yet
what speculations, what fears, what ravings, have
sprung from this word *Nihil*, — a mere word, and
nothing else! We see things grow and decay, we
witness the birth and death of living things, but we
never see anything lost or annihilated. Now, what
does not fall within the cognizance of our senses,
and what contradicts every principle of our reasoning faculties, has no right to be expressed in language. We may use the names of material objects
to express immaterial objects, if they can be rationally conceived. We can conceive, for instance, powers not within the ken of our senses, yet endowed
with a material reality. We can call them *spirits*,
literally breezes, though we understand perfectly well
that by spirits we mean something else than mere
breezes. We can call them *ghosts*, a name connected with *gust, yeast, gas*, and other almost imperceptible vapors. But a Nothing, an absolute

Nothing, that is neither visible, nor conceivable, nor imaginable, ought never to have found expression, ought never to have been admitted into the dictionary of rational beings.

Now, if we consider how people talk about the Nothing, how poets make it the subject of the most harrowing strains, — how it has been, and still is, one of the principal ingredients in most systems of philosophy, — nay, how it has been dragged into the domain of religious thought, and, under the name of *Nirvâna*, has become the highest goal of millions among the followers of *Buddha*, — we may perhaps, even at this preliminary stage of our inquiries, begin to appreciate the power of language over thought, and feel less surprise at the ancient nations for having allowed the names of natural objects, the sky, the sun, the moon, the dawn, and winds, to assume the character of supernatural powers or divine personalities, or for having offered worship and sacrifice to such abstract names as Fate, Justice, or Victory. There is as much mythology in our use of the word Nothing as in the most absurd portions of the mythological phraseology of India, Greece, and Rome: and if we ascribe the former to a disease of language, the causes of which we are able to explain, we shall have to admit that in the latter, language has reached to an almost delirious state, and has ceased to be what it was meant to be, the expression of the impressions received through the senses, or of the conceptions of a rational mind.

But to return to Locke's statement, that all names of *im*material objects are derived from the names of material objects. Many philosophers, as I remarked, instead of grappling manfully with the conclusions that are supposed to flow from Locke's observation, have preferred to question the accuracy of his observation.

Victor Cousin, in his "Lectures on the History of Philosophy during the Eighteenth Century,"[1] endeavors to controvert Locke's assertion by the following process: — "I shall give you two words," he says, "and I shall ask you to trace them back to primitive words expressive of sensible ideas. Take the word *je*, I. This word, at least in all languages known to me, is not to be reduced, not to be decomposed, primitive; and it expresses no sensible idea, it represents nothing but the meaning which the mind attaches to it; it is a pure and true sign, without any reference to any sensible idea. The word *être*, to be, is exactly in the same case; it is primitive and altogether intellectual. I know of no language in which the French verb *être* is rendered by a corresponding word that expresses a sensible idea; and therefore it is not true that all the roots of language, in their last analysis, are signs of sensible ideas."

Now it must be admitted that the French *je*, which is the Sanskrit *aham*, is a word of doubtful etymology. It belongs to the earliest formations of Aryan speech, and we need not wonder that even in Sanskrit the materials out of which this pronoun was formed should have disappeared. We can explain in English such words as *myself* or *your honor*, but we could not attempt, with the means supplied by English alone, to analyze *I*, *thou*, and *he*. It is

[1] Paris, 1841. Vol. II. p. 274.

the same with the Sanskrit *aham*, a word carried down by the stream of language from such distant ages, that even the Vedas, as compared with them, are but, as it were, of yesterday. But though the etymology of *aham* is doubtful, it has never been doubtful to any scholar that, like all other words, it must have an etymology,— that it must be derived either from a predicative or from a demonstrative root. Those who would derive *aham* from a predicative root, have thought of the root *ah*, to breathe, to speak.[1] Those who would derive it from a demonstrative root, refer us to the Vedic *gha*, the later *ha*, *this*, used like the Greek *hóde*. How the pronoun of the first person is expressed in Chinese we saw in an earlier Lecture, and although such expressions as " servant says," instead of " I say," may seem to us modern and artificial, they are not so in Chinese, and show at all events that even so colorless an idea as *I* may meet with signs sufficiently pale and faded to express it.[2]

With regard to *être*, to be, the case is different. *Être*[3] is the Latin *esse*, changed into *essere* and contracted. The root, therefore, is *as*, which, in all the

---

[1] I thought it possible, in my *History of Sanskrit Literature*, p. 91, to connect *nh-am* with Sanskrit *dha*, I said, Greek ἥ, Latin *ajo* and *nego*, nay, with Gothic *ahma* (instead of *agma*), spirit, but I do so no longer. Nor do I accept the opinion of Denfey (*Sanskrit Grammatik*, § 773), who derives *aham* from the pronominal root *gha* with a prosthetic a. It is a word which, for the present, must remain without a genealogy.

[2] Jean Paul, in his *Levana*, p. 82, says: "'I' is — excepting God, the true I and true Thou at once — the biggest and most incomprehensible that can be uttered by language, or contemplated. It is there all at once, as the whole realm of truth and conscience, which, without 'I,' is nothing. We must ascribe it to God, as well as to unconscious beings, if we want to conceive the being of the One and the existence of the others."

[3] Cf. Diez, *Lexicon*, s. v. *essere*.

Aryan languages, has supplied the material for the auxiliary verb. Now even in Sanskrit, it is true, this root *as* is completely divested of its material character; it means *to be*, and nothing else. But there is in Sanskrit a derivative of the root *as*, namely, *ásu*, and in this *asu*, which means the vital breath, the original meaning of the root *as* has been preserved. *As*, in order to give rise to such a noun as *asu*, must have meant *to breathe*, then *to live*, then *to exist*, and it must have passed through all these stages before it could have been used as the abstract auxiliary verb which we find not only in Sanskrit but in all Aryan languages. Unless this one derivative *asu*, life, had been preserved in Sanskrit, it would have been impossible to guess the original material meaning of the root *as*, to be; yet even then the student of language would have been justified in postulating such a meaning. And even in French, though *être* may seem an entirely abstract word, the imperfect *j'étais*, the participle *été* are clearly derived from Latin *stare*, to stand, and show how easily so definite an idea as *to stand* may dwindle down to the abstract idea of *being*. If we look to other languages, we shall find again and again the French verb *être* rendered by corresponding words that expressed originally a sensible idea. Our verb *to be* is derived from Sanskrit *bhû*, which, as we learn from Greek *phýō*, meant originally to grow.[1] *I was* is connected with the Gothic *visan*, which means *to dwell*.

But though on this point the student of language must side with Locke, and admit, without one sin-

[1] See M. M.'s *Essay on the Aryan and Aboriginal Languages of India*, p. 344.

gle exception, the material character of all words, nothing can be more convincing than the manner in which *Victor Cousin* disposes of the conclusions which some philosophers, though certainly not Locke himself, seem inclined to draw from such premises. "Further," he writes, "even if this were true, and absolutely true, which is not the case, we could conclude no more than this. Man is at first, by the action of all his faculties, carried out of himself and toward the external world; the phenomena of the external world strike him first, and hence these phenomena receive the first names. The first signs are borrowed from sensible objects, and they are tinged to a certain extent by their colors. When man afterwards turns back on himself, and lays hold more or less distinctly of the intellectual phenomena which he had always, though somewhat vaguely, perceived,—if, then, he wants to give expression to the new phenomena of mind and soul, analogy leads him to connect the signs he seeks with those he already possesses: for analogy is the law of each growing or developed language. Hence the metaphors to which our analysis traces back most of the signs and names of the most abstract moral ideas."

Nothing can be truer than the caution thus given by Cousin to those who would use Locke's observation as an argument in favor of a one-sided sensualistic philosophy.

Metaphor is one of the most powerful engines in the construction of human speech, and without it we can hardly imagine how any language could have progressed beyond the simplest rudiments. Metaphor generally means the transferring of a name from the object to which it properly belongs to other objects which strike the mind as in some way or other participating in the peculiarities of the first object. The mental process which gave to the root *mar* the meaning of *to propitiate* was no other than this, that men perceived some analogy between the smooth surface produced by rubbing and polishing and the smooth expression of countenance, the smoothness of voice, and the calmness of looks produced even in an enemy by kind and gentle words. Thus, when we speak of a crane, we apply the name of a bird to an engine. People were struck with some kind of similarity between the long-legged bird picking up his food with his long beak and their rude engines for lifting weights. In Greek, too, *géranos* has both meanings. This is metaphor. Again, cutting remarks, glowing words, fervent prayers, slashing articles, all are metaphor. *Spiritus* in Latin meant originally blowing, or wind. But when the principle of life within man or animal had to be named, its outward sign, namely, the breath of the mouth, was naturally chosen to express it. Hence in Sanskrit *asu*, breath and life; in Latin *spiritus*, breath and life. Again, when it was perceived that there was something else to be named, not the mere animal life, but that which was supported by this animal life, the same word was chosen, in the Modern Latin dialects, to express the spiritual as opposed to the mere material or animal element in man. All this is metaphor.

We read in the Veda, ii. 3, 4 : [1] — " Who saw the first-born when he who had no form (lit. bones)

[1] M. M., *History of Sanskrit Literature*, p. 20.

bore him that had form? Where was the life (asuh), the blood (asrik), the self (âtmâ) of the earth? Who went to ask this from any that knew it?"

Here *breath, blood, self,* are so many attempts at expressing what we should call cause.

But let us now consider for a moment that what philosophers, and particularly Locke, have pointed out as a peculiarity of certain words, such as *to apprehend, to comprehend, to understand, to fathom, to imagine, spirit,* and *angel,* must have been, in reality, a peculiarity of a *whole period* in the early history of speech. No advance was possible in the intellectual life of man without metaphor. Most roots that have yet been discovered, had originally a material meaning, and a meaning so general and comprehensive [1] that they could easily be applied to many special objects. We meet with roots meaning to strike, to shine, to creep, to grow, to fall, but we never meet with primitive roots expressive of states or actions that do *not* fall under the cognizance of the senses, nor even with roots expressive of such special acts as "raining, thundering, hailing, sneezing, trying, helping." Yet Language has been a very good housewife to her husband, the human Mind; she has made very little go a long way. With a very small store of such material roots as we just mentioned, she has furnished decent clothing for the numberless offspring of the Mind, leaving no idea, no sentiment unprovided for, except, perhaps, the few which, as we are told by some poets, are inexpressible.

[1] The specialization of general roots is more common than the generalization of special roots, though both processes must be admitted.

Thus from roots meaning to shine, to be bright, names were formed for sun, moon, stars, the eyes of man, gold, silver, play, joy, happiness, love. With roots meaning to strike, it was possible to name an axe, the thunderbolt, a fist, a paralytic stroke, a striking remark, and a stroke of business. From roots meaning to go, names were derived for clouds, for ivy, for creepers, serpents, cattle and chattel, movable and immovable property. With a root meaning to crumble, expressions were formed for sickness and death, for evening and night, for old age and for the fall of the year.

We must now endeavor to distinguish between two kinds of metaphor, which I call *radical* and *poetical*. I call it *radical* metaphor when a root which means to shine is applied to form the names, not only of the fire or the sun, but of the spring of the year, the morning light, the brightness of thought, or the joyous outburst of hymns of praise. Ancient languages are brimful of such metaphors, and under the microscope of the etymologist every word almost discloses traces of its first metaphorical conception.

From this we must distinguish *poetical* metaphor, namely, when a noun or verb, ready made and assigned to one definite object or action, is transferred poetically to another object or action. For instance, when the rays of the sun are called the hands or fingers of the sun, the noun which means hand or finger existed ready made, and was, as such, transferred poetically to the stretched-out rays of the sun. By the same process the clouds are called mountains, the rain-clouds are spoken of as cows with heavy udders, the thunder-cloud as a goat or as a goat-skin, the sun as a horse, or as a bull, or as a giant bird, the lightning as an arrow, or as a serpent.

What applies to nouns, applies likewise to verbs. A verb such as " to give birth " is used, for instance, of the night producing, or, more correctly, preceding the day, as well as of the day preceding the night. The sun, under one name, is said to beget the dawn, because the approach of daylight gives rise to the dawn; under another name the sun is said to love the dawn, because he follows her as a bridegroom follows after his bride; and lastly, the sun is said to destroy the dawn, because the dawn disappears as soon as the sun has risen. From another point of view the dawn may be said to give birth to the sun, because the sun seems to spring from her lap; she may be said to die or disappear after having given birth to her brilliant son, because as soon as the sun is born, the dawn must vanish. All these metaphors, however full of contradictions, were perfectly intelligible to the ancient poets, though to our modern understanding they are frequently riddles difficult to solve. We read in the Rig-Veda (x. 189),[1] where the sunrise is described, that the dawn comes near to the sun, and breathes her last when the sun draws his first breath. The commentators indulge in the most fanciful explanations of this expression, without suspecting the simple conception of the poet, which after all is very natural.

Let us consider, then, that there was, necessarily and really, a period in the history of our race when all the thoughts that went beyond the narrow horizon

[1] See M. M., *Die Todtenbestattung der Brahmanen*, p. xi.

of our every-day life had to be expressed by means
of metaphors, and that these metaphors had not yet
become what they are to us, mere conventional and
traditional expressions, but were felt and understood
half in their original and half in their modified character.
We shall then perceive that such a period of
thought and speech must be marked by features very
different from those of any later age.

One of the first results would naturally be that
objects in themselves quite distinct, and originally
conceived as distinct by the human intellect, would
nevertheless receive the same name. If there was
a root meaning to shine forth, to revive, to gladden,
that root might be applied to the dawn, as the burst
of brightness after the dark night, to a spring of
water, gushing forth from the rock and gladdening
the heart of the traveller, and to the spring of the
year, that awakens the earth after the death-like rest
of winter. The spring of the year, the spring of
water, the day-spring, would thus go by the same
name, they would be what Aristotle calls *homonymous* or *namesakes*. On the other hand, the same object
might strike the human mind in various ways.
The sun might be called the warming and generating, but likewise the scorching and killing; the sea
might be called the barrier as well as the bridge and
the high-road of commerce; the clouds might be
spoken of as bright cows with heavy udders, or as
dark and roaring demons. Every day that dawns in
the morning might be called the twin of the night
that follows the day, or all the days of the year
might be called brothers, or so many head of cattle
which are driven to their heavenly pasture every

morning, and shut up in the dark stable of *Augeias* at night. In this manner one and the same object would receive many names, or would become, as the Stoics called it, *polyonymous*, many-named — having many *alias's*. Now it has always been pointed out as a peculiarity of what we call ancient languages, that they have many words for the same thing, these words being sometimes called *synonymes*; and likewise, that their words have frequently very numerous meanings. Yet what we call ancient languages, such as the Sanskrit of the Vedas or the Greek of Homer, are in reality very modern languages; that is to say, they show clear traces of having passed through many, many successive periods of growth and decay, before they became what we know them to be in the earliest literary documents of India and Greece. What, then, must have been the state of these languages in their earlier periods, before many names, that might have been and were applied to various objects, were restricted to one object, and before each object, that might have been and was called by various names, was reduced to one name! Even in our days we confess that there is a great deal in a name; how much more must that have been the case during the primitive ages of man's childhood!

The period in the history of language and thought which I have thus endeavored to describe as characterized by what we may call two tendencies, the *homonymous* and the *polyonymous*,[1] I shall henceforth call the *mythic* or *mythological period*, and I shall try to show how much that has hitherto been a riddle in

[1] Augustinus, *De Civ. Dei*, vii. 16. "Et aliquando unum deum res plures, aliquando unam rem deos plures faciunt."

the origin and spread of myths becomes intelligible if considered in connection with the early phases through which language and thought must necessarily pass.

Before I enter, however, on a fuller explanation of my meaning, I think it right to guard from the beginning against two mistakes, to which the name of *Mythic Period* might possibly give rise. What I call a period is not so in the strict sense of the word: it has no fixed limits that could be laid down with chronological accuracy. There is a time in the early history of all nations in which the mythological character predominates to such an extent that we may speak of it as the mythological period, just as we might call the age in which we live the age of discoveries. But the tendencies which characterize the mythological period, though they necessarily lose much of that power with which, at one time, they swayed every intellectual movement, continue to work under different disguises in all ages, even in our own, though perhaps the least given to metaphor, poetry, and mythology.

Secondly, when I speak of a mythological period, I do not use *mythological* in the restricted sense in which it is generally used, namely, as being necessarily connected with stories about gods, heroes, and heroines. In the sense in which I use *mythological*, it is applicable to every sphere of thought and every class of words, though, from reasons to be explained hereafter, religious ideas are most liable to mythological expression. Whenever any word, that was at first used metaphorically, is used without a clear conception of the steps that led from its original to its metaphorical meaning, there is danger of mythology; whenever those steps are forgotten and artificial steps put in their places, we have mythology, or, if I may say so, we have diseased language, whether that language refers to religious or secular interests. Why I use the term mythological in this wide sense, a sense not justified by Greek or Roman usage, will appear when we come to see how what is commonly called mythology is but a part of a much more general phase through which all language has at one time or other to pass.

After these preliminary remarks, I now proceed to examine some cases of what I called *radical* and *poetical metaphor*.

Cases of radical metaphor, though numerous in radical and agglutinative languages, are less frequent in inflectional languages, such as Sanskrit, Greek, and Latin. Nor is it difficult to account for this. It was the very inconvenience caused by words which failed to convey distinctly the intention of the speaker that gave the impulse to that new phase of life in language which we call *inflectional*. Because it was felt to be important to distinguish between the *bright one*, i. e. the sun, and the *bright one*, i. e. the day, and the *bright one*, i. e. wealth, therefore the root *vas*, to be bright, was modified by inflection, and broken up into *Vi-vas-vat*, the sun, *vas-ara*, day, *vas-u*, wealth. In a radical and in many an agglutinative language, the mere root *vas* would have been considered sufficient to express, *pro re natâ*, any one of these meanings. Yet inflectional languages, too, yield frequent instances of radical metaphor, some of which, as we shall see, have led to very ancient misunderstandings, and, in course of time, to mythology.

There is, for instance, in Sanskrit, a root *ark* or *arch*, which means to be bright; but, like most primitive verbs, it is used both in a transitive and intransitive sense, thus meaning both *to be bright* and *to make bright*. Only " to make bright" meant more in that ancient language than it means with us. To make bright meant to cheer, to gladden, to celebrate, to glorify, and it is constantly used in these different senses by the ancient poets of the Veda. Now, by a very simple and intelligible process, the meaning of this root *arch* might be transferred to the sun, or the moon, or the stars; all of them might be called *arch* or *rich* without any change in the outward appearance of the root. For all we know, *rich*, as a substantive, may really have conveyed all these meanings during the earliest period of the Aryan languages. But if we look at the fully developed branches of that family of speech, we find that in this, its simplest form, *rich* has been divested of all meanings, except one; it only means a song of praise, a hymn, that gladdens the heart and brightens the countenance of the gods, or that makes their power effulgent and manifest.[1] The other meanings, however, which *rich* might have expressed were not entirely given up; they were only rendered more definite by new and distinct grammatical modifications of the same root. Thus, in order to express light or ray, *archí* was formed, a masculine, and very

---

[1] The passage in the *Vájasaneyi Sanhitá*, 18, 39, " riché tvâ ruché tvâ," contains either an isolated remnant of the original import of the root, preserved in a proverbial phrase, or it is an etymological play.

soon also a neuter, *archís*. Neither of these nouns is ever used in the sense of praise which clings to *rich*; they have only the sense of light and splendor.

Again, quite regularly, a new derivative was formed, namely, *arkáh*, a masculine. This likewise means light, or ray of light, but it has been fixed upon as the proper name of the light of lights, the sun. *Arkáh*, then, by a very natural metaphor, became one of the many names of the sun; but by another metaphor, which we explained before, *arkáh*, with exactly the same accent and gender, was also used in the sense of hymn of praise. Now here we have a clear case of radical metaphor in Sanskrit. It was not the noun *arkáh*, in the sense of sun, that was, by a bold flight of fancy, transferred to become the name of a hymn of praise, nor *vice versâ*. The same root *arch*, under exactly the same form, was bestowed independently on two distinct conceptions. If the reason of the independent bestowal of the same root on these two distinct ideas, sun and hymn, was forgotten, there was danger of mythology, and we actually find in India that a myth sprang up, and that hymns of praise were fabled to have proceeded from or to have originally been revealed by the sun.

Our root *arch* offers us another instance of the same kind of metaphor, but slightly differing from that just examined. From *rich* in the sense of shining, it was possible to form a derivative *ríkta*, in the sense of lighted up, or bright. This form does not exist in Sanskrit, but as *kt* in Sanskrit is liable to be changed into *ks*,[1] we may recognize in *riksha* the

[1] Kuhn, in the *Zeitschrift für die Wissenschaft der Sprache*, I. 155, was

same derivative of *ṛich*. *Ṛiksha*, in the sense of bright, has become the name of the bear, so called either from his bright eyes or from his brilliant tawny fur.[1] The same name *ṛiksha* was given in Sanskrit to the stars, the bright ones. It is used as a masculine and neuter in the later Sanskrit, as a masculine only in the Veda. In one passage of the Rig-Veda, i. 24, 10, we read as follows:—" These stars fixed high above, which are seen by night, whither did they go by day?" The commentator, it is curious to observe, is not satisfied with this translation of *ṛiksha* in the sense of stars in general, but appeals to the tradition of the *Vâjasaneyins*, in order to show that the stars here called *ṛikshas* are the same constellation which in later Sanskrit is called "the Seven Rishis," or "the Seven Sages." They are the stars that never seem to set during the night, and therefore the question whither they went by day would be specially applicable to them. Anyhow, the tradition is there, and the question is whether it can be explained. Now, remember, that

the first to point out the identity of Sk. ṛiksha and Greek ἄρκτος in their mythological application. He proved that *kah* in Sanskrit represented an original *kt*, in *takshan*, carpenter, Gr. τέκτων; in *kshi*, to dwell, κτίω; in *rakshas*, Lat. *pectus*. Curtius, in his *Grundzüge*, added *kshan*, to kill, Gr. κτανν; Aufrecht (Kuhn's *Zeitschrift*, viii. 71), *kshi*, to kill, κτι; Leo Meyer (v. 374), *kshan*, earth, Gr. χθών. To these may be added *kshi*, to possess, κτάομαι; and perhaps *kshu*, to sneeze, πτύω, if it stands for κτίω.

[1] Grimm (D. W. s. v. Auge and Bär) compares ṛiksha, Dir. not only with ἄρκτος, ursus, Lith. *lokis* (instead of *olkis*, *orkis*), Irish *art* (instead of *arct*), but also with Old High-German *elah*, which is not the bear but the elk, the *alces* described by Cæsar, B. G. vi. 27. This *alces*, however, the Old High-German *elah*, would agree better with *riśa* or *riśya*, some kind of roebuck, mentioned in the Veda (Rv. viii. 4, 10), with which Weber (K. Z. vi. 320) has well compared *ircus*, the primitive form of *hircus* (Quintil. i. 5, 20).

the constellation here called the *Rikshas*, in the sense of the bright ones, would be homonymous in Sanskrit with the Bears. Remember also, that, apparently without rhyme or reason, the same constellation is called by Greeks and Romans *the Bear*, in the singular, *árktos* and *ursa*. There may be some similarity between that constellation and a wagon or wain, but there is not a shadow of a likeness with a bear. You will now perceive the influence of words on thought, or the spontaneous growth of mythology. The name *riksha* was applied to the bear in the sense of the bright fuscous animal, and in that sense it became most popular in the later Sanskrit, and in Greek and Latin. The same name, in the sense of the bright ones, had been applied by the Vedic poets to the stars in general, and more particularly to that constellation which, in the northern parts of India, was the most prominent. The etymological meaning of *riksha*, as simply the bright stars, was forgotten, the popular meaning of *riksha*, bear, was known to everybody. And thus it happened that when the Greeks had left their central home and settled in Europe, they retained the name of *Árktos* for the same unchanging stars; but not knowing why these stars had originally received that name, they ceased to speak of them as *árktoi*, or many bears, and spoke of them as the Bear, the Great Bear, adding a bear-ward, the *Arcturus* (oûros, ward), and in time even a Little Bear. Thus the name of the Arctic regions rests on a misunderstanding of a name framed thousands of years ago in Central Asia, and the surprise with which many a thoughtful observer has looked at these seven bright stars, wondering why they were ever called the bear, is removed by a reference to the early annals of human speech.

On the other hand, the Hindus also forgot the original meaning of *riksha*. It became a mere name, apparently with two meanings, star and bear. In India, however, the meaning of bear predominated, and as *riksha* became more and more the established name of the animal, it lost in the same degree its connection with the stars. So when, in later times, their Seven Sages had become familiar to all under the name of the Seven Rishis, the seven Rikshas, being unattached, gradually drifted towards the Seven Rishis, and many a fable sprang up as to the seven poets dwelling in the seven stars. Such is the origin of a myth.

The only doubtful point in the history of the myth of the Great Bear is the uncertainty which attaches to the exact etymological meaning of *riksha*, bear. We do not see why of all other animals the bear should have been called the bright animal.[1] It is true that the reason of many a name is beyond our reach, and that we must frequently rest satisfied with the fact that such a name is derived from such a root, and therefore had originally such a meaning. The bear was the king of beasts with many northern nations, who did not know the lion; and it would be difficult to say why the ancient Germans called him *Goldfusz*, golden-footed. But even if the derivation of *riksha* from *arch* were given up, the later chapters in the history of the word would still re-

[1] See, however, Welcker's remarks on the wolf in his *Griechische Götterlehre*, p. 84.

main the same. We should have *riksha*, star, derived from *arch*, to shine, mixed up with *riksha*, bear, derived from some other root, such as, for instance, *ars* or *ris*, to hurt; but the reason why certain stars were afterwards conceived as bears would not be affected by this. It should also be stated that the bear is little known in the Veda. In the two passages of the Rig-Veda where *riksha* occurs, it is explained by Sâyaṇa, in the sense of hurtful and of fire, not in that of bear. In the later literature, however, *riksha*, bear, is of very common occurrence.

Another name of the Great Bear, or originally the Seven Bears, or really the seven bright stars, is *Septemtriones*. The two words which form the name are occasionally used separately; for instance, "*quas nostri septem soliti vocitare triones.*"[1] Varro (L. L. vii. 73–75), in a passage which is not very clear, tells us that *triones* was the name by which, even at his time, ploughmen used to call oxen when actually employed for ploughing the earth.[2] If we could quite depend on the fact that oxen were ever called *triones*, we might accept the explanation of Varro, and should have to admit that at one time the seven stars were conceived as seven oxen. But as a matter of fact, *trio* is never used in this sense, except by Varro, for the purpose of an etymology, nor are the seven stars ever again spoken of as seven oxen, but only as "the oxen and the shaft," *boves et temo*, a much more appropriate name. *Boötes*, too, the

[1] Arat. in *N. D.* II. 41, 105.
[2] Triones enim boves appellantur a bubulcis etiam nunc maxume quom arant terram; e quis ut dicti valentes *glebarii* qui facile proscindunt glebas, sic omnis qui terram arabant a terra *terriones*, unde *triones* ut dicerentur e detrito.

ploughman or cow-driver, given to the same star which before we saw called *Arcturus*, or bear-keeper, would only imply that the wagon (*hámaxa*) was conceived as drawn by two or three oxen, but not that all the seven stars were ever spoken of as oxen. Though, in matters of this kind, it is impossible to speak very positively, it seems not improbable that the name *triones*, which certainly cannot be derived from *terra*, may be an old name for star in general. We saw that the stars in Sanskrit were called *star-as*, the strewers of light; and the Latin *stella* is but a contraction of *sterula*. The English *star*, the German *Stern*, come from the same source. But besides star, we find in Sanskrit another name for star, namely, *tárá*, where the initial *s* of the root is lost. Such a loss is by no means unfrequent,[1] and *trio*, in Latin, might therefore represent an original *strio*, star. The name *strio*, star, having become obsolete, like *riksha*, the *Septemtriones* remained a mere traditional name; and if, as Varro tells us, there was a vulgar name for ox in Latin, namely, *trio*, which then would have to be derived from *tero*, to pound, the peasants speaking of the *Septem triones*, the seven stars, would naturally imagine themselves speaking of seven oxen.

But as I doubt whether the seven stars ever suggested by themselves the picture of seven animals, whether bears or cows, I equally question whether the seven were ever spoken of as *temo*, the shaft. Varro says they were called "*boves et temo*," "oxen and shaft," but not that they were called both oxen and shaft. We can well imagine the four stars

[1] See Kuhn, *Zeitschrift*, iv. 4 *seq.*

being taken for oxen, and the three for the shaft; or again, the four stars being taken for the cart, one star for the shaft, and two for the oxen; but no one, I think, could ever have called the seven together the shaft. But then it might be objected that *temo*, in Latin, means not only shaft, but carriage, and should be taken as an equivalent of *hámaza*. This might be, only it has never been shown that *temo* in Latin meant a carriage. Varro,[1] no doubt, affirms that it was so, but we have no further evidence. For if Juvenal says (Sat. iv. 126), "*De temone Britanno excidet Aruiragus*," this really means from the shaft, because it was the custom of the Britons to stand fighting on the shafts of their chariots.[2] And in the other passages,[3] where *temo* is supposed to mean car in general, it only means our constellation, which can in no wise prove that *temo* by itself ever had the meaning of car.

Temo stands for *tegmo*, and is derived from the root *taksh*, which likewise yields *tignum*, a beam. In French, too, *le timon* is never a carriage, but the shaft, the German *Deichsel*, the Anglo-Saxon þixl or

---

[1] L. L. vii. 75. Temo dictus a tenendo, is enim continet jugum. Et plaustrum appellatum, a parte totum, ut multa.

[2] Cæs. B. G. iv. 38, v. 16.

[3] Stat. Theb. l. 692. Sed jam temone supino Languet hyperboreæ glacialis portitor Ursæ.
Stat. Theb. l. 370. Hyberno deprensus navita ponto, Cui neque temo piger, neque amico sidere monstrat Luna vias.
Cic. N. D. ii. 42 (vertens Arati carmina) Arctophylax, vulgo qui dicitur esse Bootes, Quod quasi temone adjunctam præ se quatit Arcton.
Ovid, Met. x. 447. Interque triones Flexerat obliquo plaustrum temone Bootes.
Lucan, lib. iv. v. 523. Flexoque Ursæ temone paverent.
Propert. lii. 5, 35. Cur serus versare boves et plaustra Bootes.

þisl,[1] words which are themselves, in strict accordance with Grimm's law, derived from the same root (tvaksh, or tuksh) as temo. The English team, on the contrary, has no connection with temo or timon, but comes from the Anglo-Saxon verb teon, to draw, the German ziehen, the Gothic tiuhan, the Latin duco. It means drawing, and a team of horses means literally a draught of horses, a line of horses, ein Zug Pferde. The verb teon, however, like the German ziehen, had likewise the meaning of bringing up, or rearing; and as in German ziehen, Zucht, and züchten, so in Anglo-Saxon team was used in the sense of issue, progeny; teamian (in English, for distinctness' sake, spelt to teem) took the sense of producing, propagating, and lastly of abounding.

According to the very nature of language, mythological misunderstandings such as that which gave rise to the stories of the Great Bear must be more frequent in ancient than in modern dialects. Nevertheless, the same mythological accidents will happen even in modern French and English. To speak of the seven bright stars, the Rikshas, as the Bear, is no more than if in speaking of a *walnut* we were to imagine that it had anything to do with a *wall*. *Walnut* is the A. S. *wealh-hnut*, in German *Wälsche Nuss*. *Wälsch* in German means originally foreigner, barbarian, and was especially applied by the Germans to the Italians. Hence Italy is to the present day called *Welschland* in German. The Saxon invaders gave the same name to the Celtic inhabitants of the British Isles, who are called *wealh* in Anglo-

---

[1] In A. S. þisl is used as a name of the constellation of Charles's Wain, like temo.

Saxon (plur. *wealas*). Hence the *walnut* meant originally the foreign nut. In Lithuanian the walnut goes by the name of the "Italian nut," in Russian by that of "Greek nut."[1] What Englishman, in speaking of *walnut*, thinks that it means foreign or Italian nut? But for the accident that walnuts are no wall-fruit, I have little doubt that by this time schoolmasters would have insisted on spelling the word with two *l*'s, and that many a gardener would have planted his walnut-trees against the wall.

There is a soup called Palestine soup. It is made, I believe, of artichokes called *Jerusalem artichokes*, but the Jerusalem artichoke is so called from a mere misunderstanding. The artichoke, being a kind of sunflower, was called in Italian *girasole*, from the Latin *gyrus*, circle, and *sol*, sun. Hence Jerusalem artichokes and Palestine soups!

One other instance may here suffice, because we shall have to return to this subject of modern mythology. One of the seven wonders of the Dauphiné in France is *la Tour sans venin*,[2] the Tower without poison, near Grenoble. It is said that poisonous animals die as soon as they approach it. Though the experiment has been tried, and has invariably failed, yet the common people believe in the miraculous power of the locality as much as ever. They appeal to the name of *la Tour sans venin*; and all that the more enlightened among them can be made to

---

[1] Pott, E. F. II. 127. Itóllakas rēsutys; Gréczkoī orjech. The German *Lamberts-nuss* is *nux Lombardica*. Instead of walnut we find *welsh-nut*, *Philos. Transact.* xviii. p. 819, and *walshnut* in Gerarde's *Herbal*. In the Index to the *Herbal*, walnut is spelt with two *l*'s, and classed with wall-flower.

[2] Brosses, *Formation Mécanique des Langues*, ii. 133.

concede is, that the tower may have lost its miraculous character in the present age, but that it certainly possessed it in former days. The real name, however, of the tower and of the chapel near it is *San Verena* or *Saint Vrain*. This became *san veneno*, and at last *sans venin*.

But we must return to ancient mythology. There is a root in Sanskrit, GHAR, which, like *ark*, means to be bright and to make bright.[1] It was originally used of the glittering of fat and ointment. This earliest sense is preserved in passages of the Veda, where the priest is said to brighten up the fire by sprinkling butter on it. It never means sprinkling in general, but always sprinkling with a bright fatty substance (*beglitzern*).[2] From this root we have *ghṛita*, the modern *ghee*, melted butter, and in general anything fat (*Schmalz*), the fatness of the land and of the clouds. Fat, however, means also bright, and hence the dawn is called *ghṛitápratiká*, bright-faced. Again, the fire claims the same name, as well as *ghṛitánirṇij*, with garments dripping with fat or with brilliant garments. The horses of Agni or fire, too, are called *ghṛitápṛishṭháḥ*, literally, whose backs are covered with fat; but, according to the commentator, well-fed and shining. The same horses are called *vítaprishṭha*, with beautiful backs, and *ghṛitasnáḥ*, bathed in fat, glittering, bedewed. Other derivatives of this root *ghar* are *ghṛiṇá*, heat of the sun; in later Sanskrit *ghṛiṇá*, warmth of the

[1] Cf. Kuhn's *Zeitschrift*, i. 134, 566; iii. 316 (Schweizer), iv. 354 (Pictet).
[2] Rv. ii. 10, 4. "Jígharmy agním havíshá ghṛiténa," I anoint or brighten up the fire with oblations of fat.

heart or pity, but likewise heat or contempt. *Ghṛiṇi*, too, means the burning heat of the sun. *Gharmá* is heat in general, and may be used for anything that is hot, the sun, the fire, warm milk, and even the kettle. It is identical with Greek *thermós*, and Latin *formus*, warm.

Instead of *ghar* we also find the root *kar*, a slight modification of the former, and having the same meaning. This root has given rise to several derivatives. Two very well known derivatives are *hári* and *harit*, both meaning originally bright, resplendent. Now, let us remember that though occasionally both the sun and the dawn are conceived by the Vedic poets as themselves horses,[1] that is to say, as racers, it became a more familiar conception of theirs to speak of the sun and the dawn as drawn by horses. These horses are very naturally called *hári*, or *harit*, bright and brilliant; and many similar names, such as *aruṇá*, *aruṣhá*, *rohit*, &c.,[2] are applied to them, all expressive of brightness of color in its various shades. After a time these adjectives became substantives. Just as *hariṇá*, from meaning bright brown, came to mean the antelope, as we speak of a bay instead of a bay horse, the Vedic poets spoke of the *Harits* as the horses of the Sun and the Dawn, of the two Haris as the horses of Indra, of the Rohits as the horses of Agni or fire. After a time the etymological meaning of these words was lost sight of, and *hari* and *harit* became traditional names for the horses which either repre-

---

[1] M. M.'s *Essay on Comparative Mythology*, p. 82. Böhtlingk-Roth, *Wörterbuch*, s. v. aśva.
[2] Cf. M. M.'s *Essay on Comparative Mythology*, pp. 81-83.

sented the Dawn and the Sun, or were supposed to be yoked to their chariots. When the Vedic poet says, " The Sun has yoked the Harits for his course," what did that language originally mean? It meant no more than what was manifest to every eye, namely, that the bright rays of light which are seen at dawn before sunrise, gathered in the east, rearing up to the sky, and bounding forth in all directions with the quickness of lightning, draw forth the light of the sun, as horses draw the car of a warrior. But who can keep the reins of language? The bright ones, the *Harits*, run away like horses, and very soon they who were originally themselves the dawn, or the rays of the Dawn, are recalled to be yoked as horses to the car of the Dawn. Thus we read (Rv. vii. 75, 6), " The bright, brilliant horses are seen bringing to us the shining Dawn."

If it be asked how it came to pass that rays of light should be spoken of as horses, the most natural answer would be that it was a poetical expression such as any one might use. But if we watch the growth of language and poetry, we find that many of the later poetical expressions rest on the same metaphorical principle which we considered before as so important an agent in the original formation of nouns, and that they were suggested to later poets by earlier poets, i. e. by the framers of the very language which they spoke. Thus in our case we can see that the same name which was given to the flames of fire, namely, *vahni*, was likewise used as a name for horse, *vahni* being derived from a root *vah*, to carry along. There are several other names which rays of light and horses share in common, so that the idea of horse would naturally ring through the mind whenever these names for rays of light were touched. And here we are once again in the midst of mythology; for all the fables of Helios, the sun, and his horses, flow irresistibly from this source.

But more than this. Remember that one of the names given to the horses of the sun was *Harit*; remember also that originally these horses of the sun were intended for the rays of the dawn, or, if you like, for the Dawn itself. In some passages the Dawn is simply called *asvâ*, the mare, originally the racing light. Even in the Veda, however, the *Harits* are not always represented as mere horses, but assume occasionally, like the Dawn, a more human aspect. Thus, vii. 66, 15, they are called the Seven Sisters, and in another passage (ix. 66, 37) they are represented with beautiful wings. Let us now see whether we can find any trace of these Harits or bright ones in Greek mythology, which, like Sanskrit, is but another dialect of the common Aryan mythology. If their name exists at all in Greek, it could only be under the form of *Charis*, *Charites*. The name, as you know, exists, but what is its meaning? It never means a horse. The name never passed through that phase in the minds of the Greek poets which is so familiar in the poetry of the Indian bards. It retained its etymological meaning of lustrous brightness, and became, as such, the name of the brightest brightness of the sky, of the dawn. In Homer, *Charis* is still used as one of the many names of *Aphrodite*, and, like Aphrodite, she is called the wife of *Hephæstos*.[1] *Aphrodite*, the sea-born, was

[1] *Il.* xviii. 382: —

τὴν δὲ ἴδε προμολοῦσα Χάρις λιπαροκρήδεμνος
καλή, τὴν ὤπυιε περικλυτὸς Ἀμφιγυήεις.

originally the dawn, the most lovely of all the sights of nature, and hence very naturally raised in the Greek mind to the rank of goddess of beauty and love. As the dawn is called in the Veda *Duhitá Diváh,* the daughter of *Dyaus, Charis,* the dawn, is to the Greeks the daughter of *Zeus.* One of the names of Aphrodite, *Argynnis,* which the Greeks derived from a name of a sacred place near the *Cephissus,* where *Argynnis,* the beloved of *Agamemnon,* had died, has been identified [1] with the Sanskrit *arjuní,* the bright, the name of the dawn. In progress of time the different names of the dawn ceased to be understood, and *Eos, Ushas,* as the most intelligible of them, became in Greece the chief representative of the deity of the morning, drawn, as in the Veda, by her bright horses. *Aphrodite,* the seaborn, also called *Enalia* [2] and *Pontia,* became the goddess of beauty and love, and was afterwards degraded by an admixture of Syrian mythology. *Charis,* on the contrary, was merged in the *Charites,* [3] who, instead of being, as in India, the horses of the dawn, were changed by an equally natural

In the *Odyssey,* the wife of Hephæstos is Aphrodite; and Nägelsbach, not perceiving the synonymous character of the two names, actually ascribed the passage in *Od.* viii. to another poet, because the system of names in Homer, he says, is too firmly established to allow of such variation. He likewise considers the marriage of Hephæstos as purely allegorical. (*Homerische Theologie,* p. 114.)

[1] Sonne, in Kuhn's *Zeitschrift,* x. 350. *Rv.* I. 49, 8. Arjuna, a name of Indra, mentioned in the *Bráhmanas,* &c.

[2] Cf. Ápyâ yóshâ, *Rv.* x. 10, 4; Apyâ yóshanâ, 11, 2.

[3] Kuhn, *Zeitschrift,* I. 518, x. 125. The same change of one deity into many took place in the case of the *Moira,* or fate. The passages in Homer where more than one *Moira* are mentioned, are considered as not genuine (*Od.* vii. 197, *Il.* xxiv. 49); but Hesiod and the later poets are familiar with the plurality of the Moiras. See Nägelsbach, *Nachhomerische Theologie,* p. 160. Welcker, *Griechische Götterlehre,* p. 53.

process into the attendants of the bright gods, and particularly of Aphrodite, whom "they wash at Paphos and anoint with oil,"[1] as if in remembrance of their descent from the root *ghar*, which, as we saw, meant to anoint, to render brilliant by oil.

It has been considered a fatal objection to the history of the word *Charis*, as here given, that in Greek it would be impossible to separate *Charis* from other words of a more general meaning. "What shall we do," says Curtius,[2] with *cháris, chará, chaírô, chaírzomai, charíeis?*" Why, it would be extraordinary if such words did not exist, if the root *ghar* had become withered as soon as it had produced this one name of *Charis*. These words which Curtius enumerates are nothing but collateral offshoots of the same root which produced the *Harits* in India and *Charis* in Greece. One of the derivatives of the root *har* was carried off by the stream of mythology, the others remained on their native soil. Thus the root *dyu* or *div* gives rise among others to the name of *Zeus*, in Sanskrit *Dyaus*, but this is no reason why the same word should not be used in the original sense of heaven, and produce other nouns expressive of light, day, and similar notions. The very word which in most Slavonic languages appears in the sense of brightness, has in Illyrian, under the form of *zora*, become the name of the dawn.[3] Are we to suppose that *Charis* in Greek meant first grace, beauty, and was then raised to the rank of an abstract deity? It would be difficult to find another such

[1] *Od.* vii. 364.
[2] Curtius, *G. E.* i. 97.
[3] Pictet, *Origines*, I. 155. Sonne, Kuhn's *Zeitschrift*, x. 354.

deity in Homer, originally a mere abstract conception,[1] and yet made of such flesh and bone as *Charis*, the wife of *Hephæstos*. Or shall we suppose that *Charis* was first, for some reason or other, the wife of Hephæstos, and that her name afterwards dwindled down to mean splendor[2] or charm in general; so that another goddess, Athene, could be said to shower charis or charms upon a man? To this, too, I doubt whether any parallel could be found in Homer. Everything, on the contrary, is clear and natural, if we admit that from the root *ghar* or *har*, to be fat, to be glittering, was derived, besides *harit*, the bright horse of the sun in Sanskrit, and *Charis*, the bright dawn in Greece, *cháris* meaning brightness and fatness, then gladness and pleasantness in general, according to a metaphor so common in ancient language. It may seem strange to us that the *cháris*, that indescribable grace of Greek poetry and art, should come from a root meaning to be fat, to be greasy. Yet as fat and greasy infants grow into "airy, fairy Lilians," so do words and ideas. The Psalmist (cxxxiii. 2) does not shrink from even bolder metaphors. "Behold, how good and how pleasant (*charien*) it is for brethren to dwell together in unity! It is like the precious ointment upon the head that ran down upon the beard, even Aaron's beard: that went down to the skirts of his garments." After the Greek *cháris* had grown, and assumed the sense of charm, such as it was conceived by the most highly-cultivated of races, no doubt it reacted on the mythological *Charis* and *Charites*, and made them

---

[1] See Kuhn, *Herabholung des Feuers*, p. 17.
[2] Sonne, *l. c.* x. 355, 356.

the embodiment of all that the Greeks had learnt to call lovely and graceful, so that in the end it is sometimes difficult to say whether *cháris* is meant as an appellative or as a mythological proper name. Yet though thus converging in the later Greek, the starting-points of the two words were clearly distinct — as distinct at least as those of *arka*, sun, and *arka*, hymn of praise, which we examined before, or as *Dyaus*, Zeus, a masculine, and *dyaus*, a feminine, meaning heaven and day. Which of the two is older, the appellative or the proper name, *Charis*, the bright dawn, or *cháris*, loveliness, is a question which it is impossible to answer, though Curtius declares in favor of the priority of the appellative. This is by no means so certain as he imagines. I fully agree with him when he says that no etymology of any proper name can be satisfactory which fails to explain the appellative nouns with which it is connected; but the etymology of *Charis* does not fail here. On the contrary, it lays bare the deepest roots from which all its cognate offshoots can be fully traced both in form and meaning, and it can defy the closest criticism, both of the student of comparative philology and of the lover of ancient mythology.[1]

In the cases which we have hitherto examined, a mythological misunderstanding arose from the fact that one and the same root was made to yield the names of different conceptions; that after a time the two names were supposed to be one and the same, which led to the transference of the meaning of one to the other. There was one point of similarity between the *bright* bear and the *bright* stars to justify

[1] See Appendix at the end of this Lecture.

the ancient framers of language in deriving from the
same root the names of both. But when the similarity in quality was mistaken for identity in substance,
mythology became inevitable. The fact of the seven
bright stars being called *Arktos*, and being supposed
to mean the bear, I call mythology; and it is important to observe that this myth has no connection
whatever with religious ideas or with the so-called
gods of antiquity. The legend of *Kallisto*, the
beloved of *Zeus*, and the mother of *Arkas*, has nothing to do with the original naming of the stars.
On the contrary, Kallisto was supposed to have been
changed into the *Arktos*, or the Great Bear, because
she was the mother of *Arkas*, that is to say, of the
Arcadian or bear race, and her name, or that of her
son, reminded the Greeks of their long-established
name of the Northern constellation. Here, then, we
have mythology apart from religion, we have a
mythological misunderstanding very like in character
to those which we alluded to in " Palestine soup "
and *La Tour sans venin*.

Let us now consider another class of metaphorical
expressions. The first class comprehended those
cases which owed their origin to the fact that two
substantially distinct conceptions received their name
from the same root, differently applied. The metaphor had taken place simultaneously with the
formation of the words; the root itself and its meaning had been modified in being adapted to the
different conceptions that waited to be named. This
is *radical metaphor*. If, on the contrary, we take
such a word as *star* and apply it to a *flower*; if we
take the word *ship* and apply it to a *cloud*, or *wing*

and apply it to a *sail*; if we call the *sun horse*, or the *moon cow*; or with verbs, if we take such a verb as *to die* and apply it to the setting sun, or if we read —

"The moonlight *clasps* the earth,
And the sunbeams *kiss* the sea"; [1]

we have throughout *poetical metaphors*. These, too, are of very frequent occurrence in the history of early language and early thought. It was, for instance, a very natural idea for people who watched the golden beams of the sun playing as it were with the foliage of the trees, to speak of these outstretched rays as hands or arms. Thus we see that in the Veda,[2] *Savitar*, one of the names of the sun, is called *golden-handed*. Who would have thought that such a simple metaphor could ever have caused any mythological misunderstanding? Nevertheless, we find that the commentators of the Veda see in the name *golden-handed*, as applied to the sun, not the golden splendor of his rays, but the gold which he carries in his hands, and which he is ready to shower on his pious worshippers. A kind of moral is drawn from the old natural epithet, and people are encouraged to worship the sun because he has gold in his hands to bestow on his priests. We have a proverb in German, "*Morgenstunde hat Gold im Munde*," "Morning-hour has gold in her mouth," which is intended to inculcate the same lesson as,

"Early to bed, and early to rise,
Makes a man healthy, and wealthy, and wise."

---

[1] Cox, *Tales of the Gods and Heroes*, p. 55.
[2] L 22. 5, hiranyapânim ûtaye Savitâram upa hvaye.
I. 35, 9, hiranyapânih Savitâ vicharshanih ubhe dyâvâprithivî antar îyate.
I. 35, 10, hiranyahasta.

But the origin of the German proverb is mythological. It was the conception of the dawn as the golden light, some similarity like that between *aurum* and *aurora*, which suggested the proverbial or mythological expression of the "golden-mouthed Dawn" — for many proverbs are chips of mythology. But to return to the golden-handed Sun. He was not only turned into a lesson, but he also grew into a respectable myth. Whether people failed to see the natural meaning of the golden-handed Sun, or whether they would not see it, certain it is that the early theological treatises of the Brahmans[1] tell of the Sun as having cut his hand at a sacrifice, and the priests having replaced it by an artificial hand made of gold. Nay, in later times the Sun, under the name of Savitar, becomes himself a priest, and a legend is told how at a sacrifice he cut off his hand, and how the other priests made a golden hand for him.

All these myths and legends which we have hitherto examined are clear enough; they are like fossils of the most recent period, and their similarity with living species is not to be mistaken. But if we dig somewhat deeper, the similarity is less palpable, though it may be traced by careful research. If the German god *Tyr*, whom Grimm identifies with the Sanskrit sun-god,[2] is spoken of as one-handed, it is because the name of the golden-handed Sun had led to the conception of the sun with one artificial hand, and afterwards, by a strict logical conclusion, to a sun with but one hand. Each nation invented its

---

[1] Kaushîtaki-brâhmana, l. c. and Sâyana.
[2] *Deutsche Mythologie*, xlvii. p. 187.

own story how *Savitar* or *Tyr* came to lose their hands; and while the priests of India imagined that *Savitar* hurt his hand at a sacrifice, the sportsmen of the North told how *Tyr* placed his hand, as a pledge, into the mouth of the wolf, and how the wolf bit it off. Grimm compares the legend of *Tyr* placing his hand, as a pledge, into the mouth of the wolf, and thus losing it, with an Indian legend of *Sûrya* or *Savitar*, the sun, laying hold of a sacrificial animal and losing his hand by its bite. This explanation is possible, but it wants confirmation, particularly as the one-handed German god *Tyr* has been accounted for in some other way. *Tyr* is the god of victory, as Wackernagel points out, and as victory can only be on one side, the god of victory might well have been thought of and spoken of as himself one-handed.[1]

It was a simple case of poetical metaphor if the Greeks spoke of the stars as the eyes of the night. But when they speak of Argos the all-seeing (*Panóptēs*), and tell of his body being covered with eyes, we have a clear case of mythology.

It is likewise perfectly intelligible when the poets of the Veda speak of the Maruts or storms as singers. This is no more than when poets speak of the music of the winds; and in German such an expression as " The wind sings " (der Wind singt) means no more than the wind blows. But when the Maruts are called not only singers, but musicians, — nay, wise poets in the Veda,[2] — then again language has exceeded its proper limits, and has landed us in the realm of fables.

[1] *Schweitzer Museum*, i. 107.
[2] *Rv.* L. 19, 4; 38, 15; 52, 15. Kuhn, *Zeitschrift*, L. 521.

Although the distinction between *radical* and *poetical* metaphor is very essential, and helps us more than anything else toward a clear perception of the origin of fables, it must be admitted that there are cases where it is difficult to carry out this distinction. If modern poets call the clouds mountains, this is clearly poetical metaphor; for mountain, by itself, never means cloud. But when we see that in the Veda the clouds are constantly called *parvata*, and that *parvata* means, etymologically, knotty or rugged, it is difficult to say positively whether in India the clouds were called mountains by a simple poetical metaphor, or whether both the clouds and the mountains were from the beginning conceived as full of ruggedness and undulation, and thence called *parvata*. The result, however, is the same, namely, mythology; for if in the Veda it is said that the Maruts or storms make the mountains to tremble (i. 39, 5), or pass through the mountains (i. 116, 20), this, though meaning originally that the storms made the clouds shake, or passed through the clouds, came to mean, in the eyes of later commentators, that the Maruts actually shook the mountains or rent them asunder.

APPENDIX TO LECTURE VIII.

Dr. Sonne, in several learned articles published in "Kuhn's Zeitschrift" (x. 96, 161, 321, 401), has subjected my conjecture as to the identity of *harit* and

cháris to the most searching criticism. On most
points I fully agree with him, as he will see from the
more complete statement of my views given in this
Lecture; and I feel most grateful to him for much
additional light which his exhaustive treatise has
thrown on the subject. We differ as to the original
meaning of the root *ghar*, which Dr. Sonne takes to
be effusion or shedding of light, while I ascribe to it
the meaning of glittering and fatness; yet we meet
again in the explanation of such words as *ghriṇā́*,
pity; *hdras*, wrath; *hriṇi*, wrath; *hriṇíte*, he is
angry (p. 100). These meanings Dr. Sonne explains
by a reference to the Russian *krauka*, color; *krasnoi*,
red, beautiful; *krasa*, beauty; *krasniv́i*, to blush;
krasovatisja, to rejoice. Dr. Sonne is certainly right
in doubling the identity of *chaíro* and Sanskrit *hṛish*,
the Latin *horreo*, and in explaining *chaíro* as the
Greek form of *ghar*, to be bright and glad, conjugated
according to the fourth class. Whether the Sanskrit
haryati, he desires, is the Greek *thélei*, seems to me
doubtful.

Why Dr. Sonne should prefer to identify *cháris*,
cháritos, with the Sanskrit *hári*, rather than with
harít, he does not state. Is it on account of the
accent? I certainly think that there was a form
cháris, corresponding to *hári*, and I should derive
from it the accusative *chárin*, instead of *chárita*;
also adjectives like *charíeis* (harivat). But I should
certainly retain the base which we have in *harít*, in
order to explain such forms as *cháris, cháritos*. That
chárit in Greek ever passed through the same metamorphosis as the Sanskrit *harít*, that it ever to a
Greek mind conveyed the meaning of horse, there is

no evidence whatever. Greek and Sanskrit myths, like Greek and Sanskrit words, must be treated as coördinate, not as subordinate; nor have I ever, as far as I recollect, referred Greek myths or Greek words to Sanskrit as their prototypes. What I said about the *Charites* was very little. On page 81 of my "Essay on Comparative Mythology," I said: —

"In other passages, however, they (the Harits) take a more human form; and as the Dawn, which is sometimes simply called *asvâ*, the mare, is well known by the name of the sister, these *Harits* also are called the Seven Sisters (vii. 66, 15); and in one passage (ix. 86, 37) they appear as the *Harits* with beautiful wings. *After this I need hardly say that we have here the prototype of the Grecian Charites.*"

If on any other occasion I had derived Greek from Sanskrit myths, or, as Dr. Sonne expresses it, ethnic from ethnic myths, instead of deriving both from a common Aryan or pro-ethnic source, my words might have been liable to misapprehension.[1] But as they stand in my essay, they were only intended to point out that after tracing the *Harits* to their most primitive source, and after showing how, starting from thence, they entered on their mythological career in India, we might discover there, in their earliest form, the mould in which the myth of the Greek *Charites* was cast, while such epithets as "the sisters," and

[1] I ought to mention, however, that Mr. Cox, in the Introduction to his *Tales of the Gods and Heroes*, p. 07, has understood my words in the same sense as Dr. Sonne. "The horses of the sun," he writes, "are called Harits; and in these we have the prototype of the Greek *Charites*, — an inverse transmutation, for while in the other instances the human is changed into a brute personality, in this the beasts are converted into maidens."

"with beautiful wings," might indicate how conceptions that remained sterile in Indian mythology, grew up under a Grecian sky into those charming human forms which we have all learned to admire in the Graces of Hellas. That I had recognized the personal identity, if we may say so, of the Greek *Charis*, the Aphrodite, the Dawn, and the Sanskrit *Ushas*, the dawn, will be seen from a short sentence towards the end of my essay, p. 86 : —

"He (*Eros*) is the youngest of the gods, the son of *Zeus*, the friend of the *Charites*, also the son of the chief *Charis*, *Aphrodite*, in whom we can hardly fail to discover a female *Eros* (an *Ushâ*, dawn, instead of an *Agni aushasya*)."

Dr. Sonne will thus perceive that our roads, even where they do not exactly coincide, run parallel, and that we work in the same spirit and with the same objects in view.

LECTURE IX.

THE MYTHOLOGY OF THE GREEKS.

To those who are acquainted with the history of Greece, and have learnt to appreciate the intellectual, moral, and artistic excellences of the Greek mind, it has often been a subject of wonderment how such a nation could have accepted, could have tolerated for a moment, such a religion. What the inhabitants of the small city of Athens' achieved in philosophy, in poetry, in art, in science, in politics, is known to all of us; and our admiration for them increases tenfold if, by a study of other literatures, such as the literatures of India, Persia, and China, we are enabled to compare their achievements with those of other nations of antiquity. The rudiments of almost everything, with the exception of religion, we, the people of Europe, the heirs to a fortune accumulated during twenty or thirty centuries of intellectual toil, owe to the Greeks; and, strange as it may sound, but few, I think, would gainsay it, that to the present day the achievements of these our distant ancestors and earliest masters, the songs of Homer, the dialogues of Plato, the speeches of Demosthenes, and the statues of Phidias stand, if not unrivalled, at least unsurpassed by anything that has been achieved by their descendants and pupils. *How* the Greeks came to be what they were, and how, alone of all other nations, they opened almost every mine of thought that has since been worked by mankind; how they invented and perfected almost every style of poetry and prose which has since been cultivated by the greatest minds of our race; how they laid the lasting foundation of the principal arts and sciences, and in some of them achieved triumphs never since equalled, is a problem which neither historian nor philosopher has as yet been able to solve. Like their own goddess Athene, the people of Athens seem to spring full-armed into the arena of history, and we look in vain to Egypt, Syria, or India for more than a few of the seeds that burst into such marvellous growth on the soil of Attica.

But the more we admire the native genius of Hellas, the more we feel surprised at the crudities and absurdities of what is handed down to us as their religion. Their earliest philosophers knew as well as we that the Deity, in order to be Deity, must be either perfect or nothing — that it must be one, not many, and without parts and passions; yet they believed in many gods, and ascribed to all of them, and more particularly to Jupiter, almost every vice and weakness that disgraces human nature. Their poets had an instinctive aversion to everything excessive or monstrous; yet they would relate of their gods what would make the most savage of the Red Indians creep and shudder: — how that Uranos was maimed by his son Kronos, — how Kronos swallowed his own children, and, after years of digestion, vomited out alive his whole progeny, — how Apollo, their fairest god, hung Marsyas on a tree and flayed him alive, — how Demeter, the sister of Zeus, partook of the shoulder of Pelops who had been butchered and roasted by his own father, Tantalus, as a feast for the gods. I will not add any further horrors, or dwell on crimes that have become unmentionable, but of which the most highly cultivated Greek had to tell his sons and daughters in teaching them the history of their gods and heroes.

It would indeed be a problem, more difficult than the problem of the origin of these stories themselves, if the Greeks, such as we know them, had never been startled by this, had never asked, How can these things be, and how did such stories spring up? But be it said to the honor of Greece, that, although her philosophers did not succeed in explaining the origin of these religious fables, they certainly were, from the earliest times, shocked by them. Xenophanes, who lived, as far as we know, before Pythagoras, accuses[1] Homer and Hesiod of having ascribed to the gods everything that is disgraceful among men, — stealing, adultery, and deceit. He remarks that[2] men seem to have created their gods, and to have given to them

---

[1] Πάντα θεοῖς ἀνέθηκαν Ὅμηρός θ᾽ Ἡσίοδός τε,
ὅσσα παρ᾽ ἀνθρώποισιν ὀνείδεα καὶ ψόγος ἐστίν. . . . .
Ὡς πλεῖστ᾽ ἐφθέγξαντο θεῶν ἀθεμίστια ἔργα,
κλέπτειν μοιχεύειν τε καὶ ἀλλήλους ἀπατεύειν.
Cf. *Sextus Emp. adv. Math.* i. 289, ix. 193.

[2] Ἀλλὰ βροτοὶ δοκέουσι θεοὺς γεγενῆσθαι,
τὴν σφετέρην τ᾽ αἴσθησιν ἔχειν φωνήν τε δέμας τε. . . . .
Ἀλλ᾽ εἴτοι χεῖράς γ᾽ εἶχον βόες ἠὲ λέοντες,
ἢ γράψαι χείρεσσι καὶ ἔργα τελεῖν ἅπερ ἄνδρες,
καί κε θεῶν ἰδέας ἔγραφον καὶ σώματ᾽ ἐποίουν
τοιαῦθ᾽ οἷόν περ καὐτοὶ δέμας εἶχον ὁμοῖον,
ἵπποι μέν θ᾽ ἵπποισι, βόες δέ τε βουσίν ὁμοῖα.
Cf. *Clem. Alex. Strom.* v. p. 601 C.

their own mind, voice, and figure; that the Ethiopians made their gods black and flat-nosed, the Thracians red-haired and blue-eyed, — just as cows or lions, if they could but draw, would draw their gods like cows and lions. He himself declares, in the most unhesitating manner, — and this nearly 600 years before our era, — that "God[1] is one, the greatest among gods and men, neither in form nor in thought like unto men." He calls the battles of the Titans, the Giants, and Centaurs, the inventions of former generations[2] (πλάσματα τῶν προτέρων), and requires that the Deity should be praised in holy stories and pure strains.

Similar sentiments were entertained by most of the great philosophers of Greece. *Heraclitus* seems to have looked upon the Homeric system of theology, if we may so call it, as flippant infidelity. According to Diogenes Laertius,[3] Heraclitus declared that Homer, as well as Archilochus, deserved to be ejected from public assemblies and flogged. The same author relates[4] a story that *Pythagoras* saw the soul of Homer in the lower world hanging on a tree, and surrounded by serpents, as a punishment

---

[1] Εἷς θεὸς ἔν τε θεοῖσι καὶ ἀνθρώποισι μέγιστος,
οὔ τι δέμας θνητοῖσι ὁμοίιος οὐδὲ νόημα.
Cf. *Clem. Alex.* l. c.

[2] Cf. *Isocrates,* ii. 38 (*Nägelsbach,* p. 45).

[3] Τὸν θ' Ὅμηρον ἔφασκεν ἄξιον ἐκ τῶν ἀγώνων ἐκβάλλεσθαι καὶ ῥαπίζεσθαι, καὶ Ἀρχίλοχον ὁμοίως. — Diog. Laert. ix. 1.
'Ησίβυσε εἰ μὴ ἠλληγόρισε, Ὅμηρος. Bertrand, *Les Dieux Protecteurs,* p. 148.

[4] Φησὶ δ' Ἱερώνυμος κατελθόντα αὐτὸν εἰς ᾅδου τὴν μὲν Ἡσιόδου ψυχὴν ἰδεῖν πρὸς κίονι χαλκῷ δεδεμένην καὶ τρίζουσαν, τὴν δ' Ὁμήρου κρεμαμένην ἀπὸ δένδρου καὶ ὄφεις περὶ αὐτὴν ἀνθ' ὧν εἶπον περὶ θεῶν. — Diog. Laert. viii. 21.

PROTESTS OF GREEK PHILOSOPHERS.

for what he had said of the gods. No doubt the views of these philosophers about the gods were far more exalted and pure than those of the Homeric poets, who represented their gods as in many cases hardly better than man. But as religion became mixed up with politics, it was more and more dangerous to pronounce these sublimer views, or to attempt to explain the Homeric myths in any but the most literal sense. *Anaxagoras*, who endeavored to give to the Homeric legends a moral meaning, and is said to have interpreted the names of the gods allegorically — nay, to have called Fate an empty name, was thrown into prison at Athens, from whence he only escaped through the powerful protection of his friend and pupil Pericles. *Protagoras*, another friend of Pericles,[1] was expelled from Athens, and his books were publicly burnt, because he had said that nothing could be known about the gods, whether they existed or no.[2] *Socrates*, though he never attacked the sacred traditions and popular legends,[3] was suspected of being no very strict believer in the ancient Homeric theology, and he had to suffer martyrdom. After the death of Socrates

---

[1] Δοκεῖ δὲ πρῶτος, καθά φησι Φαβωρῖνος ἐν παντοδαπῇ ἱστορίᾳ, τὴν Ὁμήρου ποίησιν ἀποφήνασθαι εἶναι περὶ ἀρετῆς καὶ δικαιοσύνης · ἐπὶ πλέον δὲ προστῆναι τοῦ λόγου Μητρόδωρον τὸν Λαμψακηνόν, γνώριμον ὄντα αὐτοῦ, ὃν καὶ πρῶτον σπουδάσαι τοῦ ποιητοῦ περὶ τὴν φυσικὴν πραγματείαν. — Diog. Laert. li. 11.

[2] Περὶ μὲν θεῶν οὐκ ἔχω εἰδέναι οὔθ' ὡς εἰσίν, οὔθ' ὡς οὐκ εἰσίν · πολλὰ γὰρ τὰ κωλύοντα εἰδέναι, ἥ τ' ἀδηλότης καὶ βραχὺς ὢν ὁ βίος τοῦ ἀνθρώπου. Διὰ ταύτην δὲ τὴν ἀρχὴν τοῦ συγγράμματος ἐξεβλήθη πρὸς Ἀθηναίων · καὶ τὰ βιβλία αὐτοῦ κατέκαυσαν ἐν τῇ ἀγορᾷ, ὑπὸ κήρυκος ἀναλεξάμενοι παρ' ἑκάστου τῶν κεκτημένων. — Diog. Laert. ix. 51. Cicero, *Nat. Deor.* i. 23, 63.

[3] Grote, *History of Greece*, vol. i. p. 504.

greater freedom of thought was permitted at Athens in exchange for the loss of political liberty. Plato declared that many a myth had a symbolical or allegorical meaning, but he insisted, nevertheless, that the Homeric poems, such as they were, should be banished from his Republic.[1] Nothing can be more distinct and outspoken than the words attributed to *Epicurus*: "The gods are indeed, but they are not as the many believe them to be. Not he is an infidel who denies the gods of the many, but he who fastens on the gods the opinions of the many."[2]

In still later times an accommodation was attempted between mythology and philosophy. *Chrysippus* (died 207), after stating his views about the immortal gods, is said to have written a second book to show how these might be brought into harmony with the fables of Homer.[3]

And not philosophers only felt these difficulties about the gods as represented by Homer and Hesiod; most of the ancient poets also were distressed by the same doubts, and constantly find themselves involved in contradictions which they are unable to solve. Thus, in the Eumenides of *Æschylus* (v. 640), the

---

[1] Οἷς Ἡσίοδός τε, εἶπον, καὶ Ὅμηρος ἡμῖν ἐλεγέτην καὶ οἱ ἄλλοι ποιηταί· τοῦτοι γάρ που μύθους τοῖς ἀνθρώποις ψευδεῖς συντιθέντες ἔλεγόν τε καὶ λέγουσιν. — Plat. Polit. β. 377 d. Grote, *History*, I. 593.

[2] Diog. Laert. x. 123. Ritter and Preller, *Historia Philosophiæ*, p. 419. Θεοὶ μὲν γάρ εἰσιν· ἐναργὴς δὲ ἐστιν αὐτῶν ἡ γνῶσις· οἵους δ' αὐτοὺς οἱ πολλοὶ νομίζουσιν οὐκ εἰσίν· οὐ γὰρ φυλάττουσιν αὐτοὺς οἵους νομίζουσιν. ἀσεβὴς δ' οὐχ ὁ τοὺς τῶν πολλῶν θεοὺς ἀναιρῶν, ἀλλ' ὁ τὰς τῶν πολλῶν δόξας θεοῖς προσάπτων.

[3] In secundo autem libro Homeri fabulas accommodare voluit ad ea quæ ipse primo libro de diis immortalibus dixerit. — Cic. *Nat. Deor.* I. 16. Bertrand, *Sur les Dieux Protecteurs* (Rennes, 1858), p. 38.

Chorus asks how Zeus could have called on Orestes to avenge the murder of his father, he who himself had dethroned his father and bound him in chains. Pindar, who is fond of weaving the traditions of gods and heroes into his songs of victory, suddenly starts when he meets with anything dishonorable to the gods. "Lips," he says,[1] "throw away this word, for it is an evil wisdom to speak evil of the gods." His criterion in judging of mythology would seem to have been very simple and straightforward, namely, that nothing can be true in mythology that is dishonorable to the gods. The whole poetry of *Euripides* oscillates between two extremes: he either taxes the gods with all the injustice and crimes they are fabled to have committed, or he turns round and denies the truth of the ancient myths because they relate of the gods what is incompatible with a divine nature. Thus, while in the Ion,[2] the gods, even Apollo, Jupiter, and Neptune, are accused of every crime, we read in another play:[3] "I do not think

[1] *Olymp.* ix. 38, ed. Bœkh. Ἀπό μοι λόγον τοῦτον, στόμα, ῥίψον · ἐπεί τό γε λοιδορῆσαι θεοὺς ἐχθρὰ σοφία.

[2] *Ion*, 444, ed. Paley: —

Εἰ δ', οὐ γὰρ ἔσται, τῷ λόγῳ δὲ χρήσομαι,
δίκας βιαίων δώσετ' ἀνθρώποις γάμων,
σὺ καὶ Ποσειδῶν Ζεύς θ' ὃς οὐρανοῦ κρατεῖ,
ναοὺς τίνοντες ἀδικίας κενώσετε. . . . .
οὐκέτ' ἀνθρώποις κακοὺς
λέγειν δίκαιον, εἰ τὰ τῶν θεῶν κακὰ
μιμούμεθ', ἀλλὰ τοὺς διδάσκοντας τάδε.

M. Herc. fur. 338.

[3] *Herc. fur.* 1341, ed. Paley: —

Ἐγὼ δὲ τοὺς θεοὺς οὔτε λέκτρ' ἃ μὴ θέμις
στέργειν νομίζω, δεσμά τ' ἐξάπτειν χεροῖν
οὔτ' ἠξίωσα πώποτ' οὔτε πείσομαι,
οὐδ' ἄλλον ἄλλου δεσπότην πεφυκέναι.

that the gods delight in unlawful marriages, nor did I ever hold or shall ever believe that they fasten chains on their hands, or that one is lord of another. For a god, if he is really god, has no need of anything: these are the miserable stories of poets!" Or, again:[1] "*If* the gods commit anything that is evil, they are no gods."

These passages, to which many more might be added, will be sufficient to show that the more thoughtful among the Greeks were as much startled at their mythology as we are. They would not have been Greeks if they had not seen that those fables were irrational, if they had not perceived that the whole of their mythology presented a problem that required a solution at the hand of the philosopher. If the Greeks did not succeed in solving it, if they preferred a compromise between what they knew to be true and what they knew to be false, if the wisest among their wise men spoke cautiously on the subject or kept aloof from it altogether, let us remember that these myths, which we now handle as freely as the geologist his fossil bones, were then living things, sacred things, implanted by parents in the minds of their children, accepted with an unquestioning faith, hallowed by the memory of the departed, sanctioned by the state, the foundation on which some of the most venerable institutions had been built up and established for ages. It is enough for us to know that the Greeks expressed surprise

---

δεῖται γὰρ ὁ θεὸς, εἴπερ ἐστ' ὄντως θεὸς,
οὐδενός · ἀοιδῶν οἵδε δύστηνοι λόγοι.

See *Euripides*, ed. Paley, vol. I. Preface, p. xx.

[1] Eur. *Fragm. Bellerph.* 300: εἰ θεοί τι δρῶσιν αἰσχρὸν, οὐκ εἰσὶν θεοί.

and dissatisfaction at these fables: to explain their origin was a task left to a more dispassionate age.

The principal solutions that offered themselves to the Greeks, when inquiring into the origin of their mythology, may be classed under three heads, which I call *ethical, physical, historical*, according to the different objects which the original framers of mythology were supposed to have had in view.[1]

Seeing how powerful an engine was supplied by religion for awing individuals and keeping political communities in order, some Greeks imagined that the stories telling of the omniscience and omnipotence of the gods, of their rewarding the good and punishing the wicked, were invented by wise people of old for the improvement and better government of men.[2] This view, though extremely shallow, and supported by no evidence, was held by many among the ancients; and even Aristotle, though admitting, as we shall see, a deeper foundation of religion, was inclined to consider the mythological form of the Greek religion as invented for the sake of persuasion, and as useful for the support of law and order. Well might Cicero, when examining this view, exclaim, "Have not those who said that the idea of immortal gods was made up by wise men for the sake of the commonwealth, in order that those who could not be led by reason might be led to their duty by religion, destroyed all religion from the bottom?"[3] Nay, it would seem to follow, that, if the useful portions of

[1] Cf. Augustinus, *De Civ. Dei*, vii. 5. De paganorum secretiore doctrina physiciaque rationibus.
[2] Cf. Wagner, *Fragm. Trag.* iii. p. 102. Nägelsbach, *Nachhomerische Theologie*, pp. 435, 445.
[3] Cic. *N. D.* i. 42, 118.

mythology were invented by wise men, the immoral stories about gods and men must be ascribed to foolish poets, — a view, as we saw before, more than hinted at by Euripides.

A second class of interpretations may be comprehended under the name of *physical*, using that term in the most general sense, so as to include even what are commonly called *metaphysical* interpretations. According to this school of interpreters, it was the intention of the authors of mythology to convey to the people at large a knowledge of certain facts of nature, or certain views of natural philosophy, which they did in a phraseology peculiar to themselves or to the times they lived in, or, according to others, in a language that was to veil rather than to unveil the mysteries of their sacred wisdom. As all interpreters of this class, though differing on the exact original intention of each individual myth, agree in this, that no myth must be understood literally, their system of interpretation is best known under the name of *allegorical*, allegorical being the most general name for that kind of language which says one thing but means another.[1]

So early a philosopher as *Epicharmus*,[2] the pupil

---

[1] Cf. Müller, *Prolegomena*, p. 335, n. 6. ἄλλο μὲν ἀγορεύει, ἄλλο δὲ νοεῖ. The difference between a myth and an allegory has been simply but most happily explained by Professor Blackie, in his article on Mythology in *Chambers' Cyclopædia*: "A myth is not to be confounded with an allegory; the one being an unconscious act of the popular mind at an early stage of society, the other a conscious act of the individual mind at any stage of social progress."

[2] Stobæus, *Flor.* xcl. 29:—
    Ὁ μὲν Ἐπίχαρμος τοὺς θεοὺς εἶναι λέγει
    Ἀνέμους, ὕδωρ, γῆν, ἥλιον, πῦρ, ἀστέρας.
Cf. Bernays, *Rhein. Mus.* 1853, p. 280. Kruseman, *Epicharmi Fragmenta*, Harlemi, 1834.

of Pythagoras, declared that the gods were really wind, water, earth, the sun, fire, and the stars. Not long after him, *Empedocles* (about 444 B. C.) ascribed to the names of Zeus, Here, Aïdoneus, and Nestis, the meaning of the four elements, fire, air, earth, and water.[1] Whatever the philosophers of Greece successively discovered as the first principles of being and thought, whether the air of *Anaximenes*[2] (about 548) or the fire of *Heraclitus*[3] (about 503), or the Nous, the mind, of *Anaxagoras* (died 428), was gladly identified by them with Jupiter or other divine powers. Anaxagoras and his school are said to have explained the whole of the Homeric mythology allegorically. With them Zeus was mind, Athene, art; while *Metrodorus*, the contemporary of Anaxagoras, "resolved not only the persons of Zeus, Here, and Athene, but also those of Agamemnon, Achilles, and Hector, into various elemental combinations and physical agencies, and treated the adventures ascribed to them as natural facts concealed under the veil of allegory."[4]

Socrates declined this labor of explaining all fables

[1] Plut. *de Plac. Phil.* l. 30: Ἐμπεδοκλῆς φύσιν μηδὲν εἶναι, μίξιν δὲ τῶν στοιχείων καὶ διάστασιν. γράφει γὰρ οὕτως ἐν τῷ πρώτῳ φυσικῷ.

Τέσσαρα τῶν πάντων ῥιζώματα πρῶτον ἄκουε·
Ζεὺς ἀργὴς Ἥρη τε, φερέσβιος ἠδ' Ἀϊδωνεύς,
Νῆστίς θ' ἡ δακρύοις τέγγει κρούνωμα βρότειον.

[2] Cic. *N. D.* l. 10. Ritter and Preller, § 27.

[3] Clem. Alex. Strom. v. p. 603 D. Ritter and Preller, § 38. Bernays, *Neue Bruchstücke des Heraklit*, p. 256: ἐν τὸ σοφὸν μοῦνον λέγεσθαι ἐθέλει, καὶ οὐκ ἐθέλει Ζηνὸς οὔνομα.

[4] Syncellus, *Chron.* p. 140, ed. Paris. Ἑρμηνεύουσι δὲ οἱ Ἀναξαγόρειοι τοὺς μυθώδεις θεούς, τοὺν μὲν τὸν Δία, τὴν δὲ Ἀθηνᾶν τέχνην. Grote, vol. I. p. 563. Ritter and Preller, *Hist. Phil.* § 48. Lobeck, *Aglaoph.* p. 156. Diog. Laert. ii. 11.

allegorically as too arduous and unprofitable; yet he, as well as Plato, frequently pointed to what they called the *hypónoia*, the under-meaning, if I may say so, of the ancient myths.

There is a passage in the eleventh book of Aristotle's Metaphysics which has often been quoted [1] as showing the clear insight of that philosopher into the origin of mythology, though in reality it does not rise much above the narrow views of other Greek philosophers.

This is what Aristotle writes:—

"It has been handed down by early and very ancient people, and left, in the form of myths, to those who came after, that these (the first principles of the world) are the gods, and that the divine embraces the whole of nature. The rest has been added mythically, in order to persuade the many, and in order to be used in support of laws and other interests. Thus they say that the gods have a human form, and that they are like to some of the other living beings, and other things consequent on this, and similar to what has been said. If one separated out of these fables, and took only that first point, that they believed the first essences to be gods, one would think that it had been divinely said, and that while every art and every philosophy was probably invented ever so many times and lost again, these opinions had, like fragments of them, been preserved until now. So far only is the opinion of our fathers, and that received from our first ancestors, clear to us."

The attempts at finding in mythology the remnants of ancient philosophy, have been carried on

[1] Bunsen, *Gott in der Geschichte*, vol. iii. p. 532. Ar. *Met.* xi. 8, 19.

HISTORICAL INTERPRETATIONS. 415

in different ways from the days of Socrates to our own time. Some writers thought they discovered astronomy, or other physical sciences, in the mythology of Greece; and in our own days the great work of Creuzer, "Symbolik und Mythologie der alten Völker" (1819-'21), was written with the one object of proving that Greek mythology was composed by priests, born or instructed in the East, who wished to raise the semi-barbarous races of Greece to a higher civilization and a purer knowledge of the Deity. There was, according to Creuzer and his school, a deep, mysterious wisdom, and a monotheistic religion veiled under the symbolical language of mythology, which language, though unintelligible to the people, was understood by the priests, and may be interpreted even now by the thoughtful student of mythology.

The third theory on the origin of mythology I call the *historical*. It goes generally by the name of *Euhemerus*, though we find traces of it both before and after his time. Euhemerus was a contemporary of Alexander, and lived at the court of Cassander, in Macedonia, by whom he is said to have been sent out on an exploring expedition. Whether he really explored the Red Sea and the southern coasts of Asia we have no means of ascertaining. All we know is that, in a religious novel which he wrote, he represented himself as having sailed in that direction to a great distance, until he came to the island of Panchœa. In that island he said that he discovered a number of inscriptions (ἀναγραφαί, hence the title of his book, Ἱερὰ Ἀναγραφή) containing an account of the principal gods of Greece, but representing them, not as gods, but as kings, heroes, and philosophers, who after their death had received divine honors among their fellow-men.[1]

Though the book of Euhemerus itself, and its translation by Ennius, are both lost, and we know little either of its general spirit or of its treatment of individual deities, such was the sensation produced by it at the time, that Euhemerism has become the recognized title of that system of mythological interpretation which denies the existence of divine beings, and reduces the gods of old to the level of men. A distinction, however, must be made between the complete and systematic denial of all gods, which is ascribed to Euhemerus, and the partial application of his principles which we find in many Greek writers. Thus Hecatæus, a most orthodox Greek,[2] declares that Geryon of Erytheia was really a king of Epirus, rich in cattle; and that Cerberus, the dog of Hades, was a certain serpent inhabiting a cavern on Cape Tænarus.[3] Ephorus converted Tityos into a bandit, and the serpent Python[4] into a rather troublesome person, Python by name, *alias* Dracon, whom Apollo killed with his arrows. According to Herodotus, an equally orthodox writer, the two black doves from Egypt which flew to Libya and Dodona, and directed the people to found in each place an oracle of Zeus, were in reality women who came

---

[1] Quid? qui aut fortes aut claros aut potentes viros tradunt post mortem ad deos pervenisse, eosque esse ipsos quos nos colere, precari, venerarique soleamus, nonne expertes sunt religionum omnium? Quæ ratio maxime tractata ab Euhemero est, quam noster et interpretatus et secutus est præter cæteros Ennius. — Cic., *De Nat. Deor.* i. 42.

[2] Grote, *History of Greece*, vol. i. p. 526.

[3] Strabo, ix. p. 422. Grote, *H. G.* i. p. 552.

[4] Possibly connected with the Vedic Ahir Budhnya.

from Thebes. The one that came to Dodona was called a dove, because, he says, speaking a foreign tongue, she seemed to utter sounds like a bird, and she was called a black dove on account of her black Egyptian color. This explanation he represents not as a guess of his own, but as founded on a statement made to him by Egyptian priests; and I count it therefore as an historical, not as a merely allegorical interpretation. Similar explanations become more frequent in later Greek historians, who, unable to admit anything supernatural or miraculous as historical fact, strip the ancient legends of all that renders them incredible, and then treat them as narrations of real events, and not as fiction.[1] With them, Æolus, the god of the winds, became an ancient mariner skilled in predicting weather; the Cyclopes were a race of savages inhabiting Sicily; the Centaurs were horsemen; Atlas was a great astronomer, and Scylla a fast-sailing filibuster. This system, too, like the former, maintained itself almost to the present day. The early Christian controversialists, St. Augustine, Lactantius, Arnobius, availed themselves of this argument in their attacks on the religious belief of the Greeks and Romans, taunting them with worshipping gods that were no gods, but known and admitted to have been mere deified mortals. In their attacks on the religion of the German nations, the Roman missionaries recurred to the same argument. One of them told the Angli in England that *Woden*, whom they believed to be the principal and the best of their gods, from whom they derived their origin, and to whom

[1] Grote, I. 554.

they had consecrated the fourth day in the week, had been a mortal, a king of the Saxons, from whom many tribes claimed to be descended. When his body had been reduced to dust, his soul was buried in hell, and suffers eternal fire.[1] In many of our handbooks of mythology and history, we still find traces of this system. Jupiter is still spoken of as a ruler of Crete, Hercules as a successful general or knight-errant, Priam as an eastern king, and Achilles, the son of Jupiter and Thetis, as a valiant champion in the siege of Troy. The siege of Troy still retains its place in the minds of many as a historical fact, though resting on no better authority than the carrying off of Helena by Theseus and her recovery by the Dioskuri, the siege of Olympus by the Titans, or the taking of Jerusalem by Charlemagne, described in the chivalrous romances[2] of the Middle Ages.

In later times the same theory was revived, though not for such practical purposes, and it became during the last century the favorite theory with philosophical historians, particularly in France. The comprehensive work of the Abbé Banier, " The Mythology and Fables of Antiquity, explained from History," secured to this school a temporary ascendancy in France; and in England, too, his work, translated into English, was quoted as an authority. His de-

[1] Kemble, *Saxons in England*, 1. 338. *Legend. Norr.* fol. 210 b.
[2] Grote, 1. 636. "The series of articles by M. Fauriel, published in the *Revue des deux Mondes*, vol. xiii., are full of instruction respecting the origin, tenor, and influence of the romances of chivalry. Though the name of Charlemagne appears, the romancers are really unable to distinguish him from Charles Martel, or from Charles the Bald (pp. 517-539). They ascribe to him an expedition to the Holy Land, in which he conquered Jerusalem from the Saracens," &c.

sign was, as he says,[1] "to prove that, notwithstanding all the ornaments which accompany fables, it is no difficult matter to see that they contain a part of the history of primitive times." It is useful to read these books, written only about a hundred years ago, if it were but to take warning against a too confident spirit in working out theories which now seem so incontrovertible, and which a hundred years hence may be equally antiquated. "Shall we believe," says Abbé Banier, — and no doubt he thought his argument unanswerable, — "shall we believe in good earnest that Alexander would have held Homer in such esteem, had he looked upon him only as a mere relater of fables? and would he have envied the happy lot of Achilles in having such a one to sing his praises?"[2] . . . When Cicero is enumerating the sages, does he not bring in Nestor and Ulysses? — would he have given mere phantoms a place among them? Are we not taught by Cicero (Tusc. Quæst. i. 5) that what gave occasion to feign that the one supported the heavens on his shoulders, and that the other was chained to Mount Caucasus, was their indefatigable application to contemplate the heavenly bodies? I might bring in here the authority of most of the ancients: I might produce that of the primitive Fathers of the Church, Arnobius, Lactantius, and several others, who looked upon fables to be founded on true histories; and I might finish this list with the names of the most illustrious of our moderns, who have traced out in ancient fictions so

[1] *The Mythology and Fables of the Ancients, explained from History*, by the Abbé Banier. London, 1739, in six vols. Vol. I. p. ix.
[2] Vol. I. p. 21.

many remains of the traditions of the primitive ages." How like in tone to some incontrovertible arguments used in our own days![1] "I shall make it appear that Minotaur with Pasiphaë, and the rest of that fable, contain nothing but an intrigue of the Queen of Crete with a captain named Taurus, and the artifice of Dædalus, only a sly confident. Atlas bearing heaven upon his shoulders was a king that studied astronomy with a globe in his hand. The golden apples of the delightful garden of the Hesperides, and their dragon, were oranges watched by mastiff dogs."

As belonging in spirit to the same school, we have still to mention those scholars who looked to Greek mythology for traces, not of profane, but of sacred personages, and who, like *Bochart*, imagined they could recognize in Saturn the features of Noah, and in his three sons, Jupiter, Neptune, and Pluto, the three sons of Noah, Ham, Japhet, and Shem.[2] *G. J. Vossius*, in his learned work, "*De Theologia Gentili et Physiologia Christiana, sive De Origine et Progressu Idolatriæ,*"[3] identified Saturn with Adam or with Noah, Janus and Prometheus with Noah again, Pluto with Japhet or Ham, Neptune with Japhet,

---

[1] Vol. i. p. 29.

[2] *Geographia Sacra*, lib. I. l. c.: "Noam esse Saturnum tam multa docent ut vix sit dubitandi locus." Ut Noam esse Saturnum multis argumentis constitit, sic tres Noæ filios cum Saturni tribus filiis conferenti, Hamum vel Chamum esse Jovem probabunt hæ rationes. — Japhet idem qui Neptunus. Semum Plutonis nomine detruserunt in inferos. — Lib. l. c. 2. Jam si libet etiam ad nepotes descendere; in familia Hami sive Jovis Hammonis, l'ut est Apollo Pythius; Chanaan idem qui Mercurius. — Quis non videt Nimrodum esse Bacchum? Bacchus enim idem qui , i. e. Chusi filius. Videtur et Magog esse Prometheus.

[3] Amsterdami, 1668, pp. 71, 73, 77, 97. Og est late qui a Græcis dicitur Τυφὼν, &c.

Minerva with Naamah, the sister of Tubal Cain, Vulcanus with Tubal Cain, Typhon with Og, king of Bashan, &c. Gerardus Crœsus, in his "Homerus Ebræus," maintains that the Odyssey gives the history of the patriarchs, the emigration of Lot from Sodom, and the death of Moses, while the Iliad tells the conquest and destruction of 'Jericho. *Huet*, in his "*Demonstratio Evangelica*," [1] went still further. His object was to prove the genuineness of the books of the Old Testament by showing that nearly the whole theology of the heathen nations was borrowed from Moses. Moses himself is represented by him as having assumed the most incongruous characters in the traditions of the Gentiles; and not only ancient lawgivers like Zoroaster and Orpheus, but gods like Apollo, Vulcan, and Faunus, are traced back by the learned and pious bishop to the same historical prototype. And as Moses was the prototype of the Gentile gods, his sister Miriam or his wife Zippora were supposed to have been the models of all their goddesses.[2]

You are aware that Mr. Gladstone, in his interesting and ingenious work on Homer, takes a similar view, and tries to discover in Greek mythology a

---

[1] Parisiis, 1677.

[2] Caput tertium. I. Universa propemodum Ethnicorum Theologia ex Mose, Mosisve actis aut scriptis manavit. II. Velut illa Phœnicum. Tautus idem ac Moses. III. Adonis Idem ac Moses. IV. Thammuz Ezechielis Idem ac Moses. V. Πολυώνυμος fuit Moses. VI. Marnas Gazensium Deus Idem ac Moses. — Caput quartum. VIII. Vulcanus Idem ac Moses. IX. Typhon Idem ac Moses. — Caput quintum. II. Zoroastres Idem ac Moses. — Caput octavum. III. Apollo idem ac Moses. IV. Pan Idem ac Moses. V. Priapus idem ac Moses, &c. &c. — p. 121. Cum demonstratum sit Græcanicos Deos, in ipsa Mosis persona larvata, et ascititio habitu contecta provenisse, nunc probare aggredior ex Mosis scriptionibus, verbis, doctrina, et Institutis, aliquos etiam Græcorum eorundem Deos, ac bonam Mythologiæ ipsorum partem manasse.

dimmed image of the sacred history of the Jews;
not so dimmed, however, as to prevent him from
recognizing, as he thinks, in Jupiter, Apollo, and
Minerva, the faded outlines of the three Persons of
the Trinity. In the last number of one of the best
edited quarterlies, in the "Home and Foreign Review," a Roman Catholic organ, Mr. F. A. Paley,
the well-known editor of "Euripides," advocates the
same sacred Euhemerism. "Atlas," he writes, "symbolizes the endurance of labor. He is placed by
Hesiod close to the garden of the Hesperides, and it
is *impossible to doubt* that here we have a tradition
of the garden of Eden, the golden apples guarded
by a dragon being the apple which the serpent
tempted Eve to gather, or the garden kept by an
angel with a flaming sword.[1]

Though it was felt by all unprejudiced scholars
that none of these three systems of interpretation
was in the least satisfactory, yet it seemed impossible to suggest any better solution of the problem;
and though at the present moment few, I believe,
could be found who adopt any of these three systems exclusively — who hold that the whole of Greek
mythology was invented for the sake of inculcating
moral precepts, or of promulgating physical or metaphysical doctrines, or of relating facts of ancient
history, many have acquiesced in a kind of compromise, admitting that some parts of mythology might
have a moral, others a physical, others an historical
character, but that there remained a great body of

[1] *Home and Foreign Review*, No. 7, p. 111, 1864: — "The Cyclopes were probably a race of pastoral and metal-working people from the East, characterised by their rounder faces, whence arose the story of their one eye." — *F. A. P*

fables, which yielded to no tests whatever. The riddle of the Sphinx of Mythology remained unsolved.

The first impulse to a new consideration of the mythological problem came from the study of comparative philology. Through the discovery of the ancient language of India, the so-called Sanskrit, which was due to the labors of Wilkins,[1] Sir W. Jones, and Colebrooke, some eighty years ago, and through the discovery of the intimate relationship between that language and the languages of the principal races of Europe, due to the genius of Schlegel, Humboldt, Bopp, and others, a complete revolution took place in the views commonly entertained of the ancient history of the world. I have no time to give a full account of these researches; but I may state it as a fact, suspected, I suppose, by no one *before*, and doubted by no one *after* it was enunciated, that the languages spoken by the Brahmans of India, by the followers of Zoroaster and the subjects of Darius in Persia; by the Greeks, by the Romans; by Celtic, Teutonic, and Slavonic races, were all mere varieties of one common type — stood, in fact, to each other in the same relation as French, Italian, Spanish, and Portuguese stand to each other as modern dialects of Latin. This was, indeed, "the discovery of a new world," or, if you like, the recovery of an old world. All the landmarks of what was called the ancient history of the human race had to be shifted, and it had to be explained, in some way or other, how all these languages, separated from each other by thousands of miles and thousands of years, could have originally started from one common centre.

[1] Wilkins, *Bhagavadgita*, 1785.

On this,[1] however, I cannot dwell now; and I must proceed at once to state how, after some time, it was discovered that not only the radical elements of all these languages which are called Aryan or Indo-European — not only their numerals, pronouns, prepositions, and grammatical terminations — not only their household words, such as father, mother, brother, daughter, husband, brother-in-law, cow, dog, horse, cattle, tree, ox, corn, mill, earth, sky, water, stars, and many hundreds more, were identically the same, but that each possessed the elements of a mythological phraseology, displaying the palpable traces of a common origin.

What followed from this for the Science of Mythology? Exactly the same as what followed for the Science of Language from the discovery that Sanskrit, Greek, Latin, German, Celtic, and Slavonic had all one and the same origin. Before that discovery was made, it was allowable to treat each language by itself, and any etymological explanation that was in accordance with the laws of each particular language might have been considered satisfactory. If Plato derived *theós*, the Greek word for god, from the Greek verb *théein*, to run, because the first gods were the sun and moon, always running through the sky;[2] or if Herodotus[3] derived the same word from *tithénai*, to set, because the gods set everything in order, we can find no fault with either. But if we find that the same name for god exists in Sanskrit and Latin, as *deva* and *deus*, it is clear that we cannot accept any etymology for the Greek word that is not equally

---

[1] *Lectures on the Science of Language*, First Series, p. 147 seq.
[2] Plat. *Crat.* 307 C.   [3] Her. S. 52.

applicable to the corresponding terms in Sanskrit and Latin. If we knew French only, we might derive the French *feu*, fire, from the German *Feuer*. But if we see that the same word exists in Italian as *fuoco*, in Spanish as *fuego*, it is clear that we must look for an etymology applicable to all three, which we find in the Latin *focus*, and not in the German *Feuer*. Even so thoughtful a scholar as Grimm does not seem to have perceived the absolute stringency of this rule. Before it was known that there existed in Sanskrit, Greek, Latin, and Slavonic, the same word for *name*, identical with the Gothic *namô* (gen. *namins*), it would have been allowable to derive the German word from a German root. Thus Grimm ("Grammatik," ii. 30) derived the German *Name* from the verb *nehmen*, to take. This would have been a perfectly legitimate etymology. But when it became evident that the Sanskrit *nâman* stood for *gnâ-man*, just as *nomen* for *gnomen* (cognomen, ignominia), and was derived from a verb *gnâ*, to know, it became impossible to retain the derivation of *Name* from *nehmen*, and at the same time to admit that of *nâman* from *gnâ*.[1] Each word can have but one etymology, as each living being can have but one mother.

Let us apply this to the mythological phraseology of the Aryan nations. If we had to explain only the names and fables of the Greek gods, an explanation such as that which derives the name of *Zeús* from the verb *zén*, to live, would be by no means con-

[1] Grimm, *Geschichte der Deutschen Sprache*, p. 153. Other words derived from gnâ, are notus, nobilis, gnarus, ignarus, ignoro, narro (gnarigare), gnômôn, I ken, I know, uncouth, &c.

temptible. But if we find that *Zeus* in Greek is the same word as *Dyaus* in Sanskrit, *Ju* in *Jupiter*, and *Tiu* in *Tuesday*, we perceive that no etymology would be satisfactory that did not explain all these words together. Hence it follows, that, in order to understand the origin and meaning of the names of the Greek gods, and to enter into the original intention of the fables told of each, we must not confine our view within the Greek horizon, but must take into account the collateral evidence supplied by Latin, German, Sanskrit, and Zend mythology. The key that is to open one must open all; otherwise it cannot be the right key.

Strong objections have been raised against this line of reasoning by classical scholars; and even those who have surrendered Greek etymology as useless without the aid of Sanskrit, protest against this desecration of the Greek Pantheon, and against any attempt at deriving the gods and fables of Homer and Hesiod from the monstrous idols of the Brahmans. I believe this is mainly owing to a misunderstanding. No sound scholar would ever think of deriving any Greek or Latin word from Sanskrit. Sanskrit is not the mother of Greek and Latin, as Latin is of French and Italian. Sanskrit, Greek, and Latin are sisters, varieties of one and the same type. They all point to some earlier stage when they were less different from each other than they now are; but no more. All we can say in favor of Sanskrit is, that it is the eldest sister; that it has retained many words and forms less changed and corrupted than Greek and Latin. The more primitive character and transparent structure of Sanskrit have naturally endeared it to the student of language, but they have not blinded him to the fact, that on many points Greek and Latin — nay, Gothic and Celtic — have preserved primitive features which Sanskrit has lost. Greek is coördinate with, not subordinate to Sanskrit; and the only distinction which Sanskrit is entitled to claim is that which Austria used to claim in the German Confederation — to be the first among equals, *primus inter pares.*

There is, however, another reason which has made any comparison of Greek and Hindu gods more particularly distasteful to classical scholars. At the very beginning of Sanskrit philology attempts were made by no less a person than Sir W. Jones[1] at identifying the deities of the modern Hindu mythology with those of Homer. This was done in the most arbitrary manner, and has brought any attempt of the same kind into deserved disrepute among sober critics. Sir W. Jones is not responsible, indeed, for such comparisons as *Cupid* and *Dipuc* (dipaka); but to compare, as he does, modern Hindu gods, such as Vishṇu, Śiva, or Kṛishṇa, with the gods of Homer was indeed like comparing modern Hindustáni with ancient Greek. Trace Hindustáni back to Sanskrit, and it will be possible then to compare it with Greek and Latin; but not otherwise. The same in mythology. Trace the modern system of Hindu mythology back to its earliest form, and there will then be some

[1] Sir W. Jones, *On the Gods of Greece, Italy, and India.* (Works, vol. I. p. 229.) He compares Janus with Ganeśa, Saturn with Manu Satyavrata, nay, with Noah; Ceres with Śrí, Jupiter with Divaspati and with Siva (τριοφθαλμος = trilochana), Bacchus with Bágísa, Juno with Párvatí, Mars with Skanda, nay, with the Secander of Persia, Minerva with Durgá and Sarasvatí, Osiris and Isis with Iśvara and Isí, Dionysos with Ráma, Apollo with Krishna, Vulcan with Pávaka and Viśvakarman, Mercury with Nárada, Hekate with Kálí.

reasonable hope of discovering a family likeness between the sacred names worshipped by the Aryans of India and the Aryans of Greece.

This was impossible at the time of Sir William Jones; it is even now but partially possible. Though Sanskrit has now been studied for three generations, the most ancient work of Sanskrit literature, the Rig-Veda, is still a book with seven seals. The wish expressed by Otfried Müller in 1825, in his " Prolegomena to a Scientific Mythology," "Oh that we had an intelligible translation of the Veda!" is still unfulfilled; and though of late years nearly all Sanskrit scholars have devoted their energies to the elucidation of Vedic literature, many years are still required before Otfried Müller's desire can be realized. Now Sanskrit literature without the Veda is like Greek literature without Homer, like Jewish literature without the Bible, like Mohammedan literature without the Koran; and you will easily understand how, if we do not know the most ancient form of Hindu religion and mythology, it is premature to attempt any comparison between the gods of India and the gods of any other country. What was wanted as the only safe foundation, not only of Sanskrit literature, but of Comparative Mythology,—nay, of Comparative Philology,—was an edition of the most ancient document of Indian literature, Indian religion, Indian language—an edition of the *Rig-Veda*. Eight of the ten books of the Rig-Veda have now been published in the original, together with an ample Indian commentary, and there is every prospect of the two remaining books passing through the press in four or five years. But, after the text and commentary of the Rig-Veda are published, the great task of translating, or, I should rather say, deciphering these ancient hymns still remains. There are, indeed, two translations; one by a Frenchman, the late M. Langlois, the other by the late Professor Wilson; but the former, though very ingenious, is mere guess-work; the latter is a reproduction, and not always a faithful reproduction, of the commentary of Sâyana, which I have published. It shows us how the ancient hymns were misunderstood by later grammarians, and theologians, and philosophers; but it does not attempt a critical restoration of the original sense of these simple and primitive hymns by the only process by which it can be effected, — by a comparison of every passage in which the same words occur. This process of deciphering is a slow one; yet, through the combined labors of various scholars, some progress has been made, and some insight been gained into the mythological phraseology of the Vedic Rishis. One thing we can clearly see, that the same position which Sanskrit, as the most primitive, most transparent of the Aryan dialects, holds in the science of language, the Veda and its most primitive, most transparent system of religion, will hold in the science of mythology. In the hymns of the Rig-Veda we still have the last chapter of the real Theogony of the Aryan races: we just catch a glimpse, behind the scenes, of the agencies which were at work in producing that magnificent stage-effect witnessed in the drama of the Olympian gods. There, in the Veda, the Sphinx of Mythology still utters a few words to betray her own secret, and shows us that it is man, that it is human thought and human language combined, which naturally and inevitably produced that strange conglomerate of ancient fable which has perplexed all rational thinkers, from the days of Xenophanes to our own time.

I shall try to make my meaning clearer. You will see that a great point is gained in comparative mythology if we succeed in discovering the original meaning of the names of the gods. If we knew, for instance, what *Athene*, or *Here*, or *Apollo* meant in Greek, we should have something firm to stand on or to start from, and be able to follow more securely the later development of these names. We know, for instance, that *Selene* in Greek means moon, and knowing this, we at once understand the myths that she is the sister of *Helios*, for *helios* means sun; that she is the sister of *Eos*, for *eos* means dawn;— and if another poet calls her the sister of *Euryphaëssa*, we are not much perplexed, for *euryphaëssa*, meaning wide-shining, can only be another name for the dawn. If she is represented with two horns, we at once remember the two horns of the moon; and if she is said to have become the mother of *Erse* by Zeus, we again perceive that *erse* means *dew*, and that to call Erse the daughter of Zeus and *Selene* was no more than if we, in our more matter-of-fact language, say that there is dew after a moonlight night.

Now one great advantage in the Veda is that many of the names of the gods are still intelligible, are used, in fact, not only as proper names, but likewise as appellative nouns. *Agni*, one of their principal gods, means clearly fire; it is used in that sense; it is the same word as the Latin *ignis*. Hence we have a right to explain his other names, and all that is told of him, as originally meant for fire. *Váyu* or *Váta* means clearly *wind*, *Marut* means *storm*, *Parjanya* rain, *Savitar* the sun, *Ushas*, as well as its synonyms, *Urvaśî*, *Ahaná*, *Saranyú*, means *dawn*; *Prithivî* earth, *Dyávápṛithivî*, *heaven* and *earth*. Other divine names in the Veda which are no longer used as appellatives, become easily intelligible, because they are used as synonyms of more intelligible names (such as *urvaśî* for *ushas*), or because they receive light from other languages, such as *Varuna*, clearly the same word as the Greek *ouranós*, and meaning originally the sky.

Another advantage which the Veda offers is this, that in its numerous hymns we can still watch the gradual growth of the gods, the slow transition of appellatives into proper names, the first tentative steps towards personification. The Vedic Pantheon is held together by the loosest ties of family relationship; nor is there as yet any settled supremacy like that of Zeus among the gods of Homer. Every god is conceived as supreme, or at least as inferior to no other god, at the time that he is praised or invoked by the Vedic poets; and the feeling that the various deities are but different names, different conceptions of that Incomprehensible Being which no thought can reach, and no language express, is not yet quite extinct in the minds of some of the more thoughtful Rishis.

LECTURE X.

JUPITER, THE SUPREME ARYAN GOD.

THERE are few mistakes so widely spread and so firmly established as that which makes us confound the religion and the mythology of the ancient nations of the world. How mythology arises, necessarily and naturally, I tried to explain in my former Lectures, and we saw that, as an affection or disorder of language, mythology may infect every part of the intellectual life of man. True it is that no ideas are more liable to mythological disease than religious ideas, because they transcend those regions of our experience within which language has its natural origin, and must therefore, according to their very nature, be satisfied with metaphorical expressions. Eye hath not seen, nor ear heard, neither hath it entered into the heart of man.[1] Yet even the religions of the ancient nations are by no means inevitably and altogether mythological. On the contrary, as a diseased frame presupposes a healthy frame, so a mythological religion presupposes, I believe, a healthy religion. Before the Greeks could call the sky, or the sun, or the moon *gods*, it was absolutely necessary that they should have framed to themselves some idea of the godhead. We cannot speak of King Solomon unless we first know

[1] 1 Cor. ii. 9. Is. lxiv. 4.

what, in a general way, is meant by King, nor could a Greek speak of gods in the plural before he had realized, in some way or other, the general predicate of the godhead. Idolatry arises naturally when people say "The sun is god," i. e. when they apply the predicate god to that which has no claim to it. But the more interesting point is to find out what the ancients meant to predicate when they called the sun or the moon gods; and until we have a clear conception of this, we shall never enter into the true spirit of their religion.

It is strange, however, that, while we have endless books on the mythology of the Greeks and Romans, we have hardly any on their religion, and most people have brought themselves to imagine that what we call religion,—our trust in an all-wise, all-powerful, eternal Being, the Ruler of the world, whom we approach in prayer and meditation, to whom we commit all our cares, and whose presence we feel not only in the outward world, but also in the warning voice within our hearts,—that all this was unknown to the heathen world, and that their religion consisted simply in the fables of Jupiter and Juno, of Apollo and Minerva, of Venus and Bacchus. Yet this is not so. Mythology has encroached on ancient religion, it has at some times wellnigh choked its very life; yet through the rank and poisonous vegetation of mythic phraseology we may always catch a glimpse of that original stem round which it creeps and winds itself, and without which it could not enjoy even that parasitical existence which has been mistaken for independent vitality.

A few quotations will explain what I mean by

ancient religion, as independent of ancient mythology. Homer who, together with Hesiod, made the theogony or the history of the gods for the Greeks,— a saying of Herodotus, which contains more truth than is commonly supposed,— Homer, whose every page teems with mythology, nevertheless allows us many an insight into the inner religious life of his age. What did the swineherd Eumaios know of the intricate Olympian theogony? Had he ever heard the name of the Charites or of the Harpyias? Could he have told who was the father of Aphrodite, who were her husbands and her children? I doubt it; and when Homer introduces him to us, speaking of this life and the higher powers that rule it, Eumaios knows only of just gods, "who hate cruel deeds, but honor justice and the righteous works of man."[1]

His whole view of life is built up on a complete trust in the Divine government of the world, without any such artificial supports as the Erinys, the Nemesis, or Moira.

"Eat," says the swineherd to Ulysses, "and enjoy what is here,[2] for God will grant one thing, but another he will refuse, whatever he will in his mind, for he can do all things." (Od. xiv. 444; x. 306.)

This surely is religion, and it is religion untainted by mythology. Again, the prayer of the female slave, grinding corn in the house of Ulysses, is religion in the truest sense. "Father Zeus," she says, "thou who rulest over gods and men, surely thou hast just

[1] Od. xiv. 83.
[2] There is nothing to make us translate θεός by a god rather than by God; but even if we translated it a god, this could here only be meant for Zeus. (Cf. Od. iv. 236.) Cf. Welcker, p. 180.

thundered from the starry heaven, and there is no cloud anywhere. Thou showest this as a sign to some one. Fulfil now, even to me, miserable wretch! the prayer which I may utter." When Telemachos is afraid to approach Nestor, and declares to Mentor that he does not know *what* to say,[1] does not Mentor or Athene encourage him in words that might easily be translated into the language of our own religion? " Telemochos," she says, " some things thou wilt thyself perceive in thy mind, and others a divine spirit will prompt; for I do not believe that thou wast born and brought up without the will of the gods."

The omnipresence and omniscience of the Divine Being is expressed by Hesiod in language slightly, yet not altogether, mythological: —

πάντα ἰδὼν Διὸς ὀφθαλμὸς καὶ πάντα νοήσας,[2]
The eye of Zeus, which sees all and knows all;

and the conception of Homer that " the gods themselves come to our cities in the garb of strangers, to watch the wanton and the orderly conduct of men,"[3] though expressed in the language peculiar to the childhood of man, might easily be turned into our own sacred phraseology. Anyhow, we may call this

[1] *Od.* iii. 26:—
Τηλέμαχ', ἄλλα μὲν αὐτὸς ἐνὶ φρεσὶ σῇσι νοήσεις,
Ἄλλα δὲ καὶ δαίμων ὑποθήσεται· οὐ γὰρ ὀΐω
Οὔ σε θεῶν ἀέκητι γενέσθαι τε τραφέμεν τε.
Homer uses θεός and δαίμων for God.
[2] *Erga,* 267.
[3] *Od.* xvii. 483:—
Ἀντίνο', οὐ μὲν κάλ' ἔβαλες δύστηνον ἀλήτην,
Οὐλόμεν', εἰ δή που τις ἐπουράνιος θεός ἐστιν.
Καί τε θεοὶ ξείνοισι ἐοικότες ἀλλοδαποῖσιν,
Παντοῖοι τελέθοντες, ἐπιστρωφῶσι πόληας,
Ἀνθρώπων ὕβριν τε καὶ εὐνομίην ἐφορῶντες.

religion — ancient, primitive, natural religion: imperfect, no doubt, yet deeply interesting, and not without a divine afflatus. How different is the undoubting trust of the ancient poets in the ever-present watchfulness of the gods, from the language of later Greek philosophy, as expressed, for instance, by Protagoras. "Of the gods," he says, "I am not able to know either that they are or that they are not; for many things prevent us from knowing it, the darkness and the shortness of human life."[1]

The gods of Homer, though, in their mythological aspect, represented as weak, easily deceived, and led astray by the lowest passions, are nevertheless, in the more reverend language of religion, endowed with nearly all the qualities which we claim for a divine and perfect Being. The phrase which forms the key-note in many of the speeches of Odysseus, though thrown in only as it were parenthetically,

θεοὶ δέ τε πάντα ἴσασιν, "the Gods know all things,"[2]

gives us more of the real feeling of the untold millions among whom the idioms of a language grow up, than all the tales of the tricks played by Juno to Jupiter, or by Mars to Vulcan. At critical moments, when the deepest feelings of the human heart are stirred, the old Greeks of Homer seem suddenly to drop all learned and mythological metaphor, and to fall back on the universal language of true religion. Everything they feel is ordered by the immortal gods; and though they do not rise to the conception of a Divine Providence which ordereth all things by

[1] Welcker, *Griechische Götterlehre*, p. 245.
[2] *Od.* iv. 379, 468.

eternal laws, no event, however small, seems to
happen in the Iliad in which the poet does not recognize the active interference of a divine power. This
interference, if clothed in mythological language,
assumes, it is true, the actual or bodily presence of
one of the gods, whether Apollo, or Athene, or
Aphrodite; yet let us observe that Zeus himself, the
god of gods, never descends to the battle-field of
Troy. He was the true god of the Greeks before
he became enveloped in the clouds of Olympian
mythology; and in many a passage where *theós* is
used, we may without irreverence translate it by
God. Thus, when Diomedes exhorts the Greeks to
fight till Troy is taken, he finishes his speech with
these words: "Let all flee home; but we two, I and
Sthenelos, will fight till we see the end of Troy : *for
we came with God.*"[1] Even if we translated "for
we came with a god," the sentiment would still be
religious, not mythological; though of course it
might easily be translated into mythological phraseology, if we said that Athene, in the form of a bird,
had fluttered round the ships of the Greeks. Again,
what can be more natural and more truly pious than
the tone of resignation with which Nausikaa addresses the shipwrecked Ulysses? "Zeus," she says,
for she knows no better name, "Zeus himself, the
Olympian, distributes happiness to the good and the
bad, to every one, as he pleases. And to thee also
he probably has sent this, and you ought by all
means to bear it." Lastly, let me read the famous
line, placed by Homer in the mouth of Peisistratos,
the son of Nestor, when calling on Athene, as the

[1] *Il.* ix. 49.

companion of Telemachos, and on Telemachos himself, to pray to the gods before taking their meal: "After thou hast offered thy libation and prayed, as it is meet, give to him also afterwards the goblet of honey-sweet wine to pour out his libation, because I believe that he also prays to the immortals, *for all men yearn after the gods.*"[1]

It might be objected that no truly religious sentiment was possible as long as the human mind was entangled in the web of polytheism; that god, in fact, in its true sense, is a word which admits of no plural, and changes its meaning as soon as it assumes the terminations of that number. The Latin *ædes* means, in the singular, a sanctuary, but in the plural it assumes the meaning of a common dwelling-house; and thus *theós*, too, in the plural, is supposed to be divested of that sacred and essentially divine character which it claims in the singular. When, moreover, such names as Zeus, Apollo, and Athene are applied to the Divine Being, religion is considered to be out of the question, and hard words, such as idolatry and devil-worship, are applied to the prayers and praises of the early believers. There is a great amount of incontestable truth in all this, but I cannot help thinking that full justice has never been done to the ancient religions of the world, not even to those of the Greeks and Romans, who, in so many other respects, are acknowledged by us as our teachers and models. The first contact between Christianity and the heathen religions was necessarily one of uncompromising hostility. It was the duty of the Apostles and the early Christians in gen-

[1] πάντες δὲ θεῶν χατέουσ' ἄνθρωποι. — *Od.* III. 48.

eral to stand forth in the name of the only true God, and to prove to the world that their God had nothing in common with the idols worshipped at Athens and at Ephesus. It was the duty of the early converts to forswear all allegiance to their former deities, and if they could not at once bring themselves to believe that the gods whom they had worshipped had no existence at all, except in the imagination of their worshippers, they were naturally led on to ascribe to them a kind of demoniacal nature, and to curse them as the offspring of that new principle of Evil[1] with which they had become acquainted in the doctrines of the early Church. In St. Augustine's learned arguments against paganism, the heathen gods are throughout treated as real beings, as demons who had the power of doing real mischief.[2] I was told by a missionary, that among his converts in South Africa he discovered some who still prayed to their heathen deities; and when remonstrated with, told him that they prayed to them in order to avert their wrath; and that, though their idols could not hurt so good a man as he was, they might inflict serious harm on their former worshippers. Only now and then, as in the case of the *Fatum*,[3]

[1] Thus in the *Old Testament* strange gods are called devils (Deut. xxxii. 17), "They sacrificed unto devils, not to God; to gods whom they knew not, to new gods that came newly up, whom your fathers feared not."

[2] *De Civitate Dei*, ii. 25: Maligni isti spiritus, &c. Noxii dæmones quos illi deos putantes colendos et venerandos arbitrabantur, &c. *Ibid.* viii. 22: (Credendum dæmones) esse spiritus nocendi cupidissimos, a justitia penitus alienos, superbia tumidos, invidentia livklos, fallacia callidos, qui in hoc quidem aëre habitant, quia de cœli superioris sublimitate dejecti, merito irregressibilis transgressionis in hoc sibi congruo carcere prædamnati sunt.

[3] *De Civitate Dei*, v. 9: Omnia vero fato fieri non dicimus, imo nulla fieri fato dicimus, quoniam fati nomen ubi solet a loquentibus poni, id est in constitutione siderum cum quisque conceptus aut natus est (quoniam res

St. Augustine acknowledges that it is a mere name, and that if it is taken in its etymological sense, namely, as that which has once been spoken by God, and is therefore immutable, it might be retained. Nay, the same thoughtful writer goes even so far as to admit that the mere multiplicity of divine names might be tolerated.[1] Speaking of the goddess Fortuna, who is also called Felicitas, he says: "Why should two names be used? But this can be tolerated: for one and the same thing is not uncommonly called by two names. But what," he adds, "is the meaning of having different temples, different altars, different sacrifices?" Yet through the whole of St. Augustine's work, and through all the works of earlier Christian divines, as far as I can judge, there runs the same spirit of hostility blinding them to all that may be good, and true, and sacred, and magnifying all that is bad, false, and corrupt in the ancient religions of mankind. Only the Apostles and immediate disciples of Our Lord venture to speak in a different and, no doubt, in a more truly Christian spirit of the old forms of worship.[2] For

---

ipsa inaniter asseritur), nihil valere monstramus. Ordinem autem causarum, ubi voluntas Dei plurimum potest, neque negamus, neque fati vocabulo nuncupamus, nisi forte ut fatum a fando dictum intelligamus, id est, a loquendo: non enim abnuere possumus esse scriptum in literis sanctis, *Semel locutus est Deus, duo hæc audivi; quoniam potestas est Dei, et tibi, Domine, misericordia, quia tu reddes unicuique secundum opera ejus.* Quod enim dictum est, *semel locutus est*, intelligitur immobiliter, hoc est, incommutabiliter est locutus, sicut novit incommutabiliter omnia quæ futura sunt, et quæ ipse facturus est. Hac itaque ratione possemus a fando fatum appellare, nisi hoc nomen jam in alia re soleret intelligi, quo corda hominum nolumus inclinari.

[1] *De Civ. Dei*, iv. 18.
[2] Cf. Stanley's *The Bible: its Form and its Substance*, Three Sermons preached before the University of Oxford, 1863.

even though we restrict "the sundry times and divers manners in which God spake in times past unto the fathers by the prophets" to the Jewish race, yet there are other passages which clearly show that the Apostles recognized a divine purpose and supervision even in the "times of ignorance," at which, as they express it, "God winked."[1] Nay, they go so far as to say that God in times past *suffered* (εἴασε)[2] all nations to walk in their own ways. And what can be more convincing, more powerful than the language of St. Paul at Athens?[3] —

"For as I passed by, and beheld your devotions, I found an altar with this inscription, To the Unknown God. Whom therefore ye ignorantly worship, him declare I unto you.

"God that made the world and all things therein, seeing that he is Lord of heaven and earth, dwelleth not in temples made with hands;

"Neither is worshipped with men's hands, as though he needed any thing, seeing he giveth to all life, and breath, and all things;

"And hath made of one blood all nations of men for to dwell on all the face of the earth, and hath determined the times before appointed, and the bounds of their habitation;

"That they should seek the Lord, if haply they might feel after him, and find him, though he be not far from every one of us:

"For in him we live, and move, and have our being; as certain also of your own poets have said, For we are also his offspring."[4]

---

[1] *Acts* xv.   [2] *Acts* xiv. 16.   [3] *Acts* xvii. 23.
[4] Kleanthes says, ἐκ τοῦ γὰρ γένος ἐσμέν; Aratus, πατὴρ ἀνδρῶν . . . τοῦ γὰρ γένος ἐσμέν (Welcker, *Griechische Götterlehre*, pp. 183, 246).

These are truly Christian words, this is the truly Christian spirit in which we ought to study the ancient religions of the world: not as independent of God, not as the work of an evil spirit, as mere idolatry and devil-worship, not even as mere human fancy, but as a preparation, as a necessary part in the education of the human race, — as a "seeking the Lord, if haply they might feel after him." There *was* a *fulness* of time, both for Jews and for Gentiles, and we must learn to look upon the ages that preceded it as necessary, under a divine purpose, for filling that appointed measure, for good and for evil, which would make the two great national streams in the history of mankind, the Jewish and the Gentile, the Semitic and the Aryan, reach their appointed measure, and overflow, so that they might mingle together and both be carried on by a new current, "the well of water springing up into everlasting life."

And if in this spirit we search through the sacred ruins of the ancient world, we shall be surprised to find how much more of true religion there is in what is called Heathen Mythology than we expected. Only, as St. Augustine said, we must not mind the names, strange and uncouth as they may sound on our ears. *We* are no longer swayed by the just fears which filled the hearts of early Christian writers; we can afford to be generous to Jupiter and to his worshippers. Nay, we ought to learn to treat the ancient religions with some of the same reverence and awe with which we approach the study of the Jewish and of our own. "The religious instinct," as Schelling says, "should be honored even in dark

and confused mysteries." We must only guard
against a temptation to which an eminent writer
and statesman of this country has sometimes yielded
in his work on Homer, we must not attempt to find
Christian ideas — ideas peculiar to Christianity —
in the primitive faith of mankind. But, on the
other hand, we may boldly look for those fundamental religious conceptions on which Christianity
itself is built up, and without which, as its natural
and historical support, Christianity itself could never
have been what it is. The more we go back, the
more we examine the earliest germs of every religion, the purer, I believe, we shall find the conceptions
of the Deity, the nobler the purposes of each founder
of a new worship. But the more we go back, the
more helpless also shall we find human language in
its endeavors to express what of all things was most
difficult to express. The history of religion is in one
sense a history of language. Many of the ideas
embodied in the language of the Gospel would have
been incomprehensible and inexpressible alike, if we
imagine that by some miraculous agency they had
been communicated to the primitive inhabitants of
the earth. Even at the present moment missionaries find that they have first to educate their savage
pupils, that is to say, to raise them to that level of
language and thought which had been reached by
Greeks, Romans, and Jews at the beginning of our
era, before the words and ideas of Christianity assume any reality to their minds, and before their
own native language becomes strong enough for the
purposes of translation. Words and thoughts here,
as elsewhere, go together; and from one point of

view the true history of religion would, as I said, be neither more nor less than an account of the various attempts at expressing the Inexpressible.

I shall endeavor to make this clear by at least one instance, and I shall select for it the most important name in the religion and mythology of the Aryan nations, the name of *Zeus*, the god of gods (*theòs theôn*), as Plato calls him.

Let us consider, first of all, the fact, which cannot be doubted, and which, if fully appreciated, will be felt to be pregnant with the most startling and the most instructive lessons of antiquity, — the fact, I mean, that Zeus, the most sacred name in Greek mythology, is the same word as *Dyaus*[1] in Sanskrit, *Jovis*[2] or *Ju* in *Jupiter* in Latin, *Tiw* in Anglo-Saxon, preserved in *Tiwsdæg*, *Tuesday*, the day of the Eddic god *Týr*; *Zio* in Old High-German.

This word was framed once, and once only: it was not borrowed by the Greeks from the Hindus, nor by the Romans and Germans from the Greeks. It must have existed before the ancestors of those primeval races became separate in language and religion, — before they left their common pastures, to migrate to the right hand and to the left, till the hurdles of their sheepfolds grew into the walls of the great cities of the world.

---

[1] *Dyaus* in Sanskrit is the nominative singular; *Dyu* the inflectional base. I use both promiscuously, though it would perhaps be better always to use *Dyu*.

[2] *Jovis* in the nom. occurs in the verse of Ennius, giving the names of the twelve Roman deities: —

Juno, Vesta, Minerva, Ceres, Diana, Venus, Mars,
Mercurius, Jovi', Neptunus, Vulcanus, Apollo.

Dius in *Dius Fidius*, i. e. Ζεὺς πίστιος, belongs to the same class of words. Cf. Hartung, *Religion der Römer*, ii. 44.

Here, then, in this venerable word, we may look for some of the earliest religious thoughts of our race, expressed and enshrined within the imperishable walls of a few simple letters. What did *Dyu* mean in Sanskrit? How is it used there? What was the root which could be forced to reach to the highest aspirations of the human mind? We should find it difficult to discover the radical or predicative meaning of *Zeus* in Greek; but *dyaus* in Sanskrit tells its own tale. It is derived from the same root which yields the verb *dyut*, and this verb means *to beam*. A root of this rich and expansive meaning would be applicable to many conceptions: the dawn, the sun, the sky, the day, the stars, the eyes, the ocean, and the meadow, might all be spoken of as bright, gleaming, smiling, blooming, sparkling. But in the actual and settled language of India, *dyu*, as a noun, means principally *sky* and *day*. Before the ancient hymns of the Veda had disclosed to us the earliest forms of Indian thought and language, the Sanskrit noun *dyu* was hardly known as the name of an Indian deity, but only as a feminine, and as the recognized term for sky. The fact that *dyu* remained in common use as a name for *sky* was sufficient to explain why *dyu*, in Sanskrit, should never have assumed that firm mythological character which belongs to Zeus in Greek; for as long as a word retains the distinct signs of its original import and is applied as an appellative to visible objects, it does not easily lend itself to the metamorphic processes of early mythology. As *dyu* in Sanskrit continued to mean *sky*, though as a feminine only, it was difficult for the same word, even as a masculine, to become the germ of any very important mythological formations. Language must die before it can enter into a new stage of mythological life.

Even in the Veda, where *dyu* occurs as a masculine, as an active noun, and discloses the same germs of thought which in Greece and Rome grew into the name of the supreme god of the firmament, *Dyu*, the deity, the lord of heaven, the ancient god of light, never assumes any powerful mythological vitality, never rises to the rank of a supreme deity. In the early lists of Vedic deities, Dyu is not included, and the real representative of Jupiter in the Veda is not Dyu, but *Indra*, a name of Indian growth, and unknown in any other independent branch of Aryan language. *Indra* was another conception of the bright sunny sky, but partly because its etymological meaning was obscured, partly through the more active poetry and worship of certain Rishis, this name gained a complete ascendancy over that of Dyu, and nearly extinguished the memory in India of one of the earliest, if not *the* earliest, name by which the Aryans endeavored to express their first conception of the Deity. Originally, however, — and this is one of the most important discoveries which we owe to the study of the Veda, — originally *Dyu* was the bright heavenly deity in India as well as in Greece.

Let us examine, first, some passages of the Veda in which *dyu* is used as an appellative in the sense of sky. We read (Rv. i. 161, 14): " The Maruts (storms) go about in the sky, Agni (fire) on earth, the wind goes in the air; Varuṇa goes about in the waters of the sea," &c. Here *dyu* means the sky, as much as *prithivî* means the earth, and *antariksha* the air. The sky is frequently spoken of together with the earth, and the air is placed between the two (antariksha). We find expressions such as "*heaven and earth*";[1] *air and heaven*;[2] and *heaven, air, and earth.*[3] The sky, *dyu*, is called the third, as compared with the earth, and we meet in the Atharva-Veda with expressions such as "in the third heaven from hence."[4] This, again, gave rise to the idea of three heavens. " The heavens," we read, " the air, and the earth (all in the plural) cannot contain the majesty of Indra;" and in one passage the poet prays that his glory may be " exalted as if heaven were piled on heaven."[5]

Another meaning which belongs to *dyu* in the Veda is day.[6] So many suns are so many days, and even in English *yestersun* was used instead of *yesterday* as late as the time of Dryden. *Divâ*, an instrumental case with the accent on the first syllable, means by day, and is used together with *nāktam*,[7] by night. Other expressions, such as *divé dive*, *dyávi dyávi*, or *ánu dyûn*, are of frequent occurrence to signify day by day.[8]

[1] Rv. I. 39, 4: nahí .... ádhi dyávi ná bhûmyâm.
[2] Rv. vi. 50, 13: antárikshe .... dyávî.
[3] Rv. viii. 6, 15: na dyāvaḥ indram ójasâ ná antárikshâṇi vajríṇam ná vîryachanta bhûmayaḥ.
[4] Ath. Veda, v. 4, 3: tritíyasyâm itáḥ diví (fem.).
[5] Rv. vii. 24, 5: diví iva dyâm ádhi nah śrómatam dhâḥ.
[6] Rv. vi. 24, 7: nú yám jinanti śarádah ná māsáḥ ná dyâvaḥ Índram avakarsáyanti (Him whom harvests do not age, nor moons; Indra, whom days do not wither).
Rv. vii. 66, 11: ví yé dadhúḥ śarádam mấsam át áhar.
[7] Rv. I. 1:III, 5.
[8] Rv. I. 112, 25: dyúbhiḥ aktúbhiḥ pári pátam asmín. Protect us by day and by night, ye Aśvin.

But besides these two meanings *Dyu* clearly conveys a different idea as used in some few verses of the Veda. There are invocations in which the name of Dyu stands first, and where he is invoked together with other beings who are always treated as gods. For instance (Rv. vi. 51, 5):—

"Dyaus (Sky), father, and Prithivi (Earth), kind mother, Agni (Fire), brother, ye Vasus (Bright ones), have mercy upon us!"[1]

Here Sky, Earth, and Fire are classed together as divine powers, but Dyaus, it should be remarked, occupies the first place. This is the same in other passages where a long list of gods is given, and where Dyaus, if his name is mentioned at all, holds always a prominent place.[2]

It should further be remarked that Dyaus is most frequently called *pitar* or *father*, so much so that *Dyaushpitar* in the Veda becomes almost as much one word as Jupiter in Latin. In one passage (i. 191, 6), we read, "Dyaus is father, Prithivi, the earth, your mother, Soma your brother, Aditi your sister." In another passage (iv. 1, 10),[3] he is called Dyaus the father, the creator.

We now have to consider some still more important passages in which *Dyu* and *Indra* are mentioned

---

[1] Dyaùs pitar prithivi mâtar ádhruk.
Ζεῦ(ς), πατὲρ πλασεία μῆτερ άρρεκ(ές)
Agne bhrâtar vasavah mrijâta nah.
Ignis frater ——— be mild nos.

[2] Rv. l. 136, 6: Námah Divé brihaté ródasibhyâm, then follow Mitrá, Váruṇa, Indra, Agni, Aryamán, Bhága. Cf. vi. 50, 13. Dyaùh devébhih prithivi samudraíh. Here, though Dyaus does not stand first, he is distinguished as being mentioned at the head of the devas, or bright gods.

[3] Dyaùah pitá janitá.
Ζεύς, πατήρ, γενετήρ.

together as father and son, like *Kronos* and *Zeus*, only that in India *Dyu* is the father, *Indra* the son; and *Dyu* has at last to surrender his supremacy which *Zeus* in Greek retains to the end. In a hymn addressed to *Indra*, and to Indra as the most powerful god, we read (Rv. iv. 17, 4): "*Dyu*, thy parent, was reputed strong, the maker of Indra was mighty in his works; he (who) begat the heavenly Indra, armed with the thunderbolt, who is immovable, as the earth, from his seat."

Here, then, *Dyu* would seem to be above Indra, just as Zeus is above Apollo. But there are other passages in this very hymn which clearly place *Indra* above *Dyu*, and thus throw an important light on the mental process which made the Hindus look on the son, on Indra,[1] the *Jupiter pluvius*, the conquering light of heaven, as more powerful, more exalted, than the bright sky from whence he arose. The hymn begins with asserting the greatness of Indra, which even heaven and earth had to acknowledge; and at Indra's birth, both heaven and earth are said to have trembled. Now heaven and earth, it must be remembered, are, mythologically speaking, the father and mother of Indra, and if we read in the same hymn that Indra "somewhat excels his mother and his father who begat him,"[2] this can only be meant to express the same idea, namely, that the active god

---

[1] *Indra*, a name peculiar to India, admits of but one etymology, i. e. it must be derived from the same root, whatever that may be, which in Sanskrit yielded *indu*, drop, sap. It meant originally the giver of rain, the Jupiter pluvius, a deity in India more often present to the mind of the worshipper than any other. Cf. Benfey, *Orient und Occident*, vol. I. p. 49.

[2] Iv. 17, 12: Kíyat svit Índrah ádhi etí mâtúh Kíyat pitúh janitúh yáh jajâna.

who resides in the sky, who rides on the clouds, and hurls his bolt at the demons of darkness, impresses the mind of man at a later time more powerfully than the serene expanse of heaven and the wide earth beneath. Yet *Dyu* also must formerly have been conceived as a more active, I might say, a more dramatic god, for the poet actually compares Indra, when destroying his enemies, with Dyu as wielding the thunderbolt.[1]

If with this hymn we compare passages of other hymns, we see even more clearly how the idea of Indra, the conquering hero of the thunderstorm, led with the greatest ease to the admission of a father who, though reputed strong before Indra, was excelled in prowess by his son. If the dawn is called *divijâh*, born in the sky, the very adjective would become the title-deed to prove her the daughter of Dyu; and so she is called. The same with Indra. He rose from the sky; hence the sky was his father. He rose from the horizon where the sky seems to embrace the earth; hence the earth must be his mother. As sky and earth had been invoked before as beneficent powers, they would the more easily assume the paternity of Indra; though even if they had not before been worshipped as gods, Indra himself, as born of heaven and earth, would have raised these parents to the rank of deities. Thus *Kronos* in the later Greek mythology, the father of Zeus, owes his very existence to his son, namely, to Zeus *Kronion*, Kronion meaning originally the son of time, or the ancient of days.[2] *Uranos*, on the contrary,

---

[1] Iv. 17, 13: vibhanjanûh asanimân iva dyaûh.
[2] Welcker, *Griechische Götterlehre*, p. 144. Zeus is also called Kronion. *Ibid.* pp. 150, 155, 156.

though suggested by *Uranion*, the heavenly, had evidently, like Heaven and Earth, enjoyed an independent existence before he was made the father of Kronos, and the grandfather of Zeus; for we find his prototype in the Vedic god *Varuṇa*. But while in India *Dyu* was raised to be the father of a new god, *Indra*, and by being thus raised became really degraded, or, if we may say so, shelved, Zeus in Greece always remained the supreme god, till the dawn of Christianity put an end to the mythological phraseology of the ancient world.

We read, i. 131, 1:[1] —

"Before Indra the divine Dyu bowed, before Indra bowed the great Prithivi."

Again, i. 61, 9:[2] "The greatness of Indra indeed exceeded the heavens (i. e. dyaus), the earth, and the air."

i. 54, 4:[3] "Thou hast caused the top of heaven (of dyaus) to shake."

Expressions like these, though no doubt meant to realize a conception of natural phenomena, were sure to produce mythological phraseology, and if in India *Dyu* did not grow to the same proportions as Zeus in Greece, the reason is simply that *dyu* retained throughout too much of its appellative power, and that Indra, the new name and the new god, absorbed all the channels that could have supported the life of Dyu.[4]

Let us see now how the same conception of Dyu, as the god of light and heaven, grew and spread in

[1] Indrâya íd dyaúḥ ásuraḥ ánamnata indrâya mahî prithivî várimabhíḥ.
[2] Asyá ít evá prá ririche mahitvám diváḥ prithivyáḥ pári antárikshát.
[3] Tvám diváḥ bṛihatáḥ sânu kopayaḥ.
[4] Cf. Buttmann, *Ueber Apollon und Artemis, Mythologus,* I. p. 8.

Greece. And here let us observe, what has been pointed out by others, but has never been placed in so clear a light as of late by M. Bertrand in his lucid work, "Sur les Dieux Protecteurs" (1858), — that whereas all other deities in Greece are more or less local or tribal, Zeus was known in every village and to every clan. He is at home on Ida, on Olympus, at Dodona. While Poseidon drew to himself the Æolian family, Apollo the Dorian, Athene the Ionian, there was one more powerful god for all the sons of Hellen, Dorians, Æolians, Ionians, Achæans, the Panhellenic Zeus. That Zeus meant sky we might have guessed perhaps, even if no traces of the word had been preserved in Sanskrit. The prayer of the Athenians—

ὗσον ὗσον, ὦ φίλε Ζεῦ, κατὰ τῆς ἀρούρας τῶν Ἀθηναίων καὶ τῶν πεδίων.

(Rain, rain, O dear Zeus, on the land of the Athenians and on the fields!)

is clearly addressed to the sky, though the mere addition of "dear," in "O dear Zeus," is sufficient to change the sky into a personal being.

The original meaning of *Zeús* might equally have been guessed from such words as *Diosēmía*, portents in the sky, i. e. thunder, lightning, rain; *Diipetḗs*, swollen by rain, *lit.* fallen from heaven; *éndios*, in the open air, or at mid-day; *eúdios*, calm, *lit.* well-skyed, and others. In Latin, too, *sub Jove frigido*, under the cold sky, *sub diu*, *sub dio*, and *sub divo*, under the open sky, are palpable enough.[1] But then it was al-

[1] Dium fulgur appellabant diurnum quod putabant Jovis, ut nocturnum Summani. — Festus, p. 57

ways open to say that the ancient names of the gods were frequently used to signify either their abodes or their special gifts, — that *Neptunus,* for instance, was used for the sea, *Pluto* for the lower regions, *Jupiter* for the sky, and that this would in no way prove that these names originally meant sea, lower world, sky. Thus Nævius said, *Cocus edit Neptunum, Venerem, Cererem,* meaning, as Festus tells us, by Neptune fishes, by Venus vegetables, by Ceres bread.[1] Minerva is used both for mind in *pingui Minerva* and for threads of wool.[2] When some ancient philosophers, as quoted by Aristotle, said that Zeus rains not in order to increase the corn, but from necessity,[3] this no doubt shows that these early positive philosophers looked upon Zeus as the sky, and not as a free personal divine being; but again it would leave it open to suppose that they transferred the old divine name of Zeus to the sky, just as Ennius, with the full consciousness of the philosopher, exclaimed, "Aspice hoc sublime candens quod invocant omnes Jovem." An expression like this is the result of later reflection, and it would in no way prove that either Zeus or Jupiter meant originally sky.

A Greek at the time of Homer would have scouted the suggestion that he, in saying *Zeús,* meant no more than sky. By Zeus the Greeks meant more than the visible sky, more even than the sky personified. With them the name Zeus was, and remained, in spite of all mythological obscurations, the name of the Supreme Deity; and even if they remembered that originally it meant sky, this would have troubled

[1] Festus, p. 45. [2] Arnobius, v. 45.
[3] Grote, *History of Greece,* i. 501, 539.

them as little as if they remembered that *thymos*, mind, originally meant blast. Sky was the nearest approach to that conception which in sublimity, brightness, and infinity transcended all others as much as the bright blue sky transcended all other things visible on earth. This is of great importance. Let us bear in mind that the perception of God is one of those which, like the perceptions of the senses, is realized even without language. We cannot realize general conceptions, or, as they are called by philosophers, nominal essences, such as *animal*, *tree*, *man*, without names; we cannot reason, therefore, without names or without language. But we can see the sun, we can greet it in the morning and mourn for it in the evening, without necessarily naming it, that is to say, comprehending it under some general notion. It is the same with the perception of the Divine. It may have been perceived, men may have welcomed it or yearned after it, long before they knew how to name it. Yet very soon man would long for a name; and what we know as the prayer of Jacob, "Tell me, I pray thee, thy name,"[1] and as the question of Moses, "What shall I say unto them if they shall say to me, What is his name?"[2] must at an early time have been the question and the prayer of every nation on earth.

It may be that the statement of Herodotus (ii. 52) rests on theory rather than fact, yet even as a theory the tradition that the Pelasgians for a long time offered prayer and sacrifice to the gods without having names for any one of them, is curious. Lord Bacon states the very opposite of the West Indians,

[1] *Genesis* xxxii. 29. [2] *Exodus* iii. 13.

namely, that they had names for each of their gods, but no word for god.

As soon as man becomes conscious of himself, as soon as he perceives himself as distinct from all other things and persons, he at the same moment becomes conscious of a Higher Self, a higher power without which he feels that neither he nor anything else would have any life or reality. We are so fashioned — and it is no merit of ours — that as soon as we awake, we feel on all sides our dependence on something else, and all nations join in some way or other in the words of the Psalmist, " It is He that hath made us, and not we ourselves." This is the first *sense* of the Godhead, the *sensus numinis* as it has been well called; for it is a *sensus* — an immediate perception, not the result of reasoning or generalizing, but an intuition as irresistible as the impressions of our senses. In receiving it we are passive, at least as passive as in receiving from above the image of the sun, or any other impressions of the senses, whereas in all our reasoning processes we are active rather than passive. This *sensus numinis*, or, as we may call it in more homely language, *faith*, is the source of all religion; it is that without which no religion, whether true or false, is possible.

Tacitus[1] tells us that the Germans applied the names of gods to that hidden thing which they perceived by reverence alone. The same in Greece. In giving to the object of the *sensus numinis* the name of *Zeus*, the fathers of Greek religion were fully

[1] *Germania*, 9: deorumque nominibus appellant secretum illud quod sola reverentia vident.

aware that they meant more than sky. The high
and brilliant sky has in many languages and many
religions[1] been regarded as the abode of God, and
the name of the abode might easily be transferred to
him who abides in Heaven. Aristotle (" De Cœlo,"
i. 1, 3) remarks that "all men have a suspicion of
gods, and all assign to them the highest place." And
again (*l. c.* i. 2, 1) he says, " The ancients assigned to
the gods heaven and the space above, because it was
alone eternal." The Slaves, as Procopius states,[2]
worshipped at one time one god only, and he was
the maker of the lightning. *Perkunas*, in Lithuanian,
the god of the thunderstorm, is used synonymously
with *deivaitis*, deity. In Chinese *Tien* means sky
and day, and the same word, like the Aryan *Dyu*, is
recognized in Chinese as the name of God. Even
though, by an edict of the Pope in 1715, Roman
Catholic missionaries were prohibited from using
Tien as the name for God, and ordered to use *Tien
chu*, Lord of heaven, instead, language has proved
more powerful than the Pope. In the Tataric and
Mongolic dialects, *Tengri*, possibly derived from the
same source as *Tien*, signifies — 1, heaven, 2, the
God of heaven, 3, God in general, or good and evil
spirits.[3] The same meanings are ascribed by Castrén
to the Finnish word *Jumala*, thunderer.[4] Nay, even in
our own language, "heaven" may still be used almost

[1] See Carrière, *Die Kunst im Zusammenhang der Culturentwickelung*, p. 49.
[2] Welcker, *l. c.* L 137, 166. Proc. de bello Gothico, 3, 14.
[3] Castrén, *Finnische Mythologie*, p. 14. Welcker, *Griechische Götterlehre*, p. 130. Klaproth, *Sprache und Schrift der Uiguren*, p. 9. Boehtlingk, *Die Sprache der Jakuten, Wörterbuch*, p. 90, s. v. tagara. Kowalewski, *Dictionnaire Mongol-Russe-Français*, t. iii. p. 1763.
[4] Castrén, *l. c.* p. 24.

synonymously with God. The prodigal son, when he returns to his father, says, " I will arise and go to my father, and will say unto him, Father, I have sinned against heaven and before thee."[1] Whenever we thus find the name of heaven used for God, we must bear in mind that those who originally adopted such a name were transferring that name from one object, visible to their bodily eyes, to another object grasped by another organ of knowledge, by the vision of the soul. Those who at first called God Heaven, had something within them that they wished to call, — the growing image of God; those who at a later time called Heaven God, had forgotten that they were predicating of Heaven something that was higher than Heaven.

That Zeus was originally to the Greeks the Supreme God, the true God, — nay, at some times their only God, — can be perceived in spite of the haze which mythology has raised around his name.[2] But this is very different from saying that Homer believed in one supreme, omnipotent, and omniscient being, the creator and ruler of the world. Such an assertion would require considerable qualification. The Homeric Zeus is full of contradictions. He is the subject of mythological tales, and the object of religious adoration. He is omniscient, yet he is cheated; he is omnipotent, and yet defied; he is eternal, yet he has a father; he is just, yet he is guilty of crime. Now these very contradictions ought to teach us a lesson. If all the conceptions of Zeus had sprung from one and the same source, these contradictions could not have existed. If Zeus

[1] Luke xv. 18. [2] Cf. Welcker, p. 129 seq.

had simply meant God, the Supreme God, he could not have been the son of Kronos or the father of Minos. If, on the other hand, Zeus had been a merely mythological personage, such as Eos, the dawn, or Helios, the sun, he could never have been addressed as he is addressed in the famous prayer of Achilles. In looking through Homer and other Greek writers, we have no difficulty in collecting a number of passages in which the Zeus that is mentioned is clearly conceived as their supreme God. For instance, the song of the Pleiades at Dodona,[1] the oldest sanctuary of Zeus, was : " Zeus was, Zeus is, Zeus will be, a great Zeus." There is no trace of mythology in this. In Homer,[2] Zeus is called "the father, the most glorious, the greatest, who rules over all, mortals and immortals." He is the counsellor, whose counsels the other gods cannot fathom (Il. i. 545). His power is the greatest (Il. ix. 25),[3] and it is he who gives strength, wisdom, and honor to man. The mere expression, "father of gods and men," so frequently applied to Zeus and to Zeus alone, would be sufficient to show that the religious conception of Zeus was never quite forgotten, and that in spite of the various Greek legends as to the creation of the human race, the idea of Zeus as the father and creator of all things, but more particularly as the father and creator of man, was never quite extinct in the Greek mind. It breaks forth in the unguarded language of Philoetios in the Odyssey, who charges

[1] Welcker, p. 143. *Paus.* 60, 12, 5.
[2] *Ibid.* p. 176.
[3] " Jupiter omnipotens regum rerumque deûmque Progenitor genitrixque deûm."
Valerius Soranus, in Aug., *De Civ. Dei*, vii. 10.

Zeus[1] that he does not pity men *though it was he who created them*; and in the philosophical view of the universe put forth by Kleanthes or by Aratus it assumes that very form under which it is known to all of us, from the quotation of St. Paul, " *For we are also his offspring.*" Likeness with God (*homoiótēs theô*) was the goal of Pythagorean ethics,[2] and according to Aristotle, it was an old saying that everything exists from God and through God.[3] All the greatest poets after Homer know of Zeus as the highest god, as the true god. "Zeus," says Pindar,[4] "obtained something more than what the gods possessed." He calls him the eternal father, and he claims for man a divine descent.

"One is the race of men,[5] one that of the gods. We both breathe from one mother; but our powers, all sundered, keep us apart, so that the one is nothing, while the brazen heaven, the immovable seat, endureth forever. Yet even thus we are still, whether by greatness of mind or by form, like unto the immortals, though we know not to what goal,

[1] *Od.* xx. 201:—

Ζεῦ πάτερ, οὔ τις σεῖο θεῶν ὀλοώτερος ἄλλος·
οὐκ ἐλεαίρεις ἄνδρας, ἐπὴν δὴ γείνεαι αὐτός.

[2] Cic. *Leg.* l. 8. Welcker, *Gr. Götterlehre*, I. 249.
[3] *De Mundo*, 6. Welcker, *Griechische Götterlehre*, vol. I. p. 240.
[4] Pind. *Fragm.* v. 6. Bunsen, *Gott in der Geschichte*, II. 231. Ol. 13, 12.
[5] Pind. *Nem.* vi. 1 (cf. xi. 43; xii. 7):

Ἓν ἀνδρῶν, ἓν θεῶν γένος· ἐκ μιᾶς δὲ πνέομεν
ματρὸς ἀμφότεροι· διείργει δὲ πᾶσα κεκριμένα
δύναμις, ὡς τὸ μὲν οὐδέν, ὁ δὲ χάλκεος ἀσφαλὲς αἰὲν ἕδος
μένει οὐρανός. ἀλλά τι προσφέρομεν ἔμπαν ἢ μέγαν
νόον ἤτοι φύσιν ἀθανάτοις,
καίπερ ἐφαμερίαν οὐκ εἰδότες οὐδὲ μετὰ νύκτας ἄμμε πότμος
οἵαν τίν' ἔγραψε δραμεῖν ποτὶ στάθμαν.

either by day or by night, destiny has destined us to haste on."

"For the children of the day, what are we, and what not? Man is the dream of a shadow. But if there comes a ray sent from Zeus, then there is for men bright splendor and a cheerful life."[1]

Æschylus again leaves no doubt as to his real view of Zeus. His Zeus is a being different from all other gods. "Zeus," he says, in a fragment,[2] "is the earth, Zeus the air, Zeus the sky, Zeus is all and what is above all." "All was given to the gods," he says, "except to be lords, for free is no one but Zeus."[3] He calls him the lord of infinite time;[4] nay, he knows that the name Zeus[5] is but indifferent, and that behind that name there is a power greater than all names. Thus the Chorus in the Agamemnon says:—

"Zeus, whoever he is, if this be the name by which he loves to be called — by this name I address him. For, if I verily want to cast off the idle burden of my thought, proving all things, I cannot find one on whom to cast it, except Zeus only."

[1] Pind. *Pyth.* viii. 95:—
  Ἐπάμεροι· τί δέ τις; τί δ' οὔ τις; σκιᾶς ὄναρ
  ἄνθρωπος. ἀλλ' ὅταν αἴγλα διόσδοτος ἔλθῃ,
  λαμπρὸν φέγγος ἔπεστιν ἀνδρῶν
  καὶ μείλιχος αἰών.

[2] Cf. Carrière, *Die Kunst*, vol. i. p. 79.

[3] *Prom. vinctus*, 49:—
  ἅπαντ' ἐπράχθη πλὴν θεοῖσι κοιρανεῖν,
  ἐλεύθερος γὰρ οὔτις ἐστὶ πλὴν Διός.

[4] *Supplices*, 574: Ζεὺς αἰῶνος κρέων ἀπαύστου.

[5] Kleanthes, in a hymn quoted by Welcker, ii. p. 193, addresses Zeus:—
  Κύδιστ' ἀθανάτων, πολυώνυμε, παγκρατὲς αἰεί, χαῖρε Ζεῦ.
  Most glorious among immortals, with many names, almighty, always hail to thee, Zeus!

"For he who before was great, proud in his all-conquering might, he is not cared for any more; and he who came after, he found his victor and is gone. But he who sings wisely songs of victory for Zeus, he will find all wisdom. For Zeus leads men in the way of wisdom, he orders that suffering should be our best school. Nay, even in sleep there flows from the heart suffering reminding us of suffering, and wisdom comes to us against our will."

One more passage from Sophocles,[1] to show how with him too Zeus is, in true moments of anguish and religious yearning, the same being whom we call God. In the "Electra," the Chorus says:—

"Courage, courage, my child! There is still in heaven the great Zeus, who watches over all things and rules. Commit thy exceeding bitter grief to him, and be not too angry against thy enemies, nor forget them."

But while in passages like these the original conception of Zeus as the true god, the god of gods, preponderates, there are innumerable passages in which Zeus is clearly the sky personified, and hardly differs from other deities, such as the sun-god or the goddess of the moon. The Greek was not aware that there were different tributaries which entered from different points into the central idea of Zeus. To him the name Zeus conveyed but one idea, and the contradictions between the divine and the

[1] *Electra*, v. 1881:—

θάρσει μοι, θάρσει, τέκνον.
ἔτι μέγας οὐρανῷ
Ζεύς, ὃς ἐφορᾷ πάντα καὶ κρατύνει·
ᾧ τὸν ὑπεραλγῆ χόλον νέμουσα,
μήθ' οἷς ἐχθαίρεις ὑπεράχθεο μήτ' ἐπιλάθου.

natural elements in his character were slurred over
by all except the few who thought for themselves,
and who knew, with Socrates, that no legend, no
sacred myth, could be true that reflects discredit on
a divine being. But to us it is clear that the story
of Zeus descending as golden rain into the prison
of Danaë was meant for the bright sky delivering the
earth from the bonds of winter, and awakening in
her a new life by the golden showers of spring.
Many of the stories that are told about the love of
Zeus for human or half-human heroines have a similar origin. The idea which we express by the phrase,
"King by the grace of God," was expressed in ancient language by calling kings the descendants of
Zeus.[1] This simple and natural conception gave
rise to innumerable local legends. Great families
and whole tribes claimed Zeus for their ancestor;
and as it was necessary in each case to supply him
with a wife, the name of the country was naturally
chosen to supply the wanting link in these sacred
genealogies. Thus *Æacus*, the famous king of Ægina,
was fabled to be the offspring of Zeus. This need
not have meant more than that he was a powerful,
wise, and just king. But it soon came to mean more.
Æacus was fabled to have been really the son of
Zeus, and Zeus is represented as carrying off Ægina
and making her the mother of Æacus.

The Arcadians (Ursini) derived their origin from
Arkas; their national deity was Kallisto, another
name for Artemis.[2] What happens? *Arkas* is made

---

[1] *Il.* li. 445, διοτρεφέες. *Od.* iv. 691, δεῖοι. Callim. *Hym. in Jovem*, 79,
ἐκ Διὸς βασιλῆες. Bertrand, *Dieux Protecteurs*, p. 167. Kemble, *Saxons in
England*, l. p. 336. Cox, *Tales of Thebes and Argos*, 1864, Introduction, p. 1.
[2] Müller, *Dorier*, l. 372. Jacobi, s. v. *Kallisto*.

the son of *Zeus* and *Kallisto*; though, in order to
save the good name of Artemis, the chaste goddess,
Kallisto is here represented as one of her companions
only. Soon the myth is spun out still further. Kallisto is changed into a bear by the jealousy of Here.
She is then, after having been killed by Artemis,
identified with Arktos, the Great Bear, for no better
reasons than the Virgin in later times with the zodiacal sign of Virgo.[1] And if it be asked why the
constellation of the Bear never sets, an answer was
readily given, — the wife of Zeus had asked Okeanos
and Thetis not to allow her rival to contaminate the
pure waters of the sea.

It is said that *Zeus*, in the form of a bull, carried
off *Europa*. This means no more, if we translate it
back into Sanskrit, than that the strong rising sun
(vrishan) carries off the wide-shining dawn. This
story is alluded to again and again in the Veda.
Now *Minos*, the ancient king of Crete, required parents; so Zeus and Europa were assigned to him.

There was nothing that could be told of the sky
that was not in some form or other ascribed to Zeus.
It was Zeus who rained, who thundered, who snowed,
who hailed, who sent the lightning, who gathered the
clouds, who let loose the winds, who held the rainbow. It is Zeus who orders the days and nights, the
months, seasons, and years. It is he who watches
over the fields, who sends rich harvests, and who
tends the flocks.[2] Like the sky, Zeus dwells on the
highest mountains; like the sky, Zeus embraces the
earth; like the sky, Zeus is eternal, unchanging, the

---

[1] Maury, *Légendes Pieuses*, p. 39, n.
[2] Welcker, p. 169.

highest god.¹ For good and for evil, Zeus the sky and Zeus the god are wedded together in the Greek mind, language triumphing over thought, tradition over religion.

And strange as this mixture may appear, incredible as it may seem that two ideas like god and sky should have run into one, and that the atmospheric changes of the air should have been mistaken for the acts of Him who rules the world, let us not forget that not in Greece only, but everywhere, where we can watch the growth of early language and early religion, the same, or nearly the same, phenomena may be observed. The Psalmist says (xviii. 6), " In my distress I called upon the Lord, and cried unto my God : he heard my voice out of his temple, and my cry came before him, even into his ears.

7. " Then the earth shook and trembled; the foundations also of the hills moved and were shaken, because he was wroth.

8. " There went up smoke out of his nostrils, and fire out of his mouth devoured : coals were kindled by it.

9. " He bowed the heavens also, and came down: and darkness was under his feet.

10. " And he rode upon a cherub and did fly: yea, he did fly upon the wings of the wind.

13. " The Lord also thundered in the heavens, and the Highest gave his voice; hailstones and coals of fire.

14. " Yea, he sent out his arrows, and scattered

---

1 Bunsen, *Gott in der Geschichte*, ii. 352: " Gott vermag aus schwarzer Nacht zu erwecken fleckenlosen Glanz, und mit schwarzlockigem Dunkel zu verhüllen des Tages reinen Strahl." — Pindar, *Fragm.* 5.

them; and he shot out lightnings, and discomfited them.

15. "Then the channels of waters were seen, and the foundations of the world were discovered at thy rebuke, O Lord, at the blast of the breath of thy nostrils."

Even the Psalmist in his inspired utterances must use our helpless human language, and condescend to the level of human thought. Well is it for us if we always remember the difference between what is said and what is meant, and if, while we pity the heathen for worshipping stocks and stones, we are not ourselves kneeling down before the frail images of human fancy.[1]

And now, before we leave the history of *Dyu*, we must ask one more question, though one which it is difficult to answer. Was it by the process of radical or poetical metaphor that the ancient Aryans, before they separated, spoke of *dyu*, the sky, and *dyu*, the god? i. e. was the object of the *sensus luminis*, the sky, called *dyu*, light, and the object of the *sensus numinis*, God, called *dyu*, light, by two independent acts; or was the name of the sky, *dyu*, transferred ready-made to express the growing idea of God, living in the highest heaven?[2] Either is possible. The latter view could be supported by several analogies, which we have examined before, and where we found that names expressive of sky had clearly been

---

[1] Dion Chrysostomus, 12, p. 404 r. Welcker, *Griechische Götterlehre*, L. p. 946.

[2] Festus, p. 32: Lucetium Jovem appellabant quod eum lucis esse causam credebant. Macrob. *Sat*. L. 15: unde et Lucetium Salii in carmine canunt, et Cretenses Δία τὴν ἡμέραν vocant, ipsi quoque Romani Diespitrem appellant, ut diei patrem. Gell. v. 12, 6. Hartung, *Religion der Römer*, il. 9.

transferred to the idea of the Godhead, or, as others would put it, had gradually been purified and sublimed to express that idea. There is no reason why this should not be admitted. Each name is in the beginning imperfect, it necessarily expresses but one side of its object, and in the case of the names of God the very fact of the insufficiency of one single name would lead to the creation or adoption of new names, each expressive of a new quality that was felt to be essential and useful for recalling new phenomena in which the presence of the Deity had been discovered. The unseen and incomprehensible Being that had to be named was perceived in the wind, in the earthquake, and in the fire, long before it was recognized in the still small voice within. From every one of these manifestations the divine *secretum illud quod solâ reverentiâ vident* might receive a name, and as long as each of these names was felt to be but a name no harm was done. But names have a tendency to become things, *nomina* grew into *numina*, *ideas* into *idols*, and if this happened with the name *Dyu*, no wonder that many things which were intended for Him who is above the sky were mixed up with sayings relating to the sky.

Much, however, may be said in favor of the other view. We may likewise explain the synonymousness of sky and God in the Aryan languages by the process of radical metaphor. Those who believe that all our ideas had their first roots in the impressions of the senses, and that nothing original came from any other source, would naturally adopt the former view, though they would on reflection find it difficult to explain how the sensuous impressions left by the blue sky, or the clouds, or the thunder and lightning, should ever have yielded an essence distinct from all these fleeting phenomena — how the senses by themselves should, like Juno in her anger, have given birth to a being such as had never been seen before It may sound like mysticism, but it is nevertheless perfectly rational to suppose that there was in the beginning the perception of what Tacitus calls *secretum illud*, and that this secret and sacred thing was at the first burst of utterance called *Dyu*, the light, without any special reference to the bright sky. Afterwards, the bright sky being called for another reason *Dyu*, the light, the mythological process would be equally intelligible that led to all the contradictions in the fables of Zeus. The two words *dyu*, the inward light, and *dyu*, the sky, became, like a double star, one in the eyes of the world, defying the vision even of the most powerful lenses. When the word was pronounced, all its meanings, light, god, sky, and day, vibrated together, and the bright *Dyu*, the god of light, was lost in the *Dyu* of the sky. If *Dyu* meant originally the bright Being, the light, the god of light, and was intended, like *asura*, as a name for the Divine, unlocalized as yet in any part of nature, we shall appreciate all the more easily its applicability to express, in spite of ever-shifting circumstances, the highest and the universal God. Thus, in Greek, Zeus is not only the lord of heaven, but likewise the ruler of the lower world, and the master of the sea.[1] But though recognizing in the

[1] Welcker, *Griechische Götterlehre*, I. p. 104. *Il.* ix. 457, Ζεὺς τε καταχ- θόνιος. The Old Norse *tyr* is likewise used in this general sense. See Grimm, *Deutsche Mythologie*, p. 178.

name of Zeus the original conception of light, we ought not to deceive ourselves and try to find in the primitive vocabulary of the Aryans those sublime meanings which after many thousands of years their words have assumed in our languages. The light which flashed up for the first time before the inmost vision of their souls was not the pure light of which St. John speaks. We must not mix the words and thoughts of different ages. Though the message which St. John sent to his little children, "God is light, and in him is no darkness at all,"[1] may remind us of something similar in the primitive annals of human language; though we may highly value the coincidence, such as it is, between the first stammerings of religious life and the matured language of the world's manhood; yet it behooves us, while we compare, to discriminate likewise, and to remember always that words and phrases, though outwardly the same, reflect the intentions of the speaker in ever-varying angles.

It was not my intention to enter at full length into the story of Zeus as told by the Greeks, or the story of Jupiter as told by the Romans. This has been done, and well done, in books on Greek and Roman Mythology. All I wished to do was to lay bare before your eyes the first germs of Zeus and Jupiter which lie below the surface of classical mythology, and to show how those germs cling with their fibres to roots that stretch in an uninterrupted line to India — nay, to some more distant centre from which all the Aryan languages proceeded in their world-wide expansion.

[1] St. John, *Ep.* I. i. 5; ii. 7.

It may be useful, however, to dwell a little longer on the curious conglomeration of words which have all been derived from the same root as Zeus. That root in its simplest form is DYU.

DYU, raised by Guṇa to DYO (before vowels dyav);
raised by Vṛiddhi to DYÂU (before vowels dyâv).

DYU, by a change of vowels into semi-vowels, and of semi-vowels into vowels, assumes the form of

DIV, and this is raised by Guṇa to DEV,
by Vṛiddhi to DÂIV.

I shall now examine these roots and their derivatives more in detail, and, in doing so, I shall put together those words, whether verbal or nominal, which agree most closely in their form, without reference to the usual arrangements of declension and conjugation adopted by practical grammarians.

The root *dyu* in its simplest form appears as the Sanskrit verb *dyu*, to spring or pounce on something.[1] In some passages of the Rig-Veda, the commentator takes *dyu* in the sense of shining, but he likewise admits that the verbal root may be *dyut*, not *dyu*. Thus, Rv. i. 113, 14 : " The Dawn with her jewels shone forth (adyaut) in all the corners of the sky ; she the bright (devî) opened the dark cloth (the night). She who awakens us comes near, Ushas with her red horses, on her swift car."

If *dyu* is to be used for nominal, instead of verbal purposes, we have only to add the terminations of declension. Thus we get with *bhis*, the termination

---

[1] The French *éclater*, originally to break forth, afterwards to shine, shows a similar transition. Cf. Diez, *Lex. Comp.* s. v. schianiare.

of the instrumental plural, corresponding to Latin *bus*, *dyu-bhis*, meaning on all days, *toujours*; or the acc. plural *dyûn*, in *anu dyûn*, day after day.

If *dyu* is to be used as an adverb, we have only to add the adverbial termination *s*, and we get the Sanskrit *dyu-s* in *pûrvedyus*, i. e. on a former day, yesterday, which has been compared with *prōizd*, the day before yesterday. The last element, *za*, certainly seems to contain the root *dyu*; but *za* would correspond to Sanskrit *dya* (as in *adya*, to-day), rather than to *dyus*. This *dyus*, however, standing for an original *dyut*, appears again in Latin *diû*, by day, as in *noctû diûque*, by night and by day. Afterwards *diû*[1] came to mean a lifelong day, a long while; and then in *diuscule*, a little while, the *s* reappears. This *s* stands for an older *t*, and this *t*, too, reappears in *diutule*, a little while, and in the comparative *diut-ius*, longer (*interdius* and *interdiû*, by day).

In Greek and Latin, words beginning with *dy* are impossible. Where Sanskrit shows an initial *dy*, we find in Greek that either *dy* is changed to *z*, or the *y* is dropped altogether, leaving simply *d*.[2] Even in Greek we find that dialects vary between *dia* and *za*; we find Æolic[3] *zabállō*, instead of *diabállō*, and the later Byzantine corruption of *diábolos* appears in Latin as *zabulus*, instead of *diabolus*. Where, in Greek, initial *z* varies dialectically with initial *d*, we

---

[1] In *dum*, this day, then, while; in *nondum*, not yet (pas encore, i. e. hanc horam); in *donicum*, *donec*, now that, lorsque; and in *denique*, and now, lastly, the same radical element *dyu*, in the sense of day, has been suspected; likewise in *biduum*. In Greek δήν, long, δή, now, have been referred to the same source.

[2] See Schleicher, *Zur Vergleichenden Sprachengeschichte*, p. 40.

[3] Mahlhorn, *Griechische Grammatik*, § 110.

shall find generally that the original initial consonants were *dy*. If, therefore, we meet in Greek with two such forms as *Zeús* and Bœotian *Deús*, we may be certain that both correspond to the Sanskrit *Dyu*, raised by Guṇa to *Dyo*. This form, *dyo*, exists in Sanskrit, not in the nominative singular, which by Vriddhi is raised to *Dyâus*, nom. plur. *Dyávaḥ*, but in such forms as the locative *dyávi* [1] (for *dyo-i*), &c.

In Latin, initial *dy* is represented by *j*; so that *Jú* in *Júpiter* corresponds exactly with Sanskrit *Dyo*. *Jŏvis*, on the contrary, is a secondary form, and would in the nominative singular represent a Sanskrit form *Dyâvih*. Traces of the former existence of an initial *dj* in Latin have been discovered in *Diovis*, according to Varro (L. L. v. 10, 20), au old Italian name for Jupiter, that has been met with under the same form in Oscan inscriptions. *Vějŏvis*, too, an old Italian divinity, is sometimes found spelt *Vĕdjŏvis*.

That the Greek *Zḗn*, *Zênos*, belongs to the same family of words, has never been doubted; but there has been great diversity of opinion as to the etymological structure of the word. I explain *Zên*, as well as Latin *Jun*, the older form of *Janus*, as representing a Sanskrit *dyav-an*, formed like *rájan*, but with Guṇa. Now as *yuvan*, jŭvenis, is contracted to *jūn* in *jūnior*, so *dyavan* would in Latin become *Jan*, following the third declension,[2] or, under a secondary form, *Jân-us*.

---

[1] The acc. singular *dyâm*, besides *divam*, is a mere corruption of *dyâvam*, like *gâm* for *gâvam*. The coincidence of *dyâm* with the Greek acc. sing. Ζῆν is curious. Cf. Leo Meyer, in Kuhn's *Zeitschrift*, v. 373. Ζην also is mentioned as an accusative singular. As to nominatives, such as Ζήν and Ζύς, gen. Ζαντός, they are too little authenticated to warrant any conjectures as to their etymological character. See Curtius, *Grundzüge*, ii. p. 188.

[2] Tertullian, *Apol*. c. 10: "a Jano vel Jane, ut Salii volunt." Hartung, *Religion der Römer*, ii. 218.

Janus-pater, in Latin, was used as one word, like *Jupiter.* He was likewise called *Junonius* and *Quirinus,*[1] and was, as far as we can judge, another personification of *Dyu,* the sky, with special reference, however, to the year. The month of January owes its name to him. Now as Ju : Zeu = Jūn : Zēn, only that in Greek *Zēn* remained in the third or consonantal declension, instead of migrating, as it might have done, under the form *Zēnos, ou,* into the second. The Latin *Jūnô, Junon-is,* would correspond to a Greek *Zēnōn,* as a feminine.

The second form, DIV, appears in Sanskrit in the oblique cases, gen. *divas,* dat. *dive,* inst. *divâ,* acc. *divam,* &c. For instance (Rv. i. 50, 11), "O Sun, that risest now, and mountest up to the higher sky (*uttarâm dívam,* fem.), destroy the pain of my heart and my paleness!"

Rv. i. 54, 3: "Sing to the mighty *Dyu* (divé bṛihaté, masc.) a mighty song."

Rv. i. 7, 3: "Indra made the sun rise to the sky (diví), that he might see far and wide; he burst open the rock for the cows."

These forms are most accurately represented in the Greek oblique case, DiFós, DiFí, DíFa.

In Latin the labial semi-vowel, the so-called digamma, is not necessarily dropped, as we saw in *Jovis, Jovem,* &c. It is dropped, however, in *Diespiter,* and likewise in *dium* for *divum,* sky, from which *Diâna,* instead of *Divâna,* the heavenly (originally Deiana), while in *div-inus* the final *v* of the root *div* is preserved.

In Sanskrit there are several derivatives of *div,* such

[1] Gell. v. 12, 5.

as *diva* (neuter), sky, or day; *divasa* (m. n.), sky and day; *divya*, heavenly; *dina* (m. n.), day, is probably a contraction of *divana*. In Lithuanian we find *diena*. The Latin *diēs* would correspond to a Sanskrit *divas*, nom. sing. *divás*, masc.

If, lastly, we raise *div* by Guṇa, we get the Sanskrit *deva*, originally bright, afterwards god. It is curious that this, the etymological meaning of *deva*, is passed over in the Dictionary of Boehtlingk and Roth. It is clearly passed over intentionally, and in order to show that in all the passages where *deva* occurs in the Veda it may be translated by god or divine. That it may be so translated would be difficult to disprove; but that there are many passages where the original meaning of bright is more appropriate, can easily be established. Rv. i. 50, 8: " The seven Harits (horses) carry thee on thy chariot, brilliant (deva) Sun, thee with flaming hair, O farseeing!" No doubt we might translate the divine Sun; but the explanation of the commentator in this and similar passages seems more natural and more appropriate. What is most interesting in the Veda is exactly this uncertainty of meaning, the half-physical and half-spiritual intention of words such as *deva*. In Latin *deus* no longer means brilliant, but simply god. The same applies to *theós* in Greek, to *diewas* in Lithuanian.

But in Sanskrit we can watch the formation of the general name for deity. The principal objects of the religious poetry of the Vedic bards were those bright beings, the Sun, the Sky, the Day, the Dawn, the Morn, the Spring — who might all be called *deva*, brilliant. These were soon opposed to the powers of

night and darkness, sometimes called *adeva*, literally,
not bright, then ungodly, evil, mischievous. This
contrast between the bright, beneficent, divine, and
the dark, mischievous, demoniacal beings, is of very
ancient date. *Druh*,[1] mischief, is used as a name of
darkness or the night, and the Dawn is said to drive
away the hateful darkness of *Druh* (vii. 75, 1; see
also i. 48, 8; 48, 15; 92, 5; 113, 12). The Âdityas
are praised for preserving man from *Druh* (viii. 47, 1),
and Maghavan or Indra is implored to bestow on his
worshippers the light of day, after having driven away
the many ungodly *Druhs* (iii. 3119: druhúh ví yâhi
bahulâh údevih). "May he fall into the ropes of
Druh," is used as a curse (vii. 59, 8); and in another
passage we read, "The Druhs follow the sins of men,"
(vii. 61, 5). As the ghastly powers of darkness, the
Druh or the Rakshas, are called *adeva*, so the bright
gods are called *adruh* (vii. 66, 18, Mitra and Varuṇa).
Deva being applied to all the bright and beneficent
manifestations in which the early Aryans discovered
the presence of something supernatural, undecaying,
immortal, it became in time the general name for
what was shared in common by all the different gods
or names of God. It followed, like a shadow, the
growth of the purer idea of the Godhead, and
when that had reached its highest goal it was almost
the only word which had retained some vitality in
that pure but exhausting atmosphere of thought.
The *Âdityas*, the *Vasus*, the *Asuras*, and other names,
had fallen back in the onward race of the human

[1] See Kuhn, *Zeitschrift*, I. 179 and 193, where θέλγω, τελχίν, ὀτρυνώς,
Zend *Drukhs*, German *trügen* and *lügen*, are all, with more or less certainty, traced back to *druh*. In A. S. we find *dreah-læcan*, magicians;
dry, magician; *doth*, a wound.

mind towards the highest conception of the Divine; the *Devas* alone remained to express *theós, deus*, God. Even in the Veda, where these glimpses of the original meaning of *deva*, brilliant, can still be caught, *deva* is likewise used in the same sense in which the Greeks used *theós*. The poet (x. 121, 8) speaks of

"Him who among the gods was alone god."
Yaḥ deveshu adhi devaḥ ekaḥ âsît.

A last step brings us in Sanskrit to *Daiva*, derived from *deva*, and this is used in the later Sanskrit to express fate, destiny.

There is but little to be said about the corresponding words in the Teutonic branch, fragments of which have been collected by that thoughtful scholar, Jacob Grimm.[1] In name, the Eddic god *Týr* (gen. *Tys*, acc. *Ty*) answers to the Vedic *Dyu*, and the Old Norse name for *dies Martis* is *Tysdagr*. Although in the system of the Edda *Odhin* is the supreme god, and *Tyr* his son, traces remain to show that in former days *Tyr*, the god of war, was worshipped as the principal deity by the Germans.[2] In Anglo-Saxon the name of the god does no longer occur independently, but traces of it have been discovered in *Tiwesdæg*, Tuesday. The same applies to Old High-German, where we find *Ziestac* for the modern *Dienstag*. Kemble points out names of places in England, such as *Tewesley, Tewing, Tiwes mére*, and *Tewes forn*, and names of flowers,[3] such as the Old Norse *Týsfiola, Týrhjalm, Týsviðr*, as containing the name of the god.

[1] *Deutsche Mythologie*, p. 175.
[2] Grimm. *Deutsche Mythologie*, p. 179.
[3] Kemble, *Saxons in England*, i. p. 351. These had first been pointed out by Grimm, *Deutsche Mythologie*, p. 180.

Besides this proper name, Grimm has likewise pointed out the Eddic *tivar*, nom. plur., the gods.

Lastly, whatever may have been said against it, I think that Zeuss and Grimm were right in connecting the *Tuisco* mentioned by Tacitus with the Anglo-Saxon *Tiw*, which, in Gothic, would have sounded *Tiu*. The Germans were considered by Tacitus, and probably considered themselves, as the aboriginal inhabitants of their country. In their poems, which Tacitus calls their only kind of tradition and annals, they celebrated as the divine ancestors of their race, *Tuisco*, sprung from the Earth, and his son *Mannus*. They looked, therefore, like the Greeks, on the gods as the ancestors of the human family, and they believed that in the beginning life sprang from that inexhaustible soil which gives support and nourishment to man, and for which in their simple language they could find no truer name than Mother Earth. It is easy to see that the *Mannus* here spoken of by Tacitus as the son of *Tuisco*, meant originally man, and was derived from the same root *man*, to measure, to think, which in Sanskrit yielded *Manu*.[1] *Man*, or, in Sanskrit, *Manu*, or *Manus*, was the proudest name which man could give to himself, the Measurer, the Thinker, and from it was derived the Old High-German *mennisc*, the Modern German *Mensch*. This *mennisc*, like the Sanskrit *manushya*, was originally an adjective, a patronymic, if you like: it meant the son of man. As soon as *mennisc* and *manushya* became in common parlance the recognized words for man, language itself supplied the

---

[1] On Manu and Minos, see Kuhn, *Zeitschrift*, iv. 92. The name of *Sarydus*, the son of Manu, could hardly be compared with *Krka*.

myth, that *Manus* was the ancestor of the *Manushyas*. Now *Tuisco* seems but a secondary form of *Tiu*, followed by the same suffix which we saw in *mennisc*, and without any change of meaning. Then why was Tuisco called the father of Mannu? Simply because it was one of the first articles in the primitive faith of mankind, that in one sense or other they had a father in heaven. Hence *Mannu* was called the son of *Tuisco*, and this *Tuisco*, as we know, was, originally, the Aryan god of light. These things formed the burden of German songs to which Tacitus listened. These songs they sang before they went to battle, to stimulate their courage, and to prepare to die. To an Italian ear it must have been a wild sound, reverberated from their shields, and hence called *barditus* (shield-song, Old Norse *bardhi*, shield). Many a Roman would have sneered at such poetry and such music. Not so Tacitus. The emperor Julian, when he heard the Germans singing their popular songs on the borders of the Rhine, could compare them to nothing but the cries of birds of prey. Tacitus calls them a shout of valor (concentus virtutis). He likewise mentions (Ann. ii. 88) that the Germans still kept up the memory of *Arminius* in their songs, and he describes (Ann. ii. 65) their night revellings, where they sang and shouted till the morning called them to fresh battles.

The names which Tacitus mentions, such as Mannus, Tuisco, &c., he could of course repeat by ear only, and if one considers the difficulties of such a task, it is extraordinary that these names, as written down by him, should lend themselves so easily to etymological explanation. Thus Tacitus states not only that *Mannus* was the ancestor of the German race, but he likewise mentions the names of his three sons, or rather the names of the three great tribes, the *Ingævones, Iscævones,* and *Herminones,* who derived their origin from the three sons of Mannus. It has been shown that the *Ingævones* derive their name from *Yng, Yngo,* or *Ynguio,* who, in the Edda and in the Beowulf, is mentioned as living first with the Eastern Danes and then proceeding on his car eastward over the sea. There is a northern race, the *Ynglings,* and their pedigree begins with *Yngvi, Niörðr, Frayr, Fiölnir* (Odin), *Svegdir,* all names of divine beings. Another genealogy, given in the *Ynglinga-saga,* begins with *Niörðr,* identifies *Frayr* with *Yngvi,* and derives from him the name of the race.

The second son of *Mannus, Isco,* has been identified by Grimm with *Askr,* another name of the firstborn man. *Askr* means likewise ash-tree, and it has been supposed that the name *ash* thus given to the first man came from the same conception which led the Greeks to imagine that one of the races of man sprang from ash-trees (ἐκ μελιᾶν). Alcuin still uses the expression, son of the ash-tree, as synonymous with man.[1] Grimm supposes that the *Iscævones* lived near the Rhine, and that a trace of their name comes out in *Asciburgium* or *Asciburg,* on the Rhine, where, as Tacitus had been wildly informed, an altar had been discovered dedicated to *Ulysses,* and with the name of his father *Laërtes.*[2]

The third son of *Mannus, Irmino,* has a name de-

[1] Ampère, *Histoire Littéraire de la France,* III. 79.
[2] *Germania,* c. 2.

cidedly German. *Irmin* was an old Saxon god, from whom probably both *Arminius* and the *Herminones* derived their names.

The chief interest of these German fables about *Tuisco, Mannus,* and his sons, is their religious character. They give utterance to the same sentiment which we find again and again among the Aryan nations, that man is conscious of his descent from heaven and from earth, that he claims kindred with a father in heaven, though he recognizes with equal clearness that he is made of the dust of the earth. The Hindus knew it when they called *Dyu* their father, and *Prithivi* their mother; Plato[1] knew it when he said that the Earth, as the mother, brought forth men, but God was the shaper; and the Germans knew it, though Tacitus tells us confusedly, that they sang of *Mannus* as the son of *Tuisco,* and of *Tuisco* as sprung from the earth. This is what Grimm says of the religious elements hidden in German mythology:[2] —

"In our own heathen mythology ideas which the human heart requires before all others, and in which it finds its chief support, stand forth in bold and pure relief. The highest god is there a father, old-father, grandfather, who grants to the living blessing and victory, to the dying a welcome in his own mansions. Death is called 'going home,' *Heimgang,* return to our father. By the side of the god stands the highest goddess as mother, old-mother, grandmother, a wise and pure ancestress of the human

---

[1] *Polit.* p. 414: καὶ ἡ γῆ αὐτοὺς μήτηρ οὖσα ἀνῆκε — ἀλλ' ὁ θεὸς πλάττων. Welcker, *Griechische Götterlehre,* i. p. 182.
[2] Grimm, *Deutsche Mythologie,* xl. 1.

race. The god is majestic, the goddess beaming with beauty. Both hold their circuit on earth and are seen among men, he teaching war and weapons, she sewing, spinning, and weaving. He inspires the poem, she cherishes the tale."

Let me conclude with the eloquent words of a living poet:[1] —

"Then they looked round upon the earth, those simple-hearted forefathers of ours, and said within themselves, 'Where is the All-Father, if All-Father there be? Not in this earth; for it will perish. Nor in the sun, moon, or stars; for they will perish too. Where is He who abideth forever?' Then they lifted up their eyes, and saw, as they thought, beyond sun, and moon, and stars, and all which changes and will change, the clear blue sky, the boundless firmament of heaven.

"That never changed; that was always the same. The clouds and storms rolled far below it, and all the bustle of this noisy world; but there the sky was still, as bright and calm as ever. The All-Father must be there, unchangeable in the unchanging heaven; bright, and pure, and boundless like the heavens; and like the heavens, too, silent and far off.

"So they named him after the heaven, Tuisco — the God who lives in the clear heaven, the heavenly Father. He was the Father of gods and men; and man was the son of Tuisco and Hertha — heaven and earth."

[1] C. Kingsley, *The Good News of God.* 1859, p. 241.

LECTURE XI.

MYTHS OF THE DAWN.

AFTER having, in my last Lecture, gathered together the fragments of the most ancient and most exalted deity worshipped once by all the members of the Aryan stock, I shall, to-day, examine some of the minor deities, in order to find out whether they too can be referred to the earliest period of Aryan speech and Aryan thought, — whether they too existed before the Aryans broke up in search of new homes, — and whether their memory was preserved more or less distinctly in later days in the poems of Homer and the songs of the Veda. These researches must necessarily be of a more minute kind, and I have to ask for your indulgence if I here enter into details which are of little general interest, but which, nevertheless, are indispensable, in order to establish a safe basis for speculations very apt to mislead even the most cautious inquirer.

I begin with the myth of *Hermes*, whose name has been traced back to the Vedic *Saramâ*. My learned friend Professor Kuhn,[1] who was the first to analyze the meaning and character of *Saramâ*, arrived at the conclusion that *Saramâ* meant storm, and that the Sanskrit word was identical with the Teutonic

[1] In Haupt's *Zeitschrift für Deutsches Alterthum*, vi. p. 119 seq.

storm, and with the Greek *hormḗ*. No doubt the root of *Saramâ* is *sar*, to go, but its derivation is by no means clear, there being no other word in Sanskrit formed by *ama*, and with *guṇa* of the radical vowel.[1] But admitting that *Saramâ* meant originally the runner, how does it follow that the runner was meant for storm? It is true that *Saraṇyu*, masc., derived from the same root, is said to take in later Sanskrit the meaning of wind and cloud, but it has never been proved that *Saraṇyû*, fem., had these meanings. The wind, whether as *vâta*, *vâyu*, *marut*, *pavana*, *anila*, &c., is always conceived as a masculine in Sanskrit, and the same applies generally to the other Aryan languages. This, however, would be no insurmountable objection, if there were clear traces in the Veda of *Saramâ* being endowed with any of the characteristic qualities of the wind. But if we compare the passages in which she is mentioned with others in which the power of the storm is described, we find no similarity whatever. It is said of *Saramâ* that she espied the strong stable of the cows (i. 72, 8), that she discovered the cleft of the rock, that she went a long journey, that she was the first to hear the lowing of the cows, and perhaps that she led the cows out (iii. 31, 6). She did this at the instance of *Indra* and the *Angiras* (i. 62, 3); *Brihaspati* (i. 62, 3) or *Indra* (iv. 16, 8) split the rock, and recovered the cows, which cows are said to give food to the children of man (i. 62, 3; 72, 8); perhaps, to the offspring of *Saramâ* herself (i. 62, 3). *Saramâ* ap-

---

[1] See Uṇâdi-Sûtras, ed. Aufrecht, iv. 48. Sármaḥ, as a substantive, running, occurs *Rv.* i. 80, 5. The Greek ὁρμή corresponds with this word in the feminine, but not with *saramâ*.

pears in time before *Indra* (iv. 16, 8), and she walks on the right path (iv. 45, 7 and 8).

This is about all that can be learnt from the Rig-Veda as to the character of *Saramâ*, with the exception of a hymn in the last book, which contains a dialogue between her and the *Panis*, who had robbed the cows. The following is a translation of that hymn: —

The *Panis* said: " With what intention did *Saramâ* reach this place? for the way is far, and leads tortuously away. What was your wish with us? How was the night?[1] How did you cross the waters of the *Rasâ*?" (1.)

Saramâ said: " I come, sent as the messenger of *Indra*, desiring, O *Panis*, your great treasures; this preserved me from the fear of crossing, and thus I crossed the waters of the *Rasâ*." (2.)

The *Panis*: " What kind of man is *Indra*, O *Saramâ*, what is his look, he as whose messenger thou camest from afar? Let him come hither, and we will make friends with him, and then he may be the cowherd of our cows." (3.)

Saramâ: " I do not know that he is to be subdued, for it is he himself that subdues, he as whose messenger I came hither from afar. Deep streams do not overwhelm him; you, *Panis*, will lie prostrate, killed by *Indra*." (4.)

The *Panis*: " Those cows, O *Saramâ*, which thou desirest, fly about the ends of the sky, O darling.

---

[1] Parîtakmyâ is explained in the Dictionary of Boehtlingk and Roth in the sense of random travelling. It never has that sense in the Veda, and as *Saramâ* comes to the Panis in the morning, the question, how was the night, is perfectly natural.

Who would give them up to thee without fighting? for our weapons too are sharp." (5.)

Saramá: "Though your words, O *Panis*, be unconquerable,[1] though your wretched bodies be arrow-proof,[2] though the way to you be hard to go, *Brihaspati* will not bless you for either."[3] (6.)

The *Panis*: "That store, O *Saramá*, is fastened to the rock; furnished with cows, horses, and treasures. *Panis* watch it who are good watchers; thou art come in vain to this bright place." (7.)

Saramá: "Let the *Rishis* come here fired with *Soma*, *Ayásya* (Indra[4]) and the ninefold *Angiras*; they will divide this stable[5] of cows; then the *Panis* will vomit out this speech."[6] (8.)

The *Panis*: "Even thus, O *Saramá*, thou art come hither driven by the violence of the gods; let us make thee our sister, do not go away again; we will give thee part of the cows, O darling." (9.)

Saramá: "I know nothing of brotherhood or sisterhood; *Indra* knows it and the awful *Angiras*. They seemed to me anxious for their cows when I came; therefore get away from here, O *Panis*, far away."[7] (10.)

"Go far away, *Panis*, far away; let the cows come out straight; the cows which *Brihaspati* found hid away, *Soma*, the stones, and the wise *Rishis*." (11.)

In none of these verses is there the slightest indi-

---

[1] asenyá, not hurtful, D. R.
[2] anlabhavyá, not to be destroyed, B. R.
[3] *Ubhayá*, with the accent on the last syllable, is doubtful.
[4] Cf. l. 62, 7, and B. R. s. v.
[5] ûrva is called dṛilha, Rv. l. 72, 8.
[6] Will be sorry for their former speech.
[7] variyaḥ, in das Weite.

cation of *Saramâ* as the representative of the storm, nor do the explanations of Indian commentators, which have next to be considered, point at all in that direction.

Sâyaṇa, in his commentary on the Rig-Veda (i. 6, 5), tells the story of *Saramâ* most simply. The cows, he says, were carried off by the *Paṇis* from the world of the gods and thrown into darkness; *Indra*, together with the *Maruts*, or storms, conquered them.

In the *Anukramaṇikâ*, the index to the Rigvedasanhitâ (x. 103), the story is related in fuller detail. It is there said that the cows were hidden by the demons, the *Paṇis*; that *Indra* sent the dog of the gods, *Saramâ*, to look for the cows; and that a parley took place between her and the *Paṇis*, which forms the 108th hymn of the last book of the Rig-Veda.

Further additions to the story are to be found in *Sâyaṇa's* Commentary on iii. 31, 5. The cows are there called the property of the *Angiras*, and it was at their instance that *Indra* sent the dog, and then, being apprised of their hiding-place, brought them back to the *Angiras*. So, at least, says the commentator, while the text of the hymn represents the seven sages, the Angiras, as taking themselves a more active part in effecting the breach in the mountain. Again, in his commentary on Rv. x. 108, *Sâyaṇa* adds that the cows belonged to *Bṛihaspati*, the chief-priest of *Indra*, that they were stolen by the *Paṇis*, the people of *Vala*, and that *Indra*, at *Bṛihaspati's* instance, sent the dog *Saramâ*. The dog, after crossing a river, came to the town of *Vala*, and saw

the cows in a secret place; whereupon the *Paṇis*
tried to coax her to stay with them.

As we read the hymn in the text of the Rig-Veda,
the parley between *Saramâ* and the *Paṇis* would
seem to have ended with *Saramâ* warning the robbers to flee before the wrath of *Indra, Bṛihaspati,* and
the *Angiras.* But in the *Bṛihaddevatâ* a new trait is
added. It is there said, that, although *Saramâ* declined to divide the booty with the *Paṇis,* she asked
them for a drink of milk. After having drunk the
milk, she recrossed the *Rasâ,* and when she was
asked after the cows by *Indra,* she denied having seen
them. *Indra* thereupon kicked her with his foot, and
she vomited the milk, and ran back to the *Paṇis.*
Indra then followed her, killed the demons, and recovered the cows.

This faithlessness of *Saramâ* is not alluded to in
the hymn; and in another passage, where it is said
that *Saramâ* found food for her offspring (Rv. i. 62,
3), *Sâyaṇa* merely states that *Saramâ,* before going to
look for the cows, made a bargain with *Indra* that
her young should receive milk and other food, and
then proceeded on her journey.

This being nearly the whole evidence on which we
must form our opinion of the original conception of
Saramâ, there can be little doubt that she was meant
for the early dawn, and not for the storm. In the
ancient hymns of the Rig-Veda she is never spoken
of as a dog, nor can we find there the slightest allusion to her canine nature. This is evidently a later
thought,[1] and it is high time that this much-talked-of

---

[1] It probably arose from *Sâramêya* being used as a name or epithet of the dogs of Yama. See page 476.

greyhound should be driven out of the Vedic Pantheon. There are but few epithets of *Saramá* from which we might form a guess as to her character. She is called *supadi*, having good feet, or quick, an adjective which never occurs again in the Rig-Veda. The second epithet, however, which is applied to her, *subhagâ*, fortunate, beloved, is one she shares in common with the Dawn — nay, which is almost a stereotyped epithet of the Dawn.

But more than this. Of whom is it so constantly said, as of *Saramá*, that she appears before *Indra*, that *Indra* follows her? It is *Ushas*, the Dawn, who wakes first (i. 123, 2), who comes first to the morning prayer (i. 123, 2). The Sun follows behind, as a man follows a woman (Rv. i. 115, 2).[1] Of whom is it said, as of *Saramá*, that she brings to light the precious things hidden in darkness? It is *Ushas*, the Dawn, who reveals the bright treasures that were covered by the gloom (i. 123, 6). She crosses the water unhurt (vi. 64, 4); she lays open the ends of heaven (i. 92, 11), — those very ends where, as the *Panis* said, the cows were to be found. She is said to break the strongholds and bring back the cows (vii. 75, 7; 79, 4). It is she who, like *Saramá*, distributes wealth among the sons of men (i. 92, 3; 123, 3). She possesses the cows (i. 123, 12, &c.); she is even called the mother of the cows (iv. 52, 2). She is said to produce the cows and to bring light (i. 124, 5); she is asked to open the doors of heaven, and to bestow on man wealth of cows (i. 48, 15). The Angiras, we read, asked her for the cows (vi. 65, 5), and the doors of the dark stable are said to be opened

[1] *Comparative Mythology*, p. 57. *Oxford Essays*, 1856.

by her (iv. 51, 2). In one place her splendor is said to be spreading as if she were driving forth cattle (i. 92, 12); in another the splendors of the dawn are themselves called a drove of cows (iv. 51, 8; 52, 5). Again, as it was said of *Saramâ*, that she follows the right path, the path which all the heavenly powers are ordained to follow, so it is particularly said of the Dawn that she walks in the right way (i. 124, 3; 113, 12). Nay, even the *Panis*, to whom *Saramâ* was sent to claim the cows, are mentioned together with *Ushas*, the Dawn. She is asked to wake those who worship the gods, but not to wake the *Panis* (i. 124, 10). In another passage (iv. 51, 3) it is said that the *Panis* ought to sleep in the midst of darkness, while the Dawn rises to bring treasures for man.

It is more than probable, therefore, that *Saramâ* was but one of the many names of the Dawn; it is almost certain that the idea of storm never entered into the conception of her. The myth of which we have collected the fragments is clear enough. It is a reproduction of the old story of the break of day. The bright cows, the rays of the sun or the rain-clouds, — for both go by the same name, — have been stolen by the powers of darkness, by the Night and her manifold progeny. Gods and men are anxious for their return. But where are they to be found? They are hidden in a dark and strong stable, or scattered along the ends of the sky, and the robbers will not restore them. At last in the farthest distance the first signs of the Dawn appear; she peers about, and runs with lightning quickness, it may be, like a hound after a scent,[1] across the darkness of the sky. She is look-

[1] *Erigone*, the early-born, also called *Aletis*, the rover, when looking for

ing for something, and, following the right path, she has found it. She has heard the lowing of the cows, and she returns to her starting-place with more intense splendor.[1] After her return there rises *Indra*, the god of light, ready to do battle in good earnest against the gloomy powers, to break open the strong stable in which the bright cows were kept, and to bring light, and strength, and life back to his pious worshippers. This is the simple myth of *Saramâ*; composed originally of a few fragments of ancient speech, such as: " the Paṇis stole the cows," i. e. the light of day is gone; " Saramâ looks for the cows," i. e. the Dawn is spreading; " Indra has burst the dark stable," i. e. the sun has risen.

All these are sayings or proverbs peculiar to India, and no trace of *Saramâ* has yet been discovered in the mythological phraseology of other nations. But let us suppose that the Greeks said, "*Saramâ* herself has been carried off by *Paṇi*, but the gods will destroy her hiding-place and bring her back." This, too, would originally have meant no more than that the Dawn who disappears in the morning will come back in the gloaming, or with the light of the next day. The idea that *Paṇi* wished to seduce *Saramâ* from her allegiance to *Indra*, may be discovered in the ninth verse of the Vedic dialogue, though in India it does not seem to have given rise to any further myths. But many a myth that only germinates in the Veda may be seen breaking forth in full bloom in Homer. If, then, we may be allowed a guess, we

the dead body of her father, *Ikarius* (the father of *Penelope* is his namesake), is led by a dog, *Maira*. See Jacobi's *Mythologie*, s. v. *Ikarius*.

[1] *Eeriboia*, or *Eriboia*, betrays to *Hermes* the hiding-place where *Ares* was kept a prisoner. *Il.* v. 385.

should recognize in *Helen*, the sister of the *Dioskuroi*, the Indian *Saramâ*, their names being phonetically identical,[1] not only in every consonant and vowel, but even in their accent. Apart from all mythological considerations, *Saramâ* in Sanskrit is the same word as *Helena* in Greek; and unless we are prepared to ascribe such coincidences as *Dyaus* and *Zeus*, *Varuṇa* and *Uranos*, *Sarvara* and *Cerberus*, to mere accident, we are bound to trace *Sarâmâ* and *Heléne* back to some point from which both could have started in common. The siege of Troy is but a repetition of the daily siege of the East by the solar powers that every evening are robbed of their brightest treasures in the West. That siege, in its original form, is the constant theme of the hymns of the Veda. *Saramâ*, it is true, does not yield in the Veda to the temptation of Paṇi, yet the first indications of her faithlessness are there, and the equivocal character of the twilight which she represents would fully account for the further development of the Greek myth. In the Iliad, *Briséis*, the daughter of *Brises*, is one of the first captives taken by the advancing army of the West. In the Veda, before the bright powers reconquer the light that had been stolen by Paṇi, they are said to have conquered the offspring of *Bṛisaya*. That daughter of *Brises* is restored to Achilles when his glory begins to set, just as all the first loves of solar heroes return to them in the last moments of their earthly career.[2] And as the Sanskrit name *Paṇis* betrays the former presence of an *r*,[3] *Paris*

---

[1] As to Sk. ṁ = Greek s, see Curtius, *Grundzüge*, II. 121.
[2] See Cox, *Tales of Argos and Thebes*, Introduction, p. 90.
[3] I state this very hesitatingly, because the etymology of *Paṇi* is as doubtful as that of *Paris*, and it is useless almost to compare mythological

himself might be identified with the robber who tempted *Saramâ*. I lay no stress on *Helen* calling herself a dog (Il. vi. 344), but that the beautiful daughter of Zeus, (*duhitâ Divah*), the sister of the *Dioskuroi*, was one of the many personifications of the Dawn, I have never doubted. Whether she is carried off by *Theseus* or by *Paris*, she is always reconquered for her rightful husband; she meets him again at the setting of his life, and dies with him pardoned and glorified. This is the burden of many a Dawn myth, and it is the burden of the story of *Helen*.

But who was *Sârameya*? His name certainly approaches very near to *Hermeias*, or *Hermes*, and though the exact form corresponding to *Sârameya* in Greek would be *Heremeias*, yet in proper names a slight anomaly like this may pass. Unfortunately, however, the Rig-Veda tells us even less of *Sârameya* than of *Saramâ*. It never calls any special deity the son of *Saramâ*, but allows us to take the name in its appellative sense, namely, connected with *Saramâ* or the dawn. If *Hermeias* is *Sârameya*, it is but another instance of a mythological germ withering away in one country, and spreading most luxuriantly in another. *Dyaus* in the Veda is the mere shadow of a deity if compared with the

names, without first discovering their etymological intention. Mr. Cox, in his Introduction to the *Tales of Argos and Thebes* (p. 90), endeavors to show that *Paris* belongs to the class of bright solar heroes. Yet if the germ of the *Iliad* is the battle between the solar and nocturnal powers, Paris surely belongs to the latter, and he whose destiny it is to kill Achilles in the *Western gates*,

ἤματι τῷ ὅτε κέν σε Πάρις καὶ Φοῖβος Ἀπόλλων
Ἐσθλὸν ἐόντ' ὀλέσωσιν ἐνὶ Σκαιῇσι πύλῃσιν.

could hardly have been himself of solar or vernal lineage.

Greek *Zeus*; *Varuṇa*, on the contrary, has assumed much greater proportions in India than *Uranos* in Greece, and the same applies to *Vṛitra*, as compared with the Greek *Orthros*. But though we know so little about *Sârameya* in the Veda, the little we know of him is certainly compatible with a rudimentary *Hermes*. As *Sârameya* would be the son of the twilight, or, it may be, the first breeze of the dawn, so *Hermes* is born early in the morning. (Hom. Hym. Merc. 17.) As the Dawn in the Veda is brought by the bright *Harits*, so *Hermes* is called the leader of the *Charites* (ἡγεμὼν Χαρίτων). In the seventh book of the Rig-Veda (vii. 54, 55) we find a number of verses strung together as it would seem at random, to be used as magical formulæ for sending people to sleep.[1] The principal deity invoked is *Vâstoshpati*, which means lord or guardian of the house, a kind of *Lar*. In two of these verses, the being invoked, whatever it be, is called *Sârameya*, and is certainly addressed as a dog, the watch-dog of the house. In the later Sanskrit also, *sârameya* is said to mean dog. *Sârameya*, if it is here to be taken as the name of a deity, would seem to have been a kind of tutelary deity, the peep of day conceived as a person, watching unseen at the doors of heaven during the night, and giving his first bark in the morning. The same morning deity would naturally have been supposed to watch over the houses of man. The verses addressed to him do not tell us much:—

"Guardian of the house, destroyer of evil, who assumest all forms, be to us a helpful friend." (1.)

[1] In viii. 47, 14, Ushas is asked to carry off sleeplessness.

"When thou, bright *Sáraméya*, openest thy teeth, O red one, spears seem to glitter on thy jaws as thou swallowest. Sleep, sleep." (2.)

"Bark at the thief, *Sáraméya*, or at the robber, O restless one! Now thou barkest at the worshippers of *Indra*; why dost thou distress us? Sleep, sleep!" (3.)

It is doubtful whether the guardian of the house (*Vástoshpati*), addressed in the first verse, is intended to be addressed in the next verses; it is equally doubtful whether *Sáraméya* is to be taken as a proper name at all, or whether it simply means ἁιός, bright, or speckled like the dawn. But if *Sáraméya* is a proper name, and if he is meant for the guardian of the house, no doubt it is natural to compare him with the *Hermes propylaeos, prothyraeos,* and *pronaos*, and with the *Hermae* in public places and private houses in Greece.[1] Dr. Kuhn thinks that

---

[1] M. Michel Bréal, who has so ably analyzed the myth of Cacus (*Hercule et Cacus: Étude de Mythologie Comparée*, Paris, 1863), and whose more recent essay, *Le Mythe d' Œdipe*, constitutes a valuable contribution to the science of mythology, has sent me the following note on Hermes as the guardian of houses and public places, which, with his kind permission, I beg to submit to the consideration of my readers:—

"A propos du dieu Hermès, je demande à vous soumettre quelques rapprochements. Il me semble que l'explication d'Hermès comme dieu du crépuscule n'épuise pas tous les attributs de cette divinité. Il est encore le protecteur des propriétés, Il préside aux trouvailles: les bornes placées dans les champs, dans les rues et à la porte des temples, ont reçu, au moins en apparence, son nom. Est-ce bien là le même dieu, ou n'avons-nous pas encore ici un exemple de ces confusions de mots dont vous avez été le premier à signaler l'importance? Voici comment je m'explique cet amalgame.

"Nous avons en grec le mot ἕρμα, qui désigne une pierre, une borne, un poteau; ἑρμίν et ἑρμίς, le pied du lit; ἑρμακες, des tas de pierres; ἑρμάξ, un banc de sable; ἑρματίζω, veut dire je charge un vaisseau de son lest, et ἑρμυγλυφεύς désigne d'une manière générale un tailleur de pierres. Il est clair que tous ces mots n'ont rien de commun avec le dieu Hermès.

he can discover in *Sârameya* the god of sleep, but in our hymn he would rather seem to be a disturber of sleep. One other coincidence, however, might be pointed out. The guardian of the house is called a destroyer of evil, more particularly of illness, and the same power is sometimes ascribed to *Hermes*. (Paus. ix. 22, 2.)

We may admit, then, that *Hermes* and *Sârameya* started from the same point, but their history diverged very early. *Sârameya* hardly attained a definite personality, *Hermes* grew into one of the principal gods of Greece. While *Saramâ*, in India, stands on the threshold that separates the gods of light from the gods of darkness, carrying messages from one to the other, and inclining sometimes to the one, sometimes to the other, *Hermes*, the god of the twilight, betrays his equivocal nature by stealing, though only in fun, the herds of *Apollo*, but restoring them without the violent combat that is waged for the same herds in India between *Indra*, the bright god, and *Vala*, the robber. In India the Dawn brings the light, in

---

" Mais nous trouvons d'un autre côté le diminutif ἑρμίδιον ou ἑρμίδιον, que les anciens traduisent par ' petite statue d'Hermès.' Je crois que c'est ce mot qui a servi de transition et qui nous a valu ces pierres grossièrement taillées, dans lesquelles on a voulu reconnaître le dieu, devenu dès-lors le patron des propriétaires, malgré sa réputation de voleur. Quant à ἕρμαιον, qui désigne les trouvailles, je ne sais si c'est à l'idée d'Hermès ou à celle de borne (comme marquant la limite de la propriété) qu'il faut rapporter ce mot.

" Il resterait encore à expliquer un autre attribut d'Hermès — celui de l'éloquence. Mais je ne me rends pas bien compte de la vraie nature du rapport qui unit le mot Hermès avec les mots comme ἑρμηνεύω, ἑρμηνεία.

" J'ai oublié de vous indiquer d'où je fais venir les mots comme ἕρμα, etc. Je les crois dérivés du verbe εἴργω, ἔργω, en sorte que ἕρμα serait pour ἔργμα, et de la même famille que ἕρκος. L'esprit rude est-il primitif? Cela ne me paraît pas certain. Peut-être ces mots sont-ils de la même famille que le latin arceo, arctum, arculae, etc."

Greece the Twilight is itself supposed to have stolen it, or to hold back the light,[1] and *Hermes*, the twilight, surrenders the booty when challenged by the sun-god Apollo. Afterwards the fancy of Greek poets takes free flight, and out of common clay gradually models a divine image. But even in the Hermes of Homer and other poets we can frequently discover the original traits of a *Sârameya*, if we take that word in the sense of twilight, and look on *Hermes* as a male representative of the light of the morning. He loves *Herse*, the dew, and *Aglauros*, her sister; among his sons is *Kephalos*, the head of the day. He is the herald of the gods, so is the twilight, so was *Saramâ*, the messenger of Indra. He is the spy of the night (νυκτὸς ὀπωπητήρ); he sends sleep and dreams; the bird of the morning, the cock, stands by his side. Lastly, he is the guide of travellers, and particularly of the souls who travel on their last journey; he is the *Psychopompos*. And here he meets again, to some extent, with the Vedic *Sârameya*. The Vedic poets have imagined two dogs belonging to *Yama*, the lord of the departed spirit. They are called the messengers of *Yama*, blood-thirsty, broad-snouted, brown, four-eyed, pale, and *sârameya*, the dawn-children. The departed is told to pass them by on his way to the Fathers, who are rejoicing with *Yama*; *Yama* is asked to protect the departed from these dogs; and, finally, the dogs themselves are implored to grant life to the living and to let them see the sun again. These two dogs represent one of the lowest of the many conceptions

---

[1] A similar idea is expressed in the Veda (v. 79,9), where *Ushas* is asked to rise quickly, that the sun may not hurt her with his light, like a thief.

of morning and evening, or, as we should say, of Time, unless we comprehend in the same class of ideas the " two white rats," which, in the fable, gnaw the root the culprit laid hold of when, followed by a furious elephant, he rushed into a well and saw at the bottom the dragon with open jaws, and the four serpents in the four corners of the well. The furious elephant is explained by the Buddhist moralist as death, the well as the earth, the dragon as hell, the four serpents as the four elements, the root of the shrub as the root of human life, the two white rats as sun and moon, which gradually consume the life of man.[1] In Greece, *Hermes*, a child of the Dawn, with its fresh breezes, was said to carry off the soul of the departed; in India, Morning and Evening,[2] like two dogs, were fabled to watch for their prey, and to lay hold of those who could not reach the blessed abode of the Father. Greece, though she recognized *Hermes* as the guide of the souls of the departed, did not degrade him to the rank of a watch-dog of *Hades*. These watch-dogs, *Kerberos* and *Orthros*, represent, however, like the two dogs of *Yama*, the gloom of the morning and evening, here conceived as hostile and demoniacal powers. *Orthros* is the dark spirit that is to be fought by the Sun in the morning, the well-known Sanskrit *Vṛitra*; but Hermes, too, is said to rise *órthrios*, in the gloom of

---

[1] Cf. Stanislas Julien. *Les Avadânas, Contes et Apologues Indiens* (Paris, 1859), vol. i. p. 190. Dr. Rost, *The Chinese and Japanese Repository*, No. v. p. 217. *History of Barlaam and Joasaph*, ascribed to John of Damascus (about 740 A. D.), chap. xii.; *Fables of Pilpay*; *Gesta Romanorum* (Swann's translation, vol. ii. No. 88), &c.

[2] Day and Night are called the outstretched arms of death, Kaushîtaki br. II. 9: atha mṛityor bâ vâ etau vṛijabâhû yad ahorâtre.

the morning. *Kerberos* is the darkness of night, to be fought by *Herakles*, the Night herself being called Śarvarî[1] in Sanskrit. Hermes, as well as Kerberos, is called *trikephalos*,[2] with three heads, and so is *Triśiras*, the brother of *Saranyû*, another name of the Dawn.[3]

There is one point still to be considered, namely, whether, by the poets of the Veda, the dawn is ever conceived as a dog, and whether there is in the hymns themselves any foundation for the later legends which speak of *Saramâ* as a dog. Professor Kuhn thinks that the word *śûna*, which occurs in the Veda, is a secondary form of *śvan*, meaning dog, and that such passages as "śunám huvema maghávûnam Indram" (iii. 31, 22) should be translated, "Let us invoke the dog, the mighty Indra." If this were so, we might prove, no doubt, that the Dawn also was spoken of as a dog. For we read (iv. 3, 11): "Śunám náraḥ pári sadan ushásam," "Men surrounded the dog, the Dawn." But does *śuna* ever mean dog? Never, it would seem, if used by itself. In all the passages where this word *śunám* occurs, it means for the sake of happiness, auspiciously.[4] It is particularly used with verbs meaning to invoke (hve), to worship (parisad), to pray (îḍ).[5] There is not a single passage

---

[1] See M. M., "*Ist Bellerophon Vritrahan?*" in Kuhn's *Zeitschrift*, v. 149.

[2] Hermes trikephalos, Gerhard, *Gr. Myth*. 231, 8.

[3] That Kerberos is connected with the Sanskrit *śarvarî*, night, was pointed out by me in the *Transactions of the Philol. Soc.*, April 14, 1848. *Sabala*, a corruption of *śarvara*, is vindicated as the name of daybreak, *śyâma*, black, as the name of nightfall, by the *Kaushîtaki-brâhmaṇa*, ii. 9 *seq*. (*Ind. Stud.* II. 295.) This, no doubt, is an artificial explanation, but it shows a vague recollection of the original meaning of the two dogs.

[4] I. 117, 19, III. 31, 22; iv. 3, 11; 57, 4; 87, 8; vi. 16, 4; x. 102, 8; 128, 7; 160, 5.

[5] Of *śvân*, we find the nominative *śvâ* (vii. 55, 5; x. 86, 4); the accu-

where *sunâm* could be taken for dog. But there are compounds in which *suna* would seem to have that meaning. In viii. 46, 28, *Sunâ-ishitam* most likely means carried by dogs, and in *Sunâsirau* we have the name of a couple of deities, the former of which is said to be *Suna*, the latter *Sira*. Yâska recognizes in *Suna* a name of *Vâyu*, or the wind, in *Sira* a name of *Aditya*, or the sun. Another authority, *Saunaka*, declares *Suna* to be a name of *Indra*, *Sira* a name of *Vâyu*. Âsvalâyana (Srautasûtra, ii. 20) declares that *Sunâsirau* may be meant for *Vâyu*, or for *Indra*, or for *Indra* and *Sûrya* together. This shows, at all events, that the meaning of the two names was doubtful, even among early native theologians. The fact is that the *Sunâsirau* occur but twice in the Rig-Veda, in a harvest-hymn. Blessings are pronounced on the plough, the cattle, the laborers, the furrow; and among the rest the following words are addressed to the Sunâsirau:—

"O *Sunâsirau*, be pleased with this prayer. The milk which you make in heaven, pour it down upon this earth." (5.) And again:—

"May the ploughshares cut the earth with good luck! May the ploughers with the oxen follow with good luck! May *Parjanya* (the god of rain) give good luck with fat and honey! May the *Sunâsirau* give us good luck!"

Looking at these passages, and at the whole hymn from which they are taken, I cannot agree with Dr. Roth, who, in his notes to the Nirukta, thinks that

native *svânam* (L 161, 13; ix. 101, 1; 101, 13); the genitive *sûnah* (l. 182, 4; iv. 18, 5; viii. 55, 3); the nom. dual *svânâ* (ii. 29, 4), and *svânau*, x. 14, 10; 14, 11. Also *svâpadah*. x. 16, 6.

Sira may in this compound mean the ploughshare, and *Suna* some other part of the plough. *Sira* might have that meaning, but there is nothing to prove that *śuna* ever meant any part of the plough. It will appear, if we read the hymn more attentively, that its author clearly addresses the two *Sunâsirau* differently from the plough, the ploughshare, the furrow. They are asked to send rain from heaven, and they are addressed together with *Parjanya*, himself a deity, the god of rain. There is another verse quoted by *Âśvalâyana*, in which Indra is called *Śunâsira*.[1] What the exact meaning of the word is we cannot tell. It may be *Śuna*, as Dr. Kuhn would suggest, the dog, whether meant for *Vâyu* or *Indra*, and *Sira*, the sun or the furrow; or it may be a very old name for the dog-star, called the Dog and the Sun, and in that case *sira*, or its derivative *sairya*, would give us the etymon of *Seirios*.[2] But all this is doubtful, and there is nothing, at all events, to justify us in ascribing to *śuna* the meaning of dog in any passage of the Veda.

In the course of our investigations as to the original meaning of *Saramâ*, we had occasion to allude to another name, derived from the same root *sar*, and to which the meaning of *cloud* and *wind* is equally ascribed by Professor Kuhn, namely, *Saranyû*, fem.

Where *saranyû* is used as a masculine, its meaning is by no means clear. In the 61st hymn of the tenth book it is almost impossible to find a continuous

---

[1] Indram vayam śunâsiram asmin yajne havâmahe, sa vâjeshu pra no avishat.

[2] Curtius, *Grundzüge*, ii. 128, derives Σείριος from *svar*, which, however, would have given σύσιος or σύσιος, rather than σείριος.

thread of thought. The verse in which *Saraṇyu* occurs is addressed to the kings *Mitra* and *Varuṇa*, and it is said there that *Saraṇyu* went to them in search of the cows. The commentator here explains *Saraṇyu* unhesitatingly by *Yama* (saraṇaśila). In the next verse *Saraṇyu* is called a horse, just as *Saraṇyû* (fem.) is spoken of as a mare; but he is called the son of him, i. e., according to Sâyaṇa, of Varuṇa.[1] In iii. 32, 5, *Indra* is said to cause the waters to come forth together with the *Saraṇyus*, who are here mentioned very much like the Angiras in other places, as helpers of Indra in the great battle against *Vṛitra* or *Vala*. In i. 62, 4, the common epithets of the *Angiras* (*navagva* and *daśagva*) are applied to the *Saraṇyus*, and there too Indra is said to have torn Vala asunder with the *Saraṇyus*. I believe, therefore, we must distinguish between the *Saraṇyus* in the plural, a name of like import as that of the Angiras, possibly as that of the Maruts, and Saraṇyu in the singular, a name of the son of *Varuṇa* or of *Yama*.

Of *Saraṇyû*, too, as a female deity, we learn but little from the hymns of the Rig-Veda; and though we ought always to guard against mixing up the ideas of the Rishis with those of their commentators, it must be confessed that in the case of *Saraṇyû* we should hardly understand what is said of her by the Rishis without the explanations given by later writers, such as *Yâska*, *Śaunaka*, and others. The classical and often-quoted passage about *Saraṇyû* is found Rv. x. 17, 2:—

---

[1] He is called there Jaraṇyu, from a root which in Greek may have yielded Gorgô. Cf. Kuhn, *Zeitschrift*, l. 460. *Erinys* and *Gorgons* are almost identified in Greek.

"*Tvashṭar* makes a wedding for his daughter, thus saying the whole world comes together; the mother of *Yama*, being wedded, the wife of the great *Vivasvat* has perished."

"They hid the immortal from the mortals, making one like her they have given her to *Vivasvat*. But she bore the *Aśvins* when this happened, and *Saraṇyû* left two couples[1] behind."

Yâska (xii. 10) explains: "*Saraṇyû*, the daughter of *Tvashṭar*, had twins from *Vivasvat*, the sun. She placed another like her in her place, changed her form into that of a horse, and ran off. *Vivasvat*, the sun, likewise assumed the form of a horse, followed her, and embraced her. Hence the two *Aśvins* were born, and the substitute (*Savarṇâ*) bore *Manu*." Yâska likewise states that the first twins of *Saraṇyû* are by etymologists supposed to be *Madhyama* and *Mâdhyamikâ Vâch*, by mythologists *Yama* and *Yamî*; and he adds at the end, in order to explain the disappearance of *Saraṇyû*, that the night vanishes when the sun rises. This last remark, however, is explained or corrected by the commentator,[2] who says that *Ushas*, the dawn, was the wife of *Âditya*, the sun, and that she, and not the night, disappears at the time of sunrise.

Before proceeding further, I shall add a few particulars from Śaunaka's Bṛihaddevatâ. He says that *Tvashṭar* had a couple of children, *Saraṇyû* and *Triśiras* (Trikephalos); that he gave *Saraṇyû* to

[1] One couple, according to Dr. Kuhn, *Zeitschrift für Vergleichende Sprachforschung*, I. p. 441.
[2] Samkshepato Ubhâshyakâro 'rtham nirâha. Âdityasya 'Ushâ jâyâm, âdityodaye 'ntardhîyata. It is possible, of course, to speak of the dawn both as the beginning of the day, and as the end of the night.

Vivasvat, and that she bore him *Yama* and *Yami*: they were twins, but *Yama* was the elder of the two. Then *Saraṇyû* made a woman like herself, gave her the children, and went away. *Vivasvat* was deceived, and the substitute (*Savarṇâ*) bore him a child, *Manu*, as bright as his father. Afterwards *Vivasvat* discovered his mistake, and assuming himself the form of a horse, rushed after *Saraṇyû*, and she became in a peculiar manner the mother of *Nâsatya* and *Dasra*, who are called the two *Aśvins*, or horsemen.

It is difficult to say how much of these legends is old and genuine, and how much was invented afterwards to explain certain mythological phrases occurring in the Rig-Veda.

Saraṇyû, the water-woman,[1] as the daughter of *Tvashṭar* (maker), who is also called *Savitar* (creator), *Viśvarûpa*, having all forms (x. 10, 5) — as the wife of *Vivasvat* (also called *Gandharva*, x. 10, 4), as the mother of *Yama* — as hidden by the immortals from the eyes of mortals — as replaced by another wife, and again as the mother of the *Aśvins* — all this is ancient, and confirmed by the hymns of the Rig-Veda. But the legend of *Saraṇyû* and *Vivasvat* assuming the form of horses, may be meant simply as an explanation of the name of their children, the *Aśvins* (equini or equites). The legend of *Manu* being the son of *Vivasvat* and *Savarṇâ* may be intended as an explanation of the names *Manu Vaivasvata*, and *Manu Sâvarṇi*.

[1] In x. 10, 4, 1 take *Gandharva* for *Vivasvat*, *Apyâ Yoshâ* for *Saraṇyâ*, in accordance with Sâyaṇa, though differing from Professor Kuhn. In the next verse *janitâ* is not father, but creator, and belongs to *Tvashṭâ savitâ viśvarûpaḥ*, the father of *Saraṇyâ*, or the creator in general in his solar character of *Savitar*.

Professor Kuhn has identified *Saraṇyû* with the Greek *Erinys*. With this identification I fully agree. I had arrived independently at the same identification, and we had discussed the problem together before Dr. Kuhn's essay was published. But our agreement ends with the name; and after having given a careful, and, I hope, impartial consideration to my learned friend's analysis, I feel confirmed rather than shaken in the view which I entertained of *Saraṇyû* from the first. Professor Kuhn, adopting in the main the views of Professor Roth, explains the myth as follows :— " *Tvashṭar*, the creator, prepares the wedding for his daughter *Saraṇyû*, i. e. the fleet, impetuous, dark, storm-cloud (Sturmwolke), which in the beginning of all things soared in space. He gives to her as husband *Vivasvat*, the brilliant, the light of the celestial heights — according to later views, which, for the sake of other analogies, I cannot share, the sun-god himself. Light and cloudy darkness beget two couples of twins: first, *Yama*, i. e. the twin, and *Yamî*, the twin-sister (a word which suggests itself); secondly, the two *Aśvins*, the horsemen. But after this the mother disappears, i. e. the chaotic, storm-shaken dimness; the gods hide her, and she leaves behind two couples. To *Vivasvat* there remains, as his wife, but one like her, an anonymous woman, not further to be defined. The latest tradition (Vishṇu Purâṇa, p. 266) calls her *Chhâyâ*, shadow, i. e. the myth knows of no other wife to give to him."

Was this the original conception of the myth? Was *Saraṇyû* the storm-cloud, which in the beginning of all things was soaring in infinite space? Is it possible to form a clear conception of such a being, as described by Professor Roth and Professor Kuhn? And if not, how is the original idea of *Saraṇyû* to be discovered?

There is but one way, I believe, for discovering the original meaning of *Saraṇyû*, namely, to find out whether the attributes and acts peculiar to *Saraṇyû* are ever ascribed to other deities whose nature is less obscure. The first question, therefore, we have to ask is this, — Is there any other deity who is said to have given birth to twins? There is, namely, *Ushas*, the Dawn. We read (iii. 39, 3) in a hymn which describes the sunrise under the usual imagery of *Indra* conquering darkness and recovering the sun: —

"The mother of the twins has borne the twins; the tip of my tongue falls, for she approaches; the twins that are born assume form — they, the conquerors of darkness, that have come at the foot of the sun."

We might have guessed from the text itself, even without the help of the commentator, that the "mother of the twins" here spoken of is the Dawn; but it may be stated that the commentator, too, adopts this view.

The next question is, Is there any other deity who is spoken of as a horse, or rather, as a mare? There is, namely, *Ushas*, the Dawn. The sun, no doubt, is the deity most frequently spoken of as a horse.[1] But the Dawn also is not only called rich in horses, and represented as carried by them, but she is herself compared to a horse. Thus, i. 30, 29, and iv. 52, 2,[2]

---

[1] *Comparative Mythology*, p. 82.
[2] áve ná chitre aruṣhi; or, better, ásveva chitre.

CORRELATIVE DEITIES.

the Dawn is likened to a mare, and in the latter passage she is called at the same time the friend of the *Aśvins*. In the Mahâbhârata (Âdiparva, 2599) the mother of the Aśvins is said to have the form of a mare, *vaḍavâ*.[1]

Here, then, we have a couple, the Sun and the Dawn, that might well be represented in legendary language as having assumed the form of a horse and a mare.

The next question is, Who could be called their children? and in order to answer this question satisfactorily, it will be necessary to discuss somewhat fully the character of a whole class of Vedic deities. It is important to observe that the children of *Saraṇyû* are spoken of as twins. The idea of twin powers is one of the most fertile ideas in ancient mythology. Many of the most striking phenomena of nature were comprehended by the ancients under that form, and were spoken of in their mythic phraseology as brother and sister, husband and wife, father and mother. The Vedic Pantheon particularly is full of deities which are always introduced in the dual, and they all find their explanation in the palpable dualism of nature, Day and Night, Dawn and Gloaming, Morning and Evening, Summer and Winter, Sun and Moon, Light and Darkness, Heaven and Earth. All these are dualistic or correlative conceptions. The two are conceived as one, as belonging to each other; nay, they sometimes share the same name. Thus we find *Ahorâtre*[2] (not in Rig-Veda), day and night,

---

[1] Kuhn, *Zeitschrift*, I. 523.
[2] A distinction ought to be made between *ahorâtrâḥ*, or *ahorâtram*, the time of day and night together, a νυχθήμερον, which is a masculine or

but also *Ahanî* (i. 123, 7), the two days, i. e. day and night. We find *Ushâsânâktâ* (i. 122, 2), dawn and night, *Nâktoshâsâ* (i. 13, 7; 142, 7), night and dawn, but also *Ushâsau* (i. 188, 6), the two dawns, i. e. dawn and night. There is *Dyâvâprithivî*, heaven and earth (i. 143, 2), *Prithivîdyâvâ*, earth and heaven (iii. 46, 5), but also *Dyâvâ* (iii. 6, 4). Instead of *Dyâvâprithivî*, other compounds such as *Dyâvâkshâmâ* (iii. 8, 8), *Dyâvâbhûmî* (iv. 55, 1), are likewise met with in the text, *Dyunisâu*, day and night, in the commentary (iii. 55, 15). Now as long as we have to deal with such outspoken names as these, there can be little doubt as to the meaning of the praises bestowed on them, or of the acts which they are said to have performed. If Day and Night, or Heaven and Earth, are praised as sisters, even as twin-sisters, we can hardly call this as yet mythological language, though no doubt it may be a beginning of mythology. Thus we read, i. 123, 7:—

"One goes away, the other comes near, the two *Ahans* (Day and Night) walk together. One of the

neuter, and *ahorâtrî*, the compound dual of *ahan*, day, and *râtri*, night, meaning the day and the night, as they are frequently addressed together. This compound I take to be a feminine, though, as it can occur in the dual only, it may also be taken for a neuter, as is done by the commentary to Pâṇini, ii. 4, 28; 29, but not by Pâṇini himself. Thus A. V. vi. 128, 3, *Ahorâtrâbhyâm*, as used in the dual, does not mean twice twenty-four hours, but day and night, just as *sûryâchandramasâdbhyâm*, immediately after, means sun and moon. The same applies to A. V. x. 7, 6; 8, 23; Chând. Up. viii. 4, 1; Mânu, i. 65; and other passages given by Boehtlingk and Roth, s. v. In all of these the meaning, "two nycthemerons," would be entirely inappropriate. That *ahorâtre* was considered a feminine as late as the time of the Vâjasaneyi-sanhitâ, is shown by a passage, xiv. 30, where *ahorâtre* are called *adhipatnî*, two mistresses. *Ahorâtre* does not occur in the Rig-Veda. *Ahorâtrâṇi* occurs once in the tenth book. A passage quoted by B. R. from the Rig-Veda, where *ahorâtrâḥ* is said to occur as masc. plur., does not belong to the Rig-Veda at all.

two neighbors created darkness in secret, the Dawn flashed forth on her shining car."

I. 185, 1: "Which of the two is first, which is last? How are they born, ye poets? Who knows it? These two support everything that exists; the two *Ahans* (Day and Night) turn round like wheels."[1]

In iv. 55, 3, Dawn and Night (*Ushásánáktá*) are spoken of as distinct from the two *Ahans* (Day and Night).

In v. 82, 8, *Savitar*, the sun, is said to walk before them.

In x. 39, 12, the daughter of the sky, i. e. the Dawn, and the two *Ahans*, Day and Night, are said to be born when the *Asvins* put the horses to their car.

In a similar manner the *Dyáváprithiví*, Heaven and Earth, are spoken of as sisters, as twins, as living in the same house (i. 159, 4), &c.

It is clear, however, that, instead of addressing dawn and gloaming, morning and evening, day and night, heaven and earth by their right names, and as femininies, it was possible, nay, natural, to speak of light and darkness as male powers, and to address the author of light and darkness, the bringers of day and night, as personal beings. And so we find, corresponding to the former couples, a number of correlative deities, having in common most of the characteristics of the former, but assuming an independent mythological existence.

The best known are the *Asvins*, who are always spoken of in the dual. Whether *asvin* means pos-

---

[1] Or like things belonging to a wheel, spokes, &c.

scssed of horses, horseman, or descendants of *Aśva*,[1] the sun, or *Aśvá*, the dawn, certain it is that the same conception underlies their name and the names of the sun and the dawn, when addressed as horses. The sun was looked upon as a racer, so was the dawn, though in a less degree, and so were, again, the two powers which seemed incorporated in the coming and going of each day and each night, and which were represented as the chief actors in all the events of the diurnal play. This somewhat vague but, for this very reason, I believe, all the more correct character of the two *Aśvins* did not escape even the later commentators. *Yáska*, in the twelfth book of his *Nirukta*, when explaining the deities of the sky, begins with the two *Aśvins*. They come first, he says, of all the celestial gods, they arrive even before sunrise. Their name is explained in the usual fanciful way of Indian commentators. They are called *Aśvin*, Yáska says, from the root *aś*, to pervade; because the one pervades everything with moisture, the other with light. He likewise quotes *Aurṇavábha*, who derives *Aśvin* from *aśva*, horse. But who are these *Aśvins*? he asks. "Some," he replies, "say they are heaven and earth, others day and night, others sun and moon; and the legendarians maintain that they were two virtuous kings."

Let us consider next the time when the *Aśvins* appear. Yáska places it after midnight, as the light begins gradually to withstand the darkness of the night; and this agrees perfectly with the indications to be found in the Rig-Veda, where the *Aśvins* appear before the dawn, "when Night leaves her

[1] Cf. Kriśáśvinah, Páṇ. iv. 2, 66.

sister, the Dawn, when the dark one gives way to the bright (vii. 71, 1);" or "when one black cow sits among the bright cows" (x. 61, 4, and vi. 64, 7).

Yâska seems to assign to the one the overcoming of light by darkness, to the other the overcoming of darkness by light.[1] Yâska then quotes sundry verses to prove that the two *Asvins* belong together (though one lives in the sky, the other in the air, says the commentator), that they are invoked together, and that they receive the same offerings. "You walk along during the night like two black goats.[2] When, O Asvins, do you come here towards the gods?"

In order to prove, however, that the *Asvins* are likewise distinct beings, another half-verse is added, in which the one is called *Vâsâtya* (not *Nâsatya*), the son of Night, the other the son of Dawn.

More verses are then quoted from the Rig-Veda — those before quoted coming from a different source — where the *Asvins* are called *ihéhajâtâu*, born here and there, i. e. on opposite sides, or in the air and in the sky. One is *jishṇu*, victorious, he who bides in the air; the other is *subhaga*, happy, the son of *Dyu*, or the sky, and here identified with *Âditya* or the sun. Again: "Wake the two who harness their cars in the morning! Asvins, come hither, for a draught of this Soma."

[1] The words of Yâska are obscure, nor does the commentator throw much light on them. "Tatra yat tamo 'napravishṭam jyotishi tadbhâgo madhyamaḥ, tan madhyamasya rûpam. Yaj jyotis tamasy anupravishṭam tadbhâgam tadrûpam âdityah (sic). Tâv etau madhyamottamâv iti evametam âchâryasya." *Madhyama* may be meant for *Indra*, *Uttama* for *Âditya*; but in that case the early *Asvin* would be *Âditya*, the sun, the late *Asvin*, *Indra*. Dr. Kuhn (l. c. p. 442) takes *madhyama* for *Agni*.

[2] *Petvas* is explained by *mesha*, not by *megha*, as stated by Dr. Roth. Cf. Rv. x. 39, 9, ajâ iva.

Lastly: "Sacrifice early, hail the Aśvins! Not in the dreary evening is the sacrifice of the gods. Nay, some person different from us sacrifices and draws them away. The sacrificer who comes first is the most liked."

The time of the *Aśvins* is by Yâska supposed to extend to about sunrise; at that time other gods appear and require their offerings, and first of all *Ushas*, the Dawn.[1] Here, again, a distinction is made between the dawn of the air (who was enumerated in the two preceding books, together with the other mid-air deities) and the dawn of the sky, a distinction which it is difficult to understand. For though in the verse which is particularly said to be addressed to the dawn of the air, she is said to appear in the eastern half of the *rajas*, which *rajas* Yâska takes to mean mid-air, yet this could hardly have constituted a real distinction in the minds of the original poets. "These rays of the dawn have made a light in the eastern half of the welkin; they adorn themselves with splendor, like strong men unsheathing their weapons: the bright cows approach the mothers" (of light, *bhâso nirmâtryaḥ*).

Next in time is *Sûryâ*, a female *Sûrya*, i. e. the sun as a feminine, or, according to the commentator, the Dawn again under a different name. In the Rig-Veda, too, the Dawn is called the wife of *Sûrya* (sûryasya yóshâ, vii. 75, 5), and the Aśvins are sometimes called the husbands of *Sûryâ* (Rv. iv. 43, 6). It is said in a Brâhmaṇa that *Savitar* gave *Sûryâ* (his daughter?) to King *Soma* or to *Prajâpati*. The commentator explains that *Savitar* is the sun, *Soma*

[1] Rv. I. 46, 14: yuvóḥ ushâḥ ânu śríyam páriĵmanoḥ upâ acharat.

the moon, and *Súryá* the moonlight, which comes from the sun. This, however, seems somewhat fanciful, and savors decidedly of later mythology.

Next in time follows *Vrishâkapáyí*, the wife of *Vrishâkapi*. Who she is is very doubtful.[1] The commentary says that she is the wife of *Vrishâkapí*, and that *Vrishâkapi* is the sun, so called because he is enveloped in mist (avaśyâvân, or avaśyâyavân). Most likely[2] *Vrishâkapáyí* is again but another conception or name of the Dawn, as the wife of the Sun, who draws up or drinks the vapors from the earth. Her son is said to be *Indra*, her daughter-in-law *Vâch*, here meant for thunder (?), a genealogy hardly in accordance with the rest of the hymn from which our verse is taken, and where *Vrishâkapáyí* is rather the wife than the mother of *Indra*. Her oxen are clouds of vapor, which *Indra* swallows, as the sun might be said to consume the vapors of the morning. It is difficult, on seeing the name of *Vrishâkapi*, not to think of *Erikapaeos*, an Orphic name of *Protogonos*, and synonymous with *Phanes, Helios, Priapos, Dionysos*; but the original conception of *Vrishâkapi* (*vrishan*, bull, irrigator; *kapi*, ape or tremulous) is not much clearer than that of *Erikapaeos*, and we should only be explaining *obscurum per obscurius*.

Next in order of the deities of the morning is our *Saranyû*, explained simply as dawn, and followed by *Savitar*, whose time is said to be when the sky is free from darkness and covered with rays.

[1] According to Dr. Kuhn, the Evening-twilight, l. c. p. 441, but without proof.
[2] This is the opinion of Durga, who speaks of Ushas, vrishâkapáyyavasthâyâm.

We need not follow any further the systematic catalogue of the gods as given by Yâska. It is clear that he knew of the right place of the two Aśvins, and that he placed the activity of the one at the very beginning of day, and hence that of the other at the very beginning of night. He treats them as twins, born together in the early twilight.

Yâska, however, is not to be considered as an authority, except if he can be proved to agree with the hymns of the Rig-Veda, to which we now return.

The preponderating idea in the conception of the Aśvins in the hymns of the Rig-Veda is that of correlation, which, as we saw, they share in common with such twin-deities as heaven and earth, day and night, &c. That idea, no doubt, is modified according to circumstances, the Aśvins are brothers, Heaven and Earth are sisters. But if we remove these outward masks, we shall find behind them, and behind some other masks, the same actors, Nature in her twofold aspect of daily change — morning and evening, light and darkness — aspects which may expand into those of spring and winter, life and death, nay, even of good and evil.

Before we leave the Aśvins in search of other twins, and ultimately in search of the twin-mother, Saranyû, the following hymn may help to impress on our minds the dual character of these Indian Dioskuroi.

"Like the two stones[1] you sound for the same object.[2] You are like two hawks rushing toward a

[1] Used at sacrifices for crushing and pressing out the juice of the Soma plant.
[2] Tádídártham is used almost adverbially in the sense of "for the same purpose." Thus, Rv. ix. 1, 5, "We come to see every day for the same

tree with a nest;[1] like two priests reciting their prayers at a sacrifice; like the two messengers of a clan called for in many places." (1.)

"Coming early, like two heroes on their chariots, like twin-goats, you come to him who has chosen you; like two women, beautiful in body; like husband and wife, wise among their people." (2.)

"Like two horns, come first towards us; like two hoofs, rushing on quickly; like two birds, ye bright ones, every day, come hither, like two charioteers,[2] O ye strong ones!" (3.)

"Like two ships, carry us across; like two yokes, like two naves of a wheel, like two spokes, like two felloes; like two dogs that do not hurt our limbs; like two armors, protect us from destruction!" (4.)

"Like two winds, like two streams, your motion is eternal; like two eyes, come with your sight towards us! Like two hands, most useful to the body; like two feet, lead us towards wealth." (5.)

"Like two lips, speaking sweetly to the mouth; like two breasts, feed us that we may live. Like two nostrils, as guardians of the body; like two ears, be inclined to listen to us." (6.)

"Like two hands, holding our strength together; like heaven and earth, drive together the clouds. O Aśvins, sharpen these songs that long for you, as a sword is sharpened with a whetstone." (7.)

Like the two *Aśvins*, who are in later times distin-

---

purpose." As to *jar*, I take it in the usual sense of sounding, making a noise, and, more particularly, praising. The stones for pressing out the Soma are frequently spoken of as themselves praising, while they are being handled by the priests (v. 37, 9).

[1] *Niḍi*, originally that where something is placed, afterwards treasure.
[2] Rathyâ. Cf. v. 76, 1.

guished by the names of *Dasra* and *Nâsatya*, we find
another couple of gods, *Indra* and *Agni*, addressed
together in the dual, *Indrâgni*, but likewise as *Indrâ*,
the two Indras, and *Agni*, the two Agnis (vi. 60, 1),
just as heaven and earth are called the two heavens,
and the *Asvins* the two *Dasras*, or the two *Nâsatyas*.
Indra is the god of the bright sky, *Agni* the god of
fire, and they have each their own distinct personality; but when invoked together, they become correlative powers and are conceived as one joint deity.
Curiously enough, they are actually in one passage
called *asvinâ* [1] (i. 109, 4), and they share several other
attributes in common with the *Asvins*. They are
called brothers, they are called twins; and as the
Asvins were called *ihehajâte*, born here and there, i. e.,
on opposite sides, in the East and in the West, or in
heaven and in the air, so *Indra* and *Agni*, when invoked together, are called *ihehamâtarâ*, they whose
mothers are here and there (vi. 59, 2). Attributes
which they share in common with the *Asvins* are
vrishanâ, bulls, or givers of rain;[2] *vritrahanâ*, destroyers of *Vritra*,[3] or of the powers of darkness;
sambhuvâ,[4] givers of happiness; *supânî*, with good
hands; *vilupânî*,[5] with strong hands; *jenyâvasû*, with
genuine wealth.[6] But in spite of these similarities,
it must not be supposed that *Indra* and *Agni* together are a mere repetition of the *Asvins*. There

[1] Dr. Kuhn, l. c. p. 450, quotes this passage and others, from which, he thinks, it appears that *Indra* was supposed to have sprung from a horse (x. 73, 10), and that *Agni* was actually called the horse (ii. 35, 6).
[2] Indra and Agni, i. 109, 4; the Asvins, i. 112, 8.
[3] Indra and Agni, i. 108, 3; the Asvins, viii. 8, 9 (vritrahantamâ).
[4] Indra and Agni, vi. 60, 14; the Asvins, viii. 8, 19; vi. 62, 5.
[5] Indra and Agni, supânî, i. 109, 4; the Asvins, vilupânî, vii. 73, 4.
[6] Indra and Agni, viii. 38, 7; the Asvins, vii. 74, 2.

are certain epithets constantly applied to the *Aśvins* (*śubhaspatî, vâjinîvasû, sudânû,* &c.), which, as far as I know, are not applied to *Indra* and *Agni* together; and *vice versâ* (*sadaspati, sahuri*). Again, there are certain legends constantly told of the *Aśvins*, particularly in their character as protectors of the helpless and dying, and resuscitators of the dead, which are not transferred to *Indra* and *Agni.* Yet, as if to leave no doubt that *Indra*, at all events, coincides in some of his exploits with one of the *Aśvins* or *Nâsatyas,* one of the Vedic poets uses the compound *Indra-Nâsatyau,* Indra and Nâsatya, which, on account of the dual that follows, cannot be explained as *Indra* and the two *Aśvins,* but simply as *Indra* and *Nâsatya.*

Besides the couple of *Indrâgni*, we find some other, though less prominent couples, equally reflecting the dualistic idea of the *Aśvins,* namely, *Indra* and *Varuṇa,* and *Indra* and *Vishṇu,* and, more important than either, *Mitra* and *Varuṇa.* Instead of *Indrâ-Varuṇâ,* we find again *Indrâ,*[1] the two Indras, and *Varuṇâ*, the two Varunas (iv. 41, 1). They are called *sudânû* (iv. 41, 8); *vṛishaṇâ* (vii. 82, 2); *śambhû* (iv. 41, 7); *mahâvasû* (vii. 82, 2). *Indrâ-Vishṇû* are actually called *dasrâ,* the usual name of the *Aśvins* (vi. 69, 7). Now *Mitra* and *Varuṇa* are clearly intended for day and night. They, too, are compared to horses (vi. 67, 4), and they share certain epithets in common with the twin-gods, *sudânû* (vi. 67, 2), *vṛishaṇau* (i. 151, 2). But their character assumes much greater distinctness, and though clearly physical in their first conception, they rise into moral

[1] As in Latin Castores and Pollaces, instead of Castor et Pollux.

powers, far superior in that respect to the *Aśvins* and to *Indrágnî*. Their physical nature is perceived in a hymn of *Vasishṭha* (vii. 63): —

"The sun, common to all men, the happy, the all-seeing, steps forth; the eye of Mitra and Varuṇa, the bright; he who rolls up darkness like a skin."

"He steps forth, the enlivener of men, the great waving light of the sun; wishing to turn round the same wheel which his horse *Etaśa* draws, joined to the team."

"Shining forth, he rises from the lap of the dawn, praised by singers, he, my god Savitar, stepped [1] forth, who never misses the same place."

"He steps forth, the splendor of the sky, the wide-seeing, the far-aiming, the shining wanderer; surely, enlivened by the sun, do men go to their tasks and do their work."

"Where the immortals made a walk for him, there he follows the path, soaring like a hawk. We shall worship you, *Mitra* and *Varuṇa*, when the sun has risen, with praises and offerings."

"Will *Mitra*, *Varuṇa*, and *Aryaman* bestow favor on us and our kin? May all be smooth and easy to us! Protect us always with your blessings!"

The ethic and divine character of Mitra and Varuṇa breaks forth more clearly in the following hymn (vii. 65): —

"When the sun has risen I call on you with hymns, *Mitra* and *Varuṇa*, full of holy strength; ye whose imperishable divinity is the oldest, moving on your way with knowledge of everything." [2]

---

[1] *Chhad* as *scandere*, not as *sconders*.
[2] The last sentence is doubtful.

"For these two are the living spirits among the gods; they are the lords; do you make our fields fertile. May we come to you, *Mitra* and *Varuṇa*, where they nourish days and nights."

"They are bridges made of many ropes leading across unrighteousness, difficult to cross to hostile mortals. Let us pass, *Mitra* and *Varuṇa*, on your way of righteousness, across sin, as in a ship across the water."

Now, if we inquire who could originally be conceived as the father of all these correlative deities, we can easily understand that it must be some supreme power that is not itself involved in the diurnal revolutions of the world, such as the sky, for instance, conceived as the father of all things, or some still more abstract deity, like *Prajâpati*, the lord of creation, or *Tvashṭar*, the fashioner, or *Savitar*, the creator. Their mother, on the contrary, must be the representative of some place in which the twins meet, and from which they seem to spring together in their diurnal career. This place may be either the dawn or the gloaming, the sunrise or the sunset, the East or the West, only all these conceived not as mere abstractions, but as mysterious beings, as mothers, as powers containing within themselves the whole mystery of life and death brought thus visibly before the eyes of the thoughtful worshipper. The dawn, which to us is merely a beautiful sight, was to the early gazer and thinker the problem of all problems. It was the unknown land from whence rose every day those bright emblems of a divine power which left in the mind of man the first impression and intimation of another world, of power above, of order and wisdom. What we simply call the sunrise, brought before their eyes every day the riddle of all riddles, the riddle of existence. The days of their life sprang from that dark abyss which every morning seemed instinct with light and life. Their youth, their manhood, their old age, all were to the Vedic bards the gift of that heavenly mother who appeared bright, young, unchanged, immortal every morning, while everything else seemed to grow old, to change, and droop, and at last to set, never to return. It was there, in that bright chamber, that, as their poets said, mornings and days were spun, or, under a different image, where morning and days were nourished (x. 37, 2 ; vii. 65, 2), where life or time was drawn out (i. 113, 16). It was there that the mortal wished to go to meet Mitra and Varuṇa. The whole theogony and philosophy of the ancient world centred in the Dawn, the mother of the bright gods, of the sun in his various aspects, of the morn, the day, the spring; herself the brilliant image and visage of immortality.

It is of course impossible to enter fully into all the thoughts and feelings that passed through the minds of the early poets when they formed names for that far, far East from whence even the early dawn, the sun, the day, their own life, seemed to spring. A new life flashed up every morning before their eyes, and the fresh breezes of the dawn reached them like greetings wafted across the golden threshold of the sky from the distant lands beyond the mountains, beyond the clouds, beyond the dawn, beyond "the immortal sea which brought us hither." The Dawn seemed to them to open golden gates for the sun to pass in triumph, and while those gates were open, their eyes and their minds strove in their childish way to pierce beyond the limits of this finite world. That silent aspect awakened in the human mind the conception of the Infinite, the Immortal, the Divine, and the names of dawn became naturally the names of higher powers. *Saraṇyû*, the Dawn, was called the mother of Day and Night, the mother of *Mitra* and *Varuṇa*, divine representatives of light and darkness; the mother of all the bright gods (i. 113, 19); the face of *Aditi* (i. 113, 19).[1] Now, whatever the etymological meaning of *Aditi*,[2] it is clear that she is connected with the Dawn — that she represents that which is beyond the dawn, and that she was raised into an emblem of the Divine and the Infinite. *Aditi* is called the *nábhir amritasya, umbilicus immortalitatis,* the cord that connects the immortal and the mortal. Thus the poet exclaims (i. 24, 1): "Who will give us back to the great *Aditi* (to the Dawn, or rather to her from whom we came), that I may see father and mother?" *Âditya*, literally the son of *Aditi*, became the name not only of the sun, but of a class of seven[3] gods, and of gods in general. Rv. x. 63, 2: "You gods who are born of Aditi, from the water, who are born of the earth, hear my calling here." As everything came from *Aditi*, she is called not only the mother of Mitra, Varuṇa, Aryaman, and of the Âdityas, but likewise, in a promiscuous way,

[1] Rv. viii. 25, 8: tá mātā — mahí jajāna Aditiḥ. Cf. viii. 101, 15; vi. 67, 4.
[2] Boehtlingk and Roth derive *nditi* from *a* and *diti,* and *diti* from *dâ* or *do*, to cut; hence literally the *Infinite.* This is doubtful, but I know no better etymology.
[3] Rv. ix. 114, 3: Devāḥ Âdityāḥ yé sapta.

the mother of the Rudras (storms), the daughter of the Vasus, the sister of the Ādityas.[1] "Aditi is the sky,[2] Aditi the air, Aditi is mother, father, son; all the gods are Aditi, and the five tribes; Aditi is what is born, Aditi what will be born."[3] In later times she is the mother of all the gods.[4]

In an "Essay on Comparative Mythology," published in the "Oxford Essays" of 1856, I collected a number of legends[5] which were told originally of the Dawn. Not one of the interpretations there proposed has ever, as far as I am aware, been controverted by facts or arguments. The difficulties pointed out by scholars such as *Curtius* and *Sonne*, I hope I have removed by a fuller statement of my views. The difficulty which I myself have most keenly felt is the monotonous character of the dawn and sun legends. "Is everything the Dawn? Is everything the Sun?" This question I had asked myself many times before it was addressed to me by others. Whether, by the remarks on the prominent position occupied by the dawn in the involuntary philosophy of the ancient world, I have succeeded in partially removing that objection, I cannot tell, but I am bound to say that my own researches lead me again and again to the dawn and the sun as the chief burden of the myths of the Aryan race.

I will add but one more instance to-day, before I return to the myth of *Saraṇyû*. We saw how

---

[1] *Rv.* viii. 101, 15.
[2] Cf. *Rv.* x. 63, 3.
[3] *Rv.* l. 89, 10.
[4] See Boehtlingk and Roth, s. v.
[5] Eos and Tithonos; Kephalos, Prôkris, and Eos; Daphne and Apollo; Urvaśî and Purûravas; Orpheus and Eurydice; Charis and Eros.

many names of different deities were taken from one and the same root, *dyu* or *div*. I believe that the root *ah*,[1] which yielded in Sanskrit *Ahaná* (Aghnyâ, i. e. Ahnyû), the Dawn, *ahan* and *ahar*,[2] day, supplied likewise the germ of *Athênê*. First, as to letters, it is known that Sanskrit *h* is frequently the neutral exponent of guttural, dental, and labial soft aspirates. *H* is guttural, as in *arh* and *aryh*, *ranh* and *rangh*, *mah* and *magh*. It is dental, as in *vrih* and *vridh*, *nah* and *naddha*, *saha* and *sadha*, *hita* instead of *dhita*, *hi* (imperative) and *dhi*. It is labial, as *grah* and *grabh*, *nah* and *nábhi*, *luh* and *lubh*. Restricting our observation to the interchange of *h* and *dh*, or *vice versâ*, we find, first, in Greek dialects, variations such as *órnichos* and *órnithos*, *íchma* and *íthma*.[3] Secondly, the root *ghar* or *har*, which, in Sanskrit, gives us *gharma*, heat, is certainly the Greek *ther*, which gives us *thermós*, warm.[4] If it be

[1] The root *ah* is connected with root *dah*, from which *Daphne* (cf. *aí* from which *aíru*, and *daí*, from which *ddapo*.) *Curtius* mentions the Thessalian form, δαύχνα for δάφνη. (*Griech. Et.* II. 68.) He admits my explanation of the myth of Daphnê as the dawn, but he says, "If we could but see why the dawn is changed into a laurel! Is it not from mere homonymy? The dawn was called δάφνη, the burning, so was the laurel, as wood that burns easily; the two, as usual, were supposed to be one." See *Etym. M.* p. 250, 20; δαυχμόν εὔκαυστον ξύλον; Hesych. δαυχμόν εὔκαυστον ξύλον δάφνῃ (f. εὔκαυστον ξύλον, δάφνην, Abrens, *Dial. Graec.* II. 532). Legerlotz, in Kuhn's *Zeitschrift*, vii. 292.

[2] Is 'Αχιλλεύς, the mortal solar hero, *Aharyu*? The change of r into l begins in the Sanskrit *Ahalyâ*, who is explained by Kumârila as the goddess of night, beloved and destroyed by Indra (see M. M.'s *History of Sanskrit Literature*, p. 530). As Indra is called *ahalyâyai járah*, it is more likely that she was meant for the dawn. *Leuke*, the island of the blessed, the abode of heroes after their death, is called *Achilléa*. Schol. Pind. *Nem.* 4, 49. Jacobi, *Mythologie*, p. 12. 'Αχαιός might be *Ahaya*, but *Aeolus* points in another direction.

[3] Cf. Mehlhorn, *Griech. Grammatik*, p. 111.

[4] See Curtius, *Griechische Etymologie*, II. 79.

objected that this would only prove the change of Sanskrit *h* into Greek *θ* as an initial, not as a final, we can appeal to Sanskrit *guh*, to hide, Greek *keúthō* ; possibly to Sanskrit *rah*, to remove, Greek *luth*.[1] In the same manner, then, the root *ah*, which in Greek would regularly appear as *ach*, might likewise there have assumed the form *ath*. As to the termination, it is the same which we find in *Seléné*, the Sanskrit *âná*. *Athéné*, therefore, as far as letters go, would correspond to a Sanskrit *Ahâná*, which is but a slightly differing variety of *Ahaná*,[2] a recognized name of the dawn in the Veda.

What, then, does *Athéné* share in common with the Dawn? The Dawn is the daughter of *Dyu*, *Athéné* the daughter of Zeus. Homer knows of no mother of *Athéné*, nor does the Veda mention the name of a mother of the Dawn, though her parents are spoken of in the dual (i. 123, 5).

The extraordinary birth of *Athéné*, though post-Homeric, is no doubt of ancient date, for it seems no more than the Greek rendering of the Sanskrit phrase that Ushas, the Dawn, sprang from the head of Dyu, the *múrdhâ divah*, the East, the forehead of the sky. In Rome she was called *Capta*, i. e. *Capita*, head-goddess, in Messene *Koryphasia*, in Argos *Akria*.[3] One of the principal features of the Dawn in the Veda is her waking first (i. 123, 2), and her rousing men from their slumber. In Greece, the cock, the bird of the morning, is next to the owl,

---

[1] Schleicher, *Compendium*, § 125, and p. 711. Raumer, *Gesammelte Sprachwissenschaftliche Schriften*, p. 84.
[2] On changes like *nan* and *dna*, see Kuhn, *Herabkunft des Feuers*, p. 28.
[3] Gerhard, *Griechische Mythologie*, § 253, 3 b. Preller, *Römische Mythologie*, p. 260, n.

the bird of *Athênê*. If *Athênê* is the virgin goddess, so is *Ushas*, the dawn, *yuvatih*, the young maid, *arepasâ tanvâ*, with spotless body. From another point of view, however, husbands have been allotted both to *Athênê* and to *Ushas*, though more readily to the Indian than to the Greek goddess.[1] How *Athênê*, being the dawn, should have become the goddess of wisdom, we can best learn from the Veda. In Sanskrit, *budh* means to wake and to know;[2] hence the goddess who caused people to wake was involuntarily conceived as the goddess who caused people to know. Thus it is said that she drives away darkness, and that through her those who see little may see far and wide (i. 113, 5). " We have crossed the frontier of this darkness," we read; " the dawn shining forth gives light" (i. 92, 6). But light (*vayûnâ*) has again a double meaning, and means knowledge much more frequently and distinctly than light. In the same hymn (i. 92, 9) we read : —

" Lighting up all the worlds, the Dawn, the eastern, the seer, shines far and wide ; waking every mortal to walk about, she received praise from every thinker."

Here the germs of *Athênê* are visible enough. That she grew into something very different from the Indian *Ushas*, when once worshipped as their tutelary deity by the people of the Morning-city of Attica, needs no remark. But though we ought carefully to watch any other tributary that enters into the later growth of the bright, heaven-sprung

---
[1] Gerhard, *Griechische Mythologie*, § 267, 3.
[2] Rv. I. 29, 4 : sasántu tyáh árátayah bódhantu ûrá rátáyah.

goddess, we need not look, I believe, for any other spring-head than the forehead of the sky, or Zeus.

Curious it is that in the mythology of Italy, *Minerva*, who was identified with *Athéné*, should from the beginning have assumed a name apparently expressive of the intellectual rather than the physical character of the Dawn-goddess. *Minerva*, or *Menerva*,[1] is clearly connected with *mens*, the Greek *ménos*, the Sanskrit *manas*, mind; and as the Sanskrit *śiras*, Greek *kéras*, horn, appears in Latin *cervus*, so Sanskrit *manas*, Greek *ménos*, in Latin *Menerva*. But it should be considered that *mâne* in Latin is the *morning*, *Mânia*, an old name of the mother of the Lares;[2] that *mânare* is specially used of the rising sun;[3] and that *Mâtuta*, not to mention other words of the same kin, is the Dawn. From this it would appear that in Latin the root *man*, which in the other Aryan languages is best known in the sense of thinking, was at a very early time put aside, like the Sanskrit *budh*, to express the revived consciousness of the whole of nature at the approach of the light of the morning; unless there was another totally distinct root, peculiar to Latin, expressive of that idea. The two ideas certainly seem to hang closely together; the only difficulty being to find out whether "wide awake" led on to "knowing," or *vice versâ*. Anyhow, I am inclined to admit in the name of *Minerva* some recollection of the idea expressed in *Matuta*, and even in *promenervare*, used in the *Carmen saliare*[4] in the sense

---

[1] Preller, *Römische Mythologie*, p. 258.
[2] Varro, L. L. 9, 38, § 61, ed. Müller.
[3] Manat dies ab oriente. Varro, L. L. 6, 2, 52, § 4. Manare solem antiqui dicebant, quum solis orientis radii splendorem jacere coepissent. Festus, p. 158, ed. Müller.
[4] Festus, p. 205. Paul. Diac. p. 123. Minerva dicta quod bene monest.

of to admonish, I should suspect a relic of the original power of rousing.

The tradition which makes Apollo the son of Athene,[1] though apparently modern and not widely spread, is yet by no means irrational, if we take Apollo as the sun-god rising from the brightness of the Dawn. Dawn and Night frequently exchange places, and though the original conception of the birth of *Apollo* and *Artemis* was no doubt that they were both children of the night, *Létó* or *Latona*, yet even then the place or the island in which they are fabled to have been born is *Ortygia*, afterwards called *Delos*, or *Delos*, afterwards called *Ortygia*, or both *Ortygia* and *Delos*.[2] Now *Delos* is simply the bright island; but *Ortygia*, though localized afterwards in different places,[3] is the dawn, or the dawn-land. *Ortygia* is derived from *ortyx*, a quail. The quail in Sanskrit is called *vartiká*, i. e. the returning bird, one of the first birds that return with the return of spring. The same name, *Vartiká*, is given in the Veda to one of the many beings delivered or revived by the *Asvins*, i. e. by day and night; and I believe *Vartiká*, the returning, is again one of the many names of the Dawn. The story told of her is very short. "She was swallowed, but she was delivered by the Asvins" (i. 112, 8). "She was delivered by them from the mouth of the wolf" (i. 117, 6; 116, 14; x. 39, 13). "She was delivered by the Asvins from agony" (i. 118, 8). All these are but legendary repetitions of the old saying, "the Dawn or the quail

---

[1] Gerhhard, *l. c.* § 257, 3.
[2] Jacobi, p. 574, n.
[3] Gerhard, *Griechische Mythologie*, § 335, 2.

comes," "the quail is swallowed by the wolf," "the quail has been delivered from the mouth of the wolf." Hence *Ortygia*, the quail-land, the East, "the glorious birth," where Leto was delivered of her solar twins, and *Ortygia*, a name given to *Artemis*, the daughter of *Leto*, as born in the East.

The Dawn, or rather the mother of the dawn, and of all the bright visions that follow in her train, took naturally a far more prominent place in the religious ideas of the young world than she who was called her sister, the gloaming, or the evening, the end of the day, the approach of darkness, of cold, and, it may be, of death. In the dawn there lay all the charms of a beginning and of youth, and, from one point of view, even the night might be looked upon as the offspring of the dawn, as the twin of the day. As the bright child waned, the dark child grew; as the dark flew away, the bright returned; both were born of the same mother — both seemed to have emerged together from the brilliant womb of the East. It was impossible to draw an exact line, and to say where the day began and where it ended, or where the night began and where it ended. When the light enters into the darkness, as the Brahmans said, then the one twin appears; when the darkness enters the light, then the other twin follows. "The twins come and go:" this was all the ancient poets had to say of the racing hours of day and night; it was the last word they could find, and, like many a good word of old, this too followed the fate of all living speech; it became a formula, a saw, a myth.

We know who was the mother of the twins: it was the dawn, who dies in giving birth to morning and evening; or, if we adopt the view of Yâska, it was the night, who disappears when the new couple is born. She may be called by all the names of the dawn, and even the names of the night might express one side of her character. Near her is the stand from whence the horses of the sun start on their diurnal journey;[1] near her is the stable which holds the cows, i. e. the bright days following one after the other like droves of cattle, driven out by the Sun every morning to their pastures, carried off by robbers every night to their gloomy cave, but only to be surrendered by them again and again, after the never-doubtful battle of the early twilight.

As the dawn has many names, so her offspring too is polyonymous; and as her most general name is that of *Yamasûḥ*,[2] or Twin-mother, so the most general name of her offspring too is *Yamau*, the twins. Now we have seen these twins as men, the *Aśvins*, *Indra* and *Agni*, *Mitra* and *Varuṇa*. We have seen how the same powers might be conceived as women, as day and night, and thus we find them represented not only as sisters, but as twin sisters. For instance, Rv. iii. 55, 11:—

"The two twin sisters[3] have made their bodies to differ; one of them is brilliant, the other dark: though the dark one and the bright are two sisters, the great divinity of the gods is *one*."

By a mere turn of the mythological kaleidoscope,

---

[1] Hence, I believe, the myth of Aśvattha, originally horse-stand, then confounded with *niṣaṭha*, ficus religiosa. See, however, Kuhn, *Zeitschrift*, I. p. 467.

[2] Rv. iii. 39, 3. Yamasûḥ, rameṇ yamalau sûta iti yamasûr ubho'bhimânini devatâ. Sâ yamâ yamalâv Aśvinâv stroshabhāle 'sûta.

[3] *Yamyâ*, a dual in the feminine; cf. v. 47, 6.

these two sisters, day and night, instead of being the twin children of the dawn, appear in another poem as the two mothers of the sun. Rv. iii. 55, 6: —

"This child which went to sleep in the West walks now alone, having two mothers, but not led by them; these are the works of Mitra and Varuṇa, but the great divinity of the gods is *one.*"

In another hymn, again, the two, the twins, born here and there (*ihehajâte*), who carry the child, are said to be different from his mother (v. 47, 5), and in another place one of the two seems to be called the daughter of the other (iii. 55, 12).

We need not wonder, therefore, that the same two beings, whatever we like to call them, were sometimes represented as male and female, as brother and sister, and again as twin-brother and twin-sister. In that mythological dialect the day would be the twin-brother, *Yama*, the night, the twin-sister, *Yamî*: — and thus we have arrived at last at a solution of the myth which we wished to explain. A number of expressions had sprung up, such as "the twin-mother," i. e. the Dawn; "the twins," i. e. Day and Night; "the horse-children," or "horsemen," i. e. Morning and Evening; "Saraṇyû is wedded by Vivasvat," i. e. the Dawn embraces the sky; "Saraṇyû has left her twins behind," i. e. the Dawn has disappeared, it is day; "Vivasvat takes his second wife," i. e. the sun sets in the evening twilight; "the horse runs after the mare," i. e. the sun has set. Put these phrases together, and the story, as told in the hymn of the Rig-Veda, is finished. The hymn does not allude to *Manu*, as the son of *Savarṇâ*, it only calls the second wife of *Vivasvat* by that name, meaning thereby no more than what the word implies, a wife similar to his first wife, as the gloaming is similar to the dawn. The fable of *Manu* is probably of a later date. For some reason or other, *Manu*, the mythic ancestor of the race of man, was called *Sâvarṇi*, meaning, possibly, the Manu of all colors, i. e. of all tribes or castes. The name may have reminded the Brahmans of *Savarṇâ*, the second wife of Vivasvat, and as *Manu* was called *Vaivasvata*, the worshipper, afterwards the son, of Vivasvat, the *Manu Sâvarṇi* was naturally taken as the son of *Savarṇâ*. This, however, I only give as a guess till some more plausible explanation of the name and myth of *Manu Sâvarṇi* can be suggested.

But it will be necessary to follow still further the history of *Yama*, the twin, properly so called. In the passage examined before, *Saraṇyû* is simply called the mother of *Yama*, i. e. the mother of the twin, but his twin-sister, *Yamî*, is not mentioned. Yet *Yamî*, too, was well known in the Veda, and there is a curious dialogue between her and her brother, where she (the night) implores her brother (the day) to make her his wife, and where he declines her offer because, as he says, "they have called it sin that a brother should marry his sister" (x. 10, 12).

The question now arises whether *Yama*, meaning originally twin, could ever be used by itself as the name of a deity? We may speak of twins; and we saw how, in the hymns of the Veda, several correlative deities are spoken of as twins; but can we speak of a twin, and give that name to an independent deity, worshipped without any reference to its complementary deity? The six seasons, each consisting of two months, are called the six twins (Rv. i. 164, 15); but no single month could therefore properly be called the twin.[1]

Nothing can be clearer than such passages as x. 8, 4:—

"Thou, O Vasu (sun), comest first at every dawn! thou wast the divider of the two twins," i. e. of day and night, of morning and evening, of light and darkness, of Indra and Agni, &c.

Let us now look to a verse (Rv. i. 66, 4) where Yama by itself is supposed to mean the twin, and more particularly Agni. The whole hymn is addressed to Agni, fire, or light, in his most general character. I translate literally:—

"Like an army let loose, he wields his force, like the flame-pointed arrow of the shooter. Yama is born, Yama will be born, the lover of the girls, the husband of the wives."

This verse, as is easily seen, is full of allusions, intelligible to those who listened to the poets, but to us perfect riddles, to be solved only by a comparison of similar passages, if such passages can be found. Now, first of all, I do not take *Yama* as a name of *Agni*, or as a proper name at all. But recollecting the twinship of Agni and Indra, as representatives of day and night, I translate:—

"(One) twin is born, (another) twin will be born," i. e. Agni, to whom the hymn is addressed, is born, the morning has appeared; his twin, or, if you like, his other self, the evening, will be born.

The next words, "the lover of the girls," "the husband of the wives," contain, I believe, a mere

[1] As to yaman and yamih, see Rv. x. 117, 9; v. 57, 4; x. 13, 8.

repetition of the first hemistich. The light of the morning, or the rising sun, is called the lover of the girls, these girls being the dawns, from among whom he rises. Thus (i. 152, 4) it is said: "We see him coming forth, the lover of the girls,[1] the unconquerable."

Rv. i. 163, 8, the sun-horse, or the sun as horse, is addressed:—

"After thee there is the chariot; after thee, Arvan, the man; after thee, the cows; after thee, the host of the girls."

Here the cows and the girls are in reality but two representations of the same thing, — the bright days, the smiling dawns.

Rv. ii. 15, 7, we read of *Pardvṛij*, a name which, like *Chyávana*[2] and other names, is but a mask of the sun returning in the morning after his decline in the evening:—

"He (the old sun), knowing the hiding-place of the girls, rose up manifest, he the escaper; the lame (sun) walked, the blind (sun) saw; Indra achieved this when fired with Soma."

The hiding-place of the girls is the hiding-place of the cows, the East, the home of the ever-youthful dawns; and to say that the lover of the girls[3] is there, is only a new expression for "the twin is born."

Lover (jâraḥ), by itself, too, is used for the rising sun:—

---

[1] Sâyaṇa rightly explains *kavînâm* by *uśatîm*.

[2] In i. 116, 10, it is said that the Aśvins restored the old *Chyavâna* to be again the husband of the girls.

[3] Pûshan is called the lover of his sister, the husband of his mother (vi. 55, 4 and 5; x. 8, 3: svásáram jâraḥ abhí eti paśchâṭ).

Rv. vii. 9, 1: "The lover woke from the lap of the Dawn."

Rv. i. 92, 11: "The wife (Dawn) shines with the light of the lover."

What, then, is the meaning of "the husband of the wives"? Though this is more doubtful, I think it not unlikely that it was meant originally for the evening sun, as surrounded by the splendors of the gloaming, as it were by a more serene repetition of the dawn. The Dawn herself is likewise called the wife (iv. 52, 1); but the expression "husband of the wives" is in another passage clearly applied to the sinking sun. Rv. ix. 86, 32: "The husband of the wives approaches the end."[1] If this be the right interpretation, "the husband of the wives" would be the same as "the twin that is to be born"; and the whole verse would thus receive a consistent meaning: —

"One twin is born (the rising sun, or the morning), another twin will be born (the setting sun, or the evening); the lover of the girls (the young sun), the husband of the wives" (the old sun).

The following translations of this one line, proposed by different scholars, will give an idea of the difficulty of Vedic interpretation: —

Rosen: "Sociatæ utique Agni sunt omnes res natæ, sociatæ illi sunt nasciturae, Agnis est pronubus puellarum, maritus uxorum."

Langlois: "Jumeau du passé, jumeau de l'avenir, il est le fiancé des filles, et l'époux des femmes."

Wilson: " Agni, as Yama, is all that is born; as

[1] Nishkṛita, according to B. R., a rendezvous; but in our passage, the original meaning, to be undone, seems more appropriate.

Yama, all that will be born: he is the lover of maidens, the husband of wives."

Kuhn: "The twin (Agni) is he who is born; the twin is what is to be born."

Benfey: "A born lord, he rules over births; the suitor of maidens, the husband of wives."

There is, as far as I know, no other passage in the Rig-Veda where *Yama*, used by itself in the sense of twin, has been supposed to apply to *Agni* or the sun. But there are several passages, particularly in the last book, in which Yama occurs as the name of a single deity. He is called king (x. 14, 1); the departed acknowledge him as king (x. 16, 9). He is together with the Pitars, the fathers (x. 14, 4), with the Angiras (x. 14, 3), the Atharvans, Bhrigus (x. 14, 6), the Vasishthas (x. 15, 8). He is called the son of *Vivasvat* (x. 14, 5), and an immortal son of *Yama* is mentioned (i. 83, 5). Soma is offered to him at sacrifices (x. 14, 13), and the departed fathers will see Yama, together with Varuna (x. 14, 7), and they will feast with the two kings (x. 14, 10). The king of the departed, Yama, is likewise the god of death (x. 165, 4),[1] and two dogs are mentioned who go about among men as his messengers (x. 14, 12). Yama, however, as well as his dogs, is likewise asked to bestow life, which originally could have been no more than to spare life (x. 14, 14; 14, 12).

Is it possible to discover in this *Yama*, the god of the departed, one of the twins? I confess it seems a most forced and artificial designation; and I should

[1] *Rv.* I. 38, 5. The expression, "the path of Yama," may be used in an auspicious or inauspicious sense.

much prefer to derive this *Yama* from *yam*, to control. Yet his father is *Vivasvat*, and the father of the twins was likewise *Vivasvat*. Shall we ascribe to *Vivasvat* three sons, two called the twins, *Yamau*, and another called *Yama*, the ruler? It is possible, yet it is hardly credible; and I believe it is better to learn to walk in the strange footsteps of ancient speech, however awkward they may seem at first. Let us imagine, then, as well as we can, that *Yama*, twin, was used as the name of the evening, or the setting sun, and we shall be able perhaps to understand how in the end Yama came to be the king of the departed and the god of death.

As the East was to the early thinkers the source of life, the West was to them *Nirriti*, the *exodus*, the land of death. The sun, conceived as setting or dying every day, was the first who had trodden the path of life from East to West — the first mortal — the first to show us the way when our course is run, and our sun sets in the far West. Thither the fathers followed Yama; there they sit with him rejoicing, and thither we too shall go when his messengers (day and night, see p. 476) have found us out. These are natural feelings and intelligible thoughts. The question is, Were they the thoughts and feelings that passed through the minds of our forefathers when they changed *Yama*, the twin-sun, the setting sun, into the ruler of the departed and the god of death?

That *Yama's* character is solar, might be guessed from his being called the son of *Vivasvat*. *Vivasvat*, like *Yama*, is sometimes considered as sending death. Rv. viii. 67, 20: " May the shaft of *Vivasvat*,

O *Âditya*, the poisoned arrow, not strike us before we are old!"

Yama is said to have crossed the rapid waters, to have shown the way to many, to have first known the path on which our fathers crossed over (x. 14, 1 and 2). In a hymn addressed to the sun-horse, it is said that " *Yama* brought the horse, *Trita* harnessed him, *Indra* first sat on him, the *Gandharva* took hold of his rein." And immediately after, the horse is said to be *Yama*, *Âditya*, and *Trita* (i. 163, 2 and 3). Again, of the three heavens, two are said to belong to *Savitar*, one to *Yama* (i. 35, 6). *Yama* is spoken of as if admitted to the company of the gods (x. 135, 1). His own seat is called the house of the gods (x. 135, 7); and these words follow immediately on a verse in which it is said: " The abyss is stretched out in the East, the outgoing is in the West."[1]

These indications, though fragmentary, are sufficient to show that the character of *Yama*, such as we find it in the last book of the Rig-Veda, might well have been suggested by the setting sun, personified as the leader of the human race, as himself a mortal, yet as a king, as the ruler of the departed, as worshipped with the fathers, as the first witness of an immortality to be enjoyed by the fathers, similar to the immortality enjoyed by the gods themselves. That the king of the departed should gradually have assumed the character of the god of death, requires no explanation. This, however, is the latest phase of *Yama*, and one that in the early portions of the Veda belongs to *Varuna*, himself, as we saw before, like *Yama*, one of the twins.

[1] Other passages to be consulted, Rv. I. 116, 9; vii. 33, 9; ix. 68, 8, 5; x. 12, 6; 13, 2; 13, 4; 53, 3; 64, 3; 123, 6.

DEMETER, THE DAWN.

The mother of all the heavenly powers we have just examined, is the Dawn with her many names, πολλῶν ὀνομάτων μορφὴ μία, *Aditi*, the mother of the gods, or *Apyâ yoshâ*, the water-wife, *Saraṇyû*, the running light, *Ahanâ*, the bright, *Arjuni*, the brilliant, *Urvasî*, the wide, &c. Beyond the Dawn, however, another infinite power was suspected, for which neither the language of the Vedic Rishis, nor that of any other poets or prophets, has yet suggested a fitting name.

If, then, as I have little doubt, the Greek *Erinys* is the same word as the Sanskrit *Saraṇyû*,[1] it is easy to see how, starting from a common thought, each deity assumed its peculiar aspect in India and in Greece. The Night was conceived by Hesiod as the mother of War, Strife, and Fraud, but she is likewise called the mother of Nemesis, or Vengeance.[2] Æschylus calls the Erinyes the daughters of Night, and we saw before a passage from the Veda (vii. 61, 5) where the Druh's, the mischievous powers of night, were said to follow the sins of man. "The Dawn will find you out" was a saying but slightly tainted by mythology. "The Erinyes will haunt you" was a saying which not even Homer would have understood in its etymological sense. If the name of Erinys is sometimes applied to *Dêmêtêr*,[3] this is because *Dêô* was *Dyâvâ*, and *Dêmêtêr*, *Dyâvâ mâtar*, the Dawn, the mother,[4] corresponding to

---

[1] The loss of the initial aspirate is exceptional, but, as such, confirmed by well-known analogies. See Curtius, *Griechische Etymologie*, ii. 283; i. 309.
[2] M. M.'s *Essay on Comparative Mythology*, p. 40.
[3] Pausanias, viii. 25; Kuhn, *l. c.* i. 152.
[4] See Pott, in Kuhn's *Zeitschrift*, vi. p. 118, n.

SOLAR THEORY.

Dyaush pitar, the sky, the father. *Erinys Demeter*, like *Saraṇyû*, was changed into a mare, she was followed by *Poseidon*, as a horse, and two children were born, a daughter (*Despoina*), and *Areion*. Poseidon, if he expressed the sun rising from the sea, would approach to *Varuṇa*, who, in one passage of the Veda, was called the father of the horse or of *Yama*.

And now, after having explained the myth of *Saraṇyû*, of her father, her husband, and her children, in what I think its original sense, it remains to state, in a few words, the opinions of other scholars who have analyzed the same myth before, and have arrived at different conceptions of its original import. It will not be necessary to enter upon a detailed refutation of these views, as the principal difference between these and my own theory arises from the different points which we have chosen in order to command a view into the distant regions of mythological thought. I look upon the sunrise and sunset, on the daily return of day and night, on the battle between light and darkness, on the whole solar drama in all its details that is acted every day, every month, every year, in heaven and in earth, as the principal subject of early mythology. I consider that the very idea of divine powers sprang from the wonderment with which the forefathers of the Aryan family stared at the bright (deva) powers that came and went no one knew whence or whither, that never failed, never faded, never died, and were called immortal, i. e. unfading, as compared with the feeble and decaying race of man. I consider the regular recurrence of phenomena an almost indispensable condition of their being raised, through the charms of mythological phraseology, to the rank of immortals, and I give a proportionately small space to meteorological phenomena, such as clouds, thunder, and lightning, which, although causing for a time a violent commotion in nature and in the heart of man, would not be ranked together with the immortal bright beings, but would rather be classed either as their subjects or as their enemies. It is the sky that gathers the clouds, it is the sky that thunders, it is the sky that rains; and the battle that takes place between the dark clouds and the bright sun, which for a time is covered by them, is but an irregular repetition of that more momentous struggle which takes place every day between the darkness of the night and the refreshing light of the morning.

Quite opposed to this, the solar theory, is that proposed by Professor Kuhn, and adopted by the most eminent mythologians of Germany, which may be called the meteorological theory. This has been well sketched by Mr. Kelly in his "Indo-European Tradition and Folk-lore." "Clouds," he writes, "storms, rains, lightning, and thunder, were the spectacles that above all others impressed the imagination of the early Aryans, and busied it most in finding terrestrial objects to compare with their ever-varying aspect. The beholders were at home on the earth, and the things of the earth were comparatively familiar to them; even the coming and going of the celestial luminaries might often be regarded by them with the more composure because of their regularity; but they could never surcease to feel the liveliest interest in those wonderful meteoric changes, so lawless and mysterious in their visitations, which wrought such immediate and palpable effects, for good or ill, upon the lives and fortunes of the beholders. Hence these phenomena were noted and designated with a watchfulness and wealth of imagery which made them the principal groundwork of all the Indo-European mythologies and superstitions."

Professor Schwartz, in his excellent essays on Mythology,[1] ranges himself determinately on the same side:—

"If, in opposition to the principles which I have carried out in my book 'On the Origin of Mythology,' it has been remarked that in the development of the ideas of the Divine in myths, I gave too much prominence to the phenomena of the wind and thunder-storms, neglecting the sun, the following researches will confirm what I indicated before, that originally the sun was conceived implicitly as a mere accident in the heavenly scenery, and assumed importance only in a more advanced state in the contemplation of nature and the formation of myths."

These two views are as diametrically opposed as two views of the same subject can possibly be. The one, the solar theory, looks to the regular daily revolutions in heaven and earth as the material out of which the variegated web of the religious mythology of the Aryans was woven, admitting only an interspersion here and there of the more violent aspects of storms, thunder and lightning; the other, the meteoric theory, looks upon clouds and storms and other convulsive aspects of nature as causing the deepest and most lasting impression on the minds of those early observers who had ceased to wonder at

[1] *Der heutige Volksglaube und das alte Heidenthum*, 1862 (p. vii.) *Der Ursprung der Mythologie*, 1860.

the regular movements of the heavenly bodies, and could only perceive a divine presence in the great strong wind, the earthquake, or the fire.

In accordance with this latter view, we saw that Professor Roth explained *Saraṇyû* as the dark stormcloud soaring in space in the beginning of all things, and that he took *Vivasvat* for the light of heaven.[1] Explaining the second couple of twins first, he took them, the *Aśvins*, to be the first bringers of light, preceding the dawn, (but who are they?) while he discovered in the first couple, simply called *Yama*, the twin-brother, and *Yami*, the twin-sister, the first created couple, man and woman, produced by the union of the damp vapor of the cloud and the heavenly light. After their birth he imagines that a new order of things began, and that hence, their mother — the chaotic, storm-tossed twilight — was said to have vanished. Without laying much stress on the fact that, according to the Rig-Veda, *Saraṇyû* became first the mother of *Yama*, then vanished, then bare the *Aśvins*, and finally left both couples of children, it must be observed that there is not a single word in the Veda pointing to *Yama* and *Yami* as the first couple of mortals, — as the Indian Adam and Eve, — or representing the first creation of man as taking place by the union of vapor and light. If *Yama* had been the first created of men, surely the Vedic poets, in speaking of him, could not have passed this over in silence. Nor is *Yima*, in the Avesta, represented as the first man or as the father of mankind.[2] He is one of the first kings, and his

---

[1] *Zeitschrift der Deutschen Morgenländischen Gesellschaft*, iv. p. 425.
[2] Spiegel, *Érân*, p. 245. "According to one account, the happiness of

reign represents the ideal of human happiness, when there was as yet neither illness nor death, neither heat nor cold; but no more. The tracing of the further development of *Yima* in Persia was one of the last and one of the most brilliant discoveries of Eugène Burnouf. In his article, "Sur le Dieu Homa," published in the "Journal Asiatique," he opened this entirely new mine for researches into the ancient state of religion and tradition, common to the Aryans before their schism. He showed that three of the most famous names in the epic poetry of the later Persians, *Jemshid*, *Feridûn*, and *Garshasp*, can be traced back to three heroes mentioned in the Zend-Avesta as the representatives of three of the earliest generations of mankind, *Yima - Kshaêta*, *Thraêtana*, and *Kereśaspa*, and that the prototypes of these Zoroastrian heroes could be found again in the *Yama*, *Trita*, and *Kriśáśva* of the Veda. He went even beyond this. He showed that, as in Sanskrit the father of *Yama* is *Vivasvat*, the father of *Yima* in the Avesta is *Vivanghvat*. He showed that as *Thraêtana*, in Persia, is the son of *Athwya*, the patronymic of *Trita* in the Veda is *Aptya*. He explained the transition of *Thraêtana* into *Feridûn* by pointing to the Pehlevi form of the name, as given by Neriosengh, *Phredun*. Burnouf, again, it was who identified *Zohák*, the tyrant of Persia, slain by Feridun, whom even Firdusi still knows by the name of *Ash dahák*, with the *Aji dahâka*, the biting serpent, as he translates it, de-

Jima's reign came to an end through his pride and untruthfulness. According to the earlier traditions of the *Avesta*, Jima does not die, but, when evil and misery begin to prevail on earth, retires to a smaller space, a kind of garden or Eden, where he continues his happy life with those who remained true to him."

stroyed by *Thraëtana* in the Avesta. Nowhere has the transition of physical mythology into epic poetry — nay, history — been so luculently shown as here. I may quote the words of Burnouf, one of the greatest scholars that France, so rich in philological genius, has ever produced: —

"Il est sans contredit fort curieux de voir une des divinités indiennes les plus vénérées, donner son nom au premier souverain de la dynastie ario-persanne; c'est un des faits qui attestent le plus évidemment l'intime union des deux branches de la grande famille qui s'est étendue, bien des siècles avant notre ère, depuis le Gange jusqu'à l'Euphrate." [1]

Professor Roth has pointed out some more minute coincidences in the story of Jemshid, but his attempt at changing *Yama* and *Yima* into an Indian and Persian *Adam* was, I believe, a mistake.

Professor Kuhn was right, therefore, in rejecting this portion of Professor Roth's analysis. But, like Professor Roth, he takes *Saranyû* as the storm-cloud, and though declining to recognize in *Vivasvat* the heavenly light in general, he takes *Vivasvat* as one of the many names of the sun, and considers their first-born child, *Yama*, to mean *Agni*, the fire, or rather the lightning, followed by his twin-sister, the thunder. He then explains the second couple, the *Aśvins*, to be *Agni* and *Indra*, the god of the fire and the god of the bright sky, and thus arrives at the following solution of the myth: — "After the storm is over, and the darkness which hid the single cloud has vanished, *Savitar* (the sun) embraces once more the goddess, the cloud, who had assumed the shape

---

[1] *On the Veda and Zendavesta*, by M. M., p. 81.

of a horse running away. He shines, still hidden, fiery and with golden arm, and thus begets *Agni*, fire; he lastly tears the wedding-veil, and *Indra*, the blue sky, is born." The birth of *Manu*, or man, he explains as a repetition of that of *Agni*, and he looks upon *Manu*, or *Agni*, as the Indian Adam, and not, as Professor Roth, on *Yama*, the lightning.

It is impossible, of course, to do full justice to the speculations of these eminent men on the myth of Saraṇyû by giving this meagre outline of their views. Those who take an interest in the subject must consult their treatises, and compare them with the interpretations which I have proposed. I confess that, though placing myself in their point of view, I cannot grasp any clear or connected train of thoughts in the mythological process which they describe. I cannot imagine that men, standing on a level with our shepherds, should have conversed among themselves of a dark storm-cloud soaring in space, and producing by a marriage with light, or with the sun, the first human beings, or should have called the blue sky the son of the cloud because the sky appears when the storm-cloud has been either embraced or destroyed by the sun. However, it is not for me to pronounce an opinion, and I must leave it to others, less wedded to particular theories, to find out which interpretation is more natural, more in accordance with the scattered indications of the ancient hymns of the Veda, and more consonant with what we know of the spirit of the most primitive ages of man.

LECTURE XII.

MODERN MYTHOLOGY.

WHAT I mean by Modern Mythology is a subject so vast and so important, that in this, my last Lecture, all I can do is to indicate its character, and the wide limits within which its working may be discerned. After the definition which on several occasions I have given of Mythology, I need only repeat here that I include under that name every case in which language assumes an independent power, and reacts on the mind, instead of being, as it was intended to be, the mere realization and outward embodiment of the mind.

In the early days of language the play of mythology was no doubt more lively and more widely extended, and its effects were more deeply felt, than in these days of mature speculation, when words are no longer taken on trust, but are constantly tested by means of logical definition. When language sobers down, when metaphors become less bold and more explicit, there is less danger of speaking of the sun as a horse, because a poet had called him the heavenly racer, or of speaking of Selene as enamored of Endymion, because a proverb had expressed the approach of night by the longing looks of the moon after the setting sun. Yet under a different form Language retains her silent charm; and if it no longer

ABUSE OF WORDS.

creates gods and heroes, it creates many a name that receives a similar worship. He who would examine the influence which words, mere words, have exercised on the minds of men, might write a history of the world that would teach us more than any which we yet possess. Words without definite meanings are at the bottom of nearly all our philosophical and religious controversies, and even the so-called exact sciences have frequently been led astray by the same Siren voice.

I do not speak here of that downright abuse of language when writers, without maturing their thoughts and arranging them in proper order, pour out a stream of hard and misapplied terms which are mistaken by themselves, if not by others, for deep learning and height of speculation. This sanctuary of ignorance and vanity has been wellnigh destroyed; and scholars or thinkers who cannot say what they wish to say consecutively and intelligibly have little chance in these days, or at least in this country, of being considered as depositaries of mysterious wisdom. *Si non vis intelligi debes negligi.* I rather think of words which everybody uses, and which seem to be so clear that it looks like impertinence to challenge them. Yet, if we except the language of mathematics, it is extraordinary to observe how variable is the meaning of words, how it changes from century to century, nay, how it varies slightly in the mouth of almost every speaker. Such terms as *Nature, Law, Freedom, Necessity, Body, Substance, Matter, Church, State, Revelation, Inspiration, Knowledge, Belief,* are tossed about in the wars of words as if everybody knew what they meant, and as if everybody used them exactly in the same sense; whereas most people, and particularly those who represent public opinion, pick up these complicated terms as children, beginning with the vaguest conceptions, adding to them from time to time, perhaps correcting likewise at haphazard some of their involuntary errors, but never taking stock, never either inquiring into the History of the terms which they handle so freely, or realizing the fulness of their meaning according to the strict rules of logical definition. It has been frequently said that most controversies are about words. This is true; but it implies much more than it seems to imply. Verbal differences are not what they are sometimes supposed to be — merely formal, outward, slight, accidental differences, that might be removed by a simple explanation, or by a reference to "Johnson's Dictionary."[1] They are differences arising from the more or less perfect, from the more or less full and correct conception attached to words: it is the mind that is at fault, not the tongue merely.

If a child, after being taught to attach the name of *gold* to anything that is yellow and glitters, were to maintain against all comers that the sun is gold, the child no doubt would be right, because in his mind the name "gold" means something that is yellow and glitters. We do not hesitate to say that a flower is edged with gold, — meaning the color only, not the substance. The child afterwards learns that there are other qualities, besides its color, which

---

[1] "Half the perplexities of men are traceable to obscurity of thought, hiding and breeding under obscurity of language." — *Edinb. Review*, Oct. 1862, p. 378.

are peculiar to real gold, and which distinguish gold from similar substances. He learns to stow away every one of these qualities into the name *gold*, so that at last gold with him means no longer anything that glitters, but something that is heavy, malleable, fusible, and soluble in *aqua regia*;[1] and he adds to these any other quality which the continued researches of each generation bring out. Yet in spite of all these precautions, the name *gold*, so carefully defined by the philosophers, will slip away into the crowd of words, and we may hear a banker discussing the market-value of gold in such a manner that we can hardly believe he is speaking of the same thing which we last saw in the crucible of the chemist. You remember how the expression "golden-handed," as applied to the sun, led to the formation of a story which explained the sun's losing his hand, and having it replaced by an artificial hand made of gold. That is Ancient Mythology. Now, if we were to say that of late years the supply of gold has been very much increased, and if from this we were to conclude that the increase of taxable property in this country was due to the discovery of gold in California, this would be Modern Mythology. We should use the name *gold* in two different senses. We should use gold in the one case as synonymous with realized wealth, in the other as the name of the circulating medium. We should commit the same mistake as the people of old, using the same word in two slightly varying senses, and then confounding one meaning with the other.

For let it not be supposed that even in its more

[1] Cf. Locke, lii. 9, 17.

naked form mythology is restricted to the earliest ages of the world.

Though one source of mythology, that which arises from *radical* and *poetical* metaphor, is less prolific in modern than in ancient dialects, there is another agency at work in modern dialects which, though in a different manner, produces nearly the same results, namely, *phonetic decay*, followed by *popular etymology*. By means of phonetic decay many words have lost their etymological transparency; nay, words, originally quite distinct in form and meaning, assume occasionally the same form. Now, as there is in the human mind a craving after etymology, a wish to find out, by fair means or foul, why such a thing should be called by such a name, it happens constantly that words are still further changed in order to make them intelligible once more; or, when two originally distinct words have actually run into one, some explanation is required, and readily furnished, in order to remove the difficulty.

" La Tour sans venin " is a case in point, but it is by no means the only case.

From Anglo-Saxon *blót*, sacrifice, *blotan*, to kill for sacrifice, was derived *blessian*, to consecrate, to bless. In modern English, *to bless* seems connected with *bliss*, the Anglo-Saxon *blis*, joy, with which it had originally nothing in common.

Sorrow is the Anglo-Saxon *sorh*, the German *Sorge*; its supposed connection with *sorry* is merely imaginary, for the Anglo-Saxon for sorry is *sárig*, from *sár*, a wound, a sore.

In German, most people imagine that *Sündfluth*,

the deluge, means the sin-flood; but *Sündfluth* is but a popular etymological adaptation of *sinfluot*, the great flood.

Many of the old signs of taverns contain what we may call hieroglyphic mythology. There was a house on Stoken Church Hill, near Oxford, exhibiting on its sign-board, " Feathers and a Plum." The house itself was vulgarly called the *Plum and Feathers*:[1] it was originally the *Plume of Feathers*, from the crest of the Prince of Wales.

A Cat with a Wheel is the corrupt emblem of St. Catherine's Wheel: the *Bull and Gate* was originally intended as a trophy of the taking of Boulogne by Henry VIII., it was the Boulogne Gate; and the *Goat and Compasses* have taken the place of the fine old Puritan sign-board, " God encompasseth us."[2]

There is much of this kind of popular mythology floating about in the language of the people, arising from a very natural and very general tendency, namely, from a conviction that every name must have a meaning. If the real and original meaning has once been lost, chiefly owing to the ravages of phonetic decay, a new meaning is at first tentatively, but very soon dogmatically, assigned to the changed name.

At Lincoln, immediately below the High Bridge, there is an inn bearing now the sign of the Black Goats. It formerly had the Sign of the Three Goats,

---

[1] Brady, *Clavis Calendaria*, vol. ii. p. 13.
[2] Trench, *English Past and Present*, p. 223: —
  " The George and Cannon = the George Canning.
  The Billy Ruffian = the Bellerophon (ship).
  The Iron Devil = the Hirondelle.
  Rose of the Quarter Sessions = la rose des quatre saisons."

a name derived from the three gowts or drains by which the water from the Swan Pool, a large lake which formerly existed to the west of the city, was conducted into the bed of the Witham, below. A public-house having arisen on the bank of the principal of these three gowts, in honor, probably, of the work when it was made, the name became corrupted into the Three Goats — a corruption easily accomplished in the Lincolnshire dialect.[1]

In the same town, a flight of steps by which the ascent is gained from about midway of what is called the New Road to a small ancient gateway, leading towards the Minster Yard, is called the *Grecian Stairs*. These stairs were originally called the *Greesen*, the early English plural of a *gree* or step. When *Greesen* ceased to be understood, *Stairs* was added by way of explanation, and the *Greesen Stairs* were, by the instinct of popular etymology, changed into *Grecian Stairs*.[2]

[1] See the Rev. Francis C. Massingberd, in the *Proceedings of the Archæological Institute*, Lincoln, 1848, p. 58. Gowt is the same word as the German *Gosse*, gutter.

[2] See the Rev. Francis C. Massingberd, in the *Proceedings of the Archæological Institute*, Lincoln, 1848, p. 59. The learned antiquary quotes several passages in support of the plural *greesen*. Thus Acts xxi. 40, instead of "And when he had given him license, Paul stood on the *stairs*," Wickliffe has: "Poul stood on the *greesen*." Shakspeare paraphrases *grise* (as he writes) by steps: —

"Let me speak like yourself; and lay a sentence
Which, as a *grise* or *step*, may help these lovers
Into your favor." *Othello*, Act 1, Sc. III.

In *Hackluyt's Voyages*, vol. ii. p. 57, we read: "The king of the said land of Java hath a most brave and sumptuous palace, the most loftily built that I ever saw, and it hath most high *greesses*, or *stayers*, to ascend up to the rooms therein contained."

"In expensis Stephani Austenwell, equitantis ad Thomam Ayleward, ad loquendum cum ipso apud Havant, et inde ad Hertynge, ad loquendum cum Domini ibidem, de evidenciis scrutandis de *Pe de Gre* progenitorum

One of our Colleges at Oxford is now called and spelt *Brasenose*. Over the gate of the College there is a Brazen Nose, and the arms of the College display the same shield, and have done so for several centuries. I have not heard of any legend to account for the startling presence of that emblem over the gate of the College, but this is simply owing to the want of poetic imagination on the part of the Oxford Ciceroni. In Greece, Pausanias would have told us ever so many traditions commemorated by such a monument. At Oxford we are simply told that the College was originally a brewhouse, and that its original name, *brasen-huis* (braserie), was gradually changed to *brazenose*.

Brasenose was founded in the commencement of the reign of Henry VIII., by the joint liberality of William Smyth, Bishop of Lincoln, and Sir Richard Sutton. The foundation-stone was laid on June 1, 1509, and the charter entitling it "The King's Hall and College of Brasenose," is dated January 15, 1512. This college stands upon the site of no less than four ancient halls, viz., Little University Hall, described by some antiquaries as one of those built by Alfred, and which occupied the northeast angle near the lane; Brasenose Hall, whence the name of the College, situated where the present gateway now stands; Salisbury Hall, the site of a part of the present library; and Little St. Edmund Hall, which was still more to the southward, about where is now the chapel. The name of Brasenose is supposed,

hæredum de Husey, cum vino dato eodem tempore, xx. d. ob." From the Rolls of Winchester College, temp. Hen. IV., communicated by Rev. W. Gunner, in *Proceedings of Archæolog. Inst.*, 1848, p. 64.

with the greater probability, to have been derived from a *Brasinium*, *Brasen-huis*, or brewhouse, attached to the hall built by Alfred; more vulgarly, from some students removed to it from the temporary University of Stamford, where the iron ring of the knocker was fixed in a nose of brass.[1]

Instances of the same kind of popular etymology — which occasionally leads to popular mythology — are to be found in proverbs. There is an English proverb, "to know a hawk from a handsaw," which was originally "to know a hawk from a hernshaw," a kind of heron.[2]

The French *buffetier*, a man who waits at the *buffet*, which was a table near the door of the dining-hall for poor people, travellers, and pilgrims, to help themselves to what was not wanted at the high table, has been changed in English into a beef-eater;[3] and it is no doubt a vulgar error that these tall stalwart fellows are chiefly fed on beef.

One of the most curious instances of the power of popular etymology and mythology is seen in the English *Barnacle*. It is not often that we can trace a myth from century to century through the different stages of its growth, and it may be worth while to analyze this fable of the Barnacle more in detail.

Barnacles, in the sense of spectacles, seem to be connected with the German word for spectacles, namely, *Brille*.[4] This German word is a corruption

[1] Parker, *Handbook of Oxford*, p. 79.
[2] Wilson, *Pre-historic Man*, p. 68. Cf. Pott, *Doppelung*, p. 81. Förstemann, *Deutsche Volksetymologie*, in Kuhn's *Zeitschrift*, vol. i. Latham, *History of the English Language*.
[3] Cf. Trench, *English Past and Present*, p. 221.
[4] Cf. Grimm, *D. W. s. v.* Brill. Mr. Wedgwood derives *barnacles*, in

of *beryllus.* In a Vocabulary of 1482 we find *brill, parill,* a masculine, a precious stone, shaped like glass or ice (cise), *berillus* item or *bernlein.*[1] Sebastian Frank, in the beginning of the sixteenth century, still uses *barill* for eye-glass. The word afterwards became a feminine, and, as such, the recognized name for spectacles.

In the place of *beryllus,* in the sense of precious stone, we find in Provençal *berille* ;[2] and in the sense of spectacles, we find the Old French *béricle.*[3] *Bericle* was afterwards changed to *bésicles,*[4] commonly, but wrongly, derived from *bis-cyclus.*

In the dialect of Berri[5] we find, instead of *bericle* or *besicle,* the dialectic form *berniques,* which reminds us of the German form *Bern-lein.*[6] An analogous form is the English *barnacle,* originally spectacles fixed on the nose, and afterwards used in the sense of *irons* put on the noses of horses to confine them for shoeing, bleeding, or dressing.[7] *Brille* in German is used in a similar sense of a piece of leather with spikes, put on the noses of young animals that are to be weaned. The formation of *bernicula* seems to

the sense of spectacles, from Limousin *bourgna,* to squinny; Wall. *boirgni,* to look through one eye in aiming; Lang. *borni,* blind; *bornikel,* one who sees with difficulty; *berniques,* spectacles. *Vocab. du Berri.*

[1] "Berillus (gemma, speculum presbiterorum aut veterum, d. i. brill)." Diefenbach, *Glossarium Latino-Germanicum.* "Eise" may be meant for crystal.
[2] Raynouard, *Lexique Roman.*
[3] *Dict. du vieux Français,* Paris, 1766, s. v.
[4] *Dict. Prov.-Français,* par Avril, 1839, s. v.
[5] *Voc. du Berri,* s. v.
[6] In the *Dict. du vieux Français,* Paris, 1766, *bernicles* occurs in the sense of *rien, nihil.*
[7] Skinner derives *barnacle,* "frænum quod equino rictui injicitur," from *bear* and *neck.*

have been *beryllicula*, and, to avoid the repetition of *l*, *berynicula*. As to the change of *l* into *n*, see *melanconico*, *filomena*, &c. Diez, " Grammatik," p. 190.

Barnacle, in the sense of cirrhopode, can hardly be anything but the diminutive of the Latin *perna*; *pernacula* being changed into *bernacula*.[1] Pliny[2] speaks of a kind of shells called *pernæ*, so called from their similarity with a leg of pork.

The bodies of these animals are soft, and enclosed in a case composed of several calcareous plates; their limbs are converted into a tuft of jointed *cirrhi* or fringes, which can be protruded through an opening in the sort of a mantle which lines the interior of the shell. With these they fish for food, very much like a man with a casting-net; and as soon as they are immersed in sea-water by the return of the flood, their action is incessant. They are generally found fixed on rocks, wooden planks, stones, or even on living shells; and after once being fixed, they never leave their place of abode. Before they take to this settled life, however, they move about freely, and, as it would seem, enjoy a much more highly organized state of life. They are then furnished with eyes, antennæ, and limbs, and are as active as any of the minute denizens of the sea.

[1] Cf. Diez, *Grammatik*, p. 256. Bolso (pulsus), brugna and prugna (prunum), &c. *Berna*, instead of *Perna*, is actually mentioned in the *Glossarium Latino-Germanicum*, mediæ et infimæ ætatis, ed. Diefenbach; also in Du Cange, *beran*, *swinbache*. Skinner derives barnacle from *bearn*, filius, and A. S. *anc*, *oak*. Wedgwood proposes the Manx *bayrn*, a cap, as the etymon of *barnacle*; also *barnagh*, a limpet, and the Gaelic *bairneach*, barnacle; the Welsh *brenig*, limpet.

[2] Plin. *H. Nat.* 32, 55: "Appellantur et pernæ concharum generis, circa Pontias insulas frequentissimæ. Stant velut suillo crure longo in arena defixæ, hiantesque, qua limpitudo est, pedali non minus spatio, cibum venantur."

BARNACLES.   . 555

There are two families of *Cirrhopodes*. The first, the *Lepadidæ*, are attached to their resting-place by a flexible stalk, which possesses great contractile power. The shell is usually composed of two triangular pieces on each side, and is closed by another elongated piece at the back, so that the whole consists of five pieces.

The second family, the *Balanidæ*, or sea-acorn, has a shell usually composed of six segments, the lower part being firmly fixed to the stone or wood on which the creature lives.

These creatures were known in England at all times, and they went by the name of *Barnacles*, i. e. *Bernaculæ*, or small muscles. Their name, though nearly identical in sound with *Barnacles*, in the sense of spectacles, had originally no connection whatever with that term, which was derived, as we found, from *beryllus*.

But now comes a third claimant to this name of *Barnacle*, namely, the famous *Barnacle Goose*. There is a goose called *Bernicla*; and though that goose has sometimes been confounded with a duck (the *Anas niger minor*, the *Scoter*, the French *Macreuse*), yet there is no doubt that the Barnacle goose is a real bird, and may be seen drawn and described in any good Book on Birds.[1] But though the bird is

[1] Linnæus describes it, sub "Aves, Anseres," as "No. 11, Bernicla, A. fusca, capite collo pectoreque nigris, collari albo. Branta s. Bernicla. Habitat in Europa boreali, migrat super Sueciam."

Willoughby, in his *Ornithology*, book iii., says: "I am of opinion that the Brant-Goose differs specifically from the Bernacle, however writers of the History of Birds confound them, and make these words synonymous." Mr. Gould, in his "Birds of Europe," vol. v., gives a drawing of the Anser leucopsis, Bernacle Goose, l'oie bernache, sub No. 350; and another of the Anser Brenta, Brent Goose, l'oie cravant, sub No. 352.

a real bird, the accounts given of it, not only in popular, but in scientific works, form one of the most extraordinary chapters in the history of Modern Mythology.

I shall begin with one of the latest accounts, taken from the " Philosophical Transactions," No. 137, January and February 1677–8. Here, in " A Relation concerning Barnacles, by Sr. Robert Moray, lately one of His Majesties Council for the Kingdom of Scotland,", we read (p. 925) : —

" In the Western Islands of Scotland much of the Timber, wherewith the Common people build their Houses, is such as the West-Ocean throws upon their Shores. The most ordinary Trees are Firr and Ash. They are usually very large, and without branches; which seem rather to have been broken or worn off, than cut; and are so Weather-beaten, that there is no Bark left upon them, especially the Firrs. Being in the Island of East, I saw lying upon the shore a cut of a large Firr-tree of about 2½ foot diameter, and 9 or 10 foot long; which had lain so long out of the water that it was very dry: And most of the Shells, that had formerly cover'd it, were worn or rubb'd off. Only on the parts that lay next the ground, there still hung multitudes of little Shells; having within them little Birds, perfectly shap'd, supposed to be Barnacles.

" The Shells hung very thick and close one by another, and were of different sizes. Of the colour and consistence of Muscle-Shells, and the sides or joynts of them joyned with such a kind of film as Muscle-Shells are; which serves them for a Hing to move upon, when they open and shut. . . . .

"The Shells hang at the Tree by a Neck longer than the Shell. Of a kind of Filmy substance, round, and hollow, and creassed, not unlike the Wind-pipe of a Chicken; spreading out broadest where it is fastened to the Tree, from which it seems to draw and convey the matter which serves for the growth and vegetation of the Shell and the little Bird within it.

"This Bird in every Shell that I opened, as well the least as the biggest, I found so curiously and compleatly formed, that there appeared nothing wanting, as to the internal parts, for making up a perfect Sea-fowl: every little part appearing so distinctly, that the whole looked like a large Bird seen through a concave or diminishing Glass, colour and feature being every where so clear and neat. The little Bill like that of a Goose, the Eyes marked, the Head, Neck, Breast, Wings, Tail, and Feet formed, the Feathers every where perfectly shap'd, and blackish coloured; and the Feet like those of other Waterfowl, to my best remembrance. All being dead and dry, I did not look after the Internal parts of them. . . . . Nor did I ever see any of the little Birds alive, nor met with any body that did. Only some credible persons have assured me they have seen some as big as their fist."

Here, then, we have so late as 1677 a witness who, though he does not vouch to having seen the actual metamorphosis of the Barnacle shell into the Barnacle goose, yet affirms before a scientific public that he saw within the shell the bill, the eyes, head, neck, breast, wings, tail, feet, and feathers of the embryo bird.

We have not, however, to go far back before we find a witness to the actual transformation, namely, John Gerarde, of London, Master in Chirurgerie. At the end of his " Herball," published in 1597, we have not only a lively picture of the tree, with birds issuing from its branches, swimming away in the sea or falling dead on the land, but we also read the following description (p. 1391) : —

" There are founde in the north parts of Scotland, and the Ilands adjacent, called Orchades, certaine trees, whereon doe growe certaine shell fishes, of a white colour tending to russet; wherein are conteined little living creatures: which shels in time of maturitie doe open, and out of them grow those little living foules, whom we call Barnakles, in the north of England Brant Geese, and in Lancashire tree Geese; but the other that do fall upon the land, perish and come to nothing: thus much by the writings of others, and also from the mouths of people of those parts, which may very well accord with truth.

" But what our eies have seene, and hands have touched, we shall declare. There is a small Ilande in Lancashire called the Pile of Foulders, wherein are found the broken peeces of old and brused ships, some whereof have beene cast thither by shipwracke, and also the trunks or bodies with the branches of old and rotten trees, cast up there likewise: whereon is found a certaine spume or froth, that in time breedeth unto certaine shels, in shape like those of the muskle, but sharper pointed, and of a whitish colour; wherein is conteined a thing in forme like a lace of silke finely woven, as it were togither, of a whitish colour; one ende whereof is fastened unto the inside of the shell, even as the fish of Oisters and Muskles are; the other ende is made fast unto the

Fig. 29.

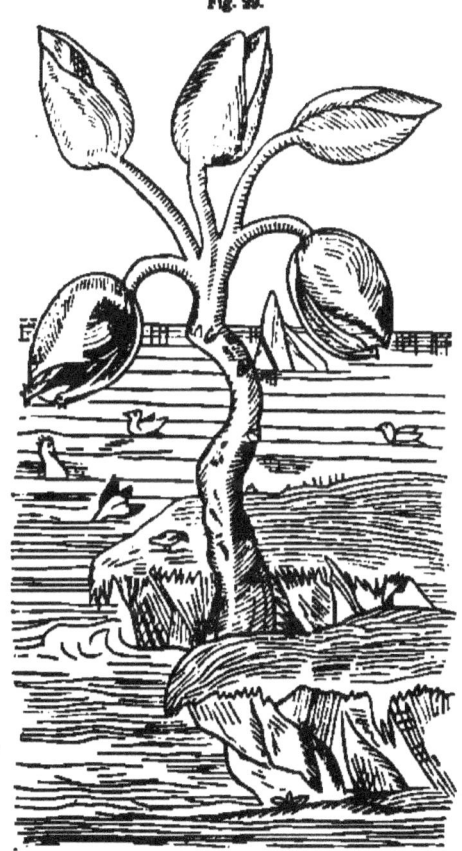

COPIED FROM GERARDE'S "HERBALL."

belly of a rude masse or lumpe, which in time commeth to the shape and forme of a Bird: when it is perfectly formed, the shel gapeth open, and the first thing that appeereth is the foresaid lace or string; next come the legs of the Birde hanging out; and as it groweth greater, it openeth the shell by degrees, till at length it is all come foorth, and hangeth only by the bill; in short space after it commeth to full maturitie, and falleth into the sea, where it gathereth feathers, and groweth to a foule, bigger then a Mallard, and lesser then a Goose; having blacke legs and bill or beake, and feathers blacke and white, spotted in such manner as is our Magge-Pie, called in some places a Pie-Annet, which the people of Lancashire call by no other name then a tree Goose; which place aforesaide, and all those parts adjoining, do so much abound therewith, that one of the best is bought for three pence: *for the truth heerof, if any doubt, may it please them to repaire unto me, and I shall satisfie them by the testimonie of good witnesses.*"

That this superstition was not confined to England, but believed in by the learned all over Europe, we learn from *Sebastian Munster*, in his *Cosmographia Universalis*, 1550, dedicated to Charles V. He tells the same story, without omitting the picture; and though he mentions the sarcastic remark of *Æneas Sylvius*, about miracles always flying away to more remote regions, he himself has no misgivings as to the truth of the bird-bearing tree, vouched for, as he remarks, by *Saxo Grammaticus*. This is what he writes: — " In Scotia inveniuntur arbores, quæ producunt fructum foliis conglomeratum: et is cum opportuno tempore decidit in subjectam aquam, reviviscit convertiturque in avem vivam, quam vocant anserem arboreum. Crescit et hæc arbor in insula Pomonia, quæ haud procul abest a Scotia versus aquilonem. Veteres quoque Cosmographi, præsertim Saxo Grammaticus mentionem faciunt hujus arboris, ne putes esse figmentum a novis scriptoribus excogitatum."[1]

The next account of these extraordinary geese I shall take from Hector Boece (1465-1536), who in 1527 wrote his history of Scotland in Latin, which soon after was translated into English. The history is preceded by a Cosmography and Description of Albion, and here we read, in the fourteenth chapter:[2]—

" Of the nature of claik geis, and of the syndry maner of thair procreation, And of the Ile of Thule, capitulo xliii.

" Restis now to speik of the geis generit of the see namit clakis. Sum men belevis that thir clakis growis on treis be the nebbis. Bot thair opinioun is vane. And becaus the nature and procreatioun of thir clakis is strange, we have maid na lytyll lauboure and deligence to serche ye treuth and verite yairof, we have salit throw ye seis quhare thir clakis ar bred, and I fynd be gret experience, that the nature of the seis is mair relevant caus of thair procreatioun

---

[1] Seb. Munster, p. 40.
[2] " The hystory and Cronicla of Scotland, with the Cosmography and dyscripilon thairof, compilit be the noble clerk maister Hector Boece channon of Aberdene. Translatit laitly in our vulgar and commoun langage, be maister Johne Bellenden Archedene of Murray, And Imprentit in Edinburgh, be me Thomas Davidson, prenter to the Kyngis nobyll grace" (about 1540).

than ony uthir thyng. And howbeit thir geis ar bred
mony syndry wayis, thay ar bred ay allanerly by nature of the seis. For all treis that ar cassin in the
seis be proces of tyme apperis first wormeetin, and
in the small boris and hollis thairof growis small
wormis. First thay schaw thair heid and feit, and
last of all thay schaw thair plumis and wyngis.
Finaly quhen thay ar cumyn to the just mesure and
quantite of geis, thay fle in the aire, as othir fowlis
dois, as was notably provyn in the yeir of god ane
thousand iiii hundred lxxxx in sicht of mony pepyll
besyde the castell of Petslego, ane gret tre was
brocht be alluvion and flux of the see to land. This
wonderfull tre was brocht to the lard of the ground,
quhilk sone efter gart devyde it be ane saw. Apperit
than ane multitude of wormis thrawing thaym self
out of syndry hollis and boris of this tre. Sum of
thaym war rude as thay war bot new schapin. Sum
had baith heid, feit, and wyngis, bot thay had no
fedderis. Sum of thaym war perfit schapin fowlis.
At last the pepyll havand ylk day this tre in mair
admiration, brocht it to the kirk of Sanct Androis
besyde the town of Tyre, quhare it remanis yit to
our dayis. And within two yeris efter hapnit sic ane
lyk tre to cum in at the firth of Tay besyde Dunde
wormeetin and hollit full of young geis in the samyn
maner. Siclike in the port of Leith beside Edinburgh within few yeris efter hapnit sic ane lyke cais.
Ane schip namit the Christofir (efter that scho had
lyin iii yeris at ane ankir in ane of thir Ilis, wes
brocht to leith. And becaus hir tymmer (as apperit)
failyeit, sho was brokin down. Incontinent apperit
(as afore) al the inwart partis of hir wormeetin, and

all the hollis thairof full of geis, on the samyn maner as we have schawin. Attoure gif ony man wald allege be sane argument, that this Christofer was maid of fir treis, as grew allanerly in the Ilis, and that all the rutis and treis that growis in the said Ilis, ar of that nature to be fynaly be nature of the seis resolvit in geis, We preif the cuntre thairof be ane notable example schawin afore our ene. Maister Alexander Galloway person of Kynkell was with ws in thir Ilis, gevand his mynd with maist erniat besynes to serche the verite of thir obscure and mysty dowtis. And be adventure liftit up ane see tangle byngand full of mussill schellis fra the rute to the branchis. Sone efter he opnit ane of thir mussyll schellis, bot than he was mair astonist than afore. For he saw na fische in it bot ane perfit schapin foule smal and gret ay effering to the quantite of the schell. This clerk knawin ws richt desirus of sic uncouth thingis, come haistely with the said tangle, and opnit it to ws with all circumstance afore rehersit. Be thir and mony othir reasonis and examplis we can not beleif that thir clakis ar producit be ony nature of treis or rutis thairof, bot allanerly by the nature of the Occeane see, quhilk is the caus and production of mony wonderful thingis. And becaus the rude and ignorant pepyl saw oftymes the frutis that fel of the treis (quhilkis stude neir the see) convertit within schort tyme in geis, thai belevit that thir geis grew apon the treis hingand be thair nebbis siclik as appillis and uthir frutis hingis be thair stalkis, bot thair opinioun is nocht to be sustenit. For als sone as thir appillis or frutis fallis of the tre in the see flude, thay grow first wormeetin. And be schort process of tyme ar alterat in geis."

Let us now go back to the twelfth century, and we shall find, in the time of Henry II. (1154–89), exactly the same story, and even then so firmly established that Giraldus Cambrensis found it necessary to protest against the custom then prevailing of eating these Barnacle geese during Lent, because they were not birds, but fishes. This is what Giraldus says in his "Topographia Hiberniæ:[1] —

"There are in this place many birds which are called *Bernacæ*: against nature, nature produces them in a most extraordinary way. They are like marsh-geese, but somewhat smaller. They are produced from fir timber tossed along the sea, and are at first like gum. Afterwards they hang down by their beaks as if from a seaweed attached to the timber, surrounded by shells, in order to grow more freely. Having thus, in process of time, been clothed with a strong coat of feathers, they either fall into

---

[1] Silvester Giraldus Cambrensis, *Topographia Hibernia*, in *Anglica, Normannica, Hibernica, Cambrica, a veteribus scripta*. Frankofurti, 1603, p. 706 (under Henry II., 1154–89).

[2] Sunt et aves hic multæ quæ Bernacæ vocantur: quas mirum in modum contra naturam natura producit: Aucis quidem palustribus similes, sed minores. Ex lignis namque ablegnis per æquora devolutis, primo quasi gummi nascuntur. Dehinc tamquam ab alga ligno cohærente conchylibus testis ad liberiorem formationem inclusæ, per rostra dependent: et sic quousque processu temporis firmam plumarum vestituram indutæ vel in aquas decidunt, vel in aëris libertatem volatu se transferunt, ex succo ligneo marinoque occulta nimis admirandaque seminii ratione alimenta simul lucrementaque suscipiunt. Vidi multoties oculis meis plusquam mille minuta hujusmodi avium corpuscula, in littore maris ab uno ligno dependentia testis inclusa et jam formata. Non ex harum coitu (ut in avibus assolet) ova gignuntur, non avis in earum procreatione unquam ovis incubat: in nullis terrarum angulis vel libidini vacare vel nidificare videntur. Unde et in quibusdam Hiberniæ partibus, avibus istis tamquam non carneis quia de carne non natis, episcopi et viri religiosi jejuniorum tempore sine delictu vesci solent. Sed hi quidem scrupulose moventur ad delictum. Si quis enim ex primi parentis carnel quidem, licet de carne non nati, fœmore comedisset, eum a carnium esu non immunem arbitrarer."

the water or fly freely away into the air. They derive their food and growth from the sap of the wood or the sea, by a secret and most wonderful process of alimentation. I have frequently, with my own eyes, seen more than a thousand of these small bodies of birds, hanging down on the sea-shore from one piece of timber, enclosed in shells, and already formed. They do not breed and lay eggs, like other birds; nor do they ever hatch any eggs; nor do they seem to build nests in any corner of the earth. Hence bishops and clergymen in some parts of Ireland do not scruple to dine off these birds at the time of fasting, because they are not flesh, nor born of flesh. But these are thus drawn into sin; for if a man during Lent had dined off a leg of Adam, our first parent, who was not born of flesh, surely we should not consider him innocent of having eaten what is flesh."

Then follows more to the same effect, which we may safely leave out. What is important is this, that in the twelfth century the belief in the miraculous transformation of the Barnacle-shell into the Barnacle-goose was as firmly established as in the seventeenth century; and that on that belief another belief had grown up, namely, that Barnacle-geese might safely be eaten during Lent.

How long before Giraldus the fable existed, I cannot tell; but it must not be supposed that, during the five centuries through which we have traced its existence, it was never contradicted. It was contradicted by Albertus Magnus (died 1280), who declares that he saw these birds lay eggs and hatch them.[1]

[1] Barbatas mentiando quidam dicunt aves: quas vulgus bomngas (baum-

It was contradicted by Roger Bacon (died 1294). Æneas Sylvius[1] (afterwards Pope Pius II., 1458–64), when on a visit to King James (1393–1437; reigned 1424–37), inquired after the tree, and he complains that miracles will always flee farther and farther; for when he came to Scotland to see the tree, he was told that it grew farther north in the Orchades. In 1599, Dutch sailors, who had visited Greenland, gave a full description of how they found there the eggs of the Barnacle-geese (whom they in Dutch called *rotgansen*); how they saw them hatching, and heard them cry *rot, rot, rot*; how they killed one of them with a stone, and ate it, together with sixty eggs.[2]

Nevertheless, the story appeared again and again, and the birds continued to be eaten by the priests during Lent without any qualms of conscience. *Aldrovandus*, in his "Ornithologia," 1603, (lib. xix.),

gans?) vocat: eo quod ex arboribus nasci dicuntur a quibus stipite et ramis dependent: et succo qui inter corticem est nutritæ: dicunt etiam aliquando ex putridis lignis hæc animalia in mari generari: et præcipue ex abietum putredine, afferentes quod nemo unquam vidit has aves coire vel ovare: et hoc omnino absurdum est: quia ego et multi mecum de sociis vidimus eas et coire et ovare et pullos nutrire sicut in ante habitis diximus: hæc avis caput habet quasi pavonis. Pedes autem nigros ut cygnos: et sunt membrana conjuncti digiti ad natandum: et sunt in dorso cinereæ nigredinis: et in ventre subalbidæ, aliquantum minores anseribus." — *De Animalibus*, lib. xxiii. p. 186.

[1] "Scribit tamen Eneas Sylvius de hac arbore in hunc modum: 'Audiveramus nos olim arborem esse in Scotia, quæ supra ripam fluminis enata fructus produceret, anetarum formam habentes, et eos quidem cum maturitati proximi essent sponte sua decidere, alios in terram, alios in aquam, et in terram dejectos putrescere, in aquam vero demersos, mox animatos enatare sub aquis et in aerem plumis pennisque evolare. De qua re cum aviditate investigaremus dum essemus in Scotia apud Jacobum regem, hominem quadratum et multa pinguedine gravem, didicimus miracula semper remotius fugere, famosamque arborem non in Scotia, sed apud Orchades insulas inveniri.'" — Seb. Munster, *Cosmographia*, p. 49.

[2] *Trois Navigations faites par les Hollandais au Septentrion*, par Gerard de Vera. Paris, 1599, p. 112.

tells us of an Irish priest, of the name of Octavianus, who assured him with an oath on the Gospel that he had seen the birds in their rude state and handled them. And *Aldrovandus* himself, after weighing all the evidence for and against the miraculous origin of the Barnacle-goose, arrives at the conclusion that it is better to err with the majority than to argue against so many eminent writers.[1] In 1629 a Count Maier published at Frankfort a book, " De Volucri Arborea " (On the Tree-bird), in which he explains the whole process of its birth, and indulges in some most absurd and blasphemous speculations.[2]

But how did this extraordinary story arise? Why

Fig. 30.

should anybody ever have conceived the idea that a bird was produced from a shell; and this particular

[1] " Malim tamen cum pluribus errare quam tot scriptoribus clarissimis oblatrare quibus præter id quod de ephemero dictum est, favet etiam quod est ab Aristotele proditum, genus scilicet testatum quoddam navigiis putrescente fæce spumosa adnasci." (P. 173, lin. 47).

[2] The fourth chapter has the following heading: "Quod finis proprius hujus volucris generationis sit ut referat duplici suâ naturâ, vegetabili et animali, Christum Deum et hominem, qui quoque sine patre et matre, ut Ille, existit."

bird, the Barnacle-goose, from this particular shell, the Barnacle-shell? If the story was once started, there are many things that would keep it alive; and its vitality has certainly been extraordinary. There are certain features about this Barnacle-shell which to a careless observer might look like the first rudiments of a bird; and the feet, in particular, with which these animals catch their food and convey it into the shell, are decidedly like very delicate feathers. The fact, again, that this fable of the shell-geese offered an excuse for eating these birds during Lent would, no doubt, form a strong support of the common belief, and invest it, to a certain extent, with a sacred character. In Bombay, where, with some classes of people, fish is considered a prohibited article of food, the priests call it sea-vegetable, under which name it is allowed to be eaten. No one would suspect Linnæus of having shared the vulgar error; nevertheless, he retained the name of *anatifera*, or duck-bearing, as given to the shell, and that of *Bernicla*, as given to the goose.

I believe it was language which first suggested this myth. We saw that the shells were regularly and properly called *bernaculæ*. We also saw that the Barnacle-geese were caught in Ireland. It was against the Irish bishops that Giraldus Cambrensis wrote, blaming them for their presumption in eating these birds during Lent; and we learn from later sources that the discovery made by the Irish priests was readily adopted in France. Now Ireland is called *Hibernia*; and I believe these birds were originally called *Hibernicæ*, or *Hiberniculæ*. The first syllable was dropped, as not having the accent, just as it was dropped in the Italian *il verno*, winter, instead of *il iverno*. This dropping of the first syllable is by no means unusual in Latin words which, through the vulgar Latin of the monks, found their way into the modern Romance dialects;[1] and we actually find in the mediæval Latin dictionaries the word *hybernagium* in the truncated form of *bernagium*.[2] The birds, therefore, being called *Hiberniculæ*, then *Berniculæ*, were synonymous with the shells, equally called *Bernaculæ*; and as their names seemed one, so the creatures were supposed to be one. Everything afterwards seemed to conspire to confirm the first mistake, and to invest what was originally a good Irish *canard* with all the dignity of scientific, and the solemnity of theological truth.

It should be mentioned, however, that there is another derivation of the name *Bernacula*, which was suggested to Gesner by one of his correspondents. "Joannes Caius," he says, "writes to me in a letter: 'I believe that the bird which we call *Anser brendinus*, others *Bernaclus*, ought to be called *Bernclacus*; for the old Britons and the modern Scots called, and call, the wild goose *Clake*. Hence they still retain the name which is corrupted with us, *Lake* or *Fenlake*, i. e. lake-goose, instead of *Fencklake*; for our people frequently change letters, and say *bern* for *bren*.'" ("Historia Animalium," lib. iii. p. 110.)

His idea, therefore, was, that the name was derived

---

[1] Cf. Diez, *Rom. Gr.* p. 109: *rendine* = hirundo.
 vescovo episcopus.
 chiesa ecclesia.

[2] Cf. Du Cange. "Bernagium, pro Hybernagium, ni fallor, miscellum frumentum."

from Scotch; that in Scotch the bird was called *Bren clake*; that this was pronounced *Bernclake*, and then Latinized into *bernclacus*. There is, however, this one fatal objection to this etymology, that among the very numerous varieties of the name *Bernicula*,[1] not one comes at all near to *Bernclacus*. Otherwise *clake* or *claik* certainly means goose; and the Barnacle-goose, in particular, is so called.[2] As to *Bran*, it means in compounds dark, such as the A. S. *branwyrt*, blackberry, different from *brunewyrt*, brownwort, water betony; and Jamieson gives us as Scotch *branded*, *brannit*, adj., having a reddish-brown color,

---

[1] The name even in Latin varies. In ornithological works the following names occur, all intended for the same bird, though I do not wish to vouch for their correctness or authenticity:—

English: Bernacle, Scotch goose.
Scotch: Clakis or claiks, clak-guse, claik-gees, Barnacle.
Orcades: Rodgans.
Dutch: Ratgans.
German: Baumgans.
Danish: Ray-gaas, Radgans.
Norwegian: Baatne-gans, goul, gagl.
Iceland: Helsingen.
French: Bernacbe, Cane à collier. Nonnette, Religieuse; Macquerolls, (?), Macrense. (?)
Latin: Bernicula, Bernacula, Bernacla, Barnicla, Bernacla, Bernecula (Fred. II. Imp., *de Arte Venandi*), Bernaca, Bernicha, Bernecha, Bernaca, Bernichla, Hranta (ab atro colore anser scoticus), Bernesta, Barnaces (Brompton, p. 1072), Barbata (Isidorus), Barbata (Albertus Magnus).

Cf. Ducange, s. v. *Menage*, s. v. *Bernacke*. Diefenbach, *Glossarium Latino-Germanicum*: "Galli has aves *Macquerolles* et *Macrenses* appellant, et tempore Quadragesimali ex Normannia Parisios deferunt. Sed revera deprehensum est a Batavis, anseres hosce ova parere," &c. (Willoughby.)

Another name is given by Scaliger. Julius Cæsar Scaliger, ad Arist. de Plantis, libr. l. 1—" Anates (inquit, melius dixisset Anseres) Oceani, quas Armorici partim *Crabrans*, partim *Bernachias* vocant. Ex creantur ex putredine naufragiorum, pendentique rostro a matrice, quoad absolutæ decidant in subjectas aquas, unde sibi statim victum quærunt; visendo interea spectaculo pensiles, motitantesque tum pedes, tum alas."

[2] Brompton, *Chronicle of Ireland*, col. 1072, ap. Jun.

as if singed by fire; a *branded* cow being one almost entirely brown. A *brant-fox* is a fox with black feet. *Branta*, we saw, was a name given to the Barnacle-goose; and it was said to be given to it on account of its dark color.

How easily in cases like this a legend grows up to remove any difficulty that might be felt at names no longer understood, can be proved by many a mediæval legend, both sacred and profane. The learned editor of the " Munimenta Gildhallæ Londinensis," Mr. H. T. Riley, tells us in his Preface (p. xviii.) that, in the fourteenth and beginning of the fifteenth century, trading, or buying and selling at a profit, was known to the more educated classes under the French name *achat*, which in England was written, and probably pronounced, *acat*. To *acat* of this nature, Whittington was indebted for his wealth; and as, in time, the French became displaced here by the modern English, the meaning of the word probably became lost, and thereby gave the opportunity to some inventive genius, at a much later period, of building a new story on the double meaning of an old and effete word.[1]

You know the story of St. Christopher. The " Legenda Aurea "[2] says of him that he was a Canaanite, very tall and fearful to look at. " He would not serve anybody who had himself a master; and when he heard that his lord was afraid of the devil, he left him and became himself the servant of the

[1] *Rerum Britannicarum Medii Ævi Scriptores, Munimenta Gildhallæ Londinensis*, vol. I. Liber Albus. London, 1859. As I have not been able to trace the story of Whittington to its earliest form, I must leave to Mr. Riley all the credit and responsibility of this explanation.

[2] *Legenda Aurea*, cap. 100.

devil. One day, however, when passing a Cross, he observed that his new master was afraid of the Cross, and learning that there was one more powerful than the devil, he left him to enter the service of Christ. He was instructed by an old hermit, but being unable to fast or to pray, he was told to serve Christ by carrying travellers across a deep river.[1] This he did, until one day he was called three times, and the third time he saw a child that wished to be carried across the river. He took him on his shoulders, but his weight was such that he could bardly reach the opposite shore. When he had reached it, the Child said to him that he had carried Christ Himself on his shoulders, in proof whereof, the stick which he had used for many years, when planted in the earth, grew into a tree." Many more miracles are said to have happened to him afterwards, till at last he suffered the death of a martyr.

It is clear, and it is not denied even by Roman Catholic writers, that the whole legend of St. Christopher sprang from his name, which means " he who bears Christ." That name was intended in a spiritual sense, just as St. Ignatius took the name of *Theophorus*,[2] " he who bears God," namely, in his

---

[1] According to a late Latin hymn, it was the Red Sea through which Christopher carried the travellers.

" O sancte Christophore,
Qui portasti Jesum Christum,
Per mari rubrum,
Nec franxisti crurum,
Et hoc est non mirum,
Quia fuisti magnum virum."

[2] " The accent placed on the penultima of θεοφόρος, as the word is written in the saint's acts, denotes it of an active signification, one that

heart. But, as in the case of St. Ignatius, the people who martyred him, when tearing out his heart, are said to have found it miraculously inscribed with the name of God, so the name of *Christophorus* led to the legend just quoted. Whether there was a real Christophorus who suffered martyrdom under Decius, in Lycia, 250 A. D., we cannot tell; but even Alban Butler, in his " Lives of the Saints," admits that " there seem to be no other grounds than his name for the vulgar notion of his great stature, the origin of which seems to have been merely allegorical, as Baronius observes, and as Vida has expressed in an epigram on this saint: —

" Christophore, infixum quod eum usque in corde gerebas,
Pictores Christum dant tibi ferri humeris." [1]

" The enormous statues of St. Christopher, still to be seen in many Gothic cathedrals, expressed his allegorical wading through the sea of tribulations, by which the faithful meant to signify the many sufferings through which he arrived at eternal life." Before he was called Christophorus his name was Reprobus; so says the " Legenda Aurea." Others, improving on the legend, represent his original name to have been *Offerus*,[2] the second part of *Christoferus*, thus showing a complete misunderstanding of the original name.

Another legend, which is supposed to owe its origin to a similar misunderstanding, is that of Ur-

---

carrieth God; but of the passive, carried of God, if placed on the antepenultima." — Alban Butler, *Lives of the Saints*, vol. ii. p. 1.
[1] *Vida*, Hymn. 20, l. ii. p. 150.
[2] Maury, *Légendes Pieuses*, p. 53.

sula and the 11,000 Virgins, whose bones are shown to the present day in one of the churches of Cologne. This extravagant number of martyred virgins, which is not specified in the earlier legends, is said to have arisen from the name of one of the companions of Ursula being *Undecimella*,[1] — an explanation very plausible, though I must confess that I have not been able to find any authority[2] for the name *Undecimella*.

It would be a great mistake to suppose that these and other legends were invented and spread intentionally. They were the natural productions of the intellectual soil of Europe, where the seeds of Christianity had been sown before the wild weeds of the ancient heathen mythology were rooted up and burnt. They are no more artificial, no more the work of individuals, than the ancient fables of Greece, Rome, or India; nay, we know that the Church, which has sometimes been accused of fostering these superstitions, endeavored from time to time to check their rapid growth, but in vain. What happened at that time was what will always happen when the great masses are taught to speak the language before they have learnt to think the thoughts of their rulers, teachers, apostles, or missionaries. What in the mind of the teacher is spiritual and true becomes in the mouth of the pupil material and frequently false.

---

[1] " L'Histoire de sainte Ursule et des onze mille vierges doit son origine à l'expression des vieux calendriers, Ursula et Undecimella, VV. MM., c'est-à-dire sainte Ursule et sainte Undecimalle, vierges et martyres." — Maury, p. 214.

[2] Jacobus a Voragine, *Legenda Aurea*, cap. 158. Galfredus, *Monumetensis*, lib. v. cap. 16. *St. Ursula und ihre Gesellschaft. Eine kritisch-historische Monographie*, von Johann Hubert Kessel. Köln, 1863.

Yet, even in their corrupt form, the words of the teachers retain their sacred character; they soon form an integral part of that foundation on which the religious life of a whole nation is built up, and the very teachers tremble lest in trying to place each stone in its right position, they might shake the structure which it took centuries to build up. St. Thomas (died 1274) asked Bonaventura (died 1271) whence he received the force and unction which he displayed in all his works. Bonaventura pointed to a crucifix hanging on the wall of his cell. "It is that image," he said, "which dictates all my words to me." What can be more simple, more true, more intelligible? But the saying of Bonaventura was repeated, the people took it literally, and, in spite of all remonstrances, they insisted that Bonaventura possessed a talking crucifix. A profane miracle took the place of a sacred truth; nay, those who could understand the truth, and felt bound to protest against the vulgar error, were condemned by the loud-voiced multitude as disbelievers of miracles. Pictures frequently added a new sanction to these popular superstitions. Zurbaran painted a saint (Pierre Nolasque) before a speaking crucifix. Whether the artist meant it literally or symbolically, we do not know. But the crowds took it in the most literal sense, and who was the bold preacher who would tell his congregation the plain, though no doubt the more profound, meaning of the miraculous picture which they had once learnt to worship?

It was a common practice of early artists to represent martyrs that had been executed by the sword, as carrying their heads in their hands.[1] The people

[1] Maury, p. 207.

who saw the sculptures could read them in one sense only, and they firmly believed that certain martyrs miraculously carried their heads in their hands after they had been beheaded.[1] Several saints were represented with a dove either at their side or near their ear. The artist intended no more than to show that these men had been blessed with the gifts of the Holy Ghost; but the people who saw the images firmly believed that the Holy Ghost had appeared to their saint in the form of a dove.[2] Again, nothing was more usual for an artist than to represent sin and idolatry under the form of a serpent or a dragon. A man who had fought bravely against the temptations of the world, a pagan king who had become a convert to Christianity,[3] was naturally represented as a St. George fighting with the dragon, and slaying it. A missionary who had successfully preached the Gospel and driven out the venomous brood of heresy or idolatry, became at once a St. Patrick, driving away every poisonous creature from the Hibernian island.[4]

Now it should be observed how in all these cases the original conception of the word or the picture is far higher, far more reverend, far more truly religious than the miraculous petrifaction which excites the superstitious interest of the people at large. If Constantine or Clovis, at the most critical moments of

[1] Maury, *Légendes Pieuses*, p. 287 : " Cette légende se trouve dans les vies de saint Denis, de saint Ovide, de saint Firmin d'Amiens, de saint Maurice, de saint Nicaise de Reims, de saint Soulange de Bourges, de saint Just d'Auxerre, de saint Lucain, de sainte Esperie, de saint Didier de Langres, et d'une foule d'autres."
[2] *Ibid.* p. 182.
[3] *Ibid.* 135, Eusebius, *de Vita Const.*, ed. Heinicher, Lipsia, 1830, p. 180.
[4] *Ibid.* p. 141.

their lives, felt that the victory came from the hands of the Only True God, the God revealed by Christ, and preached in the cities of the whole Roman Empire by the despised disciples of a crucified Lord, surely this shows the power of Christianity in a far more majestic light than when we are told that these royal converts saw, or imagined they saw, a flag with a Cross, or with the inscription, "*In hoc signo vinces.*"[1]

If Bonaventura felt the presence of Christ in his lonely cell, if the heart of Ignatius was instinct with the spirit of God, we can understand what is meant, we can sympathize, we can admire, we can love. But if we are told that the one merely possessed a talking crucifix, and that the heart of the other was inscribed with the four Greek letters, ΘΕΟΣ, what is that to us?

Those old pictures and carved images of saints fighting with dragons, of martyrs willing to lay down their lives for the truth, of inspired writers listening intently to the voice of God, lose all their meaning and beauty if we are told that they were only men of bodily strength who chanced to kill a gorilla-like monster, or beings quite different from ourselves, who did not die even though their heads had been severed from their trunks, or old men carrying doves on each shoulder. Those doves whispering into the ears of the prophets of old were meant for the Spirit of God descending like a dove and lighting upon them;

---

[1] Similar stories are told of Alfons, the first King of Portugal, who is said to have seen a brilliant cross before the battle of Ourique, in 1139, and of Waldemar II., of Denmark. The red cross of Denmark, the Danebrog, dates from Waldemar's victory over the Esthonians in 1219. See Dahlmann, *Geschichte von Dännemark*, vol. i. p. 308.

and the pious sculptors of old would have been horrified at the idea that these birds could ever be mistaken for real animals in a bodily shape, dictating to the prophets the words they should write down. Everything is true, natural, significant, if we enter with a reverend spirit into the meaning of ancient art and ancient language. Everything becomes false, miraculous, and unmeaning, if we interpret the deep and mighty words of the seers of old in the shallow and feeble sense of modern chroniclers.

There is a curious instance of mistaken interpretation which happened long before the days of Galileo. Earthquakes in later Greek were called *Theoménía*, which literally means the Anger of God. The expression was probably suggested by the language of the Bible, where we meet with passages such as (Psalm civ. 32), "He looketh on the earth, and it trembleth; he toucheth the hills, and they smoke." It was in itself a most appropriate term, but it very soon lost its etymological significancy, and became the conventional and current name for earthquake. Nevertheless it kept up in people's mind the idea that earthquakes were more immediately produced by the wrath of God, and differed in this way from thunder-storms, or famine, or pestilence. Here was the source of mischief. The name of *Theoménía*,[1]

---

[1] θεομηνία, ira divina [Eustath. p. 891, 24]; τὴν θεομηνίαν Διὸς λέγει μάστιγα (Stephani Thesaurus, Didot).

Tzetzes, *Historiarum variarum Chiliades*, ed. Kiessling, Lipsiae, 1826, v. 727 (cf. Grote, vol. i. p. 539):—

ἃν συμφορὰ κατέλαβε πάλιν θεομηνιῳ, εἴτ᾽ οὖν λιμός, εἴτε λοιμός, εἴτε καὶ βλάβος ἄλλα.

Theophanes Contin. (p. 673), (Symeon Magister, *De Michaele et Theodora*).

ἐν μιᾷ νυκτὶ συνέβη γενέσθαι σεισμοὶ μεγάλοι· καὶ αὐτὸς ὁ φωστὴρ

which was quite true in its original conception, became falsified by an inadequate interpretation. And what happened? People who, like Photius, ventured to assign natural causes that produced earthquakes, were cried down by a thoughtless multitude as unbelievers and heretics.

We have lastly to consider one class of words which exercise a most powerful influence on the mind. They rule the mind instead of being ruled by it, and they give rise to a kind of mythology, the effects of which are most widely extended, even at the present day. I pointed out in a former Lecture that, besides such abstract names as *virtue, fortune, felicity, peace,* and *war,* there are others of a slightly different character, which equally lend themselves to mythological personification. A name like the Latin *virtus* was originally intended to express a quality, manliness, the quality of a man, or rather every good quality peculiar to man. As long as this noun was used merely as a noun of quality, as an adjective changed into a substantive, no mischief could arise.

Abstract nouns were originally collective nouns, and the transition is very easy from a plural, such as "the clercs" (clerici), to a collective or abstract noun, such as "the clergy" (clericatus). *Humanitas* meant originally "all men," "mankind"; but *kind,* literally *genus,* came, like *genus,* to express what constitutes *kind,* the qualities which all members of a kind share

ἀναβὰς ἐπὶ τοῦ ἄμβωνος δημηγορῆσαι, εἶπεν ὅτι οἱ σεισμοὶ οὐκ ἐκ πλήθους ἁμαρτιῶν ἀλλ' ἐκ πληρομονῆς ὕδατος γίνονται. Joannes Malalas (Bonnae, 1831), p. 240: τῆς αὐτῆς πόλεως 'Αντιοχείας ληφθείσης ὑπὸ ἐναντίων, ὡσαύτως δὲ καὶ θεομηνίας γενομένης καὶ διαφόρων σεισμῶν καὶ ἐμπρησμῶν.

in common, and by which one particular kind or kin is distinguished from all other kinds or kins.

But when the mind, led away by the outward semblance of the word *virtus*, conceived what was intended merely as a collective predicate, as a personal subjective essence, then the mischief was done: an adjective had become a substantive, a predicate had been turned into a subject; and as there could not be any real and natural basis on which this spurious being could rest, it was placed, almost involuntarily, on the same pedestal on which the statues of the so-called divine powers had been erected; it was spoken of as a supernatural or a divine being. *Virtus*, manliness, instead of being possessed by man, was herself spoken of as possessing, as ruling, as inciting man. She became a power, a divine power, and she soon received temples, altars, and sacrifices, like other more ancient gods. Many of those more ancient gods owed their origin to exactly the same intellectual confusion. We are apt to imagine that *Day*, *Night*, *Dawn*, *Spring*, *Heaven*, *Earth*, *River*, are substantial beings, more substantial at least than *Virtue* or *Peace*. But let us analyze these words, let us look for the substantial basis on which they rest, and we shall find that they evade our touch almost as much as the goddesses of *Virtue* and *Peace*. We can lay hold of something in everything that is individual, we can speak of a pebble, a daisy, a horse, or of a stone, a flower, an animal, as independent beings; and although their names are derived from some general quality peculiar to each, yet that quality is substantiated in something that exists, and resists further analysis. But if we speak of the Dawn, what do we mean? Do we mean a substance, an individual, a person? Certainly not. We mean the time which precedes the rising of the sun. But then, again, what is Time? what is there substantial, individual, or personal in time, or any portion of time? Yet Language cannot help herself; all the nouns which she uses are either masculine or feminine, — for neuters are of later date, — and if the name of the Dawn has once been formed, that name will convey to every one, except to the philosopher, the idea of a substantial, if not of an individual and personal being. We saw that one name of the dawn in Sanskrit was *Saraṇyû*, and that it coincided literally with the Greek *Erinys*. It was originally a perfectly true and natural saying that the rays of the Dawn would bring to light the works of darkness, the sins committed during the night. We have a proverb in German: —

> "Kein Faden ist so fein gesponnen,
> Er kommt doch endlich an der Sonnen."
>
> No thread on earth so fine is spun,
> But comes at last before the sun.

The expression that the Erinys, Saraṇyû, the Dawn, finds out the criminal, was originally quite free from mythology; it meant no more than that crime would be brought to light some day or other. It became mythological, however, as soon as the etymological meaning of Erinys was forgotten, and as soon as the Dawn, a portion of time, assumed the rank of a personal being.

The *Weird Sisters* sprang from the same source.

Weird meant originally *the Past*.[1] It was the name given to the first of the three *Nornas*, the German *Parcæ*. They were called *Urðr*, *Verðandi*, and *Skuld*, Past, Present, and Future,[2] "das Gewordene," "das Werdende," "das (sein) Sollende." They expressed exactly the same idea which the Greeks expressed by the thread which has been spun, the thread that passes through the fingers, and the thread that is still on the distaff; or by *Lachesis*, singing what has been (τὰ γεγονότα), *Klotho*, what is (τὰ ὄντα), and *Atropos*, what will be (τὰ μέλλοντα).

In Anglo-Saxon, *Wyrd* occurs frequently in the sense of Destiny or Fate.

Beowulf, v. 915: — "Gæð á wyrd swá hió sceal," Fate goes ever as it must.

The *Weird Sisters* were intended either as destiny personified, or as *fatidicæ*, prophesying what is to befall man. Shakspeare retains the Saxon name, Chaucer speaks of them as "*the fatal sustrin.*"

Again, when the ancient nations spoke of the Earth, they no doubt meant originally the soil on which they stood; but they soon meant more. That soil was naturally spoken of as their mother, that is to say, as supplying them with food; and this one name, Mother, applied to the Earth, was sufficient to impart to it the first elements of personality, if not of humanity. But this Earth, when once spoken of as an individual, was felt to be more than the soil enclosed by hurdles, or walls, or mountains.

To the mind of the early thinkers the Earth became an infinite being, extending as far as his senses

---

[1] Grimm, *D. M.* p. 376. *Geschichte der Deutschen Sprache*, p. 665.

[2] Is *Elysium* another name for future, *Zukunft*, *avenir*, and derived from ἔρχομαι, ἤλυθον?

and his thoughts could extend, and supported by nothing, not even by the Elephant and the Tortoise of later Oriental philosophy. Thus the Earth grew naturally and irresistibly into a vague being, real, yet not finite; personal, yet not human; and the only name by which the ancient nations could call her, the only category of thought under which she could be comprehended, was that of a goddess, a bright, powerful, immortal being, the mother of men, the beloved of the sky, the Great Mother.

Now, it is perfectly true that we in our modern languages do not speak any more of gods and goddesses; but have we in our scientific and unscientific vocabularies none of those nondescript beings, like Earth, or Dawn, or Future? Do we never use terms which, if rigorously analyzed, would turn out to be without any substantial basis, resting like the Earth on the Elephant, and the Elephant on the Tortoise — but the Tortoise swinging in infinite space?

Take the word *Nature*. *Natura*, etymologically, means she who gives birth, who brings forth! But who is she, or he, or it? The ancient nations made a goddess of her, — and this we consider a childish mistake; but what is *Nature* with us? We use the word readily and constantly, but when we try to think of Nature as a being, or as an aggregate of beings, or as a power, or as an aggregate of powers, our mind soon drops: there is nothing to lay hold of, nothing that exists or resists.

What is meant by the expression, that fruits are produced by Nature? Nature cannot be meant here as an independent power, for we believe no longer in a *Gæa* or *Tellus*, a *Mother Earth*, bringing forth the fruits on which we live (*zeídōros*). *Gæa* was one of the many names of the Divine;—is Nature more or less to us?

Let us see what naturalists and philosophers can tell us about Nature.

Buffon says: "I have always spoken of the Creator, but you have only to drop that word, and put in its place the power of Nature."

"Nature," he says again, "is not a thing, for it would be all; Nature is not a being, for that being would be God."

"Nature is a living power," he adds, "immense, all-embracing, all-vivifying; subject to the first Being, it has commenced to act at His command alone, and continues to act by His consent."

Is this more intelligible, more consistent, than the fables of *Gæa*, the mother of *Uranos*, the wife of *Uranos*?

Cuvier thus speaks of Nature:[1]—

"By one of those figures of speech to which all languages are liable, Nature has been personified; all beings that exist have been called 'the works of Nature'; the general relations of these beings among themselves have been called 'the laws of Nature.' By thus considering Nature as a being endowed with intelligence and will, though secondary and limited in its powers, people have brought themselves to say that she watches constantly over the support of her works, that she does nothing in vain, that she always acts by the simplest means. It is easy to see the puerility of those philosophers who have conferred on

[1] See some excellent articles by M. Flourens, in the *Journal des Savants*, October, 1863, p. 623.

Nature a kind of individual existence, distinct from the Creator, from the laws which He has imposed on the movement, and from the properties and forms which He has given to His creatures; and who represent Nature as acting on matter by means of her own power and reason. As our knowledge has advanced in astronomy, physics, and chemistry, those sciences have renounced the paralogisms which resulted from the application of figurative language to real phenomena. Physiologists only have still retained this habit, because with the obscurity in which physiology is still enveloped, it was not possible for them to deceive themselves or others as to their profound ignorance of vital movements, except by attributing some kind of reality to the phantoms of their imagination."

Nature, if we believed all that is said of her, would be the most extraordinary being. She has horrors (*horror vacui*), she indulges in freaks (*lusus naturæ*), she commits blunders (*errores naturæ, monstra*). She is sometimes at war with herself, for, as Giraldus told us, "Nature produced barnacles against Nature;" and of late years we have heard much of her power of selection.

Nature is sometimes used as meaning simply matter, or everything that exists apart from spirit. Yet more frequently Nature is supposed to be itself endowed with independent life, to be working after eternal and invariable laws. Again, we sometimes hear Nature used so as to include the spiritual life and the intellectual activity of man. We speak of the spiritual nature of man, of the natural laws of thought, of natural religion. Even the Divine

Essence is not necessarily excluded, for the word *nature* is sometimes used so as to include that First Cause of which everything else is considered as an emanation, reflection, or creation.

But while *nature* seems thus applicable promiscuously to things material and spiritual, human and divine, language certainly, on the other hand, helps us to distinguish between the works of nature and the works of man, the former supplying materials for the physical, the latter for the historical sciences; and it likewise countenances the distinction between the works both of nature and of man on one side, and the Divine agencies on the other: the former being called natural and human, the latter supernatural and superhuman.

But now consider the havoc which must needs follow if people, without having clearly perceived the meaning of Nature, without having agreed among themselves as to the strict limits of the word, enter on a discussion upon the *Supernatural*. People will fight and call each other very hard names for denying or asserting certain opinions about the Supernatural. They would consider it impertinent if they were asked to define what they mean by the Supernatural: and yet it is as clear as anything can be that these antagonists connect totally different ideas, and ideas of the vaguest character, with this term.

Many attempts have been made to define the supernatural or the miraculous, but in every one of these definitions the meaning of nature or the natural is left undefined.

Thus Thomas Aquinas explained a miracle as that which happens out of the order of nature (præter

ordinem naturæ), while St. Augustine had worded
his definition far more carefully in saying that we
call miracles what God performs out of the usual
course of nature, *as known to us* (contra cognitum
nobis cursum solitumque naturæ). Others defined
miracles as events exceeding the powers of nature
(opus excedens naturæ vires); but this was not considered enough, because miracles should not only
exceed the powers of nature, but should violate the
order of nature (cum ad miraculum requiratur, nedum
ut excedat vires naturæ, sed præterea ut sit præter
ordinem naturæ). Miracles were divided into three
classes — 1. Those above nature (supra naturam);
2. Those against nature (contra naturam); 3. Those
beyond nature (præter naturam). But where nature
ended and the supernatural began was never explained. Thomas Aquinas went so far as to admit
miracles quoad nos, and St. Augustine maintained
that, according to human usage, things were said to
be against nature which are only against the course
of nature, *as known to mortals*. (Dici autem humano
more contra naturam esse quod est contra naturæ
usum mortalibus notum.) All these fanciful definitions may be seen carefully examined by Benedict
XIV. in the first part of the fourth book of his work
" De Servorum Dei Beatificatione et Beatorum Cano-
nizatione " : yet should we look in vain either there
or anywhere else for a definition of what is natural.[1]

Here a large field is open to the student of language. It is his office to trace the original meaning
of each word, to follow up its history, its changes of

[1] See an excellent article lately published in the *Edinburgh Review*, " On
the Supernatural," ascribed to one of our most eminent statesmen.

form and meaning in the schools of philosophy or in
the market-place and the senate. He ought to show
how frequently different ideas are comprehended
under one and the same term, and how frequently
the same idea is expressed by different terms. These
two tendencies in language, *Homonymy* and *Polyonymy*, which favored, as we saw, the abundant
growth of early mythology, are still asserting their
power in fostering the growth of philosophical systems. A history of such terms as *to know* and *to
believe*, *Finite* and *Infinite*, *Real* and *Necessary*,
would do more than anything else to clear the
philosophical atmosphere of our days.

The influence which language exercises over our
thoughts has been felt by many philosophers, most
of all by Locke. Some thought that influence inevitable, whether for good or evil; others supposed
that it could be checked by a proper definition of
words, or by the introduction of a new technical
language. A few quotations may be useful to show
how independent thinkers have always rebelled
against the galling despotism of language, and yet
how little it has been shaken. Thus Bacon says:—

" And lastly, let us consider the false appearances
that are imposed upon us by words, which are framed
and applied according to the conceit and capacities
of the vulgar sort; and although we think we govern
our words, and prescribe it well, — loqueudum ut
vulgus, sentiendum ut sapientes, — yet certain it is,
that words, as a Tartar's bow, do shoot back upon
the understanding of the wisest, and mightily en-
tangle and pervert the judgment. So as it is almost
necessary in all controversies and disputations to

imitate the wisdom of the mathematicians, in setting down in the very beginning the definitions of our words and terms, that others may know how we accept and understand them, and whether they concur with us or no. For it cometh to pass, for want of this, that we are sure to end there where we ought to have begun, which is in questions and differences about words."

Locke says:—

" I am apt to imagine that, were the imperfections of language, as the instruments of knowledge, more thoroughly weighed, a great many of the controversies that make such a noise in the world would of themselves cease; and the way to knowledge, and perhaps peace too, lie a great deal opener than it does."

Wilkins, when explaining the advantages of his philosophical language, remarks:—

" This design will likewise contribute much to the clearing of some of our modern differences in religion, by unmasking many wild errors, that shelter themselves under the disguise of affected phrases; which, being philosophically unfolded, and rendered according to the genuine and natural importance of words, will appear to be inconsistencies and contradictions. And several of those pretended mysterious profound notions, expressed in great swelling words, whereby some men set up for reputation, being this way examined, will appear to be either nonsense, or very flat and jejune. And though it should be of no other use but this, yet were it in these days well worth a man's pains and study; considering the common mischief that is done, and the many impostures and cheats that are put upon men, under the disguise of affected insignificant phrases."

Among modern philosophers, Brown dwells most strongly on the same subject:—

"How much the mere materialism of our language has itself operated in darkening our conceptions of the nature of the mind, and of its various phenomena, is a question which is obviously beyond our power to solve, since the solution of it would imply that the mind of the solver was itself free from the influence which he traced and described. But of this, at least, we may be sure, that it is almost impossible for us to estimate the influence too highly, for we must not think that its effect has been confined to the works of philosophers. It has acted much more powerfully, in the familiar discourse and silent reflections of multitudes, that have never had the vanity to rank themselves as philosophers, — thus incorporating itself, as it were, with the very essence of human thought.

"In that state of social life, in which languages had their origin, the inventor of a word probably thought of little more than the temporary facility which it might give to himself and his companions in communicating their mutual wants and concerting their mutual schemes of coöperation. He was not aware that with this faint and perishing sound, which a slight difference of breathing produced, he was creating that which was afterwards to constitute one of the most imperishable of things, and to form, in the minds of millions, during every future age, a part of the complex lesson of their intellectual existence, — giving rise to lasting systems of opinions, which, perhaps, but for the invention of this single word, never could have prevailed for a moment, and modifying sciences, the very elements of which had not then begun to exist. The inventor of the most barbarous term may thus have had an influence on mankind, more important than all which the most illustrious conqueror could effect by a long life of fatigue, and anxiety, and peril, and guilt.

"A few phrases of Aristotle achieved a much more extensive and lasting conquest; and are perhaps even at this moment exercising no small sway on the very minds which smile at them with scorn."[1]

Sir W. Hamilton, in his "Lectures on Metaphysics," ii. p. 312, remarks:—"To objects so different as the images of sense and the unpicturable notions of intelligence, different names ought to be given; and, accordingly, this has been done wherever a philosophical nomenclature of the slightest pretensions to perfection has been formed. In the German language, which is now the richest in metaphysical expressions of any living tongues, the two kinds of objects are carefully distinguished. In our language, on the contrary, the terms *idea, conception, notion,* are used almost as convertible for either; and the vagueness and confusion which is thus produced, even within the narrow sphere of speculation to which the want of the distinction also confines us, can be best appreciated by those who are conversant with the philosophy of the different countries."

I shall, in conclusion, give two or three instances to indicate the manner in which I think the Science of Language might be of advantage to the philosopher.

[1] Brown, *Works,* i. p. 341.

TO KNOW.

Knowledge, or to know, is used in modern languages in at least three different senses.

First, we may say, a child knows his mother, or a dog knows his master. This means no more than that they recognize one present sensuous impression as identical with a past sensuous impression. This kind of knowledge arises simply from the testimony of the senses, or sensuous memory, and it is shared in common by man and animal. The absence of this knowledge we call *forgetting* — a process more difficult to explain than that of remembering. Locke has treated of it in one of the most eloquent passages of his "Essay concerning Human Understanding" (ii. 10, 5) : — " The memory of some men, it is true, is very tenacious, even to a miracle; but yet there seems to be a constant decay of all our ideas, even of those which are struck deepest, and in minds the most retentive; so that if they be not sometimes renewed by repeated exercise of the senses, or reflection on those kind of objects which, at first, occasioned them, the print wears out, and, at last, there remains nothing to be seen. Thus the ideas, as well as children of our youth, often die before us; and our minds represent to us those tombs to which we are approaching; where though the brass and marble remain, yet the inscriptions are effaced by time, and the imagery moulders away. The pictures drawn in our minds are laid in fading colors; and if not sometimes refreshed, vanish and disappear. How much the constitution of our bodies, and the make of our animal spirits, are concerned in this, and whether the temper of the brain make this difference, that in some it retains the characters drawn on it like marble, in others like freestone, and in others little better than sand, I shall not here inquire: though it may seem probable that the constitution of the body does sometimes influence the memory; since we oftentimes find a disease quite strip the mind of all its ideas, and the flames of a fever, in a few days, calcine all those images to dust and confusion, which seemed to be as lasting as if graved in marble."

Secondly, we may say, I know this to be a triangle. Here we have a general conception, that of triangle, which is not supplied by the senses alone, but elaborated by reason, and we predicate this of something which we perceive at the time by our senses. We recognize a particular sensuous impression as falling under the general category of triangle. Here you perceive the difference. We not only recognize what we see, as the same thing we had seen before, but we must previously have gathered certain impressions into one cluster, and have given a name to this cluster, before we can apply that name whenever the same cluster presents itself again. This is knowledge denied to the animal, and peculiar to man as a reasoning being. All syllogistic knowledge falls under this head. The absence of this kind of knowledge is called *ignorance.*

Thirdly, we say that man knows there is a God. This knowledge is based neither on the evidence of the senses, nor on the evidence of reason. No man has ever seen God, no man has ever formed a general conception of God. Neither sense nor reason can supply a knowledge of God. What are called the proofs of the existence of God, whether *ontological*, *teleological*, or *kosmological*, are possible only after the idea of God has been realized within us. Here, then, we have a third kind of knowledge, which imparts to us what is neither furnished by the organs of sense, nor elaborated by our reason, and which nevertheless possesses evidence equal, nay, superior, to the evidence of sense and reason. The absence of this knowledge is sometimes called *spiritual darkness*.

Unless these three kinds of knowledge are carefully distinguished, the general question, How we know, must receive the most contradictory answers.

"To believe" likewise expresses in modern English several very different kinds of assent. When we speak of our belief in God, or in the immortality of the soul, or in the divine government of the world, or in the sonship of Christ, we want to express a certainty independent of sense-evidence and reason, yet more convincing than either, evidence not to be shaken either by the report of the senses or by the conclusion of logical arguments. It is the strongest assent which creatures made as we are can give.

But when we say that we believe that Our Lord suffered under Pontius Pilate, or lived during the reign of Augustus, we do not intend to say that we believe this with the same belief as the existence of God, or the immortality of the soul. The assent we give to these events is based on historical evidence, which is only a subdivision of sense-evidence, supplemented by the evidence of reason. If facts could be brought forward to show that our chronology was wrong, and that Augustus was emperor fifty years sooner or later, we should willingly give up our belief that Christ and Augustus were contemporaries. Belief in these cases means no more than that we have grounds, sensuous or argumentative, for admitting certain facts. I saw the revolution at Paris in February 1848: this is sense-evidence. I saw men who had seen the revolution at Paris in July 1830: this is sense-evidence, supplemented by argumentative evidence. I saw men who had seen men that had seen the revolution at Paris in July 1789: this is again sense-evidence, supplemented by argument. The same chain carries us back to the remotest times, but where its links are weak or broken, no power of belief can restore them. It is impossible to assent to any historical facts, as such, without the evidence of sense or reason. We may be as certain of historical facts as of our own existence, or we may be uncertain. We may either give or deny our assent, or we may give our assent provisionally, conditionally, doubtfully, carelessly. But we can as little believe a fact, using to believe in its first sense, as we can reason with our senses, or see with our reason. If, nevertheless, to believe is used to express various degrees of assent to historical facts, it is of great importance to bear in mind that the word thus used does not express that supreme certainty which is conveyed in our belief in God and Immortality (*credo in*), a certainty never attainable by " cumulative probabilities." [1]

To believe is used in a third sense when we say, " I believe it is going to rain." " I believe " here

[1] Dr. Newman, *Apologia pro vita sua*, p. 221.

means no more than "I guess." The same word, therefore, conveys the highest as well as the lowest degree of certainty that can be predicated of the various experiences of the human mind, and the confusion produced by its promiscuous employment has caused some of the most violent controversies in matters of religion and philosophy.

The Infinite, we have been told over and over again, is a negative idea, it excludes only, it does not include anything; nay, we are assured, in the most dogmatic tone, that a finite mind cannot conceive the Infinite. A step farther carries us into the very abyss of Metaphysics. There is no Infinite, we are told, for as there is a Finite, the Infinite has its limit in the Finite, it cannot be Infinite. Now all this is mere playing on words without thoughts. Why is infinite a negative idea? Because *infinite* is derived from *finite* by means of the negative particle *in*! But this is a mere accident, it is a fact in the history of language, and no more. The same idea may be expressed by the Perfect, the Eternal, the Self-existing, which are positive terms, or contain at least no negative element. That negative words may express positive ideas was known perfectly to Greek philosophers such as Chrysippus, and they would as little have thought of calling *immortal* a negative idea as they would have considered *blind* positive. The true idea of the Infinite is neither a negation nor a modification of any other idea.[1] The

[1] On the different kinds of Infinity, see Roger Bacon, *Opus Tertium*, cap. 51 (ed. Brewer, p. 194). Of the positive Infinite he says: "et dicitur infinitum non per privationem terminorum quantitatis, sed per negationem corruptionis et non esse." Oxford of the nineteenth century need not be ashamed, as far as metaphysics are concerned, of Oxford of the thirteenth.

Finite, on the contrary, is in reality the limitation or modification of the Infinite, nor is it possible, if we reason in good earnest, to conceive of the Finite in any other sense than as the shadow of the Infinite. Even Language will confess to this, if we cross-examine her properly. For whatever the etymology of *finis* may be, whether it be derived from *findere* or *figere*,[1] whether it means that which cuts or that which is fixed, it is clear that it stands for something which by means of the senses is inapprehensible. We admit in mathematical reasoning that points, lines, and planes can never be presented to the eye. It is the same in the world at large. No finger, no razor, has ever touched the end of anything: no eye has laid hold of the horizon which divides heaven and earth, or of the line which separates green from yellow, or unites yellow with white. No ear has ever caught the point where one key enters into another. Our senses never convey to us anything finite or definite, their impressions are always relative, measured by degrees, but by degrees of an infinite scale. It is maintained by some authorities[2] that the ear can take in 38,000 vibrations in one second. This is the highest note. The lowest number of vibrations producing musical sound is sixteen in one second. Between these two points lies the sphere of our musical perceptions, but there is in reality a *progressus ad infinitum* on either side. The same applies to color. Wherever we look, we never find a real end, a seizable *finis*. *Finis*, therefore, and the *Finite* express something which the senses by

---

[1] Bopp, *Vergleichende Grammatik*, III. p. 248. Schweizer, in Kuhn's *Zeitschrift*, III. p. 387.

[2] See p. 111.

themselves do not supply, something that in our sensuous experience is purely negative, a name of something which, in the language of the senses, has no existence at all. But it has existence in the language of reason. Reason, which has as much right as the senses, postulates the *Finite* in spite of the senses; and when we speak reasonably, the Finite, i. e. the measures of space and time, the shades of color, the keys of sound, &c., all these become to us the most positive elements of thought. Now it is our reason on which we pride ourselves most, we like to be called rational beings, and we are apt to look down on the two other organs of knowledge as of less importance. But there are, besides Reason, the two other organs of knowledge, Sense and Faith, all three together constituting our being, neither subordinate to the other, but all coequal. Faith, for I can find no better name in English, is that organ of knowledge by which we apprehend the Infinite, i. e. whatever transcends the ken of our senses and the grasp of our reason. The Infinite is hidden from the senses, it is denied by Reason, but it is perceived by Faith, and it is perceived, if once perceived, as underlying both the experience of the senses and the combinations of reason. What to our reason is merely negative, the In-finite, becomes to our faith positive, the Infinite, and if our eyes are once opened, we see even with our senses straight into that endless All by which we are surrounded on every side, and without which the fleeting phenomena of the senses and the wonderful cobwebs of our reason would be vanity, and nothing but vanity.

Not even the Natural Sciences, which generally

pride themselves on the exactness of their language, are free from words which, if rigorously analyzed, would turn out to be as unsubstantial as Nemesis and the Erinys. Naturalists used to speak of *Atoms*, things indivisible, which are mere conceptions of the mind, as if they were real, in the sensuous sense of the word, whereas it is impossible for the senses to take cognizance of anything that cannot be divided, or is incommensurable. Chemists speak of *imponderable* substances, which is as impossible a conception as that of atoms. Imponderable means what cannot be weighed. But to weigh is to compare the gravity of one body with that of another. Now, it is impossible that the weight of any body should be so small as to defy comparison with the weight of some other body; or, if we suppose a body without weight and gravity, we speak of a thing which cannot exist in the material world in which we live, a world governed without mercy by the law of gravity.

Every advance in physical science seems to be marked by the discarding of some of these mythological terms, yet new ones spring up as soon as the old ones are disposed of. Till very lately, *Caloric* was a term in constant use, and it was supposed to express some real matter, something that produced heat. That idea is now exploded, and heat is understood to be the result of *molecular and ethereal vibrations*. All matter is supposed to be immersed in a highly elastic medium, and that medium has received the name of *Ether*. No doubt this is a great advance, — yet what is Ether, of which everybody now speaks as of a substance, — heat, light, electricity, sound, being only so many different modes or modifications of it? *Ether* is a myth — a quality changed into a substance — an abstraction, useful, no doubt, for the purposes of physical speculation, but intended rather to mark the present horizon of our knowledge than to represent anything which we can grasp either with our senses or with our reason. As long as it is used in that sense, as an algebraic x, as an unknown quantity, it can do no harm — as little as to speak of the Dawn as Erinys, or of Heaven as Zeus. The mischief begins when language forgets itself, and makes us mistake the Word for the Thing, the Quality for the Substance, the *Nomen* for the *Numen*.

INDEX.

INDEX.

ACA

ACADEMY, French, its decree respecting the participles present, 27.
Accepter, origin of the French word, 287.
Acheter, origin of the French word, 287.
A-coming, *a-going*, origin of the vulgar or dialectic expression, 23–30.
Admiral, etymology of the word, 258 note.
Æacus, King of Ægina, story of his descent from Zeus, 462.
Æolus, the, of the later Greek historians, 417.
Æschylus, his remarks on the gods of Homer and Hesiod, 408.
—— his view of Zeus as the highest and true god, quoted, 400.
Estuary, origin of the word, 213.
African languages, 12.
—— Dr. Bleek's comparative grammar of South-African languages, 12.
—— with the exception of the Bushman tongue, only two families of language in Africa, 12.
—— the Hottentot language, 19, 20.
—— the vowels and consonants peculiar to each South-African dialect, and the changes to which each latter is liable in its passage from one dialect into another, 25.
—— simplicity of the syllables in the South-African languages, 202.
Africans, West, rich in gutturals, 197.
Agni, a Vedic god, meaning of the word, 430.
Aham, the Sanskrit word, 365.

ANI

Almata, Queen of Tahiti, meaning of her names, 41.
Air, vibrations of, 120.
Ale, origin of the word, 205.
Akiroraimlus on Barnacle-geese, 506.
Alfons, first King of Portugal, story of, at the battle of Ourique, 527 note.
Aloadæ, the Greek giants, origin of the name, 338.
Alphabet (ὁ ἀλφάβητος) the only word formed of mere letters, 87.
—— similar alphabetical origin claimed for *elementum*, 88.
—— the physiological alphabet, 104.
—— classification of letters, 107.
—— the alphabet of Nature, or physiological alphabet, 164–166.
—— the common alphabet proposed by Professor Lepsius, 168.
—— the alphabet of Sir W. Jones, 171.
—— Sanskrit alphabet as transcribed by Sir W. Jones, M. M., in the Missionary, and in the Church Missionary alphabets, 172.
—— rich alphabets, 173.
—— poor alphabets, 178.
—— presence and absence of certain letters in certain languages, 178–181.
—— imperfect articulation, 181.
—— number of words it is capable of producing by permutation, 88, 300.
Anaxagoras, his punishment for infidelity, 407.
—— his physical interpretation of Greek mythology, 413.
Anaximenes, his physical interpretation of Greek mythology, 412.
Animals, absence of reason in, 72.

ANI

Animus, origin of the word, 358.
Annamitic, the ancient language of Cochin-China, 37.
—— different intonations and meanings of the same word in, 38.
Annihilation, derivation of the word, 361.
Ante, table of a few of the descendants of the Latin word, 277.
Anthropology, the crown of all the natural sciences, 13.
—— Bunsen's remarks quoted, 15, 16.
Ἀπάτωρ, identity of, with the Sanskrit pitaka, 379 note.
Aphôna, or mutes, of the Greek grammarians, 151.
Aphonia, cause of, 130.
Aphrodite, the name, 390.
—— other names of her, 390, 391.
Appleyard, Rev. J. W., his work on the Kafir language, 45 note.
Arabic, number of consonants in, 180.
—— causes which produce the guttural sound of Hha (ح) and Ain (ع), 148.

Arcadians, story of their descent from Zeus, 182.
Archilochus, opinion of Heraclitus of his system of theology, 408.
Arcturus, the name, 383.
Arês and Mars, origin of the names, 341.
Argos, the all-seeing, 398.
Argynnis, a name of Aphrodite, identified with the Sanskrit arjuni, 391.
Arka, sun and hymn, the Sanskrit word, 377.
Arminius, the memory of, kept up by the Germans in the time of Tacitus, 477.
—— probable derivation of his name, 478.
-Aris and -alis, the Latin terminations, 181.
Aristotle on the elements of language, quoted, 81.
—— on words, 215.
—— his remarks on Greek mythology, quoted, 414.
—— on our first natural sense of the Godhead, 458.
—— his view of Zeus as the highest and true god, 452.

BAR

Articulation, imperfect, 131.
—— instances of utter inability to distinguish between two articulate sounds, 155.
Aryan, or Indo-European family of languages, the Polynesian claimed to be the true root and origin of the, 19.
—— other new theories, 19, 20.
—— changes caused by initial double consonants, 207.
—— treble roots of the Aryans before their separation, 212.
—— common Aryan words beginning with soft and hard checks, 222.
—— examination of a few words which form the common property of the Aryan nations, 222.
Aspirated check letters, 159.
—— mode of producing, 159.
—— probable absence of aspirates in the most ancient Aryan languages, 218.
—— aspirates in Sanskrit, Gothic, Greek, and German, 221.
Aśvins, the, of the Veda, 508, 512.
—— hymn to the Aśvins, 512, 513.
—— their later names, 514.
Athênê, the germ of the name, 521.
—— as the Dawn, 522.
Athenians, their prayer to Zeus for rain, 452.
Atlas, according to the later Greek historians, 417.
Atoms, the expression, 508.
Australian languages, number of consonants in the, 181.

BACON, Lord, on the influence of words on thought, quoted, 588.
—— Roger, his views on language and etymology, 293.
Banier, l'Abbé, his work on mythology explained from history, quoted, 418, 419.
Bank, bench, and banquet, the words, 285.
Bâ-ntu family of African languages, 202.
Bar and barrier, origin of, 285.
Barnacle, origin of the word, 552, 562.
—— the myth of the Barnacle goose, 554.

BAB

Baron, meaning of the word, 272.
Bask, formation of the participle present in, 28.
—— the Abbé Darrigol's "Dissertation" on the, quoted, 29–31 note.
Bates, Mr. H. W., his remarks on the languages of the Brazilian tribes on the banks of the Amazons, 50.
Be, to, derivation of the verb, 367.
Bears, etymology of, 215.
Bear, the Great, origin of the term, 379.
—— the Sanskrit name, 379.
—— its name of Septentriones, 382.
—— and of boves et temo, 382.
Beech, the word, in other Aryan dialects, 232, 238, 252.
Beef-eater, origin of the name, 552.
Behistún, rock inscriptions of, 12.
Believe, to, 364.
—— origin of the word, 360.
Bengali, mode of forming the so-called infinitive in, 27.
Blame, origin of the word, 280.
Bêlemer, origin of the French word, 281.
Bleek, Dr., his "Comparative Grammar of the South-African Languages," 19.
—— his treatment of the Phonology of those languages, 35.
Bless, origin of the word, 548.
Bochart, his work "De Theologia Gentili et Physiologia Christiana," &c., 120.
Bocca, Hector, his account of the Barnacle Goose, quoted, 551.
Bolza, Dr., on the analogy between speech and sounds in Italian, 111.
Bonaparte, Prince Louis-Lucien, his collection of English dialects, 10 note.
Book, origin of the word, 244.
Bootes, the name, 382.
Boves et temo, a name of the constellation of the Great Bear, 382.
Bow-wow theory, the, 98.
Brasenose, origin of the word, 551.
Brazilian tribes on the banks of the Amazons, quick corruption of language and segregation of dialects among the, 50.
Bréal, M. Michel, his note on Hermes, 493 note.

CHE

Breathings, the hard and soft, 129.
—— positions of the organs of speech in producing the various breathings, 141.
Brim, the word, in other Aryan dialects, 232.
Brisk, frisky, and fresh, common source of the words, 234.
Bronchial tubes, 122.
Brown, on language and reason, quoted, 70.
—— on the influence of words on thought, quoted, 580.
Buddhists, their Nirvâna, or Nothing, 304.
Bunsen, Baron, on the science of Man, quoted, 16.
Burnouf, Eugène, his discovery in the religion of the Aryans before their schism, 541.
Bushman tongue, 10.

CALDWELL, Rev. R., his remarks on the peculiarities of Drávidian syllabation, quoted, 205.
Chlorie, the term, 530.
Caribes of the Antilles, the different languages spoken by the men and women of the, 48.
Casirén on the languages, literature, and civilization of the northern Turanian nations, 328.
Celts, their dislike of pronouncing an initial s before a consonant, 210.
Cembilo, etymology of the word, 292.
Cenotaph, etymology of the word, 293.
Centaurs, the, according to later Greek historians, 417.
Cerberus, Hercules' explanation of the myth of, 410.
Charis, as a name of Aphrodite, 390.
—— objections to the explanation of the word Charis, 391.
—— original meaning of the word, 391.
—— Dr. Sonne's criticisms on the conjecture as to the identity of karit and charis, 469.
Checks, or mutes, class of letters so called, 151.
—— how produced, 151.
—— hard checks, 152.

CHE

Checks, soft, or media, 158.
— nasal checks, 158.
— aspirated checks, 159.
— common Aryan words which begin with soft and hard checks, 223.
Chinese language, the, grafted on the Annamitic, and formed thereby into Cochin-Chinese, 37.
— a characteristic feature of literary Chinese, 37.
— number of distinct sounds in Chinese, 38.
— instances of dialectic dispersion in, 31.
— polite phraseology of Chinese, 41.
— no outward distinction between a root and a word in Chinese, 84–90.
— the letter r not pronounced by the Chinese, 179.
— meaning of Tien, the Chinese name of God, 458.
— all syllables in Chinese either open or nasal, 202.
Chordæ vocales, office of the, 129.
— disease of the, producing aphonia, 130.
Christianity and the Greek religion, 438.
Chrysippus, his attempted accommodation between philosophy and mythology, 408.
Cicero, his remarks on the influence of our mother-tongue, quoted, 46.
Circonstance, origin of the French word, 281.
Clicks, the African, 168 note.
Cochin-China, language of, 37.
— the modern language Chinese grafted on the Annamitic, 37.
— words forming plurals in Cochin-Chinese, 40.
— formation of tenses, 40, 41.
Cohabitation, the word, 321, 325.
Consonants, no absolute necessity for them in language, 137.
— all consonants under the category of noises, 139.
— breathings, 141–147.
— trills, 149.
— checks, or mutes, 151.
— palatal consonants, 153.
— number of consonants in various languages, 154.

DAN

Consonants, liability to phonetic corruption of words beginning with more than one consonant, 201.
— entire variety of consonantal contact only in Sanskrit, 217.
— phonetic process which led to the consonantal systems of the Hindus, Greeks, Goths, and Germans, 222.
Contrition, origin of the word, 360.
Copper, period of the use of, only for weapons, armor, and tools, 245.
— names for copper in various Aryan dialects, 247.
— the copper mines of Cyprus, 249.
— first use of the word *cuprum*, 249.
Corn, the word, in other Aryan dialects, 234.
Count, meaning of the title, 272.
Country, origin of the word, 271.
Court, etymology of the word, 268.
Cousin, Victor, his views *versus* those of Locke on the names of immaterial objects, 365.
— his caution against using Locke's observation on immaterial objects as an argument in favor of a one-sided sensualistic philosophy, 368.
Crayfish, origin of the word, 285.
Creuzer, his "Symbolik und Mythologie der alten Völker," 415.
Cræsus, Gerartus, his interp[...] of Greek mythology, 421.
Cuneiform inscriptions, Grote[...] discoveries in, 11–12.
Cuprum, first use of the word, 249.
Cuvier on Nature, quoted, 334.
Cyclopes, the, according to later Greek historians, 417.
Cyrus, cuneiform inscriptions on the tomb of, 11.
Czermak, Prof., his experiments on the agency of the *velum pendulum* in producing the various vowel sounds, 130.
— his examination of the organs of speech of an Arab, 148.
— and of the causes producing the hard and soft check letters, 156.

Daiva, fate, etymological meaning of the Sanskrit word, 474.
Danebrog, or red cross of Denmark, origin of the, 477 note.

DAB

Dar, the Aryan root, in Sanskrit, Greek, Latin, Norse, and German, 219.
Dara, in the word, in other Aryan dialects, 211.
Darius, meaning of the name, 220.
Darrigol, l'Abbé, his "Dissertations" on the Bask language, quoted, 29–31 note.
Darwin on natural selection, 321.
—— his invention of a new name for a new genus of thought, 327.
Daram, name of the, in the Veda, 389.
—— myths of the, 481.
—— myth of Hermes, 481.
—— Saramâ, the Vedic Dawn, 481 et seq.
—— the riddle of the Dawn, 518.
—— legends told originally of the Dawn, 520.
—— the goddess Athênê, 522.
—— the goddess Minerva, 511.
—— Ortygia the Dawn, 523.
—— names of the Dawn and of her offspring, 527, 518.
Deaf and Dumb persons, no signs of reason given by, except by education, 79, 80.
Deer, the word in other Aryan dialects, 221.
Demeter, the name, 636.
—— as the Dawn, 536.
Democritus, his theories on language, 317, 320.
Dentals, their existence in every language, 178.
Dera, etymological meaning of, 473.
—— in Greek, Latin, and Lithuanian, 473.
Dhar, the root, its disappearance in most Aryan dialects, 210.
Dhâ, the Sanskrit root, in Greek, Latin, Gothic, and German, 225.
Dialectic regeneration, 38.
—— causes of the rapid shedding of words in nomadic dialects, 42.
Dialects of ancient Greece, researches in, 10.
—— English, 10.
—— Prince Louis-Lucien Bonaparte's collection of, 10 note.
—— Mr. Peacock's work, 10 note.
—— dialectic variation in language, 191.
Diez, value of his works in the study of Aryan speech, 181.

EAR

Dionysius Thrax —
—— quoted on the division of letters according to sound, 107 note.
Diovis, an old Italian name of Jupiter, 471.
Dis, original meaning of the Latin, 261.
DIV, a form of Dyu, 472.
—— how represented in Greek, 472.
—— and in Latin, 472.
—— derivatives of dis, 473.
Dodona, the dove of, Herodotus' explanation of, 118.
—— temple of, song of the Pleiades at, 458.
Doubt, origin of the word, 380.
Drâvidian languages, Caldwell's remarks on the peculiarities of the Drâvidian syllabation, quoted, 235.
Drub, etymological meaning of the Sanskrit word, 471.
Du, the Sanskrit root, in Greek, Gothic, German, and English, 215.
Du Cange, value of his dictionary, 255.
Duke, meaning of the word, 271.
Duo, changes to which it is liable, 264.
Dyaus, origin of the Sanskrit name, 712.
—— the bright heavenly deity of India and Greece, 444.
—— meaning of Dyu in Sanskrit, 445.
—— passages of the Veda in which Dyu is used as an appellative in the sense of sky, 443.
—— and in the sense of day, 447.
—— invocations in which Dyaus stands first, 443.
—— passages in which Dyu and Indra are mentioned together as father and son, 449.
—— other passages in which Indra is placed above Dyu, 449.
—— views of the synonymousness of dyu the sky and dyu the god, 445–447.
—— forms of the word dyu, 449.

Earl, origin of the word, 271.
Earth, the, as understood by the ancients, 552.

608   INDEX.

EGY

Egyptian language, ancient, no distinction in the, between noun, verb, adjective, and particle, 95.
Elements of language, 85.
—— Epicurus and Aristotle on the atoms, the concurrence of which was to form all nature, with letters, 86.
—— number of words which the alphabet is capable of producing by permutation, 86, 302.
—— Aristotle on element, 87.
—— origin of the Latin *elementum*, 88.
—— roots, 91.
Elementum, an alphabetical origin claimed for, 88.
—— etymological meaning of, 88.
—— *stoicheion* as rendered by *elementum*, 88.
Ellis, Mr. A. E., his essays on phonetics, 108.
Empedocles, his physical interpretation of Greek mythology, 411.
Esalia, a name of Aphrodite, 391.
Escania, etymology of the word, 293.
English language, Prince Louis-Lucien Bonaparte's collection of dialects of, 10 note.
—— origin of the termination *ing* in the, 24.
—— number of consonants in the, 181.
—— instances of phonetic changes which have taken place in the transition from Anglo-Saxon to modern English, 191.
—— Latin or French words naturalized in English, 191.
—— cause of the loss of the guttural *ch* in English, 198.
—— German elements entering into the English language, 232.
—— periods at which the Latin elements flowed into England, 283, 286.
—— double existence of the same word in English, 281.
Eas in Latin and *asi* in Sanskrit, identity of the two words, 301.
Entretenir, origin of the French word, 290.
Eos, as the god of the morning, 391.
Epicharmus, his physical interpretation of Greek mythology, 412.

FAR

Epicurus on the elements of language, quoted, 86.
—— his theories on languages, 321.
—— his remarks on the mythology of his countrymen, 408.
Epiglottis, the, 123.
Erinys, identified with the Vedic Saranyū, 503, 516.
Est, derivation of the Latin word, 309.
Estienne, Henri, his etymologies, 256 note.
Ether, the name, 592.
Ethiopians, the, as known to Homer and Herodotus, 17 note.
Être, origin of the French word, 365, 366.
Etymology, the principles of, 251.
—— Voltaire's definition of etymology, 251.
—— guessing etymology, 255.
—— etymological tests, 258.
—— change of meaning of words, 265.
—— origin of titles, 270-272.
—— different forms of the same word in different languages, 274.
—— different forms taken by the same word in the same language, 279.
—— the same form taken by different words in different languages, 298.
—— different words may take the same form in one and the same language, 301.
—— phonetic types, 331.
—— popular etymology, 518.
Euhemerus, his work, 'Ιερὰ Ἀναγραφή, 415.
—— his translation by Ennius, 416.
—— Euhemerism, 416.
Euphony, 192, 194.
Euripides, his opinions of the Homeric system of theology, 404.
Europa, meaning of the story of Zeus and, 463.
Ever, origin of the word, 265.
Experiment, the word, as showing that reason cannot become real without speech, 83.
Eye, origin of the word, 300.

F_{ARE}, to, the word, in other Aryan dialects, 227.

FAT

Fatum, the, of the ancients, 439.
F and th, change of, 182.
—— the sound of F, how produced, 182.
Feather, the word, in Aryan dialects, 237.
—— origin of the word, 297, 298.
Feridûn of the Persian epic poets, origin of, 541.
Feu, derivation of the French word, 495.
Few, the word in Aryan dialects, 237.
Filibuster, origin of the word, 285.
Finis, and the finite, meaning of, 597.
Finnish, number of consonants in, 161.
—— the name Jumala in the, 456.
—— peculiarities of Finnish, 328.
Fir, the word for, in various Aryan dialects, 238, 250.
Fire-arms and hawks, why the same terms applied to both, 245.
French language, decree of the French Academy respecting participles present, 27.
—— the French dictionary full of Teutonic words, 280.
—— and of Latin words, 287.
—— laws which govern the transition of Latin words into French, 283.
Fresh, origin of the word, 234.
Friend, the word, in other Aryan dialects, 237.
Frisky, origin of the word, 284.

GAR, the Aryan root, in Sanskrit, Greek, Gothic, and German, 221.
Garden, the word, in the various Aryan dialects, 230.
Garshasp, of the Persian epic poets, origin of, 541.
Gehrman, origin of the word, 255.
—— Roger Bacon's remarks on Brito's etymology of the word, 293.
Givre, original form of the French word, 255.
Gerard, John, his account of the Barnacle-goose, quoted, 558.
German language, great number of German words in the French dictionary, 280.
—— Romanized German, 285.

GRE

Germans, their worship of the unknown God, 455.
—— the god Tyr worshipped as the chief deity by the, 475.
—— their gods Tuisco and his son Mannus, 476, 477.
—— their shield-songs, 477.
—— their memory of Arminius, 477.
—— their night revellings, 477.
—— the names of the three great tribes, the Ingævones, Iscævones, and Herminones, 478.
—— chief interest attached to the German fables about Tuisco, Mannus, and his sons, 478.
Geryon of Erytheia, myth of, as explained by Hecatæus, 414.
GHAR, the Aryan root, in Sanskrit, Greek, Gothic, and German, 223.
—— original sense in which it was used, 387.
Ghost, meaning of the word, 383.
Giraldus Cambrensis on Barnacle-geese, quoted, 554.
Gladstone, his view of Greek mythology, 421.
Glottis, the, 122.
—— the interior and exterior glottis, 125.
God, words derived from the Sanskrit word, 445.
God, derivation of the word, 202.
—— the name of, in various languages, 455 et seq.
Gold, and not gould, 230.
Goose, the word, in various Aryan dialects, 231.
—— Barnacle goose. See Barnacle.
Gorera, etymology of the word, 210.
Greek grammarians, their division of letters according to sound, 107.
—— number of consonants in, 161.
—— names for the sea, 133.
—— the sister of Sanskrit and Latin, 436.
—— theories of the ancient Greeks on language, 315 et seq.
—— mythology of the. See Mythology.
—— problem of their excellence in the principal arts and sciences, 404.
Greeks, religion of the, independent of mythology, 433.

GRE

Greeks, Christianity and the Greek religion, 446.
—— what the Greeks of the time of Homer meant by Zeus, 451.
Grimm's law, 213 et seq.
—— general table of Grimm's law, 232.
Grotefend, his decipherment of the cuneiform inscriptions, 11, 12.
Guado, origin of the Italian word, 283.
Guastare, origin of the word, 283.
Guêpe, origin of the word, 283.
Guêre, origin of the word, 283.
Guichard, his remarks on etymological tests, quoted, 258.
Guile and wile, origin of the words, 283.
Guise and wise, origin of the words, 283.
Guttural sounds of the Arabs, as examined by Prof. Czermak, 148.
—— absence of most gutturals in poor alphabets, 177.
—— richness of the West-African dialects in gutturals, 197.
—— cause of the loss of the guttural ch in English, 198.

H, the sound of, how produced by the organs of speech, 141.
Hale, Mr., his table of the regular changes which words common to all the Polynesian languages undergo, 35.
—— his remarks on the causes of rapid changes in the Tahitian language, quoted, 44.
Hamilton, Sir W., his remarks on the influence of words on thought, quoted, 581.
Haritas, or horses of the sun of the Vedic poets, 388, 389.
Harmonics, causes of, 117.
—— discovery of the fact that there is only one vibration without harmonics, 119.
Hart, the word, in various Aryan languages, 236.
Hawaian idiom, 10.
—— specimen of "painting in sound" from Hawaian, 22.
—— consonantal articulation formerly existing in the, 132.

HOM

Hawaian idiom, probable original form of Hawaii, 132.
Hawaians, their imperfect articulation, 131.
—— almost impossible for a Hawaian to pronounce two consonants together, 201.
—— no names in Hawaian for some of the colors, 327.
"Hawk from a handsaw, to know a," 552.
Hear, the word, in the other Teutonic dialects, 276.
Heart, the word, in other Aryan languages, 230.
Hebrew, number of consonants in, 180.
Hecatæus, his idea of Greek mythology, 418.
Helena, and the siege of Troy, story of, 489, 490.
Helmholtz, Prof., 116.
—— his discovery of the absence or presence of certain harmonics, 117.
—— and of the fact that there is only one vibration without harmonics, 119.
—— his description of the production of the trilled letters r and l, 150.
Hemiphona, or semi-vowels, of the Greek grammarians, 156.
Heraclitus, his theories on language, 316-318.
—— his opinion of the Homeric system of theology, 406.
—— his physical interpretation of Greek mythology, 412.
Hermes, myth of, 481.
—— probably identical with the Vedic god Sâramêya, 492, 495.
—— note of M. Michel Bréal on Hermes, 493 note.
Herminones, the German tribe, probable origin of the name, 478.
Herodotus, his mythological interpretations, 418.
Hindu mythology compared with that of the Greeks, 447.
Hindustani, number of consonants in, 180.
Historically, the word, traced to its roots, 313.
Homer, his system of theology, 405.
—— opinion of Heraclitus of this system, 406.

HOM

Homer, insight afforded by him into the inner religious life of his age, 434, 436.
Homonymy and polynymy, 373, 374.
—— the homonymous or mythic period of language, 374. See Mythic period.
Horse, the Aryan names for, 74.
Hottentot language, a branch of the North-African class, 19.
—— one of the two great families of African languages, 19.
Huet, his "Demonstratio Evangelica," 421.
—— his endeavors to discover in Greek mythology a dimmed image of the history of the Jews, 421.
Hyperboreans, the, 17.
—— meaning of their name, 17 note.

I, the word, 366.
—— Jean Paul's remarks on "*I*," quoted, 366 note.
"*I am*," the words, in other Aryan dialects, 212.
Imagine, origin of the word, 358.
Imponderable substances, the expression, 502.
Imitative theory, the, 98.
India, Prakrit the root of the modern vernaculars of, 18.
Indo-European languages. See Aryan.
Indra, the Vedic Jupiter, 448.
—— passages in which Dyu and Indra are mentioned together as father and son, 448.
—— other passages in which Indra is placed above Dyu, 449.
—— etymology of the name Indra, 449 note.
IndrAgnî, the Vedic gods, 514.
Infants, difference between them and the lower animals, 72.
Infinite, the, 598.
Ing, the termination, in the English language, 23.
—— in forming patronymics in Anglo-Saxon, 24.
—— in forming more general attributive words, 24.
Ingævones, the German tribe, origin of the name, 178.
Interjectional theory, the, 98.

K

'Ιος, derivation of the Greek word, 309.
Irmin, the old Saxon god, 179.
Irmino, third son of the god Mannus, 178.
Iron, discovery of, marking a period in the history of the world, 240.
—— probably not known previously to the separation of the Aryan nations, 240.
Iron, origin of the word, 249, 250.
Iscævones, the German tribe, origin of the name, 178.
Island, origin of the word, 205.
Italian language, origin of its use instead of Latin in literary compositions, 46.
—— analogy between speech and sounds in the, 101.
—— laws which govern the transition of Latin words into Italian, 288.
"*I was*," origin of the words, 367.

JAN, Janus, etymological structure of the word, 471.
January, origin of the name of the month, 471.
Je, origin of the French word, 366.
—— the same as the Sanskrit aham, 366.
Jemshîd, of the Persian epic poets, origin of, 541.
Jerusalem artichokes, origin of the names, 386.
Jones, Sir William, his Sanskrit alphabet, 179.
—— his comparison between the Greek and Hindu deities, 427.
Juonela, the Finnish Thunderer, 186.
Jûnô, the name corresponding to the Greek Ζηνών, 472.
Junonius, the divinity Janus called, 472.
Jupiter, the supreme Aryan god, 422.
—— correspondence of the name with the Sanskrit Dyu, 444.

K, sound of, how produced, 151.
—— confusion of *k* and *t* in some languages, 180-182.

612 INDEX.

KAF

Kafir language, one of the great families of African languages, 20.
—— words peculiar to Kafir women, and their effect in changing the meaning of words in the Kafir language, 45.
—— other causes of changes in words among some Kafir tribes, 48.
—— number of consonants in Kafir, 180.
—— difference between Kafir and Sechuana, 187.
—— list of Kafir metaphorical words, 358.
Kallisto, the beloved of Zeus, legend of, 395.
—— the national deity of the Arcadians, 462.
—— story of Zeus and Kallisto, 463.
Kaméhaméha, edicts of, 10.
KAR, the Aryan root, in Sanskrit, Greek, Gothic, and German, 225.
Karberos, and Orthros, represent the two dogs of Yama, 490.
Kis, the word, in other Aryan dialects, 224.
King, the word, in various Aryan dialects, 272.
—— original meaning of the word, 272.
Kleanthes, his hymn to Zeus, quoted, 460 note.
Knight, meaning of the word, 272.
Knot, the word, in Old Norse and Latin, 234.
Know, to, 522.
Kronos, in the later Greek mythology, 450.
Kuhn, Prof., his explanation of the myth of Saramâ, quoted, 503.
—— his explanation of the myth of Saranyû, 542.

L, the sound of, how produced, 150.
—— confusion between *l* and *r* in some languages, 184.
—— occasional changes of *l* into *r*, 184.
Labials, deficiency of, in the languages of the Six Nations of Indians, 177.
Lady, etymology of the word, 271.
Language, science of, 8.
—— field open to the student of, 10–13.

LAN

Language, charm peculiar to the science of, 14.
—— controversies, 14.
—— the science of language a physical science, 15.
—— theories making the Polynesian the primitive language of mankind, 19.
—— Leibniz on the tests and rules to be observed in the study of languages, 21.
—— small facts and great principles, 22, 23.
—— an illustration of the principles on which the science of language rests, 23–30.
—— generalization and discrimination in treating languages, 31.
—— different languages to be treated differently, 34.
—— phonetic laws, 35.
—— dialectic regeneration, 38.
—— influence of women on language, 45, 46, 48.
—— value of Sanskrit in the study of language, 51.
—— importance which the Science of Language has for the Science of Mind, 51.
—— account of what has been achieved in framing a philosophical and universal language, 64.
—— reason and speech, 72.
—— formation of names, 74.
—— no speech without reason, no reason without speech, 78.
—— Locke on the possibility of forming mental conceptions and propositions without words, 80.
—— an instance, showing that reason cannot become real without speech, 84.
—— the elements of language, 85.
—— roots, 81.
—— the bow-wow theory, or the *Isonic*, 98.
—— analogy between the faculty of speech and the sounds we utter in singing, crying, laughing, &c., 93.
—— the physiological alphabet, 95.
—— phonetics, 109.
—— description of the organs of speech, 120–138.

INDEX.   613

LAN

Language, how the instrument of the human voice is played upon, 126.
— positions of the organs of speech in sounding the vowels, 130 *et seq.*
— consonants, 137.
— examination of eight modifications of spiritus asper and spiritus lenis, 141–147.
— trills, 149.
— checks or mutes, 151.
— aspirated checks, 159.
— phonetic change, 174, 187.
— presence and absence of certain letters in certain languages, 174–180.
— imperfect articulation, 181.
— what makes language change? 186.
— changes caused by laziness or muscular relaxation, 190.
— dialectic variation, 195.
— phonetic peculiarities, 197.
— double consonants, 211.
— twofold causes of phonetic change, 211.
— Grimm's phonetic law, 213 *et seq.*
— the principles of etymology, 234 *et seq.*
— etymological tests, 238.
— usefulness of modern languages in the study of language, 260.
— importance of the Romance dialects, in the study of the growth of language, 262.
— change of meaning of words, 265.
— origin of various titles, 270–272.
— different forms of the same word in different languages, 274.
— different forms taken by the same word in the same language, 279.
— the same form taken by different words in different languages, 298.
— different words may take the same form in one and the same language, 301.
— on the powers of roots, 313.
— Greek theories on language, 315.
— natural selection, 321.
— languages which do not possess numerals beyond four, 327.
— all names are general terms, 328.

LOC

Language, clusters of roots, 330.
— phonetic types, or "specific centres" of language, 331.
— metaphor, 351.
— Locke, on the importance which language, as such, claims in the operations of the understanding, 353–356.
— the Historical School of the 19th century, 355.
— metaphorical expressions, 359 *et seq.*
— importance of comparative philology to the study of Greek mythology, 421.
— influence which language exercises over our thoughts, 588.
— instances in which the science of language might be of advantage to the philosopher, 591.
Laryngoscope, the, 120.
Larynx, the, 122.
— its agency in producing sound, 126.
Latin, number of consonants in, 181.
— no dental aspirate like the *th* of the Greeks, or *dh* of the Hindus, in Latin, 198.
— distinction between the terminations -*aris* and -*alis*, 184.
— gradual spread of Latin over nearly all the nations of the civilized world, 258.
— history of some early Roman words, 267.
— the sister of Sanskrit and Greek, 425.
Leibniz, on the mode of studying language, 21.
— his remarks on language as the best mirror of the human mind, 51.
— his philosophical and universal language, 54.
Lepsius, Prof., his universal alphabet, 167.
Lewis, Sir G. C., his attacks on the decipherers of ancient inscriptions, 11 *note.*
Libya, the dove of, Herodotus' explanation of, 416.
Ling, the common derivative, in English, 25.
Locke, John, his supposition of the possibility of forming mental con-

LOC

ceptions and propositions without words, 80.

Locke, John, on the influence of words on thought, quoted, 351 et seq.
— on the fact that all words expressive of immaterial conceptions are derived by metaphor from words expressive of sensible ideas, quoted, 356.
— Cousin versus Locke on the names of immaterial objects, 365.
— on the influence of words on thought, quoted, 589.

Lógos, absence of, in animals, 71.
Lord, origin of the word, 271.
Lucina and *luna*, common origin of, 294.
Lyell, Sir C., on the peat deposits in Denmark, 239.

M, sound of, how produced, 158.
— Prof. Helmholtz's remarks on m, 159 note.
Male-apes, origin of the expression, 291.
Malt or *melt*, origin of the word, 247.
Manu, fable of, 629.
— his name of Sávarni, 529.
MAR, the Aryan root, history of its adventures through the world, 332.
Marcus, origin of the Latin word, 344.
Mare, the sea, origin of the word, 337.
Mars, origin of the name, 340.
— connection between Sanskrit *Marut* and Latin *Mars*, 340 note.
Marut, a Vedic god, meaning of the word, 131.
Mas, Don Sinibaldo de, his Ideography, 37.
Media, positions of the organs of speech in producing the, 141.
Melanesia, Bishop of, on the rapid shedding of words in the Polynesian dialects, 42.
Melanesian languages, number of consonants in the, 181.
Mellis, origin of the word, 346.
Mémé, origin of the word, 275.
Menage, value of his dictionary, 255.
Metaphor, 351.

MOR

Metaphor, Locke's statement of the fact that all words expressive of immaterial conceptions are obtained by metaphor, quoted, 356.
— cases in point, 358.
— Kaffr metaphors, 348.
— English and other metaphors, 359 et seq.
— Victor Cousin's views versus those of Locke, 365.
— a powerful engine in the construction of human speech, 368.
— marking a peculiarity of a whole period in the history of speech, 370.
— original general and comprehensive material meaning of most roots, 370.
— radical and poetical metaphor, 371, 372, 375.
— homonymous and polyonymous metaphors, 373, 374.
— the mythic and mythological periods, 375.
— distinction between radical and poetical metaphor, 392.

Metrodorus, his physical interpretation of Greek mythology, 413.
Mexicans, their name for metal, 248.
Mild, origin of the word, 347.
Minerva, the name of the goddess, 524.
Minister, etymology of the word, 270.
Minos, origin of the story of his descent from Zeus and Europa, 463.
Minster, origin of the word, 288.
Minstrel, etymology of the word, 270.
Miracles, definition of, 588.
Mohawks, have no labials, 177.
Moiras, or fates, originally only one deity, 331 note.
Moliōnes, the Greek origin of the name, 338–340.
Mollis, origin of the word, 346.
Monastery, origin of the word, 288.
Mongolian, number of consonants in, 181.
— the name of the Deity in, 456.
Morny, Sir Robert, his account of the Barnacle goose, quoted, 558.
"Morning-hour has gold in her mouth," 398.

INDEX. 615

MOT

Mother, the word, in the various Aryan dialects, 213.
Mother-tongue, Cicero on the influence of our, quoted, 40.
Munster, Sebastian, on the Barnacle goose, quoted, 660.
Murder, origin of the word, 338.
Mutes, or checks, 151.
— mute tenues, 152.
— mute mediæ, 155.
Mystery Plays, etymology of the term, 771.
Mythology of the Greeks, 402.
— absurdities and crudities of their religion, 404.
— protests of their own philosophers, 405.
— attempted accommodation between mythology and philosophy, 408.
— protests of the Greek poets, 408.
— origin of Greek mythology, 411.
— ethical interpretation of their origin, 411.
— physical interpretation, 412.
— allegorical interpretation, 412.
— Aristotle's remarks on Greek mythology, quoted, 414.
— attempts at finding in mythology the remnants of ancient philosophy, 414.
— historical interpretations, 415.
— the system of mythological interpretation called Euhemerism, 416.
— the Abbé Banier's "Mythology and Fables of Antiquity, explained from History," quoted, 418, 419.
— Interpreters who looked to Greek mythology for traces of sacred personages: Bochart, 420.
— importance of comparative philology to the study of the mythology of the Greeks, 422.
— a comparison of Greek and Hindu gods distasteful to classical scholars, why? 427.
— Jupiter, the supreme Aryan god, 432.
— encroachment of mythology on ancient religion, 433.
— ancient religion as independent of ancient mythology, 411.
— quotations from Homer and Hesiod, 434, 435.

NEV

Mythology of the Greeks, Christianity and the Greek religion, 438.
— Zeus, Dyaus, Jupiter, or Tiw, 444.
— what the Greeks of the time of Homer meant by Zeus, 453, 457.
— myths of the Dawn, 481.
Mythology, modern, 644.
— abuse of words, 644.
— hieroglyphic mythology of tavern-signs, 649.
— the myth of the Barnacle goose, 655.
— Whittington and his cat, 671.
— St. Christopher, 671.
— St. Ursula and the 11,000 virgins, 674.
— St. Bonaventura and his speaking crucifix, 677.
— saints with their heads in their hands, 676.
— a dove the symbol of the Holy Ghost, 676.
— sin in the form of a dragon or serpent, 677.
— the truth of myths, 678.
— Theogenis, 678.

N and ng, sounds of, how produced, 158.
— Prof. Helmholtz's remarks on n, 159 note.
NAH, the Sanskrit root, its form in Greek, German, and Latin, 310.
Name, derivation of the word, 121.
Names, formation of, 74.
— all names are general terms, 328.
Nas, the Sanskrit root, its form in Greek, 311.
Nature, the word, as popularly used, 683.
— Cuvier on Nature, quoted, 684.
Néant, derivation of the French words, 262.
Nes, the Greek word, its derivation from three roots in Sanskrit, 311.
Ne-pas, derivation of the French words, 262.
Ne point, derivation of the French words, 262.
Never, origin of the word, 261.
Newman, Prof. F. W., his essay "On the Umbrian Language," 11 note.

NIH

Nihil, origin of the Latin word, 362.
—— Bopp's etymology of *nihil*, 362 note.
Nirrdas, or Nothing, of the Buddhists, 364.
Noises and sounds, 99.
—— all consonants under the category of noises, 112.
Nomadic dialects, causes of the rapid shedding of words in, 42.
Nomadic languages as compared with State languages, 49.
Normans, their Germanized Latin language, 231.
Nothing, how expressed in language, 362.
—— under the name of *Nirrdas*, worshipped by the Buddhists, 364.
Numerals, table of the, in the various Polynesian dialects, 34.
—— alterations in the names of, since the time of Cooks, 30.
—— languages which do not possess any numerals beyond our, 327.

OAK, the word for, in various Aryan dialects, 278, 250.
Omnipresence and omniscience of the Deity, as expressed by Hesiod, 445.
Onomatopœia, 98.
—— the onomatopœia of the Greeks, 311.
Onomatopœia, secrets of, 25.
Orthros, the dark spirit fought by the sun in the morning, 498.
Ortygia, the Dawn, 525.

P, sound of, how produced, 151.
Paten and *pagan*, common origin of, 294.
Prince, origin of the word, 267.
Palestine map, origin of, 336.
Paley, Mr. F. A., his views of the mythology of the Greeks, quoted, 421.
Paragraph, origin of the word, 266.
Parts of Homer identical with the Vedic Papis, 491.

PHO

Parjanya, a Vedic god, meaning of the name, 431.
Participles present in the English language, 23-26.
—— in the French language, 27.
—— in Bengali, 27.
—— in the Dark, 30.
Patronymics, -*ing* used in forming Anglo-Saxon, 24.
Paul, Jean, his remarks on "*I*," quoted, 366 note.
Peacock, Mr., his work on the dialects of the northern counties of England, 10 note.
Pelasgians, the, had no names for any of their gods, 454.
Pen, origin of the word, 297.
Penser, origin of the French word, 360.
Perception and sensation, distinction between, 118.
Perion, his etymologies, 217.
Perkunas, the Lithuanian god of the thunder-storm, 456.
Persepolis, rock inscriptions of, 12.
Persia, rock inscriptions of, 11.
—— discoveries of Grotefend, Rawlinson, &c., 11.
—— Sir G. Lewis's attacks on their decipherment, 11 note.
Persian language, number of consonants in the, 180.
Pharynx, agency of the posterior wall of the, in producing sound, 136.
Philolaos, his theory of the origin of virtue, 320.
Phonautograph, 116.
Phonetic laws of language, 21.
Phonetics, Sanskrit works on, 108.
—— various other works on, 108 note.
—— phonetic reform, 110.
—— Mr. Pitman's labors, 111.
—— noises and sounds, 112.
—— strength or loudness and height or pitch, 113.
—— number of vibrations of a chord requisite to produce the highest and lowest tones, 114.
—— waves of sound produced by the siren, 115, 116.
—— harmonics, 117.
—— distinction between sensation and perception, 118.
—— the organs of speech, and how they are played upon, 120 et seq.

PHO

Phonetics, vibrations of air, 126.
— causes producing vowels, 127 et seq.
— consonants, 137.
— trills, 149.
— checks, or mutes, 151.
— the African clicks, 188 note.
— phonetic change, 174.
— causes of phonetic change, 190.
— muscular relaxation, 191, 192.
— dialectic variation, 193.
— phonetic peculiarities, 197.
— causes of phonetic corruption, 199, 201.
— twofold causes of phonetic change, 211.
— Grimm's phonetic law, 213 et seq.
— phonetic process which led the Hindus, Greeks, Goths, and Germans to a settlement of their respective consonantal systems, 221.
Pindar, his protests against the system of theology of Homer and Hesiod, 402.
— on Zeus as the highest and true God, 402.
Pitman, Mr., his labors in phonetic reform, 111.
Plato, his division of the letters of the alphabet, 107.
— his remarks on words, 315.
— his statement regarding Greek myths, 403.
Polynesian language, asserted to be the true root and origin of the Indo-European languages, 12.
— theories making the Polynesian the primitive language of mankind, 12.
— comparison of the numerals in the various Polynesian dialects, 24.
— Hale's table of the regular changes which words common to all the Polynesian languages undergo, 35.
— alterations in the numerals since the time of Cooke, 38.
— the Bishop of Melanesia on the rapid shedding of words in the Polynesian dialects, 42.
— a new cause of change in these languages, 42.

REL

Polynesian language, Polynesian mode of expressing thinking, 85.
— verbs used, without change of form, as nouns or adjectives, 84.
— number of consonants in the Polynesian languages, 181.
— every syllable in Polynesian must terminate in a vowel, 201.
Polyonymy and homonymy, 378, 374.
— the polyonymous or mythological period of language, 374.
Pomare, Queen of Tahiti, meaning of her name, 43.
Pontia, a name of Aphrodite, 391.
Prakrit, origin of, in literary compositions, 48.
— the root of the modern vernaculars of India, 47.
Prátiśākhyas, or Sanskrit works on phonetics, 108.
Protagoras, his remarks on the everpresent watchfulness of the gods, 133.
— his punishment for infidelity, 407.
Pythagoras, his knowledge of the cause of tone in its simplest form, 113, 115.
— his statements on language, 310.
Python, Hecataeus' explanation of the myth of the serpent, 418.

QUEEN, origin of the word, 272.
Quirinus, the divinity Janus called, 472.

R, the sound of, how produced, 142.
— confusion in some languages between r and l, 181.
— occasional changes of l into r in every language, 181.
Rançon, origin of the French word, 287.
Reason and speech, in animals and infants, 72.
— no speech without reason, and no reason without speech, 78.
Religion of the Greeks, as independent of their mythology, 414.

REL

Religion of the Greeks, Christianity and the Greek religion, 418.
—— the history of, an account of the various attempts at expressing the Inexpressible, 444.
—— our first natural sense of the Godhead, or faith, 455.
—— Tacitus, Aristotle, and Procopius, on ancient religion, 455, 456.
Rien, origin of the French word, 362.
"Rig-Veda," its importance to the study of Greek mythology, 428, 429.
—— the translation now in progress, 429.
—— the translations of M. Langlois and the late Professor Wilson, 429.
—— many of the names of the gods of the Veda still intelligible, 430.
Riley, Mr. H. T., his explanation of the story of Whittington and his cat, 571.
Ring, etymology of the word, 285.
Romance dialects, their importance in the study of the growth of language, 202.
—— note respecting the origin of the, 202 note.
Roots of language, 91.
—— Sanskrit roots, 92.
—— no distinctions in some languages between roots and words, 94.
—— roots cease to be roots when forming parts of sentences, 98.
—— the bow-wow theory, 98.
—— the interjectional theory, 103.
—— on the powers of roots, 211.
—— definite forms and meanings of the Aryan, 214.
—— the onomatopœia of the Greeks, 215.
—— clusters of roots, 220.
—— phonetic types, 221.
—— history of the adventures of the root MAR through the world, 232.
—— number of roots in Sanskrit, 241.
—— original general and comprehensive material meaning of most roots, 270.
—— radical metaphor, 278.

SAR

Rosny, Léon de, on the Cochin-Chinese language, quoted, 37.
Roth, Prof., his explanation of the myth of Sarapyû, 503, 519.

S and S, the sounds of, how produced, 145.
Sacrement, origin of the French word, 287.
Sanskrit, value and indispensability of, in the study of language, 51.
—— Sanskrit roots, 92.
—— palatal letters in Sanskrit, 153.
—— aspirates in, 160.
—— Sanskrit alphabet, as transcribed by Sir W. Jones, M.M., in the Missionary and in the Church Missionary alphabets, 172.
—— number of consonants in Sanskrit, 180.
—— rich variety of consonantal contact in Sanskrit only entire, 217.
—— number of roots to which it has been reduced by Hindu grammarians, 241.
—— Greek and Latin the sisters of Sanskrit, 427.
—— comparison between Greek and Hindu deities, 427.
—— importance of the "Rig-Veda" in the study of mythology, 428, 429.
—— the translation of the "Rig-Veda" now in progress, 429.
—— the translations of M. Langlois and the late Professor Wilson, 429.
—— meaning of the Sanskrit word Dyu, Dyaus, 445.
—— forms of the word dyu, 470.
—— hymn from the "Rig-Veda," on Saramâ, quoted, 481.
—— harvest-hymn, quoted, 492.
—— hymn on the Asvins, quoted, 512, 513.
—— hymn on the Asvins and Indragni, quoted, 518.
Saramâ, the Dawn, the Vedic goddess, 481.
—— etymology of the word, 482.
—— the character of Saramâ from the "Rig-Veda," 482.

INDEX. 619

SAR

Saramâ, her dialogue with the Panis, quoted, 481.
— Sâyaṇa's story of Saramâ, 485.
— contained in the Anukramaṇikâ, 483.
— epithets applied to her, 487.
— Helena of Troy and Saramâ identical, 490.
— the Dawn conceived by the Vedic poet as a dog, 497.
— the riddle of the Dawn, 513.
— legends told originally of the Dawn, 520.
— solar theory of the myth, 537.
— the meteorological theory, 538.
Sâramêya, the Vedic Dawn-son, 491.
— probably identical with Hermes, 491.
Saraṇyû, the Dawn, 402.
— identified by Prof. Kuhn with the Greek Erinys, 583.
Savitar, the golden-handed, a Vedic name for the sun, 380.
— meaning of the name, 411.
Schelling, on reason and speech, quoted, 81.
Schwartz, Prof., his view of the myth of the Dawn, 538.
Scylla, according to the later Greek historians, 417.
Sea, Greek names for the, 335.
Sechuana language, difference between it and Kafir, 187.
Sensation and perception, distinction between, 118.
Septentriones, a name of the Great Bear, meaning of the name, 392.
— probable meaning of triones, 382.
Serment, origin of the French word, 287.
Shield-songs of the ancient Germans, 477.
Slip and skiff, common origin of, 294.
Shunt, to, 228.
Sir, origin of the word, 271.
Sloop and shallop, common origin of the words, 294.
SNU, the Sanskrit word, its form in Greek, Latin, Gothic, and German, 210.
Socrates, his martyrdom, 107.
Sonne, Dr., his criticisms on the conjecture as to the identity of the Sanskrit word haris and the Greek charis, 400.

SYN

Sooth, origin of the word, 361.
Sophocles, his view of Zeus as the highest and true God, 461.
Sorrow, origin of the word, 548.
Sounds; analogy between speech and various sounds we utter in singing, crying, &c., 62.
— specimen of "painting in sound" from the Hawaian language, 93.
— and from the Italian, 101.
— division of the Greek grammarians of letters according to their sounds, 197.
— see Phonetics.
Speech, description of the organs of, 130 et seq.
Spirits, meaning of the word, 363.
Spiritus, origin of the word, 137.
Spiritus asper and lenis, mode of producing them, 369.
— examination of eight modifications of spiritus asper and spiritus lenis, 141–147.
Star, the word, in the various Aryan dialects, 222.
— meaning of the word, 381.
St. Augustine, on paganism, quoted, 429 note.
St. Bonaventura, and his speaking crucifix, origin of the story of, 573.
St. Christopher, legends of, 571.
St. Paul, on the religion of the Greeks, 441.
St. Ursula and the 11,000 virgins, story of, 574.
Stoicheion, meaning of the Greek word, 88.
— etymology of the word as given by Dionysius Thrax, 90.
Sub, various senses of the Latin word, 290.
Subtile, origin of the word, 296.
Sun, the golden-handed, one of the names of the, 347.
— the German Tyr and the Indian Savitar compared, 388.
Sunâsîrau, the Vedic deity, 498.
— in a harvest-hymn in the "Rig-Veda," 498.
Sundûnib, origin of the word, 548.
Supernatural, the word, as popularly used, 581.
Sûryâ, the feminine sun goddess of the Veda, 510.
Synonymes, 374.

620 INDEX.

T

T, sound of, how produced, 131.
Tacitus on the religion of the Germans, 155.
Tahiti, custom of the inhabitants of, called *Te pi*, 42.
—— effect of this custom on the Tahitian language, 43, 44.
Tar, the Aryan root, in Sanskrit and other languages, 218.
Tataria, the name of the Deity in, 156.
Tavern-signs, hieroglyphic mythology of, 548.
Te pi, custom of the Tahitians called, 42.
Team, derivation of the word, 383.
Tear, etymology of the word, 278.
Temo, meaning of the Latin word, 384.
Tengri, the Tataric and Mongolian name of God, 160.
Terms, positions of the organs of speech in producing the, 141.
Th and *f*, change of, 129.
Th (þ) and *dh* (ð), the sounds of, how produced, 130.
That, the word, in other Aryan dialects, 230.
Theomeuia, origin of the popular signification given to the word, 378.
Thirds, derivation of the Greek word, 494.
Thin, the word, in other Aryan dialects, 236.
þial, a name of the Great Bear, 385 note.
Thorax, office of the, in speech, 121.
Thou, the word, in other Aryan dialects, 236.
Three, the word, in other Aryan dialects, 236.
Thymele, origin of the Greek word, 368.
Tien, the Chinese name, meaning of the word, 450.
Tien chu, the name ordered by the Pope to be used by missionaries, 450.
Timber, the word, in other Aryan dialects, 215.
Titles, origin of various, 270-272.
Tityos, myth of, as explained by Ephorus, 418.
Tiw, the Anglo-Saxon Jupiter, 444.
Tone, the causes of the production of,

URA

known to the early framers of language, 114.
Tooke, Horne, his "Diversions of Purley," 355.
—— his statement that all abstract words had originally a material meaning, 357.
Tooth, the word, in the various Aryan dialects, 277.
Tour sens versia, la, modern mythology respecting, 380.
Trachea, office of the, 122.
Transliteration, on, 167.
True, the word, in other Aryan dialects, 234.
Trevelyan, Sir Charles, his exertions in the Anglo-Indian alphabet, 171.
Tribulation, origin of the word, 359.
Trills, the letters called, 149.
—— the sounds of, how produced, 149.
Triones, probable meaning of, 383.
True, origin of the word, 361.
Tramp, tramp card, origin of the terms, 280.
Truth, origin of the word, 361.
Tu, the Sanskrit root, in Greek, Gothic, Latin, and German, 246.
Tuesday, origin of the word, 475.
Tuisco, the German god, connected by Grimm with the Anglo-Saxon *Tiw*, 470.
Turkish language, number of consonants in the, 180.
Two, the word, in other Aryan dialects, 234.
Tyr, the German sun-god, 397.
—— worshipped as the chief deity by the Germans, 475.
—— names of places and things in England containing the name of *Tyr*, 475.

U

UKUHLONIPA, the Kafir custom called, 45.
—— its effect on the Kafir language, 46.
—— Mr. Appleyard's work on the Kafir language, 45 note.
Umbrian language, Prof. F. W. Newman's essay on the, 11 note.
Universal language, of Leibnitz and Bishop Wilkins, 64-71.
Uranos, his type, the Vedic god Varuna, 150.

URV

Urvocal vowel, the, 136.
Ushas, Urvasi, Ahanâ, Saranyû, the Vedic god Dawn, meaning of the name, 391, 411.
—— myth of, 488.
—— compared to a horse, 601.

V, the sound of, how produced, 147.
Van, in Armenia, rock-inscriptions at, 12.
Varuṇa, a Vedic deity, meaning of the name, 411.
—— the prototype of the Greek Uranos, 451.
Váyu or Vâta, a Vedic god, meaning of the name, 431.
Veda, the Dawn of the, 481.
—— correlative deities, 505.
—— the Aśvins, 502.
Vějövis, an old Italian divinity, 471.
Valum pendulum, its agency in sound. 130.
—— Prof. Czermak's experiments on the, 138.
Vid, the root, 314.
Voler, to steal, derivation of the word, 207.
Voltaire, his definition of etymology, 254.
Vowels, what they are made of, 127.
—— positions of the organs of speech in pronouncing the different vowels, 130 et seq.
—— the urvocal vowel, 134.
—— nasal vowels, 132.
Vrishâkapâyî, the Vedic goddess, 511.

W and Ẇ, the sounds of, how produced, 147.
Wallachian, peculiarities of modern, 199.
Walrus, derivation of the word, 386.
Wälsch, original meaning of the German word, 385.
Weird sisters, origin of the term, 681.
What, the word, in other Aryan dialects, 230.
Wheat, the Aryan names for, 76.
Whittington and his cat, origin of the story, 571.

ZEU

Who, the word, in other Aryan languages, 230.
Wilkins, Bishop, his scheme for a universal language, analyzed, 56–71.
Window, origin of the word, 301.
Woden, remarks of the early Christian missionaries on the god, 412.
Women, influence of, over language, 46.
—— the languages of the Caribmen and women, 48.
Words, modern abuse of, 543.
—— hollow words, 546.
—— vague words, 547.
—— popular etymology, 548.
—— abstract and collective words, 579.

Xenophanes, his idea of God, 405.

Y and 'Y, the sounds of, how produced, 144.
Yama and Yamî, the Vedic deities, 528, 529.
—— Yama as a name of Agni, 530.
—— as the setting sun, 534.
—— as the King of the Departed, 533.
Yesterday, the word, in the various Aryan dialects, 230.
Yesteresen, the word, in old English authors, 447.
Yima, in the Avesta, the myth of, 540.
Ynglings, pedigree of the, 478.

Z and Ẓ, the sounds of, how produced, 145.
Zên, Zênos, etymological structure of the word, 471.
Zeus, origin of the name, 392.
—— the word Zeus the same as the Sanskrit Dyaus, 426, 444.
—— Zeus as the sky, 452.
—— what the Greeks meant by Zeus, 453, 455, 457.
—— Zeus at one period the only god of the Greeks, 457.

ZEU

Zeus, the song of the Pleiades at Dodona, 458.
—— Pindar, on Zeus as the highest and true God, 459.
—— Aristotle's view of Zeus, 459.
—— hymn of Kleanthes to Zeus, quoted, 460 note.
—— views of Æschylus and Sophocles, quoted, 460, 461.
—— meaning of the story of Zeus and Danaë, 462.

ZEU

Zeus, origin of the "descendants of Zeus," 462.
—— meaning of the story of Zeus and Kallisto, 463.
—— and of Zeus and Europa, 463.
—— Zeus the sky and Zeus the god wedded together in the Greek mind, 464.
—— words which have been derived from the same root as Zeus, 469.

www.ingramcontent.com/pod-product-compliance
Lightning Source LLC
Chambersburg PA
CBHW021226300426
44111CB00007B/441